VICTORY AT
VILLERS-BRETONNEUX

PETER FITZSIMONS

VICTORY AT VILLERS-BRETONNEUX

WHY A FRENCH TOWN WILL NEVER FORGET THE ANZACS

WILLIAM HEINEMANN: AUSTRALIA

A William Heinemann book
Published by Penguin Random House Australia Pty Ltd
Level 3, 100 Pacific Highway, North Sydney NSW 2060
www.penguin.com.au

Penguin
Random House
Australia

First published by William Heinemann in 2016
Copyright © Peter FitzSimons 2016

Addresses for the Penguin Random House group of companies can be found at global. penguinrandomhouse.com/offices.

National Library of Australia
Cataloguing-in-Publication entry

FitzSimons, Peter, author
Victory at Villers-Bretonneux/Peter FitzSimons

ISBN 978 1 74275 952 4 (hardback)

World War, 1914–1918 – Campaigns – France – Villers-Bretonneux
World War, 1914–1918 – Participation, Australian
World War, 1914–1918 – Australia

940.4144

Jacket design by Adam Yazxhi/MAXCO
Front jacket: *(top)* Soldiers in the trenches near Monument Wood (AWM E04910);
(bottom) A soldier looks at the ruins of Villers-Bretonneux after the town was recaptured by the Australians four days earlier (AWM EO4880)
Back jacket: A corner of Villers-Bretonneux (State Library of New South Wales)
Internal design and typesetting by Xou Creative, Australia
Unless otherwise indicated, all internal maps by Jane Macaulay
Illustrations on p.533 by Midland Typesetters

Printed in Australia by Griffin Press, an accredited ISO AS/NZS 14001:2004 Environmental Management System printer

Penguin Random House Australia uses papers that are natural, renewable and recyclable products and made from wood grown in sustainable forests. The logging and manufacturing processes are expected to conform to the environmental regulations of the country of origin.

To Sapper William Charles Wilkinson – the great-grandfather of my children – a gentle and good man, who served bravely with the 58th Battalion of the 15th Brigade in the second of the battles at Villers-Bretonneux, buried many of his mates there, and like so many of the survivors, returned to Australia to rarely speak of it again. A century on, this is their story . . .

We knew you would fight a real fight, but we did not know that from the very beginning you would astonish the Continent with your valour. I have come here for the simple purpose of seeing the Australians and telling them this. I shall go back tomorrow and say to my countrymen: I have seen the Australians; I have looked into their eyes. I know that they, men who have fought great battles in the cause of freedom, will fight alongside us, till the freedom for which we are all fighting is guaranteed for us and our children.[1]

French Prime Minister Georges Clémenceau,
to the Australian soldiers, 1918

Past wars should be studied as flesh and blood affairs, not as a matter of diagrams, formulae and concepts . . . but of men. Hence perhaps an element of over-emphasis on personalities in this book and in particular on the personal ascendancy of the Australian soldier on the battlefield which made him the best infantryman of the war and perhaps of all time.

British General Hubert Essame CBE, DSO, MC, who
fought with the Australians at Villers-Bretonneux[2]

Our only disappointment is that Fritz has made such rapid advances, but it must please you to know that wherever he has met the Australians he has come, what the boys call a 'Gutzer' & has never advanced an inch . . . If only the Tommies would stand & fight like our grand boys – the state of things would be very different . . . At least I can say that I am proud to be an Australian & if history is ever truly written you will find they have done wonderful works which the English papers cannot for their own sakes mention.[3]

Lieutenant Frank Reinhard Fischer, 6th Battalion,
writing to his brother and sister in Adelaide

A Yankee who could speak German asked a German prisoner did he think they were winning the war, he replied: 'Yes, God is with us.' The Yankee replied: 'That's nothing, the Australians are with us.'

Diary of Sydney B. Young of Campsie, after 1000 American soldiers
joined 7000 Australians to capture Hamel in 93 minutes on 4 July 1918

CONTENTS

LIST OF MAPS

NOTE ON THE TEXT

For the sake of simplicity, Lieutenant-Generals and Major-Generals are referred to simply as Generals. Brigadier-Generals are referred to as Brigadiers. Similarly, Lieutenant-Colonels and Colonels are both described as Colonels. I also advise that 'left' and 'right' flank is always viewed from the position of a person within the unit under discussion and facing the enemy. German translations have been lightly edited to make their meaning clearer in English.

While British, Australian and German formations are all different, and with very broad brushstrokes, here is the rough size of the units that made up their forces in the Great War.

One Army group (Germans only) = three or more armies = up to 1,200,000 men
One Army = three to five Army Corps = up to 500,000 men
One Army Corps = three or four Divisions, plus Corps troops = 70,000–100,000 men
One Division = three Brigades and artillery = 16,000 men
One Brigade or Regiment = three or four Battalions, plus machine guns and mortars = 3,000–4,000 men
One Battalion = four Companies, plus Battalion headquarters = 900 men
One Company = four Platoons = 200 men

BACKGROUND AND ACKNOWLEDGEMENTS

Herewith, the third book of my trilogy on the experience of Australian soldiers in the Great War. It has – and I mean this sincerely – been an honour, a privilege and a fascinating exercise to track their experience through all of Gallipoli, Fromelles and Pozières, and now their greatest triumph of all, the Battles of Villers-Bretonneux.

Like most Australians, my understanding of what happened at Villers-Bretonneux was somewhere between foggy and non-existent, up until a couple of decades ago. When writing the biography of John Eales, I cherished the story of the World Cup-winning Wallaby coach Rod Macqueen taking the Wallabies to the town and then reading to them – in the last minute before they left the dressing room to go into the cauldron of Millennium Stadium, Cardiff, for the World Cup Final – the words of Lieutenant Frank Bethune to his men, in one of the battles that preceded the main event, as the Germans were about to fall upon them.

'This position will be held,' Macqueen quoted Bethune, 'and the section will remain here until relieved. The enemy cannot be allowed to interfere with this programme. If the section cannot remain here alive, it will remain here dead, but in any case it will remain here. Should any man, through shell shock or other cause, attempt to surrender he will remain here dead. Should all guns be blown out, the section will use Mills grenades, and other novelties. Finally, the position, as stated, will be held.' [1]

A dropped pin on that dressing room floor would have sounded like a clattering cymbal.

'And guys,' Macqueen finished, 'they held their position.'

RAH!

A couple of years later, while writing my book *Kokoda,* the Australian historian Neil McDonald – who had become a great friend – showed me a passage from Charles Bean's *Official History,* which thrilled me. The scene was set with the British line defending Villers-Bretonneux having been broken, the Germans were flooding west and the Australian soldiers of the 3rd Division had been sent east to plug the gap. Coming back the other way down the road were many British soldiers, shouting such warnings to the Australians as, 'You can't hold them!'[2]

Among the Brits were thousands of French refugees, many of them with all the worldly belongings they could carry in their wheelbarrows . . . and hence to the part I loved.

As documented by Bean, some of the fleeing *citoyens* took just one look at the Diggers and turned around, on the reckoning that with our blokes involved the day might be saved after all.

'*Fini* retreat, *Madame,*' Charles Bean recorded one of the Diggers saying to an old lady heading west as he sits with his mates on a brief smoko, cleaning their rifles.

'*Fini* retreat – *beaucoup Australiens ici.*'[3]

Loved it!

But detail? No clue.

Still, interest grew as I first took my three kids to Villers-Bretonneux on a family trip in 2007, to walk around the town, the battle sites and the cemetery, getting a very rough appreciation of what had happened. And then, having written books on Gallipoli and the twin battles of Fromelles and Pozières, the obvious subject of Villers-Bretonneux beckoned.

And, yes, you are right, given the rather breast-beating way I had come by the story, I would have to be on guard from writing it in a breast-beating way – something I have struggled with since. For I frankly challenge *anyone* who goes into this story not to come away amazed at how well the Australians performed in extreme circumstances.

As ever, I have tried to bring the *story* part of this his*tory* alive by writing it in the present tense and constructing it in the manner of a novel, albeit with 2000-odd footnotes as the pinpoint buttresses on which the story rests. For the sake of the storytelling, just as I noted that I did with *Gallipoli* and *Fromelles and Pozières*, I have occasionally created a direct quote from reported speech in a newspaper, diary or letter, and changed pronouns and tenses to put that reported speech in the present tense – every now and then assuming generic emotions where it is obvious, even though that emotion is not necessarily recorded in the diary entries, letter, etc. I have also occasionally restored swear words that were blanked out in the original newspaper and diary accounts due to the sensitivities of the time. Always, my goal has been to determine what were the words used, based on the documentary evidence presented, and what the feel of the situation was. For the same reason of remaining faithful to the language of the day, I have stayed with the imperial system of measurement and used the contemporary spellings.

While I prized primary documents above all else, many books were wonderful sources, and none more – as ever – than the combined works of Charles E. W. Bean, including most particularly his diaries and notebooks. On that subject, I express here my deep gratitude to Edward Bean Le Couteur and Anne Marie Carroll, the grandchildren of Charles Bean and owners of the copyright in his diaries and papers, for their kind permission to quote from the great man.

All books used are listed in the bibliography, but of the works beyond Bean, I drew particularly heavily on George Mitchell's *Backs to the Wall*, Joan Scott's *Diary of Private Edwin Need*, Jimmy Downing's *To the Last Ridge*, Peter Kilduff's *Red Baron: The Life and Death of an Ace*, Martin Middlebrook's *The Kaiser's Battle* and Robert Asprey's *The German High Command at War*.

My friend Dr Peter Pedersen has written a great book, *Villers-Bretonneux*, which acted as a compass whenever I got lost and needed to get back to the front. Ditto my friend Ross McMullin, with his wonderful biography *Pompey Elliott*.

In Germany, special thanks to Carmen Böhm from Bayerisches Armeemuseum (Bavarian Army Museum) in Ingolstadt, who went way above and beyond the call of duty; Steffi Wolf from the German

National Library in Leipzig; Frank Anton from Bundesarchiv (Department Military Archive) in Freiburg/Breisgau; the staff at Staats- und Universitätsbibliothek Hamburg (especially Marianne Meyer); the library of Helmut Schmidt Universität (Universität der Bundeswehr Hamburg); Zentralbibliothek Recht and Zentralbibliothek Philosophie, Geschichte und Klassische Philologie – Geschichte in Hamburg. In the USA, Jenny Reibenspies from Cushing Memorial Library at Texas A&M University and Damani K. Davis from the National Archives in Washington, DC.

In the United Kingdom, I thank Diana Manipud at King's College London Archives; Andrew Gough at the British Library; Tricia Buckingham at the Bodleian Libraries; and, back home, all the research staff at the mighty Australian War Memorial Research Centre . . . to name but a few!

Just as with the first two of the trilogy, and indeed with nearly all my books for the last decade, I have relied heavily on a great team of researchers, most of whom have worked with me, and substantially with each other, for many years. As with *Fromelles*, the major digger for the Diggers, trawling through diaries and letters, was Dr Noel Boreham – we respectfully think of him as 'Noel the Diary Mole' – who spent many happy *weeks* finding so many of the original accounts and quotes you will find herein, as well as doing valuable work vetting the manuscript at its completion.

Mein freund, Sonja Goernitz, meanwhile, is a dual German–Australian citizen who first started working with me for my book *Tobruk* in 2005. For this book, it was very useful that she was living back in Germany for most of the time I was writing it, enabling her to go in person to the many archives and libraries to find the material to bring to life the German experience at Villers-Bretonneux. Her ability to locate and then translate long slabs of German regimental histories, her understanding of the language and culture of the time, was crucial to turning up fresh material for this account and fine-tuning it to accuracy.

Dr Libby Effeney has worked with me on the last three books, and as a researcher and friend, she is as good as it gets – hard-working and, curiously, as intellectually strict as she is creative in working out how the story can be told better while still remaining within the parameters of *what happened*. I mentioned in the last book how, of all my favourite notations to researchers, foremost was 'LME PR', as in, 'Libby Marea Effeney, please resolve' – using the intellect and patience I don't possess to wade into this tangle of differing accounts with footnotes from everywhere and come up with a sole, solid quote sourced to an original document we ideally have a screenshot of. Bingo. Done. Move on. So too with this one. And she was also wonderful in coordinating my other researchers to work out just who was best equipped to find the answer to whichever question I posed.

Finally, my warm thanks to Dr Peter Williams, the Canberra military historian who has worked with me throughout this trilogy. He was the one to give me the first detailed 'tutorial' – involving salt and pepper shakers – on what happened during the Villers-Bretonneux battle, and as we have gone on, things have become ever more precise. Time and again I relied on his depth and width of knowledge, his 40 years of study in the field, not to mention his extensive library of wartime literature. He and I both particularly enjoyed, nearing the end of the book, putting together Sonja's translations of the German accounts of the battle and working out just where the German piece of the jigsaw puzzle should be placed in my account – to give the proper counterpoint to the Australian accounts. I give him particular credit for cross-referencing the *Leutnant* Roßbach account with other German reports, to work out exactly where Roßbach and his men must have been placed at the time, which Australians they fought and what time the scene took place. (I might say, in passing, I have long found the special joy of putting together such historical works is indeed finding the right jigsaw piece to put in the right spot. It fits! It fits! For while history itself, of course, meshes perfectly, putting together parts of different historical accounts can be a lot more challenging – and rewarding, when it brings the whole scene to life.)

As ever, I also relied on other specialists in their fields, including my wonderfully assiduous long-time researcher at the Australian War Memorial, Glenda Lynch, together with her fellow researcher, Jean Main; my dear friend Dr Michael Cooper, for medical history; Gregory Blake, for his assistance in all matters to do with firearms and artillery; and Mat McLachlan of Battlefield Tours, for vetting the whole manuscript and suggesting additional angles and stories. In this book it was a joy to revisit and refine some of the same material I first became fascinated with during my biography of Charles Kingsford Smith – most notably the life and times of the Red Baron, Fokkers, Sopwith Camels and the whole aerial war in France – and, as with that book, I relied on the expertise of aviation expert Peter Finlay to help on all matters esoterical. My thanks also to the descendants of the Australian soldier Archie Barwick, who gave their blessing to use his diarised words to strengthen my account.

As to illustrations and maps, I am once more indebted to Jane Macaulay, whose great work you will see throughout – and I might say, this book more than most needs such maps to keep it all clear.

As she has done for the last 15 books or so, my dear friend of 30 years at the *Sydney Morning Herald*, Harriet Veitch, did all the preliminary copyediting, spotting inconsistencies and errors while also untangling hopelessly twisted sentences, eliminating many grammatical errors and placing at my service her extraordinarily wide and deep general knowledge. For some reason, she knows and cares about such things as the finer points of how the Kaiser ran his court, the translation of *ersatz* in three languages, and this manuscript benefited enormously from such rare and refined knowledge.

My thanks also, as ever, to my highly skilled editor Brandon VanOver, who has always understood that I write in a particular, if unconventional, way, which he needs to keep intact 98 per cent of the time, and call in Joe's Bulldozers on the other two per cent. I understand that, but have never been sure which is the two per cent. He does, and I thank him for it.

I am grateful, as ever, to my long-time publishers Ali Urquhart and Nikki Christer, who were encouraging throughout, particularly Ali, whose instinct proved as sure as ever.

And finally, of course, my gratitude and love to my wife, Lisa, for her own passion for me trying to bring to life the experience of her grandfather, who, as you have likely read in the dedication, was one of the Australian soldiers involved in the second of the big battles at Villers-Bretonneux.

As ever, I only hope I have done the story of him and his mates justice and that the whole account moves you, as it does me.

Peter FitzSimons
Neutral Bay, Sydney
5 September 2016

PROLOGUE

Remembering that the pick of the Australians were killed
at Gallipoli, I have often wondered whatever can they have
been like. It is my considered opinion that the Australians,
even in 1918, were better in battle than any other troops
on either side . . . They were untidy, undisciplined, cocky,
not 'nice' enough for the taste even of [us Tommies]. But
it seems indisputable that a greater number of them were
personally indomitable, in the true sense of the word,
than of any other race. I am glad they were on our side.[1]
Captain Philip Ledward, of the 8th Division, reminiscing after the war
about the Australians, whom he first encountered at Villers-Bretonneux

We sighted the shores of France. Everyone was excited
and in the best of spirits; we were all thinking that at last
we had arrived in the country that was foremost in our
minds when we enlisted. For us the war was in France
and Belgium, and although Gallipoli did, and always
would, mean much to us . . . all other campaigns were of
a subsidiary nature to that in the great Western theatre.[2]
L. M. Newton, The Story of the Twelfth

That was just the way of this Great War, the most extraordinary clash
of nations the world had ever seen.

As it was just starting to gain momentum in the early months of
the conflict, Robert Buie was no more than an ordinary oyster farmer
from Brooklyn on the Hawkesbury River who joined up – one of 60
million men around the globe, 330,000 of them Australians – to take

arms against a sea of troubles, ready to do or die, or know the reason why. Harry Cobby was a mild-mannered bank teller from Melbourne, second booth from the left. George Mitchell was a country boy and larrikin from Caltowie, South Australia, while Walter 'Jimmy' Downing was a Scotch College boy from Melbourne who had been studying law and playing lots of cricket and lacrosse when he had enlisted at the age of 21.

Manfred von Richthofen, meanwhile, was a young German nobleman, a cavalry lieutenant since the beginning of the war, who was starting to toy with the idea of perhaps becoming a pilot, while a 16-year-old German lad, Erich Pernet – the youngest stepson of the most powerful military figure in Germany, General Erich Ludendorff – was not yet sure what he wanted to do in this war, only that he wished to serve the Fatherland. Wilhelm Biltz had just left his position as *Professor* Wilhelm Biltz at Clausthal University and had never heard of a young Englishman half his age, Frank Mitchell, who had been a humble bank clerk from Guernsey in the Channel Islands when the war broke out.

And Villers-Bretonneux was just another French town, one of hundreds on the edge of the growing conflict – close enough to feel the dragon's breath, but not yet engulfed by it. With just over 5000 residents, it was a picturesque and peaceful place, with spectacular farmlands lapping at its shores, and where, although not everyone knows everyone, they at least know his sister, or went to the same school as her uncle.

There seems little doubt that God has smiled on their town. Yes, the Germans had briefly come through on their way to Paris and caused some damage through looting, but after the Battle of the Marne, the *Boche* tide had just as quickly receded to dig into the line they intended to hold, come what may, just ten miles to the east of this fair and beloved burgh.

(And yet the true industrial and transport hub of the region is the city Villers-Bretonneux overlooks, the one down there on the plains, 11 miles to the west: Amiens. The cultural centre of Picardy, it boasts no

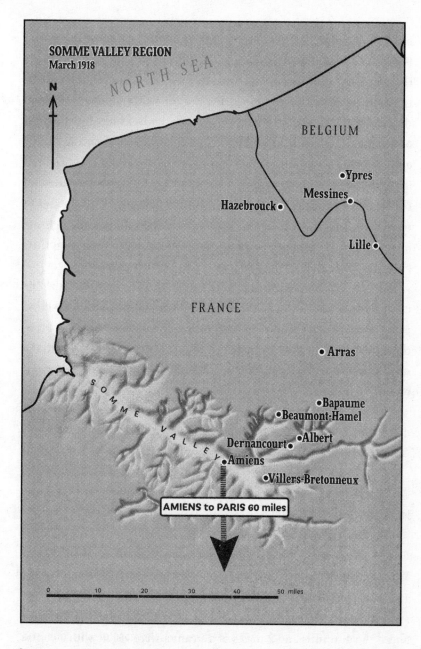

SOMME VALLEY REGION
March 1918

N

NORTH SEA

BELGIUM

Ypres
Messines
Hazebrouck

Lille

FRANCE

Arras

SOMME VALLEY

Bapaume
Beaumont-Hamel
Dernancourt Albert
Amiens
Villers-Bretonneux

AMIENS to PARIS 60 miles

0   10   20   30   40   50 miles

fewer than 100,000 people, a magnificent cathedral, and the fact that
the main railway line from Paris in the south to Arras, Lille and Calais
in the north helps make it the key rail hub for the region.)

Now, none of Buie, Cobby, Downing or the Mitchells, or anyone in Villers-Bretonneux, had ever heard of the other, nor of Baron von Richthofen or Erich Ludendorff or Wilhelm Biltz – just as the latter three had not heard of them. None of them, in the normal course of things, would ever have come across the others. None ever imagined that the survival or destruction of the others would make a blind bit of difference, one way or t'other, to the trajectory of their own exist-ence. And beyond all that, none of the Australians could even begin to imagine how the course of the war would see a few of them – some of the toughest bastards Gawd ever put breath into – *thrill* to the feel of the finest sheer silk panties under their muddy trousers while fighting in that town, even donning rouge and lipstick before proffering their cheeks to their mates, but that, too, is part of the story.

For so enormous were the forces unleashed by this catastrophic conflagration, so truly global the conflict, that many events in far-flung parts of the world, seemingly disconnected, would conspire to bring these men and Villers-Bretonneux so closely together that for each, the survival or destruction of some of the others would become of para-mount importance.

Let us take a closer look, then, at some of those disparate events that do so conspire, and some of the forces involved.

—

And there it is!

On this sunny, early afternoon of 7 May 1915, just 11 miles off the Old Head of Kinsale on the southern coast of Ireland, *Kapitänleutnant* Walther Schwieger, the 30-year-old Commander of the German U-boat *U-20* – a man of notoriously calculating and ruthless disposition – can see the most extraordinary vessel, as he would record in his log: 'Straight ahead the 4 funnels and 2 masts of a steamer were visible with a course at right angles to ours'.[3] He recognises her instantly as the *Lusitania*, a British cruiser that is the mightiest of Cunard's ocean liners.

Due to berth at Liverpool that night, she is six days out of New York on her 202nd crossing of the Atlantic, laden with meat, medical supplies, copper, oil, machinery and, Schwieger suspected, secreted war materiel. He knows she would boast about 700 crew and be carrying,[4] perhaps, 1,300[5] passengers. She's a 32,000-ton beauty, 786 feet long with engines of 68,000 horsepower pushing her beautifully through the water at an extraordinary 21 knots, making her one of the two fastest cruisers afloat.

But can he bring himself to actually fire at least one of the nine torpedoes the *U-20* is carrying, through one of its four torpedo tubes – two in the bow and two in the stern?

He can.

'Target range 800 yards . . . a British liner . . . prepare bow tube.'

The order is passed by word of mouth to the forward torpedo room. The outer cap is open and seawater fills the tube. Not a word is spoken that does not need to be spoken.

Now bringing his bow around so that the G-type torpedo – bearing 89 pounds of explosive charge – is perfectly positioned to hit the Cunard liner, he waits his moment to fire.

'500 metres . . . 400 metres . . . 350 metres . . . 325 metres . . . 300 metres,' *Kapitän* Schwieger keeps calling off the distance calmly. 'Stand by . . . stand by . . . fire bow torpedo.'

The order to fire is shouted into the forward torpedo room. The torpedo-man's mate pulls down on a lever, which releases a rush of compressed air into the tube behind the torpedo, forcing it out in an explosion of bubbles. As it exits, the torpedo's internal motor is ignited and the compact but powerful engine engages its propeller, sending it in a straight line towards its target at a speed of some 35 knots.

On board the U-boat, all is silent bar the humming of the engines as all wait for the result. Suddenly, it is as if two giant cymbals have struck on both sides of their vessel, making everything shake.

Bullseye!

Shot struck starboard side close behind the bridge.[6]

The torpedo instantly rips an enormous hole in the *Lusitania*'s hull. That first explosion causes a second, even bigger one, as the ship's boiler blows – in turn detonating the 175 tons of munitions the ship is secretly carrying. Within 30 seconds the ship is listing badly to starboard as water rushes into its shattered hull, while also sinking bow-first. Passengers jump into the sea. Lifeboats are launched. All is a frenzy of panic.

Within minutes, and with one last blast of steam, the *Lusitania* sets sail straight to the sea floor.

—

A few hours later, in the Oval Office in Washington, President Woodrow Wilson is having a cup of tea when he is handed an urgent telegram that has been sent by American Ambassador Walter Page in London: **The Lusitania was torpedoed off the Irish coast and sank in half an hour. No news yet of passengers.**[7]

Ashen-faced, though still calm, Wilson calls for more details as they come to hand, and the broad contours of the catastrophe are soon apparent. The preliminary estimates are devastating: over 1,000 of the 2,000 people on board the famed British cruise liner were thought to have died, and over 100 of them were American.

In response to the strong American diplomatic protests, the Germans express regret for the sinking of the *Lusitania* but argue that the move was nonetheless necessary in light of intelligence that the liner was carrying munitions bound to help the British war effort. Wilson skirts that issue but now gives fair warning: 'Repetition by the commanders of German naval vessels of acts in contravention of those rights must be regarded by the Government of the United States, when they affect American citizens, as deliberately unfriendly.'[8]

The message is clear: if Germany persists with the policy, they risk war with the United States.

—

And yes, for the moment, America remains out of the war, but in just over a year that war reaches a new level of carnage, as on 1 July 1916, when, using a total of two million men, the British and French forces attempt to break through the strong German trench system east of Albert in a campaign that would last four months. At campaign's end, the British and French had suffered 600,000 casualties with 200,000 of them killed, while the Germans, similarly, had 500,000 casualties with 180,000 dead.

And all for what?

The border of the Western Front – a 450-mile-long complex of trenches stretching from Nieuport on the English Channel in Belgium, across the north and east of France to the Swiss border, with four million men on each side defending it – had advanced no more than 40 miles at most since the first months of the war. In most places it hadn't moved at all as an otherwise unstoppable force met an immovable object, and the most tangible result apparent at the time had been the shedding of oceans of blood and, for the Germans, the ascension of new military leadership.

The new Supreme Commander was the warm and genial old man *Generalfeldmarschall* General Paul von Hindenburg, who took over with his Chief of Staff, the cold and ascetic General Erich Ludendorff. *Ja*, they made a strange and unlikely pairing but were still so in sync and formidable that they were even known as '*das Duo*', the Duo.

'Never,' Crown Prince Wilhelm would comment, 'have I seen any other two men of such different character furnish the exact complement of one another so as to form one single entity, as did these two.'[9]

While von Hindenburg struts the national stage, it is Ludendorff who is the driving force of the German Army, the one who rises early, works furiously throughout the day – that fury frequently ascending to incandescent rage – and then finishes late, before doing it all again the next day.

—

And what are the members of the Australian Imperial Forces in France up to at this time?

Freezing, mostly – while still holding the line on the old Somme battlefield of the previous summer and recovering from the terrible travails of 1916, when there had been six months of ceaseless battles for the three divisions of General William Birdwood's I Anzac Corps. Taking time to write up his thoughts about the boys' first winter in France, the great Australian war correspondent Captain Charles Bean had noted, 'On both sides the battle was now against the conditions of winter – a campaign which at last had a chance of making headway.'[10]

As battered as the men have been by the war to date, Bean has observed a marked transformation, as he would later write: 'From the valley of that shadow they slowly emerged, recovering in numbers, health and spirit, their area one of the best furnished, and their corps recognised as among the finest fighting machines at the disposal of the British command.'[11]

But gee it was cold, all right!

Most of them are in huts built of cheap, thin sheets of wood, that have no chimneys, where 'all the windows have an inch thick of solid ice, on the *inside*',[12] where the only thing you can do to keep the cold out is to stuff every crack you can find with paper.

'Men massed around the braziers,' one officer would record. 'Hoarfrost would form on the back of the Greatcoats of those men who were not immediately against the brazier. Men slept in pairs to get the greatest warmth from the pooled blankets.'[13]

Under such circumstances it takes a man of relentlessly sunny disposition to look on the bright side, but just such a man is Sergeant Archie Barwick, a 27-year-old farmer originally from the Tassie sticks.

'The boys are standing [the weather] splendidly, even better than a lot of the Tommies I think. Why, I have felt it far colder many a time in Tasmania . . .'[14]

Oh, and one more thing strikes Archie's whimsy on this day in late January 1917, as he mans his position in the trenches at Bazentin, a mile from Pozières.

'Kaiser's birthday,' he noted in his diary. 'Wonder what he will be up to.'[15]

—

Allied accounts, at least, will be unanimous on the answer.

The Kaiser was up to no good.

In recent weeks, the highest echelons of the German military, led by General Ludendorff, had come to a key conclusion. If they stayed with the current war of attrition, the cruel calculus of catastrophe meant that Germany must inevitably fall behind and lose for the fact that they would run out of men, munitions and food before the Allies. The harsh British naval blockade had been slowly strangling Germany since the outbreak of war, as *die Briten* and their Royal Navy controlled passage of the English Channel and the North Sea, while the French Navy blocked the Adriatic ports of the Austro-Hungarian Empire. And the one chance they had to pull off the spectacular, devastating hits on the enemy without suffering equal losses themselves was now clear. Pushed by the likes of General Ludendorff, the view grew that the best chance of defeating Great Britain lay in crippling *her* sea transport and starving *her* isles of sustenance – to give back to the Englanders what had already been done to them. And this would unavoidably include torpedoing more American shipping, despite their neutrality.

Besides, if the U-boats do wreak havoc on the high seas as expected, how likely could it be that the Americans would actually risk sending a two million man army across those seas to France? Germany's Chief of Naval Staff, Admiral Henning von Holtzendorff, was so confident of the power of the U-boats that he even put it in writing to the Kaiser. Even if the 'disorganized and undisciplined' Americans do declare war and send troops, he says, 'I give your Majesty my word as an officer that not one American will land on the Continent.'[16]

And even if it did bring war with the USA, and they did send that many troops – it is estimated it will take at least two years before the Americans will be in France *and* trained for battle – still Germany might be able to cope. Admiral Holtzendorff insisted that unleashing the U-boats would see the war concluded, as 'the campaign would be decisive in a few months'.[17]

And the revered figure of the Kaiser – referred to by General Hindenburg of the Old School as *unseren Allerhöchsten Kriegsherrn*, 'our All-Highest War-Lord' – had agreed to it all. No matter that the *very* quiet assertion of one of his generals was that he could not 'lead three soldiers over the gutter'.[18] Taking the proffered pen, he had signed the decree that would see unrestricted U-boat warfare on all shipping to the UK and her Allies, including that of the neutral Americans.

'I now expect,' the Kaiser had noted in passing, 'a declaration of war by America.'[19]

A pity, yes, but don't you see, they have no choice?

Even Admiral Georg von Müller, naval adviser to the Kaiser, who had been against the U-boat offensive as recently as a fortnight earlier, could see that now. 'I have already come to the conclusion that the general war situation demands this last shot in our locker,'[20] he confided to his diary.

And now, on the final day of January, Germany makes the announcement that the most aggressive figures in the Kaiser's military have been long advocating:

> FROM FEBRUARY 1, 1917, SEA
> TRAFFIC WILL BE STOPPED WITH
> EVERY AVAILABLE WEAPON AND
> WITHOUT FURTHER NOTICE IN . . .
> BLOCKADE ZONES AROUND GREAT
> BRITAIN, FRANCE, ITALY AND IN
> THE EASTERN MEDITERRANEAN.[21]

In short, the Germans are about to unleash unrestricted U-boat warfare. Will this prompt war with America? In all likelihood, but so be it.

'In my view,' General Ludendorff would later write, 'war with America was inevitable at the end of January 1917 . . . Disaster was on its way.'[22]

—

In Russia, meantime, things are changing at an astonishing pace. No less than revolution is in the air . . .

On 10 March 1917, in the Russian capital of Petrograd, the Tsar's troops are ordered to shoot down, in cold blood, the city's workers striking over their appalling work conditions and the fact that they and their families are starving due to the war and wartime restrictions. These protestors have even opened the gaols to liberate the prisoners, and they must be stopped! Order must be restored.

But the troops refuse to shoot, and instead line up with the workers!

That afternoon, an angry crowd of protesters at the Nevsky Prospekt is confronted by a mounted squadron. Suddenly, from out of the crowd, walks a young girl. From beneath her cloak she takes a bouquet of red roses and walks to the grim-faced mounted officer who commands this squadron.

The officer reacts.

He smiles.

He leans down and takes the bouquet.

The people cheer! Not even the Cossacks will fire upon them!

The next day, 170,000 soldiers of the Petrograd garrison join the mutiny, a new provisional government led by Mikhail Rodzianko is formed, and the announcement is made that the workers and soldiers would be represented by a 'Soviet', their own council. And yet, not even that is enough.

The Tsar, noting his officers are uneasy, takes the imperial train to his royal country residence at Tsarskoe Selo, starting out in the wee hours of 13 March, only to have his Generals effectively divert the train up a quiet branch line when the line ahead appears, as he notes in his diary, 'to be occupied by the rebels'.[23] It is in the tiny outpost of Pskov, thus, that the Tsar is informed that his personal bodyguard has now deserted and that his personal safety, and that of his family, can no longer be guaranteed. The three loyalist Generals who are travelling with him all suggest that the best course is . . . abdication. The Tsar – grown stick-thin in recent months, hollowed out from worry, and with faded, lifeless eyes, capable only of nervous glances or vacant stares

– asks to be left alone before going out for his afternoon walk, where he comes to a reluctant conclusion.

There is only one way 'to save Russia and keep the army at the front quiet', most particularly when 'all around me is treachery, cowardice and deceit . . .'[24]

After returning, he calls for the Generals.

'I have signed the abdication,'[25] he says simply.

A new provisional government, headed by Prince Georgy Lvov, is quickly formed, which promises reforms in amnesty for political opponents, freedom of the press, elections in which all citizens can vote, while also continuing the war against Germany . . .

—

In Germany, von Hindenburg and Ludendorff also watch closely the course of events. With the Tsar gone, the war effort of his country will certainly diminish, but what they really need is Russia to drop out of the war altogether. At that point, a million German troops could move to the Western Front and a great offensive launched there.

But how?

In a few days, Ludendorff – so completely colourless and lacking any trail of anecdotes behind him that he would be called 'a man without a shadow'[26] – has a possible answer, communicated to him by Foreign Secretary Arthur Zimmermann himself, that might throw a very large shadow indeed.

Herr General, we have a proposal.

You know already of the exiled Bolshevik leader, Vladimir Lenin, who is with his wife in Switzerland. If he and his core group of revolutionary comrades could be spirited back into Russia, being given papers to pass through Germany, they could act as a powerful antiwar mouthpiece there. He is the one, *Herr General*, Foreign Secretary Zimmerman insists, who will precipitate the toppling of the Provisional Government and definitively take Russia out of the war.

Ludendorff listens quietly. This might be worth trying. Both

Germany and the Allies have around four million soldiers at the Western Front and have fought each other to a bloody stalemate. If a million veteran German soldiers – hard men of enormous experience – could be freed from fighting in Russia and come to the Western Front instead, his forces would have a significant superiority there for the first time since 1914.

But it is delicate. For what if the madness of the Communist revolution spreads into Germany itself, what then? But still, the prospect of success is too intoxicating to resist.

Concluding a separate peace with Russia, getting them out of the war for good, is a top priority for Germany, and with the US soon to be on their way, it is never more urgent than right now.

The response from Ludendorff reaches Zimmermann two days later:

HIGH COMMAND OF THE ARMY INSTRUCTS ME TO TELEGRAPH AS FOLLOWS: 'NO OBJECTIONS TO TRANSIT OF RUSSIAN REVOLUTIONARIES IF EFFECTED IN SPECIAL TRAIN WITH RELIABLE ESCORT.[27]

———

The final straw for America comes on the 19 March 1917.

Mr President? We regret to inform you that another three American ships – *Illinois, City of Memphis* and *Vigilancia* – have been sunk by German U-boats. No fewer than 14,500 tons of shipping are now at the bottom of the Atlantic, and a further 15 American lives have been lost.

President Wilson sinks back into his seat, nearly as low as his spirits. This is the end, then. After everything he has done to keep America out of this dreadful war, Germany is now forcing his hand. There is no option but to go to war.

It will take over a fortnight from this point, but Congress finally agrees, and before lunchtime on Good Friday, 6 April, President Wilson is informed that the War Resolution, requiring only his signature to become valid, is on its way to the White House.

'Stand by me, Edith,' he says to his wife after she hands him the gold pen he had recently given her as a gift.

Clenching his jaw, Wilson affixes his florid signature and rises.

'In an instant, wireless operators were transmitting the news to the world. For only the fourth time, the United States of America had declared war on a foreign nation.'[28]

———

Ultimately, however, the German leadership is not *too* alarmed. It is one thing for faraway America to declare war on them, but quite another for America to raise an army, train it and transport it across the ocean through waters controlled by the U-boats.

The tone is set by Admiral Müller, who calmly notes in his diary on the day: 'News from America that Wilson has carried his proclamation of a state of war through the Senate and the Congress. So we are actually at war with the United States. No one can say where this will lead, but we hope that the U-boat campaign will bring about the end of the war in Europe before America can take a serious hand.'[29]

Yes, that is the key. They must finish the war before the Americans can arrive in force.

———

At last, all has been agreed to.

Vladimir Lenin and his party are ready to leave Zurich and head back to Russia after no less than a decade in exile.

They are going back through Germany, under German escort, with the destination of the Russian capital of Petrograd. Lenin personally negotiated the finer details and conditions of the trip with Germany's Ambassador to Switzerland, and now, on this 10th day of April, 1917, he and his entourage of 22 fellow Bolsheviks are making their way onto the platform at Zurich station, where a special train awaits.

But what's this?

Waiting there on the platform are some other 100 Russian émigrés living in Zurich. They know what Lenin and his group are up to, and while some have come to wish them well, most have come to register their disgust that Lenin – a Russian – has come to a deal with the very country that has brought his country to its knees.

Their catcalls begin at the mere sight of the Lenin group: 'Provocateurs! Spies! Pigs! Traitors!'

'The Kaiser is paying for the journey,' one Russian accuses.

'They're going to hang you . . . like German spies,'[30] shouts another.

Lenin ignores them and ushers his group onto the designated carriage, prompting some of the more aggressive in the crowd to beat on the side of the carriage with sticks, to shout even more aggressively.

'Hiss as much as you like,' says Lenin. 'We Bolsheviks will shuffle your cards and spoil your game.'[31]

At 3.10 pm, the whistle blows. The train lurches and starts to move out of Zurich Station, to yet more jeers and cheers.

'Ilyich,' shouts one supporter to Lenin, 'take care of yourself. You're the only one we have.'

When the train finally disappears around the nearest bend, the last sign of Lenin's party is a red handkerchief, streaming from the train window, like a flag.

On board, Vladimir Ilyich Lenin, at last 'leaving this cursed Switzerland',[32] relaxes a little, casually hooking his thumbs into the armholes of his vest as he always does when not outright combative – but only a little.

Six days later, as the train at last approaches Finland Station in Petrograd just after 11 o'clock on this crisp, glorious night of 16 April, a stocky figure with a luxuriant black moustache is seen pacing back and forth on the platform – at least the best he can in the crush. The editor of *Pravda*, Joseph Stalin, knows Lenin well and has been looking forward to his return. And clearly, wonderfully, Stalin is not alone. In fact, perhaps as many as ten thousand of his fellow Russians have come out to greet Lenin as well!

'The throng in front of [the] Station blocked the whole square, making movement almost impossible and scarcely letting trams through,' one eyewitness would record. 'Troops with bands were drawn up under red flags . . . Within the station, triumphal arches in red and gold, erected every few yards, stretched the length of the platform above the heads of the mass of waiting people. Banners bearing "every possible welcoming inscription and revolutionary slogan" hung above several divisions of guards of honour – soldiers from various barracks, sailors and the Bolshevik armed civilian Red Guard.'[33]

As the train pulls into the station, the crowd gazes earnestly at all the faces on the carriages, staring out, looking, looking . . .

There! On the fifth carriage, up the front, see – a man with an awed expression. It is Vladimir Lenin.

And how could he *not* be awestruck? There he was, fearing arrest by the Cossacks, and now . . . this!

Wide-eyed and grinning, the great Bolshevik leader, who has shrewdly substituted a more classic Russian worker's hat for his bowler, steps down from the carriage with his wife, Nadezhda Konstantinovna, close behind him.

Instantly, they are engulfed by the cheering, heaving mass of their fellow Russians while the band breaks into their best attempt at the revolutionary anthem 'La Marseillaise'. (A wobbly rendition, to be certain, by virtue of the fact that before the Tsar's fall they had only played songs in his honour, and with his blessing, and he had not been partial to either 'La Marseillaise' or 'The Internationale'.)

But now he is gone – and Vladimir Lenin is here! Oh, how the people cheer!

'Hurrah! Hurrah! HURRAH!'[34]

Speak to us, Vladimir, speak to us! The sailors and the honour guard and the people demand it of him.

'Sailors, comrades,' Lenin begins, 'as I greet you, I still don't know whether you have faith in all the promises of the Provisional

Government. What I know for certain though is that when sweet promises are made, you are being deceived in the same way that the entire Russian people are being deceived . . . Sailors, comrades, we have to fight for a socialist revolution, to fight until the proletariat wins full victory! Long live the world-wide socialist revolution!'[35]

'Ypa! Ypa! Ypa! Hurrah! Hurrah! HURRAH!'

Inevitably, it is Winston Churchill who summates most memorably this beginning, writing of the Germans: 'Upon the Western Front they had from the beginning used the most terrible means of offense at their disposal. They had employed poison gas on the largest scale and had invented the *"Flammenwerfer"*. Nevertheless, it was with a sense of awe that they turned upon Russia the most grisly of all weapons. They transported Lenin in a sealed truck like a plague bacillus from Switzerland into Russia . . .'[36]

—

On the same day, more than 1000 miles to the south-west, things have never been so grim for soldiers of the French Army. Now under the leadership of General Robert Georges Nivelle, one million men of France's 5th, 6th and 10th Armies begin their attack on the heavily entrenched Germans at Chemin des Dames ridge, near Soissons, on the Western Front.

It is Nivelle's firm belief that, with this one masterstroke, the war will be over in a matter of weeks, or even less.

Early success turns to disaster within days.

Over the next four weeks, the French suffer 190,000 casualties, with 30,000 killed, a result so disastrous that Nivelle is replaced by General Philippe Pétain before the month is out, even while the so-called 'offensive' goes on. And yet so devastating have been the massacres of French troops, so wantonly useless their slaughter, that the sacking of Nivelle in no way appeases the survivors, who teeter on the edge of outright revolt.

On 3 May, when 2nd French Division is ordered to attack German forces dug in on a ridge crest at Pinon, the answer comes back: *Non*. The troops, drunk and having thrown away their rifles, refuse. The revolt becomes ever more widespread as the French troops become ever more disgusted by the slaughter and aware that just about *tout le monde* feels the same.

In the end, the only way the government can quell the mutiny is to severely punish – read, shoot – 43 ringleaders and imprison another 3000 while essentially giving in to the mutineers' twin demands. From now on the authorities agree there will be more and extended home leave, and no more massive offensives requiring them to charge to their own useless slaughter. General Pétain, of course, wants to keep this embarrassing affair under wraps, and it soon becomes France's best-kept secret. The French especially want to keep it away from the Germans, who would relish news of a widespread mutiny. When questioned by more inquisitive minds about why the French weren't involved in any attacks at the end of 1917, Pétain was often heard to remark, 'I am waiting for the tanks and the Americans.'[37]

For their part, and for now, the French soldiers agree to hold their positions in the trenches against the Germans – who they hate marginally more than their own officers – but that is it. If the Allies wish to attack the Germans for the rest of the year, it will be the British soldiers and the men of their 'Dominions' – like Australia, New Zealand and Canada – who must do it.

As to the Americans, the first 14,000 of them do indeed arrive on 25 June 1917, aboard four ships that have come in a convoy, escorted by warships deployed to ward off U-boats – docking in the French port of St Nazaire and disembarking the next day to cheering crowds. True, this is only the vanguard, and it will still take another year before they are here in force, fully equipped, trained and ready to go, but it is a good start!

(The reception for the Americans was not always quite what they expected. The story will later be told of what happens when some of the first of the Americans who start to show up around this time arrive in a bar that the Australians have made their own.)

'Say, kid,' one American drawls to the nearest Australian, 'this beer is considerably flat, ain't it?'

'I suppose it is,' says the Australian. 'It has been waiting here three years for you to come and drink it.'[38])

———

In the middle of June 1917, King George V is appalled, nay, *appalled*. At a dinner party at Buckingham Palace, it has been delicately mentioned to him that, because of his family honouring their Germanic roots by being the House of Saxe-Coburg and Gotha, many British people are surmising they have sympathy for the German side of the war. He is so upset he grows pale and leaves the table. In the wake of what had happened to his first cousin, Tsar Nicholas II, just a few short months earlier – now under house arrest with his family at Tsarskoe Selo, after the British government had denied him refuge – this is no time to lose the confidence of one's people. Shortly thereafter, on 19 July 1917, King George announces that the Royal Family has dispensed with the use of German titles and will henceforth be known as 'The House of Windsor'.

The British Prime Minister, David Lloyd George, meanwhile, is struggling with a different crisis.

As ever, the Commander-in-Chief of the British Expeditionary Force, General Sir Douglas Haig, and his Chief of Staff, Sir William Robertson, are demanding yet more troops for the British offensive in Flanders, with the latter blithely estimating, 'One hundred and thirty thousand men would cover the losses on the whole British front during the period of the offensive.'[39]

And yet while military men can toss off such figures, seemingly without blanching, Lloyd George simply cannot. In this war to date, the military has chewed through hundreds of thousands of men for precious few strategic results, and always with the request for more, ever more troops. And they can never answer his central question: given that the combined manpower of the French and British on the Western

Front exceeds that of the Germans, how have they not yet stamped victory upon their enemy?

—

After their period of rest, the Australians had fought at Bullecourt in April and May, and at Messines in June 1917. They rested and rebuilt once again, then in September all five Australian Divisions were thrown into the assault to capture the key Belgian village of Passchendaele,[40] as Haig's first step in his plan to capture Flanders and the German submarine bases along the Belgian coast. It was the first time in the war that all five Divisions of the AIF had fought together, though to the immense frustration of the likes of Australian Prime Minister Billy Hughes and his leading Generals, like John Monash, they were still not under unified command, as one body, with I and II Anzac Corps able to be broken up piecemeal and sent in different directions on British whim.

Yes, just before the war had begun, Andrew Fisher – the man who would be Australian Prime Minister for a short time before Billy Hughes – had vowed that Australia would fight for Great Britain 'to the last man and the last shilling',[41] but as the war had gone on a growing sense of Australian-ness, of being more than merely the sons of Great Britain, had seen an ever stronger desire grow among the Australians to fight as one wholly Australian unit.

New Prime Minister Billy Hughes had taken up the cudgels on the issue time and again, and was slowly making progress.

Meantime, of course, those troops fought on, irrespective of what machinations were occurring at the highest levels. And what a task they had been set at Passchendaele, which heavily armed veteran German troops defended from the top of a ridge on which they had constructed many thick concrete pillboxes. Behind the ridges lay heavy German artillery, ready to lob high-explosive shells into the valleys of thick mud soaked with the blood of those who had already tried and died to make the breakthrough. Over days and then weeks, weeks and then months, the Australians continued their assault. On a good day, only hundreds of Allied soldiers were killed, and the conditions were straight from Dante's *Inferno*.

By battle's end, most of those who had survived physically were nevertheless shattered psychologically. One of them, Private Walter 'Jimmy' Downing, would note of their withdrawal, 'We were a pathetic band, with dirty faces and stubbly beards. All were hysterical in varying degrees.'[42]

As a group, the Australian troops who fought there performed magnificently well, and were particularly impressive in three successful attacks whose names would be entered in Australian military history with great pride: Menin Road, Polygon Wood and Broodseinde.

By the time Passchendaele fell to the Allies, shortly after the Australians pulled out and some thirteen weeks after the campaign had begun, the original aim – to storm down Passchendaele Ridge then push to the north-east, liberating the west of Belgium and in the process capturing the German submarine bases on the Belgian coast – had long been forgotten. The grand plans to conquer Flanders seem have become the obsessive pursuit of the British commander, General Douglas Haig, who had planned and executed the whole campaign, with the problem being that the plan was too grand.

To regain Passchendaele, a mere six miles ahead of where they had started, had cost 325,000 Allied casualties – of whom 38,093 were Australians, meaning (as infantry always suffer the highest casualties) two out of every three Australian infantrymen who fought there were killed or wounded – and 260,000 German casualties. But Haig felt that it had been worth it. The Allies got Passchendaele, all right.

By the end of the Passchendaele campaign, the Australians had confirmed their reputation – at least among French and Belgian civilians, together with their fellow soldiers from other nations, including Germany – as perhaps the best troops the Allies possessed. It was a view that did not necessarily sit easily with the British High Command, who resented the Colonials' notable lack of parade-ground polish, their disdain of discipline, and the extraordinary number of bravery awards they earned, but there was no doubting it – they could fight.

—

In Russia, all is in readiness.

As a first step, after a long night of meetings and discussion with his Bolshevik comrades, Vladimir Lenin prepares a proclamation on behalf of the Military Revolutionary Committee. Distributed through the streets of Petrograd and outwards to the people of Russia on the morning of 7 November, 1917, it reads:[43]

To the Citizens of Russia!

The Provisional Government has been overthrown. State power has passed into the hands of the organ of the Petrograd Soviet of Workers' and Soldiers' Deputies, the Military Revolutionary Committee, which stands at the head of the Petrograd proletariat and garrison . . .[44]

The downfall of the Provisional Government, however, is not yet a *fait accompli*, as many of them are still inside the Winter Palace, albeit surrounded by hostile insurgents outside, and without their leader, Alexander Kerensky, who had fled earlier that day.

At precisely 9.45 pm, the cruiser *Aurora*, at its mooring in the Neva River in Petrograd, fires a blank shot across the river at the Winter Palace.

It is the signal, organised by Vladimir Lenin, and on the instant some 40,000 Bolsheviks – half of whom are trained troops – make their move, storming in quick succession the State Bank, post and telegraph offices, rail terminals and other government buildings, all of which quickly fall.

And now, the ultimate prize. After machine guns rake the entrance and light artillery fire peppers its façade, all out-front defence of the Winter Palace melts away and the Bolsheviks are soon storming up His

Imperial Majesty's own staircase. Like a flood of fury they continue to stream through the hallways, into all the nooks and crannies, searching out and subduing the last of the last remnants of the old guard – which does not take long, as all that old guard can muster are a few Cossacks of the Russian Army and 137 female soldiers of a Women's Battalion raised by the Provisional Government.

Within five hours, the Winter Palace falls to the Red Guards.

By dawn, all of Kerensky's Provisional Government has been ousted and the Bolsheviks are in charge. The next step is everything for which the Germans could have hoped . . .

For, yes, several days later a triumphant Lenin issues a 'Decree on Peace', announcing that his newly found Soviet government will 'begin peace negotiations at once'.[45]

The Bolsheviks want no further part in this capitalist war.

With this decree, it is now obvious to the shocked Allies that, in short order, Germany will have as many as a million troops that they can move from the Eastern Front to the Western Front, giving the Germans a terrifying superiority in manpower in the finely balanced, bloody arena.

It seems likely that those million men will get there before the two million Americans will arrive from across the Atlantic, but nothing is certain. For such matters are not in the lap of the gods, but in the heads of the key men who must make these decisions.

CHAPTER ONE

THE CALM BEFORE THE STORMTROOPERS . . .

The Storm battalion is employed for specially difficult operations. Infantry are led in attack by them. Storm battalions take positions but infantry must hold them. The commander will be warned with regard to the part of the line to which he will be detailed. He will study the position thoroughly and will carry out operations on practice trenches in rear of the front, constructed exactly like the trenches in the line. After the operation is completed, the assaulting troop is withdrawn again.

Directions for a Sturmbataillon, Attack Battalion[1]

The Australians only have three interests
– wine, war and women.[2]
A French mademoiselle, about the AIF's soldiers in WWI,
quoted by Lieutenant George Mitchell in Backs to the Wall

2 NOVEMBER 1917, IN THE AIF LINES BEHIND YPRES, AUSTRALIANS ALL, LET US REJOICE

'You've heard the good news?!' Captain Charles Bean is asked by an Australian officer. Bean is excited by the very question. Perhaps the

Italians, holding on like a cat to a curtain against the Austro-Hungarians and Germans at Caporetto, have been successful at last? Or maybe the Russians or the French have secured their own big victory?

Ah, but it is even better than that.

'The five Australian divisions are to be brought together!'[3] the official Australian war correspondent is informed.

Wonderful! The long campaign, led by Prime Minister Billy Hughes and his dear friend and adviser, the journalist Keith Murdoch, has at last come to fruition.

'The decision,' Charles Bean records, 'which came as a complete surprise to the divisions emerging from Passchendaele, was everywhere hailed with delight.'[4]

Under Haig's order, all five divisions of the AIF will now be under the unified command of Birdwood, the Englishman who, to many eyes, is practically an honorary Australian. But from now on no new British officers will be appointed to the Australian Corps, with all replacements to be Australian. (These divisions, ideally 18,000 men and 4,000 horses each, are the building blocks of battle, each composed in itself of three brigades of infantry, each brigade with four battalions – all of them supported by the division's machine-gun battalion, artillery, engineers and signallers.)

Hooray! After all, a general anti-British feeling is becoming ever more pervasive among the Australian soldiers, most particularly among those who have worked most closely with them.

'Everyone here is "fed-up" of the war, but not with the Hun,' Major Garnet Adcock, a 23-year-old mining engineer from Geelong of the 2nd Australian Tunnelling Company, records. 'The British staff, British methods, and British bungling have sickened us. We are "military socialists" and all overseas troops have had enough of the English. How I wish we were with our own people instead of under the English all the time!'[5]

Other officers are even more enthusiastic as their prospects for promotion surge with the removal of the British officers. Most of the common soldiers are more circumspect, with their focus on their own platoons, companies and battalions rather than memos flying around between the 'brass-hats' and their 'bum-wipers'.

True, the Australians are not now an 'Army', as many had wanted – all of the Armies that comprise the British Expeditionary Force have at least a dozen divisions, and Australia simply cannot muster that – but to be the biggest corps in the whole of the Allied forces, with 110,000 men, is really something.

All that, and the No. 3 Squadron Australian Flying Corps, just now arriving in France, will henceforth be attached to the Australian Corps as its 'Corps squadron'.

Most pleased of all? It is undoubtedly the AIF's 3rd Division, which wasn't formed until after Gallipoli and missed the early battles on the Western Front, such as Fromelles, Pozières and Mouquet Farm, as they had still been in training in Britain at the time. At Passchendaele, they had fought along with the other divisions – and fought well – but were yet to feel a strong bond with the other Australian divisions, since they fought so often apart from them. For months, General John Monash, the highly regarded Commander of 3rd Division, has been referring to his men as the 'new chum' division. The other divisions call the 3rd the 'eggs-a-cook', for the fact that they'd never set foot in Gallipoli or Egypt – where the phrase was bandied about by street vendors selling boiled eggs – but trained in the comfort of England and had colour patches that were egg-shaped.[6]

And don't the other divvies like to remind them of it, frequently singing out a mocking verse, to the tune of 'The Girl I Left Behind Me', whenever members of the 3rd Divvie walk past.

Oh, the First and the Second are in the line
And the Fourth and Fifth are behind them
But when we look for the eggs-a-cook
I'm damned if you can find them[7]

Despite that historical divide between the divisions, however, Monash gives out a directive on the spot that the slouch hats of all his men

– which to this point have been worn with sides down, 'to create *esprit de corps* by a distinction from other divisions'[8] – be turned up on one side, like all the other Australian troops.

(And as a measure of how highly regarded the General is, as Birdwood goes back to Great Britain on three weeks' leave, it is Monash who is placed in temporary command, making him the first Australian to command the Australian Corps.)

What is most urgent now for the Allied forces is to replenish all units, to replace all the men lost in the battle for Passchendaele, but therein lies a real problem – and it is felt most acutely by the British forces.

It stems from a strong difference of opinion between the British Prime Minister, David Lloyd George, and his key commander in France, General Sir Douglas Haig. The latter is urgently demanding more men so that as soon as the winter is over his forces can attack the Germans *again*.

Lloyd George, however, appalled at the slaughter, wishes the British forces to move to a defensive posture only, *à la* the French.

Yes, there will need to be more lives lost to win the war, but if the Allies wait until 1919, they will more likely be *American* lives, not British. Perhaps, if the Prime Minister could, he would even go as far as sacking Haig for the enormous loss of life so far, for so little ground gained, but Haig retains too much support in his Cabinet and with the public – after being so lionised by the British papers – for this to be accomplished. So instead of sacking him, Lloyd George simply refuses to send more troops.

(At least Haig really does retain support in high places, with the Chief of the Imperial General Staff, Sir Henry Wilson, making a point of giving Haig's Chief of Staff a warning to pass on: 'Haig is going to face three attacks – by the Boches, by London and by Paris.'[9] Wilson still believes in his man. 'We shall want D. H. badly when bad times come.')[10]

Still, the implications of being so starved of fresh troops escapes few in the British Army High Command. Meantime, resistance to conscription grows as disillusionment with the war grows. Not for nothing does one of the most popular British pub songs of the time come to the point quickly:

I don't want to join the army,
I don't want to go to war,
I'd rather hang around Piccadilly underground,
Livin' off the earnings of a high born lady

I don't want a bayonet up me arse 'ole,
I don't want me bullocks shot away,
I'd rather stay in England, in merry, merry England,
And fornicate me fuckin' life away.[11]

All up, the situation is grim – and getting grimmer – and one of Haig's key officers, General Henry Rawlinson, even notes in his diary a devastating prediction:

'The man-power situation is really very serious and I gather there is little hope of divisions being made up to strength . . . We should be 150,000 men below establishment in the Spring . . . The Germans are bringing over divisions at the rate of 10 a month from Russia, so that by the end of February we are likely to have a lively time. We shall be thrown on the defensive and shall have to fight for our lives . . .'[12]

Inevitably, the hunger for manpower means the British Army must rely more heavily than ever on both younger and older soldiers than those who had fought in the early years of the war, and that can present challenges of its own.

At one point when Haig is inspecting the ranks, he comes across a fellow much closer to his own age of 56 than the soldiers around him.

'Well,' Haig says in a nigh fraternal fashion, 'and how did you start the war?'

But the old fellow will have none of it. Drawing himself up stiffly, he makes belligerent reply: ''Oo says I started this 'ere blinking war?'[13]

And yes, it's good to have the support of the Colonial troops, and none more so than the highly regarded, if also maddeningly trouble-some, Australians – but even they are problematic. For while their Prime Minister, Billy Hughes, is keen on sending ever more troops – he is even now championing his second unpopular conscription ref-erendum – the public mood is against him, and those who wish to volunteer are thinning. After the horrors of the last four years, there are simply not enough men in Australia coming forth to keep up with the demands of the five divisions.

11 NOVEMBER 1917, KRONPRINZ RUPPRECHT'S HQ AT MONS, A ONCE SLEEPY BELGIAN TOWN

On this day, as ever, General Ludendorff is as cold as Berlin in winter, and the only glint in his eye comes from the monocle that stares from his heavily jowled, red face as he barks orders in his high, nasal voice, his second and third chins quivering from the effort. As rigid and inflex-ible as the hairs on von Hindenburg's head, and every bit as bristling, he is punctilious, obsessed with punctuality and cleanliness. Given to sudden rages, he frequently bangs the table with as much enthusiasm as he frequently bangs the heads of his subordinates.

And yet, while such a manner of military leadership is close to tra-ditional for the Teutonic race, he is also emblematic of the rising new Germany, where even the son of a small business merchant can ascend to high position.

Prince Rupprecht, on the other hand, together with the son of *der Kaiser*, Crown Prince Wilhelm, represent all that is old gold in a Germany that is fading fast. And where two such forces meet, there is bound to be tension, perhaps all the more when it is in the magnificent Hardenpont Château, a towering white jewel set among sweeping gar-dens in a spot just outside Mons, which Prince Rupprecht has taken over as his Western Front headquarters.

For while all the officers there know that the future King of Bavaria is in nothing less than his natural habitat, while the humble Ludendorff grew up in far more modest surroundings, it is equally clear that it is

Ludendorff who must lead this discussion, and so he does – *after* Prince Rupprecht takes his leave.

The essential question before them on this day is how best to use the million German soldiers – over 30 divisions – who can soon be released from the Eastern Front with Russia, together with as many as six German divisions being able to return from the Italian Front after what looks to be a near total collapse of the Italians at Caporetto.

Though he is not as convinced as many of his peers that the Americans will soon be storming Europe, what has been clear to General Ludendorff from the first is that if Germany is to win this war then the Kaiser's forces will have to strike at the Allies before the Americans arrive en masse . . . and also before Germany is overwhelmed by *internal* forces. Though unspoken, it is understood by all at the meeting that with the example of the Bolsheviks before them, with revolution already stirring among German workers, they all need a great victory to circumvent even the possibility of the people rising, perhaps right to the point of toppling the Kaiser himself, just as had happened to the Tsar.

(It is far from certain the government can count on the support of the German soldiers, most particularly when on their own fronts they continue to receive such letters as this from the home front: 'I am so sick and tired of life that I want to cut my own and my children's throats . . . They take the breadwinner away [to the front] and let the children starve to death, they are crying for bread the whole day long . . .'[14])

Germany needs a major victory, and it needs it now.

But where on the Western Front is that victory to be achieved? There are three options: in the north, directly against the Channel ports via Hazebrouck; in the centre at St Quentin then turning north and driving the British into the sea; or against the French in the south around Verdun.

After discussion of every option, all eyes finally turn to General Ludendorff.

Speaking in short, truncated sentences, a kind of military shorthand, he agrees that they must attack with their bolstered forces from

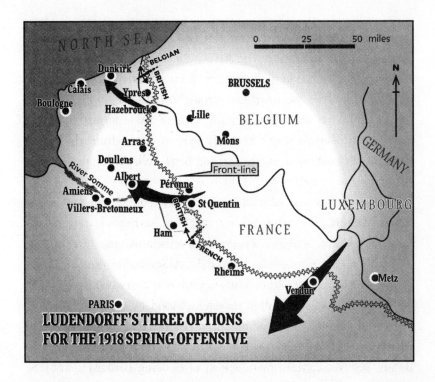

Russia and Italy. But even if the German soldiers do break through at Verdun, the terrain on the French side of the line there is wooded and hilly, hardly amenable to the kind of lightning movement the attackers would need in order to round up all Allied forces and bring the war to a close.

And so Germany's coming attack must be against the British, in country ideally suited for such rapid movement. The idea to attack up north in Flanders, around the low ground of Hazebrouck, is interesting, but the problem is if the spring brings rain that country would be too muddy to move across quickly, and their start may be delayed until mid-April. This, in view of the likely readiness of the Americans for front-line service only a few months after that, is too late.

The Germans need to attack, instead, in late February or early March, and there is only one place held by the British where the conditions will allow that: the Somme.

'It would seem,' Ludendorff starts slowly, 'an attack near St Quentin

31

appears promising. After reaching the line of the Somme . . . it might be possible . . . to advance the attack still farther in a north-western direction, and thus eventually roll up the British front.'[15]

Essentially, the German Army must reverse the British Somme Valley campaign of 1916 and push back in the opposite direction. But instead of measuring their daily advance in yards, as the British had done in pushing east, the key will be to break through and then advance a dozen miles a day to the west!

The key, of course, is to destroy the British Army and its entire supply network.

'For the success of this operation,' Ludendorff says, 'it would be especially necessary to render useless the various rail centres by means of long-range artillery and bombing squadrons. This would create difficulties for the timely arrival of the enemy's strategic reserves.'[16]

As the supreme military figure in Germany speaks, the eyes of his fellow Generals continue to dart to the maps, and it is clear what he means. Just a mile from the outskirts of the German-held town of St Quentin is the most weakly held part of the British lines. If they could push through there on a front 20 miles each side of that town, the British and the French would be definitively cleaved, and the British caught like rats in a trap. The German Army could turn north-westwards to chase the British all the way to the Channel ports of Calais and Boulogne. With Germany controlling those ports of entry for most British supplies and reinforcements, the British would have no way to supply themselves, no possibility of getting away, no choice but to surrender. What is more, the French flank would be exposed, the road to Paris open, and the Germans in possession of the French coast directly opposite southern England.

Ludendorff makes no final decision but orders further studies on the options available, working on the principles that:

1. The situation in Russia and Italy will probably enable us in the new year to strike a blow on the Western Front . . .

2. Our general situation requires an attack as early as possible,

at the end of February or start of March, before the arriving
American forces tip the scales.

3. The British must be knocked out of the war.[17]

—

In anticipation of the Germans doing precisely what they are preparing
for, on 7 December 1917, General Haig holds a meeting of his army
commanders in the French town of Doullens.

Among other things, he orders the establishment of a defensive
system composed of three zones: a front zone, a battle zone and a
rear zone. Yes, the Germans will attack, and perhaps carve their way
through the three lines, but the Brits must do everything possible to
exhaust the German resources in the process of their breaking through,
so they won't be able to go far afterwards.

—

Meanwhile, word of the Russian collapse and exit from the war makes
its way along the trench telegraph and into the Diggers' dugouts and
concerns. For Corporal Louis Avery – now in training with his 3rd
Field Company, just south of Calais – the fact that the Russians will no
longer be at war with Germany is bloody annoying.

We will be up against a powerful German offensive in the spring and
anything may happen. They will do their utmost to take the Channel
ports and drive us into the sea. I repeat, we will <u>blunder</u> through in the
mud, but we are mad with Russia deserting.[18]

For the most part, though, the Diggers are far more enraptured by
quotidian concerns . . .

In the hurly-burly of life in this war, of launching attack after attack
in this godforsaken conflict, before counting their dead, removing their
wounded, welcoming their recruits and doing it all once more . . . again
and again . . . and again, this winter starting in December 1917 will
always stand out as a period of rare respite, just when it is most needed.

In Brigadier Bill Glasgow's 13th Brigade, for example, '129 men had not taken leave for over twelve months, including forty-three for more than fifteen months and twenty-five over eighteen months.'[19]

They are desperate for a rest, and now, for the first time in many months, as December's chill sets in, the Australians are at least able to stay in the one spot, in this case on the high ground south of Ypres, including the village of Messines.

Well, at least it used to be a village, and it was likely a very pleasant one at that. Now . . . not quite. It lies on that fault line of the whole Western Front, where German thrust had met almost exactly the Allied parry. Most of the larger buildings are now rubble, and you can trace where the streets used to be – it's where the rubble is less concentrated. After the Germans had first taken Messines in 1914, they had fortified it heavily and held it until June 1917. The British (including Monash's 3rd Division, in its first big battle) had retaken it in the Battle of Messines, desperate to regain the towering heights of the ridge, where you could look out over the Flemish plains to the east and north, including the hard-fought-for Ypres itself, which has been under British control since November 1914. Who controls Messines ridge effectively controls those plains. Even more importantly, Messines also protects Hazebrouck from a German advance. Hazebrouck, 15 miles in the rear of the Australians on the ridge, is to the northern half of the British line what Amiens is to the southern half – a vital rail junction through which British supplies and reinforcements must pass, or see the British Army wither and die.

It is a prime place for the Australian Corps, one of the finest on the entire Front, to be quartered for the winter against the possibility that the Germans might try to regain this vital position from their own front-line, which is only some 400 yards to the east. Yes, the Australians are on constant rotation through those front-line trenches, and forever doing drills and training in reserve, but with the Germans on the other side being almost as exhausted and frozen as they are, there is almost a tacit understanding that this is to be a quiet time on both sides of the line.

Thankfully, the farms dotted along Messines Ridge and just south around Ploegsteert Wood are mostly intact, as are most of their barns, and it is in such places that many of the Australians are billeted. After the horrors of what they have been through, for most of the Australians it is a pleasant existence. They wake most mornings to the song of the nightingale, as 'even during the war these birds were heard to sing melodiously in the devastated woodland'.[20]

In the devastated village itself, the heavy snow that has fallen takes away much of the sheer ugliness of it and, on a good day, with your mates, you can almost imagine you are living in a winter wonderland!

It's not all play, though, as the reserve units dedicate their mornings to training drills; route marching so endless that it would kill a brown dog; bombing and bayonet practice to learn how to better kill Germans, the whole lot of it by now as routine as it is dull. One thing that helps pass the time is gazing up to the heavens, where an ever-growing number of aeroplanes dart in wasp-like movements that never cease to amaze the Anzacs. No matter what dark ends the aeroplanes' bombs and guns might mean for them as infantry, should they meet such an unlucky fate, they can't help but marvel at the topsy-turvy dogfights. It is a sight never before seen in history.

The new recruits are also issued with gasmasks, and they must learn something of the dangers they face. With one of these gas masks you can last as long as five hours. But you have to be quick in getting it on – with a favourable wind behind it, the gas can travel much faster than a man can run away from it. Lecture succeeds lecture, drill succeeds drill.

At least in the afternoon and evenings, when their time is their own, the men can relax. Despite the cold and monotony, they fill their breaks with inter-Battalion football games, snow fights and visiting mates in distant billets. By far the greatest source of excitement over the winter, though, is when – you bloody beauty – the men get precious leave. And of course the officers tend to choose the rarefied air of the South of France for their rest. The Riviera is always so nice, what? But not for the men, not for the soldiers.

Give them Paris any day, and all they ask is a few francs in their pocket and hitching a ride in a lorry to get there. What a joy it is to drink, to carouse, to hobnob in cafes, try out la vie Parisienne and, most particularly, try their luck with the French sheilas, perhaps taking them to a theatre show or a music hall, and even forgiving them the fact that most of them can only 'parleyvous', as the Diggers call speaking French, and don't understand English at all! Luckily, the men know just enough French to get by . . .

So Bill he quietly lit a fag,
He found behind his ear.
'I'll bet I make her parleyvous,
Before I go from here.

So Bill he called the tart again,
And swore he'd make her 'bite' –
'Deux beer, encore, please s'il vous plait,
I'm talkin' French tonight . . .[21]

(It is not one-way traffic, however, with a fair measure of French, after a fashion, entering the Digger's language. *'Napoo'*, for example, means 'There is no more', from the French *'il n'y a plus'*. *Napoo* beer, mate! And *'Alley toot sweet'* – adapted from *allez, tout de suite* – means 'Get moving, you bastards,' and is an alternative for the veteran Diggers' language, from their time training in Egypt, of using the Arabic *igri* for 'Fucking hurry up.' In similar fashion, *'Commong talley voo'* is for 'How you goin'?'; *'Compree?'* means 'Understood?' And *'San fairy ann,'* from *ca ne fait rien* means 'It doesn't matter.')

The more daring among the men, of course, head off to the *Folies Bergère* to see the gorgeous dancing girls. It is all so much more *soffis-tic-ated*, cobber, than the haphazard, bustling, sweaty debauchery of the Wazza red-light district back in Cairo. That had been so raw. This is so exotic . . . meets *erotic* . . . as the growing body of Digger poetry hints at:

The Signal Sergeant went to Paris
With a pocketful of dough
And 'Done' the swellest cafes
With a swagger dontcherknow
He swears he had a good time
Quite the one time of his life
But I'll lay a franc or forty
That he didn't tell his wife.[22]

For the men with as long as a *fortnight*'s leave, however, there is only one destination worth speaking of: Ol' Blighty. For the quarter of the AIF who were born there, and the well over half who have parents born there, it is even something of a homecoming, frequently with relatives to visit.

And oh, the joy of sleeping in comfortable beds, eating in swank restaurants, sitting on actual chairs and, for the wealthier among them, putting on the Ritz *at* the Ritz.

'It is a great and unique feeling to be on leave!' one Digger writes in a letter home from London. 'To ride up Bond Street in a taxi, or lie back in a stall at the Allambra smoking a fat cigar and seeing the latest revue. It is like going to one's first theatre . . . Life has a boyish zest and is well worth living on leave.'[23]

One Anzac, who already has more boyish zest than he quite knows what to do with, is Lieutenant George Deane Mitchell. Hailing from the tiny town of Caltowie in South Australia's farmland east of Port Pirie, 'Mitch' is a handsome, confident and well-loved young man. He had stormed the beach at Gallipoli at dawn on 25 April 1915 and has survived more than a year on the Western Front under Colonel 'the Bull' Leane, with the storming 48th Battalion, which had been thrown into its first battle in France at Pozières the year before. The Battalion had lost heavily in 1917, both at Bullecourt and then Passchendaele, but Mitch has come through it all – to his amazement – not only alive but unscathed.

And how good is it be alive, and in London!

'It is impossible to describe just what leave means to the soldier,' he would recount. 'For a similar depth of happiness, one must go back to childhood. The leave pass with its printed and written lines is a passport to ten days of heaven . . . We Diggers were a race apart. Long separation from Australia seemed to cut us completely away from the land of our birth. The longer a man served, the fewer letters he got, the more he was forgotten. Our only home was our unit, and that was constantly decimated by battle, and rebuilt by strangers.'

A man who has studied history, Mitch is aware that his experience is one that has been replicated through the ages.

'For a parallel, one would need to go back to some Roman Legion, serving many years in a foreign country, cut off from Rome, alien to the new land and the old, sure only of themselves . . . So, beneath the old felt hat I swaggered down the Strand with an air that inferred, "Make way for an Aussie on leave."'[24]

Ah, but careful.

Beware the English officers *insisting* on strict protocol being observed at all times. At one point, Mitch's fellow Digger, Corporal Louis Avery, is walking with a mate along Victoria Street when they are approached by a pompous git of a British Naval officer who, with two plums in his mouth, informs them that he is the 'Provost Marshal' – don't they *know*? The head of Military Police – and they have just failed to salute an Admiral.

'How are we to know who to salute in the Navy?' the mate asks. 'They have nothing to do with us and we seldom come into contact with the Navy in France.'

Avery is equally unimpressed.

'This was a deliberate trap to catch the unwary,' he records, 'and [the Provost Marshal] was following the Admiral purposely to find fault. This is one of the mean English tricks which we detest and is often practised. If this is the correct way to win the war, let them all call in the whole British Navy and we will salute the whole bally lot.'[25]

The experience of General John Monash is quite the reverse. In London at the same time, getting a fresh suit made, it is his great joy *not* to be in uniform, for the very specific benefits it offers.

'It was a new sensation,' he would write to his wife, Hannah, 'to be able to walk about the streets without having constantly to return the salutes of the soldiery. It was quite delightful to be jostled and edged into the gutter by crowds of young second lieutenants and Tommies.'[26]

Finally, of course, for officers and soldiers alike, it is over, and Mitch must head back to France, Messines, and the trenches where all his mates and fellow officers await.

'Thought you'd declared a separate peace,'[27] say the boys, making light of the news that Russia is out of the war.

For most of the men newly returned from leave, it is remarkable how quickly such pleasant memories fade as they throw themselves back into their training and their duties – to defend the line along Messines Ridge. One Digger who finds himself in the front-lines a lot over this freezing winter is Jimmy Downing, a Sergeant of the 57th Battalion in the legendary Brigadier Pompey Elliott's 15th Brigade that had been so devastated at the Battle of Fromelles but has since replenished its numbers to give sterling service at Bullecourt and Polygon Wood.

For his part, Downing, the enterprising young private who was so keen to enlist that he had stretched himself by tying weights to his feet, is continuing to prove the height restrictions for the AIF are a farce; he is awarded a Military Medal for his singularly brave actions in the Battle of Polygon Wood. It really *is* all about the 'size of the fight in the dog', not the other way around, then.

Of this winter on Messines Ridge, he would recall, 'The rains came, the frosty night bound our world in ice, it snowed. Snowstorms were the characteristic feature of this winter. They drifted unrelentingly down. The great flakes found their way through the smallest chinks in our shelters and filled our dugouts with fluffy heaps that melted and soaked us.'[28]

Like it had been at Gallipoli from late November, this is a cold unlike many of them have ever experienced, a cold that descends in the late afternoon, steals across the ravaged landscape and first settles in the trenches – where it stealthily begins turning flesh to ice, laying siege to the soul – before it starts seeping into the marrow of men's bones.

And once there, it does not leave. All the men can do is shiver and shudder, and wait it out until their long tour of duty – six or seven days in the front-line, followed by much the same in the support line just behind – is done. And in the meantime, with rumour circulating that there are scores of German divisions from Russia starting to assemble behind enemy lines, they are keenly aware that an attack could come at any time.

'We knew that when it came not many of us would survive, but we were determined that those who escaped it would give a good account of themselves. We expected [an attack] every morning and every evening. We stood to arms and waited. December passed, and it did not come.'[29]

From here, Australia seems far, far away and as Christmas approaches, many of the men are missing home more than ever. Just how long will this blasted war go on for? When will we have to fight again? Is there no chance of an Armistice?

Not for the moment, it seems.

And nor are they likely to be replaced any time soon by fresh troops from Australia, as the recruitment drives have now slowed to a trickle. Here they are, 110,000 Australians in France – about a tenth of the entire British fighting forces – reduced to getting their reinforcements mostly from those men returning from hospital after being wounded in the battle of Passchendaele.

At least for them all, far from home this Chrissie, there is the saving grace for Australian soldiers on the Western Front, the many estaminets – 'Staminays', as the Diggers say in their butchered French – small establishments set up by cash-strapped French citizens that are part cafe, part bar, even part brothel. They are places where, at base level, Madame and her minions can serve anything from piping-hot tea to *vin blanc* – inevitably referred to by the Diggers as 'Point Blank'[30] – to watery beer and, of course, delicious food from Madame's kitchen, including eggs and chips, for less than one pence (just one and a half francs).

'Quatre eggs!' calls out Madame to the cook after two Diggers walk in and place their order for four eggs.

'Cat eggs bejiggered!' one of the hungry Diggers shouts with rage. 'I want hen eggs!'[31]

And while someone is inevitably banging out a tune on an old piano, more often than not there is a different kind of banging going on upstairs, as soldiers take their turns with French girls who are *extremely* liberal with their favours in return for just five francs.

Sexual, emotional, physical, spiritual, in this freezing winter so far from home, from loved ones and lovers alike, the estaminets, as one Digger, would recall, 'gave warmth outwardly and inwardly'.[32]

And oh, the laughs!

One night, Private Jim Magee of 51st Battalion is in his favourite estaminet with his mates, and is at least three sheets to the wind, likely as pissed as *two* newts, when he decides to dance on the tabletop. No matter all the bottles and glasses, Jimmy does his best to imitate the dance of the most sensuous woman imaginable. Blokes fall about shrieking with laughter, and the bottles and glasses are sent flying everywhere! Oh, the fun.

They are Australians, far from their homes, but they have each other and that is something.[33]

———

Of course, on their side of the lines, the German soldiers enjoy exactly the same kind of establishments.

'It was very popular and had lots of visitors,' Private Heinrich Wandt would reminisce about a particular place. 'Its [French] landlord had seven daughters, the youngest 14 years old. The soldiers never called this establishment other than "*Die vierzehn Hintern*" – "The Fourteen Buttocks". Without doubt it was the most popular . . . in the rear area.'[34]

In the German Army, meanwhile, a new purpose filters among the soldiers. For, yes, although continuing to man the trenches is as wretched as ever before, manning the Western Front and being far from their families as Christmas approaches, the word spreads of the coming action.

As one soldier writes in a letter on 16 December 1917: '. . . already mighty preparations are being made for the spring. Everybody understands "spring" means "offensive", and everybody derives fresh activity from this thought.'[35]

It is a theme he returns to a week later, in a letter to the same recipient.

'Here one has only one thought – in the spring – and everyone feels convinced. Everyone feels that a damnable thorn has been removed from the flesh since Russia has opened peace negotiations.'[36]

In the meantime, the aforementioned 'mighty preparations' go on, a large part of which is to teach the most elite of the German Army the way of attacking developed by a new kind of German soldier – *Stoßtruppen*, stormtroopers – named in honour of the troops of Captain Willy Rohr, who, pursuing new tactics pioneered by him, had done so well in the battle of Verdun, and have done well since. Instead of just charging out of their trenches to attack in wave after wave, hoping to simply overwhelm the enemy by sheer weight of numbers, with more soldiers than the enemy has bullets, the stormtroopers seek to avoid a head-on attack, instead advancing through previously identified weak points. They would then attack sensitive nerve centres, like enemy HQs, artillery batteries and ammunition dumps. As they move, they must use whatever cover presents itself, and always be on the look out to provide flanking fire for other groups of stormtroopers on their right and left, *without* waiting for them if they are held up.

In sum, the German Army must finally do away with *Materialschlacht* – the battle of attrition that has marked the war to date, as it is simply a test of who will run out of resources first. In which case, Germany will definitely lose. Instead, they must move to *Bewegungskrieg* – mobile warfare – to break through, break out and, finally, break the enemy himself. No more can they afford to simply bend the enemy's line, they must make it disintegrate.

'We must not,' Ludendorff insists to his senior officers 'copy the enemy's massed tactics, which offer advantages only in the case of untrained troops.'[37]

Nein, these men are to act as highly trained individuals, working together in small teams. While the stormtroopers sow havoc behind Allied lines, the specially trained infantry battalions, using extra-light machine guns, mortars and flamethrowers, would move forward on narrow fronts – aided by precisely targeted mortar and field gun fire – to take over whatever Allied strong points the stormtroopers have bypassed. (It is the foundation stones for a famed German tactic later to be called 'Blitzkrieg'.) Finally, regular infantry battalions would come forward to secure all the territory that has been gained and kill off whatever last bits of Allied resistance remains.

'We were,' von Hindenburg would note, 'completely renouncing the mass tactics in which the individual soldier finds the driving force in the protection given him by the bodies of the men around him, a form of tactics with which we had become extremely familiar . . .'[38]

Ludendorff, typically, has used his organisational skills to bring together the masterminds of these new tactics, so they can drive the change and train the men. Notable among them is General Oskar von Hutier, the Commanding Officer of the 18th Army, who has already done so brilliantly well employing these tactics with his own men at the battle of Riga in September 1917. Also heavily involved is von Hutier's Artillery Chief, Colonel Georg Bruchmüller – a man Ludendorff will later call 'one of the most prominent soldiers of this war'[39] – who has developed new artillery tactics to go with this new form of attack.

The German troops prepare through the winter.

Those training can feel themselves getting stronger, more mobile, by the day. 'We had to drag machine guns, fling bombs, advance along trenches and crawl without a sound,' a stormtrooper will later recount of such training. 'At first, it was a severe strain on me. I sweated on every occasion and several times everything reeled around me, but only for a short time. Then, daily it grew easier. We were on duty from morning to night with only a two-hour interval at midday. I had no time for reflection and felt in good trim.'[40]

No small part of the need for this training and the whole impending attack for the German leadership is to provide the men with what it is considered they most need.

'Release from the leaden pressure of nerve-shattering trench warfare,' Crown Prince Wilhelm would note, 'was the ardent desire of the whole army in the West.'[41]

Always, the emphasis, beyond storming through and around defences, is coordinating different elements of the attack with each other.

'To that end companies, battalions and regiments were trained in the cooperation of infantry with machine guns, trench-mortars, escort batteries, aircraft and tanks, the use of searchlight and visual signals, the employment of gas, a smoke shell, etc.'[42]

And, of course, they keep to a strict timetable as much as possible, training as if they are in an actual battle.

At exactly Zero Hour – say, 5.30 am – it is the artillery's job to begin the bombardment on the targets that have been set.

5.29:30 . . .

5.29:40 . . .

5.29:50 . . .

Fünf . . . vier . . . drei . . . zwei . . . eins . . . und FEUER!

And repeat.

The infantrymen and the grenadiers have their own protocols to drill. Over the roar of the guns they listen for the sound of the bugles, the tunes they play indicating what the order is.

'*Protzen Heran!*' yells the Sergeant. Get ready to move.

There! Can you hear it? The bugles . . .

Kartoffelsuppe. Kartoffelsuppe. Potato soup, potato soup

Den ganzen Tag, Kartoffelsuppe All day long, potato soup

Kartoffelsuppe Potato soup

Und kein Fleisch And no meat[43]

It means, *advance*, and in an instant the men are doing exactly that – running.

On orders from General Ludendorff, who is following the training closely, such men are Die Besten der Besten of the German Army – no one older than 25, single and fearless, aggressive, natural-born killers and supreme athletes who are as physically hard as they are mentally tough.

Officers and soldiers alike must memorise the key elements of the handbook, *The Attack in Position Warfare*, that they are all issued with – bearing the signature of Ludendorff himself – on how to 'overrun the enemy's trench system so rapidly and penetrate it so deeply that the enemy's reserves could not arrive in time, even if they arrived at all, and finally to resume the thrust behind the broken front, vital importance was attached to the factor of surprise.'[44]

For these elements are key:

A. INTRODUCTION
This manual deals with the attack in position warfare with a limited objective and the offensive battle leading from position warfare to the break-through . . .

GENERAL PRINCIPLES
Education of the troops in that spirit of bold attack and will to conquer, with which we entered the present war, is the first guarantee of success.

The instruction of commanders and troops for the attack cannot be too minute or thorough.

Formations that are going to take part must have rehearsals of the attack against trenches specially constructed for the purpose; the smallest details must be practiced . . .

The **offensive battle** is an effort to obtain a tactical penetration and the ultimate development from there of a strategical break-through. In the latter case it works up to the **battle for a break-through**, which aims at compelling open warfare.[45]

> **Surprise** – The greatest successes in war are to be looked
> for from measures for which the enemy is least prepared.
> Therefore, in all offensive actions, surprise of the enemy is of
> decisive importance . . .
>
> **Importance of the above principles** – If the principles here
> briefly laid down receive due attention, we shall be victorious
> in attack on the Western front . . .[46]

Yes, there is an enormous amount of work to get through, but the reason they set to it with an iron will is 'primarily due to the vitalizing effect of the very idea of the offensive. It seemed to double the energies, output and devotion of everyone, even those who at first were denied the good fortune of participating in the attack.'[47]

One medico with a German battalion of stormtroopers, *Herr* Doctor Stephen Westman – a dapper young fellow with brilliant blue eyes who is highly regarded by all and sundry for his skills, notwithstanding he had not yet earned his medical degree when the war had begun – is nothing if not impressed.

'The men of the storm battalions were treated like football stars,' he would observe. 'They lived in comfortable quarters, they travelled to the "playing grounds" in buses, they did their job and disappeared again, and left the poor footsloggers to dig in, to deal with the counter-attacks, and to endure the avenging artillery fire of the enemy.'[48]

But he has no doubt. Come the next major assault, the stormtroopers are going to be very, very hard to stop . . .

LATE DECEMBER 1917, PRINCE RUPPRECHT GROUP HQ, MONS, THE PLAN CRYSTALLISES

Such is the way of these things in the German Army. No matter that *Kronprinz* Rupprecht is the General in charge of almost a million soldiers on the Western Front, he has not been invited to the conference in the charming German spa town of Kreuznach by the Rhine, held right before the New Year and hosted by General Ludendorff, to discuss the growing outlines of the Spring Offensive. Rupprecht must now get the details from his just-returned Chief of Staff, General Hermann von Kuhl, whom he trusts implicitly. The news is that the transfer of the German troops from the Eastern Front to the Western Front is proceeding smoothly. By the end of February, German forces would outnumber those of the Allies, meaning that the Germans would be in shape to launch their offensive by the middle of March, as soon as all their men and materiel are in position and the snow had melted in the spring sunshine.

The way it is all turning out, by mid-February, once the Divisions have returned from the East, the German Army will have an extraordinary 196 Divisions in the West, with 116 of them holding the line, and another 80 in reserve, ready to move where required. In short, for the first time since just after the war began, the numbers game on the Western Front is turning Germany's way.

'What entitles us to hope that in spring a breakthrough will succeed,' Prince Rupprecht writes in his diary, 'is that we believe ourselves to be operatively more nimble than our opponents, and that we never possessed so many reserves and as much artillery, than we will have in spring. The aim is to put an end to a prolongation of the war with a great blow. If it fails, then of course we are in a very bad situation.'[49]

9 JANUARY 1918, FROM THE HEAVENS ABOVE, TO HELL ON EARTH

For a British Empire pilot, it is the modern version of 'crossing the Rubicon'.

That is, after completing your training, you fly with your squadron across the English Channel into the war-zone of France. In just one flight, you pass from a green and pleasant land of bonhomie and good cheer to a place where every time you take off, the angels of death are your wingmen . . . the devil takes the hindmost and . . . you just hope that God is your observer.

Alas for Lieutenant Harold Cobby, so paltry are his own logged flying hours – a mere 'twelve or thirteen hours'[50] solo – he must suffer the humiliation of taking a *boat* across the channel, in the company of the mechanics and other ground staff in their squadron, who the cocky young pilots call 'emus'.

Soon enough, however, once they are landed a motor lorry takes them to their new aerodrome at Bruay, near Arras, with hangars that are 'contrivances of timber and canvas', while their sleeping quarters look 'more like a gypsy camp'[51] than anything else. And that booming in the distance? That, dear friends, is the guns of the Western Front!

Somehow, this war has contrived to put Cobby and his pilot mates, most of whom have 'not even fired a gun from the air', and some of whom had flown even fewer hours than him, centre stage in this notoriously deadly theatre.

'And here we were,' Cobby would recall, 'about to give battle in the air to the enemy as fighting pilots . . . We were novices almost to a man.'[52]

Given they are about to go up against the likes of the most legendary German fighter pilot of all, Baron von Richthofen himself, it certainly helps to concentrate the mind wonderfully as the men throw themselves into ever more serious training, poring over maps and aerial photographs to familiarise themselves with the lie of the land, receiving instructions about their new 'busses', as pilots are prone to call their planes. They have been assigned to fly Sopwith Camels – so named because of the hump from the cockpit forward to the nose – much to Harry Cobby's delight.

And of course they hang on every word from the grizzled flying veterans, some older than 25, who have been sent to give them the benefit of their experience. Now, whatever else happens, *'Beware the Hun in the sun!'* The Germans' preference will be to attack you with the sun right behind them, making them effectively invisible in the glare. But *constantly* look behind you, anyway. In fact, wear a silk scarf because, if you are doing it properly, it will stop the otherwise inevitable chafe from your collars.

Learn to read the signs, like when they leave traps for you: 'An unfrightened lumbering old German two-seater, or a couple of them, in the offing and low down, gave to British aerial huntsmen a direct warning of danger lurking in the sun or clouds above.'[53]

And some other things to bear in mind: 'Approach the enemy from the east, the direction he'll least expect because it's towards Germany. Sight your own guns and don't leave it to the mechanics. Attack enemy fighters from above and two seaters from below . . . Never fly straight in a dogfight except when firing. Always keep an eye on the strength of the wind, which usually blows west to east and risks taking you further over Hunland than you want to go . . . Never follow a damaged enemy down to earth.'[54]

Finally, the big day comes for No. 4 Squadron of the Australian Flying Corps to make their first sortie into 'Hunland' . . .

For Cobby, walking out to their Sopwith Camels is surreal, and as he looks around he can't help but feel that they are 'collectively about the most ignorant batch of pilots, as far as knowledge of air fighting went, that you could find in France'.[55]

His flight crew has the 'rather prosaic task of escorting a photographic machine into Hunland and back again'. Surely they can handle that!

Cobby comes up to his bus and looks up at the big aluminium cut-out of Charlie Chaplin, which he had prepared back in England and painted according to the latest screen version of the now famous comedian's get-up. Chaplin is to be his personal war mascot, and so Cobby has screwed two figures of him to each side of his Camel's fuselage. Above and below his mascot are bolted two signs, which he had 'borrowed' from a train in England. One reads, 'CAUTION – IT IS DANGEROUS TO LEAN OUT OF THE WINDOWS,' and the other, 'PLEASE DO NOT SPIT.'[56]

Cobby allows himself a smile before hopping up into the cockpit.

Within minutes the Flight Commander is leading the novice pilots up, up and away from the Bruay aerodrome 'in diamond formation', with Cobby as 'the last man of the diamond'.[57]

What a day!

Once up in the air, Cobby spends his whole time looking behind him or into the sun, certain that enemy planes are lurking, looking to kill him. He must be vigilant. The truth is, there are no enemy planes at all, and after 90 minutes of fabulous flying the puppy pilots return, exultant and just starting to growl with intent for the first time.

'We naturally felt bucked at having done the first patrol over the line,' Cobby would recall, 'small as it was. Matthews did say that we stuck so closely to him that he was frightened at times to turn his machine for fear of running some of us down, but that did not matter – we were home.'[58]

From this day on, they start to go up almost daily, weather permitting.

Most troubling to many of the pilots is the enemy ground fire, the German 'Ack-Ack' anti-aircraft fire (or 'Archie', as it is known among them) that constantly arrows its way up from the ground, seeking to blow them out of the sky. Usually the German gunners badly underestimate the height, setting their fuse so short that the shells explode a safe distance beneath them, as they have been taught to keep their planes at an altitude of at least 15,000 feet to give themselves a margin of safety. They'll just have to cope with the blinding headaches they'll get from lack of oxygen.

(For, although the Ack-Ack guns can fire up to 20,000 feet – higher than these pilots can fly – after 15,000 feet a hit is extremely unlikely because the shell takes fifteen seconds to get there. As soon as the first one explodes, the pilot changes course and the later shells will miss by a mile. Fifteen seconds later, the pilot slightly alters course again . . .)

When it comes to Ack-Ack, though, the old adage put forth by the great German philosopher Friedrich Nietzsche, 'That which does not kill us makes us stronger', does not always hold, particularly not in the mental sphere.

The truth is that some of Cobby's fellow new pilots simply cannot cope and return to the base as jabbering wrecks. They had thought they were cut out for the Flying Corps, but simply are not. Invariably, they are sent back to England with 'a case of nerves'.

Bit by bit, however, Cobby himself starts to get used to the perils and pitfalls of flying, and even enjoy the challenge, feeling a little stronger and more confident every day.

The only kind of Archie that remotely troubles him is something the pilots refer to as 'flaming onions', even though they actually resembled 'a lot of red-hot eggs strung together'. The *Licht pucker*, 'light spitter', as the German gunners call it, can set the mostly wooden planes on fire in seconds.

'Personally I think they were fairly harmless,' Coby would note, 'and that their value lay in the extremely demoralizing effect of meeting fire in the air . . .'[59]

16 JANUARY 1918, BERLINER STADTSCHLOSS, BERLIN CITY PALACE, TO AMIENS OR NOT TO AMIENS?

The very insolence of it!

On this day, in his Berlin palace on *Museumsinsel* – Museum Island on the Spree River – *der Kaiser* is suddenly confronted by *Generalfeldmarschall* Hindenburg, demanding the resignation of the Cabinet head, Rudolf von Valentini.

Hindenburg, 70 years old, is warm, genial and famous throughout Germany as the country's most trusted soldier. Just how highborn in the aristocracy he is can be judged by the length of his name – Paul Ludwig Hans Anton von Beneckendorff und von Hindenburg. But being so highborn means he can speak frankly and even coldly, even to one so high as the Kaiser, and this is such an occasion.

'The whole army,' Hindenburg tells the Kaiser, 'has lost confidence in the Government, and the fate of the whole offensive now lies in the balance.'[60]

(Admiral Müller, the faithful chronicler of all things Kaiser in his diary, would record his feelings: 'More blackmail then!')

In response, *der Kaiser* is apoplectic with rage.

'I don't need your paternal advice!'[61] he roars at his Field Marshal before slamming the door in his face.

Still, Valentini resigns within a day.

Nothing, not even insolence, can be allowed to interfere with the execution of *der Frühjahrsoffensive*, the Spring Offensive, as it has become increasingly obvious in a Germany beset with external threats and internal tensions – the Americans will soon be on their way en masse, and workers' strikes in Germany are becoming ever more virulent.

One who needs no convincing about the virtues of the attack is General Ludendorff. In fact, at this time he is visiting his front-line commanders to discuss the coming offensive so that he can make a final decision about where, exactly, to drive their spear.

By tour's end, he is convinced more than ever what the best way forward is. In a conference of his commanders held at Avesnes on 21 January 1918, they begin to work on the details.

With the Chiefs of Staff gathered, Ludendorff gets underway.

'We talk too much about operations,' he famously intones at the beginning of the meeting, 'and too little about tactics.'[62]

That is, while there has been endless discussion about where they should press their attack on the Allies, and what should be done once they have broken through, there has been altogether too little discussion about *how* they make that initial breakthrough.

He is clear about what the key is: 'We chop a hole [in the enemy line] and the rest follows. We did it that way in Russia.'[63]

So it really is obvious to the rotund Prussian officer.

A massive assault, codenamed *Unternehmen Michael*, Operation Michael, will be their opening and primary attack. With a starting point centred on St Quentin, it will roll forth across a 45-mile front, extending from Arras (via St Quentin) to just south of the Oise, straight at the British 3rd and 5th Armies.

Reflecting on his thinking at the time, Ludendorff would later note, 'If this blow succeeded the strategic result might indeed be enormous, as we should cut the bulk of the English Army from the French and crowd it up with its back to the sea. I favoured the centre attack; but I was influenced by the time factor and by tactical considerations, first among them being the weakness of the enemy.'[64]

And there really is no doubt that the weakest point of the British front lies in the southern part, just to the east of Amiens – which itself lies along the dead-straight Roman road that goes for no less than 45 miles without a bend, from St Quentin through Villers-Bretonneux.

Every bit of intelligence the Germans can gather points to the British Expeditionary Force having placed most of their defensive resources in the north, where the Channel ports lie closest to the Western Front and so must be vigorously defended. The defence gets progressively weaker and thinner on the ground as it moves to the south, from the Third Army on, held by General Julian Byng, before becoming the thinnest of all in the most southern part of its line, before Amiens, held by the Fifth Army under General Gough.

And Amiens itself – with a population of 100,000 and its vital railways running to the northern sector of the Western front – is the most important town in France when it comes to sustaining the British presence there. If ever it falls, Germany would be able to strangle the key British and Belgian supply-line, and practically guarantee the success of the German war effort. And yet, though for that reason Prince Rupprecht is eager for the plan to include the capture of Amiens, Ludendorff demurs. Because of the sensitivity of Amiens, the British will be obliged to use many resources to defend it, weakening themselves to the north. And so to his stroke of genius: instead of pushing on to Amiens, they will turn north at Albert to roll up the British line from there.

And so it is set.

The Germans will launch in the early spring, as soon as all of their forces are back from *der Ostfront,* the Eastern Front, and moved into position, ready to attack. On current reckoning, that would put *der Tag*, the day of the attack, as . . . 20 March.

The German plan Operation Michael, if not providing the knockout blow, will practically guarantee the success of a second German attack, the George offensive, due to start two and a half weeks after the first attack. In boxing terms, it is as if Operation Michael is a left hook to the body that will make the British stagger back, dazed, quickly followed by George, a straight right to the head to finish them off.

Still, 20 March may well be only just in time, if that. There are already signs that the workers' revolution that has brought Russia to its knees is beginning to stir in Germany itself! On 30 January, more than a million workers go on strike, all of it organised by a 'Workers' Council', after the Russian fashion. In the end, the only way to restore order is to militarise the factories, using precious troops to quell the revolt, placing the workers on soldiers' pay and making them subject to military, not civil, justice. But how long that will hold them is not clear.

The German Army itself is not immune from such revolt and loss of desire to continue fighting. Since the beginning of 1918, there has been an enormous increase in the number of German soldiers feigning mental problems in an effort to escape their front-line duties, including a soldier who 'pretended to be Sherlock Holmes . . . in an attempt to get discharged'.[65]

When challenged as to what on earth was going on, *Herr* Sherlock quickly cracked the case and explained, honestly, 'I have to be a free man . . . The war is a foul thing in itself. They have got everyone in a nice mess, and we have to face the music now. As I see it, they can have their war if they want to, I'm not bothered. I never wanted the war. They should not have bothered me. But now I am not supposed to be a free man any longer . . . Now I am supposed to be with the Prussians and to risk my head for no purpose whatsoever.'[66]

Success!

The soldier is diagnosed as 'permanently unfit for any form of military service'[67] and sent home. Case closed, at least for him.

Ludendorff has noted the growing revolt of workers and soldiers – for his own army has been far from immune – with some alarm.

'Thus,' he would later recount, 'a further element of weakness had developed in our own body while we were in the midst of a struggle for our very existence.'[68]

MID-WINTER, 1917–1918, MESSINES FRATERNISING WITH FRITZ

A curious episode, all up.

Across No-Man's Land, from their post at the Messines front-line, some men of the AIF's 8th Battalion can see, in the deepening dusk, an old German soldier at *his* post. Normal form on such an occasion, of course, is to take a shot at the brute, and blow his bloody head off for his trouble.

But . . . there is just something *about* this bloke. He seems so fearless, so friendly, gazing at them benignly, and so *old* – you could dinkum see his white hair at a distance of 100 yards – that it just doesn't seem right. So, for fun, the Australians wave at him and gesture. Come on over, *Herr* sport.

And be blowed if he doesn't do exactly that! *And* he speaks English.

'Hoooo are you?'[69] he asks them in his *velly* thick accent.

'We're Australians,'[70] they reply.

'No, you're not,' he says, looking them over. 'You're the same as I am, a Saxon.'

And maybe he has a point, at least in terms of their common ethnicity, because for a few of them there can be no doubt that he brings to mind their own dad, and maybe that, too, helps drive the warmth of their conversation.[71] And a few among them, perhaps, might recall that it was the Saxons of the 133rd Regiment who famously played soccer with some Scots during the Christmas truce of 1914, the Germans hooting every now and then when gusts of wind would reveal what the Scots *didn't* have under their kilts.

The Saxons, from the south of Germany, really are a different breed, and don't quite have their heart in this war.

In the here and now, after a while, it is time to go, and after hand-shakes all round, the old bloke ambles back without a shot being fired on him . . . just as an Australian officer spots him . . . and there is hell to pay. The officer puts the whole lot of his men under open arrest for allowing the old fellow to get away.

'Of course,' Archie Barwick allows, 'the proper thing would have been to collar him but it would be a rotten thing to do for they called him over & if he was game enough to trust coming across no man's land in daylight, it was up to them to let him go again.'[72]

Beyond everything else, it is a fair indication of how quiet Messines is at this point.

Walking around the Australian positions shortly after the New Year of 1918 raises its weary head above the horizon, Charles Bean and a fellow correspondent are impressed by how quiet the front is, compared to the horror of previous Australian positions at Gallipoli, Fromelles, Pozières, Passchendaele, Ypres, and so forth.

'We found the long slope on the other side unmarked by battle compared to the country we fought in at Ypres,' Bean would note. 'The old fields were covered, of course, with hoary grass. Here and there turnips still grew . . . The fore slope of this hill is crossed at intervals by camouflage screens on posts – to hide movement.'[73]

And of course the Australians are enjoying the much-needed rest, but one of the more canny Australian officers, the distinguished Gallipoli and Fromelles veteran Colonel David McConaghy, quietly wonders to Bean if there might be a hidden reason why the Germans are putting so little pressure on them.

'We are sure from the German tactics,' he says, 'that the German artillery is on a small daily allowance of ammunition, and is saving for some big stroke . . .'[74]

CHAPTER TWO

EIN MANN MIT EINEM PLAN – A MAN WITH A PLAN

I have read the German Chancellor's[1] speech with some
care, but I can see in it no indication of a settlement.
From the attitude he takes up, I deduce that the
military party [von Hindenburg and Ludendorff]
have got their way, and will be allowed to make one
more desperate attempt to win the war, by assuming
the offensive in the West at no distant date.[2]
General Henry Rawlinson, writing to British Minister
of War, Lord Derby, on 27 January 1918

The heavens are their battlefields. They are the cavalry of
the clouds. High above the squalor and the mud . . . Their
daily, yes, their nightly struggles are like the Miltonic
conflict between the winged hosts of light and of darkness.
Lloyd George in a vote of thanks to the Flying Service
in the House of Commons on 29 October 1917[3]

I suppose you can hardly realize how big a thing
a single Division is. Its 20,000 men, with all its
animals, vehicles, guns and paraphernalia, occupy
on the line of march 22 miles of road, and it

takes fifteen to twenty ordinary villages to house
them, and 32 railway trains to carry them.[4]
Monash to Felix Meyer, 3 April 1918

21 JANUARY 1918, WESTERN FRONT, DIE MICHAEL...

Together, they are gleaming giants amid the mud-men.

General Ludendorff, accompanied by the two Chiefs of Staff of the
two Army Groups, General von Kuhl for Prince Rupprecht's Army
Group and General Schulenburg for Little Willy's Army Group – all of
them impeccably turned out, of course – are on this day making a tour
of the front to be attacked in eight weeks' time, and inevitably coming
face to face with some of the hard and harried German soldiers who live
and die in these trenches.

Having decided the attack will be mid-March, Ludendorff and these
two most senior officers must now see up close the whole area, the condition of their own troops and the defences they are facing. All is in order,
and as the day goes on Ludendorff's plan, already well-formed, crystallises
further and fine details are worked out. Now, instead of one huge thrust
right at the British Fifth Army, there are to be five successive offensives,
of which '*die Michael-Offensive*'[5] is merely the first 45-mile-wide thrust.
After the Germans throw 76 German divisions – 1,500,000 men – at
the 24 British divisions in that first operation, the Allies will obviously
be forced to shift reserve divisions from other parts of the Western Front,
creating weakness wherever they do so. Hence, the subsequent series of
offensives planned from April to June. By continually thrusting as the
Allies move their divisions around, inevitably one of the thrusts must
break through, as the Germans will have, in total, some 23 more divisions than the Allies. In preparation for *der Tag*, orders have gone out to
begin amassing reserves of artillery shells in dumps opposite the parts of
the British front to be attacked, just as troops arriving from the Eastern
front are sent to be first rested and then retrained for the task ahead.

There is muted resistance to Ludendorff's plan, most notably from
the General responsible for overseeing its main thrust, *Kronprinz*

Rupprecht, who never quite trusts Ludendorff. Such a view from a Bavarian about a Prussian is far from rare. But the *Kronprinz* General has specific concerns.

'Will our forces be sufficient for a major attack? I doubt it and feel oppressed by severe anxiety . . . If we don't succeed in surprising the enemy with our attack, [then] it surely comes down to a fruitless battle of *matériel*. But if we do not gain a decisive victory this spring, the war is lost for us inevitably.'[6]

EARLY FEBRUARY 1918, LUDENDORFF WORKS AT VON HINDENBURG'S HQ AT KREUZNACH

Even for a man as habitually focused as General Ludendorff, these days are intense. He just wants this war *over* so he can get back to his wife, Margarethe, as quickly as possible, and return his two surviving stepsons safely back home. He had met Margarethe one night nine years earlier, when the new widow had been caught at a bus stop in the rain without an umbrella, and his life had changed. While as cold and ruthless as ever in his military career, once he entered the portals of the home she had made for them – initially with her three sons and daughter, whom he proudly called 'my own children'[7] – he was a different man . . . warm, genial, loving.

No man could have been prouder of his children, let alone step-children, and the fact that all three boys had become aviators in the German air force had made him glow with pride. And then the fall. In September 1917, the eldest boy, Franz, had been shot down, his body washing up on the Dutch coast. In the weeks after the funeral, Margarethe had not been able to get Franz out of her head by day or by night, when she dreamed of him.

Once, slumped in a chair, wanly looking at the pile of mail the servant had placed nearby in the hope that something would distract her, she glimpsed a familiar sight. It was the unmistakable, elegant handwriting of Franz. It was his last letter, just arrived. She had opened it, her hands shaking, to read . . .

Ach, Mutti; Oh, Mum, you cannot imagine what a heavenly feeling it is when all the battles of the day luckily are over; you put yourself to bed at night and can say to oneself while falling asleep: so, thank God, now you have still twelve hours to live. This certainty is too beautiful.[8]

Having lost one stepson already, Ludendorff knows it will nearly kill Margarethe, and himself, if they lose either of the other two. And so many German families are in the same position! There is not much more the nation can bear without breaking. And the way to finish it is clear: throw everything the Germans have, which is now considerable, in one last major assault.

But, careful! Their massing behind the front-line must be kept as discreet as possible. Surprise is to be everything, and so these troops will be kept well back from the line until at least two days before the attack goes in, and, in most cases, just the day before. Even then, they will be moved forward at night and spend the last 24 hours in carefully concealed positions at the front.

Just after dawn on *der Tag*, Germany's 17th Army, under General Otto von Below, will attack in the north around Arras. At the same time, the 2nd Army to their south, under General Georg von der Marwitz, is to attack west to Péronne, and the 18th Army, under General Oskar von Hutier – the inventor, developer and endless refiner of the whole stormtrooper concept – will attack south-west towards Montdidier.

A possible complication, true, is this new British *Superwaffe*, super-weapon – these iron monsters they call 'tanks' and the Germans call '*Panzerkampfwagen*', armoured fighting vehicles, or '*Panzer*' for short. These spitting, grinding, roaring metal behemoths had made their first appearance in the Battle of the Somme at Flers-Courcelette on 15 September 1916, and by November 1917 production had increased to the point that the British had thrown as many as 400 at once against German forces at Cambrai, to indeed smash through their front-lines. And yet *still* the British had failed – Fritz had, among other things, used their artillery as an anti-tank weapon – helping to convince the Germans that tanks were *not* an essential part of modern warfare.

'They were merely an offensive weapon and our attacks succeeded without them . . .'[9] Ludendorff opines.

Still, others within the German military hierarchy *do* believe, and, as well as using the few German tanks available – by now they have built 20 – they have also been able to recover 100 British and French tanks which, once repaired, they must learn how to use.

But it is far from certain that German crews, in German tanks, will arrive in time to take part in the Spring Offensive . . .

Some good news for the Germans comes through via intelligence reports that Haig is prepared to sacrifice ground in the south, where the southernmost of his four armies, General Gough's Fifth Army, holds the line with each of his 12 infantry divisions, with an average of just over three miles for each division, while north of Gough the average is two miles held per division. It is possible, too, that Haig has diluted the defence at this point because Gough's Army is right beside the French Army, which holds the next section to the south and can rush to his aid in force if necessary. But will they? For the only way the French can help the British is to weaken their own line, and given that the southern end of the Operation Michael attack is just 60 miles from Paris, the Germans know this is problematic.

It will be a brave French General indeed who gives the order to weaken French lines so close to Paris – when there is every chance the German drive might turn south to attack the capital – simply to go to help the British.

And, yes, Gough and his Fifth Army have a fair suspicion that they will soon be under attack and are working hard to consolidate their defences, to organise themselves. Among other things, they have started building a third line of trenches, moving stores to the front and shifting timber forward for the construction of dugouts and HQs, in the process calling heavily on the labour battalions composed of men too old or unfit for front-line service but who are still able to wield a pick or the like. But the workers are so few, and there is so much to be done!

'No amount of labour,' Gough would later say, 'nothing short of a fairy wand, could have prepared all those defences in a few weeks.'[10]

Der Rittmeister Manfred von Richthofen is beyond merely famous – much more, even, than a legend of his land. *Nein*, in a Germany struggling in this war, frequently confronted with appalling news on a daily basis, von Richthofen is nothing less than a national symbol of brilliance, of hope, of derring-do in the midst of disaster, triumphing time after time, no matter what the Allies throw at him. Every new victory makes headlines, an affirmation that however many men have been lost, the Fatherland still has the best and brightest there ever was. And, yes, von Richthofen had been badly wounded in a dogfight by a bullet that had taken a glancing chunk out of his skull back in July 1917, but that, too, had added to his story as the nation prayed for his recovery and was rewarded. And what about the time he had checked himself out of hospital prematurely so he could visit his squadron, as a prelude to taking command once more?

In the company of his comely nurse, Käte Otersdorf, von Richthofen had been in an open-top car with three others, including his father, when they had passed a long column of German soldiers on their way back to Courtrai. One of them had noted the distinguished figure in the back seat wearing the distinctive dress jacket of the *Deutsche Luftstreitkräfte*, the highest German bravery award, and . . . and . . . a head bandage. It must be him! It simply must, and the soldier cries out the name 'Richthofen!'

'The roar of the name,' one account would run, 'spread faster than [the] car and the excited and grateful soldiers waved and shouted hurrahs to the great fighter ace as he passed by.'[11]

That iconic figure, however, is just for the outside world. Here at home, on one of his rare visits, he is just his mother's adored son, and that is enough. And yet, as a mother looking closely at her son and hearing him speak – when he returns for a brief spot of leave in the first weeks of 1918 to the family's ancestral estate near Breslau – Baroness Kunigunde von Richthofen is profoundly shocked. Whereas he had once been a man full of life and love, radiating happiness and warmth, he is now aloof and distant. Some of his bearing stems from him still recovering from his terrible head wound, but this appears more to be a wound on his soul.

When the Baroness looks into her son's eyes there is something in them she has never seen before, something harsh and agonised, as though he is being tortured. Running her fingers through his hair, just as she did when he was little, she feels and sees bone – after all this time, his head wound has still not healed.

When she tries to talk to him about his future, about what he might do *nach dem Krieg*, after the war, he gives the impression that he isn't even sure if there will be a *nach dem Krieg* for him. He is exhausted, depressed and deeply, deeply pessimistic, though still trying to shield her from the worst of it.

One morning she manages to see some of the photographs he has brought home with him. One shows him in uniform, laughing with other pilots. Baroness von Richthofen, a gentle woman, points to one beaming young flyer and asks where he was now.

'Fallen in combat,' Manfred replies morosely.

'And this man?' she asks, pointing to another one.

'Also dead,' her son replies before suddenly appearing to lose patience. He puts the photo away. 'Do not ask anymore – they are all dead.'

And now, seeing the alarm in his mother's eyes, he softens and tries to reassure her.

'You do not need to worry. In the air I have nothing to fear. In the air. We are ready for them, even when there are many of them. The worst that could happen to me would be to have to land on the other side . . .'[12]

Despite this assurance from her son, it is not long after this that she overhears him on the phone, batting off someone who wants him to attend to something that afternoon.

'*Einen Zahnarzttermin?* A dental appointment?' he replies with a mixture of extreme fatigue and outright irritation. 'Really, there is no *point . . .*'[13]

And he might be right, much as his mother herself and his sister, Ilse, fight against that very conclusion.

He leaves the family home after his all-too-brief stay, to return to his waiting squadron, to take on once more the growing swarm of Allied planes that now fill the skies above the Western Front. His mother stands by the window at the top of the stairs. As Ilse drives him away, down the long, gracious driveway and back to the Schweidnitz railway station, to take a 30-mile train trip to Breslau where his plane is waiting, she is overcome with sadness but still has hope.

'*Auf Wiedersehen,*' his mother says softly as she waves goodbye. 'Until we meet again, my boy.'[14]

Though she is bereft, one thing that gives her comfort is that he is not just returning to death and destruction, the daily dancing with dangers that may kill him, but also to the love of a good woman, that same nurse who had nurtured him back to half-health the previous year . . .

Still not willing to let him go, Ilse takes her brother right to the carriage and holds his hand through the carriage window, just before it pulls away.

'Do be a little careful, please. We want to see each other again.'

'Can you envision, Ilse,' he replies sadly, 'that I could die a wretched, meaningless death?'[15]

The train pulls away from the station, and all Ilse can do is stand there watching it disappear, her brother's last words lingering.

3 FEBRUARY 1918, HARRY TAKES HIS BUS TO HEAVEN

The difference between a good pilot and a great pilot? It is a curious combination of caution and confidence, each in play at the right time; a sixth sense of where lies danger and opportunity; reaction time; simple flying skill; the capacity to overcome one's natural fears and become master of his heavenly domain. Oh, and one more thing: the ability to shoot straight, to hold your machine in exactly the right position for just long enough that it can do its deadly work. For as one 57-victory ace, James McCudden, would say, 'Good flying has never killed a Hun yet.'[16]

Lieutenant Harry Cobby, as it turns out, has all the right stuff, the right attributes, the necessary qualities. For no reason that he can work out, and despite his nervous start, he experiences a comfort and confidence in the air that is the envy of his peers. Where others have been sent back to England, he has been sent on ever more missions in his trusty 'bus'.

He is getting the knack of sticking to tight formations and shooting in the air with precision. 'My knowledge was broadening,' he later wrote of his growing confidence. 'I had learned that all German pilots were not the out and out top-line pilots that I had been led to believe, and that there were at least three of them as timid as myself.'[17] As a consequence his confidence grows, and on this day, that new-found confidence might be useful.

Flying with No. 4 Squadron in the skies above Arras, he is just swooping around to the right of a thick cloud when, suddenly, there in front of him is a German two-seater *Deutsche Flugzeug-Werke* (DFW) reconnaissance aircraft, coming straight at him, around the left of the same cloud.

Operating in the realms of emergency instinct rather than conscious thought, in a split second Cobby is able to do two things. He first presses down both levers on the underside of the horizontal bar at the top of his wooden joystick – the triggers for his twin Vickers guns – just in time to see the German lift out of his seat as the bullets tear into him. The pilot, as Cobby would recount, 'almost jumped backwards out of the cockpit'[18] and blood burst forth. Then Cobby jams the joystick forward to fly under the oncoming plane. He turns in time to see the German plane, now in flames, hurtling earthwards and disappearing into a thick cloud. It is perhaps a mercy that he is unable to see it hit the ground, but there can be no doubt as to the result – even if, because no one witnesses the end, he is not officially credited with it.

Other men, after a kill, are haunted by what they have done and cannot go on. Cobby is neither haunted nor exulted. He is cool. He is precise. As it turns out, he is as natural a killer as he is a pilot.

He has taken the first step, thus, to taking his place in a pantheon of fighter pilots in Europe who are legends in their own – oft tragically truncated – lifetime.

On the English side there had been the likes of Albert Ball, until he had been killed in action, while Billy Bishop, Mick Mannock and Jimmy McCudden all go on.

The French boasted great aces like René Fonck and Charles Nungesser, a blond 25-year-old known as 'the fighting pilot's fighting pilot', and a lady-killer to beat them all. Nungesser had an aura about him – a *savoir vivre* on the ground and a *savoir faire* in the air – that was simply mesmerising. Once, early in his flying career, he had disobeyed orders, leaving his post on the ground to go skywards and take on eight German planes that were reported to be approaching the city of Nancy. As it turned out, he had thrown himself into the fray with such gusto that he brought one plane down and made the others scatter.

The following day, he was hauled before his commanding Colonel.

'Lieutenant Nungesser,' the Colonel began, 'what would you do to an officer who deserted his post?'

'Sir,' Nungesser replied evenly, 'if he destroyed an Albatros with a Voisin and made seven others run for their lives, he deserves the *Croix de Guerre.*'

'I agree,' the Colonel said. 'The *Croix de Guerre* – plus sixteen days' arrest.'[19]

Nungesser had famously bowed low and replied: *'Mon colonel, vous êtes trop genereux.* You are too generous.'[20]

The Germans, too, have a slaughtering slew of cold-blooded aerial killers of whom they are very proud.

Early in the war, the most legendary had been Oswald Boelcke, who had famously established the *Dicta Boelcke,* a list of eight fundamental tactics of aerial warfare for the other German pilots to follow, from 'try to keep the sun behind you' to 'always attack from the rear.'

(No doubt he had observed his own dicta, but it still had not saved him. On 28 October 1916, was killed when he collided with one of his own comrades, occasioning the RFC to drop a laurel wreath over his base with the message: *To the memory of our brave and chivalrous opponent, from the British Royal Flying Corps.*[21])

And then there had been *Der Adler von Lille,* The Eagle of Lille, Max Immelmann, who is credited with inventing and employing the original version of the 'Immelmann turn', an aerial manoeuvre to change direction by 180 degrees in as quick a time as possible . . . not to mention the likes of Kurt Wolff, who was killed in September 1917 with 33 victories to his name, and Werner Voss, 48 victories, also killed in action in the same month.

All of them, however, are being surpassed in their legends now by *Rittmeister* Manfred von Richthofen, who has moved from his old-fash-ioned Albatros to *dem letzten Schrei,* the last word in manoeuvrability, the Fokker Triplane. He now rules the skies as none before him, and certainly none below him.

'Everything that is in the air beneath me,' he famously boasts, 'is lost.'[22]

A staggering 63 Allied aircraft taken down beneath his chattering guns so far is proof of the statement, a figure that no other pilot on either side is even close to. Perhaps it is not just the *Rittmeister*'s proven bravery, but his remarkable capacity for calm and patience. Never was a fighter pilot, in their short history of existence, as cool and calculating when deciding to enter a fight. He chooses his scraps wisely, and it works.

Harry Cobby is well aware of the Baron's 'celebrated boast'[23] and, like all of the Allied pilots, knows that there could be no greater glory in this war than to shoot him down.

'There seemed to be no way in which to stop him,' Cobby would recall. 'Evidently he was a dead shot, an excellent pilot and a man of superb courage and still in his early twenties. The combination seemed too much for us lesser mortals.'[24]

Still, Cobby could dream of taking him on, and does so, while also being aware that in these bad weather winter months, opportunities to fight von Richthofen will be limited, as most of his squadron's activi-ties will be, to 'flying low-reconnaissances, offensive patrols, escorting photography machines and bombing formations over the German lines and, seeking excitement to relieve monotony, in machine gunning villages in the nearer German areas between Lille and the River Scarpe'.[25]

There is also the dreadful matter of shooting whatever horses they see in German territory – to deny the brutes, literally, the horsepower they need to run their military machine – a task the pilots absolutely hate, but it has to be done.

At least, whatever happens, and for all the grisliness in the air and on the ground, once the pilots land they head to the local estaminet, the *Cerniclet*, which they swear boasts France's most beautiful young woman, Odette – the daughter of Madame who runs the place – whose attentions they vie for.

The songs! The drinking! Odette! Maman's *glares* . . .

Never mind.

Another song and more wine, ODETTE!

Harry Cobby and his mate George Malley, however, more often than not leave the other pilots to it and head to another place, 'a small shop, half estaminet, half private house, run by a Madame Brunet, a plump elderly woman,' whom they adore. She simply cannot fathom why these boys from Australia are here 'to help France fight her natural enemy', but she loves them for it.

'Madame hated the Germans with the fervidness that only the French can sustain,' Harry would recall, 'and anything in her power that she could do to damage him in any way, she would do. That we were fighting him in the air and bombing his troops was sufficient for her to take us to her ample bosom.'[26]

Madame Brunet's husband had been taken prisoner by the *Boche* – oh, how she can spit that word out, like it is a piece of putrescent *saucisson* – in the first months of the war, so now it is just herself, her elderly mother, her 17-year-old boy, Alphonse, and her able assistant Leonie in the house.

'*Ah'ree! Zheorge!*' Madame Brunet yells delightedly from the kitchen whenever they walk in the door. That's the cue for Leonie – 'a strong cheerful girl of peasant stock, with a remarkable ability to put people in their places'[27] – to prepare the boys' nightly dose of eggs, chips and coffee, while they strip down for Madame and hand over their linen, socks and uniforms for laundering and mending. She gives them full rein of the house, and even lets them turn her kitchen into their own private club.

'If any of us caught minor ailments,' *Ah'ree* would later recall, 'she would be on the job immediately with her simple remedies.'[28]

In the eyes of Madame Brunet, in helping these brave and generous young Australians who've come all the way from the other side of the world to help *La France*, she is helping to give hell to the Hun.

And she is right.

13 FEBRUARY 1918, HOMBURG, THE RABBITS RISE AS LUDENDORFF SCHOOLS THE KAISER

High, way up high.

In a high citadel on a high hill overlooking the picturesque German town of Homborg, there lies a singularly spectacular yellow castle with large turrets – a *Schloss* where *der Kaiser* and his court tend to spend a month every summer. And high in turn in the castle is a large room, on this day boasting the highest echelons of the German ruling class.

Those taking their place at this deep mahogany table, 'neath the glittering chandeliers in the *Spiegelkabinett*, the Hall of Mirrors, are all there because of their pre-eminence at the pinnacle of the monarchy, military and political classes.

His medals gleaming in the dappled light coming through the Lebanese cedars outside the windows, the rather stormy-looking Kaiser Wilhelm sits at the head of the table for this *großen Kriegsrates*, Great Council of War, with the importance of the rest of the gathering to be judged by their proximity to his royal personage. On his immediate right, the Field Marshal von Hindenburg. On his immediate left, the aged and wearied German Chancellor Georg von Hertling, with the truly most powerful man in the room, and all of Germany, General Ludendorff, just off von Hindenburg's right shoulder.

'The battle in the West is the greatest military task that has ever been imposed upon an army,'[29] Ludendorff now tells the Kaiser.[30] 'The Army in the West is waiting for the opportunity to act. We must not imagine that this offensive will be like those in Galicia or Italy; it will be an immense struggle that will begin at one point, continue at another and take a long time; it is difficult, but it will be victorious . . .'[31]

Looking at the Kaiser, Ludendorff says it straight-out: 'The Army was assembled and well prepared to undertake the "biggest task in its history".'[32]

Von Hindenburg?

Though he is not the driving force for the whole plan, he certainly agrees with it.

'I seemed to feel the longing of the troops to get away from the misery and oppression of pure defence,' he would recount. 'I knew that the German "rabbit" living underground would become the German soldier in his steel helmet who would rise from his trenches in great and overwhelming numbers to put an end by attack to the years of torment he had suffered in defence . . . let the sword flash on high and all hearts would rise with it.'[33]

Vice Chancellor Friedrich von Payer is not so sure, noting, delicately, the mood of the German people is that they have had enough of war. Though he doesn't say it, his meaning is clear. If Germany is not careful, the fate of Russia might await it, too – with the workers rising to seize power from the ruling classes.

16 FEBRUARY 1918, PARIS, GOOD OL' BEAN PUTS ON THE RITZ

Garçon! More champagne, *s'il vous plait*!

For a man who has seen more action up close than any other Australian of this war, who has been in the thick of it from the days of Gallipoli through the immediate aftermath of Fromelles, Pozières, Passchendaele and all the rest, been covered in the spattered brains of his countrymen more times than he can remember, it is a rare pleasure for Charles Bean to have what amounts to a night off with his deeply admired friend and fellow war correspondent Fred Cutlack, as they head out to Paris's most legendary cabaret music hall – did someone say dancing girls with dresses as skimpy as they are extravagant, complete with an orchestra? *Les Folies Bergère.*

And they are not the only ones. For many Allied officers in Paris have exactly the same idea, and as Bean looks around he notes that 'every nation under the sun [is represented] and you could tell them . . . by their uniform'.

Just *look* at them!

'There were French civilians and their wives and sweethearts and *cocottes*. There were Americans – scores and scores of American officers in their khaki tunics with stiff high collars; there were spruced, trimmed, polished British officers; French officers and men in their grey-blue, and in their peace time blue and red; there were big Yankee soldiers in their long overcoats and rounded hats, almost like so many monks; there were Canadians – like British soldiers except for the big square patches of colour on their back or arms; there were a few British Tommies (though, poor old fellows, they have not the money for *Les Folies Bergères* for the most part . . .)'[34]

And, of course, there is a good sprinkling of his fellow Australians. Not for the first time, and not for the last, but now with an ever-growing frequency and warmth, Charles Bean – born and raised through childhood in England, but now a passionately admiring chronicler of the wartime experience of the Sons of the Southern Cross – looks at his Australian countrymen with real pride.

'There they were in their dashing upturned hats and loose easy fitting uniform; it was not any fancy of mine that they looked so easy – they were marked amongst all the rest by their easy, frank, natural manners; their confident walk; their free unrestrained enjoyment. They made their way through these Paris crowds – either with a mate or with a girl – a woman they had picked up, no doubt, but often quite respectable in appearance as these Paris *cocottes* often are – they made their way through Paris exactly as if it were Sydney or Manly or Warrnambool. It was an Australian, up in front of the nigger orchestra, who was waving his cane to the music – dancing a half cake walk – laughing chaffing with the French men and the Canadians around . . . The Americans were stiffer and colder and restrained – our men were there to enjoy themselves and were loving every minute. If a nation with so frank and free a soul does not add something of great value to the world it will belie all its appearance and its promise . . .'[35]

—

And among the German troops, the excitement builds as preparations for the *Frühjahrsoffensive*, Spring Offensive, go on.

On this day, *Leutnant* Herbert Sulzbach of the 63rd Field Artillery Regiment arrives back to his unit – now based around the French town of La Hérie, some 20 miles due east of St Quentin.

He had been one of some 5000 German artillery officers at the Beverloo artillery training ground engaged in learning entirely different artillery tactics from those taught to them before, as outlined in Ludendorff's detailed pamphlet on 1 January.

The softly spoken 21-year-old grandson of the founder of Deutschebank – steeped in a Jewish faith requiring dedication to all serious things – and already a four-year veteran since having volunteered at the start of the war, Sulzbach is more assiduous than most, but even then there is an enormous amount to learn in a short space of time, and he is troubled even beyond that.

Before leaving for the school, everyone had told him, 'It's an honour, because it means being retrained for the great battles to come,' for, of course, everyone had been talking 'about a big German offensive which is supposed to be coming off in France'. But on the very day he had left, his entire Division had gone back 'to be trained for mobile warfare', and he feels he is missing out on a good time with his men.

'It would be just unbelievable if it came to any mobile warfare!'[36]

But the point, as explained to all the German artillery officers on their first day's instruction at Beverloo, is that there won't be any mobile warfare unless they of the artillery do their job to first neutralise the defenders to allow the stormtroopers to break through. And they must learn to remain agile, following the infantry in the advance, galloping their guns forward over any manner of terrain. Sulzbach's own job as 'Fire Control Officer' is to turn the orders into specific map coordinates and ensure the battery's rounds fall where intended.

And so to the new tactics . . .

Developed by Ludendorff's artillery impresario, Colonel Georg Bruchmüller – himself known as *Durchbruchmüller*, 'Breakthroughmüller' – the tactics turn on stunning the enemy into inactivity rather than destroying them. The Bruchmüller mode is to use gas heavily in the initial bombardment, aimed at the forward defensive troops and the crews operating the artillery batteries behind them, together with heavy artillery specifically targeted at enemy HQs and their communications systems. Wire entanglements are targeted too, so that they will pose less trouble to the advancing infantry.

No more pounding the enemy lines for days, even weeks. No, prior to the *Stoßtruppen* going over the top, there would be no 'registration' on targets – the process of determining precise ranging by firing rounds at the target – as that would give too much warning. Surprise is to be everything, and with that in mind for this particular coming attack, there will be just five hours of 'hurricane fire' – intensely focused fire on just the British Fifth Army and part of the Third Army – delivered by 6600 guns and 3500 mortars across a front 45-miles wide.

The key to success will be the efficacy of a program known as *Feuerwalze*, as in fire waltz, as in a . . . creeping barrage whereby the rain of artillery shells moves just ahead of the advancing stormtroopers, the wall of fire leaping forward 100 yards every two minutes, all detailed in the handbook the officers are given.

And it will be *intense*, with one gun pounding every 11 yards of British front-line.

As to how the storming infantry are to interact with their highly sophisticated artillery, it is . . . complicated.

'*Mein Gott*,' Sulzbach comments in his diary, 'what an incredible amount we've still got to learn! That's the first impression you get.'[37]

All up, the focus of the artillery is to neutralise the defenders but *not* obliterate the very roads and bridges behind the front that the stormtroopers would need to quickly advance.

> *The assaulting infantry must be in the enemy's position simultaneously with the last rounds from their artillery and trench mortars... A check in the advance at one place must not spread to the whole line; infantry which pushes well forward will envelop the parties of the enemy which are standing fast. Hesitation leads to failure...*[38]

In conclusion ...

> *The great attack for a break-through requires the commanders and troops should free themselves from habits and customs of trench warfare.*[39]

Quite. Sulzbach, with his comrades, had knuckled down and tried in earnest to learn the new doctrine.

For while most of the German artillerymen who have been trained after 1915 are more accustomed to battles where the guns on both sides don't move often or far, they now need to be drilled to harness the horses to the limbers and gallop their guns into action across open fields, fire 50 rounds, then repeat the process and quickly ride to a new position. Only gunners who had fought in 1914 would have any idea how to do that efficiently, and there are scarcely any such men left.

Meanwhile, in the time Sulzbach has been away training at Beverloo, La Hérie has gone from a quiet backwater to a place now flooded with German soldiers.

'There is no end to the troops stationed here,' he records, 'no end either to the troops moving past all the time ... You get the impression that we are on the brink of the most colossal action the history of the world has ever seen; it's the start of the greatest advance, and the preparation for the greatest battle that has ever been fought.[40]

From dawn the following morning, he is caught up in it himself as he joins his fellow officers and soldiers heading out on long marches beside *le* Ton River to increase their stamina, and engage in endless training drills to improve their toughness and mobility.

As they occasionally get close to the Western Front, they can see *hundreds* of new roads being built by hundreds of thousands of Russian prisoners, together with a liberal sprinkling of British, French, Rumanians and Italians. These short linking roads to the main roads – all along the front of the intended attack, from south of St Quentin to north towards Douai – are to ensure that when the time comes to move the 500,000 German soldiers from rear positions to the frontline for the attack, it can all be done with maximum efficiency. Other roads are built into forests to allow huge supply dumps to be formed near the front-line without attracting the attention of the British reconnaissance aircraft. Often, the Germans do their best to confuse the British by leaving fake guns – no more than wheels of farm carts with a wooden beam for the barrel – in prominent positions, so that their reconnaissance might convince the British artillery and bombers to waste precious resources in blowing the decoys away.

Meanwhile, on the other side, by that line that looks so very neat on the map – in reality, a shell-riddled tract of torn earth, rotting bodies and the scattered detritus of war – up on the high ground around Ypres, the Australian divisions of the AIF are doing their own tactics training to ready themselves for the German offensive, which they all feel must come in the spring. To stop the Germans, the new three-zone-deep defence system along the BEF's 126-mile front is a good start, if it can be constructed in time, but the men have to be taught how to lay out effective fields of fire and how to counter-attack in the event of a German breakthrough – should it come to that, and many feel that it will.

Among the officers charged with bringing the men up to speed is Brigadier Bill Glasgow, from Maryborough, Queensland – a tough

Boer War veteran and former Major in the 2nd Light Horse. He is a born leader whom nobody can help but respect, and he has the men of his 13th Brigade – like most of the Australian units – practising open-warfare tactics each morning.

His men, who had fought valiantly at Mouquet Farm, Messines and Polygon Wood, are, like many along the front, used to trench fighting and, in the eyes of their Brigadier, have grown 'rather sticky',[41] as in, prone to sticking to their trenches rather than coming out in dynamic, free-ranging action.

On top of that are the new 'reinstoushments', who have just arrived and need all the help they can get. It is up to Glasgow and his training officers to change their mindset. As such, each Battalion is up early, conducting 'a simple scheme in advanced guard and an attack'.[42]

Striding around his men as they train, his healthy crop of auburn hair clearly identifiable well above the heads of most of his soldiers, Glasgow – whom his men call the 'Old Man'[43] despite his tender years, for the fact it just seems like he's seen it all before, *thrice* – is a whirlwind of barking orders, and sometimes just barks alone. More than merely a matter of life and death, the result of the whole bloody war may well be riding on them getting it right, and there is no time for niceties.

Time and time again, he works them, and no one more than the Lewis gun teams, who must be able to move, set up, fire and move again! And again and again and again! The five-man Lewis gun teams roar forth, one behind the other, laden with 36 drum magazines, the Lewis (light enough to be carried by just one man), a spare barrel, smaller spare parts, a repair kit, a lubricants bag and two groundsheets. The gunner throws himself down upon one of those groundsheets, sets up the gun on its bipod, nestles the butt into his right shoulder while his No. 2 loads the first of the drum magazines on the gun and estimates the range of the target.

'400 yards . . .'

'400 yards,' No. 1 repeats, even as he moves the slider on the sight down to 400 yards, before pulling back the cocking handle. She's ready to rip.

No. 1 pulls the trigger, the gun coughs and shudders, emitting a couple of three-second bursts, the magazine making a half-revolution each time until the 47-round magazine is napoo. The groundsheet, there to prevent any telltale dust being thrown up by the gun for the enemy to sight on, now has empty copper cartridges scattered on it to the right of the breech.

No. 2 – an expert in his craft – needs a bare, hungry, sniffin' four seconds *only* to whip away the empty magazine and replace it with a full one. Meanwhile, the other three members of the crew behind them are unloading eight magazines each from their webbing pouches, laying them on the other groundsheet to keep the rounds clean. The No. 3 is sure to keep the fresh magazines up to No. 2, and so it goes. They fire, move forward, set up again.

And again and again and again!

True, if 20 magazines are fired in a short time, the Lewis gun can overheat. But even then, if you are prepared to put up with your skin blistering, you can still fire it.

Not for nothing would a January 1918 War Office Pamphlet note that 'a Lewis gun in the hands of good gunners will work as much destruction as fifty average riflemen'.[44] If they can instead use *excellent* gunners, the Lewis will be worth even more men.

When it comes to the Vickers gun, they are even *more* powerful and can take down enemy soldiers as far away as 2000 yards – the only downside being they are so much heavier than the Lewis, needing several men to carry the component parts before taking a few minutes to set up.

At Valenciennes in far northern France, meanwhile, German Ack-Ack crews are also perfecting new open-warfare tactics of their own, including having their anti-aircraft guns positioned on the back of trucks so that, once the breakthrough is achieved, they can keep pace with the troops and shoot from the skies those enemy aircraft who would seek to destroy them.

Leutnant Fritz Nagel of *Kraftwagen Flak* No. 82 is one who, from a standing start, must learn the basics, even how to drive a truck, notwithstanding the fact that the driver assigned to their crew, Eduard Rupp, had won races before the war and more than knows what he is doing. If Rupp is shot, it will be for them to take over, so Nagel must practise double-shuffle clutching and gear changes with the best of them. It is absorbing, but *Leutnant* Nagel pines more than most for his loved ones at home. In his case, it is a little particular, as immediately after returning from the Eastern Front in October, he had raced home to marry his beloved English bride, Dorothy, only to have her thereafter under strict surveillance at their home in Bremen as 'an enemy alien'.[45]

At least she is not interned, and in Nagel's view she is 'a prisoner of love more than a prisoner of war',[46] but he worries, most particularly when Dorothy tells him 'overeager "patriots"' keep accusing her 'of espionage, anti-German remarks and trying to signal enemy fliers . . .'[47]

Dummköpfe!

28 FEBRUARY 1918, FRANCE, THE AUSTRALIANS GET ZEBRA SUNTANS

'The English troops,' General von Hindenburg would note, 'were of varying value. The elite consisted of men from the Colonies – a fact which is undoubtedly to be attributed to the circumstance that the colonial population is mainly agrarian . . .'[48]

Douglas Haig does not necessarily share the same view.

Well, he certainly admires the Canadians.

'They are really fine disciplined soldiers now,' he writes to his wife, Dorothy, on 28 February 1918. 'And so smart and clean.'

But there are troops from another dominion who are a stark contrast, with their slovenly ways, their reluctance to salute their superiors and their general rebellion against authority.

'I am sorry to say that the Australians are not nearly so efficient,' Haig sadly informs Dorothy. 'We have had to separate the Australians into Convalescent Camps of their own, because they were giving so much trouble when along with our men and put such revolutionary ideas into their heads!'[49]

It is not that the Australians don't want to fight – there're no worries about that – it is that they want to fight *everyone*. The Germans. The British. The Canadians. Each other. It doesn't really seem to matter. Nor does it matter to them if they have permission or not to leave their units to go out on the town. They go anyway, and their Absent Without Leave (AWL) charges are shocking. Follow orders? Only if you ask them nicely, if you pretend to be on an *equal* footing with them. Quarrelsome be thy name. At least the British think so, for what they call 'insubordination' an Australian is inclined to call 'having a chinwag'.

The result is that the Australians are in military prison at over five times the rate of Canadians, New Zealanders and South Africans, and *nine* times more than British soldiers, who know their place.

—

On this very night, as it happens, the Australians want to – stop the presses and hold the front page – fight *Germans*.

For this specially selected group of soldiers of the 57th Battalion at Messines – from Brigadier Pompey Elliott's 15th Brigade – it is time for another trench raid, an exercise less designed to keep the Germans on their toes than back on their heels, making the bastards *reel*. Among the four soldiers making ready is Private Jimmy Downing, who waits with his mate Bot and a couple of others while their Sergeant receives his final instructions from Battalion HQ. And here he is now.

'Right-oh,' he greets them, easy as you please, as if they are all off for a jaunt to a nearby paddock. 'All got bags tied around your bayonets? All got bombs?'

Of course they have. The bags are to prevent any gleam from any flares that might be fired, the grenades for the obvious. They follow the Sergeant to one of the most forward outposts and again wait while he goes in to ensure the message makes it all along the line: they are going forward and no bastard is to shoot them on suspicion upon their return – they are not Germans.

'Come down now, boys,'[50] the Sergeant presently beckons them into the dugout, where a bottle of whisky and a little metal cup awaits, ready for them to take a few gulps before they head out.

Bottoms up – 'Happy days, Mr. Evans,' they say to the officer – and off they go. With no flares arcing skywards at the moment, it is black as pitch and they must feel their way forward along the barbed wire, the silence interrupted only by the odd bursting shell in the distance and a Stokes mortar coughing to their left. A few seconds later, rounds 'crash in a noisy heap' nearby. No matter, they keep moving. Soon, after following the Sergeant through a gap in the wire, they are in No-Man's Land. Working their way across it from shell hole to shell hole, they are so close to the German lines, just 50 yards away, that they can hear that guttural rumble of the German soldiers talking. After 30 minutes of lying completely doggo, they crawl forward with infinite care, the penalty for getting it wrong and making a noise presently showing up when they find the body of a man suspended on the wire – shrivelled and grey, rats running out of his gizzards.

A lazy flare arcs up in the middle distance, momentarily showing the poor bastard's face. Oh, Good Lord.

'It was a poor beggar reported missing after the raid a week ago,' Downing would chronicle. 'All the fingers were gone, gnawed off. Bot cut the string of his identity disc and took it. We moved on.'

Only 50 yards or so later, however, the Sergeant stops and clicks his tongue, signalling all his men to take cover, which they all do by diving into shell holes. Again, a flare reveals something horrifying – this time 14 Squareheads, literally, German soldiers with big box-like helmets on, out beyond their own wire, on patrol. And they are coming this way!

Every Australian soldier lies flat and moves not a muscle, in Downing's case 'repressing a mad desire to yell'. A harder case for one of his mates when a German boot comes down hard – 'Aaaaaaaagh!' – on his hand. Mercifully, the German soldiers pass them by, allowing the tight group of Australians from 57th Battalion to make their way through the German wire. Suddenly, they hear the German patrol coming back! This time they are caught, so there is only one alternative – taking their grenades from their pockets, they loosen the pins while still holding on tightly to the levers that prevent them exploding.

'We waited, a bomb in either hand,' Downing would recount. 'As the sergeant threw his bombs, we threw ours. There were six crashes, six flames. There were groans and wails and shouts and a medley of voices.'[51]

Now, there is fast; there is *very* fast; and then there is how fast six Diggers run when the game is up and from out of the darkness behind them German machine guns and rifles fire in their general direction. Like mad things, Downing and his mates charge back over half of No-Man's Land before throwing themselves down when the bullets around their feet become too intense. For twenty minutes they lie there as the bullets whiz over their heads, and only start to make their way back to their lines once it has stopped.

But hang on . . .

'Where's Bot?' the Sergeant asks, suddenly realising their comrade is missing. Inevitably, the code of never leaving anyone behind applies. 'He may have been knocked, we'll have to go back . . .'[52]

Carefully, quietly, they return to where they had thrown the grenades. There is no Bot to be found, but there are four dead Germans and one wounded one.

'He must have gone back alone, or else he's captured. Come on . . . We'll take this souvenir with us though.'[53]

Dragging the wounded German, they laboriously crawl back across No-Man's Land, making their way in the deep darkness in the direction where they think their own lines are to be found . . . until they hear the distinctive rattle of a rifle bolt.

'Halt!' a deep Australian voice cries out.

They are saved.

'Essendon . . .'[54] they call back, giving tonight's password.

Finally, they are safely back in their own lines and return to their dugout to find Bot, having a wound in his shoulder attended to, waiting for them.

A successful raid, all up, though not all such raids are so fortunate, and the Australians regularly suffer much heavier casualties.

'I always begrudge good men lost on these raids,' Brigadier Pompey Elliott would note, 'though they have to be attempted at times to get information that is not otherwise forthcoming.'[55]

In fact, perhaps begrudge is not quite the word. Originally nicknamed after 'Pompey' Elliott, the famous captain of the Carlton Aussie Rules team, the General is also a man of volcanic temperament, in a manner to bury old Pompeii when he blows. Never had that fury been more apparent than when he had been powerless to prevent the needless slaughter of his men at Fromelles, following insane British orders. On a bad day, his general regard for British officers as a breed sinks lower than a wombat's bottom. Since Fromelles, he has been ever more vigilant in protecting his men from suicidal orders, while still as determined as ever that they fight well.

EARLY MARCH 1918, BRUAY, SCANNING THE HEAVENS FOR THE DEVIL HIMSELF

As the frost fades and the weather warms, Lieutenant Harry Cobby can't help but notice it. No longer do they have to go looking for the German planes. More and more and more, the Germans are coming for them. No sooner do Cobby and his fellow pilots take to the skies than they are engaged in whirling dogfights – machine guns roaring, planes hurtling to earth and pilots dying.

'The technique of fighting also gradually changed,' he would record. 'No longer did we send formations of three or four machines over the line, but strengthened them to eight or ten with an occasional full squadron show.'[56]

And there is something else to quicken their pulse, stiffen their sinews and give them that wild mercury feel from the moment they lift off and push to eastern skies. The man who will go down in history as

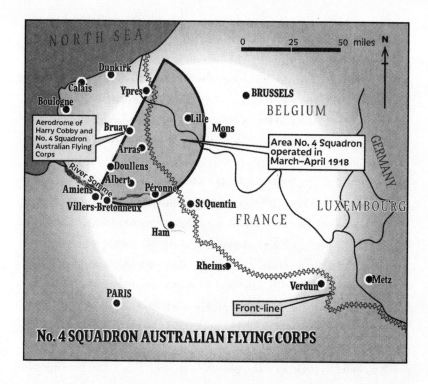

No. 4 SQUADRON AUSTRALIAN FLYING CORPS

'the Red Baron' is known to be operating on the front in which they are to fly their missions, his red Fokker triplane coming from on high, moving with lightning speed and breathtaking skill.

'The scotching of Richthofen,' Fred Cutlack would note, 'was the great ambition of every fighting pilot who had begun his ascent of the glorious ladder of "aces" in the list of "number of enemy machines destroyed". By the time the Australian scouting squadrons appeared in France, the days of the earlier crack German airmen, Immelmann, Boelcke, Wolff, Voss, had ended. Richthofen, the successor of Boelcke in command of the destroying "circus", the star of the stars in the German Air Force, was now in the zenith of his fame . . .'[57]

Beyond surviving against Richthofen – and even shooting him down if they possibly can – the Australians' main task remains: shoot down enemy reconnaissance aircraft and bombers while protecting Allied troops from the attentions of the likes of him and his circus.

5 MARCH 1918, WIESBADEN, GERMANY, LITTLE SPIKE'S BIRTHDAY

Of Margarethe Ludendorff's three sons, Erich has ever been the tallest, kindest, most handsome and . . . most loving. As a child, 'he hung tenderly to his little sister, and she to him. They were of one heart and soul.'[58]

And, of course, '*Piekchen*' – 'Little Spike' – had followed his older brothers into the air force, and she had worried every day since that he would be shot and killed, like Franz, for whom she still mourns.

But for now, Margarethe and her daughter, Margot, have had him all to themselves for two whole days. *Fliegerleutnant* Erich Pernet is home for his birthday and, tomorrow at dawn, must go back to the war. Each tick of the clock pushes him closer to departure. Now that dinner is over, they sit silently at the table, contemplating their forthcoming separation. Margarethe reaches out to slide her fingers through his short, soft hair. Then she takes his hand in hers, clearly on the point of tears.

'You must not be so sad, *mein Mütterchen*,' Erich says soothingly. 'Remember that I am wholeheartedly in my profession. Even if I've been through much hardship, I do not want to miss a single minute of the last years.'[59]

If she could speak, she would, but for now it is beyond Margarethe. All she can do is squeeze his hand as if she will never let it go.

'You know,' he goes on, 'I want to achieve something myself, and my highest and most beautiful goal is to one day become a General, like Father.'[60]

The claw around Margarethe's throat tightens.

Certainly, it has been one her 'most beautiful dreams for the future'[61] to see Ludendorff and her three boys sitting around her table as officers, but to do that they had to be *alive*, not lying dead in an unknown grave, and they have already lost dear Franz.

Erich goes on.

'I'm always sad when I hear others whispering: of course, this is Ludendorff's son. I want to be respected and recognised for my own sake.'[62]

Margarethe Ludendorff can understand. But it doesn't make the hurt of her boy's departure at dawn any easier to bear than it had been to farewell her other surviving son, Heinz, whom she had recently fare-welled to go and see service as a pilot on the Eastern Front. She cries as if she will not stop, with only Margot now for comfort, as they wave him off.

He is going to join the great Spring Offensive, taking with him the woollen scarf she has so lovingly knitted, to keep his slender neck warm in the skies above.

Möge Gott seine Seele behüten. May God protect his soul.

CHAPTER THREE
THE HUN IS AT THE GATE

For all we have and are
For all our children's fate
Stand up and take the war.
The Hun is at the gate![1]
Rudyard Kipling

Hans vos my name, und a pilot vos I
Out mit von Karl I vent for a fly
Pilots of Kulture ve vos, dere's no doubt
Each of us flew in an Albatros Scout
Ve looked for B.E.s for to strafe mit our guns
Ven last I saw Karl, I knew he was dones
For right on his tail were two little Sops
Oh hush-a-bye baby, on the tree-tops.[2]
*Popular mess song for the pilots of the Royal Flying
Corps and Australian Flying Corps*

10 MARCH 1918, NESLE, IS FRITZ FEINTING?

The Commander of the British Fifth Army, General Hubert Gough,
can feel it in his bones . . . Again and again, he has been going through
the reports, ruminatively, the heavy bags beneath his watery blue eyes

getting ever bigger as his exhaustion grows. More than ever, he has the appearance of a rather sad hound dog in uniform. But on this day it is no longer a matter of trying to discern the hidden truth behind the reports. The weekly Intelligence report issued on 10 March, using information gleaned on Gough's own front, now states the truth, black on white:

> The imminence of the offensive in the Arras–St Quentin area has been confirmed both by deserters' statements and by the enemy's activity in the construction of large ammunition dumps, light railways and the improvement of his communications [with the building of more roads]. The large concentration of artillery [observation] flights in this area continues, and night reconnaissances have seen an abnormal number of lights in back areas.[3]

Gough is so convinced that his forces will soon be in action that he has already moved 5th Army HQ to a more forward position, leaving behind comfortable quarters in Villers-Bretonneux and decamping to a more cramped building in Nesle, the small village 20 miles to the south-east. Whatever else, this will mean Gough is closer to the action, with the front-line just 10 miles away, enabling him to better direct operations when the Germans do attack.

At GHQ, Haig and his senior staff are far less sure that the attack will fall on Gough's Army. While the build-up in front of Gough is obvious, there is another equally apparent one in the far north, in front of Hazebrouck, where British intelligence reports from early March have repeatedly stated that THE GERMANS ARE PREPARING FOR OFFENSIVE OPERATIONS IN FLANDERS. Perhaps the real attack is there? Perhaps the one in front of Gough is an elaborate feint and, as Haig had already said to him, 'The German Command might be attempting to deceive us and intend to attack unexpectedly elsewhere,'[4] as they have long been expert in doing? Perhaps the

Germans will attack in both places at once? Either way, Haig mains his view. 'It is in the north I must retain my strength [to defend the Channel ports], while in the south we have some room to manoeuvre.'[5]

Whatever happens, as Bean notes, 'The knowledge that division after division of Germans was arriving from the Eastern Front, and that vast numbers of former prisoners must be daily rejoining the enemy, necessarily caused some uneasiness.'[6]

4 MARCH 1918, VALENCIENNES, FIE TO THE APPROACHING STORM

This, then, is a different kind of training for the *Stoßtruppen*, stormtroopers. While all through the winter they had trained in theory – practising tactics and rehearsing general movements – now they are preparing for *specifics*.

Working from German intelligence reports, which have themselves been informed by aerial reconnaissance observation, the men now storm forth across open fields, knowing that the models up ahead represent the British machine-gun posts they will find here, the artillery batteries that need to be knocked out and the Brigade headquarters they know will be 1000 yards back, on the right, with a wall of sandbags the height of two men protecting it.

Doctor Westman's 'football stars' are now approaching game-time. They know which team they will be playing, the weaknesses of their defence and where they will position themselves.

And they are going to turn up in force, with far more of them than the opposition can bring to the field.

'The scene,' *Leutnant* Herbert Sulzbach would note of his time by the French town of Guise, 18 miles from the front, 'is once again troops, troops, and more troops . . . We keep doing exercises to practice the tactics of mobile warfare. From far and wide, every emplacement and every hole and corner is being filled up with troops, and it looks as though we have Austrian troops here as well. The traffic on the roads is unbelievable . . . a few days later we have a large-scale exercise with one other division.'[7]

Inevitably, inexorably, the German forces really are now flooding forward on all fronts. But, *vorsicht*, careful! The Allies must not be alerted to what is happening. Nearly all the movement is to be done at night, just as the massive road repairs necessary to carry such traffic had been done by dim lanterns in the wee hours. And there are no huge ammunition dumps visible in open fields – all are secreted deep in the woods.

By now, courtesy of their gruelling training sessions at Sedan and Valenciennes, no fewer than 32 of 192 German Divisions on the Western Front have been converted into *Angriffsdivisionen*, attack divisions, with trained stormtroopers at the pointy end of the German spear.[8]

They are nearly ready to strike.

7 MARCH 1918, LONDON, AS THE MAN SAID TO THE BISHOP

Things are different in London these days for the Australian soldier on leave. Gone is the gaiety, the spontaneity, the sense of security of being in the capital city of the entire world, a place that the war cannot, at least physically, touch.

Instead, there is a strong feeling abroad of gloom and doom, of impending disaster caused by the threat of the Germans unleashing their evil forces right at the brave men holding the line on the Western Front. After four long, terrible years with dreadful sacrifices, the whole war could be over, *lost* to the Germans!

As Private Bert Bishop of the AIF's 55th Battalion strolls up the Strand towards Euston, every few yards he is accosted by clearly upset Londoners who take one look at his uniform and realise he has come from the Western Front on leave. All a-quiver, they ask the question, often with tears in their eyes: 'When is Jerry coming over, Aussie? Do you think we can hold him?'[9]

What most strikes Bishop is the fearful atmosphere, the depressive feeling over the whole city, exactly the same 'quiet tensed-up feeling'[10] he thought he had left behind at the Western Front, only to find it here, too! Sitting down for a cup of tea with an Australian mate, a sailor from HMS *Agincourt*, the mate soon asks him the same question: 'What's going to happen, Bert?'

'A big German offensive is coming,' Bert replies. 'That's accepted by everyone, but just where or when is known only to the Germans.'[11]

Worse and far more sobering than the fearful people in the street is the fact that the British Army shares their sentiment, and has for several months.

'I was returning from two week leave in England . . . and spoke to two English officers,' William Joynt of the 8th Battalion would recount. 'They told me that they dreaded going back to France to face the huge German offensive expected. One even said, "We are going to get a terrible beating."'

Joynt had been amazed, as it 'was so different from the Diggers' thoughts, whose officers were hurrying back "to be in it".'[12]

7 MARCH 1918, PRINCE RUPPRECHT'S HEADQUARTERS AT MONS

When we want your opinion we'll tell you what it is.

It is the way of a German military meeting: it is much less a discussion than a formal exchange of reports. One does not 'debate' with one's superiors, or anything even approaching that. One tailors one's report in the hope that one's superior will come to the same conclusion.

So it is with General Erich Ludendorff as he meets the five Chiefs of Staff from his five Army Groups this morning – the key organisers for four million soldiers – around a large mahogany table. Much as Ludendorff wants *der Tag* to be on or before 20 March, there are logistical impossibilities involved.

The Rupprecht Army Group – responsible for two-thirds of the attack – simply cannot get all its men and materiel in forward positions any faster, and needs a bit more time. (And, quietly, Rupprecht is less than an admirer of much of what Ludendorff says and does in the first place, noting in his diary – using a German expression to imply a certain vaingloriousness – 'that [Ludendorff] speaks out of the window is clear to me'.)[13] And Rupprecht has never been convinced that a major attack is the right option, equally noting his thoughts: 'Will our forces be sufficient for a major attack? I doubt it and feel oppressed by severe anxiety.'[14] On the other hand, he has no doubt of one thing: 'If we do not gain a decisive victory this spring, the war is lost for us inevitably.'[15]

And so it is reluctantly agreed.

The date for the launch of Operation Michael is officially set as 21 March, a neat fortnight hence. It's already an auspicious day in German history for the fact that it was on that day in 1871 that Chancellor Otto von Bismarck – whose most famous utterance had been, 'The great questions of the day will not be solved by speeches and resolutions . . . but by blood and iron'[16] – had opened the first Reichstag of the newly minted German Empire. By official communiqué from *der Kaiser* himself, the order soon goes out.

HIS IMPERIAL MAJESTY COMMANDS:

THE MICHAEL ATTACK WILL TAKE PLACE ON 21 MARCH. UNITS WILL BREAK INTO THE ENEMY'S FIRST POSITIONS 0940 HOURS. [17]

In total, 76 Divisions are slated to be put into place, just back from the British lines they are set to attack – with 32 of them set to launch on the first day, proceeding in 12 waves. It will be the biggest assault in history and three times larger than the British attack on the Somme in July 1916. The way it is planned, four-tenths of the whole German force on the Western Front will be massed to attack just one-tenth of its length. And the soldiers will be getting maximum support from the air, with 330 aircraft of the *Deutsche Luftstreitkräfte*, the German Air Force, already moving into position on the airfields between St Quentin and Cambrai. Foremost among them, of course, is *Jagdgeschwader 1,* 50 aircraft led by *Rittmeister* Manfred von Richthofen . . .

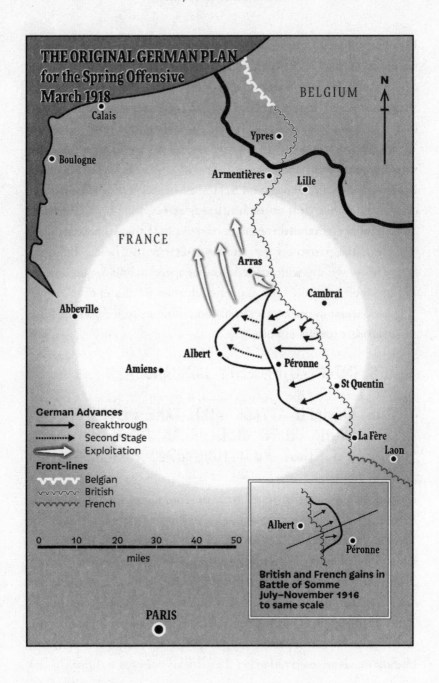

THE ORIGINAL GERMAN PLAN for the Spring Offensive March 1918

N

BELGIUM

Calais

Boulogne

Ypres

Armentières • Lille

FRANCE

Arras

Abbeville

Cambrai

Albert

Amiens •

Péronne

St Quentin

La Fère

Laon

German Advances
→ Breakthrough
▸ Second Stage
⇨ Exploitation

Front-lines
〜 Belgian
〜 British
〜 French

0   10   20   30   40   50
miles

Albert

Péronne

British and French gains in Battle of Somme July–November 1916 to same scale

PARIS

Lieutenant Harry Cobby and his comrades in No. 4 Squadron, mean-while, are doing much the same thing and suffering from the same conditions. With the clouds so thick and with such a low ceiling, all they can do is try to harass the enemy on the ground rather than fight high in the sky.

'Low flying attacks of "ground strafes" as they were known,' Cobby would record, 'were not pleasant tasks. We nearly always came home with machines shot about, and having as we did strong affection for our buses, a good deal of profanity was directed at the perpetrators of the damage. This had the effect of making the war a personal one as regards the particular part of Hunland responsible for the sacrilege, and every opportunity was taken to remind the enemy of the fact . . .'[18]

As to the enemy planes they *do* meet, one curious thing they notice is that there seems to be a preponderance of two-seater bombers, escorted by fighters who do not want to engage unless forced to. For whatever reason, it feels as though the Germans are more eager than ever to observe where the Allied strongholds and troops lie, but are reserving their resources for a bigger, more important effort to come.

Very well then.

If indeed the Germans are preparing an assault, as seems to be increasingly obvious, it behoves the Allied squadrons to do all possible to both increase their own observational flights to find the enemy's strength and to harass.

Their job, as Lieutenant Cobby would recount, was to throw themselves into 'bombing his aerodromes, taunting him to fight, probing unceasingly to discover the main secret – the selected moment of his onslaught. It was expected that the first shock would be felt in the air. The patrols sought for that shock, for the first touch of the enemy's battle-fleet. It might appear at any part of the front and at any moment. Each day . . . increased the strain.'[19]

—

Something really *is* going on.

On both 9 and 10 March, the Germans start shelling with unusual intensity – even for them – much of the area just behind the British front-lines held by the Third and Fifth Armies, sowing havoc among communications and supply dumps, and causing no end of damage. No, there is no particular shelling of the front-lines themselves, but that in itself is significant. Older heads note this is *precisely* what you do if getting ready for a big attack. You do as much damage as possible behind the lines, while keeping your powder dry and your stockpile of shells steadily building for the big attack to come on the front-lines. You damage your enemy's defensive systems without giving direct warning that you are about to go over the top.

Meanwhile, 50 miles north on Messines Ridge, things are quiet. But, perhaps, a little *too* quiet?

As one Australian diarist notes, with a view to the known transfer of German forces from Russia, it is all 'very quiet, but very electric. Because of the quietness everyone expects an attack . . . Our men don't think the Germans can get through. But they expect a bad time.'[20]

What the Australians mostly want at this time is a chance to go up against Fritz on fair terms.

At the northernmost end of the Messines ridge-line, for example, just two miles south of Ypres, the Australians are holding a post called the 'Spoil Bank', and the tension is palpable. All intelligence points to two big German build-ups: one here and one in front of Gough's Fifth Army in the south, in the area around St Quentin. But where will they strike? Perhaps both at once?

It all makes one Australian officer, Lieutenant Frank Bethune – a one-time parson now officer from Tasmania – worried for the welfare of his men. Having been given the task of defending the Spoil Bank, just one look convinces him the position is untenable if the Germans attack. With a field of fire of no more than six yards – because a bank of dirt just in front spoils their view, meaning the Germans could be right upon them with no warning – his men risk being killed before they even have a chance to defend themselves. As a good officer, Bethune points out the failing of the position to his Commanding Officer, asking to be allowed to choose a better position, only for the request to be denied.

Well then, there is only one thing for it.

And so Bethune issues his brave men an order that he puts some thought into:

> Special Orders to No.1 Section, 13/3/18.
>
> 1. This position will be held, and the section will remain here until relieved.
>
> 2. The enemy cannot be allowed to interfere with this programme.
>
> 3. If the section cannot remain here alive, it will remain here dead, but in any case it will remain here.
>
> 4. Should any man, through shell shock or other cause, attempt to surrender, he will remain here dead.
>
> 5. Should all guns be blown out, the section will use Mills grenades and other novelties
>
> 6. Finally, the position, as stated, will be held.
>
> F. P. Bethune. Lt
>
> O/C No I Section[21]

14 MARCH 1918, 10 DOWNING ST, THE IMPLACABLE VERSUS THE UNSACKABLE

And this, then, is the British version of the German dance. No matter that Prime Minister Lloyd George and General Sir Douglas Haig do not like each other – never have, never will – and that both recognise it. No matter that their relationship has never been so strained as right now, that Lloyd George has cut off Haig's supply of fresh troops from Great Britain to forestall him launching any offensives, and barely bothers hiding that fact – even though, of course, it is not written down anywhere as official policy – just as Haig knows that he is so popular with the public that he is virtually unsackable and does not much bother hiding it from the Prime Minister.

When it comes to their personal interaction this afternoon in the Prime Minister's office at 10 Downing Street, each man strains for politeness above all, in a manner befitting a Prime Minister discussing high matters of state with his Field Marshal.

In the presence also of the Leader of the House of Commons and member of the War Cabinet, Andrew Bonar Law, General Haig points out that if the Prime Minister does not release the fresh troops to him, 'the situation will be critical by June if the Enemy attacks . . .'

'But,' the Prime Minister counters in his rich Welsh brogue, 'you have given your opinion that the Germans will only attack against small portions of our front.'

'I never said that at all. The question put to me was, if I were a German General and confronted by the present situation, would I attack? And I said that if I was, I would only attack on such a limited basis. But the German Army and its leaders seemed drunk with their success in Russia and the Middle East, so it is impossible to foretell what they may attempt. In any case, we must be prepared to meet a very strong attack on a 50 mile front, and for this drafts [of new troops] are urgently required . . .'[22]

But the Prime Minister will not be moved, and Haig has no choice but to take his leave, fuming for the rest of the day and telling Lord Derby later in the evening, 'The Prime Minister by cunning argument tried to get me to commit myself to an opinion that there would be "no German offensive" and that "the German Army was done", but I refused to agree to his suggestions.'[23]

15 MARCH 1918, LA HÉRIE, NO MORE BELGIAN WAFFLE

While *Leutnant* Herbert Sulzbach has been impressed before with his Army's level of organisation, now, now he is *stupefied*. This morning, they have just received the first of their secret orders for the attack, the *precise* time they will go over the line, *exactly* what is expected of them, and the intricacies of the English defensive structure they will face, right down to the very last detail that they must overcome.

'Again and again,' he chronicles, 'you have to gaze in wonder at this careful work the Staff people are putting in, working things out right to the last detail – after all, that is the secret of our greatness . . .'

The only thing he can compare it to, in volume, was their gigantic mobilisation of 1914, but this time it is concentrated on a comparatively tiny front. This time, instead of a fist smashing into the face of the enemy, they will be a sword, expertly penetrating him, utilising 'all the things which did not exist in 1914 in the way of new weapons, new equipment and unbelievable masses of men'.[24]

Back then, it had been enough to smash the enemy, and winning the battle was enough. Not this time, though.

'Here and now, it is a question of our breaking through the enemy's gigantic fortified line and then winning the battle afterwards: in fact, it's a question of two victories . . . The preparations are getting more and more urgent, sleep is getting more and more unthinkable, every battery commander and every battery officer is a miniature General Staff. Even if you were tired, the excitement and enthusiasm wouldn't let you sleep anyway.'[25]

Tomorrow night, Sulzbach and his men – part of the Rupprecht Army Group, about to attack General Gough's Fifth Army Group – will begin moving up to the front itself, being carefully secreted in Itancourt, just back from the front-lines.

16 MARCH 1918, IN THE SKIES ABOVE FRANCE, THE CIRCUS COMES TO TOWN

Another day, another patrol.

On this fine morning, ten planes of No. 4 Australian Squadron have been given a special mission to bomb Douai railway junction and disrupt the flow of German troops who are reportedly moving through there en masse, Malley escorting. After three of the planes develop engine trouble there are just seven Sopwith Camels left, and yet it proves to be enough. Swooping from on high, they roar down upon the spaghetti of railway tracks, and await the moment.

Aware that the bombs will continue their forward momentum once they are released, the pilots know the key is to drop their loads before the intended target.

Ready . . .

Ready . . .

Now!

Nervously pushing the small lever on the joystick, there is a moment suspended in time for the pilot, rather like a bomb about to drop . . . or . . . is it? As all of them know, if all goes well the wire the lever is attached to will pull a bolt, which will release four 24-pound Cooper bombs fixed under the fuselage, just beneath the pilot's seat. The instant they are gone the plane skips up with the release of weight. But, if something goes wrong, the alternative is that the bombs don't detach, that they can be 'hung up', meaning your next thought is that it's a good thing you are 'wearing the brown underpants' – landing with your bombs still attached is a perilous exercise.

But when the bombs drop, as 99 times out of 100 they obediently do, it is wonderful.

For, oh, the *satisfaction* of seeing the explosions far below, the billowing flames and smoke as all the grey-green soldier ants run hither and thither – and you are able to get clean away.

Or at least they *think* so.

Only a short time after levelling off at 16,000 feet and beginning their journey back to Allied lines, the attacking pilots are suddenly in a dogfight for the ages as – Christ Almighty – *sixteen* brightly coloured German planes descend upon them.

It very well might be Richthofen's Flying Circus! A damned dangerous-looking bunch . . . *whoever* they are!

Suddenly the skies above Douai are filled with a couple of dozen planes looping, firing, side-slipping, diving, climbing and chasing each other across the heavens.

Two Australian pilots are soon in desperate trouble as German bullets rip holes in the fabric of their machines. One pilot, Lieutenant William Nicholls, who has only just joined No. 4 Squadron, is lucky, however, to be able to still fly his machine, and, as befitting a man whose middle name is Hurtle, does exactly that, initially outstripping his pursuers. Alas, though very nearly able to cross back over Allied lines, his pursuers finally overtake his stricken machine and force him to land, whereupon he is quickly taken prisoner.

The other, Lieutenant Percival Schafer, is in even more trouble after being fiercely fired upon and then chased as he tries to get away. With his life on the line, Schafer tries a desperate manoeuvre, allowing his bus to simply freefall, spinning earthwards, pursued all the way down by three red fighter planes.

As the patchwork of farms below spins round and round, Schafer nearly loses consciousness . . . but he holds on, knowing that if he does black out he will never wake in this world again.

And . . . *now!*

Using a technique pioneered by the great Australian pilot Harry Hawker in 1914 – putting his life on the line to prove it could be done – Schafer does something that is counterintuitive. With 3000 feet of altitude left, instead of pulling back on the joystick, to try to bring the nose up and flatten out, he does the reverse and pushes it forward (after applying pressure on the rudder opposite to the direction in which he is spinning). Hawker had proven that, when spinning downwards, your wings are no longer producing sufficient lift and the aerodynamic forces on your plane have changed to the point where, by pushing the joystick forward, the spinning stops, the plane is once again under control and the pilot can pull back the stick and level out.

Holding his breath, Schafer shoves the joystick forward – and waits, as the spinning ground below looms ever closer.

Slowly . . . the madly twirling mosaic of the world below starts to make sense and he can see . . . yes, fences, cows, villages . . . and a charming church. Jesus Christ, Saviour, Lord – there *is* a God!

The death spiral has stopped. The plane is under control. He can now level off. More importantly, the German planes that had been chasing him have been left behind as their engines simply cannot compete with the power of gravity, and no one goes into a spin unless they absolutely have to. They're not even chasing him now, to try to catch up, as he flies low over Allied lines. For in these very weeks, *Rittmeister* von Richthofen is completing his Air Combat Operations Manual, essentially a textbook for all German pilots to follow based on everything he has learned, and one principle he has spelled out in the clearest terms is now more relevant than ever, one he has in any case always drummed into his pilots:

One should never obstinately stay with an opponent who, through bad shooting or skilful turning, one has been unable to shoot down, when the battle lasts until it is far on the other side of the front and one is alone and faced by a greater number of opponents.[26]

It is madness to follow an enemy plane low over enemy lines, and Lieutenant Schafer is allowed to fly on, unhindered, finally reaching Bruay aerodrome 'with sixty-two bullet-holes in his machine, including several through the wind-screen in front of his face'.[27]

Meantime, back in the dogfight, two Australian pilots, Lieutenants George Malley and Cecil Feez, are at least able to get some revenge for the sons of the Southern Cross and shoot two of the red Albatros fighters down in flames. Lieutenant Albert Adams is also the victor in a fierce duel with a couple of enemy planes – one of them is last seen heading to the ground trailing smoke.

On returning to their aerodrome, the report that Richthofen's Circus is now open for business in the sector of the Scarpe River that runs west from Douai to Arras 'sent a thrill through local British air squadrons'.[28]

He's there!

The Red Baron and his men!

17 MARCH 1918, THE GERMAN STORMTROOPERS GATHER

Hauteville is a small French village, with a charming church, just 10 miles back from the front-lines of the Western Front and normally boasts 700 French villagers. Not today. Many of those 700 have fled, while in their place more than 15,000 German soldiers, battery after battery, battalion after battalion, are secreted in its houses and buildings, hidden in the wooden gullies that abound all around – careful to keep themselves, as much as possible, invisible to aerial reconnaissance.

This night, for example, that church alone will house as many as 500 of them, sleeping rough, between and on the pews, by and on the altar, in the vestibules and the vestry. Every square yard of God's house will be filled with a German soldier, including right up in the roof, where, even on this morning, from his bird's-eye perch, *Leutnant* Herbert Sulzbach is contemplating, chronicling in his diary a scene that had occurred the day before when he and his comrades had been about to pull out of the similar village of La Hérie, 15 miles to their east.

Many detachments move out before them, and one of them is marching to the beat of the Battalion's big brass band, complete with blaring trumpets and beating drums. The tune they gaily play as they pass Sulzbach is one familiar to him. For, *ja*, it is! Altogether, sing: '*Muss I denn, muss I denn zum Städtele hinaus?* . . . Must I go, must I go, must I leave the little town? *Wenn du weinst, wenn du weinst, Dass i wandere muß, wandere muß,* Don't you cry, don't you cry, 'cause I've got to go, Got to go.'[29]

As the men march on, many of them wave at Sulzbach and his comrades 'with such nice looks on their faces that you felt warm and enthusiastic'.

And yet, he can't help it – with an icy shudder the thought strikes: 'Which of these good men, and which of us for that matter, is going to come home from this battle which lies ahead of us?'[30]

Just a mile to the north, late that afternoon as the sun fades, stormtrooper *Leutnant* Reinhold Spengler, the Commander of a light machine-gun platoon of the 1st Bavarian Infantry Division in von Hutier's 18th Army, leaves the village of Vervins to head to the front.

'Our destination was St Quentin,' he would record. 'Endless columns of light and heavy artillery pieces, as well as ammunition wagons, passed alongside us on their way to the front. They were drawn mostly by teams of four to six horses. All of these guns were concealed from the enemy until the last moment. This display of military power made us hope that the long depressing years of war would soon come to a swift and victorious end. Perhaps now we would have the upper hand!'[31]

—

Far from being intimidated by the presence of such a formidable foe as the Red Baron in the area of the Scarpe River, where Cobby and his mates had been active just the day before, the squadrons now compete to go on missions to that area. Australia's No. 4 Squadron is in it with the best of them, searching the skies, looking for a chance to claim the scalp to beat them all.

Oh, the glory, to be able to bring down von Richthofen!

But there is no sign of him. Mysteriously, the Baron and his Flying Circus seem to have disappeared.

All men can do, in the absence of the German pilots, is to 'fire some thousands of machine-gun rounds into the German trenches near Lens and La Bassée.'[32]

But it is not the same. Where could von Richthofen and his men have gone?

—

On this day, 18 March, *Rittmeister* von Richthofen has much to contemplate. Concerned at the blow that would be dealt to German morale if ever he is killed in action, as has happened to so many other flying aces, the authorities have sent him an offer to stand down, retire, take up a desk job overseeing other pilots.

He has refused outright.

'I should consider myself the most despicable creature,' he would record, 'if, now that I am loaded with fame and decorations, I should consent to live on as the pensioner of my own dignity, and to preserve my valuable life for the nation, while every poor fellow in the trenches, who is doing his duty just as much as I am, has to stick it out.'[33]

Will there come a time when he can settle down safely with the woman whose photo he always carries with him, Nurse Käte Otersdorf?

Perhaps, but for now his place is here in the skies with his men, on this day hunting to the south, around St Quentin, and leading a prowling pack of 30 aircraft drawn from three of his *Jastas* against whatever British targets they can find.

And there is his perfect quarry now. A tight pod of British planes, heading east. As is his practice, the Baron stays well above the fray at first, allowing his men to shoot down two Bristol fighters, before he spots a lone Camel making a break for it. For a man of von Richthofen's capacity – skilful enough to get his plane so close before shooting that he just can't miss, and courageous enough to do so – it takes no more than a minute from spotting his target to blasting its cockpit and engines with lead, though, for once, not the pilot's *head*.

The plane is soon plummeting to earth for the Red Baron's 66th victory. Still, the pilot, Lieutenant William Ivamy, retains rough control and actually manages to land it, intact, in a paddock before climbing out to be immediately taken prisoner.

A German soldier from 238th Division watches what happens next.

'A German machine circled over him like a bird of prey . . . The German flyer landed right near the enemy machine, climbed out and cut the serial number from the fuselage. [The German was in] the red machine that had circled over us and everyone waved at it. It was *Rittmeister* Manfred von Richthofen.'[34]

Late that afternoon, it is time for von Richthofen's Flying Circus to pack up its tents and head west. From sundown today, when the last planes of his *Jagdgeschwader 1* – a mix of Albatros D.Va and Fokker Dr.1 – land, they will be grounded for two days. Meanwhile, all their equipment, mechanics and tent hangars are piled onto large trucks. And let's not forget the piano for the pilot's mess – together with the souvenirs on the mess wall taken from shot-down enemy aircraft that the pilots like to always have on display, the way hunters appreciate deer antlers above their fireplaces. Also safely packed away must be such things as the inevitable drinks supply, which the mess steward has to keep an eye on. And then they begin the long haul towards the town of Awoingt, just outside of Cambrai, some 35 miles north-east of Amiens. This is to be their new base from the start of *der Tag*, the big day that Operation Michael starts.

18 MARCH 1918, THE HUN READIES TO OPEN THE GATE

Now moved into his forward HQ, a comfortable house in the French town of Dourlers, General Ludendorff busies himself as never before, organising his army of 3,000,000 German soldiers – with another million deployed elsewhere – about to engage in the battle that will decide the winner of this war once and for all. Much of his time is taken up with reading endless reports informing him just how far advanced, or not, preparations for Operation Michael are, and his sending out orders accordingly.

At least with *der Kaiser*, now installed five miles down the road in Château de Merode in Trélon, things are more relaxed, and on this day His Imperial Majesty does little more than visit his loyal troops. So insistent is *der Kaiser* on keeping close to his troops, however, that he keeps on standby nearby his *Sonderzug*, his special train, to be moved about according to the military situation. Avesnes has been specially chosen by the German High Command as a town safe from the risk of enemy incursion or bombing, while still being close enough that all parts of the front are no more than a day's journey away, at most.

As noted by Admiral Müller, gilding the lily somewhat, 'The residence of several weeks in the restricted quarters on the train may serve as an example of the simple ways of our War Lord. At such time he lived entirely with his army. Regard for danger, even from enemy airmen, was quite beyond the range of our Emperor's thoughts.'[35]

—

It has been a busy day in Hauteville as both troops and artillery keep moving west through it, to the front just a few miles away, ready for *der Tag!*

'As they pass,' Sulzbach records, 'we see the latest self-propelled guns, long-barrelled giants on 100-horse-power chassis which have front-wheel drive and back-wheel drive at the same time. These great things will be ready to fire in two hours' time – they look to us like monsters raging across the country; as they drive off, the men wave at us and cheer us enthusiastically as if it were 1914.'[36]

Sulzbach works into the night, until two o'clock in the morning, with *Leutnant* Knauer, issuing last-minute movement and artillery orders, as well as ensuring that his own four-gun battery is fully apprised of the ranges, targets and times of their program. They are a small part of an artillery schedule that is as complicated as it is sophisticated, but all are determined to do their part.

19 MARCH 1918, ST QUENTIN, DELIGHTFULLY DARK DAYS

The weather is perfect! *Eine Suppe!* That is, it is dull, dark and dank, with a very low cloud cover – just made for moving troops forward without aerial reconnaissance spotting them.

General Erich Ludendorff, ensconced in his new HQ – where he is now waiting for the Kaiser to arrive from his specially fitted-out train – is pleased. While his meteorologist, *Leutnant* Dr Schaum, had warned of the likelihood of foggy mornings, which would be very problematic, this is not that. And hopefully they would have the same conditions in two days' time.

For now, the German soldiers are pressing ever closer to their designated position, four abreast across often newly constructed roads, in columns that just keep coming – for once without any worries about being spotted, strafed or bombed.

In the midst of the milling throng of German soldiers positioned just east of St Quentin – straining at the leash, *willing* their final orders to move to their attack lines to come through – is one of the commanders of a storm troop, *Leutnant* Erich Schmidt. Notwithstanding that he was a vicar before the war, devoted to spreading God's love, he is as thrilled as all the rest this afternoon when, with other company commanders, he is ushered into the presence of the artillery commander, General von Friedeburg, in Montigny.

'Now here, for the first time,' he will joyously record in his diary, 'the veil of secrecy fell. We learned that our attack section is St Quentin and our division is storm division of the first line. Our regiment is division reserve. Upon returning from the lecture we already found the attack map to be present; it was all prepared in a downright brilliant fashion.'[37]

Soon, they can attack!

———

While the Germans march towards a known objective, the Diggers wait in limbo. Most of them are still up near Ypres, in Flanders, as the 1st, 2nd and 5th Australian Divisions continue with their front-line duties.

Among them is Archie Barwick with his 1st Divvie, who takes a moment between front-line tours to jot in his diary:

'Our big guns are all in action and the air is all a quiver and everything shaking like a leaf from the concussion . . . Things can't go on much longer as they are; one side or other will have to plunge. The sector the Australians are holding at present is a most important part of the Western Front, and we are holding it strongly . . . If ever Fritz wants to try his luck and his Prussians, the shell holes, and craters stink of machine guns and we have field guns covering all our heavies – it would be a perfect massacre if ever he were to attack.'[38]

The 4th Australian Division under General Ewen Maclagan, meantime, is in support at Merris, 14 miles due west of Armentières, while General John Monash's 3rd Division is in reserve, taking 'a well-earned rest in a pleasant countryside at Nielles-lez-Blequin, not far from Boulogne . . . lying there, enjoying the first signs of dawning spring.'[39]

General Monash, on this day, is down in the Riviera, taking a long walk in the hills, drinking in the beautiful scenes and clean air, thawing out his body from a long, harsh winter.

As for the Australian Corps Commander, General Sir William Birdwood, he is over in England, leaving his Chief of Staff, General Brudenell White, the architect of the miraculous evacuation from Anzac Cove in 1915, acting on his behalf. At Australian Corps headquarters at Flêtre, just after 6 pm on this day, Brudenell White receives the daily intelligence summary from his Corps Intelligence Office. He takes it in his long fingers and scans it calmly, expertly, just as he has done thousands of times before, looking for any telltale signs of the German offensive.

Unfortunately, there is not much out of the ordinary. German preparations appear to be ongoing. One observation catches his attention, however, though it is hardly solid evidence to stand ready:

```
ENEMY'S ATTITUDE
    The left division reports the enemy much
quieter than usual, except in his artillery
opposite their right brigade front. On the left
brigade front he was slightly more aggressive.
Along the whole divisional front the enemy grows
more alert and nervy, his machine guns opening
fire at the least sound or movement.40
```

Their observers have also noted that the Germans' camouflage screening is continuing to block out ever more buildings and stations, and that new wire – 'very thick and strong'41 – is being erected along their lines.

The attack is nigh. It must be.

—

One who is sure of it: Artillery Officer *Leutnant* Herbert Sulzbach.

'Our kicking-off point for the offensive,' he records, 'is going to be

. . . St Quentin and that was once a gay, pleasure-loving rear-echelon city, and now it's a frontline position. The British trenches are hardly a mile away: but it will soon be in the rear again!'[42]

How soon, neither Sulzbach nor any of the other officers or soldiers know. Obviously, now that they are in their waiting positions, the time must be close, 'but the date and time will only be passed through at the last second. We are already imagining what it will be like when the order comes: *"Protzen heran"* – "prepare to move!" We are most conscious of the greatness of the moment, and have got into a terrific state of tension, and even when we have time for rest, we genuinely can't sleep anymore, not for a second.'[43]

19 MARCH 1918, HAIG'S HQ AT MONTREUIL, A VISIT FROM WINSTON

The Commander of the British Expeditionary Force, General Douglas Haig, lives well, as appropriate for a man in his position. When he dines, it is as if he's the Kaiser of Britain, with silver service, over several courses, with liveried waiters in white hovering and – it has to be said since he arrived in France four years earlier – what little wine he does delicately sip is very fine indeed. Far less abstemious is the generously proportioned Winston Churchill, already the size that could possibly have inspired the later line of his friend, P. G. Wodehouse: 'The Right Hon. was a tubby little chap who looked as if he had been poured into his clothes and had forgotten to say "When!"'[44]

Installed nine months earlier as the Minister for Munitions, Churchill is on a visit to the Western Front and currently talking over, during this long lunch, the current situation.

Haig is convinced that any day, and perhaps even *today*, the Germans will launch 'an attack of the first magnitude'.[45] All the signs point to it, all the intelligence reports agree that the Germans are massing their forces on just their side of the line. After dessert and cheese, Haig takes Churchill into his private room so he can better illustrate his thoughts with the use of the maps that abound there, complete with markers

– pins with cords stretched between – that show where both their own and the German strong points and front-lines are. The British positions are marked in imperial blue, the Germans in demon red.

With a single glance, thus, Churchill can see why Haig is so convinced.

The cluster of red pins particularly opposite General Gough's Fifth Army is all too obvious. And, yes, there is also a cluster in the north, opposite the British front, from Ypres to Messines.

'But the main developments,' Churchill would reminisce, 'were to be expected in the sector from Arras to Péronne and even farther south . . . More than half the German divisions in the west were ranged against the front of the British Armies.'[46]

EVENING, 19 MARCH 1918, COLONEL FRANK PIGGOTT WRITES TO HIS WIFE AS 'DER TAG' APPROACHES

At the end of a long day, collecting and collecting the 'last pieces of evidence from the Fifth Army front', General Gough is convinced. There really is an 'approaching storm',[47] as his Head of Intelligence, Colonel Frank Piggott, would describe it. A German storm, and it is heading right for them. Piggott would later detail the evidence assembled:

'A German artillery non-commissioned officer captured west of Bony, an aeroplane brought down near Fontaine, infantry prisoners captured south-west of Villers-Guislain, all told the same story, each in his own way – in some cases unwittingly . . .'

It is all strong enough that, the previous day, Piggott had written to his wife, 'I expect a bombardment will begin tomorrow night, last six to eight hours, and then will come the German infantry on Thursday 21st.'[48]

Funny he should say that. For though his expectation is that they are about to be ants in a storm – engulfed by a deluge of shell fire, gas, chattering machine guns and storming stormtroopers – they are hit sooner than he has imagined.

The drone of low aircraft overhead is quickly followed by the shattering roar of explosions just outside Fifth Army HQ. Heading outside immediately afterwards to 'see what mischief had been done', Gough is saddened to see the Germans had scored a direct hit on one of the château's sheds being used by the company of one of the BEF's labour battalions.

Following the groaning and screaming, he soon finds several dead men and a few fearfully wounded among the wreckage. One of the latter proves to be an old labourer, who is bleeding very badly but is still quite lucid.

'I . . . am . . . going,' he tells General Gough before starting to give *him* orders for once. 'Put your hand into my jacket . . . and pull out my pocket-book . . . and write down what I tell you.'

'Oh no,' Gough protests in what he hopes is a comforting fashion. 'You just keep quiet and rest yourself.'

But the old man insists. 'I want to have . . . everything settled up nicely . . . for my missus.'[49]

Gough agrees – moved by the fellow's 'coolness, his courage, his thought for others' – and takes down what is, effectively, the old man's last will and testament just before he dies.

The heavens open and it starts to rain – the first rain for eight weeks.

20 MARCH 1918, HAUTEVILLE, THE RAIN BEFORE THE FOG

Und doch es regnet. And still it rains.

For the mass of German soldiers secreted now just on their side of the line, many of them in forward trenches, the wet makes things difficult. But the upside is that the low cloud continues to keep enemy reconnaissance aircraft from observing any of their last-day movements, making things a little easier.

As *Leutnant* Herbert Sulzbach goes about his business on this day, riding his horse through the slush and mud to receive the firing lists – the precise times the men are due to fire at precise targets with designated frequency over the five hours – from the Divisional Artillery Commander, he is pleased to see 'still troops, troops and more troops moving up to the front'.[50]

And when he arrives back at the front, the concentration of troops just back from the line, ready to move forward as soon as they get the word, is extraordinary. Nearly all of the units are in their penultimate positions now, many of them, Sulzbach notes, 'with messenger dogs'.[51] (It is hoped that the British will not yet have followed the Germans' own tactic to counter messenger dogs, which has long been to position bitches on heat just behind the lines. Experience has proven that not even *German* shepherds follow orders when their primal instincts compete with their training.

No, nothing is yet absolutely confirmed, that tomorrow is *der Tag*, but with this heavy concentration of troops now in place, with everyone given precise instructions about their role once they attack, it is obvious that it must be very close. Tomorrow, they hope.

—

At Avesnes, a quick meeting between Marshal von Hindenburg and General Ludendoff, with their staff officers, receives a meteorological report at 11 am, affirming that the weather on the morrow 'would not be perfect . . . but adequate for the attack'.[52]

A bit of rain, they could live with, though too much mist would be problematic. The key is wind direction, as their gas shelling relies on it blowing from behind them, and on that count they are assured.

In the end, Ludendorff has to make the final decision, and does so.

'At midday,' Marshal von Hindenburg would recount, 'we decided definitely that the battle should begin on the morning of the following day.'[53]

With the order signed, the military machinery of the most enormous operation in history thus far is set into motion.

—

Much to the disappointment of the pilots of the Australian Flying Corps' No. 4 Squadron, stationed at their Bruay aerodrome, they are not having much luck – despite the fact that other squadrons are reporting huge numbers of enemy planes about, including the single-seater fighter 'scouts'.

As Cobby would later recall of the squadron's activity in the middle days of March, 'We anticipated that the period of quietness we were experiencing was to be of short duration, and plodded along getting into the air a couple of times a day and looking for the elusive enemy and not finding him, and then venting our frustration on anything that we could find on the ground.'[54]

On this day, Cobby is resting in the late afternoon when the flight commander calls on him and gives orders to make a reconnaissance of the sector near ours as far as Bapaume, and to get used to the layout of the country in that direction.[55]

The commander warns Cobby, an attack on a large scale is manifestly intended by the German High Command. Its actual location is unknown, but the indications are that it will commence somewhere about Cambrai or Bapaume.[56]

Cobby, having proven his natural worth as a pilot over the past few months, is detailed to lead two formations of five machines each at the crack of dawn the next morning.

It's heating up!

———

At 7 pm, 20 March, just south-east of St Quentin, *Leutnant* Herbert Sulzbach is called upon by one of his staff to take a phone call.

Picking up the receiver, he hears the long-awaited order, the words of General Oskar von Hutier as read by a superior to every officer in the 18th Army along the entire 45 miles of front to be attacked: 'After years of defence action on the Western Front, Germany is moving to the attack; the hour eagerly awaited by every soldier is approaching. I am certain that the Regiment, true to its history, will enhance its reputation in the days that lie ahead. This great objective will call for sacrifices, and we shall bear with them for the Fatherland, and for our loved ones at home. Then forward, into action! *Mit Gott für König und Vaterland!* With God for King and Fatherland!'[57]

At last it has come. Confirmation that tomorrow is *der Tag.*

Like the vast majority of his comrades, Sulzbach is thrilled, if a little overwhelmed.

'There is a terrible lot of work to do,' he notes, 'we are in the highest possible spirits, and everybody lends a hand in distributing the huge quantities of ammunition.'[58]

Not all are so thrilled. When the word spreads that the Kaiser himself, along with Marshal von Hindenburg, has arrived and intends to watch the battle unfold, one soldier greets the news with a sneer and, shivering in his damp, cold dugout, remarks, *'Ja, ja,* and he'll be doing it lying in a warm comfortable bed in his nice château.'[59]

For the *workers* of this war, it is time for their last hot meal before going into action on the morrow, one with much more meat in it than usual. (Their commanders really do think of *everything*, the soldiers note appreciatively as they wolf it down.) Nearby, volunteers are dragging 'heavy guns right up to our wire and there conceal them in shell holes'[60] so that the fingers of German artillery will be able to poke the British eyes even further back. Usually in such attacks, the heavy guns stay 2000 yards back, so this simple manoeuvre gives them the potential to pound another mile of enemy territory, and then capture it.

And now the stormtroopers of the first wave must march quietly to previously prepared concealed locations close to the lines – usually no more than a mile away, at most.

A mile north of Sulzbach, in 1st Bavarian Division, *Leutnant* Reinhold Spengler is told the news for the first time by his Commanding Officer. Tomorrow really is *der Tag* and, after the coming bombardment, he and his men are due to go over the top at precisely 9.15 am. Spengler's men clean and prepare their weapons once more and load up with extra ammunition and bombs. Once they launch their attack, the rolling barrage will move forward every five minutes. They must be ready to move forward with it, tightly behind, just as they have been trained.

'We synchronize our watches and, holding my pocket watch in

my hand, I saw that my palms had begun to sweat in anticipation,' Spengler would record. 'I passed on the information to my section leaders and NCOs, and they told the men.'[61] Once everyone is ready, Spengler's stormtroopers finally move into position at Itancourt, just a mile south-east of St Quentin. 'Just behind us, the guns of the 1st Bavarian Field Artillery Regiment were in position and a number of mortars were set up in the trench. Each gun and mortar was spaced some ten to fifteen metres apart – and this on a total front of seventy-five kilometres!'[62]

Der Tag is upon them!

———

That portly figure with the bulldog jowls picking his way gingerly through the narrow paths and labyrinthine trenches that lead to that part of the front-line near Gauche Wood being held by the 9th Scottish Division? Why, it is none other than Winston Churchill, the Minister for Munitions, come forward on a brief inspection excursion to see first-hand that all is as it should be; that, whatever else, the troops have the munitions they need for the battle that is surely to come.

The sun, which has been out most of the afternoon, is dropping below the horizon when he reaches his destination and is able to survey the British troops in all their glory.

'I can see them now, serene as the Spartans of Leonidas on the eve of Thermopylae.'[63]

Among the 9th Scots Division is 6th Battalion, Royal Scots Fusiliers, that Churchill had briefly commanded after his Dardanelles disgrace, before returning to politics, and he feels a greater empathy for them than the already great feeling he has for all British troops. Who knows what the next few days have in store for them, just how ghastly it might be?

The 9th Scottish, veterans of the Battle of Loos in September 1915, hold nearly three miles of front and are the northernmost Division of the Fifth Army, adjacent to the southernmost Division of the Third Army.

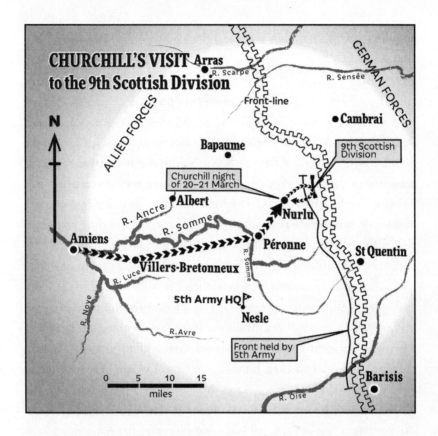

After being escorted back from the front, Churchill returns to his quarters in a still-standing habitation in the ruined village of Nurlu.

That low drone, an ever-so-faint diminuendo, like a house fly shooed out an open window – Churchill can just hear it in the distance if he cocks his ear to the east of the evening twilight?

It is the Red Baron and his fellow pilots of the Circus heading south. Straight after sundown, they have flown to a spot two miles outside Cambrai. As they ease back on their throttles to lose height, their 'aerodrome' comes into focus – a clear, flat patch of earth amid wheat fields, where their tents and mechanics await. They are part of a force that will total some 150 German fighters, all to be massed in the area to support *die Michael-Offensive*. The Red Baron and his deadly Circus are due to take off at 9 am the next day, forty minutes before the stormtroopers are unleashed, so they can wreak early havoc on Allied front-lines and just behind.

—

In his dugout at Villers-Outréaux, 15 miles north of St Quentin and 30-odd miles due east of the 9th Scottish front south of Arras, Captain Rudolf Binding takes time – like many of his comrades – to pen a few words to his family. Yes, the post has been stopped today for the sake of security, but their letters will be collected and sent on their way after their authors have gone over the top.

Captain Binding wields the pen with the practised ease of one who is a professional writer and poet in civilian life, with long, florid strokes and none of the stuttering hesitation of some of the younger soldiers. Having lived a full half-century himself, he counts himself a fatalist – what will be, will be – and unlike his fellow soldiers, many of whom are more *sons* in arms than brothers, he has a far longer lens through which to view the war.

'Tomorrow,' he writes to his family as the time passes midnight and *der Tag* has at last arrived, 'all hell breaks loose . . . It is a tremendous thing for every one of us . . . It will be a drama like a Greek tragedy . . . The troops are packed in position so tight that those in front have been there for the last ten days. For weeks past, ammunition has been hauled and hauled, night after night, to be piled in mountains round the guns. All that is to be poured out on the enemy four hours from now. One division lies behind the other to an incalculable depth, and three armies, the 18th, the 2nd and the 7th, are to attack together in unison on an infinitesimal front.'[64]

—

Before Churchill turns in, the Commander of the 9th Scottish Division, General Hugh Tudor, says to him with stoic force – perhaps aware that the shadows of the valley of death are even now growing longer and reaching out to his men – words that he will never forget: 'It is certainly coming now. Trench raids this evening have identified no less than eight enemy battalions on a single half mile of the front . . .'[65]

With those numbers it is clear that the Germans are more than massing for an attack – they have enough men to launch a massacre.

———

As his last act at the end of this long day and evening, Gough visits his four Corps commanders 'to have a final talk over everything before the battle'.[66] Before turning in, he has a brief chat with his French liaison officer, Paul Maze – a sophisticated Parisian who is a well-regarded artist in civilian life, though much in the shadow of his great friends Claude Monet and Auguste Renoir.

And the General does not mince words.

'I expect the storm to break over us tonight . . . I know for certain that we have forty-two divisions massed against us, and –'[67]

And he is interrupted by a call, which proves to be from a senior officer at General Haig's GHQ. Gough takes the opportunity to stress that his two reserve divisions should be moved forward, ready to intervene as soon as the Germans attack.

The way it appears to Maze, listening in, the GHQ officer on the other end of the line has a different view that makes Gough, after a time, close down the conversation with a defiant, 'I shall fight those blighters in my battle zone as long as we can hold them there. Good night, good night.'[68]

Enough now.

Whatever is going to happen, everyone must get some sleep. With that in mind, Gough bids Maze goodnight and tells him to come and see him early in the morning. Maze climbs atop his humble motor scooter and rides back to his lodging in the original Fifth Army HQ town of Villers-Bretonneux, that town's famed Red Château.

Before the war it had been the town's most famous residence. Owned by the Delacour family, it boasts fine gardens, greenhouses, a park and even an aviary stocked with exotic birds originating from all over the world. The Delacours' young son Jean has called it his 'earthly paradise', his own private Garden of Eden.[69] But, as is the way of such things, the early winds of war have blown the family out of the house – with 24-year-old Jean himself now serving in the French Army as a Lieutenant, and the rest of the family retreating to Paris.

Maze pushes on towards it. Not that it is easy. As he rides along, his tiny headlight penetrates ever less the thick fog rising, the first of the spring.

—

At Essigny – right opposite where Sulzbach is still directing his men, urging them to move quickly as they distribute huge quantities of ammunition – English Private Jim Brady, in a first aid post with the 43rd Field Ambulance, senses that something is up. And so do his comrades. Climbing to the top of a nearby bluff, they gaze into the darkness that blankets the flat French countryside below.

'It hung like a canopy over the front lines just over a mile away . . . mostly the guns were still, and in the distance we could quite clearly hear the rumble of enemy transport.'[70]

What to do?

Of course.

Returning to his quarters, Brady makes a cup of tea. One for him and one for the Medical Officer, Captain Duncan. But when he takes it to the Captain with a hunk of bread and jam, Duncan proves to be in a queer mood. Taking out his wallet, Duncan thrusts into Brady's hands a huge wad of francs.

'I seem to have more than I need, Brady,' he says simply. 'You'd better have some.'[71]

Brady reluctantly accepts the money and heads off to bed, miserable, full of dreadful foreboding. Perhaps everything they know, and maybe everyone, is about to be swept away by the approaching cataclysm.

'I clambered up into my bunk,' he would recount, 'which had a head room of barely two feet. Upstairs everything seemed quiet – a good deal too quiet!'[72]

Funny he should say that . . .

Over on the German side of the line, the cogs are turning and the wheels of Ludendorff's great Spring Offensive are beginning to pick up momentum.

—

The preliminaries are completed.

Now, 1 o'clock on the morning of 21 March, it is done. Just over 400,000 German soldiers are in position over a front of 45 miles, tight on the front-lines like *würste* in a tin – now to rest, the lucky ones in shelters, the not-so-lucky under bivouac sheets doubled up for warmth that never comes.

The men cradle their canisters of ersatz coffee, which they must ration throughout the cold morning, and get ready to go over the top, once the five-hour bombardment, due to start at 4 am, is over.

—

'The night of 20th March,' General Gough would record, 'every man in the Fifth Army whose duty allowed him to do so, lay down calmly enough for a night's sleep, but all of us felt perfectly certain that we would be wakened before morning by the roar of the battle.'[73]

—

On the German side of the line, they *know* so.

'Tomorrow is to be the great day,' German pilot Rudolph Stark of the *Jasta 34* at Le Cateau writes in his diary. 'Tomorrow everything will be merged into one vast battle; blood will flow and victories will be won. Tomorrow, perhaps, I shall be dead.'[74]

CHAPTER FOUR

THE KAISERSCHLACHT – THE KAISER'S BATTLE – BEGINS

When an army starts upon a campaign, it resolves
itself speedily into two parts, one that means to
keep out of harm's way if possible, and the other
that always keeps with the colours . . .[1]
General George McClellan in James Robertson's
Tenting Tonight: The Soldier's Life, 1862

It had come at last! His own stupendous hour,
Long waited, dreaded, almost hoped-for too,
When all else seemed the foolery of power;
It had come at last! and suddenly the world
Was sharply cut in two . . .
Lieutenant Max Ploughman, 10th West Yorkshire Regiment[2]

Almost everything [for the BEF] which came in
through the three northern ports had to go through
Hazebrouck. Almost everything which came through the
three southern ports had to go through Amiens . . .[3]
David Zabecki, The German Offensives 1918

21 MARCH 1918, 4.30 AM, OPERATION MICHAEL, AND THE FOG OF WAR

It was the great Prussian military analyst Carl von Clausewitz who, in 1832, put it best: 'War is the realm of uncertainty; three quarters of the factors on which action in war is based are wrapped in a fog of greater or lesser certainty. A sensitive and discriminating judgement is called for; a skilled intelligence to scent out the truth.'[4]

The '*Nebel des Krieges*' or 'fog of war', as it became known, was instantly recognised by military professionals the world over as the most apt description for the inherent confusion commanders in battle frequently experience as conflicting reports come in concerning the strength, position and intentions of the enemy.

As it happens, the fog on this still dark night is *so* thick that the German commanders immediately realise that if it does not clear in the morning, *in so einer Suppe*, in the midst of such a pea soup, the infantry attacks will be in real danger of losing direction. For how could you know which way to go when, as one German soldier, *Gefreiter* Rudolf Loss of the 210th Reserve Regiment, would record, 'Visibility was so bad that your outstretched hand couldn't be seen'?[5] It will also be impossible for the German artillery observers to be of any assistance in correcting the coordinates of fire to more accurately pound enemy targets. The planes will not only be unable to take off but, as the German Army has already found out to their cost, not even their messenger pigeons would fly!

Should they, then, perhaps delay the attack?

Nein.

For one thing, even if they had wanted to delay, the *Meldegänger*, messengers, would have no chance of finding the officers for whom their messages are intended. And for another, the actual infantry attack is not due to go in until 9.40 am, by which point surely a fair measure of the mist will have cleared.

And the mist even delivers one advantage to them meantime.

'We couldn't see anything to fire at,' *Gefreiter* Michael Pitsch of the 16th Reserve Jäger Battalion would note. 'But the English couldn't have seen any better as their bullets were flying well over our heads.'[6]

Across a front 45 miles wide, extending from Arras to Barisis, south of the Oise River, the German artillery men of the 2nd, 17th and 18th Armies are getting ready. Following their strict routine, the gunners working the 6608 artillery pieces and 3534 mortars – half of all German guns on the Western Front – carefully place shells and mortar bombs a safe distance to the rear of their pieces.

Over the next five hours, these men are set to fire 1,160,000 shells and some half million mortar rounds. It is enough to make the 1916 British bombardment on the Somme, where 1437 guns had fired 1,500,000 shells and a half million mortar rounds in seven days, look puny by comparison.

Among the usual shrapnel and high-explosive shells the Germans have ready today are a far greater number of gas shells than usual – chlorine, phosgene and tear gas. If the last makes the enemy soldiers take off their gas masks, they will hopefully inhale the other two, which will either kill or disable them. Mustard gas would disable them more, but as it does not disperse for at least a day, it would be equally devastating to the Germans' own soldiers.

Upon a hill by German-controlled St Quentin, *Gefreiter* Wilhelm Reinhard, an infantryman from 109th Leib-Grenadier Regiment, waits with his comrades – all of them with a sense of history, notwithstanding that their own may be about to end – by the artillery battery that they know is due to fire the first shot of the battle. Bemused, the gunners allow them to get within touching distance of the guns, knowing what is about to happen . . .

Suddenly, off to their right, there is a streak of light arching skywards, followed by a small crack . . . and, very dimly, a large white flare explodes against the misty heavens.

It is the signal the artillery batteries have been waiting for.

A shout goes up: '*Feuer frei*, free fire', and then the gun next to *Gefreiter* Reinhard and his comrades gives an almighty blast. The first shell of Operation Michael roars forth and soars to the east. Reinhard and his *Freunde* fall over on their backs, occasioning guffaws from the gunners. In another instant, guns all around the fallen men erupt like angry volcanos, the shells disappearing as searing streaks of flame into the darkness, lobbing towards the British lines.

And again and again and again!

'*Feuer! Feuer! Feuer!*'

Bruchmüller's artillery plan – as intricate as Chinese calculus, with no fewer than seven separate phases over the next five hours – is underway. The different phases seek to completely destroy the British first and second lines, as well as a long list of key targets behind them that have been spotted by the exhaustive air reconnaissance flights that the likes of von Richthofen's Flying Circus have been protecting. If all goes to plan, not only will the defending soldiers in the first two lines be shattered, but the nerve centres further back will also be destroyed, the ones the enemy is depending on to react in a cohesively defensive manner – the divisional and battalion HQs, ammunition and fuel dumps, aerodromes, signal centres and road junctions.

So comprehensive is Bruchmüller's plan, and so efficient the artillery, that even secure Allied positions at Bapaume and Péronne, six and 11 miles behind the line respectively, are now being shelled by long-range guns specifically targeted for the purpose.

Young *Musketier* Alwin Hitzeroth, of a *Minenwerfer* Coy with the 238th German Division – composed mostly of fresh recruits just like him, who had learned the intricacies of firing a gun not long after learning to shave – is south of St Quentin when the shocking symphony begins, most of it on bass drums, and the marrow of bones begins to quiver to its terrifying tempo.

'A rumbling, shaking, terrible noise,' he would recall of the first sign of the battle beginning. 'Some of our guns were firing Blue Cross gas-shells, and the wind brought a gust of gas back into our trenches.'

Gas! Panicking, and for good reason, the young soldiers reach for their gas masks, desperately trying not to breathe in, their fingers fumbling furiously to get the masks over their face in time. The unlucky and disorganised jump to their feet and try to find just where they have left their equipment.

Many of them will die horribly – first coughing, wheezing, choking and suffocating before feeling like their lungs are filled with red-hot needles. They inexorably weaken as the toxicity seeps into their eyes, their nostrils and ears, their mouths, the pores of their exposed skin. Then their vision goes fuzzy, a searing pain and a terrible itch spreads around their face. All that can save them is time and clean air – on the instant. But there is none of either available. And those who do have their gas masks can only watch as those who don't fall down, turn every colour from blue to green to black; their tongues hang out, their eyes turn glassy, and they cough up green froth.

'For five hours we were forced to sit this way,' Hitzeroth recalls, 'sweating in our dugout. It was naturally quite unpleasant, but to take off our masks would have meant certain death. I thought about the hellish noise outside and what our guns must be doing to the English over on the other side.'[7]

—

One second the men in the HQ of Great Britain's 36th Machine Gun Battalion, in their trenches at Seraucourt to the south-west of St Quentin, are asleep or on watch, and the next there is a distant roar followed by a high-pitched whistling getting progressively louder and shriller.

Five miles away, a German 105mm Howitzer has sent a 35-pound shell soaring skywards. Most of that weight is to be found in the thick steel casing that, by design, is creased with a pattern of deep indentations. Inside is two pounds of *Sprengeschoss* high explosive – connected to a percussion cap – so designed that when the shell lands and the percussion cap detonates the explosive will split the shell into a thousand flying fragments, each capable of taking life.

That whistling is getting *so* loud now that some of the men even look up as 'the very first shell fired at them'[8] scores a direct hit, killing three men and wounding ten.

Only a couple hundred yards away, Captain Frank Broom of the

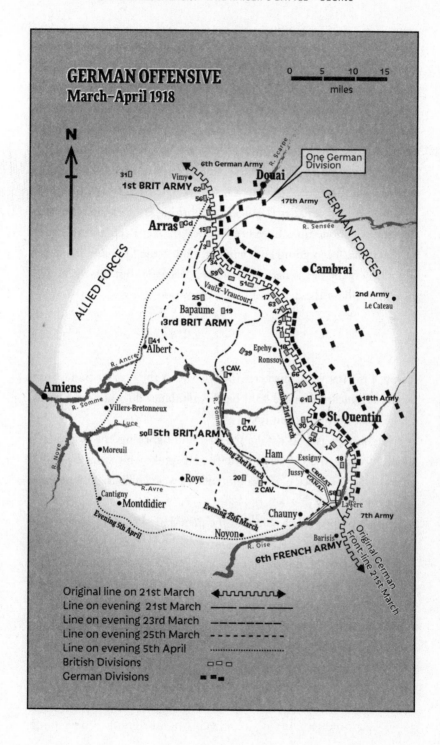

GERMAN OFFENSIVE
March–April 1918

0   5   10   15
miles

N

6th German Army

One German Division

31   Vimy
1st BRIT ARMY   62
56   Douai
17th Army
Arras   Cd
15   R. Sensée
3
34
59   R. Scarpe
51
Vaulx-Vraucourt   17
25   63
Bapaume   19   4
3rd BRIT ARMY   9
21
41   Epehy   16
Albert   39   Ronssoy
1 CAV.   66
2
Amiens   61
R. Somme   Villers-Bretonneux   18th Army
R. Luce   3 CAV.   30
50   5th BRIT ARMY   36
Ham   14
Moreuil   Essigny   18
Jussy
Roye   20   2 CAV.   56
Cantigny   Chauny   La Fère
Montdidier   7th Army
Noyon
Barisis
6th FRENCH ARMY
R. Oise

Cambrai

2nd Army
Le Cateau

St. Quentin

GERMAN FORCES

ALLIED FORCES

R. Ancre

R. Somme

R. Noye

R. Avre

Evening 21st March

Evening 23rd March

Evening 25th March

Evening 5th April

Original German Front-line 21st March

CROZAT CANAL

Original line on 21st March
Line on evening 21st March
Line on evening 23rd March
Line on evening 25th March
Line on evening 5th April
British Divisions
German Divisions

173rd Brigade Royal Field Artillery is blown clear out of his bunk 'by concussion like an earthquake'.[9] Gathering himself off the floor, he knows instantly *der Tag* has arrived. As explosions continue all around him, Broom staggers to his nearest signaller and asks to be put through to each of his batteries so he can determine if they are all right and give them firing orders. With the number of bursting shells growing by the second, the Allies must hurry to give it back to the Germans in kind.

The shocked signaller is quick to report back: he can't. No matter that the telephone lines have been buried six feet deep and the bombardment has been going less than a minute – the lines are dead. And very likely many of the battery crews are dead, too. But there is no way of telling. Under the deluge of shells, confusion reigns.

—

Private Jim Brady, his pockets still filled with the wad of francs from Captain Duncan, is in the 43rd Field Ambulance dugout near Essigny, a mile back from the front-line.

'The barrage fell on us like thunder and lightning,' he would later recall, 'causing the dugout to shiver and quake and stout beams to groan under the shock of direct hits and the waves of blast which roared down the stairway.'[10]

Plumes of dust fill the air, and the men don't know if it is better to evacuate or stay put.

Amid all the coughing and swearing, Private Jock McBarron shouts out, 'Will nobody light a sodding candle?' But before anyone can do anything, a shattering explosion right at the top of the dugout indicates a direct hit. Debris, smoke and fumes come flying and billowing down the stairs.

'My legs lost their strength, I was trembling . . .'[11]

—

Fifteen miles to the north, Captain Geoffrey Lawrence, fighting with the 9th Scottish Division, which had been inspected by Winston Churchill just the day before, is also in his dugout when the bombardment begins.

Like Jim Brady's lot, they are also in two minds about whether they are safer in here or out there, but it is soon settled when two shells fall close enough to blow in the door of the dugout.

'The candles went out . . .' Lawrence would recall. 'Splinters of metal were making sparks as they fell through just above us, and the din was quite indescribable.'[12]

And then, among the high-explosive shells falling all around, they hear the 'unmistakable plop, plop as gas-shells' fall, 'mixed with the others'. Within seconds they smell the feared but familiar 'burnt-potato or onion smell', [13] which warns them they have about ten seconds to fit their gas helmets. Some do, some don't. Some live, some die.

———

Leutnant Herbert Sulzbach, with his artillery battery in the outer streets of St Quentin – side by side with hundreds of other artillery batteries – keeps firing as never before. Sweating profusely, their muscles straining, Sulzbach's five-man crew are in their shirtsleeves in the cool morning air, operating almost like a well-oiled machine as they ram shell after shell – each weighing 16 pounds – into their *Feldkanone 16* gun, which fires them as far as five miles away.

'For the first hour,' Sulzbach will recall, 'we only strafe with alternate shrapnel, *Grünkreuz*, Green Cross, and *Blaukreuz*, Blue Cross.'

The shrapnel shells are designed to kill and maim the defenders, while the *Grünkreuz* shells, filled with phosgene, and the *Blaukreuz* shells, filled with chlorine – each marked with green or blue crosses – are designed to incapacitate the enemy so that when the German attacking infantry arrives they will be unable to fight.[14] Just one of these gas shells landing in a dugout can wipe out or disable an entire platoon of 40 men. Indeed, sent over in large enough quantities, these shells can bring a whole division to its knees – crying, coughing, blistering, red raw, burning from the inside out. And still Sulzbach and his men don't let up.

'Shell after shell is rammed into each breach, salvo after salvo is fired, and you don't need to give orders anymore, they're in such good spirits and put up such a rapid rate of fire that not a single word of command is needed. In any case, you can now only communicate with the gun-teams by using a whistle.'[15]

—

Not long before, Winston Churchill had woken in the silent watch of the night in his quarters at Nurlu, and is now lying quietly in his bed, hands crossed across his corpulent middle, musing, when the otherwise deathly silence of the darkness is shattered.

Rising quickly, he goes outside and immediately bumps into his host of the previous evening, the Commander of the 9th Scottish Division, General Hugh Tudor, who is quick to tell him, 'This is *it*. I've ordered all our batteries to open. You'll hear them in a minute.'

And, sure enough, those batteries open, for Churchill can see the flashes of over 200 British guns, firing. But he still can't hear them. Their roar has been completely drowned out by the myriad 'German shells bursting on our trench lines 8000 yards away'.

And, oh, the power of the German barrage!

'Exactly as a pianist runs his hands across the keyboard from treble to bass,' he would recount with typical eloquence, 'there rose in less than one minute the most tremendous cannonade I shall ever hear . . . It swept round us in a wide curve of red leaping flame stretching to the north far along the front of the Third Army, as well as of the Fifth Army on the south, and quite unending in either direction . . . The enormous explosions of the shells upon our trenches seemed almost to touch each other, with hardly an interval in space or time . . . The weight and intensity of the bombardment surpassed anything which anyone had ever known before.'[16]

—

General Gough, who at ten minutes past five has been awoken in his room in Nesle by the same distant roar, is not long in reaching the same conclusions.

'It was so sustained and steady,' Gough would recall, 'that it at once gave me the impression of some crushing, smashing power.'[17]

Jumping out of his bed, he wraps his dressing gown around himself and walks across the passage to the telephone in his office and quickly has the Chief of Staff of his own Fifth Army on the line.

'On what part of our front is the bombardment falling?'

'All four Corps report heavy bombardment along their front.'[18]

This must be it. This must be the big attack they have long been expecting. But *all four Corps!?*

Gough had no idea that the German blow would fall with such force, and such *width*.

'This,' he would later recount, 'at once opened my eyes to the magnitude of the attack on the Fifth Army. It dispelled with brutality any lingering hopes and ideas that I might further thin out some unthreatened part of my line and concentrate more troops against the main German attack.'[19]

He goes over to the window in his quarters now and peers out into the morning light to 'see that there was a thick fog, such as we had not experienced during the whole of the winter. We were getting into spring, and it was extraordinary to have so dense a fog at this date.'[20]

Nevertheless, as an officer not prone to great flights of emotion in any direction and with, oddly, a sangfroid grounded in his very Britishness, Gough feels that his senior officers seem to have already taken all the necessary steps. After issuing just a few more orders himself, 'and warning all concerned', he conceives the idea of what he should do next.

After all, as he would later reason, 'the German infantry would not attack for several hours . . .'[21]

There is, in short, nothing more to be done.

So Gough goes back to bed, to catch a little more shut-eye.

—

The British soldiers in the trenches are being pounded mercilessly and have no such luxury as sleep. The roar of endless explosions destroys all semblance of sanity. Their trenches shudder, shake and shatter, men all around scream and die, the blood and gore of their once best friends spatter everything all around, and shell after shell from hell continues to fall pell-mell among them, shrieking at a pitch just higher than many of the men themselves.

'Men groped through fog to their stations with shells screaming and bursting all around. A curt oath, followed by a hoarse cry through clenched teeth, came here and there from a wounded man; or someone fell with a peculiar, double-sounding thud, a rifle here, a body there, and no movement afterwards. Earth and stones and volcanic smoke fumes spouted into the fog as big new craters were scooped by explosions in and between many thousands of old ones.'[22]

—

'Monsieur . . .'

'Monsieur . . .!'

'MONSIEUR . . .!'[23]

From plumbing the depths of sleep, the French liaison officer for General Gough's Fifth Army, Paul Maze, is in his lodging just a few streets away when he awakes, just after 6 o'clock, to the blurred vision of his very annoyed landlady standing at the foot of his bed, telling him in a complaining manner, 'It's been bombarding like this since early morning.'[24]

Like . . . what?

Oh, like that.

For the first time, Maze becomes aware of the rumbling coming from the east, so strong now that it is rattling the windowpanes, 'as though heavy traffic had been continuously passing'.[25] And it is not coming from a specific spot, either, but rather from the whole misty eastern horizon. Hurriedly, Maze rises and dresses. The rest of Villers-Bretonneux is coming to life, too. From all around he can hear motorbikes roaring off in seemingly every direction.

What to do himself?

For the moment there does not appear to be a lot he *can* do. So, in the manner of his master, General Gough – intent on pursuing his normal routine in the absence of a more worthy option, whatever the crisis – Maze sits down to a substantial breakfast, served by a now *very* annoyed landlady. It is not that she can be blaming him specifically for the artillery blasts now rattling the crockery, but she is not happy, and no mistake.

Outside, the roar of motorbike messengers setting off has been replaced by a more substantial purring.

'Staff officers,' Maze would chronicle, 'were setting off in cars and immediately vanished into the fog . . .'[26]

—

Dieser verdammte Nebel! This damn fog!

At aerodromes lined along their side of the Western Front, the German pilots are all ready to go. Their mechanics have had their engines warmed up, their guns have been checked, and all of their planes are lined up in long rows, *aching* to fly. But, of course, they cannot.

'No one speaks a word,' one pilot would recount. 'With ears turned westward in the grey twilight we all listen intently. Slowly it grows brighter, but with the day comes the mist. We must wait idly. The mist spreads and grows thicker.'[27]

Few are more frustrated than *Rittmeister* Manfred von Richthofen, who stands with his fellow pilots of *Jagdgeschwader 1*, *willing* the fog to clear. Yes, at the limit, they could take off in these conditions and climb above that fog, but it would be beside the point. Not only would targets on the ground be invisible, but so would their aerodrome when it came time to land again. They simply have no choice but to wait.

—

All this time since the bombardment has started, and Captain Frank Broom of 173rd Brigade Royal Field Artillery, who had been blown out of his bunk when the first shells burst, is still none the wiser as to what the situation is with his various batteries. The signaller has still got no life from any of his smashed wires – attempts to repair them have come to nothing – and in desperation Broom sends two of his best men, Lieutenant Harold Achilles and Bombardier Arthur Jessop, out to try to get information.

At 8 am, nearly four hours into the relentless *Boche* barrage, the two return.

'Achilles,' Broom would recount, 'had gone out a boy and returned an old man, and quite unstrung . . . Poor old Achilles. He never recovered from that shaking up . . . His usefulness as a soldier ended on 21 March 1918.'[28]

At least, however, Achilles is *alive* and physically unwounded. Thousands of his fellow British soldiers are not, including 3000 dead from this initial onslaught as they become casualties of this most fearful bombardment warfare has yet known.

And still the men in the front-lines have not faced the worst of it.

—

The fog is clearing a little!

At least it is enough, at the high-country aerodrome at Bruay, that Lieutenant Harold Cobby and his comrades are quick to take the opportunity. (As preparations are always lengthy, they have been up since 2 am, heading to the mess in the freezing cold for an early cup of coffee and a bite to eat, and had known it was going to be difficult from the moment the mess had been hard to find in the mist.)

But now, the long wait is over. The mist is clearing.

Out to the planes, their Sopwith Camels that have been warmed and ready to go since dawn, and regularly ticked over since against this very moment. A top-of-the-morning wave to Charlie Chaplin and into the cockpit. Flying helmet fastened. Gloves on. Cobby, as ever, waggles his joystick to ensure that all is as it should be, and is satisfied when the ailerons on the wings react to his touch. He pushes down on the rudder bar – first with his right foot and then his left, to ensure that the rudder at the back of the plane swivels right and left, to push the nose of the plane in both directions.

He nods to the hovering mechanic, who now comes forth and grips the huge, two-bladed wooden propeller.

'Switches off,' the mechanic calls.

'Switches off,' Cobby affirms.

'Petrol on,' the mechanic calls.

'Petrol on,' Cobby affirms.

The mechanic pulls the propeller backwards a few turns to suck petrol vapour into the combustion chamber.

'Contact!'

'Contact!'

The mechanic gives the propeller a huge heave. A cough, a gurgle, and now the engine catches! In an instant, the motor gives the roar of a lion going in for the kill, blowing angry blue-white smoke out of its nostrils. After the mechanic removes the chocks, Cobby quickly gathers speed on the big grassy field that serves as a runway and then, accelerating down the strip – remembering to kick on plenty of left rudder to prevent swinging right – finally gets to that magic moment of lift-off that never fails to thrill him even when, as now, he is keenly aware that he might be racing towards his own death at well over 100 miles per hour.

It is 8 am, and Cobby and his friend Lieutenant John Courtney are leading two formations of five planes, all flown by Australians. Cobby, with his five scouts, heads off in the lead while Courtney and his pack fly above and behind, watching the tails of the leading flight to ensure that if the front runners get into trouble, their flying cavalry can swoop in to assist.

It is bitterly cold, and they all get to 4000 feet before breaking free into clear air, at which point all they can see is 'a sea of what appeared to be white cotton wool below'.[29]

So they set their course for Bapaume, down to the south and slightly east, hoping for a break in the clouds that might allow them to study the geography below and thus work out their exact position. Occasionally, as the morning sun continues to burn off some of the mist, Cobby is able to see where he is. Just beside him, in a wooden sleeve in the cockpit, he has a map pasted on a board that shows key features like towns, lakes, rivers, roads and railways and, by comparing the topography, he is able to keep a rough track of his position.

After an hour, the planes still have clear skies ahead but no visibility below. It is hopeless, and Cobby, deciding it just isn't the day for reconnaissance, swings his flight around and heads north, just east of a line of observation balloons 'just poking through the mist'. Cobby casually assumes they are their own. Suspended from each balloon – securely tethered 4000 feet above the earth – is a shivering soldier holding a pair of binoculars in one hand and a telephone in the other as he reports to those below what he can see. Though clearly in a very vulnerable position, at least these observers, unlike Cobby and the other pilots, have a parachute in case a plane brings them down.

Good luck to them. Cobby and his comrades of the air fly on.

They're still at 4000 feet, headed back to the aerodrome at Bruay, when . . .

There! What's that?

Suddenly, Cobby sees them. It is, first up, three red Albatrosses climbing through the murk in V-formation over to the west. And now, just behind them comes a whole *squadron* of planes, 'all coloured red, with the exception of one Albatros that was painted black and yellow'.[30]

Could it be Richthofen's Flying Circus? Just who has wandered into whose territory? In this fog, has Cobby led his men into Hunland?

But there is no time to deliberate. They are flying a mere hundred yards off on a parallel course now, and only the glare of the morning sun, brilliant up here with the white canvas of clouds below, is keeping the Circus unconcerned about Cobby and his men. But it is obvious that the Australians cannot have the colossal advantage of surprise for more than a few more seconds.

In this game there are fast, instinctive pilots and there are dead pilots, and Cobby rocks his wings just once to signal to the others: *follow me as I attack.* Easing his joystick forward, Cobby picks as his target the yellow-and-black Albatros and is soon hurtling down upon it, the moral equivalent of a screaming eagle diving, talons drawn, upon a slow, fat duck.

The German pilot does not even have time to recognise that Cobby and his men are there before Cobby, at a height still some 100 feet behind and the same above him, pulls the triggers. A total of 16 bullets a second from the twin Vickers machine guns pour into the German craft and its pilot. Mortally stricken, the plane flips over – a dead bee – and plummets earthwards. Cobby pulls out of his own dive and ascends to where a dogfight is taking place between the German and Australian pilots.

It is an extraordinary thing in aerial combat to pit yourself against an opponent, wheeling, cavorting through the skies, tumbling, regaining control, climbing on high for advantage, always fearful of colliding with the other pilots – friends and enemies – doing the same.

Cobby achieves his required height before engaging in the dogfight and then gets his bearings just in time to see one of his closest friends, Lieutenant Tab Pflaum, being pursued by two birds. Cobby has no time to get above his target this time and so simply hurtles forth, expertly adjusting his angle, and comes up underneath the tail of the triplane, so he will intersect with its altitude . . .

As before, it works like magic – black magic at that. The former mild-mannered bank teller from Melbourne, now the merciless Master of the Skies in France, is able to close within *ten feet* of the unsuspecting enemy before firing and unleashing hell on the German plane, which quickly heels over to go 'straight down through the mist all "arsey tarsey" . . .'[31]

Cobby has registered his second victory in almost as many minutes, and Tab Plaum is saved.

And still the men of the No. 4 Squadron are none the wiser that down below, beneath the thick blanket of fog, the biggest offensive of the Great War is now raging.

—

Private Jim Brady and his comrades, on the other hand, know only too well. At the first aid post near Essigny they have chosen, wisely, to remain hunkered in their bunker, where they have been since the barrage began. There hasn't been one window of respite in the shelling to allow them to even go up the half-decimated stairway and pop their heads out; never the remotest chance of rising up and defending their lines.

'One thing was quite certain: we were trapped by a ring of flying steel with little or no hope of escape until the barrage lifted.'[32]

And now what's this?

Through the smoke and shattering roar, a 'Red Cap'– a military policeman – rushes down what is left of the stairs, blood pouring from a right hand that has clearly taken a piece of shell fragment.

'I'm looking for battle stragglers,'[33] he announces, referring to hiding cowards, which brings roars of derisive laughter from Brady and his mates, a rare moment of levity amid the carnage.

It is a miracle they have survived this long, and anyone seeking to hide from the battle would not be hiding here.

'The point was,' Brady would recount, 'how long would it go on and how long would our weakening dugout withstand the strain? It was a thought I didn't care to dwell on.'[34]

—

By 8.30 am General Gough is up, shaved, bathed and fed, and back on the telephone, trying to work out just what the situation is.

So far there are no reports of any German advance.

But it surely cannot be long.

—

It is nearly time.

Nearly time for the Germans to lift the iron curtain falling upon the British trenches, to reveal the iron fist of massed German troops that will soon be going straight at them.

Just before going over the top, at a spot a little north of St Quentin, one of the German Sergeants of the 463rd Regiment, *Feldwebel* Wilhelm Prosch, looks at his men and notices one who does not belong – who is not meant to be in this place, at this time – about to go with them.

It is Private Baier, and his is a strange story. Before the war he had been a high-ranking regular officer in an infantry regiment – a recipient of the Iron Cross 1st Class and the Turkish Crescent for his bravery in the Dardanelles – only to be court-martialled and busted down to Private in 1916 after he had returned unexpectedly from leave to find his wife in bed with another man . . . whom he had shot for his trouble.

Prosch likes him a great deal – regarding him as 'a born soldier' – and for Baier's part, Prosch is one of the few men he trusts enough to talk openly . . .

'I am well aware I am not supposed to be here,' Baier says to him simply, 'but, as a former officer, I owe it to my conscience and my honour to be in the first line.'[35]

Na gut, fair enough then. The two shake hands.

—

'*Protzen heran!* Prepare to move!'

As the clock clicks towards 9.40 am, the order ripples down the entire first line of the German assault battalions, which extend for 45 miles from Arras in the north to south of the Oise River.

The crews of the artillery batteries, having been at work for hours already, also get the order and begin to fire the well-coordinated creeping barrage, so the first of the four waves of attackers – stormtroopers all – will have some protection as they head out.

Steeling themselves, 400,000 German soldiers prepare to charge forth from their parapets, under cover of the barrage, and straight at the 100,000 British infantry of the Third and Fifth British Armies defending their positions.

The stormtroopers who are to go over the top first unfold themselves from the shallow, tightly packed crevices in which they have spent an uncomfortable night and instinctively make one last check of their bayonets, belts and bandoliers of bullets. Some shake hands with each other, and even shout a few words of encouragement over the ongoing roar of shells landing on British positions, often no more than 150 yards away.

After all their training, all their assiduous study of their handbook, *The Attack in Trench Position Warfare*, they know, intimately, their role from here:

> The assaulting infantry must be in the enemy's
> position simultaneously with the last rounds from
> their artillery and trench mortars . . . A check in
> the advance at one place must not spread to the
> whole line; infantry which pushes well forward
> will envelop the parties of the enemy which are
> standing fast, will sweep them aside and pave
> the way for the advance of their own detachments
> which have been held up. Hesitation leads to
> failure . . .[36]

There will be no hesitation, and no lack of coordination from their synchronised watches, with now less than a minute to go.

On the southern edge of St Quentin, *Musketier* Alwin Hitzeroth and his comrades hook their trench mortars to their poles and straps, ready to carry them forward, to set up in new positions once the British first line has fallen.

The order goes out above the battle din: 'Roll assault packs and get ready to attack!'[37]

Further north, in the forward line of the German 17th Army, set to pounce upon General Byng's Third Army, *Leutnant* Hermann Wedekind waits in his assault trench with the men of his company. He has been lucky enough to procure, from a kindly mess steward, a nice bottle of vintage Burgundy wine, with which he has filled his extra water bottle. He has been sipping it discreetly all night – it keeps him warm and relieves his tension, not quite like a *Fraulein*, but not bad.

Out to their left, the men hear the familiar voice of their Battalion commander as he begins to sing, '*Deutschland, Deutschland über alles, Über alles in die Welt, Wenn es stets zu Schutz und Trutze Brüderlich zusammenhält . . .*' Others follow his lead, and soon they are all roaring the song of their fine fatherland: '*Germany, Germany above everything, Above everything in the world, when, for protection and defence, it always stands brotherly together.*'

The men's nerves settle. All along the German line, officers stare at their watches – all of which have a hand counting the seconds down.

Three, two, one, zero!

'*Protzen heran!* Prepare to move!

The order is given, the bugles sound.

In his own trenches five miles north of St Quentin, *Fusilier* Waldemar Schmielau of the 5th Guards Grenadier Regiment of Marwitz's 2nd Army, with his comrades, reacts instantly to its call:

Kartoffelsuppe, Kartoffelsuppe. Potato soup, potato soup.
Den ganzen Tag, Kartoffelsuppe. All day long, potato soup.
Kartoffelsuppe. Potato soup
Und kein Fleisch. And no meat[38]

This one means, they know, *advance* – and in an instant Schmielau is running forward, a revolver in his left hand, and, bizarrely, a bamboo riding cane in his right – which he keeps for show, as it seems to impress the men.

'I was boiling with fury,' he would recall, 'and the overwhelming desire to kill . . .'[39]

And so it is, all along the German line, as suddenly all is movement, madness and massed military murder; chattering machine guns and shattering explosions, screams and dreams . . . of death.

In the case of *Fusilier* Waldemar Schmielau, just 20 seconds after beginning their charge, he and his fellows are crossing what used to be impenetrable rolls of barbed wire but is now no more than lots of tiny pieces of metal scattered on the ground, practically paving their way forward, mere thorns in their boots. With a jump, they are over what used to be the British front-line trench but is now little more than a caved-in ditch filled with dirt, debris and death. 'The attacking waves of infantry,' he would describe, 'bobbed up and down in the white rolling smoke.'[40]

Suddenly, a figure appears just in front of him, a wounded Englishman who stares back with eyes open wide like dinner plates.

Schmielau walks slowly up to him, revolver raised. The German grinds his teeth with rage as he presses the muzzle of the revolver right to the temple of the wounded British soldier, who is powerless to move away or fight back. All that comes from him is a 'beseeching cry'. His hand fumbles in his pocket and he snatches a photograph which, with pleading eyes, he holds up for Schmielau to see. Schmielau glances at it and, with just one look, some of the blood-lust leaves him. For the photo is of the wounded soldier, in happier, healthier times, surrounded by his large, loving family. Schmielau lowers his revolver and walks on.

He is soon in the midst of furious fighting. All around him, German and British soldiers engage in a struggle to the death. It is done with fists, knives, revolvers, rifles and bombs. Schmielau jumps into a trench that is still intact and runs along it until he collides with a panicked English officer, whom he grabs by the throat and throws against the sandbags, yelling, 'Go back, you English son of a bitch!'

An instant later, the Major of Schmielau's regiment appears at his shoulder and gives him an order: '*Schlagen Sie den Hund tot, der Offizier!* Kill that dog, Officer!'[41] Again, Schmielau cannot bear to and moves on until he is suddenly confronted by a trench seething with English. This time, there is no hesitation.

This time it is not like shooting a man dead in cold blood – it is like fighting for his *own* life. He furiously pulls the trigger of his revolver, at least ten times after it is empty. The German soldier beside him throws bombs at the retreating English – one bomb exploding in such a manner that it sends a curiously dish-shaped helmet spinning fully ten yards up in the air.

Several miles further north, *Leutnant* Ernst Jünger's stormtroopers of 19th Division meet with similar success.

'A minute saw the battle ended. The English jumped out of their trenches and fled by battalions across the open. They stumbled over each other as they fled, and in a few seconds the ground was strewn with dead. Only a few got away.'[42]

For his part, Jünger is not content to let *any* of the English get away so easily and, grabbing the rifle from a nearby corporal, who is gaping uselessly after them, brings it up to fire, feeling 'an uncontrollable need to shoot'.

And so he does. A crack rings out.

No less than 150 yards away, an Englishman, fleeing as fast as his legs can carry him, suddenly goes down.

'He snapped together like the blade of a knife and lay still . . . we went on . . .'[43]

And so it goes, as the German Army continues to surge across the line of the Western Front. On the one hand the mist makes it difficult for them to get their bearings, but on the other hand it frequently allows them to pass the British guns by. In some spots where the British resistance does remain strong, German tanks do the honours in mopping them up. Just 2000 yards to the north of Essigny, at a place called Pontchu Farm, for example, where a battalion of the London Rifles refuses to budge, two German tanks, *Mephisto* and *Gretchen*, grind slowly forward like hesitant giants to . . . crush several machine-gun nests, then open fire on the infantry with canister rounds from 100 yards.

(The first of those tanks constructed – and there had been just 20 in total – the A7V, had rolled off the production line in October the previous year. Bristling behemoths, A7Vs weighed in at 35 tons, boasted a crew of 18 and were armed with six *Maschinengewehr 08* machine guns and a 57mm Maxim-Nordenfelt cannon.)

It is a persuasive argument that is quick to bring the London Rifles around to the German viewpoint. They surrender.

That accomplished, the German soldiers and the tanks move on to Essigny, where Private Jim Brady and his comrades of the 43rd Field Ambulance have noted that the barrage had 'stopped as if it had been switched off by a giant hand. The silence was deafening.'

One of the ambulance drivers goes up the ruined stairs – now more like a well-laid pile of debris that happens to lead up and out of an opening at the top – to report that, although all is quiet upstairs, the village of Essigny is 'completely flattened'.[44]

Brady and his mates decide to settle down the best they can by playing a game of whist while they await events. Not easy under the circumstances, but after a couple of hands they are able to steady their nerves and play properly, *hoping* that their mates in the front-lines are all right.

———

A mile and a half east of Brady, on the Essigny front-line, Corporal Ted Gale is a little unnerved. The fearful barrage on them has stopped, which is to the good. But the fog is so thick that they can't even see the sentry next to them in the trench. They peer forward, expecting any moment to be attacked, but . . . nothing!

Finally, the company Captain comes along and tells them: 'Funny thing going on. It's very unusual. There's no sign of an attack. You'd better all go down in the dugouts and have something to eat, something to drink. Leave a couple of sentries up here.' After nearly four years of war, none of them have heard anything like it. The custom: after the barrage comes the attack, just as day follows night. Not today, it seems. Odd. Maybe it's a ruse? That long, infernal, hellish barrage?

Come what may, Corporal Gale, a Cockney like they don't make them anymore, does as his Captain says and goes down into the dugout. He gets a brew going, and just as the water is about to boil, some ten minutes later, the Captain pops his head in and says very quietly, with deathly calm, 'You can all come up. You won't want your rifles.'[45]

Emerging from the dugout, suddenly they are surrounded by armed Jerry soldiers!

'Of course, we realized what had happened. Jerry had broken through on the right and left of us. This was a mopping-up party coming. They'd never attempted a frontal attack. That was the strategy, you see, they went through on the right and the left. Our whole battalion was caught.'[46]

Success! It has, in fact, been for the German soldiers of General von Hutier's 18th Army a textbook manoeuvre straight out of Ludendorff's playbook, *The Attack in Position Warfare*:

Surprise — The greatest successes in war are to be looked for from measures for which the enemy is least prepared. Therefore, in all offensive actions, surprise of the enemy is of decisive importance.[47]

One German soldier looks Corporal Gale right in the eye and says in the most perfect Cockney accent imaginable: 'The war's finished for you, ain't it?'

(*Well, blow me down wiv a fevva for a fiver!* 'He said it just like that,' Gale would recount. '"*Ain't it,*" he said, Cockney-like.')

Gale looks at him and says, 'You speak good English, don't you?'

'Yes,' the Jerry soldier replies. 'I was a barber in London.'[48]

—

A mile and a half back, in the dugout, a short time later, Private Brady has an unbeatable hand, and is about to win a whopping five francs, thank you very much, when . . .

The crack of a pistol from the top of the stairs and a bullet smacks into the ground at Brady's feet an instant before two Jerry soldiers, with field-grey uniforms, bucket helmets and a real attitude, appear.

'Come up, Tommy!' one of them shouts. '*Los! Los!* Go on! Get going!'[49]

Of course, they lay their cards down and put their hands in the air, heading straight up the stairs with the German pistols trained upon them. They are soon marching back to German positions, their eyes agog.

'As far as the eye could see in the thinning mist,' Brady would recall, 'were vast waves of German soldiers trudging forward over what until a few hours before were the British front-line trenches. Behind them came the scores of small field guns, tended by boy soldiers seemingly barely out of their teens, youngsters with flamethrowers, canisters and hoses at the ready, engineers, signallers, field guns dragged by retching mules, heavier 5.9s on tractors, ammo limbers and gun carriages . . . And all the time the German guns thundered as they continued to pound away at our rear positions.'[50]

About to be among that tide of German boy-soldiers moving west, squiring the men in his artillery battery, like a cross between a caring mother hen and a strutting rooster, is *Leutnant* Herbert Sulzbach, now starting with the second wave.

An officer shouts the order: '*Nach vorwärts – protzt auf!* To the front – limber up!'[51]

And to the front they go, jog-trotting by their horse-drawn guns through St Quentin, all of them amazed at receiving almost no British fire, all the while quickly passing over 'ravaged, shell-torn battle grounds'[52] as they approach the area that they had all fought so bitterly over in 1916.

—

It is the experience common to many British soldiers on the morning, as the day grows warmer and the fog continues to thin and dissipate.

The shattering explosions all around have subsided and they can hear
. . . *what is that in the distance?* . . . bugles!

Among his comrades of the 61st Machine-Gun Battalion positioned at a high point overlooking the Omignon River, just four miles
north-west of St Quentin, Private William Ware is the first to see the
marauders looming from the gloom.

'Eh, Sergeant,' he warns, 'they're coming.'

'*Och*, they're the Gordons,' replies the Sergeant, referring to a nearby
Scottish regiment.

'Not in them tin hats,' says Private Ware. 'Shove that belt in!'[53]

In an instant they have their machine gun firing, but in the swirling
mist it is impossible to tell the effectiveness of their fire and . . . even
before Ware can work out what has happened, three German soldiers
have rushed in from the left, hit his mate the machine gunner over the
head with a rifle butt and knocked Ware to the ground. They are about
to finish him off with their bayonets when, as Ware would later recall,
'a German officer with a beard and his left arm in a sling came into the
post from the right . . . He stopped his men finishing me off.'[54]

—

Similar scenes are occurring all along the British line. Forward posts
do their best to hold their positions, only to realise that somehow the
Germans have got past them and are coming at them from the rear and
flanks.

Such is the case at Fampoux, on the Scarpe River five miles east
of Arras. Private Thomas Bickerton and his chums have been firing
forward into the mist, only to hear shots out to their left and right, and
screams, meaning that in all likelihood, both of their flanks have been
breached.

What to do?

Quickly, Bickerton's Sergeant sends back runners to Battalion HQ
to seek instructions, taking precautions to send three of them, in case
they don't get through. It is as well, for one of them is killed, another

taken prisoner and only the third returns, wild-eyed, to advise, 'The Germans are cooking breakfast in our battalion headquarters.'[55]

By Jove!

Running low on ammunition; mentally, physically and emotionally exhausted; and now surrounded – it is obvious to the British that the end, in one fashion or another, is near. Private Bickerton is unsure what to do and goes into the next firing bay to seek orders from his platoon commander.

And there the commander is, sitting on the fire-step, revolver in hand.

Dead.

The Lieutenant has killed himself in preference to being taken prisoner.

A thickly accented voice suddenly rings out: 'Come out! Come out! Surrender, put your hands over your heads and run towards us.'[56]

Bickerton, together with other survivors from his platoon, do exactly that. Their war is over.

And they are far from the only ones.

As subsequent records will show, of the 650 soldiers of the 2/8th Worcester Regiment, defending the line at Fayet, near the western edge of St Quentin – 20 miles south from the positions of Bickerton and Ware – just 26 were killed, about 25 fled and got away, and almost all the rest, 600, surrendered and were captured. In truth, they had barely fought at all.

As for Herbert Sulzbach, he couldn't be happier!

'Everything has gone brilliantly,' he scribbles in his diary, 'the sappers have already thrown bridges across the British trenches, the whole supply column is working successfully . . . The first prisoners are coming through, well-built chaps, with very good uniforms and equipment, in hard training for field sports, all thorough-going 'Tommies' walking along cheekily with a fag in their mouths. I had a quick word with a few British gunners, they had been completely surprised and were speechless at our massed infantry assault. . .'[57]

His men have limbered their guns up at expert speed and are almost as far as Essigny, where, not long before, Private Jim Brady and his buddies had been playing cards, safe in the knowledge that they were well behind the front-lines.

AUSTRALIAN CORPS HQ, THREE MILES EAST OF HAZEBROUCK, 10 AM, 21 MARCH 1918, BRUDENELL WHITE RECEIVES THE NEWS

A sober-suited military man to his bootstraps, General Cyril Brudenell White has rarely received a more sobering cable than this one. The Chief of Staff of the Australian Corps is behind his desk in Australian Corps HQ when the cable comes through at 9.59 am, informing him of a large ENEMY OFFENSIVE ON THIRD AND FIFTH ARMIES.[58]

Glancing at the map, the implications are obvious. The Third and Fifth Armies hold over 45 miles of the line, the top part of which is just 30 miles from where Australian Corps is now situated. An attack on *both* of them has to be a *huge* one, and the obvious likelihood is that the Australian soldiers will be drawn into it.

It is for Brudenell White to inform the Commanding Officers of all five Australian Divisions that they may well soon be called on to fight, depending on how far the Germans advance and just how well the British Third and Fifth are able to hold on.

(Getting word to General John Monash of the 3rd Division is a little problematic. He remains on leave down Monaco way and is not immediately contactable, but at least Brudenell White can get the message through to 3rd Division HQ, whose task it will be to find him.)

—

For the 100,000 British defenders, it is a nightmare. The shocks come so thick and fast that they are hard to comprehend, let alone react to. Most of the men have been woken from a deep slumber to find their positions being hit by the Hammers of Hell, with artillery shells bursting upon them with an intensity never before conceived, let alone experienced. Comrades are torn asunder, lifelong friends from the Pals Battalions – so-called because they have been specifically formed by men who knew each other in civilian life – are suddenly spattered with each other's brains, just before they are themselves splattered all over the trench walls.

And then . . . ?

And then in an instant the shells stop falling. In the whole seconds when the explosions have ceased and all that is heard is the searing screams of dying men, from out of that fog of war – smoke and mist combined – suddenly emerges . . . what?

Men!

Big men!

Running at them. Phantoms of the fog, angels of death, soldiers, German soldiers. Many British soldiers have no time to even bring their guns to bear on these figures coming out of the fog before the Germans are suddenly thrusting bayonets at them, firing pistols, rifles, whatever comes to hand.

The British defend the best they can, but the Germans are so many and their attack so well-planned and sudden that there is all but no stopping them – at least on the front of the Fifth Army, which takes the German blow with full force.

Those British forces that can, fall back.

—

Suddenly this is an entirely different kind of warfare.

After nigh on four years of being stuck in bitter trench warfare, measuring their advances and retreats by yards alone, now everyone is out in open country! The Germans have so quickly overwhelmed the British positions, advancing well beyond even their enemy's deepest fallback trenches, that Fritz now finds himself on open roads, advancing rapidly across open fields.

As Brigadier William Croft of the 9th Scottish Division puts it, 'The whole countryside was grey with moving Boches, like lice on a trench sodden kilt.'[59]

And for the British and French forces trying to stop them, there is no time to truly dig in, nor anywhere to construct new and substantial trenches. All they can do is hope that the furious momentum of the German thrust will soon abate before they get to the Channel ports, and then, *then* they can choose the place to make their stand.

MORNING, 21 MARCH 1918, HAIG AT MONTREUIL REACTS TO THE ENEMY ATTACK

While General Haig and his highest officers had expected an attack, the *scale* of this one is quite shocking, and Haig immediately pens an urgent note to Chief of the Imperial General Staff, Sir Henry Wilson:

'This morning at 4 a.m. the enemy started his attack on the wide front we expected. It is hardly necessary to urge the CIGS (for I have repeatedly done so) to insist on the Government producing men for drafts!'[60]

They need men, and they need them as quickly as possible. And there is no time to quibble over their youth, or the fact that their training might not be finished.

For now, Haig must get back to reading and soaking in the piles of reports and messages growing taller around him – evenly divided between those that snarl, those that cry in fright, and those that weep.

—

For his part, in the War Office at Whitehall, Sir Henry Wilson and the other members of the Army Board are profoundly shocked. Yes, they had been expecting a German attack. But on *this* scale? Nigh on 80 German Divisions are attacking just 24 depleted British Divisions across 45 miles. No one knows more than Wilson just how thin their numbers are in the area the Germans are attacking. After four years of war, Britain had been reduced to raising regiments of boy-soldiers – and even then, the Prime Minister Lloyd George had refused to send them to France. The days of the Somme campaign, when British soldiers had seemed limitless, are now long gone. As Chief of the Imperial General Staff, it had been Wilson's task to counter all the pleas coming from France for more men by steadfastly refusing to send them. At this time, the British forces are down 150,000 men on what's needed at the front, and yet, courtesy of bringing back their soldiers from the Eastern Front, the Germans are suddenly throwing in *seven* times that number of extra men on their side against them. What had been a rough balance of exhaustion is now totally in the Germans' favour. The extra million *men*, not mere boys, as the British have been calling on, but tough veterans of enormous capacity – together with the accompanying artillery, shells, gas, transports, horses, supplies and planes – has suddenly given the Germans the chance to deliver one devastating hammer-blow that could end the war in their favour. Suddenly, with the news, the clock is ticking. On the instant, the mindset of CIGS changes. They can no longer afford to formulate airy-fairy policy on how best to win the war in 1919. They now must withstand this attack, which might end the war in Germany's favour *next week* if it is not stopped!

Sir Henry Wilson – a rather curmudgeonly figure who labours under the nickname of 'Ugly Wilson', courtesy of a striking facial scar left over from the Third Burmese War of 1887 – gets busy. His first step is to write a letter to Lloyd George asking him to immediately send to France the troops he has held back.

—

And, yes, such are the ways of this extraordinarily modern world that at much the same time as both General Haig and Sir Henry Wilson are reading the first reports of the German attack, much the same news is hitting the streets of London – and all of it before soldiers in the back areas in France have the first clue.

Charles Bean has just gone out this morning to Charing Cross to cable the report he has written back to the *Sydney Morning Herald* when he notices a gnarled old news vendor has just scrawled something on his blackboard leaning by a huge pile of papers:

Bombarding on the whole front from near St Quentin to the Scarpe[61]

Oh the sheer joy of it!

Certainly Londoners are shocked by the news, and there is great fear abroad as to what might happen, but Bean's reaction would prove to be very much that of the Diggers he has come to adore. 'My heart and spirits jumped up 100 degrees,' Bean would later recount. 'So the German was attacking after all – he was really going to do it. The bombardment was on a front of over 50 miles!'[62]

It is such a relief. Ludendorff and Hindenburg are now launching, Bean feels, 'in order to justify the army, and the mailed fist method, and the inflated brutality and pompousness by which they and their system stand or fall. One hoped almost beyond hope that they would fling themselves upon our army here in order to justify their boasts to their people and end the war by an offensive this year. And they are doing it. One does not for a moment believe that they will succeed . . . They will get 5, 10, perhaps 15 miles.'[63]

But then, he is sure, they will be brought up against an unbroken wall. 'They will have lost a million men; the German people (and the soldiers) will begin again to cry louder and louder – To what end? . . . But one cannot help rejoicing that the best has happened.'[64]

Bean does his quick calculations. Today is Thursday, so if the Germans follow usual form and bomb for four days, he should plan to be in France, on the front-lines, by Sunday at the latest.

———

For their part, *Generalfeldmarschall* von Hindenburg and Ludendorff wait with their entourage in their HQ, 40 miles east of Arras, at Avesnes, where from the west comes only 'the distant indefinite roll of thunder coming from the battlefield'.[65] The Kaiser, sitting in his Court train, can hear the same thing and glories in it, perhaps even more than his Generals. It is the sound of his power asserting itself.

All of them, of course, are desperate for solid information but, this early in the action, that is impossible.

'The first reports back are only vague,' Marshal von Hindenburg would recount. 'Things seem to have progressed well, [but] it was only gradually that the atmosphere of uncertainty cleared . . .'[66]

———

For the most part, the tactic of the stormtroopers to push through where there is least resistance before doubling around and coming at the British defenders from behind, works.

'We were in action for some time and we hit many Germans,' Private John Parkinson of the 16th Machine Gun Battalion, fighting in Ronssoy, would recount. 'Then it went quiet and I thought that we had stopped them.'

Victory! Perhaps . . .

Still not sure, Private Parkinson is just loading another belt into the machine gun, to get ready for another German surge, when he feels a bump in his back. Looking around, he is confronted by a German officer nudging a revolver right into his spine.

'*Komm mit!* Come along, Tommy,' the German says, not without kindness. 'You've done enough.'[67]

The truth? He has a point.

Putting his hands in the air, Private Parkinson turns around and says, 'Thank you very much, sir.'[68]

He is now a prisoner, but he is also impressed. 'I know what I would have done,' Parkinson would later recount, 'if I'd been held up by a machine gunner and had that revolver in my hand. I'd have finished him off. He must have been a real gentleman.'[69]

———

Other British divisions – particularly those of the Third Army around Arras, where they hold the line with one division every two miles, as opposed to the one division per three and a quarter miles of Gough's Fifth Army – are able to give a better account of themselves.

'We saw *Boche* in fair numbers coming down the hill out of the mist towards us,' Captain Robert Johnston of the 16th Battalion Royal Scots would recount. 'There was no need to give fire orders. Rapid fire was opened by rifles and Lewis gunners – the noise was deafening. The enemy just disappeared, going down into the cover of the shell craters. Several times the attack seemed to get going again, but inevitably stopped before it reached our front line.'[70]

—

At last, at a village two miles south-east of Cambrai, the mist is fully burned off by the midday sun, and Baron von Richthofen and his *Jagdgeschwader 1* are able to take off. With a syncopated series of roaring crescendos, he and eleven other planes take off, eager to create havoc among the surely retreating British. Alas, such is the luck of the draw that, as they hunt along the Bapaume–St Quentin road, the only targets that present themselves are two observation balloons, which are quickly shot down, but that is all. It is the equivalent of a tiger easily killing two mice – leaving the tiger very hungry indeed.

—

At his HQ in Mons, *Kronprinz* Rupprecht continues to go through the reports now starting to flow in from the battlefront. Though up until midday such reports had been only sporadic about the progress of the 17th, 2nd and 18th Armies – attacking the southern half of Byng's Third Army and all of Gough's Fifth Army – there is no doubt that big progress it is.

'The strong morning fog,' Rupprecht records in his diary of such reports, 'seems to have favoured strongly the gasification of the enemy artillery, which gave no effective *Sperroder Vernichtungsfeuer*, counter barrage.'

There had been a problem in some areas when the wind had changed and the gas had flowed back on his troops, meaning they had to don gasmasks, which slowed things down, but still 'the British had offered precious little resistance, particularly in the first line'.[71]

An English radio message had even been intercepted: '*Wir sind in höchster Not!* We are in dire need!'[72]

As for Crown Prince Wilhelm, the Army Group commander for von Hutier's 18th Army, which is the key force smashing into Gough's Fifth Army at the Somme, he is thrilled with progress.

'The eleven divisions of the first wave of the 18th Army stormed forwards from the line Bellenglise-Hamégicourt, close behind[73] the barrage,' he would recount, '[and] the enemy's first position was quickly captured at all points. There was hard fighting for the intermediate position, but in the afternoon this, too, had fallen and the second position had been broken through in many places.'[74]

Short of an outright British surrender, things could hardly be going better.

—

For many of the marauding German soldiers, it is like pushing through a thick, thorny forest, only to suddenly break through into glorious, green, open country. That is, after a late morning and early afternoon spent fighting and killing their way through the three lines of the British trench system and wiping out the remaining pockets of often still heavy resistance, they are *through*, to the other side of *Der Ostfront*, the Western Front.

Space! Greenery! And something else . . .

Stillness.

Leaving the explosions of grenades, the roaring machine guns, the rifle shots, the screams of dying men behind them, the stormtroopers of the 79th Regiment – attacking towards Seraucourt, six miles south-west of St Quentin – are suddenly met by a strange, almost eerie silence. They have emerged from that hell on earth into a beautiful day, into something not that far from the popular conception of *Himmel*, heaven.

Ah, but pockets of hell still remain.

Leutnant Hermann Wedekind is, at this moment, leading his men forward, with the words of his Battalion Commander's triumphant song still marching through his mind – *Deutschland, Deutschland über alles, Über alles in die Welt.*

Indeed, moving onward, ever onward, for the glory of *Deutschland*, they approach some farmhouses that sit near a copse of trees when, without warning, heavy machine-gun fire suddenly rips into his men.

'*VERTEIDIGT EUCH!* Defend yourselves!' *Leutnant* Wedekind screams. '*Oder Ihr werdet abgeknallt wie die Hasen!* Otherwise you'll be killed like hares. *Reichweite 600!* Range 600!'

In short order, his men have started to return fire, plastering the copse with so much lead that even branches start crashing down on the British defenders therein, but still the fire on the Germans remains heavy.

In desperation, Wedekind shakes the strangely inactive man next to him and shouts,

'*Feuer!* Shoot!'[75]

Still the soldier doesn't. But his excuse for disobeying is every bit as bulletproof as . . . well, as he isn't.

For he is dead.

Leutnant Wedekind is just kneeling to examine the man, a Hannoverian like himself, when he feels as if a giant of a man has struck his left shoulder a massive blow. Wedekind has now been shot himself. His part in this battle is over, and he begins to crawl backwards.

—

Similar pockets of resistance remain for nearly all the German soldiers who have managed to get through the initial trench system, as their fleeing British counterparts are frequently rallied by an officer to set up ambushes.

Such proves to be the case for most of the men of Germany's 18th Army in the far south, up against Gough's Fifth Army. For it is, at the end of *einem wunderbaren Tag* for Wilhelm Prosch's 463rd Regiment, who have fought through the day towards Seraucourt and are still advancing now, just on dark.

Yes, they have taken some casualties and lost some good soldiers, but they are as nothing to the Britishers they've killed, wounded and captured, nor against the extraordinary advances they have made. From starting the day at Itancourt, they have now advanced all of five miles and more, and still they are not done!

Up ahead are 50 British soldiers, trapped but still armed and with plenty of ammunition. There is no chance they can get away, and ultimately all seem likely to be killed, but it is equally certain that a lot of German soldiers will be killed trying to dislodge them.

Suddenly, a shout.

It is the disgraced Private Baier, the former *Captain* Baier brought low for having shot his wife's lover. On his own initiative, taking his life in his hands, he has fashioned a 'white flag' from some light-coloured undergarments and is walking towards the enemy and the 50 muzzles now pointed at him.

A few minutes later, the 50 British soldiers put down their weapons, put their hands in the air and allow themselves to be shepherded back to German lines by Private Baier. An educated man and fluent English speaker, he has managed to convince them of the hopelessness of their position and the virtue of simply staying alive. On the strength of his initiative, the divisional commander will put in a formal request to higher authorities that Baier 'be reinstated as a regular officer'.[76]

The request is declined – only the Kaiser can allow such a move – but brave Baier is at least awarded the *Goldene Tapferkeitsmedaille*, the Gold Medal for Bravery . . .

A small parenthesis here: the decision by these particular British soldiers has no doubt been a wise one. When the Hannoverians of *Leutnant*

Wedekind's 79th Regiment seven miles to their north are confronted by a similar group of perhaps 500 British soldiers, they are stunned by the ferocity with which the British continue to fight against all odds, exacting a terrible toll on the Germans, who continue to flood forward regardless. This continues to the point when the Germans are right upon them. An order in English is given. The British soldiers throw down their weapons, and walk towards the Germans, hands held high.

Shots ring out.

Several German soldiers, enraged by the British presumption that they can shoot Germans right to the last, then simply say 'We give up *now*,' expecting their own hides to be saved . . . exact a terrible revenge.

'I cannot blame our men for their bloodthirsty conduct,' one German officer would recount. 'The defending force, after driving their bullets into the attacking one at five paces distance, must take the consequences. A man cannot change his feelings again during the last rush with a veil of blood before his eyes. He does not want to take prisoners, but to kill. He has no scruples left; only the primeval instinct remains . . .'[77]

—

Hauptmann Rudolf Binding has seen little action on this first day, and is mostly just amazed at how well kitted out the English prisoners are. The memory of one, in particular – a devastatingly handsome young Englishman – who is 'just waiting, with a smiling, interested face, for me to speak to him,' would stay with Binding ever afterwards.

'This officer wore the most wonderful riding boots. When I looked him up and down he apologised for not being properly dressed for marching. He said he had just been going for a ride. He appeared to take it rather amiss that our attack had not left him time to dress himself in proper style with boots and puttees to be taken prisoner.'[78]

—

Among the soldiers of the five divisions of the Australian Corps, the word starts to spread from late afternoon, at first within senior officer ranks. Something's up. Fritz is on the move down south.

And of course the men themselves soon get wind of it.

'The Officers seemed uneasy,' Private John Hardie, a young farrier from Grong Grong, resting on this day with his 9th Brigade comrades of the 3rd Division, would recall. 'Several dispatch riders came to the camp today and it is easy to see that something is wrong.'[79]

No furphy this time, it is soon confirmed as dinkum. The brass are saying the Squareheads have started their big push along a 45-mile front, west of St Quentin. What's not sure is how they are going.

'There were wild and contradictory reports of terrible disaster to our arms,' Private Jimmy Downing, of Brigadier Pompey Elliott's mighty 15th Brigade, would later relate, 'or bloody repulse of the enemy. Rumours ran fast from lip to lip.'[80]

Of course, among a few timid souls there is trepidation about what might await, but, as ever, Elliott stands in strict contrast. Recovered from his winter blues only in the last fortnight or so – having suffered a nasty facial rash caused by German mustard gas at Polygon Wood – and now on the road to being his true, ruddy-cheeked, straight-talking self, he is nothing less than elated to hear that the Germans are finally having a go. 'There is a feeling in the air that we are all glad he is coming, and that we will hit him up to some tune before he wins through.'[81]

The upshot across the Australian Corps is a strong feeling that we might be back in action soon, Dig, and the most likely of all to be called on are those of us lucky enough to be in the 3rd and 4th Divisions.

Even if the 3rd Division's commanding General, John Monash, is taking a peaceful walk in the hills overlooking the Mediterranean at this very moment, that won't stop the 3rd Division being sent forward.

And, sure enough, at 5.20 pm the Brigadiers of the 3rd Division receive word from General Monash's Chief of Staff, Colonel Carl Jess, warning the commanders that they 'might be required to move on 48 hours notice'.[82]

Just three hours later, the 3rd Division commanders are ordered to send billeting parties to Watou, north-west of Messines and eight miles directly west of Ypres, at 6 the next morning.

What's more:

THE 3RD AUSTRALIAN DIVISION (LESS ARTILLERY) WILL MOVE TO THE STEENVOORDE AREA ON THE 22ND AND 23RD INSTANT. [83]

Interesting. The attack appears to be in the south but they're sending us to Flanders in the north. Perhaps the southern attack is a diversion? Who knows. Orders are orders and Colonel Jess moves quickly to obey them.

'At nine o'clock that night,' Private Hardie records, 'we got orders to be ready for the road at any moment. The German Army was furiously attacking right from the coast to the Somme. I may tell you that I thought the enemy had about one chance in a hundred of breaking the line anywhere between Passchendaele and Armentières.'[84]

And certainly not when the Australians are on their way!

—

At least the most northerly of General Gough's twelve infantry divisions, the 9th Scottish Division, have fought valiantly throughout the day and, for the most part, have held their position against the marauding Germans.

As darkness approaches, one of the division's officers, Captain Peter Howe, takes advantage of a brief lull in the battle to not only retire to his dugout to write a report, but also have a cup of cocoa, which he hopes will revive him and . . .

And as soon as he starts to sip it . . . he starts to nod off . . . pausing only to place the cocoa on the rough stool beside him . . . when he is suddenly awakened.

The first thing he sees is a small mouse balanced on the rim of the cocoa mug, having a sip . . . as you do.

Behind him, a breathless runner begs to report: 'Sir, the enemy is behind us on both the right *and* the left and you must retire as quickly as possible . . . destroying everything as you go.'

Right you are.

Instantly wide awake now, Captain Howe moves almost as quickly as the runner, who has now disappeared in the night. Gathering his things, Howe races up the stairs, pausing only to throw a phosphorus bomb behind him to destroy the whole dugout.

'As I did so I thought, "poor little mouse."'[85]

This general order from General Douglas Haig's HQ to 'proceed to the rear, because a general retreat has been ordered'[86] is not well received by most of the Scots, and some even come close to mutiny. One would recount, 'as our boys, far from retreating, were expecting to go over the top and finish the bloody-nose treatment they had given Jerry . . . [We learned later] that the retreat had been caused by the collapse of the division on our right flank, who had simply disappeared. But the language from the front-line must have taken years off Douglas Haig's life. The names he was called were the most ferocious and original that one Scot ever called another.'[87]

—

For the 400,000 German infantry who have crossed No-Man's Land this day, the experience of *Gefreiter* Adolf Renschler of the 185th Regiment is typical. There is grief for comrades who have not survived, exultation for how well the whole advance has gone and a search to find shelter for the night. Renschler and his comrades settle on a small, ruined cottage, clearly recently abandoned by the British. That much is evident from the huge barrel of red wine in the kitchen surrounded by glasses. One of Renschler's comrades helps himself to the wine with such gusto that, for a reason only he can understand, he takes *all* of his clothes off and is now entirely nude in the chilly night.

Finally, he shouts, *'Ich will ein' Engländer.* I want to find an Englishman. *Ich will ihn töten!* I want to kill him!'[88]

He charges off into the night, straight towards the English positions . . . never to be seen again.

—

With General Hubert Gough there has long been a question among his closest colleagues about whether he is an inveterate optimist or . . . a touch delusional.

On this occasion, his entire Fifth Army front has been decimated. After just a day, the Germans have pushed a bulge into Gough's line, advancing an extraordinary five *miles* westwards at some points, like on the Essigny plateau. They are well into formerly safe Allied territory, engulfing towns previously untouched by war while also recapturing some 'forty-six French villages that they had abandoned under duress in 1917'.[89]

And yet, the good General, harried as he is in the moment, with an infinite stream of communications and conflicting updates, would later recall in his memoir: 'The result of the first day's battle could be considered satisfactory and as a magnificent effort. We had identified over forty German divisions actively engaged against the Fifth Army. Their losses had been very heavy . . .'[90]

As a commander, Gough has unwavering faith in the men below him. But even he must acknowledge on this day that there are simply not enough of them! There are nearly 40,000 British casualties. Over half of them are captured, 7500 are dead and there are 10,000 wounded to cope with. After dinner on this night, with the racket of fighting unabated outside, Gough places a telephone call to Haig's Chief of Intelligence to report the day's events, stretching the truth a little where required.

'The Army,' he asserts, surely with a quiet blush, 'has done splendidly in holding against such enormous odds, practically the whole of its Battle Zone with the exception of the three breaches in our line, at Essigny, Maissemy and Ronssoy.'[91]

Some 40 German divisions are in the attack against the Fifth Army, he informs General Herbert Lawrence, adding that there are yet more German units massed in the rear, which leads him to his most crucial point: They must have reserves. And they must have them NOW!

'The Germans will certainly continue to push their attack tomorrow . . . and it will undoubtedly continue with unabated fury for many days.'[92]

Without reserves coming forward, not even he is sure they can hold.

Unfortunately for Gough, Haig's man does 'not seem to grasp the seriousness of the situation'. He tells Gough that, in his opinion, 'The Germans will not come on again tomorrow, after the severe losses they have suffered.'[93] Lawrence thinks that the Hun 'will be busy clearing the battlefield, collecting their wounded, reorganizing and resting their tired troops'.[94]

Gough, mouth agape, disagrees emphatically.

But, as he would later recall, 'I failed to make much impression. It has always been my opinion the GHQ did not fully grasp the magnitude of the assault on the Fifth Army . . .'

Hanging up, Gough is dissatisfied. But, for the moment at least, he must make do – and dispose his men as best he can for the fight that will surely continue with fervour on the morrow.

—

Far more calm on this evening is Crown Prince Wilhelm, who has received reports from his 18th Army, which has been sticking it to Gough's Fifth all day and has sound cause for optimism.

'By the evening,' he would later recount, 'the infantry of the divisions of the first wave, closely followed by their escort batteries, had penetrated to an average depth of 6 kilometres into the enemy's defensive system . . . A large labour force was industriously engaged in repairing roads and railways so that supplies could be sent up to the divisions. The way to an extension of the break-through had been opened. The English had suffered terribly heavy losses, both in men and in prisoners, guns and war material. The vital thing was to give the sorely shaken enemy no time to recover. The impetus and enthusiasm of the troops was such that they did not need the Army Order I issued in the evening of March 21 enjoining them to keep up[95] the pursuit without respite.'[96]

—

Meantime, at GHQ in Montreuil, Haig sends a letter to the British Military Representative at the Supreme War Council. Though careful not to *formally* blame the British front's near-collapse on the refusal of Prime Minister Lloyd George to send more drafts, as per Haig's requests, there is no mistaking in which direction his finger is pointing:

> This morning at 4 a.m. the enemy started his attack on the wide front we expected. It is hardly necessary to urge CIGS (for I have repeatedly done so) to insist on the Government producing men for drafts![97]

The British front, stretched some 126 miles, has never been so thinly defended as now. Gough's Fifth Army, menaced by fog, handicapped by rushed preparations for defence and a lack of men, is on the verge of losing all three of its defensive zones.

While waiting for those drafts to arrive – if indeed they are to be sent – all Haig can do is send what few reserves he has to the most critical points. One of the two reserve divisions ordered forward is the British 8th Division under General William Heneker, a Canadian-born martinet and veteran of many British colonial wars in Africa, who, it would be noted by one of his Brigadiers, is an officer who 'expected to be saluted by everyone within eye range'.[98]

On this day, things move quickly.

'Suddenly,' Heneker would later recall, '[we were] put on 6 hours to move . . . At about 7 p.m. orders to entrain tomorrow for the south and come under Gough, Fifth Army . . . Gough wanted to see me tomorrow morning at breakfast. Had a quick dinner and started for Nesle via Doullens and Amiens at 8 p.m.'[99]

After midnight, Haig also requests that the French commander, General Pétain, send three French divisions to plug holes in the line along the Somme bend, which Gough hopes to hold. (Though the 152-mile-long Somme runs west into the English Channel, at Ham it turns north for 20 miles to Péronne, providing a natural obstacle for the whole German thrust to the west, if it can just be held, with particularly heavy guards on every bridge along that stretch.)

—

There is an odd thing about General Ludendorff, noted by his staff officers who have been with him for a long time. At mealtime, he likes to break his bread into small balls and roll them on the table.

'If he rolled the balls slowly things were all right,' his favourite portrait artist, Hugo Vogel, had noted, 'but if he did it violently there was a storm approaching.'[100]

Tonight? Tonight, General Ludendorff has every reason to roll the balls *slowly*.

At his HQ at Avesnes this evening, General Ludendorff talks to the staff officers returning from the battle and sifts through the reports coming back from the front-line – a front-line that has moved more on this single day than on any other day in the war to date. True, it isn't *exactly* where the Germans had hoped, with targets that had been nigh on impossible, but the achievements are still spectacular.

Having crushed the first of the British defenders, his forces had burst into open country and taken over 21,000 British soldiers as prisoners, together with 500 pieces of artillery. Some 7500 men are thought to have been killed.

Yes, Ludendorff's own forces have suffered 40,000 casualties – with around 11,000 soldiers killed and 29,000 wounded – to make a total of 78,000[101] casualties on the day, if both side's losses are added together, the most terrible toll of the war to date. But on the German side, it has been more than worth it. In the words of General Hans von Plessen to the Kaiser and his entourage, in their nearby château at Avesnes, it is clear 'that the English have taken a terrific pasting.'[102]

For in this 18 hours so far, the German army has reclaimed as much French ground as the British forces had so bloodily clawed in the whole of the Battle of the Somme, lasting five months and suffering over *half a million* casualties!

'The results of the day seemed to me satisfactory,' Marshal von Hindenburg would record. 'Such was also the opinion of the General Staff officers who had followed the troops and were now returning from the battlefield [to report to us]. Yet only the second day could show whether our attack would share the fate of all those which the enemy had made on us for years, the fate of finding itself held up after the first victorious breakthrough . . .'[103]

CHAPTER FIVE

AUX ARMES AUSTRALIENS, FORMEZ VOS BATAILLONS!

My principal trouble was that I could not eat, but champagne and brandy with an odd biscuit seemed good enough. It was nothing more than overstrain, nervousness, and a mixture of fear and high tension. Added to this was the feeling that the war was going the wrong way and that our efforts were wasted. The line literally jumped forward miles daily and there did not seem to be sufficient troops or guns to stop the German advance . . .[1]
Lieutenant Harold Cobby, Australian Flying Corps

The AIF must be thought something of by the Higher Commands, when they are used to stem the flood in the North as well as in the South.[2]
Lieutenant Ben Champion, of 1st Battalion, 1st Brigade, AIF 1st Division

22 MARCH 1918, MESSINES, SONS OF THE SOUTHERN CROSS TO HEAD SOUTH

There is movement at the station, for the word has passed around . . .

The Squareheads are on the rampage, they've broken through in a dozen spots at once, and there is a good chance *we're* going to be called on – and I mean 'alley toot sweet' – to help to stop the brutes!

For the 110,000 Australians up around Messines, there is an instant 'stiffening of the sinews, a summoning up of the blood'[3] as rumours swirl.

But wait, what's this?

Although those in the highest echelons of the 3rd Division, at rest near Hazebrouck, are not surprised that they had been the first to receive a movement order the night before, it is not the direct order that surprises, but the *direction* it sends them.

Not south but east, to Flanders!

And so today, the 9th Brigade are the first to get the word: they will soon be moving out, quick march, to be followed by the rest of the 3rd Division throughout the day and tomorrow.

Meanwhile, it is true that, in the frenzy of the moment, this instruction for the 3rd Division to split from the command of the Australian Corps to bolster the British forces at Ypres is in contravention of the whole idea of that Corps, that from the time of its formation, Australian soldiers would be under Australian commanders – but there is nothing for it. In the extremity of the situation, who is to argue the niceties of national protocols when the whole war might be in the balance?

Certainly not General Birdwood, the Commanding Officer of the Australian Corps, who is still on leave in London, and certainly not the Commanding Officer of the 3rd Division, General John Monash, because he is still – to Colonel Jess's frustration – out of contact.

As it happens, Monash is having a wonderful time in the south with one of his Brigadiers, Commander of the 9th, Charles Rosenthal – or 'Rosie', as everyone from Monash down to the humblest Privates knows this officer, a successful architect in civilian life. No matter that Rosie is on three weeks' sick leave with congested lungs, he is slowly coming good and their joyful days together hiking, dining and general sightseeing is testament to the old adage that ignorance is bliss.

'Altogether,' Rosie notes in his diary, 'a very interesting day and full of pleasure, and not the least being conversation on many topics with General Monash.'[4]

22 MARCH 1918, ROAMING ABOVE THE ROMAN ROAD

On this bright late morning, eager as he is nervous, *Leutnant* Erich Pernet of the *Deutsche Luftstreitkräfte, Feldflieger Abteilung* No. 29 Flying Company, is piloting his LVG CV two-seater with his observer, *Leutnant* Karl Westphal, right behind him. When everyone knows your stepfather is the most important military man in Germany, General Erich Ludendorff, of course you have to constantly prove yourself and demonstrate that you are worthy of piloting a plane in a war zone – while you are still only just gone 20 years old. And when your own beloved brother has already been shot down and killed the year before, and your mother has not stopped weeping to this day, you have a *Pflicht*, a duty, to stay alive. Occasionally, his hands reach to the scarf their mother has knitted for him, almost in a manner to give him strength. As *Leutnant* Pernet looks down, far down, to the ground, he is thrilled to note that the German forces have moved an extraordinary six miles forward just in the last day – whole long columns fill the roads heading west – but so too is it apparent from the many ambulance wagons heading the other way that the British still have plenty of fight left in them.

The French town of Villers-Bretonneux shows up 20 miles ahead, which means he is now just in enemy territory. His particular mission today is to conduct reconnaissance of the area south of the old '*Römerstraße*',[5] Roman road, leading to Villers-Bretonneux, to see if the British are bringing up more troops and note supply dumps, transport hubs and artillery batteries so they can be bombed later. Of course the enemy is expecting them to do exactly that and will send out fighters to stop the German eye in the sky, so Erich is being especially vigilant.

But such is the capricious whim of this war that, all too often, being 'careful' has nothing to do with whether you follow the fate of your brother or get back to your mother, one way or another.

For, on this morning, flying a Sopwith Camel, Captain Tom Sharpe of the Royal Flying Corps No. 73 Squadron – with already three victories to his credit – simply swoops down from on high and blasts the German plane amidships with his twin Vickers guns.

There is the chattering, there is the shattering, there is a long spiral downwards – the shuffling off of a mortal coil all the way to the ground – and then the crumpling as the plane meets earth and bursts into flames, just one mile east of General Gough's HQ for the Fifth Army, by the Ham-to-Nesle road.

Both *Leutnant* Pernet and *Leutnant* Westphal are found by a British soldier, dead in the wreckage.

Their bodies are respectfully removed and buried on the spot. A makeshift cross is affixed atop the grave, bearing the inscription:

Here rest two German flying officers.[6]

Following along behind the troops, a German Regimental medico, Dr Erich Schmidt, will be as pleased as he is surprised to see it. Usually, he finds, the Brits just don't care that much, and even use wooden crosses for firewood.

'How different is the German mentality,' he notes. 'Many graves of the enemy greeted us too, each on which the German soldier had placed the inscription: *'Hier ruht in Gott ein tapferer Engländer!* Here rests with God a brave Englishman!'[7]

———

After a morning being driven all along his section of his front – to visit all four of his corps commanders – General Gough is disconsolate. He has started the day hoping to work up a plan of counter-attack, but now he knows it is out of the question. All of his commanders are in agreement – there is no chance of holding the Somme bend now; the best they can hope for is to slow the German advance by holding on to what they have for as long as possible.

They don't have the men or the munitions to push back against the German flood, and probably not even the *will*. The situation is so grim that, once back at his forward HQ at Nesle, Gough's first order is for his staff to pack up so they can 'get back to the next knot of communication wires . . . at [the] original Headquarters in Villers-Bretonneux'.[8]

Afterwards, he heads there himself, with his driver, via a roundabout route along the Somme. Across every bridge, British soldiers are retreating. They seem cheerful enough, and even assure him they are still full of fight. But there is no doubt just how exhausted they are, nor the direction they are heading – in full retreat.

Once across the Somme, he notices many of them sinking down and immediately falling asleep.

Overall, Gough finally must face it: his men have been falling back since yesterday morning. And given that reserves are not assured – last night the French had promised to send reinforcements for his right flank but are now stalling – there is no telling when and where the Allies will be able to make a stand.

So confused is the situation that nobody really knows what's going on or exactly where the Germans are, let alone their own troops. Most importantly, it is impossible to know the positions of the thousands of British Empire soldiers who *are* trying to flood forward, but are only able to drip, slow as honey, along heavily congested roads to fill gaps in the front – gaps that are God knows where!

'It was now evident that the German attack was so serious,' Gough would recall, 'that I could not hope to fight it out successfully in the Battle Zone, but must carry out a delaying action, which would aim at saving the Army front from complete annihilation, but which would enable it at the same time to maintain an intact, though battered and thin, line in face of the German masses until such a time as the British and French Commands could send up sufficient troops to hold the ground.'[9]

And so he has his staff write up orders to be sent to all his corps commanders straightaway:

In the event of serious hostile attack corps will
fight rear-guard actions ... Most important that
corps should keep close touch with each other
and carry out retirement in complete cooperation
with each other and corps belonging to Armies on
flanks.[10]

3RD DIV, NEAR BOULOGNE, SUNDOWN, 22 MARCH 1918, THE 9TH BRIGADE BEGINS THE LONG JOURNEY EAST

After a whole day standing around doing three-fifths of bugger-all, bar waiting for the expected orders to move, near sundown they finally get them.

The bugler sounds 'fall in', and no more than ten minutes later the column is on the road, leaving the men of the 10th and 11th Brigades, who are to follow the next day. They push on through the twilight and into the dark night . . . marching, marching, marching . . . oh so rhythmically . . . to the train, the train, the train . . . which will take them to Watou.

'I don't think I will ever forget that night march,' Private John Hardie of the 33rd Battalion would recount. 'The Battalion was well over strength and all the boys were in great condition. The Unit never looked better and both Colonel [Morshead] and the Major showed that they were proud of it.'

For Hardie, it is particularly difficult. He is still limping badly, courtesy of a bullet through the knee the previous year, but, in the grand traditions of his new-found craft, there is nothing for it but to soldier on.

And these men are going to a big blue, make no mistake. For as they continue to march, they can hear the constant pounding of the guns to the south and even smell the cordite at this distance – *sixty* miles away – just like the smell bushfires carry at home.[11]

(Of which, they know more than most. They are 'New England's Own', the men of Morshead's 33rd Battalion, drawn from Armidale, Tamworth, Bingara, Uralla, Barraba, Manilla, Walcha, Moree, Inverell, Narrabri, Guyra, Glen Innes and Tenterfield. Oh yes, they know a bit about bushfires alright.)

Keep going, Diggers!

And still they do, with even more enthusiasm nearing midnight as the cold wind, getting colder, goes right through them, and the only hope of staying even a *little* warm is to march faster. At last, at two o'clock, the call comes along the line . . . '*Companyyyyy*, halt!' and they find themselves near a railway siding.

'As there didn't appear to be any likelihood of a move for a while, the good doers found some brushwood to warm the rest of the troops. The band struck up, *Keep the home fire burning*, and everyone had a jolly half hour or so.'[12]

Soon enough, however, they are ordered onto the train – 50 Australian soldiers to each 'horse box', designed for eight horses, or 40 men.

They are off to the railway station at Watou, *ta-woot-tee-woo!*

—

Herr . . . General?

Herr . . . General . . . We have news of *Leutnant* Erich Pernet.

He is . . . missing in action.

In his HQ at Avesnes, on this second day of the battle, General Ludendorff takes the news hard.

He dreads being the one to break it to his wife, Margarethe, that the second of her sons might now be gone. But it must be done . . .

Margarethe picks up on the other end of the line.

'Erich has not returned from his flight,'[13] says General Ludendorff.

There is a drawn-out crackle on the other end of the line, an ominous thud and then . . . nothing.

In her home, Margarethe lies on the ground, unable to move or make a sound. Her *Piekchen* is gone. The claw is back around her throat. She is in shock.

For his part, General Ludendorff cannot allow himself to indulge too much in grieving. He must focus on the battle at hand – and at least that continues to go as well as he could possibly have hoped for.

Marshal Paul von Hindenburg is certainly of that view. 'The evening of the second day saw our right wing in possession of the enemy second position,' he would recount. 'Our centre had even captured the third enemy line, while the army on the left wing was [racing ahead] and now miles away to the west. Hundreds of enemy guns, enormous masses of ammunition and other booty of all kinds was lying behind our lines. Long columns of prisoners were marching eastwards.'[14]

The key now is to be able to follow up the breakthrough by rushing soldiers forward. All this, however, and they still haven't brought their biggest weapon of the war into play. That is due for dawn on the morrow . . .

7 AM, 23 MARCH, MONT-DE-JOIE, 70 MILES NORTH OF PARIS, TIME FOR THE BIG GUNS . . .

It is nearing time.

The German ballistics and gunnery officers and their technicians and gun crews rouse from a restless night and look out of their huts to see a light fog draped down the side of the small mountain and blanketing the valleys below, shutting out the skies above and heralding perfect conditions for a bombardment. Just down the slope, HQ is already astir. The carefully calibrated final preparations are being performed. Finally, it is here – the day all of their long labours will come to a climax.

The great offensive – *Der Kaiserschlacht* – is going to plan. The German infantrymen, behind a curtain of artillery fire, have rolled over the front-line, waves of storm battalions leapfrogging over and around each other and, to their delight, straight through the British Fifth Army!

And now, let the Allies deal with *this* . . .

For two years Germany's best and brightest have been working on the '*Kaiser Wilhelm Geschütz*', the Emperor Wilhelm Gun (aka the Paris Gun). At 250 tons, with a barrel 112 feet long, it is the largest and most powerful artillery piece the world has ever seen. Over the last six months, their men have excavated the necessary land and prepared the gun emplacements, built a special railway and moved three versions of this extraordinary armament here to little Mont-de-Joie, just north of the otherwise quiet village of Crépy-en-Laonnois, some 70 miles north of Paris. Put together on a design provided by an eccentric

German scientist, Dr Otto von Eberhardt, under the auspices of the German Navy and led by Krupp's technical manager, Professor Fritz Rausenberger, it has been slumbering for the last few days . . . but on this morning the giant awakes! As the gun is on rails, it is now rolled out of the enormous excavation in the side of a mountain where it has been hiding and hauled forward to its firing pit. There, the whole enormous armament can turn on a steel base ring, no less than 27 feet in diameter. Primed by an overall crew of 70, this extraordinary weapon is ready to unleash its unholy cargo on the enemies of the German Empire.

Two German officers stare at the enormous metal beast above them and – carefully watched by the beast's two proud fathers, von Eberhardt and Rausenberger – begin their gruesome work. They determine true north, check it in relation to the City of Light, make adjustments according to the prevailing wind direction and velocity, temperature and air density – just as allowance has been already made for the curvature of the earth and how much the planet will spin while this shell is above it – and then make a small mark on the gun's turning circle so the gunners know in which direction to fire. The German officers and engineers alike are satisfied now to note thick plumes of blanketing smoke rise from positions around them, right on schedule. The smoke pots will keep the Paris Gun hidden from the eyes of French pilots, who will shortly be coming to look for it.

The enormous barrel of the gun – with a structure like a suspension bridge at its far end to prevent droop – is elevated, raised foot by torturous foot, until it has reached a precise 50-degree angle and its muzzle is the height of a ten-storey building.

A shell weighing 230 pounds is now brought to the breech of the gun on the bed of a special carriage and winched up to the loading platform 20 feet above. The shell is inserted through the long powder chamber and slowly turned anticlockwise until its screw thread is in line with the thread of the gun's barrel . . . and the two threads lock . . . before it is turned some more, until the projectile is fully loaded and can go no further. Two bags and a cylinder – a three-part powder charge system – are loaded into the gun's breech behind the shell, a larger than normal load of 432 pounds to counteract the nitroglycerine propellant almost frosting over in the chilly morning.

The Commanding Officer's watch reaches 16 minutes past seven. Sixty seconds to go. Everyone into the four-foot-thick concrete shelters set back from the guns, and make sure your earplugs are in.

Silence. After all their long training, the Commanding Officer knows that all the protocols have been observed and all is as it should be, but still runs through his mental checklist. Only when completely satisfied does he give the command:

FEUER!

With a deafening crack of orange hellfire, just a 50th of a second later, a 'huge cloud of orange-red smoke and incandescent gas [burst forth]. The projectile had gone. The great gun recoiled violently in its cradle, came to rest, and then slowly slid forward into the battery.'[15]

Meanwhile, the shell the size of a fat man that rocketed out of the gun's blackened maw is now speeding towards the cloudy sky at a mile a second, revolving clockwise 100 times a second as it goes.

It rises and rises, taking 90 seconds to reach the pinnacle of its arc 24 miles above France – when building the prototype, the Germans had succeeded in propelling the first man-made object into the stratosphere – before it begins its deadly descent and lands 80 seconds after that. It is one of many shells that day, each of them requiring more gunpowder than the last to overcome the damage that each shot does to the barrel of the Paris Gun. Each subsequent shell has to be screwed a little higher in the barrel before it locks.

Where do the shells land?

Other artillery crews are able to find out by direct line of sight or by forward observation officers using binoculars. In this case, the Paris Gun crew will have to find out by perusing the French and Swiss newspapers on the morrow, hoping to have sown panic and struck a devastating psychological blow against the morale of the French. Time now to prepare the next shots, and 15 of them are fired over the next four hours, before a pause, as *der Kaiser* himself is due to arrive!

7.20 AM, 23 MARCH 1918, QUAIE DE SEINE, PARIS, HELL COMES FROM THE HEAVENS

Saturday is the busiest day of the week in Paris. *Les Parisiens* are up early to get to the store, or heading to the markets to stock the larders and prepare for the traditional family meal the next day. And so it goes today. People fill the streets and subway cars, getting on with their lives. The war is far away and the French Army is protecting them from all bar air raids. Ever since 30 German planes had flown over Paris on the night of 30 January, dropping 144 bombs – the most formidable raid of the entire war thus far – warning sirens had become commonplace, if for the most part false alarms. More air raids on the nights of 8 and 11 March have kept the population on edge. *'C'est la guerre'* is a now daily remark, accompanied by a shrug.

And so it is with a weary intent that *Parisiens* shuffle into the streets this morning. In the north-east section of the fortified area of Paris, a few people are walking along the Quai de Seine. Suddenly, violently, they are startled by the crash of an explosion on the stone pavements in front of house number six.

QU-EST-CE QUE C'EST?

Exactly. The bold and the curious among the onlookers hurry to the scene. To the soldiers, it sounded like a high-explosive shell. To civilians, it is surely an air bomb. But during the day? How odd!

They brace themselves for more explosions, for the air-raid sirens to sound, but nothing comes. There are no sirens because observers have seen no enemy planes. *Très curieux.*

Twenty minutes later, a second explosion occurs a mile and a half away at the bustling Gare de l'Est, on the cobbles of Boulevard de Strasbourg, as commuters make their way to the Metro.

Windows blow, cobbles fly through the air, hot metal fragments spray out in every direction and a newsstand and several carts are flung about. People scream and scatter. As the cacophony of catastrophe subsides, local shop owners peer out to see dead and wounded strewn across the street. They run to the aid of the injured, perplexed, wondering where the explosion had come from and why the *Boche* are raiding in daylight. The Germans could not have picked a better target – attacking the busy hub of the Gare de l'Est has struck the exact chord they wanted. The gendarmes urgently inform police headquarters, and the news continues to go up and up, all the way to the office of Prime Minister Georges Clémenceau and President Raymond Poincaré.

Back on Quai de Seine, the crowd around the explosion site is growing thicker. Yet, across Paris, most people are oblivious to the attacks, and the business of the city continues uninterrupted. More 'bombs' continue to fall in disparate parts of Paris, causing limited casualties, but soon the damage will grow, along with the panic.

In the 90 minutes since 7.20 am, six bombs have fallen on spots that are unremarkable, to say the least. Unlike the air raids the *Parisiens* have grown used to, which have definite targets to cause definite disruption – electric power plants, munitions factories, etc. – these bombs seem to be falling somewhat indiscriminately. It is all very odd. Some speculate that it must be Germans firing a gun, but that is easily dismissed because the Germans are still 70 miles away.

An official communiqué to the press is written up at 10 o'clock and sent to the newspaper offices and displayed on various bulletin boards:

At 8:20 some German planes that were flying at a very great altitude succeeded in crossing the lines and in attacking Paris. They were at once pursued, both by the Paris Defence airplanes and those of the Front. Several . . . bombs have been registered. There are a few victims. A later communiqué will specify . . . detail of the raid.[16]

Meantime, projectiles continue to fall.

Late in the morning, French President Raymond Poincaré and Prime Minister Clémenceau, as a show of solidarity with the people, visit an all-girls school of some 600 students, all huddled in underground shelters. They are heartened to find the girls singing 'La Marseillaise'.

As the day passes, most *Parisiens* get on with their lives the best they can, on this otherwise beautiful spring day. Shopkeepers open for business once more; the Metro rumbles to life; the housewives get on with their day, procuring and preparing lunch; while factory workers who have been released from their duties head home. And yet, in the course of it all, people are seen to suddenly stop and stand in the street, eyes glued upon the sky above, each hoping to spot the elusive German planes.

Conversations rest upon one topic alone: the bizarre bombardment. The last of the projectiles falls at 2.45 pm. It causes no real damage. Within the hour the bugles and bells sound the 'all's well' tune, and those people still in the shelters make their way out to the street to learn what has happened. For about eight hours from 7.20 am, there had been 25 explosions in and about Paris, killing 16, wounding 29 and damaging many buildings. Still, it seems no one understands *how*? It is late afternoon before an explanation is offered by the government, with a second communiqué sent to the newspapers at four o'clock and soon pasted up on the boards outside their headquarters:

```
The enemy fired on Paris with a long range gun
starting at 8:00 a.m. At intervals of a quarter
of an hour, shells of 240 millimetre calibre fell
on the capital and its suburbs. There are about a
dozen dead and about fifteen wounded. Measures
are being taken to counter-shell the gun.[17]
```

A gun? *A gun?* From 70 miles away? *Mais, ce n'est pas possible!*

Not even many of the Germans can believe it when the report breaks.

'Today's army report,' Richard Stumpf, a sailor in the Kaiser's High Seas Fleet, writes in his diary, 'as if it were the most natural thing in the world, stated, "Today we shelled the fortifications of Paris from a distance of 120 kilometres." Was it a premature April fools joke? This was my response at first until Havas News Agency issued a similar report.

120 kilometres? Why doesn't the whole world go mad? I simply cannot understand how this is possible.'[18]

When he reads the same reports, Herbert Sulzbach cannot help but agree: 'It's just unbelievable, and what an impression it must be making on the morale of the people in Paris.'[19]

Charles Bean himself agrees, when he hears the news, noting in his diary that the German Army, *has actually (the Paris papers say) been shelling Paris today with a long range gun which their planes have located at St Gobain - over 70 miles. . . scarcely believable. Someone even suggested that the French Government had had it done to cover a retirement.*[20]

———

It was Field Marshal Helmuth von Moltke, Chief of the General Staff in the 1890s and the mentor of so many of the current German generals – including Ludendorff – who said it best. 'No plan of operations,' he ever and always insisted to his underlings, 'survives the first collision with the main body of the enemy.'[21]

You had to expect that, and adapt accordingly.

That is what Ludendorff feels he must do now, and the precise reason why, on the third day of Operation Michael, he has gathered to his HQ at Avesnes the two Chiefs of Staff for his two Army Groups – General Hermann von Kuhl and General Friedrich von der Schulenburg – to go through the reports and examine the maps.

It is soon obvious that, while most of Operation Michael is going exactly to plan, the glaring exception is the attack on Arras, which has seen the tide of battle crash on the shores of the British Third Army . . . all to no effect. This is a problem. If Arras does not fall, the German Army will not be able to roll up the British by pushing north.

The alternative? Change the plan. Reinforce success. Forget Arras and pursue a different goal. The *Schwerpunkt*, the centre of gravity of the attack, will change to that most important railway hub: Amiens. If the German Army can push through just 40 miles from its present position and take Amiens to seize control of that line – or just get close enough to use artillery to destroy the big complex of Amiens station and rail yards – it will be able to strangle the key British supply-line as well as divide his enemies.

'The object now,' Ludendorff makes clear to his subordinates, 'is to separate the French and British by a rapid advance . . . in order to drive them into the sea . . . In so doing the Second Army must push forward on both sides of the Somme, on to Amiens.'[22]

Ja, on to Amiens. It is an incontrovertible argument.

The course of this war has proved beyond doubt that control of the railways is even more important than control of key roads and, as both Amiens and Hazebrouck boast essential rail junctions, control of them is of paramount importance. When you understand that it takes no fewer than 30 rail wagons to supply all the needs of one Division *for one day*, you understand how quickly that Division could be strangled if those rail wagons could be stopped.[23] While almost everything that comes through the northern ports destined for the Allies passes through Hazebrouck, *everything* coming from the southern ports passes through Amiens. And, yes, should those railway junctions fall, the British could try to get some supplies through by road, but given that it takes 150 motor lorries to carry the same freight as one rail wagon, it would take 5000 lorries a day to supply just one Division, and there are simply not that many drivers or lorries available, let alone roads.[24]

'Thus,' General Hermann von Kuhl, Chief of Staff to Army Group Prince Rupprecht, would summate, 'there was a complete change of plan. Hitherto the main feature had been the attack on the British . . . Now the French and British were to be separated.'[25]

All obstacles in the path of that goal must be destroyed or brushed aside. Starting with Albert and Villers-Bretonneux . . .

—

As for General Haig, it is also time to come to grips with what is actually happening on his 45-mile-long front-line. And so, starting early, first he visits the Third Army's General Julian Byng at Albert – where the reports are not all that bad, as the northern half of the Third is holding easily; Arras is safe – and then heads to the Red Château at Villers-Bretonneux to see General Hubert Gough at the Fifth Army's HQ. Here, things are not so good.

The once-genteel surrounds of French privilege are now as busy as a beehive, with the château walls covered with a maze of telephone wires, and each of the grand rooms given over now to various branches of the Fifth Army. Grim-looking staff officers hurry hither and thither.

Much of Gough's hopes had been pinned on holding off the Germans at the Somme bend, that part of the Somme where, for 20 miles, it flows from the south to the north, and he had positioned his remaining forces accordingly, but . . .

'[But I was surprised to learn,]' Haig would recount, '[that] his troops are now behind the Somme and the River Tortille. Men very tired after two days fighting and long march back. On first day they had to wear gas masks all day, which is very fatiguing.'[26]

For the life of him, though, General Haig, in his own words, 'cannot make out why the Fifth Army has gone so far back without making some kind of a stand.'[27] He doesn't ask Gough this in so many words, as it would be rude, but they are his thoughts, as recorded in his diary. All this and yet he finds Gough 'confident and cheerful.'[28]

As to Gough, more sad hound-dog in his appearance than ever – the heavy bags beneath his watery blue eyes surely holding back his tears of frustration – he is equally *deeply* dissatisfied with his meeting with Haig. Here he is, completely overwhelmed by German forces flooding forward on all fronts, and all Haig can do is ask a few questions, offer a few aphorisms, while remaining 'calm and cheerful'.[29]

But actual advice, strategy, an offer of help, more Divisions coming to his aid? Of the last, there is none closer than a three-day march. As to the rest, all that Haig can do is tell Gough that it appears that there are now 45 enemy Divisions ranged against them on a front some 45-miles long – an extraordinary concentration of a massive force. Gough, by his own later account, keeps waiting for Haig to offer up what he intends to do, but when nothing is forthcoming he doesn't like to ask. It would be . . . rude.

'The Fifth Army,' Gough assures Haig, 'will go on fighting as long as there are men to do so, but my casualty rate exceeds by far the accession of my reinforcements . . .'[30]

'Well, Hubert,' Haig replies diffidently, 'you can't fight without men.'[31]

The question that Gough has, even if there is no record of him voicing it, is where is he to get those men from, and how quickly can he get them?

——

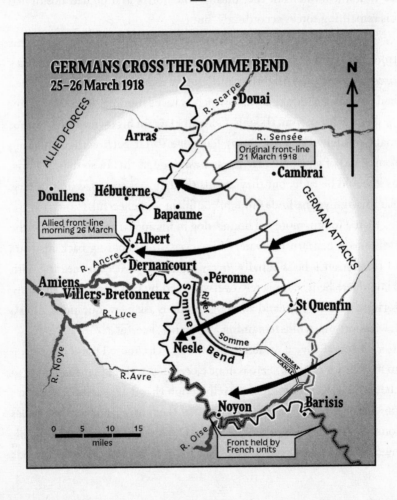

GERMANS CROSS THE SOMME BEND
25–26 March 1918

The word starts to spread rapidly among more of the Australian soldiers up in Flanders. They really *are* going to be called in.

For Private Edwin Need of the 59th Battalion – perhaps the finest battalion of Brigadier Pompey Elliott's 15th Brigade of the 5th Division – it is a red-letter day.

'Great alarm everywhere,' he would chronicle, 'the news coming through of the smashing by the Germans of the British Fifth Army down on the Somme . . . The whole western front in a state of alarm, the air electric, big movements of troops taking place, guessing that we too would soon be on the move, the Australians generally being used at most vital points, being classed as storm or shock troops . . .'[32]

And the reaction of him and his comrades to the news that they are likely to be thrown at a marauding German army that has apparently already shattered the British?

'This really puts the fellows in better spirits . . . a little action being welcome, everyone having long waited for the opportunity to get out into the open and have a go, this sitting behind sandbags, having lumps of metal hurled at you from miles away, didn't seem a fair go.'[33]

And now they might be able to get a fair go and take on the Germans in open country? You bloody *beauty*.

In fact, for the moment, Private Need's 5th Division remains stuck at Messines – together with the 1st and 2nd – while it is the 4th Division lucky enough to get the word that they must prepare to move within 24 hours.

Colonel Alexander Imlay, Commanding Officer of the 4th Division's 47th Battalion, is thrilled, noting in his diary: 'Received orders to hold ourselves ready to proceed to battle front – always our luck to be in first. But this time the eggs-a-cook crowd are caught and have to go in too.'[34]

At least a few soldiers of the 4th Division, like Lieutenant George Mitchell of the 48th Battalion, are more sanguine at the prospect of heading back into serious battle.

'Orders to prepare to move,' he records in his diary. 'I stand in the sun. A stout old Frenchman sows his field . . . [while] all with us is

activity. What matters the personal shock of combat to him? I antici-
pate it all. The roar of the shells, the wounds, the stink of the explosives
and the infernal jabbering of the machine guns. The farmer steadily
goes on with his sowing. We go to the reaping.'[35]

And so, as it happens, do the men of the 3rd Division. After being
rushed east towards Watou, getting on and off trucks and trains,
marching around in ever-decreasing circles, being turned around,
rerouted, detrained, entrained and stuffed around before being turned
around once more, at last come clear orders: they, too, are now heading
south, on the track winding back . . . to the Somme!

—

For most of the Germans soldiers, particularly those attacking the Fifth
Army at the Somme, the progress is amazing.

'We are going on like hell, on and on, day and night,' *Hauptmann*
Rudolf Binding records in his diary. 'The sun and moon help. One or
two hours halt, then on again. Our baggage is somewhere in the rear,
and nobody expects to see it again. We are glad if ration carts and field
kitchens can get up to us at night; then men and horses feed for the
next twenty-four hours in one sitting . . . Another wonderful spring
day with an early mist, which helps us. Our cars now run on the best
English rubber tyres, we smoke none but English cigarettes, and plaster
our boots with lovely English boot-polish – all unheard of things which
belong to a fairyland of long ago.'[36]

—

At four o'clock that afternoon, 23 March, Haig receives General Pétain
at GHQ at Dury, just south of Amiens.

Pétain is clearly somewhat shocked at the rapid turn of events, but
still resolute. The situation is dangerous but still manageable. What is
obvious to both men is that the Germans must *not* be allowed to drive
a wedge between the French and British forces.

'Pétain is most anxious to do all he can to support me,' Haig records in his diary. 'The basic principle of [our] co-operation is to keep the two armies in touch. If this is lost and the Enemy comes in between us, then probably the British will be rounded up and driven into the sea!'[37]

4 PM, 23 MARCH 1918, 10 DOWNING ST, THE CRISIS COMES CALLING

And so it has come to this. For four months, Prime Minister Lloyd George has deliberately held back the reserve soldiers in Britain that General Haig has been demanding be sent to France, specifically to prevent Haig from launching any more mass murderous offensives. But now that the Germans have launched an offensive of their own, it seems equally clear to Lloyd George that he has no choice. Sitting at the head of the green baize-covered mahogany table in the Cabinet Room – at the same time Haig is meeting Pétain on the other side of the Channel – Prime Minister Lloyd George takes a sounding from all the other ashen-faced members of the War Cabinet and they all agree. In the words of the Prime Minister, the situation requires 'to send from England every man that was needed to strengthen the line in France . . .'[38]

Within hours, the word suddenly comes through to, among others, the young men earmarked to reinforce the British 8th Division. In their camps across England, 18- and 19-year-olds must begin packing immediately and be ready to embark on their journey as soon as the following day. The Division that awaits them in France, they know, has seen some of the toughest action of the war, having served in the battles of Neuve Chapelle, Aubers Ridge, the Somme in 1916 and Passchendaele in 1917. So much bloody *bloody* action, in fact, that by now nearly all the 'old Bills' – the tough, pre-war, mustachioed soldiers with skins tanned by ten years in Burma or India – are dead, as are most of the veterans of the early years. All that is left are those who were sent as replacements before Lloyd George put a stop to their wanton slaughter on needless attacks, and now the new boys are going to join them to form one of the youngest, least experienced Divisions in the British Army. But, so be it, the young'uns set to with a will and are very shortly on their way, irrespective of the fact they have not completed their training, wouldn't know a Mills bomb if it climbed up the toilet bowl and bit them on the bottom, and many have not even fired a single live round from their rifles. Nor are they even fully equipped, lacking such things as mess kits. Within two days of the Cabinet Decision, the 5000 young soldiers destined for 8th Division – callow youths, some of them born *this century*, if you can believe it! – will be on their way. They are to join the tens of thousands of reinforcements heading for France.

———

Der Kaiser is in as high spirits as he has been since August 1914, when it appeared the war had already been won. Having spent the day inspecting the men at the front, south-west of St Quentin, he is bursting with pride, eager to share the news of the success of his troops far and wide.

In fact, as his special train pulls back into the platform at Avesnes, a startled guard on the platform suddenly sees the head of the Kaiser poking out the window as he shouts the news he wishes all of Germany could hear: '*Die Schlacht ist gewonnen, die Engländer total geschlagen!* The battle is won, the English have been utterly defeated!'[39]

There is champagne for dinner, and a communiqué is released to the people, highlighting the personal role His Imperial Majesty has played in the great victory, something that is, Müller notes, 'a well-meaning lie issued by the Von Hindenburg and Ludendorff firm which the German people will not believe for one moment.'[40]

No matter. It is the temper of the times, and all understand it.

And, of course, *Seine Kaiserliche Majestät*, His Imperial Majesty the Kaiser, is the first to raise his glass and propose a toast: '*Auf die Armee und ihre großen Heerführer*, to the Army and its great leaders!'

Rising to the occasion, the Kaiser's great confidant, General Hans von Plessen, replies with a toast of his own, even more heartily embraced by the gathering: '*Auf unseren Kriegsherrn und Führer*, to our War Lord and leader!'[41]

In a German tradition dating back centuries, they toast only with their left hands, so as to keep their right hand free for their rifles.

—

At his HQ in Montreuil, on this evening, Sir Douglas Haig has called for an emergency meeting with General Henry Horne of the First Army and General Herbert Plumer of the Second Army – the two Armies holding the northern half of the Western Front that have not yet been attacked. As it will still take some time to get reinforcements from England to bolster the lines of the Third and Fifth Armies, and as the infernal Americans *still* refuse to throw even what forces they have into a serious fight until their men are better trained, Sir Douglas asks both Generals, with no little urgency, what forces they can spare to send south.

After discussion, Haig achieves the result desired. General Plumer has 11 Divisions but agrees to hold his section of the line with just

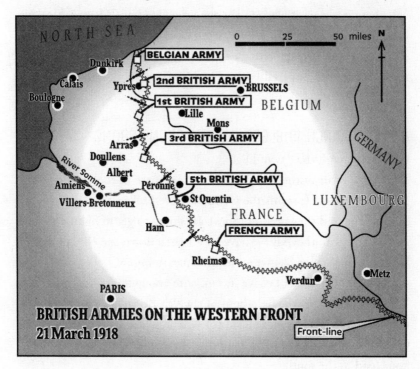

eight divisions and let Haig have the best three divisions he has, thus releasing the 3rd, 4th and 5th Australian Divisions.[42]

Perfect. The Australians can be troublesome, and no doubt about it when it comes to fitting in with British discipline and the like, but, more importantly, they also have a strong record of being more than troublesome to the Germans. Haig can ask no better than to send for the Australians in these extreme times.

—

Heaven should make such a day. After crossing the English Channel from Folkestone to Calais by steamer, the now famed Australian war correspondent Charles Bean arrives, at last, at the Australian Corps HQ in the town of Flêtre, just eight miles from Messines.

Of course there is no bed available for him, but the oldest rule of war correspondence applies: wheresoever there is a fellow correspondent, there is always a place to lay one's sleeping bag. After waking his bleary-eyed friend Fred Cutlack, Bean does exactly that. (Apart from everything else, the fact that Bean holds the nominal rank of Captain in the Australian Imperial Force gives him some bunk rights.)

8 AM, 24 MARCH 1918, GOING GOING GRONG GRONG

Great news with the dawn, Dig!

Instead of us of the 3rd Division waiting here in the north, we are being sent south! It seems the Germans have broken through, around St Quentin, and they need us. So we are going to get to fight, after all. Never again can they say we have 'never been down the old Somme!'[43] Not only that, looks like we're the first ones going in!

Some soldiers don't believe it, but, sure enough, at 8 am, with one 'Quiiiiiiick march!', the battalions of the 9th Brigade are on their way to their congregation point outside of Watou, where motor lorries await to carry some of them forth . . . another step on the long and oft circuitous road to the south.

Among the men marching is the farrier from Grong Grong, Private John Hardie, who will tell his parents in a letter: 'About daylight we marched out again, and were picked up by motor lorries on the main road. Eventually we were joined by the rest of the 3rd Division and I can tell you it was some sight. The string of lorries seemed to be miles long. In fact, I couldn't see either end as our Battalion appeared to be in the centre.'[44]

By 10 am, each battalion, jammed in 30 to a truck, is in a string of 60 trucks on the next phase of their long journey, to where half a million marauding Germans have broken through.

—

Far, far in the south, a long journey to the north is about to begin for the Commanding Officer of their own 3rd Division.

General John Monash – who, as a 14-year-old schoolboy during the Kelly Gang raid on his home town of Jerilderie, had talked to Ned Kelly, later saying 'a Sunday school superintendent couldn't have given me better advice as to human conduct'[45] – is still on the Riviera, and still oblivious of events. The news finally reaches him and his companion, Brigadier Charles Rosenthal of the 9th Brigade, via urgent cables from Colonel Jess.

Monash moves quickly and arranges for a special carriage to be reserved the following morning to take him and Rosie north to Paris, also wiring to Jess to send his valued aide-de-camp, Captain Paul Simonson, together with his driver and car, to pick them up from Gare de Lyons in Paris on Monday morning.

Rosenthal is sanguine, at best, about his return. Still with no real idea of the seriousness of the situation, his primary feeling is one of exhaustion, recording in his diary, 'As usual my luck is out – my leave seems further than ever from realisation.'[46]

With a whistle and a jolt – just as it ever was, just as it ever will be – their train starts the long haul north.

—

Most of those soldiers falling back before the German onslaught are British, but not all. Members of the 2nd Australian Tunnelling Company, who have been attached to the Third Army under Byng since November 1917, are right in the thick of it.

'Still on the retreat,' one of the Australian sappers writes in his dairy on this, the fourth day of the German assault. 'Now back to Seltra and going still back on Martinpuich. Fritz coming fast in as we fall back. He has now got back what we took from him last year.'[47]

Martinpuich is just less than two miles north-east of Pozières, and the hope is that their combined forces can stop the Germans before they get to that sacred Australian site.

That evening, the word spreads among the Australian troops that the Germans have crossed the Somme, south of Péronne.

How fast they are moving!

—

The bulk of the five divisions of the Australian Corps have yet to be ordered south. At least, on this crisp morning of 24 March, the men of General Monash's 3rd Division are on their way to the action, even if – with so many lorries trying to make their way along skinny provincial roads – it is slow going.

The men of 4th Division, meanwhile, are packed and ready to depart, but still wait in billets west of Messines for marching orders from their commander, General Ewen Maclagan. As to General Joseph Hobbs's 5th Division, they are yet to receive any orders to move from Messines Ridge but have been told they're soon to be 'whirled into the maelstrom'.

Wonderful!

One Digger records the enthusiasm of his mob, who are heard to remark:

'Wish they would hurry us down!'

'I suppose that we'll be sent.'

'We'll have to go down and stop them.'

'The old Somme, eh? We'll be back there.'[48]

Ah, yes, the Somme. The very word conjures myriad memories, bitter and joyous, but all of them strong.

'Much Aussie blood had been spilt there,' one Digger would reminisce, 'more was to be spilt in helping stop Fritz, more to be spilt regaining the lost territory. Despite the catastrophe down south the AIF were in great spirits and their morale was rising higher and higher. We were feeling in great form, the weighty responsibility about to be thrust on us served but to make us more confident. The AIF was a magnificent body of fighters. Courage and brains combined.'[49]

The 1st and 2nd Divvies, also still stuck on Messines Ridge, feel much the same. As a fellow Digger remarks to Archie Barwick when he hears the news of the attack down south, 'Guess it means the bally old Somme & beaucoup stunts!!'[50]

Archie himself, disciplined diarist that he is, writes, 'So the Great Hun offensive has been launched at last. They surprise me; I honestly thought they had better sense than come at that game, for come what may they have not the slightest chance of winning.'[51]

—

Now the 40 German reserve divisions, not used on the first day, are flooding forward. Another day, another 15 miles. That's six hours marching to the west, with a ten-minute break each hour and an hour off for lunch. They could have marched faster and with fewer breaks, certainly, but it is important not to wear troops out, in the admittedly unlikely case that they will suddenly have to fight.

Neuer Tag, neues Glück: new day, new luck. Up ahead, the division of *Leutnant* Herbert Sulzbach continues to advance against what is only spasmodic British defence, and his artillery battery is continuing to perform well, accurately targeting whichever points of resistance observers determine can be best quelled by shells landing down their spouts.

On this afternoon, Sulzbach and his battery are continuing to push to the west and are some 20 miles east of Villers-Bretonneux, on the Ham-to-Nesle road, when the young German artillery officer happens to notice a burned-out German plane. Right beside it is a freshly dug grave, complete with cross, upon which is affixed a sign:

Here rest two German flying officers.[52]

Sad.

Sulzbach and his men move on.

—

It is passing high noon, high up on the ridge above Pozières, right by the legendary windmill site where – as the monument of large white stones topped with a large dark wooden cross attests – some 7000 Australian lives had been lost to take it from the Germans in mid-1916, when one of the official Australian war photographers, Lieutenant Hubert Wilkins, passes by.

And what is this?

Right by the summit, he is thrilled to find fellow Australians, members of – who are you? – the 2nd Australian Tunnelling Company. Right now they are furiously digging both a trench across the line of the ridge and a small tunnel under the road to pack with explosives.

They're going to blow the whole thing up, sport!

The Germans are just to the east, heading this way, and the hope of the Australians is that making a huge crater on this narrow pass of road will at least slow down their wheeled transport. Beyond that, there are no plans to make a serious stand here. It is conceded that Pozières will fall within a day or two, perhaps even *hours*. As they dig, hundreds of British infantry stream past, heading west. The Tommies are exhausted but still in good order. There is no major panic apparent, but they appear directionless, apart from the one general point on the compass they are following: *away* from the Germans.

The British officers that Wilkins asks confess that they are without orders now about where they are to go. So they just follow the road, away, away, away . . .

One Commanding Officer tells Wilkins in passing, in fact *while* passing, that – not to put too fine a point on it – '51st Division ran first . . . and let the Germans through . . .'[53]

As Wilkins walks past the summit where the Australians are digging and heads down the lee side of Pozières slope, he walks through huge numbers of British soldiers bivouacked there, nominally ready to fight the Germans, now said to be just five miles away. But as far as Wilkins can determine, they are even less disposed than their brethren to provide serious resistance.

Wilkins is unimpressed with the lax attitude – and he is a man whose own bravery has already become the stuff of legend. Twice in this war he would find himself in action so thick he'd put down the camera and get involved himself, and on both occasions win the Military Cross for his trouble. General John Monash himself would call Wilkins 'the bravest man in my command'.[54] It is bravery, of course, that has helped with his photography, and just a couple of months earlier, when the Western Front was still stable, Wilkins has told Bean he intended to use flash photography out in No-Man's Land to get a photograph of a German night patrol, 'as they sometimes do with wild animals in America'.[55]

Now, *that's* brave!

For their part, after digging their trenches, laying their charges and blowing the bastard up – leaving a deep crater that will surely take the Germans half a day to fill in – the 2nd Australian Tunnelling Company falls back with all the rest. Yes, it is demoralising to be falling back before the German onslaught, but there is an upside.

'The retreat,' their Commanding Officer, Major Garnet Adcock, would record, 'was a relief after the stagnation and monotony of trench warfare. At last we got out of the mud into the open country and could lie in the clean, if wet, grass, and take a shot at Fritz. It was hard work but it was <u>fighting</u>.'[56]

And for the first time in yonks, they have plenty of fresh tucker, 'commandeering stores abandoned by other troops who had long since vanished over the western horizon . . . Other days we picked up odd scraps or 'cleaned out' the rabbits and chickens left behind by civilians.'[57]

—

It is happening!

The Germans are *still* advancing, and the news just gets worse and worse. Now the brutes are in High Wood, which, as the veterans know, is almost within range of a .303 bullet from the old windmill atop Pozières Ridge.

It cannot be long now before they are called upon!

And, sure enough, the word indeed comes through to 4th Division that they are to head south in the morning and join the 3rd Division, who are already en route, even if *still* a little stalled.

'We're off. Just saw the order,' one Digger says as he walks into his billet to tell the boys the news. 'We're to embus at 10 o'clock on the 25th of March. That's tomorrow. Goin' in motor buses, that means goin' a long way. Must be off down Amiens way because they reckon Fritz'll have that in a few days' time.'[58]

'Hooray,' another responds blithely from where he is lying, trying to get some sleep on his hard bed, 'we'll soon be dead.'[59]

For some time thereafter, the Diggers in the room chat about the German breakthrough until another friend drops by and tells them that the Squareheads have 'taken all the old joints we fought over from November 1916 to April 1917'.[60]

'And he's flaming welcome to them,' pipes up the voice from the bed.

The men sit in silence as their minds flash back to 'memories of mud! Of Pozières and Mouquet Farm . . . of Bapaume and Bullecourt – of blood!'[61] So many thousands of Diggers had died taking Pozières and Mouquet Farm alone, and it is just not right that Fritz should take it back – at least not without a major stink.

They talk long into the night, speculating about 'the big Fritz attack and the hundreds of spare battalions Fritz must have now that Russia is no longer hammering at his eastern frontier'.[62] They talk of the joys, they presume, of open warfare once they are out of the trenches, what it will be like, and just what they'll do to any mass Fritz formation attacks.

For his part, George Mitchell sits solemnly with his fellow Diggers of the 48th Battalion at their local estaminet, now a cherished local watering hole, discussing 'the breakthrough'.[63]

'How could it possibly have happened? New tanks, and gases?'[64]

They shall see.

'To the men of the two divisions,' Bean would write of the 3rd and 4th, 'the orders came as a direct summons, quite different from any previously made on them, to act decisively for the winning of the war.'[65]

And *this time*, instead of risking all to gain a trench of dubious value, it is going to be up to them to directly stop the Germans in an open fight. Perfect.

'Here,' Charles Bean would note, 'was a situation in which it was obvious that every effort must help directly towards beating the *Boche*. This, at last, was the job for which they had come overseas.'[66]

11 PM, 24 MARCH 1918, DURY, WILL FRANCE FACE THE FRAY?

General Douglas Haig has seen tough times before, but rarely like this.

The southern third of his British forces on the Western Front are in full retreat, led by Gough's Fifth Army, which appears to have just about disintegrated. Britain is now experiencing its worst day of the war since the First Battle of Ypres, over three years earlier. Every fresh report shows the better part of British forces receding before the storm, suffering terrible casualties along the way.

And now, just before the midnight hour, Haig has one more meeting remaining in his château at Dury, just three miles south of Amiens – this one with Marshal Pétain.

A meeting of minds, it is not.

From the moment that an ashen-faced Pétain is gravely ushered into Haig's study, it is obvious that the Frenchman is even more seriously shaken than he had been the day before. Then, the situation had been manageable. Now, it seems, Pétain has come to the conclusion that, for the British at least, the situation is perilously close to being beyond retrieval. If that is the case, then clearly it is time Pétain started thinking only about the interests of France . . . and Pétain. A position, it seems, not altogether foreign to him. Just in the last day, the Germans have leaped forward six miles and captured Péronne. The clear danger is the enemy now taking Amiens – just 20 miles further along the road – which boasts the rail network that carries over half the supplies for the British Expeditionary Force, coming in through the ports of Rouen, Dieppe and Le Havre. If Amiens falls, it will be all but impossible to hold the rampant Germans off.

'Pétain,' Haig will later recount, delicately, 'struck me as very much upset, almost unbalanced and most anxious.'[67]

'General Pétain,' Haig addresses him formally, 'I ask you to concentrate as large a force as possible about Amiens, astride the Somme, to cooperate with my right.'[68]

Pétain demurs. 'But I expect every moment to be attacked in Champagne, and I do not believe that the main German blow has yet been delivered.'[69]

Good Lord! The French have not even been attacked yet, and this is the best they can do?

Oui. The best Pétain can promise is that he will instruct his leading General in this field, Émile Fayolle, to position all available French troops at Montdidier, 20 miles south-east of Amiens and the Somme – perfect for moving to defend Paris, but blooming hopeless to help Haig's British forces.

And now Pétain completely, unashamedly, even tells Haig straight out: 'I have directed Fayolle in the event of the German advance being pressed still further, to fall back southwards to Beauvais [30 miles south of Amiens in the direction of Paris], in order to cover Paris.'

Haig can barely believe it.

'It was at once clear to me,' he would recount, 'that the effect of this order must be to separate the French from the British right flank, and so allow the Enemy to penetrate between the two Armies.'

Perhaps he has misunderstood?

'Do you mean,' he asks Pétain plaintively, 'to abandon my right flank?'[70]

Pétain nods his head in the manner of a man who agrees, *c'est vrai*, that Haig's words are a very fair summation of his own intent.

'It is the only thing possible,' the Frenchman says by way of expiation, 'if the enemy compel the Allies to fall back still further.'[71]

To emphasise the point, Pétain now shows Haig the order he had issued to his forces at nine o'clock that evening:

The primary [French] task is to maintain unity of
the French armies .. Secondly, if it is possible, to
maintain liaison with the British forces.[72]

So Pétain has told his force to maintain contact with the British, *si c'est possible?* The whole battle hangs in the balance; everything rides on stopping the German wedge dividing them; and the French will only hold on, *SI C'EST POSSIBLE?*

Unable to convince the rattled Frenchman to change his mind, Haig takes his hat, his cane and his umbrage, and leaves in high dudgeon at one o'clock in the morning, returning on his own train to his principal HQ at Montreuil, where he arrives two hours later on the 25th.

Two hours later, Haig sends a telegram to Sir Henry Wilson, Chief of the Imperial General Staff, in London, urgently requesting that Wilson and Lord Milner COME TO FRANCE AT ONCE IN ORDER TO ARRANGE THAT GENERAL FOCH, OR SOME OTHER DETERMINED GENERAL WHO WOULD FIGHT, SHOULD BE GIVEN SUPREME CONTROL OF OPERATIONS IN FRANCE.[73]

As it happens, it is not the first communication that Wilson has had on the subject, as only hours earlier he had also taken a phone call from General Foch himself . . .

—

Exactly what is going on? Where are the Germans now, where are the British forces, and just who is being sent forward?

Exactly. No one is more desperate for solid information about what is happening than Charles Bean and Fred Cutlack. Trying to sort through the mass of conflicting reports, rumours and outright furphies to work out what is fact and what is fiction means they must go to a central fount of sure information. It is for this reason that on this day – after making their way through endless streams of refugees, panicky officers and haunted-looking men – they arrive at the Allied Press HQ in Amiens. Surely the Press Officer assigned for this purpose will know? Stamping their feet after the cold drive, they knock on his door and are warmly welcomed. Of course, there is only one question to be asked . . .

'Well, they're past Combles,' the Press Officer replies equably, despite the fact that the village is just five miles due south of Bapaume and only 25 miles from where they now stand. That means the Germans must have advanced 20 miles in just the first four days.

'Past Combles! You mean on the old Somme battlefield!'

'Yes.'

'Not truly! Then do you mean they're *past* Bapaume?'

Seeking firmer information, the two correspondents go to see the Chief Censor, Major Neville Lytton. One look at his face and it is clear that he really does grasp the seriousness of the situation.

'Where's the nearest point they have got to?' Bean asks.

'Delville Wood,' Lytton replies glumly, naming a wood within view of the Pozières windmill, just 20 miles away!

'Haven't we any reserves? Surely we must have!' Bean says.

'No, I don't think there's a division between the Germans and here,' the Press Officer says morosely.

'Our divisions will surely be coming, and the New Zealanders,' Bean insists.

'How can they get here in time?'

Only time will tell.

Ah, but how that time passes, in the wee hours of the night, in his nearby lodgings, as Bean tries to settle down for some sleep . . . only to be woken by the explosions of German bombs being dropped on Amiens. He rises quickly to find a general alert to go with rumours everywhere – 'there was mention of the German cavalry getting through,'[74] unleashing troops on horseback to wreak havoc far and wide behind Allied lines. Still, like everything, it is unconfirmed.

Bean makes one last notation in his diary before turning in once more:

I hope that Germans don't arrive here to wake us in the morning.[75]

For Bean, as for them all, there is the genuine fear that dawn will come with the German Army in tow. All through what little remains of the night there is the constant roar of heavily laden lorries. But which way are they going? Heading to the front, with supplies and reinforcements, which would be good? Or coming back from the front, with retreating soldiers, which would be disastrous?

It is difficult to say.

Several times, Bean goes to the window to peer through the trees on the boulevard, trying to work it out. East, they are still going *east*, which is something. And now some of the trucks are stopping for a moment, close enough that Bean can hear snatches of their conversation travelling to him in the night air.

'70 miles! . . . Gun which is firing on Paris . . .'[76]

Sure enough, that extraordinary gun the Germans have is still the thing that everyone is talking about, and Bean reflects on what a fortunate thing it is at the moment – it gives everyone something to talk about that *isn't* the flood of German soldiers heading their way.

Exhausted, he returns to bed in the vain hope of getting some sleep before awaking once more as dawn breaks to the sound of troops marching. It only takes a couple of snatches of overheard conversation, and a brief glimpse of their size and their uniforms, for him to know it.

They are New Zealanders.

'I can't say how glad I was to see them,' he would record of his thoughts in his diary. 'They are the solidest, calmest looking troops in France.'[77]

But the Australians run them pretty close.

Where *are* they?

———

The day of 25 March dawns as cold and dull as a trigonometry class in Bathurst High School on a Monday morn in June. Such an atmosphere clashes sharply with the bright and fiery spirit of the men of the 4th Division, who are now ready to move south!

Oh, the fervour with which the men of the division's brigades proudly march towards their waiting lorries – or towards their 'Tommy route march', as the Diggers have labelled any such mechanical military transports. In their vanguard, regimental bands play the thumping Australian marching song, to the tune of 'Waltzing Matilda' . . . with more gusto than ever:

> *Fighting the Kaiser, fighting the Kaiser*
> *Who'll come a-fighting the Kaiser with me?*
> *And we'll drink all his beer,*
> *And eat up all his sausages,*
> *Who'll come a fighting the Kaiser with me!*[78]

Everywhere, the officers are being briefed by their superiors so they can pass on to their men just what is happening.

George Mitchell and the men of the 48th are ready.

It is, surprisingly, the Maman of his billet who is perhaps less ready for Mitch and the boys to leave.

'When I said goodbye to Madame,' Mitchell would recall, 'she wept and wished us Godspeed.'[79]

She says to Mitch, with a look so forlorn, so miserable it could break the heart of Satan himself, 'The *Boche* will come now.'

Recovering, she shoves a 'lucky five-franc Napoleon' in his hand, saying with a momentary sparkle in her eye, '*pour bon chance*,'[80] and they bounce out the front door, waving at Madame as they go.

They march along the road to the 'motor lorries . . . waiting in a great line down the road. Dust was blowing in clouds and the sun went out.'[81]

They climb up into their allotted lorries, squeezed in tight, and start to move off at the pace, and with seemingly the same meandering moves, of a sick snail.

'It was a long, long slow journey,' Mitchell jotted in his diary later. At one point they stop for a bite, and 'the mademoiselle of an estaminet was telling the Captain that the Huns were shelling Paris. We did not believe it!'[82]

'Impossible,' the boys tell her. 'Im-bloody-possible!'[83] they refrain, yet with a tinge of a twinge of doubt . . .

These days, Dig, you just never know.

As they continue along the road, they notice new shell holes around and see the occasional flare fly up, 'unpleasantly close'.[84]

But still they are up for it!

—

At the same time as the 4th Divvie trundle south, *bumperty-bump-bump*, over war-torn turf, the men of the 3rd Division – now all together again, camped in spots between Hazebrouck and St Omer – are being briefed on the situation.

The officers of the 10th Brigade, for one, are all assembled – right in the middle of the road at a spot near the tiny village of Campagne. The brigade's Commanding Officer, General Walter McNicoll, a distinguished Gallipoli veteran known by his admiring men as 'Fire-eater McNicoll',[85] gathers them around to give them a very quick and to-the-point briefing – there is no time to waste!

Loved by his soldiers for the fact that, like them (and unlike the other Brigadiers), McNicoll was born with a *tin* spoon in his mouth and is *Australian* to his bootstraps, the Victorian is usually found with his beloved 'Karl', a captured German messenger dog who has switched sides. That tin spoon background means McNicoll doesn't bullshit, calls it as it is, and here is a case in point, as his whole manner now indicates that things are *not* middle-of-the-road at all.

'The Fifth Army has been driven back,' McNicoll tells them gravely, urgently, 'and we are retreating *everywhere*. The British front is broken and the British and French armies are in danger of separation. The German divisions are pushing forward with great rapidity . . . and a long-range gun is shelling Paris.'[86]

The upshot?

'You are to entrain tomorrow morning [at St Omer]. On arrival at [Mondicourt], you will go straight into action. It will be the fight of your lives – the result of this war now hangs in the balance!'[87]

Now, gentlemen, look here on the map.

The general plan, as it seems at this point, is that the Australians of the 3rd and 4th Divisions are to be placed on the British right wing – the traditional post of honour on battlefields, dating from the ancient time of Thucydides onwards – and, in this case, already familiar ground to the old hands along the Somme Valley.

The 1st and 2nd can hold Messines until GHQ can find a way for them to join us. Meantime, the 5th is on its way and will be here soon. They need as many Australians as they can get in this crisis.

So, let's get to it. The men need to quickly place in storage everything but the bare essentials – and essentials starts with Lewis and Vickers machine guns with ammunition bandoliers and two grenades each, which the Quartermaster will be issuing to every man.

The eggs-a-cook's 9th Brigade, camped just a few miles to the east, are told that, so as not to clog the arterial roads headed for the front, they are to march out – *of course, why didn't they think of that solution!?* – at 2 am, heading for the station at Steenbecque, bound for the town of Doullens.

Still, Private John Hardie is pleased to have some semblance of solid information, jotting in his diary that night, 'The authorities don't seem to know what to do with us. I really believe that Fritz has got them thinking. Anyway, the Colonel seems very uneasy.'[88]

—

The Australian soldiers of 4th Division, still on their way, packed in 30 to each lorry, continue to rumble down the chokka roads to the south, many of them with their mouths and noses tucked into their shirts as they try to breathe without taking in 'the white powder which wrapped the whole route like a fog, and dusted the wagons and the men as with snow'.[89]

And yet, as Charles Bean would note, 'Dust, jolting, crowding could not abate the spirit of the troops. When, late in the afternoon, the lorries with the leading brigade, the veteran 4th, turned sharply off the main road at St Pol into the countryside south-eastwards, it came into an atmosphere of suppressed excitement.'[90]

When the Germans had launched this latest battle, the picturesque St Pol had been 22 miles behind the lines and had made it through the war unscathed. But not now, as German long-range guns set it in their sights and start shelling. Far to their south, the Australians can see a single column of black smoke against the impossibly blue sky, showing where the British had set fire to their massive ammunition dump, in preference to leaving anything behind for the marauding Germans. Everywhere they look they see French citizens sadly piling carts sky-high with all their valuables before beginning the long haul to the west and, hopefully, safety. Of course, as the Australians bump past, 'lorry-load after lorry-load of cheerful men . . . each crowd shouting and waving to the old folk', the French pause and gaze back.

The word spreads as the villagers call to each other from house to house, the one bit of good news of the day: *'Les Australiens!'*

Yes, as unaccustomed as they are in these parts, the reputation of the AIF precedes them.

'A few minutes later, spontaneously,' Bean chronicles proudly, 'the

French villagers began unloading their carts, and the furniture was carried indoors again.'[91]

—

Another day, another *five* miles of advance.

It is late in the afternoon and *Leutnant* Fritz Nagel and his comrades of *Kraftwagen Flak* No. 82 are at full tilt with their anti-aircraft artillery battery heading down the Bapaume–Albert Road. They come to the crest of a ridge, to the right of which are the ruins of an old windmill. The map shows that just over this next rise is a village called Pozières, and beyond that, Albert!

And there it is! As they come to the top of the hill, Albert lies before them, just five miles away and . . .

And suddenly there is a blinding blaze of light and an explosion right by their side. Nagel and his comrades jump from their truck and into a narrow ditch by the side of the road, which feels 'like a haven of safety', at least in comparison to being exposed and vulnerable in the truck. Those in the trucks behind have come under similar fire, and as Nagel looks out from the ditch he can see that many of them have left the road and are now swarming down the slopes towards Pozières, both to escape the concentrated shelling and to keep advancing, to keep pushing west.

Heartened, *Leutnant* Nagel gives the order – *Schnell! Schnell! Schnell!* – and he and his men are quickly back in their truck, back on the road, heading down towards Pozières, Nagel still shaking at how close he had come to making Dorothy a widow. It is times like these that he is more grateful than ever that their truck has been so lovingly looked after by its usual driver and mechanic, Rupp, the former racing car driver. Its engines roar as never before and it surges forward like an angry bull.

And yet still they are not out of it.

'I had never driven the gun at top speed,' Nagel would recount, 'but all I could do was put my foot down and let her go . . . Looking behind we could still see geysers of dirt shooting up as high as trees.'[92]

Are 7000 Australians rolling over in their graves to see the earth they gave their lives for back in July–August 1916 now back in German hands?

Perhaps.

More certainly, their bodies are being blown from them.

—

At 10 Downing Street, the situation is being monitored closely, and by no one more than the Cabinet Secretary, Maurice Hankey, who has barely slept since the German offensive began.

'This has been a really terrible day,' he notes in his diary. 'Although the gap between Third and Fifth Army has been filled in, our troops everywhere are being driven back and must be extremely exhausted. The Australians and New Zealanders are due tonight at Albert, and may hold up the enemy until the French arrive to cover Amiens . . . All day I kept thinking of Briand's saying during the drawn out Verdun attack – *Nous sommes crucifiés . . .*'[93]

—

After a long day on the trucks moving south, before wearing out their boot leather, the men of the 4th Division are finally approaching their billets around Basseux, seven miles north of Hébuterne.

Everyone off the buses!

'Got out and lined up,' George Mitchell would recount. 'Oh, it was good to get warm. For an hour and a half we marched heavily laden in the moonlight.'[94]

The fact that they are nearing the Gates of Hell is emphasised by the fact that, even as they start their march to the east, heavy German shells begin falling nearby and the first of the billeting parties tell them that the enemy is only four and a half miles away!

It takes damn nigh on two hours, but at last, nearing two o'clock in the morning, they arrive at their billets and are able to put their kits and the blasted guns down before quickly turning in to try to get some shut-eye.

But sleep does not come easily, and not just because the cold night seeps into their bones now that they have stopped marching.

While it is one thing to be drop-dead exhausted, it is quite another to be able to drift off into the Land of Nod when, just to their east, they can hear the constant *boom-BOOM-boom-BOOM* and angry rumble of the German artillery, together with the constant drumming of machine guns. It is all close enough that Divisional HQ sends out pickets on all roads approaching from the east so that any for'ard German patrols will receive an appropriate message that the Australians are here, so this nonsense must stop. Meanwhile, officers and NCOs are sent to the ridge-line above to reconnoitre against an emergency that would see them have to stop an advance *in extremis* in the next few hours.

The 48th Battalion, meanwhile, must stand-to, denied rest, and remain 'ready for instant action'.[95]

All they know is, somewhere to the east, the Germans are continuing to flood towards them.

CHAPTER SIX

THE EMPIRE STRIKES BACK

One is proud to be an Australian anywhere, but especially
here. It was splendid to see the welcome the French people
gave us. Some that were about to leave remained, saying
that now they were safe, as the brave Australians would stop
the *Boche*. They have little confidence in the English but
trust the Scotch and Colonials. That is our opinion too.[1]
Major Garnet Adcock, 2nd Australian
Tunnelling Company, 3 April 1918

Diggers, as sober as saints in a grotto;
Diggers half shot, and Diggers quite blotto;
Church-going Diggers, and Diggers that swore –
Those were the Diggers that went to war.[2]
Lydia O'Neil, in 51st Battalion Newsletter, No. 43

26 MARCH 1918, BINDING TIES, UNDERDRESSED

Captain Rudolf Binding and his men of the 50th Reserve Division can
barely contain themselves. After five days of battle, leaping an enormous five miles forward with every cycle of the sun, suddenly all is
green again as they are 'through at last, through the awful crater-field
of the [1916 battle of the] Somme. After 25 miles of unbroken waste
the first house, ruined though it was, was saluted like a vision from the

promised land . . . Now we are in the English back areas . . . a land flowing with milk and honey. . .'[3]

And chickens! And pigs! And calves to be slaughtered! And weeping French families, who hand them over . . . Now, even, the German horses can feast on masses of oats.

Reinvigorated, they move on again, scarcely believing the lack of British resistance so far. In four years at the Western Front, progress had been measured in yards alone, each one of them paid for with young lives lost. Now, suddenly, it is measured in miles alone as the British continue to fall back. The advancing Germans have to pay only minimally in casualties. In all the confusion, it has to be said, some of the British soldiers and their officers seem to . . . simply lose heart.

On this fine morning, Captain Binding and his men continue to advance in open formation, marching forward along the road just five miles east of Albert, when they see the strangest thing. Marching towards them, easy as you please, almost as if on a morning stroll is . . . *was ist das?* . . . 'an English general, accompanied by a single officer'.[4]

The German soldiers hold their fire – the men approaching are clearly unarmed, and besides, if you killed them, you couldn't get an explanation for this 'extraordinary sight'.[5] *Hauptmann* Binding, the one noted English speaker among the Germans, is called to come forward.

Binding is stupefied by the vision of the General now standing patiently before him.

'About 35 years old, excellently – one could say wonderfully – dressed and equipped, he looked as if he had just stepped out of a Turkish bath in Jermyn St. Brushed and shaved, in breeches of the best cut and magnificent high lace boots, such as only the English bootmakers make to order, he came to meet me easily and without the slightest embarrassment.'[6]

It is all enough that Binding himself feels quite underdressed for the occasion of taking this fine fellow prisoner, but he still tries to rise to it.

'Good morning,' the German officer begins, before straining to reach by high courtesy what he cannot by *haute couture*. 'You have given us a lot of trouble . . . you stuck it for a long time.'[7]

'Trouble!' the Englishman expostulates. 'Why, we have been running for five days and five nights! And when I could no longer get my brigade to stand and fight, I have taken charge of a machine gun myself, to set an example to my retreating men.'[8]

But, now, old chap, he surrenders, what?

'What is your name?' Binding asks him.

'I am General Sir Bertrand Dawson, Equerry of the King.'[9]

Put in the charge of two soldiers, Sir Bertrand and his fellow officer are taken prisoner and moved to the rear, where they can be extensively interrogated before being shipped to a prisoner-of-war camp to see out the war.

Binding and his men keep moving west.

Albert, a key stepping stone to Amiens, is just five miles ahead. The Germans continue flooding to the west while the Allies in the area, including, now, the first of the Australians, try to work out where they are and what can be done.

—

On this late morning of 26 March, the Commanding Officer of the 4th Division, General Ewen Maclagan, in his new HQ at Basseux, six miles north of the town of Hébuterne, dispatches ever-changing orders to his brigades as he walks the wire between the orders he is getting and just what is possible.

As ever, when the best of the best is required, he is inclined to go to his 4th Brigade, under the command of Brigadier Charles Brand – a Boer War and Gallipoli veteran from Queensland, so trusted and liked by his troops that they have given him the ultimate accolade, the nickname of 'Digger'.

At 11.15 am, Digger Brand is in his 4th Brigade HQ at Saulty when he receives urgent word that the enemy has 'broken through with armoured cars at Hébuterne'. His men must 'occupy the line from Souastre to Bienvillers-au-Bois',[10] just north of the besieged town.

The 4th Brigade are on their way shortly afterwards.

———

Fifty miles to their east, Kaiser Wilhelm is returning in his special carriage to his HQ at Avesnes after a brilliant day spent at the front. As ever, Admiral Müller is there to greet His Imperial Majesty, together with the appropriate toast once they are back in their château.

Lassen Sie uns trinken Champagner! Let us all drink champagne!

Say what you will about the French, there is no doubt they make a good drop.

'Spirits were so high,' Müller records, 'that His Majesty declared that if an English delegation come to sue for peace it must kneel before the German standard for it is a question here of a victory of monarchy over democracy.'[11]

———

For all the confusion, at least by this point the Commanding Officer of the 4th Division, General Ewen Maclagan, knows more or less where his Division is situated. Which is all right for some . . . For while an army famously travels 'on its stomach', an army commander in search of his army must travel on information on where exactly to find them. Maclagan's counterpart in the 3rd Division is Monash, and the problem he has on this same late morning is that there is precious little solid information to be had. In all of the confusion of so many Armies and HQs moving, official communiqués are out of the question, and all that remains is the khaki grapevine, which pulsates with, as Monash would note, the 'wildest and most contradictory rumours', making it 'very difficult to locate anybody'.[12]

Which is why he is here now.

Monash has further learned that his division has been placed under the command of 10th Corps, whose HQ he now must find, even though they are 'rapidly on the move backward and did not remain more than a few hours in any one town'.[13]

After being driven from town to town, frequently against the flow

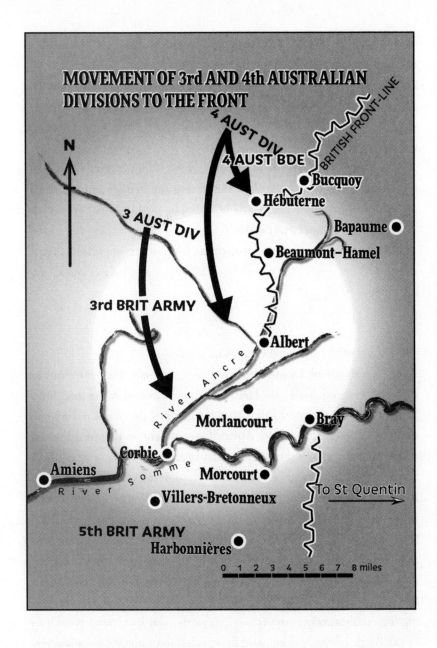

MOVEMENT OF 3rd AND 4th AUSTRALIAN
DIVISIONS TO THE FRONT

4 AUST DIV

4 AUST BDE

BRITISH FRONT-LINE

N

3 AUST DIV

Bucquoy

Hébuterne

Bapaume

Beaumont–Hamel

3rd BRIT ARMY

Albert

River Ancre

Morlancourt

Bray

Corbie

Somme

Morcourt

Amiens

River

To St Quentin

Villers-Bretonneux

5th BRIT ARMY

Harbonnières

0 1 2 3 4 5 6 7 8 miles

of British soldiers retreating from the front, Monash is finally able
to locate his rattled Corps Commander at Frévent, General Thomas
Morland, who tells Monash that he is to get his 3rd Division 'to the east
of Doullens and there await further orders'.

If all goes well, the 10th Corps just might be able to 're-establish a line between Arras and Albert'.[14]

And now, arriving with his driver and staff officer in the tiny town of Doullens, just 18 miles north of Amiens and 18 miles north-west of Albert, Monash 'tumbles into a scene of almost indescribable confusion'.[15]

Passing by *La Mairie*, as in Doullens Town Hall, Monash notes the town square chock-a-block with motor cars and brilliantly uniformed French and British officers, clearly hovering by the cars while even more important personages meet inside.

'I had, however, no time for them as I had more important things in hand.'[16]

—

The gravity of the situation escapes no one.

In *La Mairie* of Doullens at this very moment, the Chief of the Imperial General Staff, Sir Henry Wilson, General Haig and Lord Milner – one of the most influential members of the War Cabinet and the sole representative of the British Government in this forum – are receiving reports from their Army commanders in France, and it is bad, very bad. Yes, up north, the First and Second Armies are intact, for they have not been attacked, but further south, the right wing of General Byng's Third Army has caved in, while further south still, General Gough's Fifth Army has had to fall back at almost 20 miles, across a front 25 miles wide, while the Germans continue to advance. Since the beginning of the attack, the Germans have been moving forward an average of *five miles a day*. For British Generals accustomed to measuring their daily advances in yards – 200 yards a day had been a good leap in the Battle of the Somme, and more often than not it was only a few blood-drenched yards if that, if not nothing at all – it is as shocking as it is unprecedented as it is . . . *incomprehensible*. Somehow, they must find a way to stop the Germans.

Now, strange as it might seem, Gough has not only *not* been invited to this meeting, but, as he would later note, 'I was not even informed that it had taken place . . .'[17] And so he can offer no explanation for such a disaster.

But, oh, how capricious are the Gods of War to war's commanders. General Horne and General Plumer's First and Second Armies have not even been tested, so their reputations remain intact. And at least the left flank of Byng's Third Army, firmly holding on to Arras, remains securely attached to them. But Gough, whose forces have been stretched more thinly than any of them – through a policy not of his making, that he has been forced to accommodate – is facing the full might of the German attack, with a left British flank that is receding (the southern half of Byng's Third Army) and a right French flank doing the same. All that notwithstanding, the assumption of most of the men around the table at *La Mairie* is that 'the Byng boys had been let down by Gough's men',[18] a notion that drives a number of subsequent decisions. A large part of their deliberations, too, involve working out just where the remnants of the Fifth Army are situated . . .

Following this meeting of the British Expeditionary Force, another is held to include the French political and military leaders, and the tone is set early. The first two French to arrive are Prime Minister Georges Clémenceau and the lugubrious General Philippe Pétain, the one-time giant of Verdun, now worn down by the war, the deaths, the lack of resources, the mutinies, the *hideous* spectre of an extra million German soldiers arriving on this front, and him incapable of matching or stopping them. Catching sight of Haig, Pétain points the British General out and whispers forlornly to Clémenceau, 'There is a general who will have to surrender in the open field, and I after him.'[19]

The contrast with Foch – who arrives a few minutes later, bouncing around with energy and seeming confidence – could not be greater.

The most regal of the throng remains *le Premier Ministre*, Georges Clémenceau, known as *'Le Tigre'* for the sustained ferocity of his political manoeuvrings, not to mention complete lack of mercy for his enemies. Yes, at 76 years old Clémenceau has lost nigh every hair atop his head, but he more than makes up for it with his bushy eyebrows and absurdly luxuriant white moustache, which seems to have a life of its own whenever he is making thunderous speeches, which is mostly. But he is sharp, speaks good English, courtesy of having lived for four years in New York as a young man, and follows the discussion effortlessly, with no need of the translators whispering into the ears of many of the other French figures.

Foch, too, has no need of translators, having received a notably full Jesuit education, which insisted on 'God's soldiers' having fluency in English, among other things.

The discussion that ensues between them all quickly becomes animated, and never more so than when General Pétain waxes lugubrious and intimates that the battle is all but lost, even going so far as to compare Britain's current position with the complete collapse of the Italians at Caporetto the previous November, when Germany and the Austrians had closed to within 70 miles of Venice before Britain had sent five divisions to save them.

In response, Sir Henry Wilson is apoplectic with rage – his facial scar positively *glowing* in a manner to make him more menacing still – and even Foch is ropable with his countryman. *Malheureusement*, unfortunately, *le* lugubrious Pétain does not back down, asking Haig what *he* would do in the same situation?

'I have no more men fit to go into the line,'[20] Haig replies simply, implying that Pétain does.

Exactly. Right ready to explode now, Wilson – who appreciates perhaps more than most that the entire war hangs in the balance, and if the Germans are not stopped, all is lost – follows up, insisting it won't be lost if we British get *more* help from you French, *more* reinforcements.

'We have sent all the help we can,' Pétain protests, pointing out that he has already sent 24 French divisions into the area, 'and the aim now must be to defend Amiens.'[21]

Amiens?! *Amiens*?!?!

But that is *20* miles back from the current German position! Of course they want to defend that crucial city – if it falls, the Allies will likely lose the war – but not from the *outskirts*! It must be defended by stopping the Germans where they are *now*.

As it turns out, no one is stronger in their condemnation of this approach than Pétain's fellow Frenchman General Foch, who leaps to his feet to insist in his thickly accented English that, 'It *ees* essential not to retreat any further, not to yield an *eench* of ground without fighting. We must hold on at all costs *where we are . . .*'[22]

For Haig, it is confirmation that General Foch – he of the pugnacious chin, who is forever guided by the maxim that 'the will to conquer is the first condition of victory'[23] – '*la victoire c'est la volonte*' – is just what *le docteur* ordered. After all, this is one and the same French officer who so famously during the First Battle of the Marne in September of 1914, as Commander of the Ninth Army, had sent a message to his commander, General Joffre: 'My centre is giving way, my right falling back; *la situation est excellente. J'attaque.*'[24]

That, as it happens, precisely summates the position of Haig's forces at this minute. His right is falling back now all the way to the town of Bouchoir, just 20 miles south-east of Amiens. Haig's château HQ for the battle of the Somme in 1916, at Beauquesne, is today being looted by German infantry. And if bloody General Pétain had had his way, Haig's right would have been ankle-deep in the English Channel as his men scrambled into the boats to take them from France and obliteration.

The worst impact of all will come on whichever troops are placed on the British right wing.

And so Haig seizes the moment.

'If [General] Foch will consent to give me his advice,' he says quietly, 'I will gladly follow it.'[25]

Alors! A British General, agreeing to follow orders from a Frenchman? It is no small offer and, in fact, is far from spontaneous. An elevation of Foch to the role of overall Allied commander is precisely what Foch has been angling for. He has already been in touch with these British leaders, having telephoned Wilson, whom he knew well from before the war, in London two nights earlier. Foch had insisted, *mon ami*, that someone other than Pétain must take charge over all the Allied forces on the Western Front or they are done for. Given that as long ago as six months earlier one of Foch's own military colleagues had noted that Foch 'wants to direct the war and be the *Generalissimo*' and 'wants to replace Pétain',[26] it hadn't taken long to work out who he had in mind. And for the British, it makes sense, as Foch is likely the only one who can restore French aggression to match their pride, and it will be worth it – the one chance they have of saving the day, stopping the Germans and giving themselves time to turn the tide.

And now Haig has made the offer, it must be seized upon.

Gentlemen, *Monsieur le Premier Ministre, Messieurs les Generaux*, a short break.

Lord Milner – still completely appalled by Pétain's contemplation of a retreat and inspired by Foch's attitude – requests a brief private meeting with Prime Minister Clémenceau and a proposal is quickly put. If General Foch is immediately, this very minute, placed in charge of the French forces, the British will agree to having him in charge of *all* the Allied forces on the Western Front, including, of course, their own. He can be the Allied Commander-in-Chief on the Western Front.

Clémenceau, *le Tigre*, agrees and immediately has an agreement drawn up which, on behalf of their governments, both he and Lord Milner sign.

Foch beams; the suddenly humiliated Pétain glowers. Clémenceau sparkles and even reaches over and pats the venerable Sir Henry Wilson on his 54-year-old head and tells him he is '*un bon garçon*,'[27] a good boy.

Wilson's thoughts have gone unrecorded, though the reviews of the British soldiers were mixed, with one of them heard to remark, 'Lets us down sharp, doesn't it? And what a smack in the eye for Haig, and a knock out for Gough and Byng it is. Yet the noospapers are all a-bubble with their old eye-wash!'[28]

There is no Australian in the room, but the view of the AIF's leadership mirrors that of Charles Bean who, when he hears of the change at the top, notes with relief in his diary:

General Foch has at last been made . . . Commander in Chief of the whole British French and American force on the Western front . . . He is responsible for the plan and therefore for the first time one is certain that there is a plan.[29]

Entirely unfussed with the Allies rearranging their Generals like deck-chairs on the *Lusitania*, the Germans keep moving. Apparently, they have now *passed* the old areas of the Somme battlefield!

For the men of the Australian Corps, most particularly the veterans of 1st, 2nd and 4th Divisions, it is like watching a herd of elephants, uniformly grey, tramping all over the grave of your dearest friend.

'In the mind of every man of the old I Anzac,' Charles Bean would record, 'the same question arose: "Will [Fritz] retake Pozières?"'[30]

Reports start dribbling in from the British troops in the tattered front-line north and south of the old Somme town of Albert that they are seeing German troops moving down the slopes of the Ancre valley towards them, which means Pozières must now be in Hun hands. With the Cambrai–Amiens road cutting through the town and forging a straight path to the strategic location of Amiens – straighter than even a crow could fly – there is no doubt the Germans are intent on approaching Albert and capturing the town!

What's more, the exhausted British troops of the 9th Scottish Division had retreated back through the town the night before – it had been a brutal journey under the spotlight of a bright full moon – and are now weakly holding a new line just behind it.

As the confused situation stands, coming up to midday on this fine Tuesday, 26 March, the Scots' line stretches along the railway running north–south through Albert some two miles to the south, to the town of Dernancourt.

Five miles north from Albert, at a poorly defended section of the front just south of Beaumont-Hamel, the 1st New Zealand Rifles have just arrived to go into the line. Among them is Private George McKay, who walks up to the ridge-line, from where he can see 'the country for a thousand yards all around'.

He looks out and, as he would later recall, 'We hardly got settled when over they came. Band out in front and all, just marching . . . They had taken France, in other words, and they were home and dry. So I gave the first blast [of my Lewis gun] at a thousand yards . . . They scattered, broke up their formation and took to the long grass.'[31]

But, still, they are coming. Even if a little more warily this time, now led by men bearing guns, not trombones.

McKay knows it: the Allied line urgently needs to be reinforced or Amiens will very shortly end up as a feather in the hat of a hugely expanded Hunland.

NOON, 26 MARCH 1918, HÉBUTERNE OR BUST

The Diggers of the 48th are renowned as being a tough bunch. They are, for the most part, from the country, and as their Chaplain William Devine would later write, 'They were not a kid glove kind of men.'[32]

No indeed. They are men who are more comfortable on the goldfields of Western Australia than in the urban offices of Sydney or Melbourne. They are log splitters and timber cutters from the backblocks; they are rural storemen, blacksmiths, mining engineers – or 'ginger beers', as the Diggers call them in rhyming slang – and railway workers.

Lieutenant George Mitchell from the South Australian town of Caltowie – the tall, tough and quick-witted natural leader – is in their image. Sure, at first glance he *looks* like a dandy city slicker with his fine features, but his gnarled hands tell the story of one who has done much hard yakka in his rural upbringing and the years since, including in this brutal war.

On this day, those hands are helping themselves to lunch in his latest billet, for his first meal of the day – the men of the 48th, along with their brother battalion in the 12th Brigade, the 47th, had arrived around Basseux in the wee hours of the morning after a gruelling trip from the North, and are just rising – when he suddenly hears a shout.

'Company commanders wanted at the double.'[33]

And they mean, *at the double.*

So much so, that just seven minutes after leaving their billets, the company commander, Captain Lionel Carter, rushes back from the brief company commanders' meeting, shouting, 'Turn out! Turn out!'[34]

The men are quickly on their feet, grabbing rifles, buckling on equipment, tying boots, hoisting up kits, as Captain Carter gives them the dinkum oil: German armoured cars have been spotted, approaching, just three miles away.

'With a sensation of being about to die in the last ditch,' Lieutenant Mitchell would recount, 'we got the men out in an incredibly short space of time. Stood to. Part of our battalion moved to their trench positions.'[35] They must make ready to meet the attack.

The 47th Battalion march out first, up the road towards Hébuterne. Their commander, Colonel Alexander Imlay, takes the precaution of commandeering the first empty lorry he can find and puts it in the charge of a couple of his men. His instructions are clear: head a couple of miles down the road and, in the narrowest, most impassable spot you can find, disable it so it completely blocks the road.

Slow the bastards down; give us more time to get into position!

'We waited, lined up,' Mitchell would record of his own 48th Battalion, who line up along the roads in support. 'The strained feeling vanished, and we all licked our lips in anticipation.'[36]

It shouldn't be long now, with word coming through that the Germans had made their breakthrough east of Hébuterne, on the closest edge of the old Somme battlefield.

—

Feeling rather left behind on this day, back on Messines Ridge, are the men of the 1st Division, including Archie Barwick, who writes in his diary:

Bad news continues to trickle through. The latest is that the Germans are within 2 miles of Albert. Just think of that after all the blood and agony spent in winning that

*hellish piece of country [in the Somme battles of 1916] &
now it has all gone for nothing & the Hun is still going
strong. The 3rd, 4th and 5th have gone down there, and
2nd is following . . . We are in the line and they say we
are stopping here for a time. I would much rather go down
there and sink or swim with the rest of the lads. I'm certain
that once the old Colonials get into the line again, they'll
check his run.*[37]

All that Archie and his mates want to know is, when will the mighty
men of the 1st Division get to show what they can do?

While it is agreed that, indeed, 'Amiens has to be saved at all costs
and the fate of the war depends on it,'[38] the men intend to fight with
everything they have so the Germans don't even get close to Amiens in
the first place.

LATE LUNCHTIME AT DOULLENS, 26 MARCH 1916, JE T'ADORE, AND SHUT THE DOOR

And the French, being the French, decide that no great moment in
history can be complete without . . . a three-course lunch at a place legendary for its local cuisine, the Hotel des Quatre Fils Aymon, across the
rue from *La Mairie*. (Only Haig declines. He is not fussed on French
food and prefers to dine out of the luncheon box his own English chef
had prepared earlier in the day, and he has brought with him in his
staff car.)

Tant pis, too bad for him.

'Well,' Prime Minister Clémenceau says to his longtime favourite
military man, Foch, over the roast *canard*, turning to him, 'you've got
the job you so much wanted.'[39]

This is, *plus ou moins*, true.

On the other hand, Foch is tempted – he will later recount – to
reply: '*Monsieur le Premier Ministre*, assuming the direction of a battle
which during six successive days has been largely lost, can hardly be

the object of any great desire on my part, but rather constitutes, by reason of its risks, an act of duty and sacrifice in the service of my country.'[40]

But he decides not to.

Whatever else, the new Supreme Commander for the entire Western Front has a clear understanding of the situation.

'The situation can be likened to a double door,' Foch had already written to the French Minister of Munitions on this day. 'Each of the generals [Haig and Pétain] is behind his half of the door without knowing who should push first so as to close the door. I quite understand their hesitation: the one who pushes first [risks] having his right or left wing turned.'[41]

And just which unit to throw into the gap as the Germans crash on that double door is yet to be determined. Some troops are going to have to be sent forward immediately, to stop the Germans breaking through and give Foch the time he needs to coordinate the simultaneous shutting and *locking* of that double door.

Still, as the meeting concludes, the distinct tones of a familiar song, at least to the British, can be heard, coming from outside . . .[42]

It's a long way to Tipperary,
It's a long way to go.
It's a long way to Tipperary
To the sweetest girl I know!
Goodbye Piccadilly,
Farewell Leicester Square!
It's a long, long way to Tipperary,
But my heart's right there.[43]

It is the Australian soldiers of the 3rd Division who have been marching, bussing, marching, waiting, train-ing, marching, waiting, and on the train once more – with just a little resting thrown in, where they can find it – for well over three days straight, just to get here. The first lot are just pulling into the station.

Preparing to alight from one of the carriages is Colonel Henry Goddard, an English-born man who migrated to Brisbane at the age of 21 and had so risen through the ranks of the armed forces that he had not only been in command of Brisbane defences at the outbreak of the war, but later, after joining the AIF as an officer in 1915, had performed particularly well in command of Quinn's Post at Gallipoli. In fact, so highly regarded is the 49-year-old Goddard that, still in the absence of Brigadier Rosenthal, it is he who has been bumped up from his usual role as commander of the 35th Battalion to now be in temporary command of the 9th Brigade.

As the train starts to slow and his men line up behind him with their kits on their shoulders, Goddard looks over at Doullens Town Hall, just over yonder, and notices 'General Haig's car and a car bearing the French Commander-in-Chief's colours'.[44]

Must be 'a conference of the GOC's in chief', he thinks to himself.

A British Major walks up and demands of Goddard, still standing in the open doorway, 'Are you 9th Brigade?'

'I am,' Colonel Goddard replies, matching the Major's curmudgeonly tone with ease.

'What troops have you got?' the harried British Major demands once more.

'Brigade Headquarters, 100 fatigue men, a machine-gun company and a light trench mortar battery,'[45] Goddard replies, omitting that the rest of his 9th Brigade are due to come in on trains behind him.

The British Major nods and says, 'Our line is broken. The Germans are coming on . . . and their cavalry are now approaching. You are to proceed with what troops you have and hold them.'[46]

Goddard is shocked.

'It was an extraordinary order,' he would later recall, 'considering the total troops in my hand were not more than 200, to be asked to face an enemy that had the Fifth Army on the run.'[47]

And a dangerous enemy it clearly is, as evidenced by the severely wounded men now pouring into the station in the hundreds, many of them on their last legs and some of them missing a leg. Overworked stretcher-bearers have commissioned Hun prisoners to help, carrying the worst cases from the ambulances to the hospital train, trailing blood all the way.

There is some negotiation concerning under whose authority such an extraordinary order comes – finally it is established that it is from General Byng – and when Goddard is satisfied he orders the advance guard of the 9th Brigade to move out along the road.

Goodbye Piccadilly,
Farewell Leicester Square!

And *au revoir* Doullens . . .

But, yes, what the soldiers see first-up is nothing if not confronting – coming the other way down the road that leads to the Germans are streams of French civilians mixed with British soldiers, travelling rearwards from the village of Pas-en-Artois some two miles away.[48]

Most of the British soldiers are panicked and have abandoned their equipment and weapons to allow them to move more quickly away from the danger.

'You're going the wrong way, Diggers,' a group of English gunners heading west call sarcastically to the Australians marching east, 'Jerry'll souvenir you and your bloody band too.'[49]

—

And still the trains keep coming. During the afternoon, the 9th Brigade's 33rd Battalion arrives into the station to find Doullens 'in a very battered state . . . The roads were badly congested with traffic both military and civilian.'[50]

Private John Hardie stares out the train window, wide-eyed, wondering at the cause of so much bustle and confusion this far behind the front-lines. 'We weren't long in ignorance of the cause of the confusion,' he jots in his diary shortly after, 'for we soon had the last man detrained when we were ordered to load our rifles and prepare for action . . . Word had just come in that the German cavalry were just over a mile[51] out along the road towards Arras.'[52]

And so they start marching east, steeling themselves to meet the enemy, though first they meet an unending stream coming back along the Arras Road, as John Hardie would record: 'flying refugees, runaway Tommies, broken up artillery and disabled motor vehicles which were being towed by motor lorries'.

Hardie looks closely at their faces. Without exception, 'all of the people had that hunted peoples look on their faces. Old and young, rich and poor were all on the same footing and were carrying bundles most likely containing their most cherished belongings. It was a most pitiful sight and I don't think I will forget it till my dying day.'[53]

All of the Diggers feel badly seeing the French fleeing their villages like this, but perhaps Hardie feels it more than most. Clearly, the villagers love their villages the way he loves Grong Grong – and the way Grong Grong loves him. Before he left his Riverina town, the good citizens of that burgh had given him a fob watch, a decorative copper disc with a wreath around the outside of the face and the portrait of a Digger standing in the middle. Not many Diggers have a fob watch, but *he* does, and is proud of it. He constantly toys with the fob as he marches along. The other Diggers are following the latest fashion, the wristwatch – but theirs is not from the good people of Grong Grong.

———

Back at Doullens railway station, Colonel Henry Goddard is still putting every successive batch of men to arrive in order to be sent east when a welcome sight approaches. It is General John Monash himself, his Divisional Commander, shortly afterwards followed by the good Brigadier, Charles Rosenthal, who is making a quick visit to the line to see how bad things truly are. The old band is back together. Goddard happily hands command of the 9th Brigade back to Rosie and gives them a quick summation of their journey.

Even while in the act of *hail fellow, well-met*, yet another excited

British officer rushes up to report that, 'A number of German armoured motor cars have broken through at Hébuterne, and the German cavalry are within ten miles of the town!'[54]

It is perhaps true, perhaps not. If so, it is grim. But Monash has heard too much nonsense on this day already to be sure of anything. He can at least trust Brigadier Rosenthal, however, who has seen with his own eyes a 'disgraceful withdrawal'[55] of British forces at nearby Mondicourt, to the east, and knows that it is more than possible. Clearly, the most important thing now is to ensure that he can get his full division on the march and in position as quickly as possible.

'Collect all the troops you can,' Monash orders Rosie, 'and temporarily take up a position to cover Doullens, so that my detrainment from all the numerous trains to come can be carried out without interference.'[56]

That process is already begun, and the 9th Brigade continue to flood to the east from Doullens train station to the cheers of the local population, who know from just one look at the distinctive turned-up slouch hats that these men are Australians – and they will *fight*.

Now arriving at the station are the Diggers of the 3rd Division's 11th Brigade.

It's a long way to Tipperary,
It's a long way to go.
It's a long way to Tipperary,
To the sweetest girl I know!

They include the 42nd Battalion from Queensland, known as the 'Australian Black Watch' – after the famed Scottish 42nd Regiment, the Black Watch. And it is for this reason that the band they are marching to includes bagpipes, which, though beloved by the Scots, are more often thought by the French to sound like old cats fighting.

Still, on this occasion, over and above their singing and the bagpipes can be heard what one 42nd Battalion soldier, Private Vivian Brahms, describes as 'the wild cheers of congested throngs of French refugees'.[57]

General Monash, meanwhile, motors on to Mondicourt, some six miles to the east, hoping to catch up to the commander of the 10th Division, whose unit his men have been placed under.

———

At a rest stop an hour later, the men of Brigadier Rosenthal's 9th Brigade, now a few miles east of Doullens, see a group of retreating British soldiers crowd around a weird mob of Australian soldiers having a smoko, to cadge some ciggies of their own. In return, one of the British soldiers gives the Aussies fair warning: 'It's impossible to stop the German push as they are coming in *swarms*.'[58]

One of the Australians, his gasper hanging off the corner of his mouth in typical gravity-defying manner, is thrilled to hear it, turning to his mate and exulting, ''Struth, Bill, we'll get some souvenirs now.'[59]

And so now, onwards.

However far Tipperary, their destination for that night is confirmed now to be east of Thièvres, and they head off towards it, their faces to the foe that awaits.

'In the garden beside me two small girls in clean pinafores played shuttlecock in the bright March sunshine,' one soldier would recall, 'while just over the paling on the road stood a deserted handcart, with a very old woman strapped upon it, dead and abandoned.'[60]

Push on!

———

Push back. The Commanding Officer of Britain's 8th Division, General William Heneker, feels he has no choice. It has been an exhausting five days. His division, in reserve behind Ypres when the hostilities had broken out down south, had been put under Fifth Army command on the night of the 21st, and then ordered into the line on the Somme, directly east of Amiens and west of St Quentin.

Since 24 March, his men have been conducting that most difficult of all military operations – a fighting withdrawal while still in contact with the enemy. Perhaps if their young reinforcements on their way from England had arrived in time they might have been able to make more of a stand of it, but the new men are still at least 48 hours away. They are half-trained 18-years-olds, Heneker knows, but better than nothing – just a tiny percentage of the 190,000 British soldiers who've been rushed across the English Channel to France since the German attack began, of whom 50,000 are *just* 18, and all of whom should already have been here if Lloyd George had not been playing games! In the meantime, Heneker and his men have been trying to cover a front of over nine miles, coming up against some ten German divisions! They had watched from the west bank of the Somme as German soldiers crossed over and penetrated their line. By the 25th, they had moved back to Pargny, on the banks of the adjacent Somme Canal, only to witness the same again. Germans everywhere!

For four solid days now the 8th Division have been in retreat. And despite promises of French reinforcements on their right flank, none have arrived. It is no wonder some of the men have been so spooked they've deserted and are all the way back to Amiens. But, despite the apparent tragedy of the situation and the highbrow views of the high brass who had deliberated in safety at Doullens, casually castigating the failures of the Fifth Army and labelling them stragglers, there are countless men who are doing their darnedest to not retreat at all. They stay resolute, holding desperate positions despite terrible odds. Even the personnel of several brigade HQs are being thrown into the gaps, finding what pluck they can in a most ominous situation.

Major William Duncan at 8th Division headquarters, reading report after report, would later write, 'I would like to draw a veil over this depressing period. Our infantry had been worn out; more than 90 per cent of them were conscripts, and whereas in 1914 no battalion ever left a trench until it was blown out of it by shell-fire, now it only needed a few salvoes to start an infectious trickle to the rear . . .'[61]

Despite being forced back time and time again, troops are found and rallied, harried and parried into the many, many gaps. Though

desperately tired, hungry and exhausted, they who stay carry out holding actions – even counter-attacks. Often they are supported by only
one or two field guns firing over open sights, with direct vision of the
target, almost a return to the tactics of the African bush campaigns of
the Empire or those used in the Napoleonic Wars.

Somehow, strength is found to carry on, often thanks to individual
men or small groups. As one officer would later recount, 'What had
really stopped the rot was the personal courage of the officers and men
in the remnants of the units and the battle groups. Miraculously, faith
in discipline at all costs, the Army's tradition since the days of Cromwell
and pride of race had survived: without sleep, without hot food, frozen
stiff by night, they fought on until they dropped.'[62]

And so it is that General Heneker, once again establishing a new HQ,
this time at Vermandovillers, is 18 miles due east of Villers-Bretonneux.
For there is no way around it – the Germans have pushed 25 miles past
St Quentin and, since the start of the battle, the 8th Division has lost
200 officers and 4000 other ranks. What it most needs is sufficient
time to rebuild with the 5000 18- and 19-year-old soldiers on their way
to join it. But as with so many instances during the division's time on
the Western Front, time is one commodity that is in very short supply.

———

What is in plentiful supply for all soldiers on the Western Front, by
the by, is lice – known to the Diggers as 'chats' – and the process of
removing them, 'chatting', albeit with etymological roots from many
centuries earlier. A frequent activity for all is to sit around talking as
they painstakingly remove the biting little bastards from where they
most like to congregate – in the seams of their clothes. By running your
finger and thumb along both sides, you can squeeze them out and crush
the life from the brutes.

———

Back at the late lunch, the joy at the decision aside, the ongoing gravity of the situation is underlined by an unconfirmed report that, as Sir Henry Wilson would describe it, '*Boche* tanks and cavalry are through Pas-en-Artois, and we had better clear out!'[63]

No matter that the report proves to be false.

With discretion the better part of valour, and so many more things to accomplish in such little time for all of them, the French dignitaries head back to Paris while the likes of Sir Henry Wilson and Lord Milner must begin their journey back to London, pausing only at Haig's HQ at Montreuil.

As Charles Bean would note, 'Douglas Haig is 10 years younger tonight than he was yesterday afternoon.'[64]

It is not just the usurping of Pétain that pleases the General, vaulting Foch over and above him. Sir Henry Wilson has also proposed removing Gough and his senior staff from command of the retreating Fifth Army and replacing them with General Henry Rawlinson, together with his old Fourth Army staff.

Haig has vigorously agreed. Just as they need the French to fight, they need the Fifth Army to stop retreating and push back, and Rawlinson could be just the man for the job.

Exeunt Sir Henry Wilson and Lord Milner, knowing that a British destroyer is waiting for them at Boulogne, ready to take them across the Channel.

—

As for the new *Generalissimo*, first things first, he heads straight to see General Hubert Gough in his new HQ at Dury in a small château he had moved to from Villers-Bretonneux the previous day. All Gough knows of the impending storm is a brief telephone message to the effect that 'Marshal Foch had been appointed *Generalissimo*' and he is coming to meet Gough, so 'stay in to meet him'.[65]

Unaware of the full and frank views exchanged about his performance up at Doullens that day – broadly, that 'the Gough boys have let down the Byng boys (who would not have lost a yard but for Gough and his men)[66] – nor *even* that the conference had taken place, Gough follows orders and continues to work as he waits, confident in his belief that 'the Army had faithfully carried out the terrible and heavy task that Haig had set it'.[67]

Foch walks in, ramrod straight, all a-quiver with righteous rage and just *busting* to say something, which does not take long . . .

'Why are you at your headquarters and not with your troops?' he begins in fast French. 'Why don't you fight as we fought at the first battle of Ypres? Why is your army retiring? What are your orders to your army?'[68]

These prove to be merely his opening remarks. The furious Frenchman goes on, spouting out questions for which there are no answers, raising his voice higher and higher.

Gough is profoundly shocked, and the stiffness of his upper lip is tested.

'He waited for no replies to any of these questions' the English General would later recall. 'This was just as well, for any explanation would have probably led to an altercation.'[69]

Nearly spent, and asking nothing of the state of the Fifth Army from Gough's own perspective or the current disposition of his forces, Foch shouts, 'There must be no more retreat, the line must now be held at all costs!'[70]

And with that, the Frenchman – a bristling man-o'-war with every sail straining under the storm of his own words – tacks into the falling twilight.

As for Foch's incredible orders, which Gough feels are impossible to be carried out, he nevertheless sends forth word that the men are not to retreat, 'in accordance with military discipline'.[71]

———

In a long line above the green fields that lie just to the east of Souastre, clods of dark earth are flying skywards in the late-afternoon sunshine.

Just as they have been ordered, the men of the 4th Division's 4th Brigade are now digging in. As they continue their furious shovelling – and pass the pick, can you? – Brigadier Digger Brand receives new orders from General Byng of the Third Army: they must separate from their own division and 'occupy Hébuterne which is reported to be held by the enemy'.[72] The town is just four miles south-east of the 4th Brigade's current positions and seven miles north of the strategically vital town of Albert. Either the Germans have already taken it, or at least the British have already abandoned it – no one is sure.

Either way, a dangerous gap in the line has appeared, and the Australians must plug it by positioning themselves on the ridge that lies just beyond Hébuterne and then defending that ridge at all costs.

Oh, and one more thing: it is *urgent*. Just on 200 lorries have been sent for them, and in short order all 4000 of the 4th Brigade have piled on with their kit and are rumbling along the roads to the south-east. The extraordinary French countryside floats past, as if in a dream.

One British Artillery Brigadier, who watches the Australians pass by with enthusiasm, cautions Lieutenant Colonel John Lavarack, a staff officer of the 4th Division: 'You Australians think you can do anything, but you haven't a chance of holding them.'[73]

Ah, but we are sure we can, we new recruits and veterans alike . . .

There is naked excitement among most of the 4th Brigade, particularly many of the new recruits who've just arrived, and they want nothing more now than to have a go and get stuck into Fritz! Most of the veterans, however, like Colonel[74] Harry Murray – 37 years old, born in Tasmania but latterly a proud Western Australian – are too old, and have seen too much and done too much to feel anything like that. For he has been around, all right.

When he first enlisted in 1914, having worked at Manjimup, Western Australia, employing sleeper cutters, he had described himself as a 'bushman'. Before that he'd been an armed escort for a mining company north of Kalgoorlie. Though he had started the war as a humble private, it was obvious to all that he was not only a soldier but a leader of men, and now he's not only a Colonel but also one of the most highly decorated infantry soldiers of the British Empire. Victoria Cross? Yup. Distinguished Service Order? Two of those. Now Colonel Murray has much on his mind as the trucks rumble their way to the south, but the primary emotion he feels is less excitement at the bugle's call than a world-weary sense of duty that they may as well get on with it.

As to the other brigades of the 4th Division, they are also ordered to move in this mid-afternoon, with the 12th Brigade ordered by their Commanding Officer, Brigadier John Gellibrand, to march east to a small village some two miles north of Hébuterne.

The men form up and lead out, and are just 500 yards up the road when a cyclist comes puffing up from behind, telling them the order has been reversed – they are to return from whence they came and await further instruction.

And so the men, bemused and a little frustrated to say the least, turn on their heels and head back to town.

———

At Versailles, General Henry Rawlinson puts the phone down, a little overwhelmed in spite of himself. Gough is to be sent home, and it is Rawlinson himself who is to 'reconstruct the remnants of Fifth Army as the Fourth Army', under his command. He is under no illusion about the challenge ahead, with 80,000 British soldiers having been killed, wounded, captured and, yes, deserted, in the last *week* – with nowhere near enough men on call to replace them. He records his thoughts in his diary: 'It is quite evident that the *Boche* means to get Amiens, and if he does he will cut the British Army from the ports of Rouen and Le Havre, as well as separating us from the French Army. We can manage with Boulogne and Calais at a pinch, but it will not be easy . . . It will then be open to the Germans to turn either on us, or on the French. Personally I think he will turn on us and endeavour to drive us into the sea. I think he will then turn on the French, with Paris as his objective. Anyhow, we shall have some ding-dong fighting but, with our backs to the wall we shall, I know, give a good account of ourselves.'[75]

—

It has been a long day for General John Monash, and a particularly long afternoon as he races from spot to spot trying to gather his 3rd Division to him, not to mention trying to get some solid orders so he can direct the men to the right positions.

Making it all the worse is that the roads are 'simply packed with wild-eyed Tommies, refugees on foot and in every conceivable conveyance, with their furniture and wheel-barrows, hand-carts, farm-wagons, and the like . . .

Everybody that was interrogated appeared to have the idea that the *Bosch* was just behind him on his very heels.'[76]

Monash is sympathetic, watching the French civilians flee westward, but, like Brigadier Rosenthal, he is so appalled by the retreating British that he assigns Military Police to establish 'straggler-posts', whereby those stragglers can be gathered together and formed up into makeshift but coherent units capable of making a stand. In the meantime, as the sun begins to wane, he and his staff officers requisition a château at Couturelle on the north side of the Doullens–Arras road, which he intends to make his HQ, and establishes, as best he can, communications with his chain of command, both upwards and downwards.

While making contact with his own command is easy, finding Sir Walter Congreve, the Commander of VII Corps – to whom 3rd Division has just been assigned – and who has just called for him to report in, is the task that Monash must now tackle. Congreve's HQ has been falling back before the German storm, so it may not be easy.

—

And that must be Hébuterne up ahead.

Colonel Harry Murray and his men are soon jumping off the trucks just two miles from the village of Souastre, which is in turn just three-and-a-half miles from Hébuterne. Best to get out here and proceed carefully on foot – in defensive formation, with scouts at the front and on the flanks – rather than open themselves to the possibility of an ambush when they are tightly grouped in the trucks.

Forming themselves up into company columns, the Australians of the 4th Brigade are soon marching down the cobbled road in the bright afternoon sunlight, not at all sure what they are about to face, only that it is likely formidable.

As Private Walter Kennedy of the 4th Brigade's 15th Battalion later recalled, 'When we reached Hébuterne on the Somme, a terrible sight met our gaze, the British Army was in full retreat, indeed everything looked desperate, they [threw] us Aussies into this huge gap . . .'[77]

Panic is in the air, with several of the British officers shouting as they pass, 'The Germans are in Souastre with armoured cars!'[78]

Beyond the panic, the faces of those exhausted British soldiers tell much of the story. They have done their dash, fought the good fight, but now . . . they can no more. These men have been retreating for six days, have seen their comrades uselessly slaughtered, and know that nothing can stop the Germans. What they most want now is sleep, and safety. Those few common soldiers who have the energy to speak to the Australians going forward have just one theme: 'Jerry is close behind us. And he has tanks!'[79]

(There is certainly a consistent theme developing.)

Perhaps most rattled of all are the British officers, with the Australians noting one motor car speeding down the road carrying – count 'em, Blue! – *nine* staff officers, the driver leaning on his horn in the vain hope of clearing those straggling masses that lie between them and safety.

Of course, this means those British officers fleeing for their lives have to run the gauntlet of Diggers coming the other way, many of whom are happy to share their views that the British officers would be – in broad summation of the sentiment – probably inclined to sit down when they piss. The Diggers are far more forgiving of the weeping French civilians, whole families shocked at how quickly the German storm has hit them, the powerlessness of the British to stop them, the fact that they have just had to walk out on their whole lives with so little notice.

'One old man carried his wife on his back,' Charles Bean would relate, 'other villagers carted their aged sick in wheelbarrows. As everywhere, they welcomed the swinging Australians.'[80]

As they push towards Hébuterne, Captain Thomas White of the 13th Battalion sees the old folk among the French take one look at the Australians, unload their carts and begin to place the contents back in their houses.

An old man explains their actions to one of the Diggers: *'Pas necessaire maintenant, vous les tiendrez.'*[81]

Inevitably, such words are put first into English by those few Diggers who speak Frog, and then into rough Australian, which boils down to: 'Now that you Aussies are here, we don't need to go. You'll hold these bastards.'

———

But what of these tanks said to be heading this way?

Colonel 'Mad' Harry Murray takes the lead, not for the first or last time. Commandeering a stray platoon, he orders them to accompany him forward so they can go out for a spot of tank-hunting.

In short order, the other Australian soldiers see the platoon haring along after Colonel Murray, at least the best they can, their kit and rifles jiggling as they jog along. The only solid information Murray can get comes from a hurrying British staff officer, who tells him in passing – fast, down the road – that 'the Germans are coming on in numbers',[82] and . . .

And everyone down! Get into the ditches either side of the road!

Up ahead in the distance, at the end of a long stretch of straight road, Colonel Murray can see, just behind a red car, some kind of extraordinary contraption flanked by eight men in grey.

'If these are the tanks,' Murray thinks to himself, 'then Providence has delivered them into our hands!'[83]

The 13th Battalion's commander, Colonel Douglas Marks – the youngest Battalion commander in the whole Australian Corps at just

23 years old – is close by and can see them too. He tells the men near him, 'I think we can fix their drivers if they remain on top like that.'[84]

The *phut-phut-phut* of the armoured cars' engines grow louder.

Barking instructions to his men, Murray sets up an ambush whereby, on his signal, the Australians will first shoot down the soldiers flanking the tank, before having a go at the tank itself.

(The Australian veterans hate tanks, just on principle, and are not afraid of them. Who can forget how the tanks let them down in 1st Bullecourt, back on 11 April 1917, when the men had been relying on them to blunt the enemy defences, only for the *bloody* tanks to break down, get lost and delayed on the way – resulting in so many of their mates being slaughtered?)

They steel themselves as the quiet, bucolic scene – butterflies flutter by all around and birds gaily sing in the spring sunshine – is suddenly invaded by the roar of clanking machinery and the sight of the grim-faced Germans protecting their brutal behemoth on tracks, until . . .

Until Murray suddenly realises.

'Don't fire!'[85] he shouts.

There has been a mistake.

Instead of a red car, it is a tractor.

Instead of a tank, it is a number of disc ploughs.

Instead of fierce German soldiers, the men are sad-looking members of the French Agricultural Corps, retreating from the land they had been tilling around Bapaume.

Instead of being shot to pieces, as had been planned, they are allowed to proceed between the lines of Australian soldiers on each side of the road, 'all smiles and "*bonjours*" at knowing they now had their motors safe',[86] never knowing just how close they came to lying dead in a ditch.

Colonel Murray and his men continue their push towards the tiny village of Souastre – which proves to have just 100 homes at best – and find two fresh battalions of British troops already there, for, despite the general British retreat, still General Haig has managed to send some reserves forward. One of the battalions, a Yorkshire regiment, is even dug in, while the other regiment has, a tad bizarrely, positioned itself in an open field on the German side of Souastre, protected only by *piles of grass*. (It's a sure sign of incompetence, the Australians know. If the Brits had time to gather grass, they should have spent the time digging in.)

For their part, the Diggers dig in like mad things and start to carve out their trenches on the south-east corner of the village, from which point they look down the gently sloping ridge to the shattered village of Foncquevillers, recently pulverised by the Germans' artillery.

'And, as far again beyond, high on the edge of the brown moorland of the old Somme battlefield,' Charles Bean would recount, 'a cluster of battered trunks marked the village of Hébuterne.'[87]

Of course, patrols are carefully sent forward to try to determine just where the Germans are, and in what numbers, when word comes that not only is Hébuterne in the hands of the Germans, but Brand has been ordered to have the 4th Brigade recapture it!

While they make ready – assembling by an old windmill, as directed, and checking their weaponry and ammunition – Brigadier Brand personally heads forward after the patrols to, as the official 4th Brigade war diary would have it, 'bring clarity to all the obscurity so that he can give his men clear orders and a fighting chance.'[88] Or, in the Old Brig's own vernacular, he's going to 'get the dinkum oil . . .'[89]

His men watch him ride off calmly on his magnificent chestnut steed, with a small group accompanying him, and 90 minutes later . . . yes, that's *him* . . . see his grizzled form galloping back, calling for the commanders of each battalion to come forward so he can address them.

'I rode right through Hébuterne, men', he says triumphantly, 'and there is not a fucking Fritz in it.'[90]

There is no need to dig in where they are. They can move forward, secure Hébuterne and make their stand in a line just beyond it, with the 62nd British Division holding their left flank and the remains of the British 19th Division, some 500 strong, off to their right. Or so the patrols have informed him.

Still, before moving, what about some grub, given that the men have not eaten since the morning? The Old Brig insists. 'Give the men a good hot meal, replenish their ammunition, and be in the allotted sectors by 7 pm. We have no artillery behind us.'[91]

A curious move, perhaps, to delay the *crucial* move while the cooks bring up their grub carts, but there it is.

(Captain Charles Bean himself would be delicately critical. 'It was then 5.40, and, considering the tension of the moment and the vast issues at stake, he was indeed a cool commander – the future student may think too cool – who, with other commanders possibly in desperate straits on either flank of the gap, left this vital point open to the enemy while the cookers, then back with the transport, marched up with their chimneys steaming and gave his troops their evening meal.'[92])

Still, with tucker now in their tummies, it is the scouts who head off first, followed at a safe distance by the brigade . . . which is as well. For the Brigadier is proved wrong when – look out! – the scouts discover that Fritz is indeed in the village, just not in force. Mercifully, they are quickly picked off, meaning that the brigade itself is able to sweep through the village in what amounts to 'a weird advance through the dark streets, yards, houses and cellars of the deserted village . . . at the point of the bayonet'.[93]

Alas, though most of the German fire upon them is no more than unaimed Parthian shots, one of them causes the first Australian battle casualty of the German Spring Offensive when Lieutenant Morven Nolan is felled with a mortal wound.

'In spite of his painful and dying condition,' the 13th Battalion history would record, Lieutenant Nolan was notable for 'remaining cheerful and giving some valuable information before "going west".'[94]

Nevertheless, now in full darkness, the brigade is digging in across a 2000-yard front on the eastern side of the village.

'Hébuterne was secured,' Charles Bean would proudly report, 'by troops who were not likely to give way if it was humanly possible to hold on.'[95]

The difference between General Ludendorff when he is angry and a happy bird chirruping its contentment as the sun goes down? Considerable.

'The 17th Army *leistet nichts*, does not perform!' he roars down the phone to Prince Rupprecht. 'It *kommt nicht vorwärts*, doesn't advance! It hasn't even reached Boyelles and Puisieux!'[96]

Whereas all else is going very well and his forces continue to advance across most of the front, the fact that they continue to struggle to make headway on Arras is deeply disturbing. It confirms his view that the best way forward is to double their efforts to go after Amiens – at least that advance *is* working.

Ludendorff is aware, too, that the British 'seem to be anxious to cram, with troops vacated from elsewhere, the gaps in the middle of the attacked front'.[97]

Ludendorff, however, is of the view that those troops have been put there 'too late, hopefully'.[98] For once, Rupprecht agrees. The most interesting thing is that 'the *Mischung*, mix within the English Divisions, has reached a worrying level already, and there seems to be *eine ziemliche Unordnung*, quite a mess on the enemy side'.[99]

—

The rest of the 4th Division, the 12th and 13th Brigades, meanwhile, are still waiting at their billets around Basseux, exhausted, to be told where to go. Finally, on this night, they receive word that they must leave their 4th Brigade at Hébuterne and march due south some 20 miles to Senlis where . . . a situation has arisen.

It seems the British soldiers of VII Corps have abandoned the Albert–Bray line to the advancing Germans, leaving the approach to Amiens wide open! It is into this vital gap to the south of Albert that the 12th and 13th Brigades must now move at all haste.

And so it is that on this early evening, Colonel Bull Leane of the 48th Battalion calls his officers to him and tells them straight up: 'Gentlemen, there is no front line between us and the enemy. His position is not known. We start at midnight on a twenty-mile march toward Albert. We do not even know that the road is clear or whether we can beat him to Albert. We must protect our own flanks and be prepared for anything.'[100]

CHAPTER SEVEN

'FINI RETREAT – BEAUCOUP AUSTRALIENS ICI'

As an Australian he [Monash] realised that he must
appeal to [his soldier's] intelligence, their imagination,
their adaptability, their high sense of comradeship,
their capacity for independent judgement and their
aggressive instincts. He would feed them on victory.
He would teach them to believe, because of success,
that they were invincible. He would make every man
feel that what he was and what he did was vital.
Major-General Hubert Essame.[1] *Essame, a Brit with the 8th*
Division, fought with the Australians several times in 1918

Thank Heavens – the Australians at last.[2]
General Congreve (CO VII Corps) to John Monash

MIDNIGHT, 26 MARCH 1918, MONDICOURT, ALL RIGHT FOR SOME

It has been a long haul, but after a long march from Doullens, the men
of the 9th and 11th Brigades join the 10th and are billeted around
Mondicourt, meaning General Monash's 3rd Division is now complete. The 11th Brigade, which had come in to Doullens later than
scheduled, are finally allowed to stop, nearing midnight. They are at the

small village of Thièvres, five miles east of Doullens, and the third-best Australian restorative of all – after bed and beer – awaits.

'We were unable to occupy our billets that had been allotted to us,' Private Vivian Brahms would recount, 'for the simple reason that the territory was apparently in the hands of the enemy.'[3]

So, no bed.

All that remains is a drink of hot tea for everyone, and they more or less drop where they stand, to get whatever kip they can, using their packs – and even each other's stomachs – for pillows.

As the soldiers settle in for the night, word comes through that, come tomorrow, the 3rd Division will again move further south and take up positions around Heilly, south-west of Albert, near the Amiens road.

For now, let us rest, as we move off again by bus at 4 am.

———

Twelve bells. It is time.

Lieutenant George Mitchell, with the 4th Division's 12th Brigade, stirs from his position on a rough bed of straw that he has laid out for himself beneath the kitchen table at his billet. Around and about there is the 'bustle of impending departure', which includes Madame rushing to the Captain and asking, in a fearful voice, *'C'est retraite encore?'*

'Non, Madame,' says the Captain rather grandly, proud of his French-speaking abilities, his men and their country. *'Les soldats d'Australie ne font jamais retraite.'* Australian soldiers don't do retreats.

Madame, alas, is not yet convinced, and becomes hysterical.

'C'est retraite encore, c'est retraite, c'est retraite . . .' she wails. 'We have lived here for thirty-six years, and through all the bombardments. Now you go, we must go.'

Mitch listens, all while gathering his pack and rifle, glad that the Captain has the job of pacifying Madame, and not him – while also glad that his own family, 12,000 miles away, safe in Australia, does not have to face such agony. Crying all the while, the young Frenchwoman gathers her little daughter and her surprisingly aged husband to her and dashes from cupboard to cupboard, picking from them, 'the most precious possessions of their lifetime'.[4]

As Mitch and his mates line up outside on this dark night, Madame and her family are finished; their wheelbarrow is fully loaded. Right at the top is a large crucifix, seemingly averring that, despite it all, they still have faith in a benevolent Saviour watching over them. Sobbing, they move off into the night, only calling back their hope that the good Lord will look after the Australians, too. It is a pitiful sight and one voice rings out from the ranks, expressing all of their thoughts: 'Damned awful – that!'[5]

But to the business at hand.

Orders have just been confirmed that they are to march down to Albert . . . which is now in the possession of the Hun!

Very well, then.

By the riiiiiiiiight . . . quick . . . *march!*

Mitchell's 48th Battalion is underway by just after midnight, bringing up the rear of the 12th Brigade's column, right behind the 47th Battalion, which had left an hour earlier.

Not for nothing would the 48th Battalion diary record of the last 24 hours, *This was certainly a day of rumours which proved false and of orders which were soon cancelled and it was not pleasant for weary men to be messed about in this way.*[6]

———

As soon as Sir Henry Wilson and Lord Milner arrive back at Victoria Station, after taking an express train from Dover, they are joined by none other than the Minister for Munitions, Winston Churchill – bursting forth along the platform, scattering people and porters like chickens before a fox, as he is ever wont to do – and all hustle straight to 10 Downing Street. Arriving, they are greeted by Prime Minister Lloyd George, together with the members of his five-man War Cabinet he trusts most, Andrew Bonar Law and Cabinet Secretary Maurice

Hankey. It is now for Wilson and Milner to give a full report on the results of their meeting with the French, and the situation with Foch now taking supreme command over and above Pétain, which will hopefully give the French the ginger they need to make a fight of it.

'The chances,' Lord Wilson sums up for Lloyd George, 'are now slightly in favour of us.'[7]

—

Oh, the agony of it all. For while the 4th Brigade of the 4th Division are dug in to the east at Hébuterne, the 12th and 13th Brigades continue to march through the night, on and on towards Albert.

'Men fell as they walked,' Lieutenant Mitchell would note, 'got up unaided or were hoisted to their feet. At each hour halt every man dropped where he stood. At the end of the ten-minute interval the stronger shook or booted the weaker till they woke.'[8]

In short order Mitchell finds himself walking alongside one of the battalion's characters, the 'inimitable Lieutenant Potts', who starts to not only stagger all over the road, but also, to Mitchell's consternation, call him 'Suzanne', not to mention several endearing terms that Mitchell finds most discomforting.

When Mitchell abuses and shakes him, it is only to discover that Potts is more or less sleepwalking.

'[I] took his arm and led him for miles while he slept.'[9]

The main thing is they keep moving towards Albert.

—

Generally, the Australians make an extremely favourable impression on their British counterparts. There's something distinctly *different* about them, the way they carry themselves.

'Their total lack of swank or class distinctions among them is most refreshing,' Private Reginald Wilkes the 16th Royal Warwickshires would record of the men of the 4th Australian Brigade, whom he comes across near Hébuterne. 'It is fine to hear their officers calling their men by their Christian names. It is very funny to see one of these colonials go up to a young English officer and say, "Mate, can you tell us the time, please?" Their conventions and ways of speaking to officers would send some of our old soldiers crazy. It's Tom, Dick and Harry with them, no Sirring and saluting.'[10]

Odd, that such a breed as that should generally prove to be such fine soldiers, but there you go.

27 MARCH 1918, VII CORPS HQ, IN A CHÂTEAU AT MONTIGNY

It has been a long haul. After a solid three days of travel, always searching for the right HQ to report to so he can know precisely where his 3rd Division are required to deploy themselves, John Monash is extremely pleased to have at last arrived at Montigny, the VII Corps HQ, in a once-grand château. True, at the time of his arrival, in that wee-est of wee hours represented by 1 am, the HQ is still being set up and he is a little underwhelmed by finding VII Corps' most senior officers 'sitting disconsolately in a dark building',[11] but at least he is here. (Most disconsolate of all is General Sir Walter Congreve, VC, Commander VII Corps, the poor cove who has seen his four divisions fall back in a flood, not a trickle, hence the damn *pickle* they find themselves in now, with a gaping hole in the line near Albert.)

But as pleased as Monash is, there is little doubt that Congreve is every bit as pleased to see him, and probably more.

'Thank heavens,' he says, beaming at the sight of Monash stepping into the room, 'the Australians at last.'[12]

After a bare minimum of inquiries about his trip and general health, Congreve gets to the point. 'General,' he says to Monash, pointing to the map spread before him on the mahogany table, 'the position is very simple. My corps at 4 o'clock today was holding the line from Bray to Albert when the line broke, and what is left of the three divisions in the line after four days' fighting without food or sleep is falling back rapidly. German cavalry have been seen approaching Morlancourt and

Buire. They are making straight for Amiens. What I want you to do is to get into the angle between the Ancre and the Somme as far east as possible and stop them.'[13]

And that . . . is . . . it.

A quick glance at the map makes it clear.

Amiens, the key city the Germans are driving towards, sits at the western-most point of a lateral triangle, formed, clear-cut, by the two Roman roads that extend from it heading east. When the battle had begun, the Fifth Army's VII Corps had held nine miles of that front and, as recently as today, had indeed held the six miles from Albert to Bray. But now that VII Corps are shattered and falling back, leaving a gaping hole in the line, it is for the Australians to plug the hole, to get between the Germans and the apex of the triangle, and hold them back.

This is so far removed from the usual military way of issuing precise orders – at least two pages, with numbered paragraphs, followed by appendices . . . The division will occupy the position marked

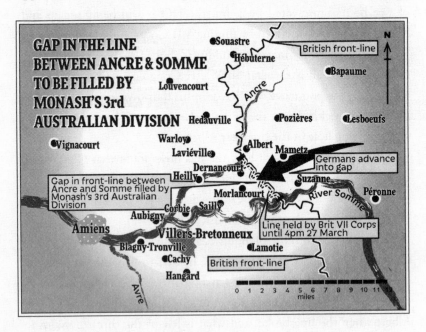

GAP IN THE LINE BETWEEN ANCRE & SOMME TO BE FILLED BY MONASH'S 3rd AUSTRALIAN DIVISION

British front-line

Souastre
Hébuterne
Bapaume
Louvencourt
Ancre
Hedauville
Pozières
Lesboeufs
Vignacourt
Warloy
Albert
Mametz
Lavieville
Germans advance into gap
Dernancourt
Heilly
Suzanne
Gap in front-line between Ancre and Somme filled by Monash's 3rd Australian Division
Morlancourt
River Somme
Péronne
Aubigny
Corbie
Sailly
Line held by Brit VII Corps until 4pm 27 March
Amiens
Villers-Bretonneux
Blagny-Tronville
Lamotie
Cachy
British front-line
Hangard
Avre

0 1 2 3 4 5 6 7 8 9 10 11
miles

on maps 22 and 23 . . . the objective of the move is . . . establish contact with 4th Division, who will be on your left and 25th on your right . . . arrangements for cooperation with artillery (see appendix 4) . . . the division will be in position by no later than 11 am . . . that Monash is quite stunned. It really amounts to little more than: 'General! The Germans have broken through and we can't stop them, so you will have to.'

Nevertheless, rising to the occasion, Monash promises that he will do his best, sir, to have his men do exactly that. He asks only for his masters to 'place a small room at my disposal and give me the use of a telephone',[14] so that he might work through the night to make the necessary arrangements.

MIDDLE OF THE NIGHT, 26–27 MARCH 1918, HOBNAILS AND COBBLESTONES

There! Down in the dark valley, where that strange rumbling is coming from . . .

Are they some kind of giant fireflies?

No, these are Australian men, Australian *soldiers* of the 4th Division's 12th Brigade, marching through the night, their hobnailed boots striking sparks against the cobblestones, often after they stumble under the weight of their full kit. With the 47th Battalion at the front of the column, they keep moving south, right across the gaping maw of the German advance. But it's exhausting, all right.

Colonel Alexander Imlay notes his concerns in the war diary:

Men were very tired after being all previous days in cars, very little sleep during the night and moving about all day and to bring a 17-mile march on them was testing them.[15]

True enough. Marching in full kit at 108 paces per minute, the 47th continue through the cool, clear night towards Albert, with the threat of battle ever present.

They really must be careful.

'As it wasn't known where the Germans were on the march south,' Charles Bean would chronicle, 'the flank guards . . . protected [the column]. The only instructions were – "the Germans are in front of you, you have rifles and bayonets – at him!"'[16]

Onwards, ever onwards they march, even now as a curious moon rises over them. Flashes and booms out to their left show where the battlefront lies – close.

Together with the metallic beat of hobnails and horseshoes on cobblestones, shouts of Sergeants and Corporals along the column keep the men in time and *on* time. Every so often a soldier starts up a marching song, which flares briefly before fading away, replaced once more by rattling gear and swooshing legs, and the endless restless rumble of bursting shells, just beyond reach, out there, somewhere in the dark. The Diggers march on.

In the next battalion along, the 48th Battalion, Lieutenant George Mitchell is still propping up his sleepwalking comrade, the 'inimitable Lieutenant Potts'.[17] Mitchell's diary tells the story: 'On. On. On. A halt every hour. The grey dawn light showing in the east. Poor old Potts fell with fatigue. I helped him. He slept as he walked, and talked in his sleep. Tank tracks everywhere and tanks lay about.'

Light from the sun now well below the horizon continues to slowly seep into the sky above, bringing the mysterious surrounds gradually into focus.

There is a bare white road before them. Occasionally, huge black bombers buzz above, menacing them, but, strangely, not actually bombing them. They keep moving through the scattered, shattered villages . . .

'The last of the fleeing inhabitants would regard us silently. Guns moving, moving back,' Mitchell would reminisce after the war. 'God! Would the retreat never stop! There is nothing left today but steel and fire and stone. Did we know what the day held?' [18]

And, of course, there are the frightened residents of the villages they pass through, 'in silent groups in unlighted doorways . . . Fear – terror was in the air.'[19]

As ever, coming the other way, retreating British soldiers and lots of artillery units. 'Small parties of aimless, mostly unarmed, men getting back. Always back . . . The menace of the unseen, incalculable enemy was as of an avalanche. We felt like Lilliputian actors in some gigantic drama of the gods

Hark to the galloping horse,
The crash of rending gun;
The stars are off their courses,
The hour of doom has begun.[20]

———

Not even the sparrows have farted.

It is still only four o'clock in the morning when the clarion call of the bugle shatters the pre-dawn hours for the Diggers of the 3rd Division, unaware as yet that they are bound for Morlancourt Ridge.

Some groan, others pull their sheepskin jackets over their heads, desperate for just another couple minutes of shut-eye before the Sergeant comes shouting at them, as Sergeants – a bastard breed – have been wont to do since the dawn of time. A noble few soldiers sit up, rubbing their eyes.

And now, sure enough, here he comes.

'Full marching order in twenty minutes!'[21] is the Sergeant's cry.

'Oh,' Private John Hardie would recount in his diary, 'you ought to have heard the language when the boys understood what was wanted. Still, a soldier doesn't as a rule need long to complete his toilet and everyone was out on the road within the time allowed.'[22]

The men of the 3rd Division are on their way again. At last, they're going into the line to fill the gap between the Ancre and the Somme on Morlancourt Ridge.

'In the grey light of dawn we were met by a convoy of motor lorries which took us down towards Albert.'[23]

DAWN, 27 MARCH 1918, THE 4TH BRIGADE AT HÉBUTERNE, ALL QUIET ON THE WESTERN FRONT

And the truth of it?

This ain't too bad, Dig!

For the bulk of the Australian soldiers used to fighting in the trenches, amid the mud and the blood, it is an extraordinary pleasure to find themselves in a just-abandoned village, with their trenches right beside it.

It means that while a few blokes can man the for'ard positions, the rest of them can help themselves to the well-stocked cellars, pantries and, later, the soft beds. Many catch and kill the ownerless fowls and rabbits running around the village, and the ground is soon lined with feathers and furs.

Later on, Captain Thomas White of the 13th Battalion would report how his men had found a sole Frenchman who had refused to leave.

'Ah, Monsieur,' he had explained to the Digger who'd encouraged him to go, 'my fowls and my pig, our beautiful things . . .'

Still, he was finally prevailed upon to leave, with two Diggers even escorting him to the rear.

'We had his pig and fowls that night for tea,'[24] Captain White finished his account.

The luckiest even find fully prepared meals sitting on the kitchen tables, ready to be eaten, their former owners have clearly fled unfed . . . Now pass the wine, please.

Yes, there is the sound of the odd angry shot in the dark distance, but here in this village there is more often than not the sound of corks popping as cheery campfires appear all around, and the aroma of roasting chickens fills the evening air.

'Such conditions of warfare,' Bean notes, 'had never before been known in the A.I.F., and the campaign took on the complexion of a picnic, or of a children's escapade, a world removed from the experiences of previous years. The conditions of the previous month in Flanders faded in memory like an evil dream.'[25]

As the sun rises, the Australians, dug in on the fringes of Hébuterne, are able to look out over the old Somme battlefield. And what a sight it is!

'Its flanks and depressions were clothed in long grass which waved in the gusts like the coat of a Shetland pony,' Bean would describe it, with uncharacteristic colour. 'Across the foreground, a roughness in the grassy surface, like the unevenness of some dug-out rabbit-burrow in an Australian paddock, indicated the site of the British support line of pre-Somme days, and beyond it the old network of trenches, British and German, extended in a belt two miles wide. Their grassy undulations were still deep enough to give useful cover, and the rusty wire-entanglements, looking like belts of russet weeds, still formed in parts a formidable obstacle.'[26]

As the Diggers peer closer and are able to discern just what they are seeing, they realise that, far from a scene of bucolic beauty alone, inert and harmless rolling grasslands, the vista before them is alive, *crawling* with German activity. Look there! Over there, on the moor, to the east, those are German wagon lines. And those little ants are soldiers, preparing to advance – to come here and try to kill us.

'In the distance a German battery, in the open, blazed at some movement behind the Australian line; the flash of each gun could be detected.'[27]

With one battalion held in reserve behind, three battalions of the 4th Brigade are now dug in on a 2000-yard front facing south-east, with Kiwis on their right flank and Brits on their left, though all up it is far from a complete defensive line and there are clear gaps.

Meantime, the Diggers get ready for the forthcoming visit from Fritz, and so clean their rifles and check their ammunition clips.

—

As the first strokes of colour streak forth from the glowing horizon way out there beyond Hunland somewhere, it is the men of the 47th Battalion – trudging at the head of the 12th Brigade column – who are the first to arrive in the town of Senlis-le-Sec around 6 am. In peacetime, of course, chirruping birds are the usual orchestral accompaniment to the birth of the new day. Here, it is heavy drums in the distance, scattered shelling coming from the direction of Aveluy, just north of Albert.

So be it. The Diggers keep moving through the town.

Yes, the residents are long gone, but oh what memories are coming back for those veteran Diggers who had been posted here back in 1916, back when the Pozières show was on the go. Over there is *La Mairie*, more battered than it was last time; there the cobbled back alleys leading off from the main street; and just up there a little ways, of course, will be Madame Laval and her estaminet, with her *belles filles*. I wonder if they are still there?

For many of the veteran Australian troops now gazing down into the long valley of the sparkling Ancre River, where they can soon see the red-roofed town of Albert before them – a hub of hospitals, warehouses, roads and railways, crucial to the British cause and so loved by the veteran Diggers that they refer to it as 'Bert' – it is almost something of a homecoming. Rather than *déjà vu* all over again, they really have been here before, most notably on first approaching Pozières in mid-July 1916, and in the weeks thereafter, as they had been rotated through the line.

Not for nothing do many of the remaining villagers come out to greet them and even refer to them as '*nos Australiens*', 'our Australians', with wonderful warmth.

'The reception of the Australians by the local population,' one Digger would recount, 'was unmistakable and made their return to the Somme a high romance. In many of the farms and village houses were found still pinned to the walls photographs of individual Australians and flags commemorating Anzac Day 1916. For this hereabouts had very nearly come to be a little bit of Australia by association during the summer and winter campaigns of that year. Some of the Diggers here found themselves known by name and remembered like intimate friends. They had fought and played, lived and died, about this countryside, not merely as soldiers, but like patriots defending their own homes. And not in vain.'[28]

And look way over there, Dig, to Albert in the far distance! 'Fanny' is still there.

Of course she is. Way up high, leaning out at an impossible angle from the top of the red-brick church tower of Notre-Dame de Brebières, the statue of the Virgin Mary had first looked to Charles Bean's eyes, among others, as if she was prostrate with grief at the sheer tragedy of what was happening to her children . . . but in fact she had been put that way by a German shell in the early part of the war. With typical irreverence, the Australians had nicknamed her 'Fanny', after Fanny Durack, the famed Australian Olympian who had won the gold medal for the 100-yard swim at the 1912 Stockholm Games, because, to a certain extent, it also looks as though Mother Mary was diving forward.[29]

Either way, the legend had grown among the local French and the Allied soldiers that when 'the Virgin falls into the street, the war will end',[30] and even the Germans had picked it up, though in the version they nurtured, as one of them would recount, was 'a superstition that the nation which shot down the Virgin would be vanquished'.[31]

Either way, the point is that the war goes on, so of course Fanny is still there.

Colonel Imlay orders his men to go into the empty houses so they can attend to their feet, change their socks and have some breakfast.

'If the day might bring forth anything,' Imlay noted in the battalion war diary, 'it was just as well to be prepared.'[32]

Colonel Bull Leane and the men of the 48th begin to arrive soon after, and the Bull firstly confers with Brigadier John Gellibrand on their next move.

'The Brigadier and the Bull were studying maps. Runners were dashing everywhere . . .'[33]

Congreve's orders are for the 12th Brigade to divert from Albert itself – reports say it has fallen – and proceed some four miles to their south to hold the Dernancourt railway embankment, with the 13th Brigade in support behind.

Yes, sir.

But first the Bull orders his tired men into the billets – 'not the most comfortable in France',[34] it is noted by the men, who have stayed in countless billets with countless gracious madams all across the northern end of France, and so feel fit to judge – to get what rest they can.

Mitchell and the sleepy Lieutenant Potts, who is no longer in his reverie, amorous for the affections of Suzanne, but dozing silently, slouched over his comrade, come into Senlis-le-Sec around 8 am. They quickly find a house to settle into for a bit of rest.

They start a fire. The cooks slaughter the chooks for the men to eat for breakfast, which they do with gusto.

And just as Mitchell has found himself a nicely scented boudoir with the laundered sheets turned down, inviting him to catch some shut-eye, a runner bursts in informing him that the battalion 'will move for Hénencourt at 10.15'.[35]

Outside, Imlay is sending the word out to his men of the 47th: at 10 am they are to move out of Senlis and concentrate with the rest of the 12th Brigade at Hénencourt, in preparation for movement to the Laviéville Heights above Dernancourt.

—

That distinguished figure of high military rank, walking purposefully towards the high ground just east of Franvillers on this early dawn? It is, of course, General John Monash – the puffs from his ubiquitous pipe mingling with the last wisps of mist. He has been working through the night, giving orders to his brigade commanders as to where to position his men of the 3rd Division once they arrive around Heilly. Now he has come forward himself to see that all is as it should be and that they are ready for the Germans. Taking his binoculars, he earnestly scans the area to his east.

And there they are!

'From the high ground at Franvillers, we could plainly see the German Cavalry operating on the high ground to the south of Morlancourt. It was really a question of an hour one way or the other whether we could intercept him or not.'[36]

On just the next ridge across, near Morlancourt, he can see *'Bosch Armoured Cars,'* together with the 'Bosch Cavalry', pressing forward, taking only desultory fire from whatever remnants of the British forces are there to stop them. It is along this Morlancourt Ridge that he must position his men.

'For two hours,' Monash would recount, 'I was momentarily expecting to get mopped up [by the *Bosch*].'[37]

Mercifully, at 8.30 am, however, there is the rumble of roaring engines coming from behind, and Monash's own motorised cavalry, the Australians of the first two battalions of the 11th Brigade, arrive from Mondicourt.

'This convoy,' Monash would recount with some pride, 'consisted of 60 motor buses – old London motor bus type – all crowded with troops, all armed and with plenty of ammunition. It was a miracle of good management.'[38]

Quickly now, Monash directs them into position with orders to march along the road to Heilly, cross the Ancre there, and dig in on the other side, with trenches dotted along for two-and-a-half miles, extending along the ridge-line that lies between the villages of Mericourt and Sailly-le-Sec, neatly configured to face an attack from the east. The topography of such a position has been wisely chosen, with a clear field of fire to the front and good views out to both flanks, in turn protected by the Ancre on the left and the Somme on the right.

Yes, the men are still spread thin, but it is something that the Germans will still have to conjure with as they try to push east to the apex of the triangle, and in the meantime more lorries are pulling up, more buses – more Australians arriving to hold the line.

At ten o'clock another roar of engines signals the arrival of another bus convoy, this one bearing two battalions of the 10th Brigade, under the command of General McNicoll.

——

Brigadier Rosenthal's 9th Brigade, meanwhile, are still in their busses, still rattling their way to the south, towards the Ancre River. Handed out the day's rations, Private John Hardie, with his 33rd Battalion, despite his better judgement gobbles up every last crumb in 60 seconds flat.

Around 9.45 am, he would recount, the 'busses dropped us . . . rather close to the new line and stray shells were falling around. After another bit of a march we were halted behind a steep embankment to prepare for battle. You see usually when going into the line we shed a lot of our gear, and always have a church parade, which is attended by those who wish. This was just outside a village called Heilly.'[39]

While the men prepare themselves for the fight that is surely to come, Brigadier Rosenthal, together with Colonel Goddard and other key officers, heads off into Franvillers to receive orders from 3rd Division's commander, General Monash, to find out just what contours the fight will be fought on, what they are expected to do. It is very simple – they're expected to stop the Germans. The 10th and 11th Brigades will hold the line between the Ancre and the Somme. The 9th Brigade will be in reserve behind them, and Rosenthal immediately begins to dispatch orders for his men to that effect.

Henry Goddard, before heading back to where his 35th Battalion are waiting outside Heilly, scans the latest report: **Enemy . . . have crossed Ancre at Dernancourt and Buire.**

That is unlikely to be too much of a problem, Goddard knows, as the 4th Division will be in position to stop them going further. We Australians will handle it. The real worry, though, is south of the Somme where **the left flank of the Fifth Army is not known with certainty.** Goddard knows that's bad – to send out a report like that means not a soul at HQ has a clue where the Fifth Army is right now, so even now Fritz may be getting around their southern flank in the vicinity of Villers-Bretonneux.

With every hour that passes without a German attack, the Australians are getting stronger in the triangle as the British let go.[40]

The Diggers of the 9th Brigade, meantime, have grown bored sitting idle, waiting. As Hardie would jot down later that day, 'About half an hour [after we arrived] most of the Battalion was out grub hunting and quite a lot of us were successful in locating food fit for the troops to eat.'[41]

Ah, the Somme. The land of milk and honey. They are back!

———

Despite reports on both sides of the lines that the German Army has 'captured' Albert, Fritz Nagel, on arrival in Albert this morning at six, is not sure. 'I expected to find the streets filled with marching troops and vehicles of all descriptions,' he would later recount.

Not so.

The streets are empty, the buildings lie silent, and just the sound of aeroplanes, recently taken off and now scouting the front-lines low overhead, taking shots at what they can, prevents the place from being silent.

'We sensed that something was wrong,' Nagel would continue, 'and we became apprehensive. If the town had already been taken, where were all the soldiers . . . ?'[42]

Nagel and his crew look at each other, confused. Perhaps they are in No-Man's Land, he suggests. Or perhaps the British have laid a trap for the Germans, allowing them to come in, only to launch the well-known tactic of a pincer movement, launching an attack on both sides of the town to cut them off and then come in and encircle them for the final kill. It is with great wariness that the Germans slowly drive on through the town. The sound of the motor never seemed louder, no matter that the driver and mechanic, Sergeant Eduard Rupp, can make any car purr like a cat in the spring sunshine.

They turn a corner and Nagel, to his great relief, sees soldiers dressed in German grey lying in position some 50 yards away. He walks up to them and begins to speak in a whisper before he realises the truth on their faces.

Cold. Unblinking. Dead.

Out of respect they move the bodies over to the side of a building before pushing on slowly, 'sure we had not yet reached our front-line'. Further along the road they come across 'a wounded German Marine propped against a house . . . shot through the foot.' The British are 'just around that corner', the man warns, looking down at his foot for emphasis.

Nagel and his crew continue on, and the next moment, a German soldier comes flying out of the front door of one of the houses lining the street, waving at them frantically, as if to say, 'Get back! *Los! Los!*'

Nagel walks towards him, leaving the crew behind.

As he approaches, the German soldier shouts in a whisper, 'British soldiers are holding houses at the end of the street.'

Out of another house comes a buff German officer, who, in a softly spoken, professional tone, tells Nagel, 'I am the commander of the 3rd Battalion of the 1st Marine Infantry Regiment . . . Thank you for coming to our aid.'[43]

Fritz has heard of his unit, which has a 'top-notch' reputation, but he still can't understand why they are not fighting. The officer goes on to tell him that, though his unit has been in action since the beginning of Operation Michael, and had taken most of Albert yesterday, now, on the edge of the town, it had encountered fierce resistance that has stopped them cold.

'We attacked them yesterday without success,' the officer says, 'and suffered terrible losses . . . Most of our casualties were caused by a machine-gun nest that is installed in a factory building about 400 yards in front of our line.'[44]

And, now, the commander explains, their orders are to attack again at 8 am.

'I can see only complete failure and very bloody losses ahead of us if that machine-gun nest dominates the sector. The windows are well protected by sandbags and there are machine-guns in all six windows, easily visible through binoculars. We need artillery to knock them out, but there is no supporting artillery in sight. But, now, you have arrived.'[45]

Nagel asks the commander, 'Why is the enemy artillery not in action?'

'They don't dare shoot so long as our lines are close together,'[46] comes the reply.

And now the commander has one of his aides take *Herr Leutnant* Nagel up to the attic window to see the situation for himself. They must go quietly and move slowly. Reaching the window, they ease it open and Fritz Nagel looks out.

'I was flabbergasted,' he later recalled, 'to see the flat tin hats of British infantry below us in the garden only fifty yards away. The enemy seemed to be everywhere – some in foxholes, some in short trenches, some hidden behind trees, hedges and so on. What I saw was not a fixed line. We could not tell where their line began or where it stopped, but we were certain an attack would be a desperate undertaking.'[47]

—

Among the Allied troops manning the more official front-line, which is just behind Albert – behind the few machine-gun nests that remain in the town itself – is the South African Lieutenant Geoffrey Lawrence with the 9th Scottish Division.

He and his men have been in the thick of it for days, and they are exhausted. Word has come through that the Australians are to relieve them, but for now they continue to hold this line between Albert and Dernancourt. Thankfully, those in the advanced possies, like Lieutenant Lawrence, had never received Congreve's mistaken retreat order and so had not fallen back with the rest of the men. It's one of those rare mistakes that turns out for the best.

As the sun rises, so too do the Flying Corps boys continue to lift their aircraft up and up to inhabit the skies.

Lieutenant Lawrence, sitting in a shallow trench on the rising land behind Albert, watches as British planes zoom into Hunland, drop bombs and zoom back around . . . all while German planes menace them.

—

Seventeen miles to the north-east of Albert, on this bright spring morning, a red German Fokker takes off and soars into the heavens with five triplanes of *Jasta 11*, No. 11 Fighter Squadron, closely in its wake.[48] The Red Baron and his Flying Circus are back in their natural habitat, like lions on the open veldt – and hungry ones at that, looking for prey. Baron von Richthofen, of course, is in the lead, scanning the skies ahead for enemy aircraft that are riding the wave of clear weather to strafe and bomb the advancing German infantry down near Albert. Sure enough, just after 9 am, the Red Baron sees what he has been looking for – a single Sopwith Camel biplane flying low. True, the Camel is a faster plane than his Fokker, but he knows his own skills will make up the difference.

Swooping from high above, giving him the advantage of the blinding sun as cover, Richthofen tears down, coming close above the Camel to let out a few quick bursts from his twin Spandau machine-guns. He fires 150 bullets, and it proves to be enough. A stream of white vapour pours out from the Camel's fuel tanks – two of which are located just behind the unfortunate pilot, with the third nestled above his knees.

Inside the Camel is the 31-year-old Gloucester farmer Captain Tom Sharpe, a flight commander in the 73 Squadron with six victories under his belt – the most important, of course, being Erich Pernet, General Ludendorff's stepson, whom he'd killed just a few days earlier.

Sharpe feels the jolt of his aeroplane as the bullets strike and looks over his shoulder to see the vapour trail. He switches off his engine immediately, so as to avoid his craft going up in flames. With as much control as he can bring to bear upon his stricken craft, he careers down, down towards the earth, heading straight for a stretch of the Ancre River just northeast of Albert.

With a shuddering crash, the plane plunges into the water. Sharpe, shaken to the core and unable to move, looks around and knows instantly that he is on the wrong side of the line.

It is not long before he is plucked from the machine and taken prisoner by the *Boche*.

The Red Baron stalks on, hungry for more prey.

A short time later, Lieutenant Geoffrey Lawrence happens to be watching as several British RE8s – nicknamed 'Harry Tates' – fly overhead, pushing towards the Hun side of Albert, when . . . out of the blue sky, from way up on high, come three red triplanes.

Down in Albert itself, Fritz Nagel and his crew have just finished a good late breakfast of corned beef from plundered British supplies and are now getting back to their 'routine duty of shooting at low-flying planes'.[49]

Of course, with so many enemy planes about, all eyes are on the prize in the skies as they continue through town, looking for a spot where they can operate their gun. Passing through the open marketplace, they are fascinated to see 'a British shell has hit the golden Madonna on Albert's medieval church . . . She was hanging head down from a wire, as if plunging to her death.'[50]

Pushing up a side street, they suddenly come under heavy attack from British planes. Looking up, *Leutnant* Nagel sees 'several Bristol double-deckers carrying two men and two machine-guns . . . milling around over our heads looking enormously big.'[51]

The planes continue dropping bombs while also machine-gunning German troops. It is precisely the situation that Nagel and his Ack-Ack soldiers have been trained for, and he is quick to react.

'*An die Flak!* Man the gun!' Nagel cries.

In an instant, his six-man crew are up on the truck and have their 77mm Krupp anti-aircraft gun pointed straight up and primed with a shell ready to explode no higher than 150 feet after being fired from the barrel. They now all look expectantly to Nagel, awaiting his signal as the roar of a low-altitude plane gets closer.

There!

The wings of a Bristol coming over the rooftops appear. Nagel drops his arm and his brave boys blaze away.

'We blasted away so fast,' Nagel would chronicle. 'I thought the gun might topple over. Within seconds I saw one plane hit, coming down squarely, as if it would fall on top of us . . .'[52]

Ah, but there are still more enemy fighters to come.

The crew reload and await Nagel's signal. The screaming engines of an approaching British plane grow louder.

And . . .

WARTE AB! WAIT!

Just before Nagel is about to give them the signal to unleash their deadly load, the German officer recognises that the planes coming over are not Bristols – they are much smaller, multicoloured triple-deckers. They are Fokker Dr.1s. It is Baron von Richthofen's Flying Circus!

Nagel shudders at how close they have come to making a terrible blunder.

'I was thankful the crew were disciplined enough not to have started firing before I gave the signal. To shoot down Richthofen, the national hero, would have been awful.'[53]

Lieutenant Geoffrey Lawrence, from across the line, watches, enthralled yet appalled, as the action unfolds in the skies above Albert. Five of the British planes are brought down with apparent ease by the mighty Circus, or perhaps the bursts of Ack-Ack. And, look here, as another Bristol fighter-bomber enters the scene, all casual, as if accidentally strolling into a den of wolves . . . only for the wolves to all pounce upon him!

Ah, but the brave British lion fights back!

Lawrence and all of his soldiers watch closely; it is a wonder to behold. While the pilot throws his machine around the skies with expert ease, swivelling and swerving, skiving and diving, throwing the German gunners off their aim, his observer in the rear cockpit blazes away at the flying Fritzes. He's brought down one of them! And *another*! With every German plane that plummets, a roar goes up from the Australian soldiers.

But wait . . . *now* look! It starts with a little spark in their petrol tank, which grows bigger and bigger until a mass of flames surrounds the pilot's cockpit – but do you think that stops him?

It does not!

The men below stare 'in very fear' as the pilot climbs out onto the bottom left wing of his biplane and, with one leather-clad arm, manages to keep control of the joystick and keep flying, all while his observer keeps firing and brings down ANOTHER German plane.

Oh, those magnificent bastards! The pilot with supreme skill manages a manoeuvre known as 'side-slipping' to keep the flames away from his side of the plane – and away from the observer – all while circling lower, bringing his kite in for a landing, right near where Lieutenant Lawrence and his men are dug in on the rising slope behind Albert. Even before the plane has stopped rolling, the pilot and observer jump down and race as far away from the plane as they can get, aware that the both the petrol tank and all the ammo on board will surely explode in seconds. But wait! While the pilot has made good ground, the observer, badly wounded, has collapsed near the plane and is feebly trying to crawl away. He lets out a cry.

The pilot hears him, turns, runs back, grabs the observer by the scruff of his flying coat as a bitch might grab one of her errant puppies, and then *drags* him like a mad thing away from the plane, which is now in flames.

'It was,' Lieutenant Lawrence would record, 'one of the most remarkable and exciting things I ever saw in the war.'[54]

BOOOOM! The plane explodes, bringing the pilot down, too. And now, as soldiers burst from their trenches and go to the two men's aid, it is the pilot's turn to be dragged to their shallow trenches. Both the flyers are burned and wounded – the pilot with three bullet holes, the observer with six – but *alive!*

'Don't worry,' Lieutenant Lawrence assures the pilot, Lieutenant Alan McLeod, a Canadian, 'you'll be in Blighty in a few days.'[55]

'That's just the trouble!' McLeod replies. 'I'd like to have a crack at that bugger that brought me down.'

The young man – staggeringly, he proves to be just 18 years old! – falls silent once more and the smell of burned flesh fills the air. The wounded flyers must remain in the trench all day while the soldiers do the best they can for them before the stretcher-bearers can get to them after dark and shuttle them back to a dressing station.

High above, the Red Baron stalks on, *still* looking for fresh meat.

LATE MORNING, 27 MARCH 1918, MORLANCOURT, BEAUCOUP AUSTRALIENS ICI

South of the high adventure up near Albert, many of the 3rd Division soldiers continue moving into position along Morlancourt Ridge, tracing a line between Mericourt on the southern bank of the Ancre River, to Sailly-le-Sec on the northern bank of the Somme. Looking around, they are simply thrilled with the sheer *aching* beauty of this place – a real change from the frosty swamps of Flanders. There are no Germans to be seen as yet.

Even for those with little experience of the trenches, the greenery, the flowers, the butterflies, the neat hedges, neater cottages, hares breaking cover, lowing cattle and gentle, rolling hills here would be a delight. But if, like so many of these men, you have spent much of the last three years (including Gallipoli) amid the mud, blood, barbed wire and sheer devastated and devastating ugliness of the trenches, then this place looks a lot like heaven. In this early spring, the snow has long melted away, the wheat has been planted five weeks before and is already coming through some four- to six-inches high, green and beautiful, an affirmation of life returning after this long winter of their discontent. It is all so beautiful that the many farmers among them are reluctant to walk over it, to scrunch it under their clodhoppers. But scrunch they must, and within minutes those clods made of chalky, wet soil are sticking to the boots they intend to give Fritz right up his backside.

Of course, as the Australians move forward, trying to get into position, they pass by roads becoming ever more clogged with the ragtag remnants of the shattered British forces.

As ever, many yell warnings to the Australians – 'You can't hold them!'[56]

Au contraire, mon petit Tommy . . . The Australians think they can. (One British Officer would later write of the advancing mob, 'They were the first cheerful stubborn people we had met in the retreat.'[57])

Friends, it is their record. For the last four years of this war, the Australians have done – to use their newly in vogue expression – 'fucking well'. Time and again, from Gallipoli onwards, but most particularly in the battles of Pozières, Bullecourt, Messines and Passchendaele, they have demonstrated themselves a force to be reckoned with. They are physically formidable, morally courageous and filled with crack shots and blokes who'd sooner a fight than a feed. Confidence is part of the Australian nature, and pride at how well they are doing is growing.

For Charles Bean, it is all proof positive of something he had written in the *Sydney Morning Herald* well before the war had started: 'The Australian is always fighting something. In the bush it is drought, fires, unbroken horses, and cattle; and not unfrequently strong men . . . We look upon all this as very shocking and unruly in England nowadays; but there is no doubt that having to fight for himself gives a man pluck . . . All this fighting with men and with nature, fierce as any warfare, has made of the Australian as fine a fighting man as exists.'[58]

As yet another unit of the 3rd Division marches into Heilly they are greeted by the French residents, not as conquering heroes but as heroes who are going to prevent the locals from being conquered by *les Allemands*, who, all the villagers know, are now within a cannon's roar of them.

Many of the locals burst into tears at the mere sight of the Australians moving forward.

The murmuring among them starts . . .

'*Qui sont-ils?* Who are they? *De quel pays viennent-ils?*' What country are they from?

And the answer: '*Ce sont les Australiens* . . . They are Australians.'

And then the cry is taken up, first by a few and then by many: '*Vive l'Australie! Vive l'Australie! Vive l'Australie!*'[59]

Standing by *la rue*, there is even a gnarled old parish priest – dressed in his black cassock and white surplice, with swinging crucifix – raising his hand to make the sign of the cross, blessing the passing Australians. May God be with you as you go forward in our country, so far from your own home, to help save us from the invaders.

Still other *citoyens* react in even more inspiring fashion as the men of the 3rd Division move forward.

Some take one look and turn around, heading home on the reckoning that the day is saved. It is a move the Diggers themselves encourage.

'*Fini* retreat, *Madame*,' Charles Bean records one of the Diggers saying to an old lady heading west with all her worldly possessions in a wheelbarrow,[60] as he sits with his mates, cleaning their rifles. '*Fini* retreat – *beaucoup Australiens ici.*'[61]

And it is demonstrably true, as yet more Australians continue to flood forward to sort Fritz out.

———

Up at Hébuterne, on 28 March, the soldiers of the 4th Brigade are still waiting.

At 11 am, they see the grey swarm on a ridge-line just three-quarters of a mile to their east. Colonel Marks, Commander of the 13th Battalion, which is at the south-east edge of the town, records in his diary, 'At 11.20 am aeroplanes reported the enemy massing.'[62]

Their bayonets couldn't be sharper, their machine-guns are *thump-thump-thumping* – their nostrils are filling with that acrid though not totally unpleasant smoke thrown off by a Lewis gun in full flight as it works through its 47-round ammunition drum in two or three short bursts – and the artillery boys are doing their best to lob shells over to disperse the Hun.

In the meantime, the Old Brig – Brigadier Charles Brand – is sitting in his headquarters at Foncquevillers with his beloved German shepherd, Karl, curled cosily at his feet, when he receives an order from on high.

'It is to be distinctly understood,' it reads in an unambiguous tone, 'that no retirement from our present position is permissible. All officers and ranks are to be made to understand this. Most stringent orders must be issued by all commanders to this effect, and officers who fail to observe the spirit of this order are to be relieved of their commands.'[63]

Though Brand has no doubt that his boys wouldn't dream of retiring, he passes the word forward.

The hour hand tick-tocks past midday, past one o'clock and . . . *there!*

To the south-east of Hébuterne, waves of grey.

They are out in the open. No need for bayonets, boys. We've got this covered. Within seconds the Lewis guns are raging and the grey blobs disappear into the grass.

As Australia's official keeper of such moments, Charles Bean, would later note of the action, the Germans 'came on in wave after wave, advancing obliquely across the summit and flank of the spur in a direction which would take them past the southern edge of Hébuterne, as if they were making, as indeed they were, for the village of Sailly-au-Bois, some miles behind the junction of the Australians and New Zealanders. As these lines tried to sweep past the Australian front, the 15th and 13th poured into their flank at long and moderate ranges a fire which completely broke the attack.'[64]

Hun troops, surely as they came, are now seen running low to the ground, *away* from their objective, as fast as their sturdy Fritz legs can carry them!

———

By now, in the early afternoon, General Monash, at his headquarters at Franvillers, is feeling stronger. His troops have continued to arrive, and by two o'clock he has 5000 men digging in across the rough ridge-line that passes 'in the angle between the Ancre and the Somme',[65] each company carefully sending out patrols to determine just where the Germans are and what they are doing.

One thing they don't need to inquire about is the enemy artillery, which is now falling mostly behind the newly established Australian front-line, onto the rear areas. There is contact with the Germans up front, but, to Monash's surprise, for once they don't seem set on attacking with everything they have.

What could have happened to them?

Could it be that they have taken one look at his own fine soldiers streaming into the sector, obviously there to block their advance, and

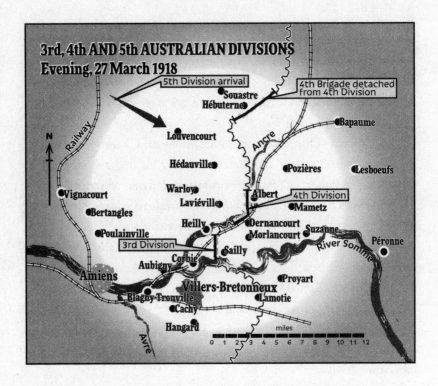

decided they need to regroup before advancing once more?

Whatever the reason, it at least gives Monash a moment to have a smoko – in his case, of course, a pipe – and to look at the situation through the calmest, most objective lens he can conjure.

While the general danger is the Germans regrouping to make another big push for Amiens, for him personally the risk is the Hun slipping around behind his 3rd Division, first via Villers-Bretonneux then via the bridge that cross the Somme at Corbie, and taking the road all the way to Amiens that way, leaving the Australians in their wake. Beyond that, this single bridge is the main avenue of communication between Monash's 3rd Division at Morlancourt and the Australians at Villers-Bretonneux. So, clearly, whatever else happens, his men must – MUST – hold both this Somme bridge and the other Somme bridges nearby. Not a Hun is to cross them, and he issues his orders accordingly.

A company of men from the 11th Brigade's 44th Battalion are quickly on their way to Corbie to act as the trolls of their childhood nursery rhymes, making sure that not a single German Gruff may cross the bridge.

Two miles north of Corbie, Colonel Goddard is in his new HQ at Bonnay, on the bank of the Ancre. Goddard, a six-footer built like a thermometer, can not only look like a 'long streak of misery' but sometimes sound like one. Yet there is no doubt that the great care and respect he has for his men is returned in kind by his fellow officers and men alike. He is not sure what awaits, bar the fact that his men will acquit themselves well.

—

Monash's other brigade, the mighty 11th, has arrived at long last. Dumping their packs at Heilly, they assume fighting order before crossing the Ancre and pushing on south towards Sailly-le-Sec on the Somme.'

'Although we had not known a hot meal in forty-eight hours,' the 42nd Battalion's Vivian Brahms would recall, 'and we did not know when we were likely to get one, our spirits were of the best.' [66]

How could they *not* be feeling good?

Monash's line between the Ancre and the Somme is complete when the stunningly picturesque village of Sailly-le-Sec is reached at noon. The 11th Brigade start to dig themselves into the rudimentary trenches that have been left to them on the eastern side of the recently abandoned hamlet. Gazing to the east, for the moment there is little sign of the Hun, and so the Australians do the obvious . . .

'Never had we seen such an abundance of wine,' Brahms records of what they find in Sailly-le-Sec. 'More plentiful than water . . . Every available vessel capable of holding liquid was utilized for carrying away the luscious beverage. With poultry, eggs, sheep, pigs and wine all to be had for the taking, the men of the 42nd had the time of their lives . . .'[67]

And they keep going until there is '*napoo*' left.

This, friends, *this* is the way to fight a war!

27 MARCH 1918, FROM PARIS, WITH IRRITATION

Had the blasted Germans not launched their attack, Charles Bean would have had the exquisite pleasure of watching the famed opera *Carmen,* with its story of a young soldier and the fiery Gypsy girl, the previous evening in Paris and still be *tra-la-la-laaaaa* thrilling to it now.

Instead, all of that has now gone by the board, and he must scramble through the day and into the night – every day and every night – to keep track of just where all the Australian divisions are, what action they have seen, what action they are likely to see, and then put it into 1000-word reports before finding a way to send those reports back to the *Sydney Morning Herald* and papers around Australia.

On this day, Bean and Fred Cutlack are able to secure a brief interview with General Monash, who Bean finds 'as lucid as usual'.[68] The General explains where he has placed his men, in a strong position on Morlancourt Ridge, and how the 3rd is now a rock the Germans will break themselves upon, should they be so foolish as to attack.

Bean and Cutlack head off along the Albert–Amiens Road, talking to any men they meet, as has been Bean's way from the first day at Gallipoli. Among other things, they are able to establish that the Germans have not only taken Pozières back at the cost of practically *no* lives but have reportedly walked in and captured Albert too, which would place them only two miles ahead on this road, now choked with refugees coming back the other way? It scarcely seems fathomable. Good Lord!

Now Bean can even *see* the Germans.

There, see? Taking Bean's proffered telescope, Cutlack agrees that those ant-like figures moving on the crest behind Morlancourt – two miles to the south-east – must be Germans, likely the advance screen moving ahead of the main mass of troops.

The situation looks grim and yet, given that he is so close to his old digs in these parts, Bean decides to very briefly drop in on his old landlady, Madame Leuwers, the venerable old soul in the village of Heilly with whom he had stayed during all of the Pozières battle and its aftermath. And there it is, the old, unprepossessing tenement on the main street, standing just as it was.

Bean knocks on the door and, to his amazement, is rewarded by the quavering voice of the old lady within.

'*Qui est-ce?*'

'*C'est Monsieur le Capitaine,*' Bean replies in his fluent French, '*qui était avec vous l'hiver dernier,* who was with you last winter.'[69]

'I was at my wits end what to do,' he would relate in his diary. 'I couldn't leave her there – and yet I couldn't risk alarming the village and causing a stampede.'[70]

'What can I do, *Monsieur?*' Madame replies simply. 'I should have to walk there – and I cannot walk . . . Do you think there is any danger?'

'Not unless the Germans advance.'[71]

'Well, I suppose we should have to stay *pour les Allemands,* for the Germans to take us.'[72]

Even while they are speaking, three shells explode outside, shells that Bean recognises from the sound must be coming from a high-velocity gun typically used by the Germans to shell rear areas, villages and crossroads – anywhere that British troops might be gathered.

Not one of the three French old folk even blinks; they keep talking as if it is nothing but the whistling wind outside. Oh, but Madame feels it, all right.

'Alas,' she goes on, tearfully but not fearfully, 'then I can do nothing but stay here for ruin and death. What *misère*, what a time. That this little house where I have kept all my little belongings intact, so far, must be ruined like those other villages of the Somme, and I killed in the ruins.'[73]

Bean and Cutlack take their leave, promising to return *demain*.

———

Was im Himmel ist mit dem Rittmeister los?! What on earth is going on with the Captain?! *Leutnant* Ernst Udet is not sure. But on this day, Udet is one of the ten planes of *Jasta 11* under the command of *Rittmeister* von Richthofen, cruising along the Roman road between Amiens and Villers-Bretonneux, when the Baron does something entirely uncharacteristic. Instead of hugging the heavens as is his wont, descending only when a safe target has been established, something gets into him. Spotting a column of British guns being hauled along the road towards the east, *der Rittmeister* – positioned in the lead so all other members of his *Jasta* can see him – suddenly waggles his wings once and swoops down. With no choice but to follow despite the danger, the others, too, push their joysticks forward and are soon flattened back in their seats as their planes hurtle down.

Der Rittmeister is without mercy. Expertly pulling out of his dive and levelling off just 30 feet above the ground, he roars along above the whole column, spitting death from his dual machine guns at the British soldiers, the survivors of whom desperately run for cover. In quick succession, the other nine German fighters follow suit, exacting a terrible toll and . . .

And now what? Once the *Rittmeister* reaches the end of the column, he turns and goes back the other way, making *another* attack! It is against every dictum he has ever taught his men and insisted upon, exposing himself and them to ground attack as all the defences now get a bead on them – but he does not appear to care. 'Machine guns posted in roadside ditches fired viciously at us as we flew overhead,' *Leutnant* Udet would chronicle. 'Yet, despite the fact that his wings were riddled with bullets, the *Rittmeister* still continued to fly just as low as he had before.'[74]

Udet knows Richthofen doesn't believe in flying constant, long patrols, 'standing sentry duty in the air'[75] when there is little prospect of a fight. 'We only go up to fight,' he says. But this is a savage attack, seemingly without care for his own safety.[76] It's all quite out of character for the usually calm, calculating German ace, whose patience in the past has served him well.

Was ist bloß mit dem Rittmeister los? What is *going on* with the *Rittmeister*?

(A decent man is *Leutnant* Udet. The following day, after shooting down a Sopwith Camel, he goes to visit the fallen pilot at the German field hospital where he has apparently been taken, only to find that the pilot had been killed instantly by a bullet to the head. The doctor hands Udet the wallet, revealing the dead man to be a Canadian: **LIEUTENANT CHARLES MAASDORP, ONTARIO**. Inside the wallet is the picture of a distinguished old lady, with a letter from her: *You mustn't fly so many sorties. Think of your father and me.*

'I drove back to the squadron base,' Udet would recount. 'One must not think about the fact that a mother will cry for every man one brings down.'[77]

—

Thank the good Lord. The Australian 5th Division, under General Talbot Hobbs, is finally moving south. Among them, of course, is Brigadier Pompey Elliott's 15th Brigade.

That morning at Messines, Private Jimmy Downing and his mates of the 57th Battalion had been suddenly ordered on parade and then told to return to their billets to begin to pack, leaving behind 'every surplus article'.[78] Within the hour they had been marching the six miles to the railway station at Bailleul, with the whole town under heavy shelling, and then boarded a series of trains that pulled into the station. One of those trains, alas, was soon hit, with many killed.

And now, here they are still, shivering in the back of a crowded cattle truck as northern France moves backwards in the twilight.

'The carriages rattled and bumped as we smoked and wondered towards what dreadful things we were being taken,' Downing would ruefully recount. 'We drowsed and were wakened by the jolting of the truck, or by the discomfort of the hard corners of the heaps of rifles and equipment on which we were huddled, forty men in a space of fifteen feet by nine . . .'[79]

Still, there is general contentment that they are on their way. All they know is that the Australians of the south have been thrown into the line and need their support, and that is enough. This is certainly the view of a runner in the 5th Division's 14th Brigade, Edmund Street.

'Despite the catastrophe down south,' Street would recount, '[we of] the AIF were in great spirits and . . . morale was rising higher and higher . . . We were feeling in great form, the weighty responsibility about to be thrust on us served but to make us more confident. The AIF was a magnificent body of fighters. Courage and brains combined . . . the mob was full of fighting spirit.'[80]

LATE AFTERNOON, 27 MARCH 1918, DERNANCOURT, KILTS WILT AS SLOUCH HATS TILT

The 9th Scottish Division's 6th Royal Scots Fusiliers that Churchill characterised on the eve of the battle as being 'serene as the Spartans of Leonidas on the eve of Thermopylae'[81] have met much the same fate in the end. Though they fought nobly, they are now completely devastated.

Having fallen back an average of four miles a day from 22 March, they have lost 10,000 of the 16,000 soldiers they'd started with – all killed, wounded or captured – and are now more than relieved to be relieved by the Australian Division.[82]

If only the Australians can find them!

So devastated have the Scots been that for the Australians moving forward it is unclear just where the front defensive lines actually are. All they can do is proceed carefully, *feel* out where both the Scots and the enemy are, and dig in accordingly.

A case in point is the fraught line in front of the village of Dernancourt, just 2000 yards from the houses marking the southern edge of Albert, barely held by the embattled Scots. Less a defensive line than a scattering of defensive outposts spread out along the railway, it risks being hopelessly exposed when the Germans make their next thrust forward, to move beyond Dernancourt, which they are now thought to hold.

Imlay and his men of the 47th are arriving now at the nearby village of Hénencourt, on the other side of a crest to the west of the position, and before they can even take their loads off they are ordered by Brigadier Gellibrand to 'move forward at once and stem the tide'.[83]

As has always been his fashion, Imlay heads out to reconnoitre the ground ahead, and comes under sporadic fire for his trouble. This is not going to be easy. Actually, he realises it will be downright difficult. Coming over the crest and looking down upon Dernancourt, Imlay sees for himself that High Command's so-called 'defensive line' – which had looked so neat on the map – is practically non-existent and poses no serious obstacle to the Germans. The few trenches are shallow and dug into the lower part of the slope above Dernancourt, complete exposed to the German artillery. As to the brave Scots below, if there are any left at all, the truth is that they are less defending a front-line than seeking what shelter they can in the shallow holes that have been dug. The only upside is they get plenty of shell holes for free, with more coming all the time as the German big guns continue to pound them.

Stone the bloody crows! But leave them alone.

Even for Imlay to get his men down the exposed slopes that extend well over a mile to take over from the Scots is a fraught exercise, but by mid-afternoon they are ready with the two battalions – the 47th and 48th – lined up behind. They give it their best shot.

Sadly, the Germans do the same, with many of those shots hitting.

As recorded in the 47th Battalion unit diary: '2:30 pm. Ordered by Brigade to advance frontline ... This necessitated movement on the forward slope of hill in full view of the enemy who shelled us, causing casualties which were minimised by adopting loose formations and dribbling men through.'[84]

It takes some doing, and casualties are heavy, but by 5 pm – after scampering down the slope like scalded crabs through the barrage of shells and machine-gun fire – the men of the 47th are at least dug in on the low side of the slope.

Not so Lieutenant George Mitchell and the men of the 48th

Battalion, who remain mostly at the crest of the hill, a point Colonel Imlay notes with a hint of annoyance in the 47th diary:

> *48th Battalion, who were to have moved at the same time, had not yet put in an appearance.*[85]

The 48th's CO, Leane, always one to do as he deems fit rather than what he has been told, has taken a gamble that there would be no German attack on the railway line this day and decides to ignore Brigadier Gellibrand's orders. Instead, he will wait until dark to move the battalion down the slope. Given the carnage below, it is clear to the experienced officer that his men cannot move all the way down to the railway line just in front of Dernancourt until the safety blanket of night arrives.

Meanwhile, at least the Colonels Imlay and Leane are able to meet up with the COs of four Scottish units that they are taking over from.

'[They] asked us,' Imlay will record, 'to take over their line running along the railway line . . . but they could give us no information regarding the position.'[86]

It is not until night falls that they will reach any further and see what they are in for. The men pause where they are, and wait for darkness.

———

As the day begins to fade, *Kronprinz* Rupprecht in his HQ at Mons, takes stock of his Army's progress.

As near as he can work out, there seems to be a pause in the advance as the enemy moves its reserve forces forward, but reports also indicate that in those positions, 'the enemy initially was only weak and had thrown partial, scraped-together-from-everywhere forces at us'.[87]

Rupprecht is convinced that Ludendorff has erred in sending three reserve divisions towards Villers-Bretonneux instead of committing them north of the Somme. 'Pity,' he jots in his diary this evening. 'Today or tomorrow, [had we the three divisions] we would get through at Hébuterne if we went all out.'[88]

Without the reserves, Rupprecht's attack for the morrow will be on a smaller scale than he had hoped. But the enemy is still on the defensive, so not all is lost. He orders his men to keep pushing forward – 'attack the railway embankment [at Dernancourt and Albert] next morning. The artillery preparation [to] begin at 5.15 am and the assault . . . delivered at 6.00.'[89]

The rough plan is to smash through the Australians along the railway then drive up the slope and take the high ground, on Laviéville Heights, which, if they can capture it, will offer ideal views for German artillery observers in the direction of Morlancourt, Corbie, Villers-Bretonneux and Amiens.

With the men waiting in shoddy, muddy positions in the pouring rain on this night, the regiment's commander is ordered back to a meeting at 50th Division Headquarters. Upon arrival he is informed that, on the morrow, the 229th and 230th Regiments, brothers in arms, will assault along a front with Dernancourt at its centre.

'The artillery preparation should begin at 5.15 am, the infantry attack 6 am.'[90]

When the Regiment Commander asks if the artillery could prepare in such short time, Brigadier von Maltzahn concurs with the concerned sentiment but reassures his Commanders 'that the attack could succeed against weak rear guards . . . the order remains'.[91]

As per their duty, they ride back through the rain to distribute orders to their sodden men: prepare for attack in the morning.

At least with the pause, for the German troops it is more than a saving grace to now find plenty of provisions – British provisions! – that they can not only ingest but wear, too.

Rudolf Binding records in his diary, 'Our men are hardly to be distinguished from British soldiers. Everyone wears at least a leather jerkin, a waterproof either short or long, English boots or some other beautiful thing.'[92]

The French locals – those who chose not to flee – are unimpressed, but nonetheless they are forced to 'deliver up chicken and pigeons with

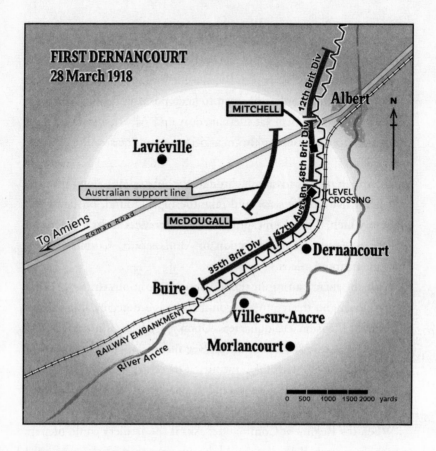

the usual tears. Cows, calves and pigs find their way unobtrusively out of their farmyards into the field kitchens . . .'[93]

It is not easy providing for the enemy. And the locals spend much of their time with their heads firmly in their hands, tears streaking down their faces. Not least because the Germans are also 'looting with some zest'.[94]

—

A soft knock on the door once more. There is now no time to return for Madame Leuwers at Heilly on the morrow, as Bean had promised. He has just found out the nearest Germans are little more than a mile away and will likely attack at dawn. So he must go *tonight*. Again she answers the door, and now it is Bean doing all the talking. The Germans are close, very close. Most villagers are leaving on foot, as the roads are being kept free for Allied military vehicles alone. He knows she cannot walk far, so he has come with a car to get her and her sister. The problem is there is no room for her sister's husband – which is admittedly problematic, as he, too, cannot walk far.

'If he stays, I stay,' the sister says calmly, 'and we will die together… [But] *merci*, thank you *Monsieur*, for your kind thought.'[95]

It takes some doing, and *les Mesdames* must leave behind some precious possessions that they want to take with them, but ultimately room is made for the most precious possession of all: *Monsieur le 'usband*.

Madame Leuwers's final words before they pull away are to another old woman, a neighbour who refuses to leave, calling out the window as Bean pulls away: 'Now Clemence – feed the fowls . . . tomorrow.'[96]

In short order, Bean has dropped the old trio at the much safer town of Vignacourt, where they have friends, before rushing back to 4th Division HQ at Baizieux Château, where there is news. Two brigades of the 4th Division have been sent to hold the railway embankment at Dernancourt, three miles east of Heilly, and an attack is expected there tomorrow.

CHAPTER EIGHT

HOLD THOSE BASTARDS

It almost looked as if the whole British Army in
this part of the world was in a state of rout.[1]
John Monash at Doullens on the afternoon of 25 March

They could be led easily, but the officer who
tried to drive them died of exhaustion.[2]
Captain Longmore, 44th Battalion, on his men

RISING EVENING, 27 MARCH 1918, BY THE LIGHT OF A SICKLE MOON

As the sun dips below the horizon after this glorious spring day, which
appears to be turning into a wet night, so too do the men of the 48th
Battalion finally move over the crest of the hill and dip down the gentle
slope towards an elevated section of railway line that lies just north
of Dernancourt and a little over a mile south-west from the edge of
Albert. They are to occupy the left, or northern, flank of the brigade's
sector. The railway line that slashes its way through the undulating hills
in these parts – elevated in the valleys in cuttings through the tops of
the hills – is the obvious spot to make a stand. To their right, the 47th
Battalion is already in position along the rail line.

Those behind the railway embankment have a decent defensive line,
while those guarding above the cutting may merely drop grenades onto

enemy troops venturing along or across it, and the enemy will be blown apart. And yet, if the Germans do get over the embankment they are free to go *anywhere*. The fields are so flat and open that it would be only supply wagons restricted to the roads; the infantry, cavalry and field artillery could go in any direction they like.

For the most part, however, the thought of serious battle recedes just a little with the fading light, as the sound of rumbling shell fire dies down.

Lieutenant George Mitchell, as ever, is with the leading platoon, taking up the new position to relieve an exhausted group of Scots, who are thrilled at their arrival.

'Who are you?' they ask.

'Forty-Eighth Australians.'

The Scots rejoice – The Australians are here! – and the 48th starts to spread out along the line, relieving the weary men as they go.

One wee laddie who has not slept a wink for two full days is fighting the urge to let his heavy eyelids close when he sees the silhouette of a large figure loom over him and then jump down into his ditch.

Has his end come?

And then the laconic drawl is unmistakable.

'Get the hell out of it, Jock,'[3] says the Australian soldier, nudging him up onto his feet. And so the Private does, quickly joining his mates.

'Jerry's little promenade is finished,' they tell each other in their thick Scottish accents. *Now* them Squareheads will be getting the 'lick in the lug' they so richly deserve! The Scots can do no more, and a burly Sergeant with a raspy voice tells Mitchell in clipped tones – his sentences die out about halfway through before he gathers strength for the next one – just how shattered and battered they have been over the last six days, how they have buried good men, fought, fallen back, buried some more, and so on, until here . . . they . . . are.

'These,' he says pointing to the ragtag group of kilted soldiers assembling around him, 'are all that is left of our brigade.'[4]

Even while Mitchell and the Scottish Sergeant talk, however, up on the bank a voice with a broad Scottish accent calls into the night to something or *someone*, maybe many of them, on the other side. 'Halt, who goes there?'

'Shoot, ye silly bastard,' roars the Sergeant, 'and challenge after!'[5]

With that, the sentry on high fires his rifle, waking hollow echoes in the night. The Sergeant and Mitchell charge up the bank, with the fresher man, the Australian, inevitably making it to the top first. Lieutenant Mitchell grabs the sentry's rifle and blasts away at all flickering shadows in the twilight that even *might* be approaching Germans. In response, there is no return fire, no screams, no thud of a falling body – no nothing.

Satisfied, Mitchell and the Sergeant descend to their own side of the bank and complete the formalities of the handover, allowing the weary and grateful Scots, the 'poor gallant blighters',[6] to depart.

Do the Australians wonder what the Scots are wearing under their kilts? Of course. But such questions are better left for the estaminet, when you're both so drunk that skunks would look askance. Here, the poor grizzled Jocks look so exhausted that it doesn't seem right to ask such a jocular question. And, as it happens, the Australians are done in themselves . . .

'Our exhausted men dropped into the ready-dug rifle possies against the rails,' Mitchell would recount. 'Officers and stronger NCOs patrolled up and down, straining eyes into the darkness, in this our most dangerous hour.'[7]

Just who or what is in front of them? No one has any idea, as the Scots who have left, the official 48th Infantry Battalion history records, 'could give no information whatsoever.'[8]

Late that night Colonel Imlay's staff record the situation of the 47th:

Spasmodic shelling and machine-gun firing throughout the night, everybody on alert and confident of resisting any attack by the enemy.[9]

———

Across from them, the German soldiers of the RIR 229 and 230 are also moving 'in great haste and strongly affected by the pouring rain' to the *'Bereitstellungsplätze* [deployment places]' that have been set up 'in the vicinity of the paths leading from Méaulte to Morlancourt. Despite the darkness the men were in position by around 4 am.'[10]

There on the muddy flats beside the Ancre River, a few hundred yards from the Australians, they wait.

—

At least the Australians of the 48th know that their right flank is covered, with the men of their brother battalion, the 47th. The 47th know as little specifically of what is in front of them as the 48th do, but they have more general reason to be wary. Right in front of them, just on the other side of the railway embankment, is the village of Dernancourt itself, now all still and empty, its trees and buildings providing a perfect covered approach for hostile Huns.

Even more troubling, the Scots they have relieved haven't been there long enough to dig any trenches along or behind the railway line – all they have managed are a few shallow indentations carved out of the embankment.

And so the men of the 47th follow their training and start to dig trenches, including some further back – 500 yards up the hill – against the possibility of the Germans breaking through, with still another trench dug in near the heights of the slope.

All up, with the 12th Brigade following the usual system – two battalions forward and two battalions in reserve, ready to move forward if necessary – the 48th Battalion now holds 1000 yards on the left while the 47th Battalion holds 1000 yards on the right. Each of those battalions has some 750 soldiers in forward positions. The other two Battalions – the 45th and 46th – hold a second line 1000 yards back up the slope, in the direction of Laviéville Heights, near 12th Brigade HQ. To the right of the 47th is 13th Brigade's 52nd Battalion, holding the embankment for another 1200 yards to the west.

—

Meanwhile, five miles to the west at Bonnay, the 9th Brigade's Commanding Officer, Brigadier Rosenthal, gives orders to Colonel Henry Goddard and Colonel Leslie Morshead, of the 35th and 33rd Battalions respectively. They are to immediately march their men to the Somme bridges from Sailly-le-Sec to Corbie, 'to prevent the enemy from crossing the Somme and from taking Corbie'.[11]

In this war of fluid movement, back and forth, controlling the bridges across the most fluid thing of all – the Somme – will be crucial in hindering the Germans.

Toying with his fob watch, as ever, Private John Hardie of the 33rd is soon on the move.

'We were hurriedly marched on down the bank of a river,' Hardie would recall, 'which I believe was the Somme. We arrived at a large town at sunrise where we were halted for breakfast and do you know several cows which had been following the column were now milked by the boys. Instead of having water to drink we had fresh milk for once. After an hour's halt the march was resumed . . .'[12]

So much for the milk. Now, where is the honey?

—

Praise the Lord and pass the hay. Meanwhile, 50 miles north of the river, Private Edmund Street has been trundling south with the rest of the 5th Division, the third of the five Australian divisions to head south to the Somme, sitting on the hard floor of a carriage usually reserved for horses. Sometimes the train races; sometimes, as Street would recall, it crawls 'like lame snails along the metals'.[13]

And *now* what? As the train nears the town of St Pol, it starts 'to race in the most frenzied manner'.[14]

Something is very wrong.

St Pol station flashes by and, having just cleared the town, the men feel 'a mighty concussion'. Above the roar of the speeding train comes the unmistakable 'burst of a monster shell'.[15]

The train keeps moving and a sigh of relief goes 'up from every Horse Box'.[16]

'The concussion of those fifteen-inch shells live with me yet,' Street would later write.

Private Eric Russell and his 58th Battalion, aboard a train behind Edmund Street, are not so lucky. 'On our journey down,' he later recalled to his mother, 'we had a horrible experience when passing through St Pol, which was being shelled. One shell hit the rear of the train, smashing three trucks to atoms, killing & wounding about 40 men & 15 horses. This was . . . pretty awful.'[17]

Brigadier Pompey Elliott, already safely arrived at Doullens, knows nothing of it, but his boys in the 58th Battalion have been hit by a long-range shell. Sixteen of his fine men are killed before the battle has even begun.

27 MARCH 1918, ALBERT, SCHICKERED SCHWEINHUNDE

Was um Himmels Willen ist da los? What, for heaven's sake, is going on here?

Hauptmann Rudolf Binding and his men had been roaring forward, advancing as never before against the remnants of the British defence, when suddenly, just outside Albert, they have to stop. They are not being fired on from the ground, and there is no strafing from the air. Their own airmen report there are no obstacles and no enemy to speak of between Albert and Amiens. The road to the city they are now targeting lies at their mercy, but they are not moving on it. And it cannot be because their division, on the prow of the attack, is tired – they have seen little real fighting to this point. And yet, they are as stationary as statues.

'Nobody could understand why,' Binding would comment. 'Our way seemed entirely clear.'[18]

Binding and a fellow officer requisition a car and carefully mosey their way into Albert itself, past all the army vehicles and soldiers standing around smoking.

The first clue as to the problem comes on the outskirts of town, when he begins to see 'curious sights' – German soldiers who . . . don't *look* like German soldiers. Some have top hats atop their military garb. Some are staggering drunkenly, while still others are 'driving cows before them . . . a hen under one arm, a bottle of wine and another open in their hand . . .'[19]

When Binding gets into Albert proper, it is even worse: 'The streets were running with wine.'

Suddenly, out of a cellar comes a *Leutnant* of the 2nd Marine Division – likely the same soldiers Fritz Nagel encountered just the day before – who is every bit as sober as he is, 'helpless and in despair'.[20]

'*Leutnant*,' Captain Binding says to him sharply, 'it is essential to get the men forward immediately.'[21]

Solemnly, emphatically and despairingly, the *Leutnant* makes reply as the sounds of drunken revelry continues to come from the cellar below: 'I cannot get my men out of that cellar without bloodshed.'[22]

The only possibility is if *der Hauptmann* Binding himself would like to try his hand?

'But it was no business of mine,' the 51-year-old Binding would acknowledge sadly of his chances of dealing successfully with drunken 20-year-olds. 'And I saw too that I could have done no more than he.'[23]

The only thing for it, for now, is to allow the men – once-great German soldiers now reduced to a bunch of *Trunkenbolde*, drunkards – to gorge themselves on drink and food, and then restore order, and move on.

———

Meanwhile, for the forward companies of the 47th Battalion, the first order of business on this evening of 27 March is to see if there is *any* sign of the marauding Germans. If so, the key is going to be to work out just where their broadest mass is, because, so far, the Australians are too few to be able to defend this whole line. Though they have their own small groups of men in key spots, much of the railway line embankment is held by no more than sentries, whose job it is to give as much warning to the others as they can about where the brutes are.

On the left of the 47th Battalion's sector, Captain Charles Symons, the Commanding Officer of D Company, closely studies the positions along his line and organises his defences accordingly.

Expertly surveying the ground and putting himself in the position of the enemy, he sees there are two obvious spots that the Germans are most likely to attempt to cross. One is an underpass, a narrow tunnel that goes beneath the tracks just south-west of his company's sector. The other is the level crossing where the road rises up gently to meet the railway, neatly intersecting it at right angles. If you had to get a large body of men across the barrier formed by the railway and the embankment, then this is precisely where you would send them. It is up to him and his men to make sure that does not happen for the Germans. To help hold it, Symons gives an order for his Scout Sergeant, 27-year-old Stan McDougall, to watch the crossing with two of his men. Good choice. Sergeant McDougall is a soldier like they don't make 'em anymore. He was a Tasmanian blacksmith before the war – an expert horseman, bushman, boxer and marksman to boot – who had already distinguished himself in the battle of Pozières, and his men seem to follow him in much the same way that summer follows the spring. That is, it is just the natural order of things, and there is a great deal of warmth all round. (And his family has always known it: before he had left for the war, in August 1915, his brother had half-jokingly said, using the family nickname for him, 'Well, Jerry old boy, goodbye and good luck. Mind you, win the Victoria Cross.' Rising to the occasion, Stan had replied, 'You can depend upon it that if it comes to the pinch I'll do my best.'[24])

There is a calm resolution to Stan that inspires confidence, in recent times stiffened to a certain steeliness for the fact that another younger brother, Private Wallace McDougall, had been killed by the Germans here on the Western Front.

Symons leaves them north of the level crossing on the lee side of the railway embankment, which is where they intend to dig in, Diggers.

They know that the Germans are very close. Will they attack?

Perhaps, and it is for this reason that McDougall and his men strain their eyes and their ears through the still tepid light.

—

The Western Australians at Hébuterne assume their natural position. Deciding to hit rather than waiting to *be* hit, they carefully push forward on this night of 27 March with the aim of taking out the nest of Huns in the village cemetery. First they outflank the Germans with the aid of suppressing fire from Lewis guns, before rushing in to do their best bayonet work and send the Fritzes below ground, where they belong. Then the Australians set to, finding 'possies' for their guns and setting up a defensive system, just as they had been training to do, so they have the best chance of holding the town when the Hun next come a'knocking on the gate in force.

In the first glow of dawn on the 28th – slowly, carefully – patrols inch forward to have a stickybeak at just where the *Boche* lines beyond the crest now lie.

Not there.

And not *there*.

Not anywhere!

They're *gorn!* Their midnight stunt had scared the Germans off! Whereas the closest Huns had been dug in just 20 yards ahead of the Diggers' line, the Germans' positions now lie vacant. Of course, the exultant Western Australians quickly push their own line over the crest.

They *have* held those bastards – pushed 'em back a bit too.

FIRST LIGHT, 28 MARCH 1918, DERNANCOURT, WHEN MCDOUGALL TOPPED THE SCORE

It's been a long and restless night, watching out for a German attack. At 6 am, however, with still no sign, McDougall decides to give his two men a spell.

They may 'stand down' – in fact, curl up for a kip behind the embankment – while he takes over the watch.

Footsteps!

Where?

Over there. Coming from along the railway line!

It proves to be two officers of the 47th Battalion, ensuring that all sentries are in place. With Sergeant McDougall in this spot, they know they have no worries, that all is as it should be. After a few friendly words, they move on, northwards and . . .

And now what?

Just to the east, where he knows the Germans are, McDougall now hears another sound.

There!

It is a familiar noise; he knows it instantly. It is 'the sound of bayonet scabbards flapping on the thighs of marching troops'.[25]

Christ.

As quietly as he can, but still with urgency, he calls to his two comrades to wake up.

One of the officers who has just left, Lieutenant George Reid, hears him and is the first to respond, calling back through the mist.

'Is that you, Mac?'

'Yes,' Sergeant McDougall replies, 'come up here quick. I think they're coming at us.'

The flapping is getting louder now, and a second after Lieutenant Reid clambers up the embankment, to look out into the mist, he exclaims, 'By Jove, they are!'[26]

What the Australians need now – and quickly – is more men to help. Now joined by his two comrades, McDougall runs to summon the rest of their platoon. The easiest way to cover the 100 yards to where the platoon lies is to hop up the embankment and skip along the top of the railway line, giving him an elevated, if exposed, position.

And there they are!

Out to his right as he runs, he can see them emerging from the mist, coming on in a long line towards the railway line, along the battalion's entire front: German soldiers, on the move. Mercifully, they haven't yet seen him, and McDougall and his two companions are able to get to the nearest section of his platoon, instantly rouse them and, with Lieutenant Reid now joining them, get seven men and rush back to their original spot at the crossing, which had been momentarily undefended.

But it ain't now.

On McDougall's signal, the nine Australian soldiers open fire – a vicious burst right into the heart of the approaching Germans. Screams and groans are heard, followed very quickly by return fire and, soon, something else. From out of the melee emerges a German grenade that arcs high and, an instant before it explodes, lands right by two Australian soldiers firing their Lewis gun. Both men are thrown off the gun, bleeding profusely.

McDougall races forward along the embankment, desperately alarmed.

Does the gun still work?

There is only one way to find out.

Gripping it with the familiarity of one who had been a Lewis gunner earlier in the war, and the passion of one who has long dreamed of a moment such as this, he runs *down* the slope like the Man from Snowy River – *ride boldly, lad, and never fear the spills* – straight at the Germans now going through at the level crossing, well ahead of his men. If it doesn't work, he is going to be dead. He cocks the weapon – being careful to angle it slightly away from him on his right side, to prevent the revolving magazine on top from catching in his clothing – then squeezes the trigger. The machine gun bursts into life, chattering and scattering the coming Germans straight in front. McDougall keeps going, as his admiring Captain would describe, 'firing the gun from his hip into the Hun, inflicting heavy casualties and causing confusion in their ranks.'[27]

Watching closely, McDougall's men are open-mouthed with admiration.

'When the Hun saw him running towards them at close quarters,' a Sergeant would recall, 'and firing the gun, the formation was broken by his daring.'[28] McDougall quickly changes the magazine on the Lewis, sliding it in with an expert hand. But, just as he does so, out to his left two German light machine-gun teams have made it to the top of the embankment and are firing into his own men!

With every moment precious, McDougall swivels the gun across his chest and presses the trigger. On the split instant, half the head of the nearest German explodes, splattering those behind him. Before they can react, McDougall is gunning *them* down, too. No fewer than seven dead Germans fall at his feet, allowing McDougall's men of the 47th to rush forward and grab their guns.

With such devastation falling on this pack of Germans trying to cross the ramparts, those following are not following long and quickly turn on their clicked heels.

Verrückte, madmen, up ahead!

With the battle blood-lust upon him – a kind of murderous, maniacal madness – McDougall is not content to leave it there and runs further along, on the chance of finding more of them.

Suddenly, he finds himself 'looking down on some twenty Germans, crouching in pot-holes and shell-holes on their side of the bank, obviously waiting for the signal to cross the line'.

Christ almighty! He is one, and they are many, and it is a moment . . . suspended . . . in . . . time . . .

If the Germans take cover and fire, there is no doubt about the result. McDougall would be hit by one of them and the line would be crossed. But McDougall simply does not give them that chance, and reactsontheinstant!

Bringing his gun up once more, he is immediately spraying them, ten bullets a second pouring forth. The survivors quickly flee, 'McDougall then standing on the bank, with his gun at the hip, chasing them with its fire.'[29]

Although the actions of McDougall and his men have prevented the Germans from breaking through the northern half of the Australian line, the southern half has already fallen. The German soldiers are brazenly crossing the line, a veritable first splash of enemy lapping over the barrier that risks becoming a flood if it is not stopped and those who have crossed dealt with.

Worse for McDougall's 47th, the Germans attack them from both behind and in front, making their position untenable.

Again, the whole battle hangs in the balance.

McDougall, accompanied by his mate, Sergeant James Lawrence, charges south-west, firing first along the line to stop the flow and then down onto the 50 German soldiers who have already crossed. By now the barrel of this new gun is so hot that his left hand has blistered and he can no longer hold it, but there is a way around this.

Sergeant Lawrence steps forward and, with his thick leather gloves for protection, holds the gun steady while the blacksmith from Tassie continues to fire with his uninjured hand, the sweat pouring off him, his muscles screaming for relief, but never wavering.

After some minutes they cease fire, sensing the German onslaught has been demoralised. Lawrence and another Sergeant start to move forward to detain the Germans scattered on the ground in front of them.

In the corner of his eye, on the very periphery of his peripheral vision, McDougall catches movement. Swinging his head around, he sees a German officer pop up from a hidey-hole, a crevice in the embankment, to take one silent step forward and level his revolver at Sergeant Lawrence's head.

'Look out behind you!' McDougall shouts, and only just in time. Lawrence reacts like a scalded cat and, in the process of swinging around to bring his rifle to bear, trips over just as the German fires.

The bullet misses.

Another 47th Battalion Sergeant does not, and guns the German officer down.

McDougall and Lawrence resume firing on the Germans below and, as they do so – alternating their fire by shouting 'reloading!' once the shooter's ammo is spent, keeping their fire constant – two of their men race around the left flank of the Germans who have crossed, so as to come at them from behind.

The instant McDougall pauses, these two step forward, point their revolvers at the German officer's head and order them to surrender.

Perhaps rarely in this war have so many German officers and soldiers been so absolutely delighted to do so.

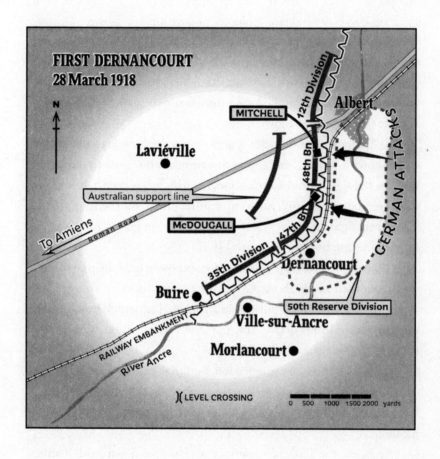

This part of the battle is over.

'If it hadn't been for McDougall,' Sergeant Bill Brown would note, 'the enemy would have got through. He did most of the work.'[30] And an extraordinary effort from the 47th Battalion, having succeeded in stopping a major German attack stone-dead – at least for the moment.

—

Further north along the line, the flanking 48th Battalion are facing a similar attack in front and just south of Albert. Alerted by the firing to their south, it is a fairly sure bet that 'shits are trumps' to their east. Sure enough, it doesn't take long before German soldiers start coming at them from out of the mist.

The Australians of the 48th spread out on the lee side of the railway embankment, watch them approach and take aim. Well-trained, they wait for the signal from Captain George Mitchell – even as the Cap'n calls out the range '200 yards' to remind those who've forgotten to lower their sights to do so – while still keeping an eye on him, waiting for him to drop his arm to signal 'FIRE'.

As Mitch drops his arm, his men rise, exposing only the tops of their torsos and their heads above the railway embankment.

'Lewis guns and rifles blended in a chorus,' Captain Mitchell would proudly record in his diary. 'The grey mobs on our front wavered and broke at a hundred yards.'[31]

Among those Germans is Rudolf Binding, who is surprised at his own lack of panic or fear as he calmly watches comrades fall around him, a kind of unearthly feeling that endures . . . even when . . . he is hit too!

It feels like the 'blow of a hammer' and he goes down hard, instinctively putting his hand where the bullet has struck. To his amazement, there is none of the gushing blood that he has seen so many times when other soldiers have been hit. On inspection, he finds he has suffered no more than 'a weal'. Miraculously, the rifle bullet has gone through the two thick coats he is wearing because of the freezing conditions before hitting 'a pair of riding-breeches of English cloth, against which the English bullet stopped respectfully and fell to earth. I picked it up almost like a friendly greeting and stuck it in the pocket of the breeches which it had failed to pierce.'[32]

The battle goes on.

With a shout of warning, Captain Mitchell looks to his right rear.

Bloody hell!

It is a line of men coming over a rise and moving towards them from behind, where it was thought the Allied defensive line was. This is either reinforcements coming up or *another* group of Germans who have broken through and are now rolling up the Australian resistance, pushing in behind them.

Mitchell moves quickly.

Plunging down the embankment to reach his Commanding Officer, he tells Captain Lionel Carter of the 48th Battalion, 'Captain, I'll go across and find out the strength of these birds . . .'

'All right,' Carter, a former blacksmith turned Methodist missionary, says grimly. (No turning the other cheek for him. He wants to *hammer* the brutes.)

As Mitchell hurries off, the line of men in front coming their way are even thicker in the half-light.

'You are sure they are our chaps?' Carter calls out after him, almost hopefully.

'No,' Mitchell yells back, drawing his pistol. 'I'm damned if I am.'

And be damned. Carter is right upon them before he can see clearly enough, by their square helmets and grey uniforms, that they are indeed Huns! As close as he is, he has no choice.

Bursting forward, he thrusts his pistol at the officer's head, just as that officer – seemingly unaware, like all of his men, that the Australians are so close – is trying to take his pistol from its holster.

'Up! Up! Up! Damn you!'[33] Mitchell yells.

In the end, the episode is proof positive that the old adage of the Wild West – 'A Smith & Wesson beats four aces every time' – still holds true in this modern world.

Pistol in his face, the officer has long given up all notion of resistance. All he can do is babble his apologies in a mixture of broken English, French and German. As Carter's men have now come up, the other Germans surrender with equal resignation, and the Australians are soon able to hear something of their story. They had been a platoon of 52 Prussian soldiers when they had started out – from an original regiment of the 50th Division boasting some 3000 men – but the cards had not fallen their way, and they had already been involved in a vicious battle where they had lost two of their officers and twenty of their men.

Some of them are still so shaken that it almost seems like they are glad to be taken prisoner – at least that means they have a good chance of staying *alive*.

———

Scheiße.

Far on the 48th's left, in the houses at the edge of Albert beyond Mitchell's view – facing C Company of the 48th Battalion – *Leutnant* Fritz Nagel and his comrades of *Kraftwagen Flak No. 82* have come up with an unorthodox plan.[34]

It's risky, but it's the best they can do to help the isolated Marines with their attack, scheduled for 8 am, and doomed to failure if the one pod of Australian machine-gunners are not dealt with. For their worst fears have been realised and it has been confirmed that the British soldiers formerly there have been relieved by the brutes from the far south.

This machine-gun nest is HOT and entirely oblivious to rifles, machine-gun fire and charging Germans soldiers, whom they pick off like rabbits.

The Marine *Hauptmann* has called for the big guns to take them out. Specifically, the *Hauptmann* wants *the* big gun – the 77mm Krupp anti-aircraft gun of *Kraftwagen Flak No. 82*. In these narrow streets on the western edge of Albert, the machine-gun crew is holding up the whole German advance, and they must be destroyed.

Jawohl, Hauptmann.

But there is a real problem. The only way the Germans can be sure of hitting their target is to bring their gun forward and shoot horizontally by line of sight. And yet . . .

'The minute our barrel was visible to the Australian riflemen – some only 50 yards away – they would fill us full of lead before we could fire the first shot.'[35]

Nagel puts a new plan to the *Hauptmann*. Why not send the infantry in first, to subdue *die* riflemen who are defending their machine-gunning comrades in the house, and then follow up hard with the gun? Once we get our gun close enough, several hundred yards past the riflemen, a 77mm round through the house will blow it apart.

Der Hauptmann is not at all keen. Nagel himself thinks 'the whole thing . . . rather terrifying . . .'[36] but there is no other way, even if, again, he must risk making Dorothy a widow.

Still, best not to explain the whole thing in too much detail to the crew for fear of *sie unnötig zu beunruhigen*, putting the wind up them.

The exception is the driver, who must be fully apprised, and Nagel takes him to the roof of the house they have been sheltering behind to show him the machine-gun nest 400 yards away – and the crossroads, about 200 yards before it, that they must get to before firing. Obviously, they are going to have to race. Any firefight with the enemy soldiers in the house, and the riflemen all around, and they will lose.

Strangely, the driver – an odd fellow, inordinately proud of his truck and the power of its engine – seems entirely untroubled by the prospect ahead. And it *is* odd. At 35 years old, the tall, strong Sergeant Eduard Rupp, with his broad red face, is much older than the rest of the crew and a man whose passions are as limited as they are *deep*. A racing driver before the war, 'his conversation was exclusively about racing, women, motors and more women'.[37] Oh, and his truck, a standard-issue 1912 Opel army truck, which nevertheless he has souped up to coax every last ounce of horsepower it has in it . . . and some more besides!

It can be done, Rupp assures Nagel. He can roar in with the gun atop their flatbed, the crew can fire, and he can get them out, 'without fail'.[38] Nagel then briefs the crew, and he is only half-joking when telling the gunner that he must make sure he and Rupp have jumped from the cab and their heads are *well* out of the way before he actually fires the gun straight ahead. (That should go without saying, but you can never tell with gunners, who, as a breed, are always keen to pull whatever trigger is before them. In any case, neither the gunner nor the crew laughs, as all realise the size of the task ahead.)

Half an hour before Zero, all is in readiness.

Fifteen minutes before Zero, the heavy artillery bombardment comes over from somewhere behind the town. 'The big shells coming from behind us,' Nagel would recall, 'some seemed to shriek as if they were tumbling over on the air. Salvo after salvo exploded on the other side. The geysers of mud and debris could be seen easily, but we were disappointed because none of the shells landed on the enemy directly in front of us.'[39]

At Zero, the call goes up – '*Vormarsch!* Advance!' – although so loud is the motor that the order is more seen than heard.

The German soldiers rush forward, blazing away as they go. Some fall to the enemy marksmen, but they send enough firepower back the other way that the fire of those marksmen on the road is diminished.

Und JETZT, and NOW!

Sergeant Rupp stamps on the accelerator, shifts through the gears and within seconds they are belting down the street, the scattered *pings* of bullets on metal indicating that they are taking fire, but so far it has been ineffectual.

They reach the crossroads. Rupp slams on the brakes.

Jetzt, jetzt, JETZT!

Und . . . Feuer!

'My feet had barely touched the ground,' Nagel would recount, 'when our first shell came screaming out of the barrel. The flash and crack almost flattened me . . . The very first shell had slammed right into the nest, as did every one of the following shots. Men could be seen jumping out of the windows. The house seemed to explode and started to burn. The target existed no more.'[40]

The riflemen start to take a fearful revenge on them as the bullets hitting all around 'reach a crescendo . . . A rifle bullet had knocked off one of our gunners.'[41]

The problem facing them now is to get back to safety, which is difficult given the truck is 'pointed in the wrong direction . . . To go back and reach the safety of the first house in reverse gear would not be possible because the truck was too slow.'[42]

Nagel waves his arm for his men to follow him, and they quickly take shelter in the nearest ditch. The key, now, is whether the rest of the German soldiers can catch up with them. If not, they are behind the Australian front-lines and able to be finished off with one grenade. For the moment, no sign . . .

They are in 'a tight spot'.[43] And then it happens.

Just as the fire starts to hit the truck, *Leutnant* Nagel is suddenly aware – even over the roar of the battle – that the worthy Sergeant Rupp is shouting something in his ear. And now Rupp leaps from the safety of the ditch, grabs the crank and, with two massive turns, has the motor roaring into life. Leaping back up into the driver's seat and turning the truck on a penny, he is barrelling back towards them!

Now! Now! Now!

With a roar of their own, Nagel and the gun crew leap from their trench and pile onto the back of the truck as Rupp makes like the racing driver he was, down the final straight at Le Mans.

'I have never understood why nobody got hurt in that wild ride . . .'[44] Nagel would recount.

Within twenty seconds they are back to safety behind the first house, with everyone clapping Rupp on the back and laughing that maniacally joyous laugh of those who have faced death . . . only to find themselves alive, alive, ALIVE. Can you believe we are *alive?*

Rupp is the hero of the hour, for what Nagel characterises as his 'magnificent performance'[45] will later be recognised with an Iron Cross First Class.

'What made you jump on the truck?' Nagel asks over the roar of the ongoing battle, now diminishing a little as the German soldiers push forward.

'The motor is in fine shape,' Sergeant Rupp replies simply, 'and I am not letting those *Hurensöhne*, sons of bitches, shoot it up.'[46]

—

Never a dull day in Doullens, lately.

And it is an odd thing, but there it is. Just as the swaying of a railway carriage can rock grown men to sleep like babies in the cradle, so too does the slowing sway of the train preparing to stop tend to wake them again.

And so it is in the cold light of this morning, as the men of Jimmy Downing's 57th Battalion gradually come to in a place that seems to have a scattering of brick houses and large chimneys. Lightly they grumble as they rise, in the same manner as robins chirp and dogs growl, because that is just what comes naturally at this hour.

Where are we, Dig?

The sign on the platform has it: ***Doullens***.

The 5th Division are nearly there.

'A bugle blew a note and we stretched our cramped limbs and scrambled stiffly from the train . . . We began a march of which we knew not the goal, of which we knew only that it would be long and weary.'[47]

—

Less a changeover than an invasion in itself, at 4.30 pm on 28 March, General Rawlinson arrives at General Gough's Fifth Army HQ at Dury to take command of what will now be called the Fourth Army – complete with all of Rawlinson's staff, 300 strong! Once installed, he rings around his corps commanders to get a feel for just where Fritz is and what he's up to and . . .

And General Rawlinson, we have reached General Herbert Watts, your Commanding Officer of XIX Corps, and he is on the line.

Watts's men, Rawlinson already knows, are just hanging on, a little to the east of Villers-Bretonneux.

But now things are *really* grim, Watts tells him, emphasising that he is expecting a big push from the Germans on the morrow.

How grim?

'They may well get us by lunch-time and you by teatime.'[48]

—

As for Monash's men of the 10th and 11th Brigades, up at Morlancourt, they are still advancing cautiously, trying to push the line out as far as they can. They advance by section rushes, with the force of 2000 riflemen breaking into small groups, similar to the stormtroopers, and rushing forward in short bursts across a front of 4000 yards. The idea is to rush to whatever cover they can, bring fire to bear on the enemy ahead – forcing them to keep their heads down and their rifles un-aimed – and then rush again.

With some dozens of cricket-team-sized groups doing the same, they are able to bring constant fire on the Germans, even while giving them the smack in the snout, and worse, they so desperately deserve. Remember, every smack drives them back. The ultimate aim is to shock the Germans, to suddenly rise up when they are least expecting it, to go from reeling backwards (as the British have been doing) to charging forwards (as Australians do) and, ideally, get right among the Squareheads with the bayonets.

In truth, however, the eggs-a-cook boys don't come across nearly as many Germans on their move forward as the Tommies had led them to expect, meaning that this, their first action down on the Somme – their own baptism of fire – turns out to be relatively easy work.

They continue to push forward slowly.

—

Still stupefied by how quickly the Germans have moved west and how seemingly powerless the British forces are to halt them, on this late afternoon of 28 March the French liaison officer at General Gough's

HQ, Paul Maze, is on the road just south of Amiens when he sees, up ahead, a line of cars surrounded by French officers in blue uniforms.

Venturing forward, on the reckoning he might be able to give them some information on the road he has just travelled down, he is suddenly accosted.

'*Qui êtes vous?*' one of the officers, with a chin like a clenched fist, snaps at him. '*Et à quelle unité appartenez-vous?*'[49] Who the hell are you? And what unit do you belong to?

The speaker is a high-ranking French officer, with a uniform that positively *shines* with the medals sewn into two rows on his chest, just as do the two rows of gold leaf all around his peaked cap.

Maze explains that he is the liaison officer at General Gough's headquarters.

'He's not in command anymore,' snaps the officer.

And it suddenly clicks with Maze. He is speaking to General Foch.

Maze salutes sharply and races back to Dury, through streets clogged with lorries of the Fourth and Fifth Army, all heading west, away from the battle.

In the small garden in front of the house in Dury that General Gough is using as Fifth Army HQ[50] – where Haig also has his HQ – Maze finds the man himself, deeply immersed in his thoughts.

'I am no longer in command of the Fifth Army,' Gough says rather sadly, 'but before I tell you what has happened, if you have any urgent news you must give it to General Rawlinson, who is now in command . . . He is a fine soldier; you will like him.'[51]

Maze is soon told the story.

General Foch had paid a visit to Gough two days earlier and unleashed some 'abrupt . . . short and deprecatory'[52] remarks about the Fifth Army before summarily dismissing him. Still the gentlemanly Gough will utter not a word against Foch or the man who has replaced him, General Rawlinson. As Maze and Gough take their leave of each other with a handshake, the English General simply says, 'We must win the war. We must not let our personal feelings distract us for a moment from our purpose.'[53]

Gough climbs into the back of his staff car and is driven away, to head home to England where his wife, Daisy, awaits.

Privately? Gough is all of hurt, bewildered and seething.

'I cannot say that I approved of the Fifth Army being handed over body and soul to the French,' he would later allow, 'even if Foch was Generalissimo.'[54]

———

After a long journey lasting 48 hours by train and foot, the remaining battalions of the 5th Division arrive in their cramped horse and cattle carriages to Mondicourt, east of Doullens, where Jimmy Downing's battalion had disembarked.

Everybody off!

Out they get, not forgetting to have some fun as they do so.

'Here and there,' Edmund Street would record of their experience, 'a chap remembered that we were out of trucks generally used for livestock. Some bellowed and tossed their heads, others neighed and whinnied, others still, bleated like lambs and sheep. The mob was in good fettle.'[55]

At least they are now.

In short order the mood changes somewhat. In front of the men – full packs up and on their shoulders, together with their rifles – the long, war-weary road beckons. As soldiers proceed to the south towards Louvencourt, they are confronted by hundreds of devastated French refugees crossing their path from the east.

Among them, of course, are Tommy soldiers.

'Ah've lost me unit, *Choom!*' they frequently offer as they pass, by way of explanation.

'Your mates are ahead,' the Australians retort. 'You won't find them in the rear.'[56]

Still the Australians push on, push south, with good-natured chaffing soon returning.

'Won't our pyjamas feel nice tonight!' they call.

'Get off and walk, you cow!' they call to a mounted and retreating British officer. 'Your horse is getting tired!'

(What's he going to do? Arrest them? Him and whose army? Not his. He doesn't have one anymore.)

'This is better than Aussie!'[57]

The last is hard to argue with, at least in terms of scenic beauty. Picturesque village after picturesque village falls to their tread, until in the middle of one of them, Louvencourt, the blessed cry rings out.

'Companyyyyyyy . . . halt!'

Battalion intelligence men soon appear and guide them to their billets – what else but barns that usually house cows, horse and sheep?

But no one is complaining. Private Edmund Street and his mates of C Coy have a barn to themselves and soon take the opportunity to have a much-needed kip before getting up an hour or two later to have a look around. A few French civilians still remain and, of course, 'a crowd of Tommy stragglers'.

And what's that they're calling?

Of course. Once again they hear what will soon become a familiar refrain.

'Ah've lost me unit, *Choom!*'

Of course they have.

Edmund Street is just one who is unimpressed.

'The crooks of the Fifth Army had bolted. The wasters in the Battalions had made for the rear.'[58]

Careful, though. They're not all like that.

'But it must be kept in mind,' Street would equally note, 'that many thousands of the Fifth Army at that moment were fighting like heroes, to the death.'

And not even all the wasters are all bad.

'Our presence seemed to inspire most of the timid men and I think that many went back to the line. And were probably killed there.'[59]

—

It has been a long and arduous day at Dernancourt for the German 50th Reserve Division, but after trying to press forward on all fronts, only to be stymied at every turn, finally as the sun wanes so too does their attack. They wait for darkness before withdrawing, less 800 men lost, killed, wounded or taken prisoner.

'The attack stalled at the railway embankment,' the RIR 229 history would ruefully record. Meanwhile, the story, and the subsequent historical account, is the same for the RIR 230 on their left.

'It was no longer possible . . . to renew the attack. The Englishman sat unmoved on the railroad embankment, between himself and the village a completely open terrain. Who showed himself there, became victim to *englischen Scharfschützen*, English snipers.'[60]

Unbeknownst to the Germans, the defenders are not English but Australian snipers – many of them farm boys who've grown up with a rifle as practically an extension of their left arm.

———

Kronprinz Rupprecht is thrilled as report after report comes in of successful attacks, with an extraordinary *four* English divisions captured on just his own front. He is sure that, after all, they are 'standing just before the success of the final breakthrough'.

Ah, but the Gods of War are nothing if not fickle.

'In the late afternoon,' he notes in his diary, '*die Hiobsbotschaft*, the crushing news, came in that today's attack . . . has failed . . .'[61]

It seems the English have thrown everyone, from cooks and bottle-washers to even worker battalions, to hold the enemy. What is more, so many horses have been killed in recent weeks by enemy planes, and particularly today, that the Germans cannot get their artillery forward in sufficient mass to continue the attack.

And yet, surely, the thin replacement forces cannot last long? Rupprecht retains hope.

'Thus, it will require probably only a final push to get them to collapse!'[62]

As for General Ludendorff, he is looking at the situation north of the Somme with growing concern, particularly where the advance has been slowed by moving over the old Somme battlefield, replete with so many shell holes – some of which can swallow tanks whole. Plus, the arrival of the Australians on the scene has had a real effect.

'The [Australians] formed a new front north of the Somme,' he would note, 'which was sure to be difficult to overcome . . . while our armies were no longer strong enough to overcome them unaided. The ammunition was not sufficient and supply became difficult.'[63]

On a purely personal note, if Ludendorff is somewhat distracted at the moment, it is principally because there has still been no trace of dear Erich found. It is with this in mind that he puts a notice out to German soldiers in the area, offering a high reward for any information leading to 2/Lt Pernet's whereabouts.[64]

EVENING, 28 MARCH 1918, MORLANCOURT RIDGE, A PARLIAMENT OF OWLS, A PUSH OF PATROLS

General Monash commands, they do.

At noon, his orders had been very clear, and now the men execute them. Yesterday they'd probed the Germans in tiny groups and succeeded in advancing the line a good 500 yards. But today? Well, today, for the first time since the whole wretched German advance began just a week earlier, the Australians are going to push back in a BIG way, heading east away from Amiens. Monash's two brigades, 8000 men, will break free from their trenches and attack Fritz full-on.

RAH!

With that in mind, just after 5 pm, the first patrols are sent carefully forward from the current line being held, seeking to find exactly where the Germans are strong, where they are weak. A first wave of soldiers follow behind them, pushing forward accordingly. (For Charles Bean, who chronicles the exercise, it resembles nothing so much as the 2nd Battle of Krithia in the Dardanelles. 'The enemy was distant, the ground was open pasture, almost as level. As at Krithia, the advance was made towards the end of the afternoon in plain daylight . . .'[65])

Still the inevitable happens as an Australian patrol of the 42nd Battalion – Queenslanders all, under Sergeant Alston Wheeldon – creeps close to the village of Sailly-Laurette, lying on the northern bank of the Somme River, and which may or may not be in German hands. For suddenly the Australians come under fire from a German patrol stalking west – seeking to find out where the Australian front-line is – and throw themselves to the ground.

Emboldened, the Germans continue to move forward. One of them even cries out in his thick Teutonic accent to the Australians: 'Hands *oop!*'

Ja?

Nah.

'Hands *oop* be buggered,'[66] cries a Queenslander in return.

In an instant, the men from north of the Tweed have jumped to their feet and are pouring fire into the massed Germans, who drop their rifles and run as fast as they can. The final score is Queensland 9, Germany 0, with the Queenslanders having killed six German soldiers, wounded two and taken one prisoner.

Similar clashes take place across the line, with mixed results, but the outcome is clear. The first Australian wave takes up a position 1000 yards forward of the original line, followed by a second wave moving through the first and advancing another 1000 yards again – sometimes against intense machine-gun fire.

By this evening of 28 March, as the Diggers are digging in on the ridge, now only a mile west of the village of Morlancourt, the 3rd Division has pushed its line 2000 yards to the east, ready for whatever the Germans throw at them next. Most importantly, from the point of view of morale, for the first time since Operation Michael began, the senior staff officers at GHQ whose job it is to mark the front-line positions by use of pins and red cotton move both to the *right* on the map.

RAH!

And, of course, the ever-confident General Sir John Monash is proud as punch.

He writes to wife, Hannah, on this evening: 'You will see that I have been in the thick of it. A half dozen of the best Divisions in France are rapidly assembling, and there is every possible reason to believe that we shall succeed in stopping the *Bosch* attempt to get to Amiens. If we can hold out for two or three days longer, events are expected which will transform the situation.'[67]

The effect of the Australians bolstering the shattered British 35th Division along the line has been heartening.

'We thus had [north of the Somme],' Monash would proudly recount, 'a sprinkling of stout first class Divisions at various parts of the line and the effect of their arrival was electric and remarkable. The advent of my own Division . . . had an astonishing effect in stiffening up everybody on both flanks, and the tendency to run was checked; people began to regain confidence, and measures for re-organization of the whole line were commenced.'[68]

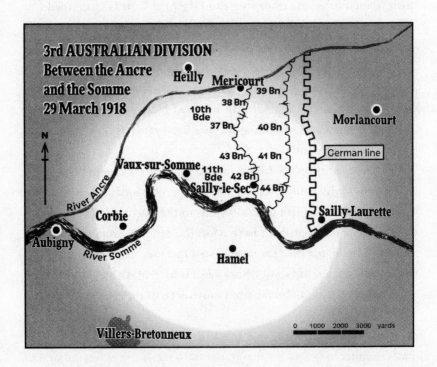

EVENING, 28 MARCH 1918, GENERAL HENRY RAWLINSON GETS TO GRIPS

In his quarters at Dury, the newly installed Commanding Officer of the Fourth Army, General Henry Seymour Rawlinson, GCB, GCSI, GCVO, KCMG, is somewhere between coming to grips with the situation that he has inherited . . . and having that same situation grip *him* by the throat and start to strangle him.

On this same day he's taken over, what's left of his army – half what it had been just a week ago – has fallen back south of the Somme another six miles. So totally demoralised and nearly leaderless are those who remain that Rawlinson has no formation that he can rely on to stand and fight. The enemy are now closing on Villers-Bretonneux. He knows if that village falls too, the German thrust must succeed, because Amiens will fall – likely by tomorrow, unless he can throw determined soldiers who will *fight* onto the line.

Most disturbing of all is the position of XIX Corps, which is holding six miles of front extending south from the Somme to the Luce River, some three miles east of Villers-Bretonneux. In the last week, the corps has lost no less than two-thirds of its infantry – 20,000 men killed, wounded and taken prisoner, many of the latter without firing a shot – so it is really only 'holding' that front conceptually, rather than actually. One tap on the snout and the fight will surely be all over.

'The situation is serious,' General Rawlinson writes this night to General Foch, 'and unless fresh troops are sent here in the next two days, I doubt whether the remnants of the British XIX Corps which now hold the line to the East of Villers-Bretonneux can maintain their positions . . . I feel some anxiety for the security of Amiens and draw your attention to the danger in which this place will be if the enemy renews his attacks from the east before fresh troops are available. I fear that the troops of the XIX Corps are not capable of executing a counteroffensive.'[69]

In fact, most of the British troops directly to the south of the Somme are no longer from the original XIX Corps, which has been effectively shattered. Rather, they are men from an ad hoc army formation dubbed 'Carey's Force' – named for the British martinet, General George Carey, who is charged with throwing together 'every cook, batman, driver, messman, artilleryman, unmounted cavalryman, any of the odds and sods who, though wearing uniform, have never used a rifle in their life. What a bewildered lot they looked, lying there wondering what was going to happen next.'[70]

Some 3000 strong, their job is to help the XIX Corps defend that *arc de défense* south of the Somme that radiates out from the hub of Villers-Bretonneux. Of the remaining Tommies of the XIX Corps' crumbling 61st Division, who have been in the line since *der Tag*, many of them are the ones assigned the task of teaching Carey's men how to shoot – while also, nominally, trying to hold the line, less for grim death than among grim death. The remnants of one of its battalions, which has lost over half its men so far, are at the village of Marcelcave, a mere two miles east of Villers-Bretonneux. It is obvious, most of all to them, that they will not last long.

As the battalion history records of this evening's fighting, '6.00 pm. Enemy attacked the Eastern end of the village and the troops on our right poured into the cutting. Every effort was made to force these units to return to their defences or to take up position North and South of the railway line, but it was quite useless and they continued to pour into the cutting.'[71]

The Brits are being run out of the town by Fritz. New troops must be sent. And now!

Who to send? Not only have the Australians already done remarkably well at Hébuterne, north of the Somme, but there are equally crack Australian troops, the 9th Brigade under General John Monash, who are now positioned some three miles north at Corbie.

The answer is obvious: Rosenthal's 9th will have to go to Villers-Bretonneux.

—

The Australians of the 14th Brigade at Louvencourt, meanwhile, behind the line west of Hébuterne, are about to have breakfast.

'An Anzac wafer each,' Private Edmund Street would ruefully recall. 'A loaf of bread and a tin of jam to 25 men. We tossed for the bread and jam . . . This tossing up was decided so that at least two men could have a feed. Our stomachs began to think our throats were cut.'[72]

Still, they're not Australians for nuttin' and – always a fair fist of living off the land – they send foraging parties out to scour the local farms, only to find, in one particular case, those buggers of A Company have beaten them to it! Just as they arrive, the B Company men see half a dozen men in the farmyard just before the shot of a rifle rings out and a headless chook is suddenly running hither and thither. The Digger who fired the shot steps forward to claim his prize when suddenly the farmhouse door is flung open, revealing Madame, a picture of disgust, disdain and dismissal all in one.

With 'a furious flurry of skirts', the stout old lady swoops forward, claims her chook and, pausing only to 'fling a withering glance at the gaping Digger',[73] goes back inside. She slams the door, a final exclamation mark for her views on the subject.

'The whole thing was so sudden,' one Digger would recount. 'It was a full minute before the dazed Digger woke up. Gradually a grin spread over his face and off he went elsewhere to scrounge . . . Everywhere hungry men were looking for food.'[74]

—

Meanwhile, 15 miles to the south at Corbie, Colonel Henry Goddard, Commander of the 35th Battalion of the 9th Brigade, is worried. He has received word that his men, along with the rest of the 9th Brigade, might soon be leaving their guard over the Corbie bridges to move south of the Somme to Cachy. On this misty morning, he has taken two officers with him to reconnoitre and, on horseback, they cross the river at Sailly-le-Sec.

Everywhere now they find rack and ruin and the shattered remnants of British units of the Fifth Army, whom, true to reports, 'appear to have been having a bad time'.[75]

Pushing off along the road to the town of Hamel, they are soon having a bad time themselves. As they approach the village, a scattered rain of death begins to fall upon them.

'The Huns were still furiously shelling the town. It had been abandoned by the British, evidently without waiting for a fight.'[76]

As they continue, they come across an old French couple trudging into town.

'Where are you going?' Goddard asks in his best schoolboy French.

'Hamel,' the old man says tiredly.

'That is madness,' the Australian remonstrates. 'You will be killed immediately if you enter.'

'We no longer care,' says the old man. 'We fled two days ago, and have tried to sleep in outhouses, on the ground, but my wife cannot sleep without her bed and will only die of exposure. So we are going back to die in our bed.'[77]

Colonel Goddard tries to persuade them not to do it, but it is a task beyond him. They continue on their way to Corbie, leaving behind 'an inferno of shell fire'[78] and lamenting the imminent death of the old couple.

Arriving at Corbie just after noon, Colonel Goddard finds Brigadier Charles Rosenthal and they ride back to their headquarters at Bonnay, where they find a flurry of activity and many sighs of relief that the Brigadier is back.

Rosenthal receives the news shortly afterwards, direct from General Monash: the whole of the 9th Brigade must move south of the Somme, *tonight*, to bolster the British forces there. They are to be under the command of the British 61st Division.

It is believed, General Monash explains to the Brigadier, that the Germans are going to make a concerted thrust at Amiens via Villers-Bretonneux, just three miles south of their current position. And so Brigadier Rosenthal must get his men into position at the town of Cachy, just west of Villers-Bretonneux, as quickly as possible to act as reserve, ready to counter-attack quickly should any part of the front-line collapse.

Rosenthal, a man who has already been wounded five times in the war to this point, including at Gallipoli, and whom Charles Bean would say 'loved not only to be in the front line, but to be seen there',[79] is quick to give the orders accordingly.

(His men admire Rosenthal for his courage. One time he had been out in No-Man's Land inspecting his wire when he had seen a few Germans – and promptly captured three of them for their trouble!)

The order goes out, to **ALL UNITS OF 9TH BRIGADE GROUP**, that they must **MOVE AT ONCE VIA CORBIE TO CACHY**.[80]

The first in the Order of March are the Diggers of Colonel Morshead's 33rd Battalion, who have been in Corbie for the past two days, among them Private John Hardie, who would record the mood of the morning. 'My word some of the men were having high times. Plenty of champagne and some of them were strutting about with top hats instead of their tin lids. Some actually had the cheek to wear girly overcoats.'[81]

But, having received word that the battalion is to move out within hours, the men now trade their top hats for tin hats, their female overcoats for khakis and leather jerkins once more. By nightfall of this Good Friday, they are on their way to becoming the first Australian brigade on the south side of the Somme, moving on Cachy.

'I may state,' Hardie recounts, 'that all along the road we saw gun pits but not one gun in position. A chap out of the Royal Artillery afterwards told me that they couldn't leave their guns in position at night as they didn't know where Fritz was.'[82]

Hardie soaks it all up and gets his bearings, his major distress coming from seeing so many dead horses. As a farrier back in Australia, he'd prospered because of his gentle way with them – they somehow knew he didn't want to hurt them – and it now hurts *him* to see so many slain.

Brigadier Rosenthal, meanwhile, at 8 o'clock this night, is pleased to report to 61st Division HQ at Gentelles – just a mile south-west from Cachy and two miles back from Villers-Bretonneux – that his men are

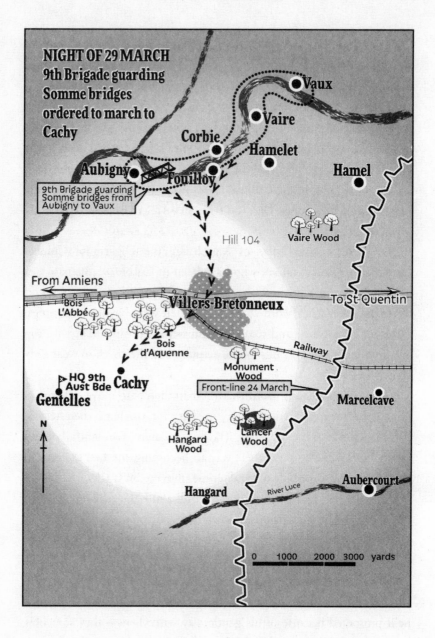

on their way. The Commanding Officer of the 61st Division, General Colin Mackenzie, is pleased to hear it and informs Rosenthal that the key task of his 9th Brigade will be to prepare themselves so that if the line is broken, his men can immediately counter-attack. Oh, and one more thing, Brigadier. You will set up your own HQ here with me at Gentelles, rather than up front with your men at Villers-Bretonneux, where the action is likely to be.

Such an order is anathema to Rosie. He had been at his best on the first day of the Gallipoli landing, leading from the front throughout. And he had been with his men through many scrapes ever since, always where the action is. And now his British commander wants him to stay here with him, well removed from the action? Rosie can barely stand it but, still, he must obey orders and does the only thing he can. He puts his finest battalion commander, Colonel John Goddard, right up front, in temporary command. That way, in the event of an attack – and even should the telephone lines between Gentelles and Villers-Bretonneux be cut in a battle, as they would likely be – Goddard can coordinate the moves of all the 9th Brigade's battalions, should that prove necessary.

('A sticky British general would not allow any of us out of his sight,' is how Rosenthal would later describe it, 'so that it was left to Goddard to keep the brigade together . . .'[83])

Colonel Goddard moves quickly, catching up with his men of the 35th Battalion in Corbie and marching them four miles to Cachy – just a coo-ee's call from Villers-Bretonneux – where they finally arrive at 2.30 am to find shelter and get some much-needed kip in the empty sheds of the abandoned aerodrome nearby.

—

With Rosie and the 9th Brigade now gone south to Cachy, who better to replace them guarding the bridges over the Somme around Corbie than Pompey Elliott and his equally first-class 15th Brigade?

Elliott gets the phone call from 5th Divisional HQ at 7.29 pm and is simply told – without a skerrick of paperwork offered or asked for – to get his mob moving on the march to Corbie within the hour. His men are going on almost no sleep as it is and have been forced to change their billets twice today alone. But too bad.

And too bad that Jimmy Downing and his mates of the 57th Battalion are profoundly immersed in sleep on this late afternoon, billeted in barns around Hédauville, some eight miles north of the Somme. Suddenly and unwillingly, they become dimly aware that one of their Sergeants is stumbling through their pigsties, shouting in a thick voice, 'Reveille! Reveille!'

It's 8.30 pm. Christ on a cross, they've only had a couple of hours sleep. On the third day *He* might have risen again, but they can barely bear to in their exhaustion. Still, orders are orders – despite having had only a coupla hours kip, they are to march out that night. As in, *now*.

So too with the other 3000 soldiers of the 15th Brigade.

And so off they go, on the march, under the gun, on the cobble-stones, bound for Corbie.

Like a massive khaki centipede winding its way south, all of their feet pounding in rough rhythm, the 15th Brigade keeps pushing south until at last, in the early morning, they arrive at the crest of a hill. Far to the south-west they can see 'Amiens cathedral, touched with fire in the glory of the morning, outlined against a pale green sky. Here was surely something to fight for, a symbol of France, the strong pillar of our alliance.'[84]

They keep moving and, before long, the jingle of stirrups, an urgent *clip-clop* and the snorting of horses signal the coming passage of a magnificent-looking squadron of French cavalry, all 'sky blue cloaks and blue enamelled helmets'.[85] There's a certain Gallic haughtiness about them, making them look quite the part. True, they are trotting *away* from the front, but they look the part regardless.

And now, coming slowly into sight are the bridges over the Somme they are to guard . . .

———

The French remain a problem, as only the French can be. Despite General Foch's grand talk of not ceding an inch of French soil, the truth is that they have barely struck a blow in anger since the Germans launched this latest assault. All that happens is more talk of a big fight to come. After General Foch meets General Haig on this day at Abbeville, Haig notes in his diary, *By 2 April I gather that the French should have sufficient troops concentrated to admit of them starting an offensive. But will they?*[86]

EVENING, 29 MARCH 1918, ST GRATIEN, PASS THE PORT

This, then, is how to fight a war. In his four years of this catastrophic conflict to date, General John Monash has lived in dugouts, humpies, dumpies, tents and trenches. He's slept in trains, trucks and potato patches – while at Gallipoli he had even slept in 'a hole in the side of a hill, about 6' x 7" and 4' deep'.[87]

On this evening, however, he is in a Louis XI château just outside the village of St Gratien, usually occupied by *le Comte de Thielloye*. Pass the port. Monash and his senior officers are nothing if not comfortable as they all come to grips with just how the situation lies now, courtesy of the large maps spread out on *le Comte*'s vast mahogany dining room table. When the reports that continue to come in are all put together with Monash's own knowledge – having spent most of the day, as he would describe it, 'flying about in my motor car visiting parts of my own line, and those of my neighbours; so as to keep close touch with every development of the situation'[88] – the knowledge of their position is comprehensive.

All up, Monash is satisfied to report of the whole of the Australian Corps in the vicinity, the 3rd, 4th and 5th Divisions, 'We now present a strong united front over a frontage of some 12 miles and the enemy will batter himself against it in vain.'[89]

At least he hopes so. After the tumultuous events of the last few days, the mood is one of exhausted elation. There is a strong sense of how well the Australians have done to re-form a defensive line so quickly, confirmed by the many messages of 'most flattering congratulations from everybody that matters'[90] that they have received.

The worry is not them; it is the Brits . . .

'You must understand the failure of the Fifth Army which held the line South of the Somme,' he writes to Hannah. 'The Fifth Army has been practically pulverized into fragments and its commander [General Gough] has been sent home.'[91]

As to the French, they are supposedly holding Rawlinson's right flank south of Villers-Bretonneux 'but have moved slowly'[92] to get themselves into position. Still, he is filled with hope, as are other senior Allied officers, that they 'will make their great counter-attack, but where and when this will take place no one knows definitely'.[93]

Further good news is that the 2nd Australian Division has now left their billets west of Messines and will arrive on the morrow at Amiens, while the last Australian division in the north, 1st Division, will be following them shortly. If all goes well, Monash continues to Hannah, 'I expect it will not be many days before our own [Australian] Corps Headquarters also arrives and we will again be a happy family.'[94]

Thus, as the last of this month of March starts to sink through the year-glass of time, the news is good. On the area assigned to them – from Albert in the north to Villers-Bretonneux in the south (not to forget the 4th Brigade at Hébuterne sandwiched in the north of Albert between the Kiwis and the Brits) – the Australians have held the Germans. The only question is for how long, and what will the Germans do to regain their momentum in the area?

—

In these tumultuous days, as the German storm approaches Villers-Bretonneux – now less than two miles away – most of the town's residents grab whatever worldly possessions they can easily carry and start off to the west. The town has been steadily drained of its people all week.

Among those fleeing are the many household staff of the Red Château, Château Delacour. As they carry their bags down the stairs and load them into carts, a distinguished-looking young French Lieutenant is seen walking the grounds.

Mais, c'est le fils du patron! C'est Monsieur Jean!

Indeed, it is the youngest son of the owner, the well-liked 25-year-old Jean, who is now an officer in the French Army. Stationed nearby, and realising that Villers-Bretonneux (and with it the family's beloved château) is likely about to be engulfed by the German advance, Lieutenant Jean Delacour has paid the place a quick visit. 'The town was still intact,' he would recall, 'but empty, and the first shells were beginning to fall. I entered the grounds of the château.'[95]

For an hour the French Lieutenant wanders out and about through the gardens, the aviaries and the park, always with visions flooding back of himself and his brothers and sisters playing as happy children in this very spot, then without a care in the world. And now it is likely to soon thunder to the tread of the German jackboot.

As the shells continue to fall nearby, he heads back into the old home, past the laden servants now streaming out of it – many of them greeting him with tears running down their cheeks – and into the château's grand salons, filled with artistic treasures surely about to be lost or destroyed.

'I took a long look at those cherished possessions,' he would recount, 'but there was such a short time to stay and so little room in the car that I did not take with me a single souvenir . . . I said goodbye to the beloved place.'[96]

Together with much of the French and British Armies, he heads west, away from the Germans. If the village is to be saved, and Amiens defended, it will have to be done by others.

29 MARCH 1918, TRÉLON, WITH GOD ON THEIR SIDE

All continues to go well for the German troops, and *der Kaiser* is more convinced than ever that God is with them. Such is his strong feeling after attending a church service at Trélon – just five miles north-east of St Quentin – conducted by a simple chaplain from the local German troops.

Shortly afterwards, however, the Kaiser complains at the news that one of the leading German newspapers, *Kölnische Zeitung*, has taken to calling this major spring offensive: *Die Kaiserschlacht*, 'The Kaiser's Battle'.

'It makes it seem,' the Kaiser fumes to his underlings, 'as though none of the *previous* battles had had anything to do with me.'[97]

In fact, however, it is on this day that the Kaiser's battle, after a week of oft-spectacular leaps forward, stalls for the first time, rather in the manner of General Ludendorff's bread-balls, which have been getting ever slower. All along his line, it not only feels to General Ludendorff as if his forces are stalled . . . they are stopped outright! *Kaput*. It is at its worst just north of the Somme, certainly – at Albert, Dernancourt and, now it seems, Morlancourt Ridge. And even where the news is better, where his soldiers really have broken through – south of the Somme against Gough – there is a real problem getting supplies through to his most forward men, meaning that across the line it is the best troops who are *least* supported. And yet, with that thrust south of the Somme having succeeded so well so far, bringing them within a stone's throw of the key stepping stone of Villers-Bretonneux – from where they can destroy Amiens – it is obvious that they must hurl everything they have to give them that final surge.

And so it is with some purpose and steely resolve that at 6.55 this evening he issues orders over the phone for General von der Marwitz's 2nd Army, to drive hard on Amiens south of the Somme . . . To accomplish these missions the Second Army [will] be reinforced by two divisions from the Seventeenth Army.[98]

General Marwitz is glad to have more men. If all goes well and those reinforcements arrive in force, then, as soon as the morrow, Villers-Bretonneux will be in German hands.

—

After a long day's march and even longer evening – still going, 'still shambling along . . . literally walking in our sleep . . .'[99] – the men of the 15th Brigade are at last getting close. There, in the faint moonlight, down in the dreamy valley filled with the lagoons of the Somme, they can see two towers reaching to the heavens, which they are told belong to Corbie church. And Corbie, they know, close to a town called Villers-Bretonneux, is their destination.

Well ahead of them, of course, and visiting Monash's HQ at nearby Bonnay, a staff officer says to Pompey Elliott, 'They will never get here.' Such comments, mere throwaway lines to most, rile the loyal and competitive leader, who is thrilled only a short time later when the 15th does arrive, 'intact, in close and beautiful order, no man or horse missing from his place . . .'

Such pride!

'I have seen them triumph in battles . . .' he would later recount, 'but I have never been prouder than when, on one occasion in France, we marched, at night, 26 miles [into Corbie].'[100]

And no matter that it is 4.15 am.

'That night,' Jimmy Downing would relate, referring to the bare hour or two that remain till daylight, 'we slept in houses. The inhabitants had fled, leaving the bread in the oven, the fire in the stove, the soup in the pot . . . We found good wine and slept well.'[101]

The unit commanders, however, are less fortunate, being immediately

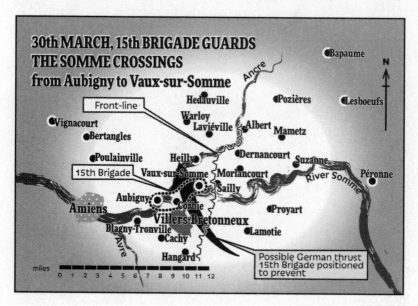

called together by Brigadier Elliott for a conference. They arrive with bags under their eyes, drooping and dark, and a tired shuffle in their gait.

Too bad.

Now that 9th Brigade has crossed the Somme to Cachy, Pompey tells them, we of the 15th are taking up their previous positions, guarding the Somme crossings from Aubigny to Vaux-sur-Somme . . .

There is more, much more, but the essence of it is that the situation in these parts, particularly south of the Somme, is highly unstable. The real danger will come if the Germans capture Hamel or Villers-Bretonneux then try to cross the Somme from there. It is up to 15th Brigade to prevent that . . .

CHAPTER NINE

THE FIRST BATTLE OF VILLERS-BRETONNEUX

I told Maclagan and Elliott – the 9th Aust. Inf. Brigade was
making the fight of its history in defence of that village . . .
I thought Villers-Bretonneux had gone – indeed, though I
did not say so, I thought the position there quite hopeless.[1]
Charles Bean, in his diary entry for 4 April 1918

30 MARCH 1918, FIE, THE BATTLE CRY

By now, it is like clockwork. A new day, a new attack.

The German artillery roars forth, the stormtroopers roar forward . . .

This time, the two have Villers-Bretonneux in their sights.

Brigadier Charles Rosenthal of the 9th Brigade is asleep in the
village of Gentelles, just two miles south-west of Villers-Bretonneux,
when the barrage begins. The instant he goes outside to see the myriad
flashes on the eastern horizon, he is certain the attack they have been
expecting is *on*.

As much is confirmed when all the telephone lines go dead, no
doubt destroyed by the shells. Rosie is eager to go forward himself
but – to his great chagrin – permission is firmly denied by the 61st
Division's General Colin Mackenzie. He wishes to have the Australian
officer close by him, whatever happens on this day.

Thus, it is most urgent that Rosie gather his battalion commanders, and he immediately sends out a message for them to meet him in the church square at Gentelles. Above the train-approaching-at-speed sound of heavy shells arriving from afar, followed by their shattering explosions, Rosie gives his orders. The men must move out of their billets in the aerodrome, which the Germans are clearly intent on destroying, and go 1000 yards 'northwards to the edge of a wood'[2] – Bois l'Abbé – where they are to await further instructions.

At this moment, one of Rosie's men, Private John Hardie of Colonel Morshead's 33rd Battalion, is sitting outside one of the concrete buildings in that aerodrome, resting his gammy left leg and listening to the roar of battle, when over the top come 'a squadron of Hun planes', soon followed by a squadron of Sopwith Camels.

A dogfight breaks out. One of the Camels is getting absolutely hammered when the pilot pulls off a famous manoeuvre, a 'tumbling nosedive', which puts the plane into freefall fast enough to get away from its pursuers. And the plane *keeps* falling as the onlookers hold their breath . . . until, yes, magically, seemingly just 50 feet from a shattering death, the pilot pulls back on his joystick!

'Then,' Hardie would recount, 'he straightened out and planed down just like a bird alighting.'[3]

Back home at Grong Grong, they would read the newspapers over their brekka or tea. Here, he can see the major news happening before his eyes. And, sure enough, before long there is more fresh news from the skies – coming right at him!

'Fritz started to shell us,' he would recount, 'Some of the [high-explosive shells] struck the building my platoon was in. Some more landed in the backyard and wounded a mule.'[4]

The Australians scatter and hit the ground like spring lambs, limbs akimbo but at least down, which is all that counts. In the ruckus, a staff officer runs over and passes on Rosie's order, translated into terms everyone can more quickly understand.

'Scatter and take to the open fields,'[5] he yells, waving his arm to the north.

Compree?

They *compree*, and they obey. Alas, some of the shrapnel shells are quicker than they are, and 'some of the other lads weren't so lucky for several were wounded and a few paid the supreme sacrifice'.[6]

——

Right on 0800 hours, Brigadier Rosenthal's battalion commanders of the 9th Brigade – the 33rd's Colonel Leslie Morshead, the 34th's Colonel Ernest Martin, the 35th's Colonel Henry Goddard and the 36th's Colonel John Milne – gather in front of him in the church square at Gentelles.

'The enemy have taken Aubercourt [the village just east of Hangard Wood],'[7] he reports to his officers, who look at each other knowingly.

This is a worry. The battle has only just begun and *already* the Germans are less than two miles from Villers-Bretonneux. For the time being, Rosenthal explains, be 'prepared to counter-attack at Villers-Bretonneux'.[8]

Yessir.

——

Back in the abandoned aerodrome at Cachy, the shelling has subsided. The troops of the 9th Brigade are doing what they always seem to be doing these days – getting ready to move again. Soon enough, Hardie marches out into the nearby wood of Bois l'Abbé.

In the cold. In the rain. In the mud. With the sound of booming artillery in the distance. (Hardie at least is warmed by his escapade of the previous afternoon where, after searching Cachy for a couple of hours, he had found what he was looking for, a large French flag, which he proceeded to hang from the tallest building in the town – *La Mairie* – just on principle, just to give the Germans the shits.) Somehow, despite it all, there is an innate cheerfulness to the 33rd as they make cubbyhouses out of their waterproof sheets and crouch together in the rough shelter provided, the rain now thundering down.

'The lads,' Private Hardie would note, 'were singing the usual songs; "Oh, it's a lovely war", "Australia will be there" and "Keep the home fires burning".' [9]

Still, as the songs ring out, the thoughts of many of the men inevitably turn to home. It doesn't feel like it here in France, in the middle of this hellish war, but it is Easter Saturday, and – let's see, yes – nearly Easter Sunday back home. A day usually spent with parish and family.

Maybe next year, boys.

Sing it:

Keep the Home Fires Burning,
While your hearts are yearning,
Though your lads are far away
They dream of home.
There's a silver lining
Through the dark clouds shining,
Turn the dark cloud inside out
'Til the boys come home. [10]

Not far away, Colonel Goddard's 35th are doing much the same. Huddled in their own makeshift bivvies and with the threat of the Hun so close, a few take the opportunity to study their **LIST OF GERMAN PHRASES WITH APPROPRIATE PRONUNCIATION,** handed out a few days earlier, as a refresher.

'Hands Up!'

'*Hände hoch*' pronounced, '*Hender Hoch*' ('o' as in 'hole').

'Throw away your revolver!'

'*Revolver Weg!*' pronounced, 'revolver veck!'

'Halt!'

'*Halt!*' pronounced, 'Halt'[11]...

That one, at least, is easy enough.

—

Eleven-odd miles west of the wet Diggers, Paul Maze, General Gough's French liaison officer, is on the approach to Amiens, shocked by the number of German shells that suddenly start falling on this once-elegant town.

'The bombardment of Amiens had begun,'[12] he would recall.

On arriving in the town, he notes the empty railway tracks, the holes in the station's roof, the sandbags in front of the cathedral, the ransacked shops, the way the entire façade of the patisserie had been torn open by a shell, and how rubble and Military Police are now all over the streets. There is a strong sense of impending doom.

And yet, when Maze walks around a corner, there standing out the front of her restaurant, Chez Josephine, is the famous Madame Josephine herself, renowned for her *pomme frites* and juicy roast chickens. She is hurriedly packing the last of her cooking utensils into a cart, together with easily moveable foodstuffs. The indomitable Madame chats with him briefly and, deeply admiring her pluck, he bids her good luck and farewell.

As he walks away, Madame Josephine yells out, '*Tiens, grand,*' and throws him 'one of her last cooked chickens, which I held like a Rugby pass'.[13]

Paul Maze smiles at this pillar of a woman, stoical to the last, all while shells hurtle down on her home town. He tucks the chicken under his arm and moves on, sidestepping rubble and shell holes as he goes, darting left and right, war's answer indeed to a rugby fly half on the boil, but certainly not passing *this* ball.

—

At 2.15 pm, after half a day of nonstop shelling and bedraggled, shell-shocked Tommies hauling themselves west, away from the Germans, Rosie gets the word. The men of the 9th Brigade are ordered to 'counter-attack and re-establish the line immediately . . .'[14]

Rosie, having expected this order all day, rides off immediately to inform the troops.

—

Colonel Leslie Morshead . . . Brigadier Rosenthal would like to see you.

The 28-year-old Morshead, Commander of 33rd Battalion – a 'dapper little schoolmaster'[15] from Ballarat who had landed on the shores of Gallipoli on the first day and had been the only officer of his battalion not wounded or killed at Lone Pine – is quick to answer the call. The experienced officer, of whom Bean says, 'the traditions of the British Army had been bottled from his childhood like tight-corked champagne',[16] rides up to the Brigadier.

The Hun, Rosie explains, are through the British line. As near as we can work out, they are now no more than two or three miles to the south-east of Villers-Bretonneux. And so, you and your men are 'to capture and establish a line from . . . Marcelcave to Aubercourt, and to capture Aubercourt, which is in possession of the enemy . . . You are to work in conjunction with the [cavalry unit, the] 12th Lancers, who are 400 strong . . .'[17]

'When are we to do it?' Morshead asks.

'Now.'

'Any artillery?'

'No.'

'Do you know where the British line is?'

'No.'

'Can I have some troops to support me?'

'Yes, the 34th . . . but don't use the 34th if you can avoid doing so.'[18]

You are to advance three-and-a-half miles from Bois d'Aquenne, and on a front of some 2700 yards. Under normal circumstances this would be regarded as an impossible task if there are many Germans in the way, but, in the foggiest of wars such as this, no one knows if there are.

It is just as well that Morshead had learned to ride like a bushman while working as a jackeroo around Ballarat in his teens. For, shortly after being given the order, there he is on his horse, galloping across the open field, heading north to give his men their orders.

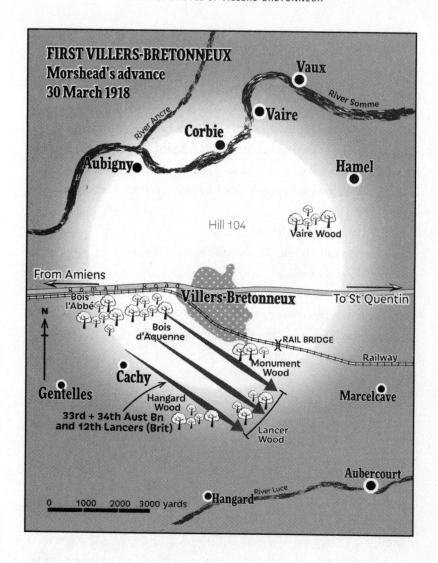

Only a short time later, the Australian soldiers of the 33rd Battalion are roused mid-song from beneath their dripping shelters and lined up along the south-western edge of the woods, to stand before their Colonel atop his snorting steed.

Among the men on foot is Private John Hardie, who would recall that Morshead 'gave us a lecture and laid on plenty of soft soap'[19] about what fine soldiers they are and how confident he is that they have the ability to do the difficult task set before them.

Blah, blah, blah. This might inspire some soldiers, but not Hardie. Just tell us what you want done, Colonel.

That is much simpler to explain if far more difficult to achieve.

'[You must] hunt the enemy out of Hangard Wood and capture the village on the other side.'[20]

Colonel Morshead finishes up with his usual line: 'Play the game as men of the 33rd always do!'[21]

And that, mates, is the cue, as ever.

The bugle sounds and a Sergeant's voice rings out from somewhere down the line: 'Faaallll-in!'

'The march began,' Hardie would recount, 'towards the battle line or rather to the place where we imagined Fritz to be. You see there was absolutely no infantry facing the enemy here.'[22]

The Tommies have *gorn*.

—

Morshead is conferring one last time with his company commanders when up rides a British cavalry officer who introduces himself as Lieutenant Edward Barron of the 12th Lancers. With the classic clipped cadence of the military on a mission, he says, 'My regiment have been ordered to assist the 9th Brigade by supporting its northern flank.'[23]

Colonel Morshead smiles as he sees the 400-strong regiment not far behind the Lieutenant, all looking fierce on their horses, nerves steeled for battle, lance pennants fluttering along with their hearts.

'The approach march was an unusual sight,' Morshead would much later recount to Charles Bean. 'There we were, headed by the 12th Lancers, mounted, marching across the open in daylight in full view of the enemy – a lone body of men going into the blue . . . We were well forward of anyone and uncomfortably isolated.'[24]

Marching in formation down the Cachy–Villers-Bretonneux Road, songs begin to ring out from the 'poor bloody infantry' (as they are known in the cavalry units, flying squadrons, navy, and any other units in the armed forces that aren't the poor bloody infantry). Colonel Morshead, ever the 'fighting leader',[25] rides out ahead with the Lancers by his side, certainly understanding how odd it all is.

Before them lies 'the open plateau, copse and ploughland, between the Somme and the Luce'. As Morshead continues to ride forward at the head of his men, he keeps his bearings by the twin towers of the church of Villers-Bretonneux over to his left front, with some of the town's many gracious villas visible through the trees.

On any other day, in peacetime, it may have been quaint. Not so today.

Morshead can't help but notice that the *Boche* bombardment appears to be falling everywhere around, except for on the 'château along the Villers-Bretonneux–Amiens Road, the idea doubtless being to have good accommodation for themselves when they occupied the town'.[26]

Riding alongside the Lancers' commander, Colonel Cecil Fane, Colonel Morshead feels honoured 'beyond his wildest dreams'.[27]

'It was a proud privilege to be allowed to work with such a fine regiment as the 12th Lancers,' he would report to Brigadier Rosenthal the next day, 'Their approach march instilled in the men the utmost confidence and enthusiasm, and I am glad to say greatly counteracted the effect of so much straggling.'[28]

His own men, though, marching and singing, drenched by the rain, are in fine fettle.

This vision of their Colonel, galloping past in such magnificent fashion at the head of such a splendid squadron of horsemen – somehow recalling the days of yore, like a scene from a Tennyson poem, *half-a-league, half-a-league, half-a-league onwards, into the valley of death, rode the six hundred* – would not leave his men unaffected.

'Never shall I forget that march,' Private John Hardie would recall. 'The Battalion was in columns of threes and alongside was a square of cavalry about 400-strong. It was a sight I had often read about but never expected to see. One thing I would like to know was what poor old Fritz thought when he first caught sight of us for it must have scared him a bit.'[29]

—

Colonel Morshead and the 12th Lancers, meanwhile, still out in front of the 33rd Battalion, reach a wood east of Hangard Wood at about 4.15 pm, which, as it is nameless, Morshead soon gives the name of . . . Lancer Wood. The 33rd and the Lancers easily take the wood against very thin defence. Beyond, across the fields, they spy Germans coming their way.

One young, unbridled officer of the cavalry who is standing with Colonel Morshead as the Germans get closer urges him to let the Lancers charge the enemy.

'Oh, let's have a go at them, sir,' the cavalry officer pleads. 'We'll dish them straight away.'

'Not I,' replies Morshead with an amused look at the young British officer. 'What would your Colonel say?'

'Don't ask him. He's under your command and if you order him he'll have to do it.'[30]

Instead, Morshead subscribes to the Shakespearean adage that 'the better part of valor is discretion, in the which better part I have sav'd my life'[31] and orders the Lancers to dismount to get into positions at the edges of the wood so they can protect the 33rd Battalion's flanks, allowing the Australians to move forward to the attack.

The infantrymen, meantime, have organised themselves into skirmishing order and move up to an assembly point on the western edge of Lancer Wood, ignoring the shells now falling all around them. All they need now is the order to move forward in attack and it'll be *on*, Blue.

At 5 pm it comes, and the Australians push on like a line of beaters going to flush snipe.

'The movement forward was splendidly carried out,' Morshead would subsequently report to Brigadier Rosenthal, 'On the right slight opposition was encountered but easily disposed of.'[32]

Indeed. The official history of that 'slight opposition', as ruefully noted by the 91st Regiment of the German 19th Division, is that Morshead's soldiers 'made a strong counter-attack and tried to surround our men. Since both companies there were isolated, they were able to escape only by a *schleuniges*, immediate and very fast [retreat] to avoid captivity.'[33]

Despite the Germans looking for a *schleuniges,* there are enough left, dug in further back, to give the Australians curry as they press further ahead. Emerging from the eastern edge of Lancer Wood, rain still bucketing down, Private John Hardie is with his platoon, venturing forth into the open unknown, when they come under heavy fire.

'We kept advancing by short rushes,' he would later recall, 'and of course were losing men every yard. I couldn't help noticing the little puffs of steam the red hot bullets sent up striking the sodden wheat fields, sometimes they were all round me, other times just in front. My mates fell on either side and I expected my turn any moment, but felt as though it was no concern of mine what happened.'[34]

About 200 yards beyond Lancer Wood the men come under 'very heavy machine gun and rifle fire'.[35]

Do they baulk? Do they, *hell!*

'They deployed at once and moved forward without flinching,' Colonel Morshead would delight in reporting. 'All ranks displayed the greatest determination and eagerness to get to the *Bosch* with the bayonet.'[36]

And Private John Hardie is there with the best of them, on the left of the counter-attack, continuing to advance though soldiers all around him are crying out and going down. The slaughter is unimaginable, but still he and the survivors push forward.

'By the time the line had advanced to a position about three hundred yards in front of the enemy,' he would record in his diary, 'there was about twelve men left, one sergeant, one corporal, and a lance corporal out of a Company which had been over strength.'[37]

It wasn't as bad as Hardie believed, but a devastating half of the company has gone down, and it is up to them to make the sacrifice count for something. It will not be easy. Beyond the withering

German fire, all of their Lewis guns are out of action through mud blocking their mechanisms. Many of their rifles are also jamming from over-heating and dirt.

Hardie's rifle is so hot he can barely hold it. What should they do? Continue to attack or hold on to the ground they have won? In the end it is the Sergeant who takes the lead, deciding the best thing will be to dig in and hold on.

'Well,' Hardie recounts, 'we stopped in that position in the sodden wheat fields until dark (as we were cut off from the rest of the Unit) and then sent word back to H.Q. of the plight the remnants of B Company were in.'[38]

Fortunately, as Morshead would report, the rest of the Australian line has been able to push forward, 'in spite of heavy losses, and the enemy hurriedly retired . . .'[39]

—

Colonel Goddard, back near Cachy, has had his plans foiled.

He is just about to order his cold, drenched men back to the aerodrome 'where at any rate they would be dry',[40] when he receives new orders.

The 35th Battalion are to relieve **THE WHOLE OF THE 61ST DIVISION FRONT OF VILLERS-BRETONNEUX**.[41]

Seriously? One Australian battalion to take over a whole British Division's front? Things are either more desperate than I thought, or the British High Command think that one Australian battalion is all it takes to do the work of an entire British division.

For the second time that day, now in search of the British troops he is to replace, Goddard rides east with his nucleus of officers to 'Villers Bret', as the men are calling it by now.

What is apparent to Goddard is that the 184th Brigade's current commander – commanders come and go as fast as 5.9-inch shells in this part of the world – General Alexander 'Patsy' Pagan, is a little 'too keen on looted champagne'.[42]

Frankly, everyone Goddard finds is delirious, confused and somewhat hopeless, and 'if relief was to be complete before daylight (and movement was impossible after dawn) ordinary hand over was out of the question'.

So, led by his inherent sense of both responsibility and initiative, Goddard takes it upon himself to go 'over the area and give authority for all troops other than our own to withdraw'.[43]

———

Those battlers out there in the freezing-cold wheatfields, just east of Lancer Wood?

They are Morshead's men – the eggs-a-cook boys showing their worth on the Somme at last!

They are wet as water but stick fast as glue to their newly established line. They have had it out with Fritz, bayonet to bayonet, and caused a retirement of the *Bosche* line to beyond Lancer Wood. But Colonel Morshead is looking on the situation with growing concern. He knows that as soon as the enemy wises up to the actual numbers of men out there – a fifth of blooming well *nothing* when compared with the Germans across from them – they will mount a counter-attack of their own.

'The enemy was well entrenched and in strong forces,' Colonel Morshead would later report to Brigadier Rosenthal. 'As we had no artillery support his fire was consequently extremely heavy and unfortunately very accurate. Owing to such strong opposition we were not able to reach our objectives.'[44]

They are some hundreds of yards from where they were supposed to be, and they have not recaptured Aubercourt, but on a positive note their line is 'well sited and is a very good defensive position. With determined troops the enemy could easily be held, and any advance he attempted would be very expensive'.[45]

And so Colonel Morshead, at 8 pm, sends back word for his reserve to move up and reinforce the right flank, and for the 34th Battalion 'to send forward a company to reinforce the left flank'.[46]

—

Private John Hardie is there when the boys of Colonel Martin's 34th Battalion arrive. 'I don't think there was ever a more pleasing sight,' he later recalled.

Hardie looks back over his shoulder and, through the charcoal haze of a rainy night, can see their silhouettes moving stealthily forward. 'There looked to be thousands of them.'[47]

But the men of the 34th don't stop there. Following Moreshead's orders, they push on through the night, past the line. Within minutes it seems to Private Hardie, who can faintly hear the action through the deluge, that they have captured a line of newly made German trenches some 250 yards ahead of where the 33rd are entrenched.

'You could imagine the surprise that Fritz would get,' Hardie would later recount of the night-time advance, 'for they were on top of his trenches before he knew what was doing. I don't think he fired fifty bullets altogether and the 34th used nothing but the bayonet, and I'm afraid they were rather merciless as they advanced . . . without taking any prisoners.'[48]

And, yes, it may seem merciless, but these boys of the 34th have come up through a bloody trail of dead and wounded comrades. The suffering they saw and were forced to leave behind without lending a hand 'had the same effect that a red rag would have on a bull'.[49]

They have not come to take German prisoners – they have come for blood, and their vision actually takes on a red tinge.

Having mercilessly cleared the trenches and captured two machine guns along with four lucky prisoners who are, in the end, spared, the blood returns to the brains of the men, along with its attendant common sense. They fall back to the main defensive line being held by Morshead's battalion.

And now 'every Tom, Dick and Harry set to work to dig trenches', as Hardie would recount. 'I can assure you that it was no light undertaking, especially as we had nothing better than our entrenching tools which are as useful as a tablespoon.'[50]

But wait!

Shortly thereafter, Hardie finds the most blessed of all things just lying there in a field – an actual *shovel* – and busies himself with his mates, digging their Lewis gun into position, when . . .

They look up to see the orderly of one of the 34th's company commanders, advising that his Captain had heard they have a shovel. He wants it so he can dig his dugout for the night.

That's easy. Tell him to fuck off. It's *our* shovel – and we're using it for our Lewis gun, which is more important than his dugout. The orderly nods and leaves. The men well know he'll likely temper their remarks in translation to his Captain.

Hardie and his mates keep digging, with one or other of them occasionally going for a prowl forward to see what they can see. And here is a bloke now, a sleeping soldier, with his back to a mound. Hardie gives him a nudge to wake him, 'but it was the poor fellow's last stop. At having a good look at him I could see that he was a Jock and must have been acting as sentry when killed.'[51]

A short time later, two officers and a private head out, and Hardie and his mates can suddenly hear the guttural cry of a German sentry challenging them. 'Then there was a couple of shots and a scream, but all our men came back alright.'[52]

It has already proved to be a productive night's work for Morshead's command. They have pushed Fritz back no fewer than 2000 yards on the south side of Villers-Bretonneux, even if, most regrettably, they've lost a lot of fight-ready men in doing it.

—

Somewhere behind Private Hardie, way back in the darkness, Goddard's men of the 35th Battalion are arriving into 'Villers-Bret' to find most everyone bar the very old folk, and one mother with her children, gone. Upon seeing that mother tearfully loading her cart, an Australian soldier says to her kindly, 'You needn't go, Ma. The Aussies are here. Best stay where you are.'[53] He helps unload the cart and carry her things back inside. (It remains to be seen whether this is a good idea or not . . .)

Now, the Diggers have heard of this town, but they are the first Australian soldiers to march into it with intent, ready to defend it to the last. As Colonel Henry Goddard has given the ghostlike British sentries their marching orders – *Git!* – his men are now ordered to fan out to the east of the town and take up positions to defend it.

Captain Gilbert Coghill of the 35th Battalion is among the officers who go forward to the small railway embankment that lies on the south-eastern edge of the town. He soon finds five junior British officers 'crouched in a burrow in the side of the embankment . . . covered by a waterproof sheet'.[54]

'Where are your men?'[55] Captain Coghill asks, trying to keep his temper.

'Out there,' one of them replies despondently, pointing with a casual, dismissive wave of his hand into the dark void.

Coghill cringes. These junior officers, every one of them a platoon commander, should not only *know* where their own men are *but be with them*, instead of tucked away in their little hidey-hole a few hundred yards back from the line. It is a blatant and unforgivable dereliction of duty.

The Tommies sense the disgust of their antipodean ally, but they simply don't care. Not one bit.

(Not for nothing would General John Monash write of this time, 'Some of these Tommy Divisions are the absolute limit, and not worth the money it costs to put them into uniform . . . Bad troops, bad staffs, bad commanders.'[56])

But Captain Coghill cares; he moves off again with his company in the direction indicated.

All he finds is one little group of British soldiers lying next to each other like sad sausages in a sodden hole, cuddling each other for warmth. Well, this is as good a place as any to make their stand, and Coghill gives orders for his company to dig in.

—

Just as Colonel Morshead had predicted, the Hun have re-formed and are quick to launch an attack on the battalion's embattled left flank at the north end of Lancer Wood. In his dugout, Private Hardie no sooner receives word that Fritz is coming – which roars along the line like a bushfire with a hot westerly behind it – than, like all of them, he risks a quick stickybeak above the trench parapet.

And there is Fritz hisself!

'In the dim light', Hardie spies 'a great mass of men on the skyline about three hundred yards away'.[57]

Thank Gawd they have dug their Lewis gun into a good position – now is the time.

'Every machine gun and rifle opened up in a murderous fire,'[58] he would recount.

Across the line, the Germans go down heavily.

'Needless to say,' Hardie notes with a kind of jaunty bravado that is growing in him, just as it is growing in his comrades, 'we were left in peace to strengthen the position.'[59]

As for Colonel Morshead, he is inordinately proud of his men, as he recounts in his report to Brigadier Rosenthal: 'Heavy rain fell from early in the afternoon to late at night. Working over the ploughed fields under such conditions affected the Lewis guns and rifles. Every man was drenched to the skin and very cold, but this did not dampen his ardour.'[60]

And although after midnight their flanks are still 'somewhat in the air'[61] and they have made no contact with any British unit, they have at least re-established a front-line that is now 'well protected by Vickers and Lewis Guns. We had five Vickers Guns from the 9th Australian Machine Gun Coy. – two covered either flank and one the centre, and we had 25 Lewis Guns.'[62]

Around 2 am the 10th Essex comes up to relieve the tired Australians. Private John Hardie is among the men now moving back. He's been carrying a mate with a broken leg for the last mile. 'The poor fellow never whimpered,' he later recalled, 'and we must have hurt him for we were stumbling and slipping all the time. You can imagine how tired we were as for several days we hadn't had a decent sleep and then the stunt on top of it all just crowned things.'[63]

And with the boys of Goddard's 35th Battalion all but done taking up the line in front of Villers-Bretonneux, Amiens is still safe. For now.

30 MARCH 1918, MORLANCOURT RIDGE, THE 3RD DIVISION COMES FIRST

General Monash will be proud of his 9th Brigade, just across the Somme from Morlancourt Ridge at Villers-Bretonneux. But at this point he knows little of their action; he is sleeping in his headquarters after a long day of his own. That morning everything had been rustic beauty, birds and butterflies. The next thing, it was all bullets, bandages and bombs as the German assault on the Australian lines defending Morlancourt Ridge got underway around 12.30 pm. Then came a further peppering from long-range machine guns. Mercifully, it only lasted for a few minutes and there was little damage done – *are the Germans, perhaps, running low on ammunition in forward positions?* – before it fell away and, peering over the edge of their trenches, the Australians had seen them.

The cry had gone up: 'Fritz is coming over!'[64]

And so he was.

In fact, *heaps* of Fritzes! Suddenly the Australian soldiers of the 3rd Division could see 'waves of enemy troops'[65] heading their way, a total of three German regiments, at least 8000 infantry in all, in long lines, 'one following the other at 100 yards distance'.[66]

They were coming forward in such numbers it was clear there would be little chance of stopping them, unless . . .

Unless the soldiers of the 3rd Division could get artillery support . . . . and, right on cue, their guns roared a response! Showing great courage under fire, a few minutes after the German soldiers appear, so too did the batteries of 3rd Division artillery, their horses snorting and straining as they hauled the guns into position. And now the 3rd's artillery was firing over open sights 'and poured a devastating volley into the advancing masses . . .'[67]

Not to be outdone, Fritz had also brought his guns forward.

'They wheeled their teams round bold as brass . . . The teams trotted off and the guns were left just beyond the skyline. You could see with the naked eye the [German] gunners walking round on the skyline, quite carelessly . . .'[68]

But not for long. Taking aim at these distant ducks in a shooting gallery – just a little like being back at the Goulburn Show, when they could impress their best girl by their proficiency in knocking over so many that the showman must give her whichever prize she desires – the Australians brought their Vickers machine guns to bear, and the cheers went up as the Germans went down.

Got him! Got another one! And *another* one!

'The morale of the 42nd,' Vivian Brahms would record of his brethren situated at the southern end of the line, 'was never at a higher pitch. Men were actually laying wagers in francs as to which of them would be the first to hit a specified German.'[69]

Perhaps even higher in morale were the men of B Company, 44th Battalion. 'Lewis gunners with coats off and one boot on, just roused from [a daytime nap], were using their weapons with splendid effect. Rifles became hot, but the fire never slackened. In ten minutes time the Hun attack was completely demoralised, and in less than half an hour it was driven to earth and shelter . . . There was no doubt now in the firmness of B Company's belief that all the Fritz's in Germany could not shift them . . .'[70]

By 3 o'clock it had all been over. Though the Australians had lost some 150 men, the Germans suffered the loss of at least ten times that number.

As Captain William Uren of the 41st Battalion would report: 'Improved morale was the result of the day's sport.'[71]

Major General Harold Grimwade, Commander of the 3rd Division Artillery, is also pleased, writing in his diary this night, 'Our artillery did splendid work today, and inflicted heavy casualties . . . the Bosch were held along the line.'[72]

Now, in the quiet of night, the eggs-a-cook boys in the front-line along Morlancourt Ridge become aware of the effects of the day's sport as the misty darkness carries the sound far from darker places still. 'The enemy evidently realised the hopelessness of making any further progress,' one of the relieved Diggers would recount. 'His wounded were heard moaning through the night . . .'[73]

For his part, Monash could not be more pleased. 'The battle was a walk-over for us,' he would write in a letter afterwards, with no little pride. 'We simply slaughtered the enemy wholesale . . . After an hour, the whole attack had petered out, and this, up to the time of writing, is the end of the German attempt to capture Amiens by direct approach . . .'[74]

Monash will soon receive a warm note from the Commander of the 1st Cavalry Division, thanking him for the fine work of his 9th Brigade over at Villers-Bret: 'It was a very real relief to know that I had your stout-hearted fellows on my left flank, and later also on my right flank and that all worry was therefore eliminated . . . It was a pleasure and an honour to be fighting alongside troops who displayed such a magnificent morale.'[75]

'After two days fighting,' Monash would write to his wife with great satisfaction, 'we have stood firm, the road to Amiens is closed, and we, and the Fourth Australians and the New Zealanders further north steadied up the whole British line.'[76]

—

For their part, the Germans of the 18th Division at Morlancourt are both bloodied *and* bowed.

'There was little time for preparation,' their official history would accurately and ruefully recount, even if going on to mistake the nationality of their enemy. 'Poor artillery support and the English machine guns were so well hidden that they could not be knocked out. The power of our attack was exhausted. Spirits sank to zero. The Division suffered a reverse the like of which it had not yet experienced.'[77]

One of the division's regiments, the 86th, would go even further in its own official history, noting that the Australians 'had proved themselves a tough opponent who was not easily made to get up and run . . . This realisation was bitter. Was this the end? Was this whole offensive beyond our strength? These questions were *auf vielen Lippen*, on many lips, that night.'[78]

30 MARCH 1918, GERMAN GHQ, AVESNES, FRITZ LICKS HIS WOUNDS

In the wake of the successful counter-attack by Australia's 9th Brigade, his forces are stalled and Ludendorff must decide what to do next at Villers-Bretonneux.

Meanwhile, it's time to put the last pieces in place for Operation George – the second part of the overall plan to completely *wipe out* the British Expeditionary Force, this one to break through their lines around Hazebrouck and push on to the Channel ports. Hazebrouck is, after all, effectively the Amiens of the north – occupy it and the key to victory is secured.

With this end in mind, at 6.45 this evening, General Ludendorff, from his quarters in Avesnes, sends word to *Kronprinz* Rupprecht, informing him that, as the General has decided that Operation George will definitely go ahead in ten days or so, he will be needing some of *der Kronprinz*'s heavy artillery to be shifted to the north to Hazebrouck. This includes some of the batteries of General Marwitz's 2nd Army that Rupprecht had been counting on to subdue Villers-Bretonneux, but there is no choice.

And it is not as if Ludendorff wants them to stop the assault on Villers-Bretonneux because of it. In fact, only three hours later, he telephones General Marwitz to tell him that the 2nd Army must redouble their attack on the village as soon as *tomorrow*.

In response, General Marwitz is underwhelmed. Instead of the huge daily progress they had made to this point, the reports this evening have indicated that the 2nd Army's results are 'even less than at first believed'[79] and 'widely behind expectations'.[80]

And what's more, he is being given these orders on the day that his forces have been handed their helmet by the Australians, and told by them with no little force to *halt*. Never mind that the enemy is now better dug in than ever.

Choosing his words carefully, as one must to a General of Ludendorff's power, Marwitz delicately points out that the troops simply cannot attack again without a few days' preparation and additional resources.

'Such an attack required careful preparation,' Marwitz will later characterise the position. 'The troops were tired, reserves had not yet arrived and artillery ammunition was short.'[81]

For the moment, Ludendorff has little choice but to back down, agreeing that Marwitz and the 2nd Army can have more time, while still insisting that Marwitz will have to make do without the artillery Ludendorff insists must go north.

Kronprinz Rupprecht, writing in his diary that night, is more positive about the push towards Amiens than General Marwitz. And he is pleased that Ludendorrf has ordered the Operation George[82] attack, noting, 'Because the enemy has weakened his front to the south of Armentières considerably, the George Attack is definitely on at last.'[83]

———

Instead of relying on the telephone, General Haig prefers a face-to-face encounter on such important matters and so travels to Sir Henry Rawlinson's HQ at Dury.

In his office, filled with maps covered with their ubiquitous imperial blue pins and cotton *receding* and demon red pins and cotton *advancing*, Rawlinson explains the current situation to Haig. 'There are nearly 20,000 remnants of divisions in the Villers-Bretonneux sector,' he explains in his Eton College accent, which bespeaks his privileged background. 'The majority are very tired indeed, most having been fighting since the beginning of the battle . . .'[84]

There is no way around it, sir. My men must be allowed time to rest and reorganise, and we must bring forward strong reserves to take over the line and give them a break.

Just where the reserves can come from is not yet apparent. But what is obvious is that the 9th Australian Brigade will have to be retained near Villers-Bretonneux until that problem is solved.

CHAPTER TEN

STORM ON THE HORIZON

Altogether [Villers-Bretonneux] was a delightful
setting for anything but grim war.[1]
Private Ralph Keegan, Australian gunner

31 MARCH 1918, VILLERS-BRETONNEUX, GODDARD GETS HIS GINGER UP

Easter Sunday dawns grey and cold, but at least it is not raining.

Overnight, the British 61st Division has handed the sector over to the 18th Division, under whose command Brigadier Rosenthal and his men now come. Unfortunately for Rosie, his new commander – like General Mackenzie of the 61st Division – still insists that he keep his brigade headquarters well back from the front-line, at the village of Gentelles. At least he is able to make inspections of front-line positions, and on this morning he rides east with a group of staff officers to visit his battalion commanders, including the 35th's Colonel Henry Goddard, who reports that his men are in the line and everything is satisfactory.

In return, Rosie informs the likeable Queenslander that the 'enemy have captured Hangard and the French are relieving on the right . . . I have warned the remaining battalions of the 9th Australian Brigade to be ready to counter attack.'[2]

With the *Boche* in possession of Hangard Wood, two miles to the south, Goddard knows that Villers-Bret is under more threat than ever, and Rosie confirms it with a heavy nod, telling him, 'The position looks very blue.'[3]

A nod back. There is not a whole lot more to be said.

As Brigadier Rosenthal takes his leave, Goddard calls over his Staff Major and tells him to collect his things – they are going to establish a battalion HQ elsewhere in town, closer to the men in the front-line.

'Just as we were going out of the door and immediately as I left the room I was in,' Goddard would jot in his diary later that night, 'a shell came through the roof and a good few fell round.'[4] Dust flies up, covering Goddard in a fine, light-grey film, giving him a distinctly pallid look. Shortly afterwards, picking himself up and readjusting his helmet, he heads off to find General Evans, the latest commander of the 61st Division's 184th Brigade, to let him know that he is moving his HQ elsewhere. Making his way through scattered groups of the 184th, it doesn't take long for this old soldier to realise what a slovenly and disorganised bunch they are, and he is soon to find a significant part of the reason why.

When he is finally able to locate General Evans, instead of being in his HQ surrounded by staff officers and maps, Goddard finds him in the open, next to a haystack, beside a man who is asleep, while he, a senior British General – looking 'tired and dirty and unshaven' – has a shovel in hand and is digging a trench for his own protection, never mind the troops.

'Good morning,' Goddard says equably, snapping off a salute.

Alas, all General Evans can do is scream out, 'We are under observation!'[5] His obvious fear is that a German sniper will shoot him now that he has been identified as a senior officer.

Goddard looks around and sees that, on the contrary, Evans is quite safe. The good General, Goddard realises, is 'thoroughly rattled'.[6]

Far too rattled to continue as a commander. And so he puts it delicately to his senior officer, 'You can go back to the rear as soon as you like . . . I will take all responsibility.'[7]

The point is, sir, the Australians will take it from here.

The General mumbles something incoherent. Goddard takes his

leave, gingerly, so as not to rattle the man any more. He heads back to find his staff and establish the new HQ.

—

A couple of miles to the west, in the village of Cachy, all the boys of the 33rd Battalion who had counter-attacked so brilliantly the night before are now back from the front-line[8] and seeking out their latest billets.

Private Hardie is walking through the streets with the fellow survivors from his company, looking for a bed – and a hot meal, if possible – when he sees their 'platoon officer who hadn't been in the stunt'.[9]

The platoon officer takes one look at the handful of mud-soaked men, then looks at Hardie, as if imploring him to say, 'The boys are just round the corner, they'll be here in a mo'!'[10]

Alas, Private Hardie can only shake his head.

The officer 'breaks down completely on learning that we represented the total strength of B Company,' Hardie later recalled. 'No doubt we must have looked a miserable and disreputable bunch for one could hardly drag one foot after another and it was impossible for any more mud to cling to our clothes (or rather rags).'[11]

Finally, the platoon officer pulls himself together, wipes his face with his sleeve and motions for them to follow him to their billets. Private Hardie walks through the door of a quaint house and sees 'the billy boiling and also our beds made'. The boys have 'a drink and a bit of a snack'[12] then toss in to get some sleep.

—

Pompey Elliott is at this moment on the banks of the Somme, marching with purpose through the town of Corbie, his ruddy cheeks bright as beetroot, eyes peeled for looters. And that's exactly why he's here now.

A couple of days earlier, you see, Elliott had come across a British officer of the 14th Division with a mess cart full of looted champagne.

Trundling along, the officer looked well chuffed with himself. Until he saw the corpulent figure of an Australian officer standing in his road.

Without hesitation, and universally deaf to any kind of excuses, Pompey had handed the Tommy officer over to the military police. And then, as only Pompey can, he makes two orders known to all the men in or near the town of Corbie.

One: 'Any officer seen taking wine out of Corbie is to be publicly hanged in the marketplace!'[13]

And two: 'Anyone spreading rumours of orders to retire is to be taken before the nearest commanding officer and, unless he can give a satisfactory account of himself, he is to be shot forthwith!'[14]

One officer standing nearby, not from Pompey's 15th Brigade, watches on in disbelief. 'It was all very reminiscent of the Red Queen in Alice in Wonderland,' he would later write. 'The men of his brigade were said to laugh at these things but others found them embarrassing.'[15]

As a Digger later recalled of the episode, 'If the Tommies were not running, they were breaking all records for the walking championship . . . Most of the Tommies were rounded up by Australian officers, who did not mince words about what they would do if the runaways did not stand to.'[16]

Pompey himself later wrote of his orders *extremis*: 'None seem inclined to make of themselves a test case under the circumstances.'[17]

But still, he knows the men are tired and want to slack off and indulge in a tipple too many. And it is for this reason that he is next touring the outposts of his own 15th Brigade to see that all is shipshape.

He comes across a small, isolated group.

'What the devil are you doing?' he thunders.

'Outposts, sir,' the bravest of them replies.

'What are your instructions?'

'To look out for you, sir.'[18]

The men's commander had obviously told them to warn him if Pompey was about, so he could have time to conceal whatever needed concealing. The men were too dim to realise that they shouldn't tell Pompey that!

And so Pompey storms off in a rage – the type of rage that only Pompey can maintain and never regret – to have a little parleyvous with this unnamed officer. Following closely behind is one of his staff officers, Captain Bob Salmon.

'On arrival at the company headquarters,' Captain Salmon later recalled, 'we first met the cook and his offsider. The cook was dressed in a long frock coat, lavender trousers, high-coloured flowing tie, fancy waistcoat and bell topper, and his offsider was dressed as a female . . . Both were inebriated.'

Pompey's blood boils. In this instant he may hate these boys – his *own* boys – more than he hates the Hun across the line.

Slow to catch up, the drunk Diggers look up.'When they recognised Pompey,' Salmon would recall, 'they sprang to attention in a sort of way and saluted. It was the most ludicrous sight, but Pompey almost bellowed with anger.'[19]

Pompey finds and replaces their Commanding Officer within the hour.

—

Back at Villers-Bretonneux, the men of Henry Goddard's 35th Battalion are still in the line to the east of the town. Apart from the odd shell landing nearby, it is relatively calm. The rest of the brigade is in reserve back at Cachy.

Goddard himself is looking forward to a decent sleep. 'Our new quarters are much more comfortable. The house is well furnished[20] and is a large one. Everything is just as the people rushed away from it except that it appears to have been looted though much valuable stuff remains. I had a nice bedroom on the ground floor at the back of the house...'[21]

He turns in.

Outside, some of his men, along with other Diggers from various units – like the field ambulance – are acquainting themselves with the town. And they like what they see! Having travelled light, they are now met with cupboards full of new clothes, larders full of food, cellars full of wine and liquor!

Forthwith, they partake of these new treasures.

1 APRIL 1918, MESSINES, NO FOOLS THEM

You bloody beauty. It might be April Fool's Day but this is dinkum.

At long last, after ten days of waiting, the foot-sloggers of the AIF's 1st and 2nd Divisions have got the word. They can join the rest of the Australian soldiers in the south, make a stand in front of the approaching Germans and at last get a real crack at Fritz – and they are moving as soon as 10 o'clock this morning!

After the frantic stowing of gear, cleaning of billets and issuance of extra ammunition, Archie Barwick's 1st Battalion of the 1st Division are among the first to be on their way. They are excited, true, but also soon aware – once Barwick starts to think about the news 'that we were hopping in for our cut at the earliest opportunity' – that there is an inevitable consequence of their move south.

Yes, there is no way around it: 'There will be a few of the lads missing in a week or so, worse luck.'[22]

They push on, push south, beginning a cycle that will see them marching to rail yards, getting on trains, getting off again, marching to billets, arriving late at night . . . rushing breakfast the next morning and away on motor buses . . . Same again the next day, but this time it's Shanks' pony, moving all the time, moving south.

Their positions on Messines Ridge are taken by a couple of British Divisions that the high authorities consider better suited to that quiet sector – one of them being the shattered remnants of the 9th Scottish Division, which has been sent to Messines for desperately needed rest and so they can receive reinforcements to build back up to full strength. What is most important is to get the crack Australian troops to where they are most needed.

—

John Hardie has just got up on this Easter Monday morning in his billet at Cachy, just 2500 yards to the south-west of Villers-Bretonneux, when German shells start pounding the town. Several men of the 33rd go down hard, requiring stretcher-bearers on the DOUBLE!

'One Officer gave the order to take to the open immediately [after] the first shell came shrieking over,' Hardie would recount, 'but several of us disobeyed as it was mostly shrapnel and it was amongst those who obeyed that the casualties occurred.'

When this bout of shelling is over, Hardie and his mates start prowling around. One of them finds a French flag. Hardie himself discovers 'a gasmask stuffed with loot from a jeweller's shop'.[23] Wonderful! Hardie wisely throws the bangles and rings onto the roadway, treasuring the new gasmask as if his life depends upon it – because it does. His own mask had been damaged in recent days, and all the Australians know only too well what happens to the poor bastards who get gassed without protection.

On this same day, another Australian soldier, Private Sydney Young of the 36th Battalion, notes in his diary:

1st April. Saw two Tommies tied to trees as part of 28 days F.P. for being drunk.[24]

F. P. stands for field punishment, a brutal concept left over from the previous century. When flogging had been abolished in 1881, this method of disciplining the troops in the field had replaced it: being bound by handcuffs or rope and tied to some immovable object for two hours a day, often in an uncomfortable position, as in with your feet barely touching the ground.

The Australians always looked on such barbarity with horror. Not only would they have rebelled outright if their own officers had tried such cruel and humiliating punishment on them or any of their mates, but they also frequently cut down the Tommies they found suffering it.

Bloody British.

—

The Germans?

After ten days of continual battle – surging forward, moving men and materiel to the west, all while coping with a flood of wounded and prisoners coming back the other way – the result is inevitable.

The men of Germany's 91st Infantry Regiment, who had taken Aubercourt with relative ease on 30 March before being brought to a standstill by Colonel Morshead's 'fierce resistance,'[25] are, for the moment at least, perilously close to *kaput*. Exhausted, exposed, low on supplies, the best they can do is just hold on in the muddy, shallow ditches and holes in front of Aubercourt as hellfire rains upon them from the enemy's artillery. At least their situation is recognised by those higher up. The stormtroopers' progress has far outstripped the supply lines.

'Our strength exhausted . . . we had to take breath,' Marshal von Hindenburg would ruefully recount. 'The infantry needed rest and the artillery ammunition.'[26]

Wunderbar!

'No attacks on our part were ordered,' the regimental history of the 91st gratefully records of this first day of April. 'The day should be exploited primarily for refreshing the combat troops . . . The enemy artillery fire was like the strength of the previous day. Apparently, however, new long-range guns had arrived, who sent their iron greetings from far behind their terrain.'[27]

Such greetings are being extended to the Hun soldiers all along the line. They must now work furiously to build better trenches. The shallow shell holes and undulations in the earth they've been making do with simply cannot protect them.

The key question is, what now? And on this morning of 1 April, General Ludendorff is at St Quentin, trying to determine the answer, his heavy brow ever more furrowed. In recent days, Ludendorff has been so worried that his balls of bread at breakfast, lunch and dinner tend to fly around like marbles in a bucket.

After Operation Michael had started so promisingly, with such huge advances, in the last couple of days that momentum has come to a halt. In the north, around Arras, the British Third Army is continuing to hold the line, while in the south, in front of Amiens, the colonials have arrived to stiffen the British resistance and the German 2nd Army has itself all but stalled. In total, they have captured over 1000 guns and nearly 100,000 prisoners – but no vital strategic objective, no place that will inevitably shift the course of the war in Germany's favour.

Ludendorff calls a meeting so they might come to a decision, and General von Kuhl is quick to express his view once more: 'The main objective is the British, therefore Second and Seventeenth Armies should attack north of the Somme.'

Ludendorff demurs, correcting his *Generalleutnant*. 'The main objective,' he insists, 'is first to split the British from the French, *then* the main objective becomes to destroy the British.'[28]

Ah, yes, Villers-Bretonneux. It is a town upon a small, elevated plateau, before which, for once, the Allies really have mounted some serious resistance, digging themselves in and obliging the German Army to take pause in positions still some two miles outside the town.

('Perhaps,' the Chief of the German General Staff would record of his thoughts after the war, 'Amiens means decisive victory. Capture Villers-Bretonneux whatever happens, so that from its heights we can command Amiens with masses of our heavy artillery!' It is a view entirely in agreement with Marshal von Hindenburg's.[29])

It is possible they will call off Operation Michael, but not yet. First they must throw their all into capturing Villers-Bretonneux, in which case Amiens really would be inevitably pounded into submission – and they would press on to take it the day after the attack on Villers. The timing for the attack is tentatively set for dawn, 4 April, three days hence. In the meantime, the 2nd Army, which will have carriage of the attack, must shift forward their reserve divisions now trickling in, ready to take over. The divisions that have been in the line since the beginning of the *Kaiserschlacht* urgently need to be rested. If Villers-Bretonneux is captured, then Operation Michael remains alive. If not, then the Germans will have no alternative but to call off the offensive and shift even more of their heavy artillery north for Operation George, which is due to start on 9 April.

———

General Haig can feel it in his bones: the Germans are about to attack once more. As to where, he is not positive. But he *is* positive that, whatever else happens, his side must hold Villers-Bretonneux. At a meeting with Prime Minister Georges Clémenceau on this day, in Rawlinson's Fourth Army HQ at Dury, he points out the importance of this, again.

Holding Villers-Bretonneux, he says, covers the British right flank and the French left flank, and, most crucially, keeps the Germans from taking or destroying Amiens.

But, Monsieur le *Premier Ministre*, there is now an urgent need for the French – yes, the *French* – to do more, to take over the line just south of Villers-Bretonneux 'from Moreuil to the village of Hangard . . .'[30]

Clémenceau immediately instructs an orderly to call for General Foch, and after Foch arrives a short time later – flags afluttering in his motorcade – it doesn't take long. Clémenceau speaks to him quickly in private, then Haig explains exactly where he wants the French positioned, on the right flank of the British lines in front of Villers-Bretonneux, taking over the front presently held by 8th and 14th Divisions. These two divisions can now be shifted north to Haig's line, also in front of the village.

'Foch,' Haig later notes with some satisfaction in his diary, 'quickly put his name to a document ordering General Fayolle to take over the line I wanted.'[31]

No, it is not the French actively involved in the fight, as Haig would prefer, but at least it has them more involved in defending the line, allowing the British to more heavily concentrate their forces.

1 APRIL 1918, BATTLING THE BULGE AROUND VILLERS-BRETONNEUX

Driving along the roads around Villers-Bretonneux on this afternoon, noting 'the new wheat just springing 5 or 6 inches high',[32] is none other than Charles Bean, and after a day visiting Australian positions and talking to senior officers, he has much to ponder.

The bulge made in the Allied line, with the prow directed at Amiens, is now 50 miles wide and 40 miles at its deepest. Around the curve of the bulge the French hold the southern third, but the rest is defended by the British. For the most part, senior officers of the AIF to whom Bean has spoken are satisfied, with the exception being the ongoing thorn of having Australian units under English command – particularly after all the exultation in early November at the Australian Corps coming together. The Commander of the 4th Division, General Ewen Maclagan, for example, reluctantly had to cede his 4th Brigade, still at Hébuterne, to the command of the 37th British Division, and he wants his men back as badly as they want to come back. (Among other things, the 'old Brig' of the 4th, Colonel Charles Brand, has told Bean, 'I do not wonder that the British soldiers came back so fast considering the way they were fed.'[33])

Two other questions are commonly put to Bean on the day: what on earth are the French doing, and what will the Germans do next? For all the brouhaha made by Foch about how his forces would not cede an inch of French territory, they have yet to strike a blow in anger at this latest German attack.

The next move by the Germans is not known, but the way Bean sees it, after examining the situation on maps, the problem the Germans have is that, after attacking initially on such a wide front, '[their] drive is getting down to a pencil point, very dangerous looking . . . rather like the ram of a battleship. They must widen [the salient] . . .'[34] Otherwise, with no forces flanking those on the prow, they are in danger of the point of the pencil breaking off – if they come up against a force sufficiently strong enough to do it.

As to just why the British have been so atrocious in resisting the

German assault to this point, one of the officers he has consulted, Colonel Arthur Butler, had told Bean that 'the men are universally blaming Haig for this reverse – [while] the Australian officers blame Gough, whom they have never liked since Pozières. It is wonderful how true that intuition is. Everyone whom I speak to is glad that Foch has been made C in C.'[35]

———

It is not as if the problems the Australians are having with British officers are not sometimes reversed in these troubled times – far from it.

On this evening, Lieutenant Jim Davies of the British Army's 9th Fusiliers is with his men west of Albert, close to Dernancourt, when he sees a lone soldier walking towards him in the near darkness.

'Who are you?' Davies calls.

'Fucking Australian,' the robust, belligerent and clearly drunken voice comes back. 'Who are you?'

'You realise you are talking to an officer?' the shocked Davies replies, mustering as much authority as he possibly can.

'Go fuck yourself,' comes the reply.

Davies takes pause. What to do now? His own troops are watching him very carefully, very coolly. This is going to be interesting.

In the extremity of the situation, with the Germans about to attack, it is clearly going to be counterproductive to say to his own men, 'Take his name and number.'

So there appears only one alternative. Davies punches the Australian with enough force to fell an ox, and this son of the Southern Cross drops like a sack of spuds.

That settles *that* brief insurrection.

'I never saw him again,' Davies would recount. 'I didn't want to . . . It was the only thing to do.'[36]

In terms of general bad behaviour, like looting, there will be many accusations made against the Australians, not *all* of which are true. Some such charges are hotly denied by officers in particular, including

Captain Alexander Ellis of the 5th Division's 29th Battalion, who would go on to add: 'Lest there may be some . . . who are troubled by widely advertised English views of Australian discipline generally, it may be as well to admit that the average Australian private has not the lynx-eyed deference which detects officers from afar, and confers on them an extravagant salute at a range of fifty yards or more. In this respect Australian discipline is tested best by steadiness on the field of battle and by reliability in circumstances of great strain and danger.'[37]

And that really is something.

But there is, and make no mistake, a good deal of bald-faced looting by the Australians, too . . .

In Villers-Bret, where for the last couple of days the 9th Brigade boys in support have had the run of the town, 'the warehouses were stocked, the shops likewise, and the cellars and estaminets were not by any means stripped of liquors and champagnes.'[38] So they've done the obvious and have set up a black market to trade their looted goods. Grog, clothes, bicycles, lingerie – you name it – one of the Diggers has hoarded a supply and is open for trade. Everything must go! Come and get it!

'For instance,' one soldier would later explain, 'a Digger with a hoarded supply of old champagne would swap a couple of bottles of it away to another Digger for a souvenired bicycle, would ride it perhaps for a couple of days, and in turn would exchange it for a loaf of bread.'[39]

Finally, though, an officer of the 9th Brigade wises up to the game and orders all bottles of grog to be smashed. As one Digger would lament, 'Those who were in the town that day saw something that had never been seen in the town before and it is hoped will never be seen again – the gutters running red with wine!'[40]

The Diggers assure the officers that it is all gone.

Still, you never know . . .

—

Enemy shelled Cachy and Gentelles again this afternoon with 5.9, Rosenthal notes in his diary this night. *Our battalions now living in huts and in the open away from the village of Cachy.* Of all the decisions that Rosie has made, perhaps the most significant is also recorded in his diary:

> *Instructions given late tonight regarding the construction of a switch line in front of Gentelles and Cachy.*

To be known as the Cachy Switch Line – a switch line being a fighting trench that connects your front-line to your second line, to be used if the enemy captures a section of your front-line – the construction of this singularly deep trench will begin the next day, and it will extend for 2000 yards from north of Cachy, in front of Bois d'Aquenne, almost to Villers-Bretonneux.

Yes, the Australians want to hold Villers-Bretonneux, and they think they can. All this day Fritz has been probing forward against Australian positions, and all day long the brute has been beaten back, not least because 'the artillery got on to him, drove him back in disorder and caused him heavy casualties'.[41] But if, perchance, the Germans *do* break through, then it is as well to have a trench line to fall back upon, to set up as the next line of defence.

Among the artillery positioned to act as sentinel over the town of Villers-Bretonneux is that of the Monash's 3rd Division. General Monash writes to Hannah, explaining, 'for several days the situation on my right flank was very obscure. I therefore made all preparations to defend the line of the Somme west of Sailly-le-Sec as far as Aubigny, in case the enemy tried to get behind me.'[42]

That includes, of course, positioning some of the 3rd Division's field batteries so that they have sights over the ground south of the Somme, extending to Villers-Bretonneux.

—

While it is one thing for an officer to simply draw a line on a map indicating where a particular trench should be positioned, it is quite

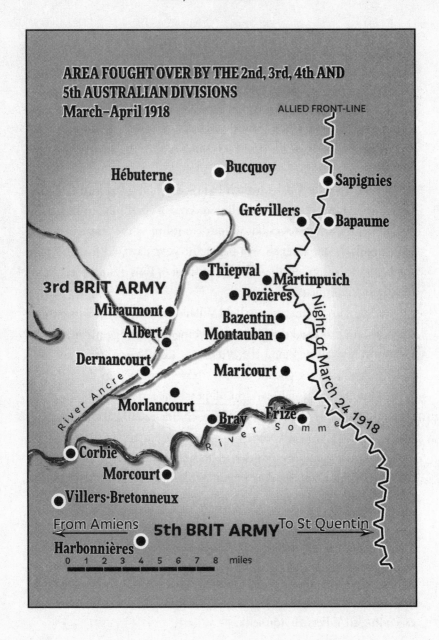

AREA FOUGHT OVER BY THE 2nd, 3rd, 4th AND
5th AUSTRALIAN DIVISIONS
March–April 1918

ALLIED FRONT-LINE

Hébuterne

Bucquoy

Sapignies

Grévillers

Bapaume

Thiepval

Martinpuich

3rd BRIT ARMY

Poziëres

Miraumont

Bazentin

Albert

Montauban

Dernancourt

Maricourt

Morlancourt

Bray

Frize

Night of March 24 1918

River Ancre

River Somme

Corbie

Morcourt

Villers-Bretonneux

From Amiens

5th BRIT ARMY

To St Quentin

Harbonnières

0 1 2 3 4 5 6 7 8 miles

another to actually dig the bloody thing, *as well as* its support line, a
parallel trench several hundred yards behind – the fall-back position
should the first line be breached. There is something of a support line
in existence here – 200 yards behind the front-line and parallel to the

9th Australian Brigade's front – built by the Brits who've abandoned it, but it is judged as manifestly inadequate.

For the 35th Battalion, positioned in the front-line just 3000 yards to the east of Villers-Bretonneux, the truth is they just don't have the manpower required, and it is for this reason the 9th Brigade's Brigadier Rosenthal has ordered the 33rd Battalion forward on this late evening of 2 April to assist in the digging.

The one upside of the messy task in the rain is that at least it is easy to make headway in the soft, ploughed soil – so fertile you could plant a matchstick and grow a pine tree. Even those who don't have their 'banjo' entrenching tool are able to move heaps of wet earth with their hands and helmets. All are aware that, with the Germans coming on strong, every effort they make at this moment might soon mean the difference between life and death.

Quietly now. Marching first into Villers-Bretonneux in the fading light, the 465 soldiers of the 33rd Battalion gaze around them. Clearly this had been quite a picturesque town once, with neat houses, cobble-stone streets, carefully tended garden patches and . . . perhaps even a certain French smugness that, while there might exist a world beyond this beautiful place, it was a good thing that God had blessed them to be right here.

Colonel Morshead reports to Colonel Goddard, under whose com-mand he now comes, and is told to billet the men in 'the south-east portion of the town'.[43] As for Morshead and his staff, they are to stay and set up headquarters here with Goddard.

The Diggers are close behind.

'After dark,' Private John Hardie records, 'we marched out to a large town on top of the ridges which is called Villers-Bretonneux where we were billeted for the night . . .'[44] By now all but the oldest and most stubborn of the inhabitants of Villers-Bretonneux have fled, leaving their homes and, most pertinently, their once well-stocked cellars to soldiers.

Bit by bit, the lights, or at least the lanterns, come on again in Villers-Bretonneux as the Australians make themselves comfortable – always a strong point for those men from the south – in once-grand

An elderly resident of Villers-Bretonneux who remained in her house throughout the fighting of 4 April.[45]

châteaus and humble cottages alike. Naturally enough, the Diggers are not long in referring to the town as 'VB', after the famed beer Victoria Bitter from south of the Murray River, or just 'Villers' or 'Villers-Bret.'

Once the men are settled, working parties are sent forward to help the 35th dig trenches – with eight hours digging each night to be the aim, and back by dawn so as not to be seen by enemy observers.

—

Given that Private Hardie and his comrades are no longer there, how surprising can it be that his aforementioned 'booze artists' are quickly on the job once more, going after the undoubted cache that VB still possesses.

Among them are a couple of mates, Private Alfie Holton and Private Reggie Dilley, from the 36th Battalion, who have heard there is grog freely available, and so they do the obvious. The two leave their make-shift huts in the woods at Bois l'Abbé, three miles from VB, and make their way into town when it is dark. Sure enough, as soon as they arrive they find 'a cellar full of every sort of wine and beer and champagne and also full of men, Tommies, Aussies, etc.'.

As a labourer from the back of Bourke, Alfie had been *born* thirsty, and to his eyes this looks as close to heaven as he will ever get. 'The cellar,' he would recount dreamily, 'was a room 100 ft by 20 ft and about 14 ft or so high and I can remember even now seeing men on top of cases 10 and 12 ft from the floor and singing and shouting like mad. I am sorry to say now that it was not long before I was like the rest of them and in the early hours of the morning you could have seen Dill and I staggering home.'[46]

—

Tough duty, but someone has to do it.

As it turns out, Private John Hardie finds himself on guard duty, protecting against looters the contents of a large building in VB found to contain huge amounts of food and booze, not to mention 'tangle-foot', the Diggers' nickname for rolls of barbed wire.

The German shelling of Villers goes on, all day long, killing many soldiers and officers, and maiming many more. And, wouldn't you know it, right at the height of the worst of the shelling an old lady – she musta been at least 80 years old with wrinkles on her wrinkles – closes the front door of her house, which she has probably lived in all her life. Cheerfully holding a swag containing all her worldly belongings, she walks on down the shell-torn road towards Amiens.

'She was the last inhabitant to leave Villers-Bretonneux,'[47] Private Hardie records, 'and seemed quite cheerful as she hobbled along . . .'[48]

Anyway, back to defending against the dastardly looters. Hardie heads inside the building and remarks to one of his mates, Corporal Tommy Polson, about the pleasures of a soldier's life, nodding to two of their other mates who have just finished a fine meal of roast chicken with tinned vegetables, washed down by a couple bottles of the finest champagne.

Tommy laughs, and then dies.

For at that instant, a German shell crashes through the roof and explodes.

When Hardie comes to a few seconds later it is with some surprise that he finds himself still alive and seemingly unhurt, though it is obvious that Tommy and another bloke who was standing next to him are dead. Staggering through the smoke and dust, Hardie is trying to remember where the door is when one of the guards from outside appears and suggests they get out. Genius! But now comes another shell, another explosion, and the guard is hurled into the street. Hardie makes it outside anyway, alive, and even gets 30 yards up the street before somehow . . . the cobblestones . . . rise up . . . to meet him . . . and he collapses. Private Hardie is gathered in, taken to a dressing station and soon evacuated to a field hospital 15 miles behind the lines. His part in the Villers-Bretonneux campaign is over.

—

The two well-cut, impeccably turned out military figures moving through the town this morning stand in stark contrast to the devastation they see all around them. Colonel Morshead of the 33rd Battalion and Colonel Goddard of the 35th are reconnoitring on the instructions of their brigade commander, Brigadier Rosenthal, who had dropped by their HQ this morning after having 'visited the new [Cachy] switch line and found all units had work well in hand'.[49]

Rosie had been very pleased with his battalion commanders' efforts and had spent ten minutes talking over the situation and giving them his orders: the '35th Battalion [are] to use all companies in the front line, while the 33rd are to be responsible for construction of the support line. The 33rd Battalion is to provide a party of 50 NCOs and men . . . as a picket for the town'.[50]

Then, before he had left, he also handed front-line command over to Colonel Goddard, given that the British Generals have ordered him to stay further back at Gentelles, from where he has no hope in hell of commanding his men.

Colonel Goddard had taken on the responsibility with his signature equanimity, assuring the Brigadier that he would not let him down.

And now Goddard and Morshead are hunting out the best observation posts, the concealed routes through the town and any large cellars where they can shelter their men.

Most impressive is the town church, with its large, dark-red twin towers, perfect for positioning observers. From up on top they can see the whole surrounding terrain, including, most particularly, the railway running along the south side of town. It is flat, sometimes slicing through undulations in the ground in cuttings, sometimes perched atop high embankments – in both cases forming a strong defensive feature against attacks from that direction.

They also note a scattering of small woods, *les bois*, gathered in green puddles around the town, places of mostly scrubby growth on ground not considered suitable for farming – but ideal for Fritz to dig himself into as he forges his way west. The woods will have to be closely watched and heavily defended.

One of these spots of growth, Monument Wood, some 1500 yards to their south, is particularly significant – a chapel in an apple orchard surrounded by a wall of trees marks the furious battle fought right here during the Franco-Prussian War in 1870. On 27 November, the great French General Charles Bourbaki, with 17,000 newly raised soldiers, had fought valiantly against twice that many German veterans under General Edwin von Manteuffel, who was leading the march along the Roman road from Péronne in an effort to take the nearby town of Amiens. If they could get to that town and destroy its rail line, the French capacity to move their reinforcement and supplies along it would be strangled and their army would wither and die. On that occasion, the French had lost the battle and the Germans had successfully gone on to take Amiens. This time, the Australians are here.

As to the Villers-Bretonneux church itself, it is in remarkably good condition. 'A fine old building,' Colonel Goddard would note in his diary, 'and except for one or two shells, untouched.'Alas, the same cannot be said for all the soldiers now inhabiting Villers. 'A dead man or two and a pool of blood just inside the door gave it a tragic aspect.'[51]

As the two officers come out of the church, a distant, high drone adds some pepper to their worst fears. It is German aircraft, up there, surely doing reconnaissance on just where the Australians are dug in.

Brigadier Rosenthal, meantime, is trotting back to his own head-quarters in Gentelles. As he leaves Villers-Bret he can't help but lament the devastation, noting in his diary later that day, *The condition of this and every other town through which our British troops have returned is too awful for words. Looting and drunkenness has been the order of the day and in my opinion have been directly the cause of so much falling back. We are trying our best to straighten up the towns again but it is a Herculean task.*[52]

———

Up Dernancourt way, the 4th Division blokes are getting a little dis-concerted by all the . . . peace! Sure, there remain so many shells flying from both sides that it is a wonder some of them don't collide midair, and there is still the odd local skirmish and raid around the front-lines. Apart from that, the men in the forward positions are finding things just a little . . . well . . . *dull*.

'We are getting a glum lot,'[53] George Mitchell notes in his diary, writing on the front-line after a day in which three-fifths of bugger-all has happened. The only bit of excitement comes at the end of the day, when Mitch takes a fatigue party forward, carrying bundles of tangle-foot so that if Fritz comes on again, he'll be slowed down and more easily shot.

Nearby, on Mitchell's right flank, Private Stanley Sutcliffe of the 51st Battalion is finding events equally unspectacular.

'Things were so quiet,' he would record of this period. 'We hardly knew the Germans were there at all . . . We had nothing to do, only a little bombing in the streets of Dernancourt.'[54]

For all that, well behind the lines at 13th Brigade headquarters, Brigadier William Glasgow is just one who knows this period of relative peace won't last. 'It looks as if all the Colonial troops are to be sacrificed to check this advance,' one of his staff records in his diary of the feeling among the Australian officers. 'They certainly have brought Fritz to a standstill, but cannot last forever.'[55]

3 APRIL 1918, 2ND ARMY HEADQUARTERS, GUISE, THE BATTLE TO END ALL WARS

For General Georg von der Marwitz, the tall, grey-tipped, purse-lipped, well-clipped commanding officer of Germany's 2nd Army – whose troops are due to launch the last great breakthrough to Amiens in the morning – it has been a hectic few days. He is keenly aware that, while winning the battle and losing the war is one thing, sometimes, rarely, there are battles that can win a war in their own right, and this is one of them. And it is so close!

'You could measure the distance that separated the Germans from final victory, *in Schritten*, in steps,' he would note of this time. 'It is the small distance from the German front to Amiens.'[56]

It is now up to his men to close that gap.

And others, among them General Marwitz's own commander *Kronprinz* Rupprecht, share his concern that they simply won't have the material strength to pull off the breakthrough; the very problem Ludendorff has been trying to avoid since he first started planning.

But they must try.

'We must get our heavy field guns in the triangle at Longeau, east of Amiens, to take the city under fire,' he writes in his diary this evening. 'The more terrain we gain, the more effectively we can carry out our bombardment of the city, the bombardment of the central station of Amiens, and the railway bridge over the Somme. If we succeed in making the railways in Amiens unusable, a very important advantage is achieved . . .'[57]

It is all so neat when written down like that. A little too easy, perhaps. So it is that he balances his entry with his characteristic caution: 'But who knows whether it'll happen that way!'[58]

—

Privates Reggie Dilley and Alfred Holton – known as Dill and Alfie to their mates and each other – have gone back for second helpings. They'd had such a good time the night before; it's the obvious thing to do, isn't it? Years of this blasted war, in blasted trenches all the time, and suddenly you have a chance to be merry with mates, guzzling gallons of the finest grog there ever was? Of course they skip their trench-digging duties and go back to Villers-Bret after dark on this third day of April – even if, this time, they have to dodge the MPs who have been placed on duty to keep out the scurvy likes of them.

No matter, in short order they are in a cellar and knocking it back with the best of them, so much and so quickly that they soon empty it and move to another cellar, whereupon . . . *aw, shit* . . . here comes the Captain of their company. And he is pissed off.

'Drop that,' the Captain nods to Dill and the gallon jar of wine he is holding.

Dill, however, will do no such thing, and rises to the occasion.

'I am going to take it home,' says he.

'You're not,' replies the Captain. 'Drop it.'

So Dill drops it – plenty more where that came from – and he and Holton quickly scurry off, ignoring the Captain's cries for them to go straight back to camp. They duck into the first cellar they find, just around the corner, only to be pursued by the Captain again, now backed by a Corporal, both of them with 'their balls in a knot'. Well, the *both* of them can get nicked. Alfie and Dill get away once more and head into yet another cellar.

This time the Captain sends out after them a Lieutenant with several soldiers, and one of the Sergeants would later tell Alfie how they arrived to find him flat on his back with his mouth open while Dill poured the grog straight down his gullet. When one of the other Sergeants pulls Alfie to his feet, that gentlemen is so aggrieved that he takes a wild swing at the officer and falls over once more. He and Dill are placed under arrest and led away – only to be interrupted by German shells falling all around and Holton wanting to fight a Frenchman for his tin hat, only narrowly avoiding being shot for his trouble.

'You're a fine state to be in,' a passing Australian officer says to Holton. 'Suppose Fritz was to come now, what would you do?'

'I'd fight the lot of them,'[59] Alfie says, and he means it.

If they'd been Brits, of course, the two brawling booze artists would likely have been given field punishment. As it is, they are instantly given ten days' fatigue duty – burying dead horses will be the nicest of their tasks – and suspension of pay as punishment.

———

All quiet on the Western Front on this late night of 3 April.

But for how long?

As the soldiers of the 9th Brigade's 35th Battalion settle into their haphazard trenches 3000 yards east of Villers-Bretonneux – most of them getting some kip in their shallow dugouts, leaving just a few comrades on sentry duty – there is little tangible sign of any forthcoming attack. Yes, there is an awareness that the German Army is just over yonder fields, many of the soldiers secreted in the villages of Marcelcave and Aubercourt, but there is no particular sign that they are readying for another 'stunt'. And, yes, there is discomfort, but it is more physical than spiritual. For much of this war the trenches occupied by the Australians had been sophisticated affairs, deeply zigzagging across the terrain, with a large parapet on the enemy side providing extra protection, as did the many rolls of barbed wire.

This is not like that. These trenches – a platoon-length series only 50 yards or so long, with gaps in between each platoon and no communication trenches to get to the men under cover – had been dug only yesterday and are unfinished and ramshackle at best. Shallow as a birdbath, they are constructed so that you have to stoop as you walk along, for fear of Fritz knocking your bloody block off. A latrine? Unless you want to be standing in it, the best you can do is to crap in an empty Maconochie's stew tin and throw it Fritz's way, into No-Man's Land, giving him some small change for the shells he's been sending you.

All of them recognise these trenches for what they are – somethin' that is better than nuttin', and just a little better again than a poke in the eye with a burnt stick, but not by much. They're not built to withstand a serious German assault, and all the men will be able to do is the best they can. Tonight they are making small fires to warm their Maconochie stew and boil their billies, trying not to think of the lucky bastards of 33rd Battalion, back there in VB, no doubt having the time of their lives in some Frenchie's cellar.

Meanwhile, the digs of the 34th and 36th Battalions are further back still, in a reserve in the woods just west of town. One of the boys of the 36th – one who hasn't snuck into Villers-Bret to raid the booze supply – is having a grand time, a rare occasion where being in the woods is better than being out. 'It was raining pretty heavily so we made a tent out of our two waterproofs,' he records in his diary, 'lined it with straw from an adjacent haystack, caught the rain off the roof in dixies, and made tea, and lay back in comfort & enjoyed it.'[60]

Heaven!

All right for some. Back up front, Major Henry Carr – a civil servant from Parramatta before the war – is in charge of all four companies in the front trench. There will be no tea for him tonight. Doing his rounds near midnight, making sure that all sentries are awake and alert, he comes across Captain Hugh Connell from 35th Battalion HQ. The two have a chat as brief as it is quiet. And Major Carr is firm.

'The enemy will attack tomorrow morning,'[61] he says flatly. All day he has noted low-flying German planes observing them, most particularly flying laterally *along* their trench system, tracking its layout. Like dark clouds before the coming storm, this is a sure sign of trouble ahead. Carr is insistent that Connell be extra vigilant, that their ammunition supplies are fully stocked and the men have got the word that Fritz should be here shortly.

As the long boom of artillery in the far distance rolls over them, Carr moves further along the line to the right and gives the same view to Captain Raleigh Sayers of D Company, and then 200 yards further again to Captain Gilbert Coghill of A Company, a 30-year-old professional soldier from Kempsey who is and always has been notably dedicated to the cause. Carr knows Coghill to be the best kind of officer, one who is not only unbending in maintaining high standards in his own behaviour, but who also inspires those around him to try to reach the benchmark he has set.

Because of Carr's insistence, the sentries are on high alert throughout the night. The remainder of the men are to sleep – Carr wants them rested and ready for whatever the Germans might throw at them in the morning. In the early hours a raid instituted by the 7th Buffs, the East Kent Regiment, over on the far right of the Australians, brings further evidence of German intentions. They are able to take a German prisoner who, on interrogation, spills a bean. Just one bean. Not all of them. The German Army, he says, is indeed 'about to attack'.[62]

Two companies of the 9th Brigade's 33rd Battalion are moved into the same support line behind the 35th Battalion that they had been so assiduously digging 36 hours earlier.

Ready for anything . . .

CHAPTER ELEVEN
A DAY OF RECKONING

Some of the English divisions had been badly broken and we
passed a number of derelicts who regarded us with a sort of
unwilling admiration, as men going up to do the impossible
. . . It makes one feel proud to be an Australian to see our
boys after all this passing through a village singing. They are
magnificent and wherever they go they inspire confidence,
both in the Tommies and in the French civilians.[1]
Captain Francis Fairweather of the 10th Brigade
in a letter home, 4 April 1918

The personal ascendancy of the Australian
soldier on the battlefield . . . made him the best
infantryman of the war and perhaps of all time.
British Major-General Hubert Essame, CBE, DSO, MC,
who fought with the Australians at Villers-Bretonneux[2]

Ein harter Kampf entbrannte, a tough battle ensued.[3]
A German newspaper report, in Vossische Zeitung, of the events of 4 April

DAWN, 4 APRIL 1918, EAST OF VB, THE CLOCK IS TICKING

All is in readiness. Fifteen German divisions, with seven more in reserve,
will attack along a 21-mile front against the British from the Somme

southward through Villers-Bretonneux to Hangard Wood and against the French 1st Army further south from Hangard to Grivesnes – rather similar in size to the first day of the Battle of the Somme in 1916, while still only a third of the opening day of *der Kaiserschlacht*.

The key part of the attack is directed at the 14th and 18th British Divisions, with the 35th Australian Battalion tucked in between them in the trenches along 8000 yards of the front, some two miles east of Villers-Bretonneux. Here, almost 50,000 German soldiers from the 4th Guards Division, the 228th Division and the 9th Bavarian Reserve Division – all belonging to General Marwitz's 2nd Army – are now in position. The first of the German waves to cross the 400 yards of *Niemandsland*, No-Man's Land, are already crouched or lying in the makeshift trenches that have been hastily dug where their advance had ended on 30 March. Most of the next waves are secreted in hidden locations, like woods and folds in the ground as much as a mile further back, ready to move forward when the first wave rolls forth to break over the enemy defences.

Nearby – in some cases no more than 1500 yards away and equally secreted – are 500 artillery pieces, their battery commanders now anxiously looking at their watches, all carefully synchronised.

—

As dawn creeps over the trenches in front of Villers-Bretonneux, the soldiers of the British 14th Division, the Australian 9th Brigade and the British 18th Division – 19,000 soldiers in all – 'stand to'. That is, following the strictest military protocol, they stand in their trenches, weapons in hand. When there is just enough light to see, they ensure there is nothing and no one in No-Man's Land before 'standing down', leaving the sentries to it while they make tea and get ready for a brekka of biscuit and jam, with a thick, greasy slice of bacon if the gods smile on them.

—

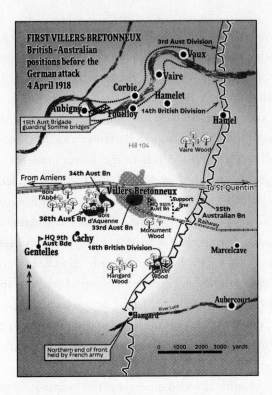

FIRST VILLERS-BRETONNEUX
British–Australian
positions before the
German attack
4 April 1918

3rd Aust Division

Vaux

Vaire

Corbie

Hamelet

14th British Division

Aubigny

Fouilloy

Hamel

15th Aust Brigade
guarding Somme bridges

Hill 104

Vaire Wood

From Amiens

34th Aust Bn

Villers-Bretonneux

To St Quentin

Bois
l'Abbé

HQ 35th
Aust Bn

Support
line

35th
Australian Bn
Railway

36th Aust Bn

Bois
d'Aquenne

33rd Aust Bn

Monument
Wood

HQ 9th
Aust Bde

Cachy

Gentelles

18th British Division

Marcelcave

N

Hangard
Wood

Lancer
Wood

Aubercourt

River Luce

Hangard

Northern end of front
held by French army

0   1000   2000   3000   yards

They are just seconds away. At exactly 5.30 am, it is the German battery commanders' job to launch the bombardment on British front-line
positions. It will last for exactly 60 minutes.

5:29:30 . . . 5:29:40 . . . 5:29:50 . . .

Fünf . . . vier . . . drei . . . zwei . . . eins . . . und FEUER!

—

In one trench of the Australians' 35th Battalion, right in front of
Villers-Bret itself, Captain Gilbert Coghill's batman is serving a breakfast of freshly roasted chicken and a bottle of champagne that is nicely
chilled, courtesy of a cold night spent in the fields. No use wasting the
local supplies, what? Suddenly there comes a dirty crack of doom from
the east, and a thousand more on the instant. The subsequent heavy
rumbling is soon followed by the inevitable whistling . . . and then
the ghastly explosion of shells all around. It is, no doubt, the Germans

doing what they have always done so bloody well – ruining an otherwise pleasant morning, the light rain notwithstanding.

Captain Coghill abandons his champagne and gives the orders. With shell fire this intense, it can only be a matter of time before the Germans attack en masse. The likelihood of this is confirmed when gas shells enter the deadly artillery mix – the classic prelude to an infantry attack. As the 35th's Colonel Goddard would recall, the whole town 'was smothered in high explosive and gas'.[4] The men whip on their masks.

With the Germans' cue, the symphony starts up in the west, too, as the British artillery pounds away, returning shell fire in kind.

The time is just after 7 am when, through their blurry gasmasks and plumes of clearing shell smoke, the Australians in the front-line can suddenly see what at first appears to be the ephemeral will-o'-the-wisp swirling towards them. The village of Marcelcave on fire behind gives these strange phantom silhouettes the appearance of Satan's hellhounds let loose to rip out their throats. But these figures all too quickly turn out to be grey masses of German Infantry on the charge.

Still, rising to the occasion, Captain Coghill calmly tells his men that they are to allow the Germans to keep coming and not fire a shot until he lifts his arm. He even climbs atop the embankment they have been using as their principal defence and repeats the order, ensuring that every man jack in his company can see him.

'All right,' one of the men at his feet agrees equably, gazing up at him, 'but Christ couldn't make me stand up there.'[5]

———

The German soldiers of the 9th Bavarian Reserve Division, some 8000 infantry strong, continue to surge forward – the 228th Division on their right and the 4th Guards Division further to the right again. Yet they are not without wariness. The night before they had learned, somewhat to their chagrin, that the soldiers they would be attacking are *Australier*, Australians, and the veterans among them know what that means.

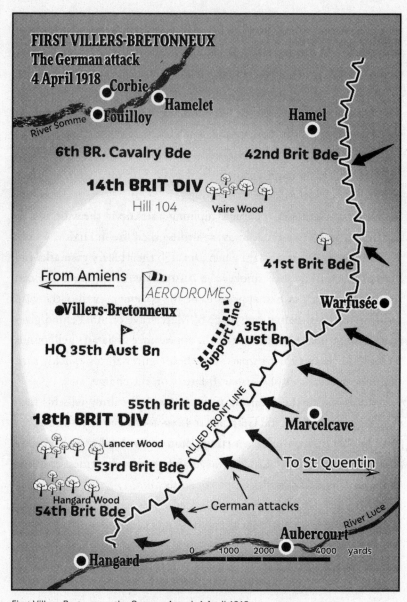

First Villers-Bretonneux the German Attack 4 April 1918

—

For the Germans of 48th Regiment, the attack is going well, albeit with a few problems . . .

As planned, at precisely 7.30 am, 650 soldiers of the 2nd Battalion of the 48th Regiment charge forth from their trenches, when 'short shots of our *Feuerwalze* . . . threaten to derail the joined attack.'[6] To be killed or maimed by the enemy is one thing, but nothing is more demoralising or embittering for surviving troops than to see comrades killed by their own. In such circumstances, it takes great leadership to put things right, and in this case the 2nd Battalion of the 48th Regiment is well provided.

'Then Capt. [Rudolf] Teichmann,' as the 48th Regimental History would record, 'who has watched closely all the developments, places himself at the head of this company, and pulls the hesitating men with him, leading by example. Closely behind the *Feuerwalze*, the battalion penetrates into the enemy position, and all who do not surrender are shot when trying to flee. Only a [few of the British soldiers] manage to escape in the direction of Bois de Vaire. Without faltering, the infantry attack is carried out to the ordered objectives.'[7]

This is typical of Teichmann, one of the most outstanding officers in the German Army. As his divisional commander, Major-General von der Heyde, would later note, 'Captain Teichmann is an excellent officer, who already several times had been active decisively by rapidly detecting the situation and personal intervention. On 4 April 1918, he again has *den Sieg an die Fahnen des Regiments geheftet*, stapled victory on the flags of the regiment by quick decision, by fully inserting himself and by his great influence on the troops . . .'[8]

And still the German attack goes on, proceeding well.

'At 10.05 am,' the official history will record, 'the 2nd Battalion of the 48th Regiment has reached the outskirts of Villers-Bretonneux . . .'[9]

Trouble.

For they had come across the Australians the year before at Passchendaele, when they had been defending their trenches and doing well against all comers, until the night of 26 September 1917, at Polygon Wood, when the Australians had attacked them in force and beat them soundly. The 9th was obliged to retreat, dragging their wounded with them. In this campaign, the 9th have been kept fresh and thrown into the line for this, their first battle in Operation Michael – only to find themselves up against the Australians again.

Scheißen!

—

And still Coghill waits, intent on giving the Germans no warning until they are right upon his men.

60 yards . . .

50 yards . . .

45 yards . . .

40 yards . . .

And . . . *now!*

Coghill raises his arm. A burst from a Lewis gun hammers out, quickly drowned out by the roar of many guns opening up. Alas, the first German shot has hit Coghill in his elevated arm, and he is now bleeding heavily. For the moment he will have to look after himself, as the Australians *pour* fire into the approaching Germans, whose approach is shattered.

'We were ready for them,' Colonel Henry Goddard would recount, 'and every rifle, Lewis gun and machine gun came into action . . . We had no wire defences but the German troops sagged and withered under our fire.'[10]

Fritz does not dispute it, even if he will be mistaken in the nationality of who is stopping them.

'At 6:30 am the attack begins,' one Regiment's history records, 'but the resistance of the enemy is not broken, the firing lines of the *Garde-Ersatz-Division* do not come out of their positions, because the heaviest artillery fire comes against them. The attempted attack is *im Keim erstickt*, nipped in the bud, by the Englishman.'[11]

The German officers, of course, continue to rally their men. Barking orders like snarling Alsatians on short leads, they get the next line moving, including Infantry Regiment 78, who have the objective of taking Hangard Wood to the south of Villers-Bret.

Grey-clad and muddy Fritzes struggle forward, cursing *quietly*, lest the Alsatians turn on them. With the air a-whir with randomly ranging shell fragments and rather more expertly aimed bullets from machine guns secreted in places unknown, they can manage only to 'get into a very awkward position'. They are in the open, lying in unprotected troughs – 'no shelter against losses'.[12]

'The situation is awkward,' the Regimental history records, 'but it requires endurance, yet every minute calls for new victims. Individual groups collect in the shell holes and, with their spades, try to expand the holes into makeshift trenches.'[13]

Captain Coghill, now recovered enough to control his men – his left hand trying to stem the flow of blood from his right arm – shouts 'cease fire' as the German attack fades away, survivors go to ground and no profitable targets can be seen.

But now, rallied by their officers, the Germans come on again, and once more Coghill allows the soldiers to approach just close enough so his men can't miss before giving the order, *verbal* this time, to cut them down again. Similar resistance is provided by the other companies of the 35th Battalion, making the result familiar to Fritz, if he is still confused as to who stands in his way.

'German guns roar thunderous battle cries across to the enemy,' the 78th Regiment historian would chronicle, 'again the riflemen of the *Garde-Ersatz-Division* face the storm, but again the hidden English Machine Gun nests are not gripped effectively.'[14]

Too bloody right. 'Three times they came on,' Colonel Goddard would proudly recount, 'and on each we held them though, in places, our line was several times penetrated but in each instance without set back.'[15]

Inevitably, the Germans swing away from the ferocity of the Australian fire and attack the British forces of the 18th Division on Captain Coghill's right flank, where the going is easier. When the British start to retreat, it is Coghill himself who races to them and practically *shames* them into returning. After all, a man pleading almost as much as he is bleeding is hard to say no to when he implores you to do your duty – and all the more so when he promises that his Lewis gunners will give the Brits covering fire if they return to their posts.

Yes, sir. Very good, sir.

Coghill races back to his own position, with German bullets flinging up dirt all around him . . .

Alas, by the time returns, not only have the Brits on his right flank fallen back once more, but so too have the Brits on their *left!*

By Colonel Goddard's account, they 'went back at the run, abandoning everything. The enemy was quick to take advantage coming round our left flank with enfilade and reverse fire.'[16]

In fact, the British 14th Division, positioned immediately north of the Australian 9th Brigade – which is to say on the Australian left – has completely collapsed under the weight of the German attack, leaving a hole extending all the way to the Somme, through which the Germans of the 228th Division are now *pouring.* Already the key village of Hamel, bitterly contested since 29 March, risks falling to Fritz.

Colonel Goddard, aware of the yawning gap opening on his left, brings forward two companies of the 33rd Battalion from within the town to protect the left flank of the 35th, but he knows it can only be a temporary measure.

Captain Coghill's men are soon taking fire from both flanks, as well as in front – with the obvious danger being that the German stormtroopers will work their way behind them, and they will be cut off.

—

Colonels Goddard and Morshead are in the former's HQ in Villers-Bretonneux, poring over maps, reading reports and sending out orders hither and thither, trying to stay on top of the situation, when a breathless runner arrives from the front with the news that 'the [35th] Battalion's left flank is in the air'.[17]

There's no one bloody there!

Colonel Goddard now realises the problem can't be solved by the

German stormtroopers advance through the Allies' front-line during the Spring Offensive – the *Kaiserschlacht* – in northern France, March 1918. (The Art Archive/Alamy stock photo)

German reserves amassing in the town of St Quentin, the starting point of Operation Michael, directed at the British Third and Fifth Armies. The deployment of reinforcements from the Eastern Front enabled the Germans to launch a massive offensive in the West. (Sueddeutsche Zeitung Photo/Alamy stock photo)

The German cavalry advances as part of Operation Michael, the opening offensive of the *Kaiserschlacht*. (Interfoto/Alamy stock photo)

British soldiers of the Fifth Army killed during the German offensive of 1918, Albert, France. The failure to withstand the assault led to the dismissal of the army's commander, General Sir Hubert Gough. (Hulton Archive/The Print Collector/Getty Images)

The German emperor, Kaiser Wilhelm II (*centre*), on his way to visit German troops in the battlefield with Crown Prince Rupprecht of Bavaria (*left*) and General Sixt von Armin (*right*). (AWM H13191)

The Kaiser (*centre*) studying maps with General Paul von Hindenburg (*left*) and General Erich Ludendorff (*right*). (AWM H12326)

The 'Paris Gun', mounted on its specially constructed rail. The 112-foot barrel bombarded Paris from the wood near Le Gateau at a distance of 80 miles. Its shells could reach a height of nearly 25 miles. It was the largest and most powerful artillery piece the world has ever seen. (AWM A03671) (*inset*): A German soldier happily poses in the barrel of the Paris Gun.

Various types of Allied artillery ammunition used to battle the German onslaught. (AWM E05483)

A Vickers machine-gun team wearing gasmasks. One man would feed the ammunition belt while the other fired the water-cooled weapon. The whole crew typically comprised six to eight men. (Pictorial Press Ltd/Alamy stock photo)

A tripod-mounted Lewis machine gun and its Australian crew. The No. 2 man (*right*) was in charge of reloading the top-mounted drum magazines. (AWM P00826.007)

Messenger dogs and their handler, near Villers-Bretonneux. (WS Collection/Alamy stock photo)

Manfred von Richthofen, the daring and deadly ace known as The Red Baron. Flying with the Imperial German Army Air Service (*Luftstreitkräfte*), he is officially credited with shooting down 126 Allied airmen in 80 aircraft. (GL ARCHIVE/ALAMY STOCK PHOTO)

Von Richthofen, seated in the cockpit of his Albatross DV. Among other members of *Jasta* 11 is his brother, Lothar, seated cross-legged in front. (PICTORIAL PRESS LTD/ALAMY STOCK PHOTO)

Dogfight! A German gunner zeros in on a diving British plane. (INTERFOTO/ALAMY STOCK PHOTO)

Die with your boots on. Von Richthofen, Germany's most successful fighter pilot during the First World War, is laid to rest after being shot down on 21 April 1918 in action above Morlancourt Ridge, near the Somme River. Allied soldiers honoured him with a 14-man firing party, thundering a three-volley salute into the air. (AKG-IMAGES/ALAMY STOCK PHOTO)

Three British soldiers on a captured German A7V tank. Part of a *Sturm Panzerkraftwagen Abteilungen*, Armoured Assault Vehicle Detachment, these tanks caused havoc and devastation across the front-lines around Villers-Bretonneux. (AWM A03978)

Opposing the German A7V in the battlefield is the British Mark IV tank. The Second Battle of Villers-Bretonneux featured the first tank-on-tank warfare in history, on 24 April 1918. (AWM E05424)

Casualties from the front pass destroyed tanks outside Villers-Bretonneux. (The Print Collector/Alamy stock photos)

View of the ruined church of Villers-Bretonneux. The Germans initially tried to keep the town intact, hoping to shelter troops in it for the push to Amiens. This strategy quickly changed and the town was relentlessly bombarded and set alight by heavy artillery fire coming in at a thousand high-explosive shells an hour. (AWM E02158)

Members of an Australian burial party standing among the bodies of several German prisoners killed the previous morning by a German shell while being escorted to a prisoner-of-war cage. The men were captured at Villers-Bretonneux on 24–25 April during the night of the counter-attack by the 13th and 15th Australian Infantry Brigades, which drove the German forces from the town. (AWM E04768)

Private A. G. Townsend, a member of the 46th Battalion, making a meal of vegetables salvaged from a ruined garden near Villers-Bretonneux. (AWM E02185)

Australian soldiers of the 28th Battalion in a front-line trench at Dernancourt, 27 April 1918. (AWM E02295)

View of the railway cutting near Villers-Bretonneux, where the Australian 12th Infantry Brigade Headquarters was located, 3 May 1918. (AWM E04881)

Sergeant W. Joyce (*left*) and Driver Simister, standing on the Fouilloy-Villers-Bretonneux Road, watching the German shells bursting on the ridge of Hill 104. (AWM E02330)

An Australian soldier standing at the entrance of an archway built through the embankment of the Amiens Railway. During the fighting in this area between April and August 1918, the tunnel was used as a regimental aid post by successive battalions operating on the Villers-Bretonneux front. (AWM E05416)

Soldiers of 28th Battalion in the front-line trenches on the edge of Monument Wood, a scene of fierce fighting and devastation during its occupation by the Germans, who, at the time, had been forced by the Australians to evacuate the portion of the wood facing Villers-Bretonneux. (AWM E02674)

A large group of German prisoners, captured by the Australians near Villers-Bretonneux. (AWM E03074)

A group of Australian soldiers who had been gassed in operations in front of Villers-Bretonneux, lying in an open field at a crowded aid post near Bois l'Abbe. The effects of mustard gas were especially devastating and included painful blisters on exposed skin and in the lungs. (AWM E04851)

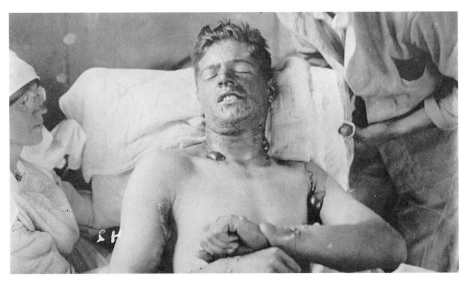

A Canadian soldier in a field hospital, with mustard gas burns. (WORLD HISTORY ARCHIVE/ALAMY STOCK PHOTO)

Field Marshal Sir Douglas Haig, Commander-in-Chief of the Expeditionary Forces in France and Belgium from 1915 to 1919. (AWM A03713)

Lieutenant-Colonel Leslie James Morshead, 33rd Battalion. (AWM H19231)

Sergeant Stanley Robert McDougall, 47th Battalion. McDougall was awarded the Victoria Cross for 'most conspicuous bravery and devotion to duty when the enemy attacked' on 28 March 1918 at Dernancourt. Eight days later he repelled another enemy attack at the same location, for which he was awarded the Military Medal. (AWM A05155)

The 'Red Château', which served as the Fifth Army's HQ in Villers-Bretonneux while the town was held by the Allies. After being initially spared, by the end of the heavy German artillery fire loosed upon the town, the building was reduced to a smouldering ruin. (AWM E05496)

Australian soldiers of the 5th Machine-Gun Battalion with French civilians about to return to their damaged homes in Villers-Bretonneux. (AWM P01543.001)

French children tending the graves of fallen Australians at Adelaide Cemetery, Villers-Bretonneux. (AWM E05925)

two companies of Morshead's 33rd that he just sent forward 'to take up a support position north of the railway'.[18]

Goddard is under no illusions: 'Their position as it stands is hopeless.'[19]

He has no choice but to pull both the 35th and half the 33rd right out of it before they are surrounded, back to the support line where the rest of Morshead's 33rd are already in position. Goddard knows that 'this will shorten our front and make it possible to still deny the town to the enemy'.[20]

The fearless runner sprints back out the door to get the message through and succeeds in reaching Captain Coghill, who, just after 8 am, gives out a reluctant order for his men to pull back 1000 yards to the rear to the support line, kindly dug for them by the 33rd three days ago for just such an eventuality – whereupon the good Captain is also shot in the knee for his trouble.

This is going to be a long day.

—

As the morning wears on, the 15 German divisions continue to make good advances as the exhausted and mostly inexperienced British forces retreat before their onslaught. The triumphant soldiers of the 78th Infantry Regiment have their sights set firmly on their objectives: Hangard Wood and Monument Wood.

Over to their right, the Prussian General Friedrich von Gontard, the Commander of XIV German Corps, riding to a vantage point can now see the dark-red twin towers of the church of – *Was ist das . . . name auf der* map? – what he knows must be *der Stadt auf* Villers-Bretonneux ahead, on a small plateau, with another broad hill to its right. This plateau and that hill, he knows, are the keys. If they can just control the high ground, they will be able to start shelling Amiens with fire guided by direct observation. ('*Ja*, 200 metres more, Hans, and 50 metres to your left, and you will be right on the railway station.')

General Gontard believes in this attack, believes in the future of

Germany, believes in *den Kaiser* – in fact, he wears a moustache exactly like His Imperial Majesty's, in his honour – and knows just what is at stake.

He watches carefully and with no little pride as his men – almost all of them on foot, as both motor vehicles and horses are at a premium – continue to march forward. Most of those coming up from the rear are on the *Römerstraße*, Roman road, which runs gun-barrel straight from St Quentin to Amiens via Villers-Bretonneux, and the fire upon them is admittedly getting stronger the closer they get to VB.

—

It is for good reason that Colonel Goddard is now a blur of military moves – dispatching orders, demanding updates, reading reports and generally trying to make up in astute command what he is lacking in actual boots on the ground.

By 9.30 am the fog of war has cleared a little, despite both rain and shells continuing to teem down in equal measure, and the situation becomes more apparent.

All four companies of the 35th Battalion are now back in position in the support trenches, forming a continuous line with the troops of Morshead's 33rd Battalion on their left. They are further bolstered by ten Vickers guns that troops of the 33rd are digging in on their left flank to counter whatever might be coming at them.

There is no doubt that the coming clash is going to be ugly, as the rain-soaked, muddied men of Morshead's battalion come under ever heavier fire from the right flank of the German attack on Villers-Bretonneux. Advancing towards them are the German soldiers of the 228th Division, who continue to make relatively easy headway towards that large lump on the landscape that the British know as 'Hill 104' – so named because on the French maps it is marked as being 104 metres above sea level.

For the Australians, the question has to be asked: where is the *real* cavalry when you need them to save the day? Why, here! At the veritable

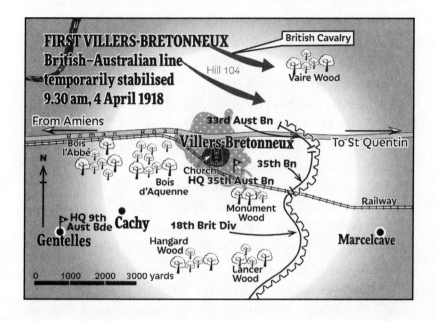

FIRST VILLERS-BRETONNEUX
British–Australian line
temporarily stabilised
9.30 am, 4 April 1918

British Cavalry

Hill 104

Vaire Wood

From Amiens

33rd Aust Bn

To St Quentin

Bois
l'Abbé

Villers-Bretonneux

N

35th Bn

Church

Bois
d'Aquenne

HQ 35th Aust Bn

Railway

Monument
Wood

HQ 9th
Aust Bde

Cachy

18th Brit Div

Gentelles

Hangard
Wood

Marcelcave

0   1000   2000   3000 yards

Lancer
Wood

last minute, as the Germans start to swarm Hill 104's lower slopes, to the left of the 33rd Battalion a stampeding team of horse-borne soldiers thunders forth. Riding four abreast, it's Britain's answer to the 'Four Horsemen of the Apocalypse' – Conquest, War, Famine and Death, with War and Death in the lead. Their collective hoofs make the ground quake for hundreds of yards in every direction, the jingling of their spurs and bits are music to the ears of the merely earthbound soldiers. The sight of their leather bandoliers filled with ammunition slung across their left shoulders and under their right arms, even around their horses' necks, is a wonder to behold.

All the King's horses and all the King's men, 900 strong, come from such famous British cavalry regiments as the Prince of Wales's 3rd Dragoon Guards, the Royal Horse Guards and the 10th Hussars. They are nearing the crest of Hill 104 from the west at full gallop when the order goes out: 'Trooooooop halt' followed by 'Trooooooop dismount'.

Once their horses are taken to the rear, the cavalrymen cross the summit and begin to pour down the other side, each troop of 30 men forming a thin line of posts on the slope of the exposed eastern face of the hill, just as – from on high – C Battery Royal Horse Artillery fires on the Germans caught in the open. For the moment, and for a nice change on the day, the Brits are holding

Thank God for the British cavalry. As one Digger of the 58th Battalion would later recall, 'The flight of the 14th British Division infantry came as a shock to the reinforcing troops, but the Captain in charge of "A" Company of the 58th Battalion was full of admiration for the Cavalry. "No men," he said, "could have done more than these cavalry men did."'[21]

The men of Morshead's 33rd Battalion couldn't agree more. The cavalry now secures their left flank and continues to bring fire on the Germans who would otherwise be coming straight at them. They are the precious glue between Brigadier Pompey Elliott's 15th Brigade on the Somme and Rosie's 9th at Villers-Bretonneux.

The German stormtroopers, for Kaiser and Fatherland, attempt to get around the newly reinforced Australian left flank further to the north, only to – unbeknownst to them – come under the scrutiny of more binoculars than the favourite at the Melbourne Cup. For, up on Morlancourt Ridge, just a couple of miles to the north across the river, the artillery observers of the Australian 3rd Division have spotted the creeping Krauts. Artillerymen dream about targets like this.

In an instant, the five-man battery crews are going at it like navvies on the 54 powerful 18-pounder field guns spaced ten yards apart across the slope. And load! And . . . *fire!* And ignore the puff of acrid smoke that blows into your face every time a breech is opened to eject the shell casing and insert another shell.

Take that, you bastards! And that! And *that!*

At this 'rapid-fire' rate of six shells per minute, it is exhausting

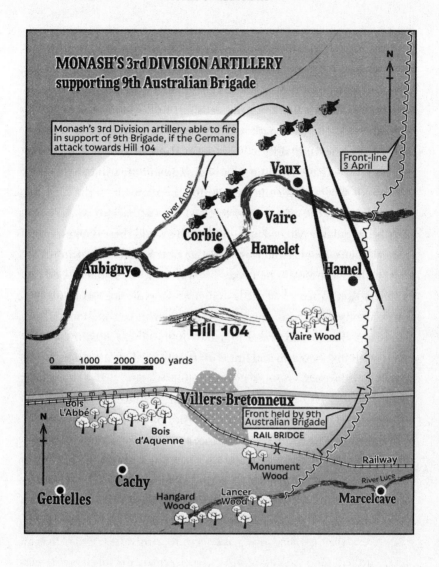

MONASH'S 3rd DIVISION ARTILLERY
supporting 9th Australian Brigade

Monash's 3rd Division artillery able to fire
in support of 9th Brigade, if the Germans
attack towards Hill 104

N

Front-line
3 April

Vaux

River Ancre

Vaire

Corbie

Hamelet

Hamel

Aubigny

Hill 104

Vaire Wood

0   1000   2000   3000 yards

Roman Road

Bois
L'Abbé

Villers-Bretonneux

Front held by 9th
Australian Brigade

N

Bois
d'Aquenne

RAIL BRIDGE

Monument
Wood

Railway

Cachy

River Luce

Gentelles

Hangard
Wood

Lancer
Wood

Marcelcave

work, but the gunners never waver, following exactly the orders issued
through a loudhailer of each battery commander standing 20 yards
to the rear of his gun. They continue to fire on the swarm of Huns
over 'open sights'[22] to great effect. Far to the south, they can see the
German ants run every which way – less many who now lie curled up
on the ground – just as if the Australians had been 12-year-old boys
who had kicked an ants' nest. But, collectively, the Germans are no
longer moving towards Australian positions.

Much to Commander Goddard's relief, back at his HQ in Villers-Bret, he soon hears news that the enemy are falling back. It is hard going, though, as the 9th Brigade boys, hidden in various machine-gun posts, take shots at any movement, causing 'numerous casualties'.[23]

Meanwhile, to the south of the Australians defending Villers-Bretonneux, the 18th British Division in front of Lancer Wood and Hangard Wood have given up a lot of ground but are still hanging on.

Captain Coghill's men are secure for the moment as the fighting lulls, so he takes the opportunity to crawl his way back to an aid post. After being quickly patched up – in Coghill's world there is no problem so great that enough bandages, elbow grease and fencing wire can't fix it in the short term – he makes his way back to Colonel Goddard in Villers-Bret to see what needs doing. As Coghill hobbles into HQ, Goddard raises his head towards the doorway, takes one look at his bloody wobbliness and *orders* him out of the line. Captain Coghill salutes with his good arm and limps off to seek medical attention, trailing blood as he goes.

Back at his HQ at Gentelles, Brigadier Rosenthal is relieved to receive reports from his 35th Battalion: 'They had beaten off the attack, inflicting heavy casualties on the Boche, and . . . they feel quite capable of dealing with any further attacks.'[24]

It is late morning and still the Australian line is holding its own, just.

—

South of Hangard Wood the situation is not so favourable. The German attack on French 1st Army has pushed two miles westward.

The whole situation for the Allies hangs in the balance, and as Marshal Paul von Hindenburg would later report, 'The first reports of the progress of our attack on that day were very promising . . .'[25]

As it is, they are now approaching the slopes that lead to Hill 104, and if they take that high ground then the fall of Amiens will be the most likely result . . . There are just three competent forces that lie in the German path – Brigadier Rosenthal's 9th Brigade near Villers-Bretonneux, the 6th British Cavalry Brigade now on Hill 104 and Elliott's 15th Brigade holding the Somme bridges, two miles west of Hamel.

The Australian soldiers of the 15th Brigade are spectators to the battle underway to their south. At 10.30 am they send a report to Elliott at his HQ that 'the enemy are coming over the top in front of Hamel'.[26] Just before midday, Pompey – who has been monitoring the situation closely – receives more news from Captain Harold Ferres guarding the bridge at Vairé, a mile north-west of Hamel. German soldiers can now

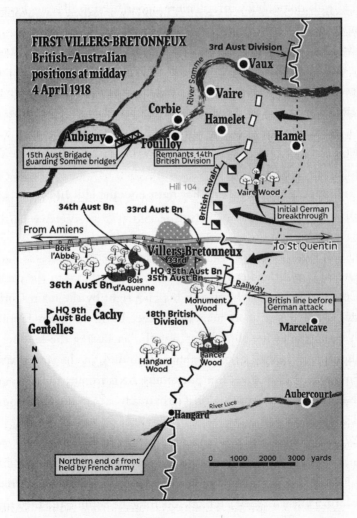

be seen coming out of this side of Hamel – the town has fallen! – and 'the English troops are falling back'.[27]

Ferres also reports, 'I am stopping [fleeing] English troops and sending up ammunition,'[28] but there is no doubt that the situation is more than passing grim.

'As I expected from the manner in which they were holding the line,' Elliott would recount, 'they gave way very badly . . . great numbers flung down their arms and ran away . . . the situation looked disastrous.'[29] He confirms that Captain Ferres should keep doing what he is already doing, but with still more vigour, 'to stop all stragglers and compel them to fight'.[30]

At 12.30 pm, once Captain Ferres reports that his men are under long-range machine-gun fire from the still-advancing Germans, Elliott orders two companies of his 59th Battalion – currently in reserve in the nearby village of La Neuville – to move forward to support the 58th. By 1 pm the situation is so grim that Elliott orders the entire 59th and 60th forward to form a line, with Vairé on their left flank. The Germans must be stopped!

And most important of all, they must not take Hill 104!

—

Whatever else, Brigadier Pompey Elliott knows that – in the person of Colonel Herbert Layh, now in his HQ right by the main Corbie Bridge – he has a good man in charge. Layh has been familiar with being under fire since stopping a bullet during the landing at Gallipoli, and he had been notably outstanding in the tragic battle of Fromelles. Elliott gives him his orders: he is to take the 59th and 60th Battalions. He is to stop the German advance to the west around Hill 104.

Within 15 minutes Layh is marching at the head of over 1000 men as they move in artillery formation, spread out to minimise casualties should a shell land among them across the open fields. Upon arrival, they form a line with their left flank touching the Somme and their right flank meeting with the left flank of the British cavalrymen now digging in in front of Hill 104. The cavalry's right flank, in turn, touches the Australian 33rd Battalion's left in front of Villers-Bretonneux. The lines is as skinny as a sick dingo, but it is a line established in place of what had previously been disintegration.

Colonel Morshead, meantime, is taking advantage of the improved visibility and heads up to the battalion's observation post, from where 'considerable enemy movement'[31] is observed all along the front. As Morshead would later note in his report of the day's activity, 'We made most use of the comparative lull around noon in getting forward supplies of ammunition. Our mobile reserve of [.303 rounds] and tools reached us at 1 p.m. and a dump was formed near Battalion H.Q . . . Our line was in ploughed fields, consequently the Lewis guns and rifles were all in a very muddy state. The men all availed themselves of this opportunity to clean them.'[32]

As for Colonel Goddard, he, too, is more than satisfied with the advance made by the 33rd and the cavalry, and now turns his attention to his right flank, where the enemy are concentrating their artillery fire, signalling their intent to attack there. He hopes the 18th can hold tight but is not filled with optimism.

Meantime, Brigadier Rosenthal, beyond frustrated that he is not up in the village with his men but more cognisant than ever that 'my responsibility was to hold Villers-Bretonneux',[33] makes his own move.

The men of Colonel Martin's 34th Battalion and Milne's 36th had been warned to stand ready earlier this morning, and now Rosenthal orders them to move forward.

The 36th Battalion are to head to the south of the town. And that means ALL MEN. Even those brawling, boozy bastards Alfred Holton and his mate Reggie Dilley are relieved of their fatigue duty – as part of their punishment they have spent the morning 'digging small trenches in the ground alongside of the big guns for the gunners to get into, in case of danger'[34] – and told to rejoin their company. Alfie can see all his mates already a quarter mile ahead. The pair grab their kit and run after them, demanding, 'What's the matter?'

'Fritz is coming!'[35] their mates yell in disbelief that this fact could have been lost on anybody in this part of France!

Elsewhere, the 34th Battalion are to bolster the lines on the north side of Villers-Bretonneux. One Lieutenant among them is glad to be on the move in artillery formation. They had been too long 'waiting in a terraced field',[36] out in the open, where they 'suffered a number of casualties'.[37] And though the shells continue to fall, at least they are moving, not just sitting like ducks.

———

To the south of Villers-Bretonneux, the German soldiers of the 78th Infantry Regiment are ready to make their next push on Hangard Wood so they can break through and envelop Villers-Bretonneux (just as the vigilant Colonel Goddard suspects is their intent).

The artillery has finished preparations and the bombardment is starting.

Kommt, Jungs! Die greifen wir uns! Come on, lads, up and at 'em!

Under a cold rain, the stormtroopers charge out of their makeshift trenches. Instantly, they are 'smothered again in the defensive fire of the hidden enemy Machine Guns, *aber es soll und muß geschafft werden*, but it should and must be done!'[38]

At 12.50 pm, 'a new storm is carried out by Regiment 78, which is in turn repulsed by the tenaciously defending British'.[39] Many of the men are now dead in a ditch. The rest are shivering, muddy and hungry.

There is a silver lining, though. By now the surviving stormtroopers have figured out just where 'almost all pockets of resistance of the enemy'[40] are hidden. And so they 'designate the front line exploratory artillery- and mortars-officers'[41] the role of taking out said pockets.

One by one, they begin to do just that.

Once that task is complete, their push on Hangard may yet prove successful.

———

General Count von Finkenstein, the Commanding Officer of the 4th Guards Division, is more than pleased with how his troops, proud Prussians all, have performed on this auspicious day so far – they have advanced well over a mile – but now he has a problem. Reports have come in that the enemy appears to be increasing his force on and around Hill 104.

And so von Finkenstein, after galloping forward to the Wolfsberg (a hill behind Hamel) to see for himself, quickly makes his way to Bayonvillers to see General Friedrich von Gontard, the Commander of XIV German Corps. He snaps off a salute, clicks his heels together and respectfully suggests that the time is opportune to throw the 1st Division, now waiting in reserve just a short distance in the rear, into the ferocious fray to overwhelm the defenders of Hill 104 and take that position, too.

Gontard demurs. Among other things, 1st Division is the last reserve he has, and against the possibility that the enemy launches an attack of his own, it is important that he has a division to throw into whatever gap might emerge.

And it may not be necessary. If the troops now attacking Villers-Bretonneux directly keep up their rate of progress, that town will fall shortly anyway, and Amiens will be the next to go.

So, for now, the 4th Guards Division can keep attacking Hill 104, but they will have to make do without another division in support.

It is a decision that will be bitterly regretted, particularly by Marshal von Hindenburg.

—

Aware that a battle is underway and Australians are defending against a major German assault, Charles Bean wishes to be there, right in the thick of it. He and AIF photographer Lieutenant Hubert Wilkins quickly pack their things and go. Leaving their cottage quarters in a tiny village five miles north-west of Corbie, they instruct their AIF driver to steer the little tin car – a 1915 'Swift 10' with all of ten horsepower and two cylinders under the bonnet – to the south-east, towards the sound of the artillery, driving so that the balls of dirty thunder continually rolling over them get progressively bigger, louder and dirtier. (And they *sound* angry. Not for nothing do the Germans themselves call this 'the grumble' – '*das Grummeln*'.)

As they get close to Villers-Bretonneux, Bean and Wilkins suddenly realise that they are *in the middle* of a battle. All along the road, from the Somme River onwards, up through Fouilly and right to the outskirts of Villers-Bretonneux, artillery batteries – 60-pounders and six-inch howitzers positioned in the fields to the left – are POUNDING enemy positions. The reverberations from their thunderous fire are so strong that it almost feels as if the sound alone will blast the men from the road. Things are particularly willing just 500 yards out to their left as they drive towards Hill 104. At least what they can now see is heartening: Australian soldiers with their distinctive, loping, relaxed manner of marching. It is almost a statement in itself – 'We are doing this part of the military malarkey, but don't actually believe in it.' Bean is proud of being able to spot the Australian-ness of the way they move at a distance of 200 yards, and this is a case in point, as the last of Colonel Herbert Layh's two battalions of the 15th Brigade get into position. Bean and Wilkins keep moving, amazed that the horses that dragged the artillery forward can graze on the new spring corn to their right, while others lie slaughtered on the ground, stinking enough to curl a man's nose hairs.

———

This time as the Germans of the 4th Guards Division approach, they receive fire from both the British cavalry and the Australians – a stiff combination – and take pause. No matter that they are one of the finest units in the German Army, that in the war to date they have crushed British, French and Russian troops – and completely routed the British 24th Division in the opening days of the *Kaiserschlacht* – so severe and accurate is the fire upon them that they simply cannot go on.

Pompey would be more than happy with the results. 'The reception the leading files [of Germans] got,' he would proudly recount, 'turned the stomach of all who should have followed from the fight. One of my machine guns . . . placed slightly forward of the line and protected by a swamp, fired across the front and piled 200 German corpses in a ghastly rampart of slain before the survivors of the column concluded that they had urgent business elsewhere.'[42]

Though the German shelling on the defenders of Hill 104 is strong enough that the Australians must quickly dig in, for the moment their advance is stopped. They have already shown good progress for the day, taking the much-coveted Somme village of Hamel and its bridges. It remains to be seen whether they will make another serious push on Hill 104.

——

The closer Bean and Wilkins get to Villers-Bretonneux, the thicker the shell holes become, including on the road, which the men must navigate their way around and, had they been in the mood to flog a dead horse, there are more and more of them scattered about.

Once into the town proper, they see soldiers taking shelter in doorways and keep going until they get to the completely empty main road – which is empty for good reason. On both sides of the road, German shells are shattering buildings, sending blasts of bricks everywhere. Both men tell the driver to go as fast as he can until at last they leave the village behind, descending the hill towards Amiens. Out to their left, big woods appear, Bois l'Abbé, and, feeling a little safer for the first time in 20 minutes, they pull over to reconnoitre, instructing the driver to continue for a mile down the road to Amiens and wait for them there. Making inquiries, they work out that Brigadier Rosenthal and the 9th Brigade are in Cachy or thereabouts, and so begin to walk across the open, rolling fields towards that village.

——

Colonel Goddard now has a fair grip on what has happened. The Germans have advanced for just over a mile along a front 4000 yards wide. In the unusual position of commanding both his battalion and all 9th Brigade operations, he must work out what to do to stop the rot right there, despite being 'without staff, except for a roughly improvised one, all too few and inexperienced in staff work' and with 'no communications, and no hope of more support from anywhere'.[43] Compounding his problems is that his men 'are tired and had suffered much from exposure to the bad weather – they were without shelter of any sort'.[44]

With all his reserves now engaged – bar one company of the 35th Battalion and the 6th Londons Regiment (a Tommy unit that had come up the night before and is, as fate may have it, commanded by a son of the Southern Cross, Colonel Charles B. Benson) positioned on the eastern edge of VB – Colonel Goddard is feeling increasingly desperate, wondering just when the Germans will launch their next assault and just how his men will stop them. Then he hears it.

It is the blessed sound of the iconic Australian Army's 'Blundstone boots' on the cobblestone road outside his headquarters. And in walks Colonel Milne, commander of the 36th Battalion, come to get instructions about where to place his troops. Goddard is happy to see him. Milne, too, is a 'fighting leader',[45] highly prized in these trying circumstances. Strong, broad shouldered, fearless, with a powerful voice and a marked Scottish accent, Colonel Milne, DSO – the coveted Distinguished Service Order given courtesy of the 'great capacity and initiative' he'd displayed at Passchendaele – is a force to be reckoned with, all on his own.

With no time to waste, Goddard orders Milne to bring his men up to a position to the south-west of the town, while also sending word for Colonel Martin, who should be arriving shortly with his men, to place his 34th Battalion on the west side. Goddard also decides to keep Colonel Milne close by, 'handy to my headquarters in order that he might be kept posted with events and be ready to act quickly on the right which I felt sure would be the threatened flank'.[46]

So stay with me, Colonel, if you would.

Milne nods and sends a runner out to pass along the orders to his men. The runner ducks out the door and heads south, hugging the buildings on the eastern side of the street on the reckoning that it is the most sheltered from the shell fire.

Under such circumstances, it is with no little relief that he soon finds the Diggers of the 36th Battalion tucked away in a dip along the road to Hangard. Among them are Alfie and Dill, and both are grateful for the order to lie down – the hammering in their head has been perhaps even louder than the shattering artillery, and stronger still than the hammering they'd given themselves the night before on the grog. Gawd almighty.

Word is quickly passed down the line that Fritz is going to try it on. He's going to attempt to push through the southern approaches to Villers-Bret – where they now lie – so as to envelop and capture the town. The 36th Battalion's task is simple: stop the brutes.

—

Meanwhile, the boys of the 34th Battalion have followed orders and got themselves into position on the north side of Villers-Bret, in a sunken road, which is great for getting away from the machine-gun bullets flying overhead. But it is *terrible* when artillery shells land in what becomes the bottom of a bucket. Australian blood flows into the rich soil of France at a rate of knots; somehow the German artillery has drawn a bead on them. Still, they've had it far worse many times before, and for the moment all they can do is tend to their many wounded and try to keep their heads down.

And then terrible news comes down the line: their Commanding Officer, Colonel Ernest Martin, has been wounded, along with all of the 34th Battalion HQ staff officers, including his second-in-command and his adjutant.

In the sunken road, Lieutenant Alfred Fell is devastated to hear the news, but he knows he must get on with it. Craning his neck above a thick tuft of dripping grass, he squints through the falling rain at 'the horrible carnage all around, the toll of Officers and men of the English Artillery, dismounted Cavalry and Infantry regiments being very heavy, and the slaughter of the horses being a most pathetic sight. German planes were spotting for their own Artillery, who were making things most unpleasant.'[47]

For those still unscathed, the time is coming to get on with what they have come here to do, what they have lost so many lives for – to stop Fritz from winning the war *this week*, by preventing him from breaking through to Amiens. 'Once more unto the breach, dear friends, once more; Or close the wall up with our English dead.'[48]

With Colonel Martin now gone, it is Major Leroy Fry who takes command, and he sends a runner to Colonel Goddard at his battalion HQ, telling him that they are in position. Let the Germans come on. Even decimated as they are, the 34th Battalion will be ready for them.

—

Colonel Morshead, whose boys of the 33rd are continuing to hold the line on the left of the 35th boys, is back at Goddard's HQ when the panting runner arrives with welcome news that lightens the tense atmosphere no end: both the 34th and 36th have arrived and are in position. Probably just in time. As Morshead would later report to Brigadier Rosenthal, it is obvious that as 'the enemy's artillery concentrated their fire south of the railway and, as so much movement could also be seen there . . . they would next attack Villers-Bretonneux from the south'.[49]

—

Back on the German side of the lines, down in front of Hangard Wood, the gunners, helped by forward observers with binoculars and a field telephone, have been successful in pinpointing and destroying the most troublesome of the hidden British machine-gun posts, one by one.

After several failed attempts so far to push through the enemy line, this time they are sure they will get there with this last surge, that their patience is about to pay off.

And so as the *Landser*, the low-ranking German infantrymen, steel themselves, the preparatory bombardment rises up once more to its devastating climax before the clock ticks down to zero.

Fünf . . . vier . . . drei . . . zwei . . . eins . . . null!

At 2.30 pm exactly, the whistle blows and the mighty German stormtroopers rise up again to attack once more. Seemingly endless waves of German soldiers now charge forward along a front that extends from Hangard village in the south to the Roman road in the north. As the 78th Regiment's history would record, 'Despite the efforts of the previous weeks, despite all the failures of the day, despite the cold rainy weather, despite the soggy soil in which sank the assailants low, the companies collect in the late afternoon in the pouring rain to the decisive impetus. And this time it succeeds, though it must be fought step by step and bloody . . .'[50]

The infantry charge on, helped by their artillery, which throws out an iron curtain advancing in front of them, helping to keep the enemy defenders' heads down.

Across from the German 78th, on the Australians' right flank, is Britain's 18th Division, which has been holding on so far. But now under attack, with their machine-gun posts no longer scything down the oncoming Huns, they find themselves reeling under withering fire. And . . . gas! With the wind blowing from the east, just before the stormtroopers had charged the German artillery dropped gas shells – blue cross, green cross, make a sign of the cross and hope you're not sent to the Red Cross – in the English trenches. And so now, the 18th Division, coughing as if to bring up a lung, can just see through their red-raw eyes and the dripping wet air the unmistakable figures of German stormtroopers, approaching the eastern edge of Hangard Wood itself, and they look to be coming on in the thousands!

Charging over a rise in the ground that hides the battalion from German view, Alfred Holton and the Diggers of the 36th suddenly see an English soldier doubled over without a gun, his khakis dripping mud, scurrying back towards their line at speed. Holton hopes the man is an exception to the rule, that this lone Tommy is just that – a lone Tommy.

Alas, the hunched soldier soon turns out to be the first of many. What starts as a trickle soon flows like a stream. Holton can't believe it and would later recount, 'The Tommies began to come back in crowds coughing and spitting. There were 2 or 3 times as many as us and had the wind up proper. Fritz had gassed them first and then came over and the Tommies had cleared out. When they came to where we were, we held them up for a few minutes and then they went on behind the whole of them spitting and coughing.'[51]

Within minutes there is a flood of retreating British soldiers – seemingly coming from *everywhere* – now swirling past and around the Australians like leaves being picked up and hurled before an oncoming storm front. Most alarming is that most of these British soldiers are not carrying their rifles, indicating that this is less a tactical retreat than an out-and-out rout, with every man for himself. And, sure enough, as ever more British soldiers with haunted, red-rimmed eyes come closer, it is clear they are all but *running* back, pausing only to report in their thick accents, *choom*, that, 'The Germans are coming in their thousands!'[52]

———

Goddard's worst fears are now becoming a reality as the Germans indeed push so hard on the British to his right that they break. This time, the Germans are nigh on unstoppable, and by 4.30 pm, after the whole British line defending it has disintegrated, Lancer Wood has been lost, as has Hangard Wood. South of there, the French have also been driven back.

The Hun troops of the 78th Infantry Regiment, now in Hangard Wood, are ecstatic, scarcely believing how easy it has all been. As their history would record, 'At dawn . . . the target is reached, the forest of Hangard south of Villers-Bretonneux in the possession of the regiment, the opponent in front of this section *in voller Flucht*, in full flight.'[53]

Against that, there is no doubt that they are also exhausted, barely able to lift their arms for a handshake or a pat on the back. So they sit, dripping wet, and take pause before regrouping for the next leap forward – the one that will secure them what they have come for, Villers-Bretonneux.

——

As the light begins to wane, so too do the Australian fortunes. The German attack goes on unabated – both from in front and soon from their right flank – and threatens to become overwhelming. Still, the Australians of the 35th and 33rd Battalions keep at it, firing on anything that moves in front of them.

More! More! More! The men carrying the ammo can barely keep up with the pace.

When, as happens frequently, an Australian gunner falls with a bullet to the head, his No. 2 steps forward and takes over the gun. When, as happens frequently, the Lewis guns become jammed with mud from the bullets and shrapnel landing all around, throwing the wet earth everywhere, another solution appears . . .

Goddard is advised of the problem; Colonel Charles Benson of the 6th Londons barks out sharp orders; and in even shorter order 18 of his own men are on their way to the front-line, carrying ammunition and clean Lewis guns. An exchange is made – bless the Brits' cotton socks. They soon return with the Australians' guns and set to work cleaning and unjamming them.

Some 2000 yards in the rear, Milne's men of the 36th Battalion witness the same British soldiers with haunted, red-rimmed eyes continuing to retreat through the Australian positions, losing their sense of direction, pausing only to repeat the now popular Tommy refrain: 'The Germans are coming in their thousands!'[54]

And off they go. At speed. Officers, too.

'A Tommy Brigadier,' one Digger will later write home, 'is reported to have overtaken a hare on the road towards Amiens.'[55]

And then the 35th see it too – the Brits on their right have *gorn*. The Hun is in Monument Wood . . .

As that wood is just 500 yards south of Goddard's headquarters on the edge of Villers-Bretonneux, the critical point has been reached. Moving quickly, Lieutenant Wynter Wallace Warden, the officer in command of the 35th Battalion's right flank – in the front-lines on the south-east corner of Villers-Bret – shouts orders for his men to urgently form a defensive flank facing where the marauding Germans have broken through. The intent is not to give up their for'ard position entirely but to do what they can to hold what they can.

Alas, the men of the 35th Battalion who are further off to the left in that most for'ard line, noting the men on their right falling back, assume the order has been given for the whole battalion to withdraw and begin to fall back themselves. Just like the Brits; first there is a trickle and soon enough it becomes a solid stream of Australians moving back to and through Villers-Bret.

They have been in the line for five days without a spell and under direct attack for over 12 hours. They are muddy, wet, cold, hungry, exhausted and running low on ammunition. Perhaps if Captain Coghill had still been with them they might have held, but it is not to be.

'As the movement spread northwards,' Charles Bean would sadly but dutifully note in his *Official History of Australia in the War*, 'Major Carr and Captain Hawkins tried desperately to stop it, but some of the junior officers, in spite of their appeal, "would not heed . . ."'[56]

Truthfully, it is all they can do to get out of the way in time to avoid being trampled in the rush. 'The whole line of the 35th went. The two leaders were left alone. The Germans could be seen south of the railway streaming towards Villers-Bretonneux . . .'[57]

Appalled at the sudden disintegration of what had moments earlier been a strong line – *what happened to the bloody 35th??* – Major Carr races back to the town to tell Goddard.

Meantime, the furphy about orders to withdraw suddenly becomes even more damaging as it reaches the ranks of the 33rd Battalion to the left, whose men are already eager to do exactly that. They, too, start to slowly withdraw, many crossing the abandoned aerodrome by the Roman road as they head towards the town.

As the 34th's war diary faithfully records:

4:30 p.m. An order was received from Colonel Goddard, temporary commanding 9th Brigade operations, that 34th was to withdraw to high ground in rear of the village.[58]

Of course, Colonel Goddard has issued no such order.

Nevertheless, the men of the 34th withdraw – and don't think twice about it, either. Lieutenant Alfred Fell is there, and is grateful for the order. As he would later note, 'The situation looked so black that no surprise was shown when Major Fry, who had assumed command of the Battalion, was ordered to move to a position on the ground behind the town.'[59]

It seems clear to all that, barring a miracle, man-made or otherwise, the German Army is about to engulf Villers-Bretonneux . . .

CHAPTER TWELVE
A TWILIGHT OF FIGHT

I am awfully jolly; awfully happy. It is good to be of
service and feel – I was going to say 'British', I think
I'll say 'Australian'. Australia saved the day [at Villers-
Bretonneux, defending] Amiens. She will save it again . . .
I am proud and you must be proud to be Australian.'[1]
Robert Austen Goldrick, 36th Battalion, in a
letter to his father, 10 April 1918

LATE AFTERNOON, 4 APRIL 1918, A DERELICT HOUSE IN VILLERS-BRETONNEUX, GODDARD'S FINEST HOUR

At his headquarters, Goddard motions Milne to the map, explaining that should it be necessary for Milne's 36th to counter-attack, then along the north side of the railway would be best. All of a sudden there is a commotion outside. Major Henry Carr of 35th Battalion bursts through the door in the manner of a man with something so important to say that it trumps his lower rank and he can speak without first begging the Colonel's pardon. Carr is dishevelled, perspiring profusely and covered in the grime of battle. There is no time for even such preliminaries as saluting as he shouts the news: 'The line has gone.'[2]

There is a momentary, shocked silence that allows Carr to take a breath before adding, just a little more calmly, 'Captain Hawkins and I were absolutely the last of the 35th to leave it.'[3]

Yes, the Australians have abandoned their posts, and as this spot – this HQ – is now the foremost position, it will be the next to fall. There is a pause, then Goddard turns to Milne. 'Colonel, you must counter-attack at once.'[4]

Milne leaps to his feet, salutes his commander and immediately heads out the door. A hardened Army professional – once a private in the British army and with 11 years' service all told – he has all the information he needs.

Colonel Henry Goddard settles himself.

It is times such as these when a man proves whether or not he is fit to fight, born to battle and capable of command *in extremis*, when the chips are down and the Germans are up you for the rent as never before . . .

'Lancer Wood was lost and the whole line in that vicinity was broken through,' Goddard would later summarise the situation. 'The French were driven out of Hangard and the British from Hangard Wood. The enemy struck with great force straight for Cachy and the Bois l'Abbé to envelop Villers Bret from that flank. By 4:30 p.m. the position was desperate.'[5]

The Hun is truly at the gate. Again.

Colonel Goddard's next priority is to block the Germans from entering the town from the east. He has just the crew for the job. He turns to Captain Raleigh Sayers, a 26-year-old engineer from Geelong who is in command of the 35th's D Company, still in reserve in the town.

'Go out at once,' he barks, 'and hold them.'[6]

Sayers is to take with him men of the 9th Machine Gun Company and the 6th Londons and go to the railway cutting at the south-east corner of town. They are to stay there and *hold on!*

Captain Sayers walks briskly out of the HQ and sets off to ready his men.

Goddard now looks across to Colonel Leslie Morshead, as if looking for a third good idea . . . and wouldn't you know it? The 34th Battalion are also not far away. Morshead suggests to Goddard, 'I should go out and find the 34th and take them round the northern flanks of the town and launch a counter-attack from there.'[7]

Done!

Exit Colonel Morshead in search of 34th HQ.

—

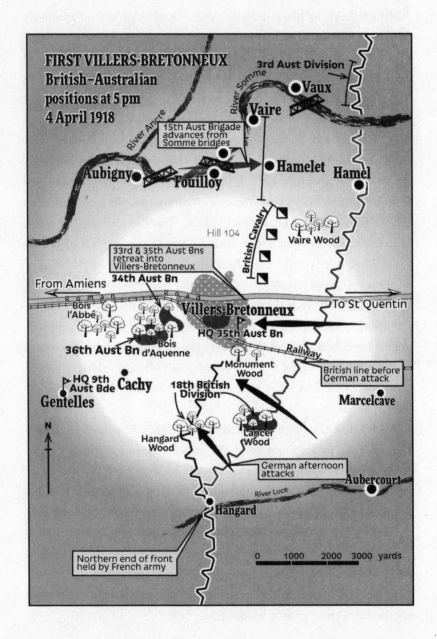

Thankfully, Captain Sayer's 170 men are moving quickly into position. Perhaps a little too quickly – in the hubbub Captain Sayers has forgotten to grab a revolver. He strides confidently forward with just a 'battle bowler' – a tin hat – for protection. Perhaps the notion is that if fortune favours the brave it must positively *love* supremely courageous leaders of men in battle.

Meanwhile, Colonel Morshead goes surging through the streets of Villers-Bret, trying not to gag at the overpowering stench of rotting horseflesh, dodging the portly British engineer Sergeant supervising the loading of a wagon with timber taken from the houses for use in fitting out the newly dug trenches, and urging every man he sees – without stopping himself – to get back to their lines, to defend! Familiar with the area, he is heading towards the sunken road at the north-eastern edge of town, where he knows the Commanding Officer of the 34th Battalion, Colonel Martin, *should* be with his men.

Before he gets there, however – and even as the German shelling becomes ever more fierce, roaring down from on high and sending scything shrapnel ricocheting everywhere – he keeps coming across knots of Diggers coming back from that direction, whom he identifies as Martin's men. Half are wounded, and the other half are helping them back. Clearly, they have been punished.

Morshead finally runs into Major Fry, who gives him the unwelcome news that Colonel Martin has been wounded and sent back to a field hospital, meaning that Fry himself is now in charge of the 34th.

As it happens, Major Fry is more than glad to run into Colonel Morshead, in the hope he can clear up . . . *what the hell is going on?* Fry had been on his way to see Goddard to confirm an extraordinary order he'd received, 'for the battalion to withdraw to high ground in rear of village south of railway line,'[8] which seemed more than passing odd – they would be giving up without a fight when Villers had not yet been taken! Colonel Morshead is quick to put him right. Fry must move the battalion forward and prepare to counter-attack.

Morshead also tells Major Fry to 'post Lewis guns to cover all roads',[9] which Fry orders on the spot, before naming the very spots

they are to go. To ensure that all is done, Colonel Morshead decides
to accompany Fry, to reconnoitre the position themselves and work
out where best to place their men.

The word goes around, the Diggers of the 34th begin to form up
and march back east along the Amiens Road, behind the figures of
Colonel Morshead and Major Fry pushing into the grey distance ahead
of them. Dragoons and Lancers appear from nowhere and offer to ride
in support of them.

Rah!

As the grateful Colonel Morshead would report to Rosie the next
day, the cavalry had sent 'a squadron to cover the 34th Battalion's
movement to the railway'.[10] A blessing, pure and simple. There is no
other immediate support in sight.

With that, Major Fry and Colonel Morshead ride out to take stock
of the position in front of Villers-Bret.

———

Having seen enough, at 5 pm Captain Charles Bean and Lieutenant
Hubert Wilkins start to walk back across the fields to their car when
they suddenly notice many groups of men off to their left, walking
away from the battle. Most of the men have no weapons with them!
And then the newspaper men see more and more of them – *but it was
gradually borne in upon us that the whole countryside was retiring.
Wilkins, whose eyes are better than mine, said he could see men running
on the further horizon.*[11]

Bringing his telescope to bear, Bean can even see a rather stately
looking British officer calmly riding back with his men. Above and
behind the officer, white star flares are soaring. To Bean's eyes, 'Evidently
the Germans were advancing and marking their advance for their own
artillery by this signal which meant "Here we are!".'[12]

Appalled, Bean and Wilkins watch as the groups of retreating
soldiers, 'poor little figures of modern day Englishmen', keep passing,
one of them particularly catching Bean's eye as he appears to be little

more than 'a weak looking child . . .'[13]

'Which is the road, sir?' one of the soldiers asks.

'What road?'

'Which is the road to Amiens?' the soldier means to ask, though he actually pronounces it 'Aymeens'.

'Why are you retreating?'[14] 'There were too many Germans for us,'[15] the soldier replies simply.

As Bean and Wilkins, completely dispirited, are making their way back to the Roman road west of Villers-Bretonneux, where their car and driver are waiting for them, they suddenly see 'bunches of men, 12 to 25 strong, walking [away from Villers-Bretonneux] . . . and a few men with bayonets still fixed to their rifles. These were Australians, the first we had seen in the crowd.'

And, yes, these men of the Australian 9th Brigade – 35th Battalion boys, it seems – are completely exhausted and filthy, but at least they're all carrying their rifles – even if these appear to be clogged with mud.

'We've been in five days without a spell,' one of the soldiers tells them upon questioning, 'and we are pretty well done up.'[16]

When it becomes apparent that the men are not quite sure where they should be heading, Bean – who after all boasts the rank of Captain – makes something more than a suggestion and something less than an order as they stand by a crossroads:

'Look, men, you Australians here. It's no good going on without knowing where you're going to. Hang on here a moment until an Australian officer comes along.'[17]

Great idea, Captain Cobber. (Bean really has come a long way in the Diggers' estimation. In 1915 they had called him a teetotalling wowser, thought him a shocking dobber for his reports on the Battle of the Wazza in Cairo's red-light district, and now they are taking orders from him!)

'Well as we're going to stop,' one of them says as he unslings his rifle and throws down his pack, 'we may as well sit down.'[18]

The platoon grabs the opportunity for some well-earned rest, either sprawling by the road and using their haversacks as pillows to rest their weary heads or leaning back against one of the many heaps of man-gold-wurzel that abound all around – the root vegetable is perfect for feeding livestock in these parts. They've barely settled in when there is a familiar whistling . . . and then a 93-pound shell from a German 5.9-inch Howitzer explodes just ten yards away. They are only saved from being killed to a man by the fact that the shell buries itself in the mud before exploding, though one man still standing by Bean and Wilkins is wounded. Why a shell in this particular patch, well beyond Villers?

Bean strongly suspects it is because the German guns have registered the crossroads, hoping to catch cross-traffic. Either way, the result is the same. It is a miracle they are still alive, and none of them is inclined to press his luck further. Captain Charles Bean wears the heavy weight of responsibility for the orders he has just dished out; his decision has injured the men.

So as the troops of the 35th Battalion keep straggling back, Bean and Wilkins head off to find their car 'in great gloom',[19] stopping only to quickly visit Brigadier Elliott of the 15th Brigade at Corbie. Bean informs him that the '9th Australian Infantry Brigade is making the fight of its history in defence of the village'.[20]

For all that, and though Bean is careful not to say so, he thinks their position quite hopeless. 'The one thing that cheered us was the difference between our men and the British in the retreat . . . The British . . . were clearly panicked and quite spiritless.'[21]

—

So quickly has Colonel Milne moved, so urgent the situation, that he arrives back among his men of the 36th Battalion, still positioned on the reverse slope of a hill on the south-west corner of Villers-Bretonneux, quite out of breath.

'Company Commanders to assemble at the double!'[22] he roars as soon as he arrives.

Goddard's order had been for them to advance astride the railway cutting, but it has become obvious to Milne as he hurriedly heads back that that is not where the Germans are at their most menacing. In fact, the danger point is to the *south* of the railway, right by Monument Wood, where the Germans are preparing to launch on Villers-Bretonneux proper.

And so let the Devil take the hindmost and the Gods of War be with him, Colonel Milne decides to ignore Goddard's order and organises his whole battalion – some 700 men in all – to attack south of the railway, towards Monument Wood, where even now he can see figures in deathly grey moving inexorably forward.

And if the Gods of War have sent Goddard a very bad hand to play right now, they've at least sent him a very capable leader of men deeply respected by them. The Scottish lilt in his voice as he barks orders is because he had been born and raised in Aberdeen before going to Australia at the age of 18, where he had done everything from farm labouring to mining, to driving engines on the Gympie goldfields, to 'marrying my Mary' and raising three fine sons before joining the Wide Bay Regiment in 1908 and then, of course, the Australian Imperial Force.

Landing at Gallipoli at dawn on 25 April 1915, in charge of a company of the 9th Battalion, Milne had fought valiantly throughout the day and was so in the thick of the action that he had been wounded *five* times, the fifth so severely he had been left in a row of dead on the beach until someone noticed he was alive. Returning to Australia to see his family, any other man would have stayed there – content to have demonstrably done his bit and more – but not Milne. He'd come back as soon as he was able, to first be gassed at Messines and then shot once more at Passchendaele – earning his Distinguished Service Order in August 1917, as well as being mentioned in dispatches in December 'for keeping the front line well supplied with stores, munitions and water, although his party was constantly depleted by casualties and exhaustion'.[23]

Standing here in the thick of it once more, what is obvious to Colonel Milne is that speed is everything, both in terms of how quickly they can mount the attack and then how rapidly they can advance to get at the Germans, who are now threatening to engulf the town the Australians are being counted on to defend. Again, there is no time to write down orders. Once the company commanders are gathered in the sunken road that runs by where the 36th Battalion is concealed, he just tells them straight, in truncated military sentences. He is not panicked but leaves them in no doubt as to just how perilous the situation is: 'The Boche have broken the English line and are advancing on the village.'[24]

As if to prove his point, the Huns spray a 'heavy burst of machine gun fire'[25] at a rise between them and the Huns, just missing them. Milne goes on speaking without missing a beat. 'English troops have been retiring for half an hour through our lines, but efforts to stop them are in vain.'[26]

He tells his men that they are going to counter-attack by 'sweeping along the southern end of the railway line'.[27] In the distance, but getting ever closer, is the sound of gunfire and the odd *zzzzips* of machine-gun bullets passing overhead and *cracks* for close ones.

'Bushelle,' he says to the commander of A Company, 'your company will be on the left. Rodd, B Company will be in the centre. Tedder, C Company will take the right, and I shall send immediately to the OC of the Queen's to ask him to cooperate. Bushelle, your left flank will rest on the railway embankment. The 35th are on the other side. Attack in one wave. D Company under Captain Gadd, I shall hold you in reserve here in the sunken road. Get ready, there's no time to waste.'[28]

'How far shall we go?' Captain John Bushelle, a 42-year-old station overseer originally from Sydney's Paddington, asks.

'Go till you're stopped,' replies Milne grimly, 'and hold on at all costs.'[29]

There is really nothing more to say. There is clearly a job to be done, and they are equally clearly the only men who can do it.

The briefing over, the company commanders race off to shout orders in turn at their Lieutenants, Sergeants and Corporals, whom they must form up into their platoons and then companies, and make ready to move in no more than ten minutes.

Toot sweet, you bastards. It's on.

And now, for Milne, here is a bit of good news. Though the 18th Division has disintegrated, there are still some brave officers and men left over, and one of those officers, Brigadier Edward Wood, a career soldier, Boer War veteran and Commanding Officer of the 55th Brigade, has stayed on – even after telling his Brigade HQ to pack up and retreat – so that he can rally whatever troops he can. Finding two intact companies of the 7th Queen's Regiment, Wood starts to gather them for the cause, at which point Milne spies him in the distance – 'a stoutly built figure, with overcoat and walking stick, rallying some British troops'.[30]

Quickly, Milne sends 'a cordial invitation to cooperate, operating on the right flank of C Company'[31] via his adjutant. To Milne's surprise, Brigadier Wood agrees!

'A similar request was made to the officer rallying the Buffs,' Charles Bean would record, 'but was declined.'[32]

A pity, but having 180 brave British soldiers joining them is really something.

Within minutes, the 7th Queen's men gather with the Australian soldiers, who are forming up by their companies, checking for grit or mud that might jam the cartridge in the breech, putting a round up the spout, fixing their bayonets, nodding to mates for perhaps the last time, sneaking a quick glance at the family photo in their wallet, and even dashing off a very quick note to 'Jenny' or 'Jill', sometimes to both.

The mood is grim but purposeful. They have all said often enough that they want a chance at the Germans in a fair fight, in an open field. Well, this is now bloody well it.

Alfie Holton and his drinking cobber Reggie Dilley are there with the best of them – and a good thing, too. Their particular skill, beyond drinking and raising hell, is expertly operating a Lewis gun for B Company, with Dill the No. 1 holding and firing the gun while Alfie, his No. 2, keeps feeding fresh 47-round magazines. A part of Alfie's preparations is to wrap a sandbag around the barrel, so if Dill has to fire from the hip, he can hold it even if it's red hot.

The order comes to advance. Dill lifts the Lewis onto his shoulders, and he and Alfie get into position.

'As there were not enough of us for two lines of attack,' Holton would recount, 'we had to advance in . . . just one line of men across, the usual way was to have at least 3 lines of attack.'[33]

Ah well, *c'est la guerre*. The pair shake hands. They're mates. And this might be it.

As they make their final preparations, Colonel Milne walks along the line, talking to the men and telling them straight, as he has ever been wont to do: 'Good-bye boys. It's neck or nothing.'[34]

All up, the worthy Colonel has done remarkably well to so quickly assemble a force of 700 soldiers from his 36th Battalion, bolstered by the 180 men from the 7th Battalion Queen's Regiment attached on his right flank. Meanwhile, Captain Sayers, with 170 men of the 35th on the railway's north side, has been told to keep pace with Milne on the south side – making just over 1000 soldiers in all who will be attacking. Further support will be provided by a small second line formed by the remnants of two companies of the 6th Londons, some 100 men, whose role is to follow up hard, ready to strike the enemy wherever and whenever the first line meets heavy resistance.

All must be in readiness for the attack to go in at 5.15 pm.

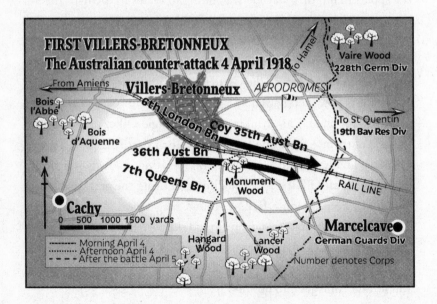

—

As the Diggers of the 36th Battalion get ready to lead the decisive coun-ter-attack to the south-east, Colonel Morshead and Major Fry consult again on how to position their own men coming up behind them. Some diehards of the 33rd will join the left of their line. Morshead and Fry are confident that, as the Hun's attention turns to the 36th Battalion, there will be time to set up their own offensive. Major Fry rides back to his men to give them the new orders while Morshead heads back to HQ in town.

As Fry would record in the battalion war diary, the whole 9th Brigade (or what's left of it) will, if all the attacks work, reclaim a line 2500 yards long, back in the same support trench east of Villers-Bretonneux that had been lost that afternoon.

Milne and Sayers can make the main attack, with Moreshead and Fry standing ready with their men to support them in the north later.

—

South of Morshead and Fry is the company commander of 35th Battalion's D Company, Captain Raleigh Sayers. The first inkling of his military and leadership skills had come in the cadets at the Shore School in North Sydney, where he had also excelled at cricket and rugby, but now comes a real test. And, typically, he does not beat around the bush. Bringing the remnants of the whole shattered battalion to where he is standing in the sunken road at the railway cutting, Sayers explains the situation: 'A bayonet charge is our only hope, and I will lead it.'[35]

—

South-west of Sayers, all is hustle and bustle as Milne's counter-attack prepares to step off, with grim-faced men telling jokes that no one finds funny at this moment . . . all while grey clouds of Germans are forming on their eastern horizon, complete with menacing bolts of lightning, represented by artillery shells that start to land in VB and take their toll. Once prepared, the men dump the haversacks with their personal belongings in a pile for later retrieval – they hope – giving a quick nod to comrades, steeling themselves to move forward for this job o' work to be done . . .

For his own part, Colonel Goddard hurries out of his HQ so he can watch the counter-attack unfold. He positions himself on a slight swell in the ground 500 yards east of the railway station, a point where he can see much of the action. It is not a sheltered position and, like all spots near the front-line, is now 'swept by shell fire and machine guns'.[36] But Goddard feels the need to keep on top of the situation – notwithstanding that he is all out of reserves, and if this counter-attack fails there will be nothing between him and 3000 German soldiers intent on taking Villers-Bretonneux. It *must* succeed.

And there they are now, Milne's 1000, moving forward in splendid order, spread out laterally. True, Milne is clearly making his main thrust south of the rail line, not north as Goddard had ordered, but knowing Milne as he does, there'll obviously be a good reason for that, so Goddard is not concerned.

In fact, as he would later recall, 'It was one of the most inspiring sights imaginable.'[37]

And with them, of course, Colonel Milne, keeping stride with the second wave of the 6th Londons as the first wave now starts up the small crest that will bring them into view of the Germans coming out of Monument Wood.

'At 5:15 p.m.,' Milne would proudly report to Rosie, 'the counter attack was launched, the Battalion moving forward with great dash and in fine formation.'[38]

On the left of Milne, Captain Sayers and his men advance with two parts vigour to one part stealth – moving fast but trying to stay as low to the ground as possible – to make themselves harder to see for as long as possible, so the dog *won't* see the rabbit.

To their right, on the south side of the rail line, the 36th Battalion's A Company under Captain John Bushelle, who imbues his men 'with

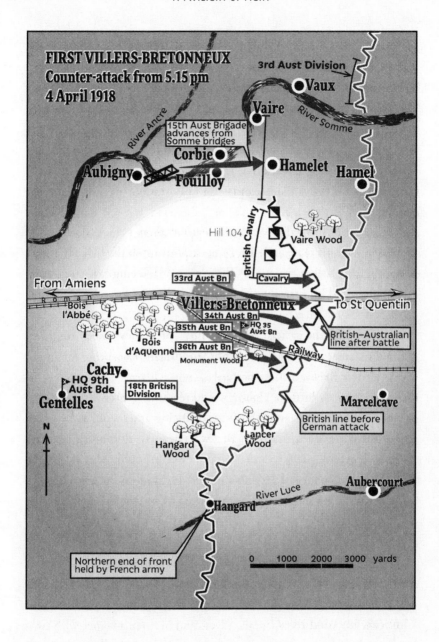

wonderful spirit and confidence',[39] are making fast progress. Within minutes they have closed to within 200 yards west of the railway bridge.

The 36th Battalion's B Company, a further 200 yards again to A Company's right, are also pushing ahead with confidence, when they suddenly strike an early obstacle: 'organized opposition from special Machine gun points'[40] hidden in Monument Wood.

Among Bushelle's men, of course, are Alfie Holton and Reggie Dilley, the latter always a step in front of Holton, since he is carrying the Lewis gun. All of a sudden 'Dill' drops low. A 'sharp shooter'[41] is 'having a go'[42] at him. Bloody Fritz is aiming for all the men carrying a Lewis.

Dill yells at Holton, 'Just get in front of me will you, that bloke will get me.'[43]

No questions asked, Holton does just that and ducks in front of Dill to protect his mate and, most importantly, 'stop the bloke that was shooting from seeing the gun'.[44] They move on, staying extremely close to the ground, Dill carrying the gun well below his knees to obscure it from Fritz as much as possible.

As they pass the eastern edge of Villers-Bret, they 'sweep round to the right'[45] and head straight towards Monument Wood.

And there they are, those bastards!

'As soon as we turned,' Holton would recount, 'we saw Fritz in front of us about 500 yards away. He was advancing and laying a telephone line at the same time. As soon as he saw us he started his machine guns; he had them about 200 feet apart and he was firing like this so you see he had a good chance of getting all of us. He used to fire knee high so that he would shoot us in the legs and then as we dropped get us in the body or head.'[46]

Instantly, the whole of B Company drop to their bellies with a thud. They let the *Boche* troops opposite them 'have it with guns and rifles and then after a few rounds', when there is a lull, they lift themselves up 'and run about 50 or 100 yards and then drop down again and into him with guns and rifles'.[47]

It is a lethal affair with instant death now closely stalking them all. Out there in the field in front of them are two large haystacks from behind which the Hun are sending out particularly heavy machine-gun fire. Over to the right Holton notices C Company and the Brits beyond them are keeping pace with the advance.

Colonel Milne, watching from his observation post, sees B Company come under such a flanking fire that the result is 'rather disastrous'.[48] As he would later report to Rosie, 'Wide gaps were left between all the company frontages by reason of the extended front on which it was necessary to deliver our counter attack.'[49]

He sends out orders for his reserve company to get ready to move up and bolster the line.

———

For the German soldiers of the 9th Bavarian Division, the day has gone fairly well so far, and now the division's fresh reserve regiment is being brought forward to finish the job. They emerge from Monument Wood to head for Villers-Bretonneux proper, filled with confidence.

The 3rd Bavarian Ersatz Regiment is 2500 strong, and over the course of the day they have listened to the sound of the battle ahead, heard reports of the many great victories of their *Kameraden* and wait for their *own* chance to kill *die Tommys*. All the word is that the British are hopeless, have lost the will to fight, and it is almost a shame to stick bayonets into them – it's not a fair fight. But they will *force* themselves to!

And now, by a stroke of good fortune, it is their own regiment that is about to have the honour of taking the ultimate prize, the one they have been told all along was their major goal – Villers-Bretonneux. As they emerge from Monument Wood, the men of the 3rd Bavarian Regiment can now see the town just a few hundred yards up ahead, the dark-red twin towers of the church providing a sure landmark of where they are heading. Doing it by the book, they advance with five waves of men, 300 yards apart, their machine guns well in the rear, protected until such a time as they can be sure that the situation for'ard is secure.

Fanned out, going in for the kill, the soldiers grin to each other at the lack of resistance so far. The British have simply evaporated at their mere sight, and . . .

Und . . . Was ist das?

One second there is nothing between their five waves and Villers-Bretonneux, and the next there are 1000 soldiers, bayonets forward, jogging – *nein* – *running* STRAIGHT AT US!

And their Lewis guns are blazing!

Four hundred yards away, and getting closer all the time.

The orders ring out: *Fünfter Zug, hinlegen! Reichweite 400 Meter. Feuer frei!* Fifth platoon! Hit the dirt! Range 400 metres. Open fire!

While some brave German soldiers do exactly as ordered and immediately bring their guns to bear, cutting a swathe through the oncoming line of madmen, it is only to see that after the oncoming line falters momentarily . . . *still* they come on regardless!

They're now just 200 yards away!

—

At the same moment, north of the railway, Captain Raleigh Sayers is leading his D Company of the 35th, staring ahead . . . when he sees the most extraordinary thing.

The Germans' line, which had been charging towards them with equal intent, suddenly falters! A flutter in their hearts, a stutter in their steps, and the first wave of Germans – shaped thinly for attack and not thickly for defence – are turning!

Given the choice between facing madmen with flashing bayonets charging at them like mad dogs or getting back to the seeming safety of the woods, there is no choice. And indeed, like mad dogs who have suddenly seen a juicy quarry make a run for it, a collective guttural roar goes up from the Australians. A red mist of blood-lust rises.

Into 'em, boys!

For now, even the brave German soldiers who have held their ground, finding themselves now abandoned, leap to their feet and turn. The gun fire on the advancing Australians has fallen away to near nothing. Had the Germans brought just one machine gun into these for'ard ranks closest to Villers-Bretonneux, the battle would have been quite different. But in an instant the whole situation changes as the

Australians close in on the now terrified Germans . . . their bayonets fixed.

—

Over to the right, Milne's men Holton and Dilley continue their jack-in-the-box advance. Down on your bellies! Up and run! Down! Up! Down!

And, of course, they are firing meantime.

In extreme situations like this, the whole process of reloading takes no more than four seconds, meaning the bursts of bullets from the Lewis guns tearing into the Germans are all but constant.

Ah, but so are the German bullets coming back. Holton is going for his life when he hears a seemingly innocuous *ping* and notices that one of his mates in the Lewis gun crew has had something hit his tin hat. Holton is just going to ask him if he is okay when his mate's jaw kind of goes slack and he falls forward. Holton leans over to take the man's helmet off, at which point the blood simply pours out of his head . . .

And that's the end of that mate. It doesn't take long.

By this time, as the Australians struggle under the withering fire still coming from the haystacks in front of them, Colonel Milne has ordered the reserve company forward. And now they respond, bent low as if against the wind, to 'reinforce the centre, link up the companies, and as far as possible, straighten out the line'.[50] Two small companies of the 6th Londons – the Brits are coming good! – also appear and, just when they are needed most, fill the gap between A and B Companies to stiffen the lines and consolidate the gains already made.

Milne, watching the battle unfold, looks over to Hunland and notices 'considerable bodies of the enemy commence to form at distances from 500 to 700 yards in front of our line'.[51] Down in the front-lines his men have seen them too, for within minutes the proud commander would report, 'These parties suffered very heavy casualties from our Lewis Guns and rifle fire.'[52]

(Among them, Dill and Alfie are still going hell for leather.)

—

Back on the left, Captain Sayers is in the thick of battle with his men. Some officers in such circumstances choose to stay back from the fray, but not him. At the head of the troops, his first major contact is to jump into a shell hole containing three Germans manning a machine gun. Once his revolver – taken from a dead fellow officer – jams, he does the next best thing.

'He throttled two Germans,' one of his men would recount, 'and with his tin helmet split the skull of a third, thus putting the team out of action.'[53]

Over on their right, across the rail embankment, Captain Bushelle's A Company finally encounters a bloodier resistance as their wave meets intense small-arms fire from German soldiers with revolvers, shortly followed by riflemen who have joined the furious fray and, yes, now some machine guns that have been rushed forward to line the edge of the orchard . . .

Even though many of the swarming Australians do go down, there are enough of them who keep coming, who can get close enough before throwing themselves down, that they can bring heavy fire, in turn, on the German machine gunners.

In the centre of the Australian attack, Major Brent Rodd – a 39-year-old father of six from North Sydney – spies his friend, Captain Bushelle, some 100 yards to the left, and sends a messenger (who is extraordinary for how fast he can run while bent so low, his jaw practically touching his flying boots) to enquire as to whether his company will keep pushing forward. The answer comes back just as quickly: you bloody betcha.

And Bushelle is as good as his words; his men keep up their withering fire. After all, the genesis of the 36th Battalion had been when the NSW Minster for Public Information, Ambrose Carmichael, sponsored a recruiting drive to raise a battalion from NSW rifle club members – hence their nickname, 'Carmichael's 1000' – and they boast many members who can shoot a cigarette from the mouth of a passing sparrow at 100 yards on a windy day. In fact, their fire is so devastating that the surviving German soldiers – who had been more inclined to join the Goethe and Beethoven clubs – turn and run, hotly pursued by Bushelle's men.

First the Germans crash through the branches back into Monument Wood, and then into the oncoming waves of their own soldiers as the pursuing mad dog Australians close on them. A furious bayonet battle ensues, mixed with grenades.

In the gloom, after the first flurry of explosions, all is suddenly a weirdly punctuated quiet, a ballet of death filled with flashing, slashing blades; groans; death rattles; grunts of exertion; the sucking sound when blades are removed from pierced lungs; gurgling geysers of blood spouting up and then falling away; those distinctive thuds that the human body makes when it goes down, dead before it hits the ground.

With the Bushelle breakthrough on the left, the German soldiers holding their own in the centre suddenly find themselves outflanked, and they, too, start to give way. A similar battle breaks out as Major Rodd's men turn into screaming, whirling dervishes – bounding, leaping, spinning beasts who seem to flash bayonets from every limb – savaging every German they can catch, which is many.

Alfie and Dill are in it with the best of them. They are running forward again when one of their mates, Charlie, gets hit. Against orders – *nothing* is supposed to get in the way of an attack – Holton goes back to find him on the ground, blood pouring from his knee. Alfie tries for a few seconds to get Charlie's trouser leg up so he can get a bandage on it to stem the flow, but he soon gives up. In all likelihood his mate won't die – though it might be touch and go – but others forward really will perish if he doesn't get there to do his bit. On such decisions do the course of entire battles run.

'I'll have to go,' he says to his mate. 'I cannot do anything for you.'[54] The mate nods, he gets it. They shake hands and Alfie is quickly on his feet once more, running to catch up with the rest of his crew.

And there they are, just up ahead. 'Alfie! Alfie!'[55]

He's just in time. Alfie throws himself to the ground right by the spot where Dill has positioned himself in a shell hole with three others from the crew, leaving no room for him. And no matter that a big tuft of grass is the only thing protecting him from the guns of Fritz, Alfie still whacks the magazine on and Dill is firing again in no time. Yes, they take a pounding, with man after man going down – 'I can say that there was only Dill and I on our gun that came out of this counter attack,' Holton would recount of the fate of the dozen men of two Lewis gun crews they'd begun the attack with – but in military terms it is all worth it. 'We held Fritz at that place which was about two miles from where we had started.'[56]

And when the Australians over on the far right break through to the other side of the wood, the Germans give the game away and run. The Australians jump in the enemy trenches where they can. Monument Wood has been retaken!

Those in exposed positions stay down, waiting for darkness to fall. The gaps are plugged and the Australians' line is looking solid.

As Holton settles in behind his life-saving tuft of grass and the gun fire briefly subsides, he can hear 'a big shout on our left'.[57]

It is Captain Sayers and the boys of the 35th, of course, who have had equal success and have come to much the same conclusion. Their advance has ended just a hundred yards short of the railway bridge – the fire on them had become too strong – and they dig in to hold the ground they have won.

A little over an hour later and a short way to the north, Morshead with the 34th and elements of the 33rd launch their part of the counter-attack. Using three Canadian armoured cars – essentially 1914 Rolls-Royce Silver Ghosts covered with armour plating and a machine-gun turret on top – they 'barrel up the Roman Road with Vickers guns blazing to lend a hand'.[58]

The German resistance offered to this mechanised cavalry is as token as it is brief, and by dark Morshead and his men are able to link with Sayers. All up, the Australians and British have advanced an extraordinary 2000 yards on a 2500-yard front, almost as Fry had predicted. They didn't quite get back into their support trench of the morning, but the threat to Villers has been stopped cold.

The bold Australian counter-attack has not only shattered the German Regiment that had to suffer the worst of it, the 3rd Bavarian Ersatz Infantry Regiment, but also those on its flanks. As the war diary of the German 48th Regiment would note, 'At 6 pm the enemy attacks on both sides of the village. He succeeds. The troops on our left are pushed back; thus is no longer possible for our regiment to advance further.'

In fact, it is soon apparent that their situation is far worse. As the 48th Regiment is now totally exposed to flanking fire from *den Australiern*, they have no choice but to fall back themselves, in all the wretched 'deep mud, which made a lot of the weapons . . . unusable and command communications difficult. Despite all this, and *unter den schwierigsten Verhältnissen*, under the most difficult circumstances, it was possible to once again make a connection with [our left] flank.'[59]

By continuing to retreat they finally get to the spot where the remnants of the next regiment to their left have dug in, meaning the German line is secure once more – albeit a long way further back than it was before they commenced the attack on the Australian lines.

To secure the newly captured position, Colonel Milne orders 'tools and ammunition' to be 'hastened forward by a small party from headquarters – signallers, batmen, police and gas personnel'.[60] At this desperate hour, everyone must roll up their sleeves and pitch in, the Australians' own answer to Carey's Force – when chief cooks and bottle-washers became gunners and bombers.

On the far right flank of the Australians' line, just as they have regained some semblance of an upper hand – though it is anyone's guess whether they are about to be engulfed by a German *counter*-counter-attack – a curious incident takes place.

The Australians in the front lines are settling just a little, with the red mist lifting a bit. With the light of battle still in their eyes they are finding what cover they can, digging ditches deeper when not exchanging shots with the Germans close by . . . as Sergeants and Corporals move among them, getting them organised . . . with no one sure if some Germans have got past them and might be coming at them from the rear . . . or if both of their flanks are secure, for that matter, and . . .

And who is this now suddenly come among them? It is a British officer, ordering the Australians to retire! But is he *actually* a British officer? Listen, pompous Pommy pricks ordering them around don't sit well with the Australians at the best of times, but on this occasion it is outrageous to order them to give up ground that has been so hard won. Not only do the Australians refuse the order, but they ask to see the man's papers, to prove that he is indeed a British officer and not a German spy. (There have been infamous cases throughout the war of Germans pretending to be British and pulling off this kind of stunt.)

This fellow is wearing an officer's tunic, all right, but a private's hat, bearing the Queen's Regiment badge, with the name *G. E. Martin* written inside, but that is all! He has no papers. Further, he can offer 'no satisfactory explanation of his conduct and presence', nor for why he carries a pack instead of ordinary fighting kit, like other *genuine* officers.

A Lance-Corporal is so convinced he is a spy that he brings his revolver to bear, points it at this maybe-maybe-not British officer's head and – no, *no, NO!* – shoots him.

Dead.

'But,' as Captain Charles Bean would recount, 'there was found on the dead stranger no definite evidence that he was German, and it seems all too possible that he was not, and that the rough justice of his end was one of the million minor tragedies of the war.'[61]

By 8 pm it is all over. The Australians have established a new defensive line from the Roman road on their left to south of Monument Wood on their right, with the 7th Queen's holding their flank south of there. And the wood itself is once again in Australian hands.

Well done, Australians.

All up, it has been an extraordinary day for the Australians defending Villers-Bretonneux. In the final casualty count, they have lost 1400 men, more than a third of the 9th Brigade. But, as Rosenthal will proudly report to Monash, 'The Brigade . . . covered itself with glory and on a conservative estimate from all C.Os. accounted for over 4,000 enemy on our own front, irrespective of casualties caused by our artillery.'[62] Colonel Milne had conducted a 'magnificent counter-attack', and Rosie informs his Commanding Officer, 'I am very proud . . .'[63]

Colonel Charles Benson, the commander of the 6th Londons, would record his own view of Milne: 'The greatest credit is due the OC of the 36th . . . This officer undoubtedly retrieved a very awkward situation.'[64]

Good judges are of the view that he should be awarded a significant medal for his bravery and leadership.

And while the officers are proud, the Diggers – the ones who do the actual *digging* – like Alfred Holton and Reggie Dilley, are still lying out there in the mud and cold, feeling only a soft, warm glow of pride, which is trumped by a profound sadness for the friends they have seen fall along the way. As Holton would later recall, 'It was a bad day fighting and at the finish we only had about 80 men in our Company which should have been about 250.'[65]

But they stopped Fritz all right, *and* drove him back.

'In brilliant fashion,' Brigadier Rosenthal would report with no little satisfaction to General Monash, 'they did their job, drove the enemy back, captured 6 machine guns and 3 prisoners (the conditions making it impossible to deal with numbers of prisoners) and re-established the line.'[66]

A short translation of the parenthetical remark? They shot dead even those Germans who surrendered, for they simply did not have the spare troops necessary to deal with prisoners in the middle of a battle.

—

For the moment, the Germans must accept the reality of it. Their attack has been turned back by the jog-trotting Australians, they've lost Monument Wood, and for the moment Villers-Bretonneux remains in Allied hands. All they have to show for the day in this area is the village of Hamel and Hangard Wood, now occupied by Germany's 78th Infantry Regiment. For their part, the 78th IR is glad to have held on to those positions, even if, as their war diary records, 'Throughout the course of the war, the regiment has never been as mentally and physically strained as on 4.4.18.'

All the 78th can do is settle down the best they can in the darkness and fog of their own exhaustion, midst the pounding rain, 'without being able to find shelter, without food, tired of struggle and march . . .'

In fact, it is 'only with extreme effort' that they can keep the ground they have gained against enemy counter-attacks. 'So a resistance line has been established by the Regiment through the forest of Hangard and bent back on the wings.'[67]

The Germans in Hangard Wood are isolated from support on their flanks, but they remain determined to hold what they have.

———

General Gontard's XIV Corps report on the results of 4 April is stark and makes sober reading for General Georg von der Marwitz:

> The Bavarian [9th] Division was forced to withdraw in the face of strong counter-attacks [and] the Guards Ersatz Division, on its left, had reached Cachy, but also lost the ground that it had gained that afternoon.[68]

The rest of the German attack, which had been against French positions from the village of Hangard, six miles to the south, has fared a little better as the French defence demonstrated a certain round-heeled quality, and the German forces advanced two miles before being stopped.

———

While relieved that his men have held the Germans off from Villers-Bretonneux so far, Goddard is under no illusions. The advance has not quite made its objective: the same support line trench they had held this morning, which would have provided a better position to hold if the enemy wanted to try for VB again tomorrow.

'I had to appreciate,' he would recount, 'that the troops available to me were quite inadequate to meet a fresh attack on the morrow which was almost certain to come. The troops had suffered heavy casualties, were worn out with the continuous fighting and were in a miserable condition from exposure to the mud and severe weather. I felt another night under the conditions obtaining would leave them stiff and in bad form to meet an early morning attack.'[69]

The solution?

To Goddard it is obvious. In consultation with Rosenthal, who comes forward at dusk to warmly shake the hand of every man he can, it is decided they must attack, *again*. Specifically, Rosie orders 'an advance of about 1000 yards to resecure our old support line trenches'.[70]

Goddard is in full agreement.

'I felt,' he would recount, 'my only possible chance was to affect some surprise which would mislead the enemy as to our strength. The only way to accomplish this was to ourselves attack – he had been advancing on a retreating army and I felt it would be the last thing he would expect.'[71]

Further encouraging this line of thinking is the notion that if they could just *take back* some of the ground the Germans had won, it would surely 'cause him to pause before making further attack, thus giving us breathing space until relieving troops arrived'.[72]

The orders, when they come, are clear. The Diggers of the 35th – who have shot their bolt and are now eyeballs-rollingly exhausted – are to come out of the line. They will be replaced by a composite force of the 36th, 34th and 33rd Battalions, with some soldiers from the 7th Queen's Regiment and the British cavalry. Together, they will attack in the dark along a 2500-yard front. The aim, as Rosie later explains to Monash: 'Secure for ourselves and deny to the enemy the line of trenches we had dug as support to our original front line of yesterday morning.'[73]

—

At 1 am on 5 April, 1500 men jump up from their trenches and race forward with every intent to stun the Hun, expecting an opposition that . . . isn't always there. There are certainly a few scattered strong points manned by German soldiers who do indeed stand their ground and fight, but there are not enough to stop the Australians. After a short, sharp tussle – most of which centres on Huns dug in around the aerodrome until they, too, are overwhelmed – the Diggers are quickly back in the very support line trench that had been Colonel Goddard's original objective when he had ordered Milne to counter-attack at 4 pm the previous day.

As recorded in the war diary of the 35th Infantry Battalion, 'Strong opposition was encountered but our losses were not severe. Our Lewis Guns fired from the hip and heavy fire was brought to bear by this means and by our rifles.'[74]

There is great satisfaction with the result: 'about 50 enemy . . . killed and 19 prisoners taken'.[75] They could not have asked for better – and the prisoners are soon on their way, under escort, to an open field in the rear surrounded by a wire fence, where they can be held under guard for a day or two before being transferred to a prisoner-of-war camp.

'It was a complete success,' Colonel Henry Goddard would record, 'the enemy being taken quite unprepared as it was certainly the last thing expected. The most important part of our task next to denying the enemy the Villers-Bretonneux position, that of gaining time, was effected.'[76]

Still, the Australians have now lost 1440 men, and there will be enduring bitterness that it need not have happened had the Tommies held the line that morning. As Pompey Elliott would write to his cousin Milly: 'A number of the British officers should be cashiered for gross neglect of duty and incompetence. A number of them have been under me of late and their apparent indifference is astounding. I actually over-heard one say "Well, if the Boche does get Amiens it won't matter to us, it's not our country."'[77]

The bottom line, however, remains. They have held Villers-Bretonneux and Hill 104. As Brigadier Rosenthal notes in his diary on this day, with evident satisfaction, '[The 5th Division] holds from main Amiens road at Villers-Bretonneux to the Somme while 3rd and 4th Aus. Divs. hold up to Albert. Thus the lines of approach to Amiens are all controlled by Australian troops who hold about 15 miles of front.'[78]

Rah!

It is something of which the Germans themselves are very much aware, with the next morning's edition of Berlin's finest newspaper, *Vossische Zeitung*, reporting, with a mixture of pride and regret:

> *Between Ancre and Avre the Englishman makes feverish efforts to keep his position and the Germans push back again. Since his own completely disordered troops are not sufficient for this purpose, he has brought Australische und Neuseeländische Kontingente, Australian and New Zealand contingents, and inserted them into the front line . . .*[79]

Even General Ludendorff must acknowledge, in his official communiqué, that the assault, specifically around Villers-Bretonneux, had not gone according to plan.

'. . . *Australier [geben] keinen Fußbreit Boden frei* . . . Australians give away no inch of ground.'[80]

As to Prince Rupprecht's Chief of Staff, General Hermann von Kuhl, he is convinced that the chance for Germany to strike a decisive blow has now been missed, while Crown Prince Wilhelm goes so far as to advocate that the attacks planned for the next day be cancelled and Operation Michael ended.

But General Ludendorff will not hear of it. There is one last chance for the offensive to triumph after all, one last attack. If it works, the whole situation will be saved and they'll reach Amiens after all, but via a different route, on the north side of the Somme. The assault planned for 5 April, along nine miles of front from Dernancourt to Hébuterne, will go ahead.

—

What remains is to continue the evacuation of the wounded Australians, to get them serious medical treatment. And, oh, how startled many of the nurses are when receiving the wounded men back at 3rd Australian General Hospital at Abbeville, some 40 miles to the north-west. As one Australian nurse – there are some 2000 of them in France with the Australian Army Nursing Service – clips away the patient's pants to tend to a bullet wound through the leg . . . hello, hello, what do you know? A pair of pastel pink lace panties that she would *kill* to be wearing herself! And the situation is far from uncommon. Mostly they just leave the panties be. No point in getting the Diggers' knickers in a knot.

CHAPTER THIRTEEN

THE SECOND BATTLE OF DERNANCOURT

After the lull, the storm. . . .What has happened so far
is that the Boche has taken back at considerable cost
the ground he gave up voluntarily a year ago – and
very little else. He possibly hoped to get to Amiens, but
I don't think he will get there now. The Boche hasn't
advanced one yard on our front, and I hope he won't.[1]
Brigade Major Thomas Louch, 12th Brigade

The dead and wounded of the 47th
lay everywhere underfoot.[2]
History of the AIF's 47th Battalion

10 PM, 4 APRIL 1918, DERNANCOURT, THEY SHALL NOT PASS

After the Germans made such enormous strides against the British in
the first ten days of the *Kaiserschlacht*, it has not escaped their notice
– among both officers and soldiers – that every time they have been
stopped, it seems to have been the Australians on the other side of the
parapet.

And so it risks being once again . . .

Since the battle at Dernancourt a week earlier, the Australians have

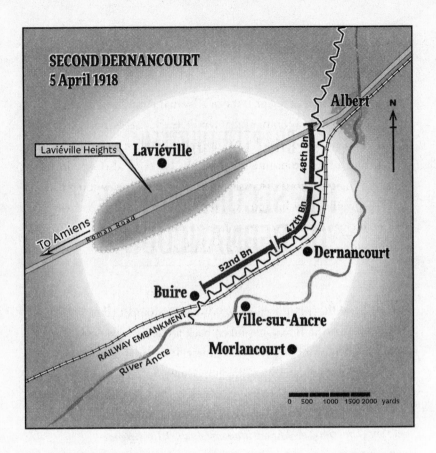

SECOND DERNANCOURT
5 April 1918

Albert

N

Laviéville Heights

Laviéville

48th Bn

To Amiens

Roman Road

47th Bn

Dernancourt

52nd Bn

Buire

Ville-sur-Ancre

RAILWAY EMBANKMENT

Morlancourt

River Ancre

0   500   1000   1500 2000   yards

entirely relieved all British forces in the area and dug themselves in along the railway line. Colonel John Whitham's 52nd Battalion is on the right for roughly 1200 yards from Ville-sur-Ancre, stretching north-east to the railway bridge at Dernancourt. The 47th Battalion occupies the line from that bridge for roughly another 1000 yards, and finally the 48th Battalion holds it from there to Albert.

All have the support of the newly formed 4th Machine Gun Battalion under the command of the redoubtable Colonel Harry Murray, VC, nothing less than the most decorated soldier in the AIF and a man most Australian soldiers would be happy to follow through the gates of Hell. And sometimes, if you do what Colonel Harry says, you can visit Hell upon others . . . For Murray has 36 Vickers guns, each able to douse an area the size of an Aussie Rules oval with so much flying lead that no enemy without protection could live.

Which might be as well, for there is no doubt the Australians are expecting Fritz to try again.

On the evening of 4 April, the tall Tasmanian officer strolling along the foot of the railway embankment at Dernancourt is more than familiar to his men. Colonel John Whitham of 52nd Battalion is making a final tour of his front-line before dark. He reminds Captain Albert Fraser of their previous discussion that 'there will be no going back'.

Fraser replies that he understands the orders – *come what may, there will be no retreat, and you must fight to the very end* – and is content, adding with quite inspiring sincerity, 'I hope they come.'[3]

DAWN, 5 APRIL 1918, ANCRE VALLEY, SHADOWS IN THE MIST

The Germans are not done in these parts, as the final phase of Operation Michael is launched as planned, codenamed *Sonnenschein*, sunshine . . . Nine German divisions are now set to attack along a front nine miles wide – including 6000 yards held by the 12th and 13th Brigades of the AIF's 4th Division around Dernancourt, and 3000 yards still held by their brother brigade, also of the 4th Division, the 4th Brigade at Hébuterne.

The Australians see no sign of the expected attack, and at dawn it seems unlikely that Captain Fraser will see his wish fulfilled – the Germans on the other side of the embankment don't appear to be stirring. Lacking anything better to do, his battalion commander, Colonel Whitham, shaves, breakfasts and begins reading the newspaper.

For the Australian soldiers at Dernancourt, the first clue of what is to come had been heard through the misty night, when sound travels furthest. The likes of Sergeant Stan McDougall would later report that he and his mates observed 'the tramp of feet of Germans'[4] as if thousands of enemy soldiers were being moved into position. And now, sure enough, a barrage for the ages bursts overhead at 6 o'clock on the morning of 5 April.

In familiar fashion, the barrage goes for two hours and the

Australians keep their heads down. For the 48th Battalion's Lieutenant George Mitchell, the attack comes as no more of a surprise than it had for the 47th's Stan McDougall. The previous day Fritz had also unleashed an hour-long barrage from 12.30, so strong that all the Australians had been able to do was lay low in the trenches, waiting for it to pass, biding their time by playing with a quivering rabbit that preferred them to the shrapnel. 'It would run all over us,' Mitchell had noted in his diary. 'After a tour outside it would come in and shake water all over us.'[5]

The previous day, however, had felt like merely a softening-up barrage. This feels like the real thing, like the Germans are about to burst upon them.

'It was the heaviest shell fire I have ever seen . . .' Mitchell would record, which is saying something. 'I passed my water bottle full of rum along the line after having a good swig myself.'[6]

What better thing to have for breakfast under the circumstances?

'Shells were exploding everywhere and pieces of metal falling in singing showers all round us. No news came to us.'[7]

Over to the right, in the reserve line behind the 52nd Battalion, Private Stanley Sutcliffe of the 13th Brigade's 51st Battalion notes just how heavy *and* expert it is: 'Such a barrage . . . as I have never seen before or since. Jerry had his guns registered on all our batteries, and was even knocking guns out miles behind our lines.'[8]

Again and again, the guns would pound the front-lines, move back to the artillery, and then come back to the front-line again, clearly 'with the idea of killing every living thing in its way'.[9]

Three times, heavy shells explode within 30 yards of where Sutcliffe and his mates are dug in, and three times they are miraculously left shaken up but otherwise unhurt. It proves to be the first flurry of what will amount to the largest set-piece attack ever faced by Australians.

In all, three German divisions, totalling some 50,000 soldiers, are being hurled at just 6000 Australians. Fritz's intent, as it had been the week before, is to take the Laviéville Heights, which lies 2000 yards up those gentle slopes. The vantage point would not only provide an open road to Amiens but offer ideal views for the German artillery observers to direct devastating volleys in the direction of Amiens – together with, in this case, the Australian positions at Morlancourt, Corbie and Villers-Bretonneux.

And as the last of the murky mist starts to fade at around 9 am, the Australians can now see the first of these Germans advancing on the railway embankment from the south.

Among the soldiers of the 47th Battalion lining the embankment, the cry quickly goes up.

'They're coming!'

'Give it to 'em!'

They give it to 'em all right, firing at a distance of just 500 yards with a potent mixture of their pinpoint .303 rifles and wide-net machine guns. At this range, with so many densely packed Germans coming at them with just about no cover, the Australians cannot miss. Every bullet counts. They are also helped by 4th Division artillery batteries positioned just on the other side of the crest of Laviéville Heights, where the Germans can't see them.

'Thousands of Fritz are rushing the railway embankment from everywhere,' one Digger would recount. 'We're bowling them over, but nearer to the embankment they draw. The ground behind is carpeted with grey figures that lie still, that twitch and kick, lashing the ground with agony . . .'[10]

For those Germans out in the open trying to attack the Australians, it is Hell on Earth.

One minute Private Hubert Schroeter of the 3rd *Jägerbataillon* of the 3rd Marine Division had been simply moving forward without problems, and the next it happens. 'We were met by a terrific explosion of machine-gun fire,' he would recount. One bullet hits him in the upper left arm. Two more hit him in both legs, just below the knees. Right beside him, one of his best friends, Ludwig Krause, takes a bullet to the chest and dies before his eyes. There is no time for their comrades to help; they must continue to charge forward against the Australian guns, only for them to all fall, too.

All that Schroeter can do is crawl into a deep furrow that presents itself as he tries to get away from the deadly, incessant machine-gun chatter. Convinced he is going to bleed to death from the gushing wound in his arm, he tries to bind it with his rifle sling.

'To do this,' he would recount, 'I had to move about, and every time my helmet jutted above the lip of the furrow the [Australians] fired their machine guns at me. Due to a heavy loss of blood, I lost consciousness many times.'[11]

On the far right of the Australian positions, the 52nd Battalion are more than holding their own. As Private Sutcliffe would report, 'He came over in full marching order, evidently with the idea of reaching Amiens without a stop . . . The first wave of Germans came in massed formation, and they were cut down by machine-gun fire just like a scythe cuts grass.'[12]

But here comes the second wave, so fast and so strong that they get right through to the line of 52nd Battalion, who must now rise to meet them with the mixed fury of bullets and bayonets at close quarters.

'That was the first time I experienced hand-to-hand fighting with the bayonet,' Sutcliffe records, 'and it was heavy! But the German kept being reinforced with the result that we were pushed back about 1000 yards.'[13]

The situation is the same across the rest of the line. The German forces are so many and so committed that they really are able to advance as the battle rages through the early morning and beyond, with successive waves continuing to roll thunderously forward. The first German breakthrough comes just before ten o'clock, when a concerted attack on the middle of the 47th Battalion sees the Australians forced to pull back. The *Boche* are now swarming over the railway line in such numbers that they not only take over the 47th's front-line positions, but also their support lines, even reaching their battery of machine guns.

Most significant for the Australians is that the retreat of the 47th sees the Germans secure access to the small tunnel that goes through the embankment on the road from Dernancourt to Laviéville Heights, which allows them to bring two field guns through the tunnel and open direct fire on the rest of the Australians at 1000-yards range, causing their own devastating toll of casualties.

Though the 12th and 13th Brigades keep fighting with everything they have in them, by late morning the tide of German soldiers is so strong that something must give – the defensive situation worsened by the fact that, in this particular hollow, the mist remains thick. 'Except Germans . . . seen at close quarters, it was impossible for the defending troops to tell what was happening.'[14]

Of the three battalions in the front-line – the 48th on the left, the 47th in the centre and the 52nd on the right – it is the 47th that continues to receive the brunt of the attack. Indeed, they are the ones who must continue to retreat to more secure positions up the slope. This further exposes the flanks of both the 48th and the 52nd, and, though the latter holds on for dear life, the former must fall back as well. The situation is grim and getting grimmer as the hole in the centre of the Australian line widens, and Australian soldier after soldier falls.

To even slow the Germans is going to take a Herculean effort, but, as it happens, the 47th have a proven Hercules among them. And no, Sergeant Stan McDougall, the Tasmanian blacksmith, has not yet been awarded the Victorian Cross for his heroics the first time the Germans attacked at Dernancourt – insufficient time has passed for the recommendation to be considered, let alone approved – but there is plenty of speculation among his many mates in D Company that that is precisely what he deserves. So, we'll see.

For now, you can see him there!

Isolated near the now German-held support line, some 1000 yards north of the tunnel, McDougall is not just taking punishment from the 'enemy's arty', which is 'very hot', but also being enfiladed with machine-gun fire from the flanks – in one direction from Albert and in the other from the church tower in Dernancourt.[15]

Won't these bastards be told?

And, yes, the Germans are there in overwhelmingly superior numbers, but being outgunned has never remotely bothered McDougall. Back in Tassie, as a 13-year-old, he had first got in trouble for belting a bullying schoolmaster, and at 16 he had fought the great Ted Luttrell for the middleweight championship of Tasmania, only narrowly going down on points. This is just more of the same. He must have a go.

Perhaps with the heavy sigh of one who finds himself having to do exactly the same job as a week before, even though he thought the job done, McDougall once again grabs the nearest available Lewis gun and takes it to what will subsequently be described as 'a very exposed position where he could enfilade [the] enemy at close quarters up to 30 yards'.[16]

Again, it is like a fireman with a hose, defying the flames to wildly spray everything within coo-ee in one particular direction – that of the invading Germans. The red mist descends once more for McDougall, and his sheer brazenness is staggering as he keeps firing from the hip, releasing a primal roar from deep in his belly.

The Germans he is firing upon are bowled over like ninepins, and the only hesitation in his aim as he sweeps back and forth is when he spies an enemy soldier bringing a gun to bear upon him, in which case that soldier is eliminated with a concentrated spray. Finally, however, one German soldier does have his gun aimed right at McDougall's belly, and squeezes off a shot.

The bullet flies true and . . . hits McDougall . . . right in his Lewis gun, instantly rendering it useless. Throwing both it and himself to the ground, he comes back around and realises that he is perhaps a tad close to the surviving Germans after all. As his mates further up the slope, awestruck at his bravery, give him cover, he is able to crawl a remarkable 300 yards to safety.

Done now?

Not yet, Cobber.

Taking yet *another* Lewis gun, 'he returns to his post in No Man's Land' – right where he had previously been – and starts firing once more for all he is worth, which is plenty, and is 'responsible for many dead'.[17]

When his ammunition runs out, McDougall crawls back to his men once more to find that his platoon commander has been killed. He, naturally, takes command, moving his men into ever-better positions, ensuring that the fire on the Germans remains constant.

Yet *still* the grey German tide comes on, hitting the remnants of the 47th Battalion so hard that they have no choice but to fall back even further up the slope, dragging their wounded with them.

One Digger of the 45th Battalion, Private Eddie Lynch – a 21-year-old from Bourke – would chronicle it clearly: 'We've got a score of Fritz for every one of us who gets hit . . . They've made a fair advance, but every yard of it is marked by a fallen man . . . He still has to shift us if he wants all the ridge, which he undoubtedly does . . . It's our turn next and we know it. Can we hope for better luck than the 47th?'[18]

—

At the same time as the 12th and 13th Brigades of the 4th Division are fighting for their lives against the three swarming German divisions at Dernancourt, eight miles to the north their brother unit, the 4th Brigade, is equally engaged at Hébuterne. The nine German divisions launching across a nine-mile front have struck Australians at the northern and southern end of their assault – which happen to be the very spots where they are being held up.

At 9.27 am Lieutenant Charles Aherne is in the front-line with the 16th Battalion 1000 yards south of Hébuterne, about to be relieved, when he suddenly sees a mass of German troops heading their way, over Serre Ridge from the south-east, just before a rain of Fritz's artillery comes down upon the Australians. The only thing slowing the Germans is that instead of charging down the hill, they must carefully pick their way through the myriad old shell holes of the 1916 Somme battle, now overgrown with long grass – not to mention the odd overlooked skeletal remains of both enemies and friends, swathed in pieces of tattered cloth that had once been their proud uniform.

Again, watching them come, Aherne is not panicked. He simply dashes off a note to the 16th Battalion commander:

Things are very hot. Postpone relief until further
notice. It is impossible [because of artillery fire]
for them to come up. He is massing in front of the
quarry to my right ... They are about 150 yards in
front of me, but we can kill them as fast as they
come. Keep lookout for SOS ...[19]

As good as his word, when the barrage lifts at 9.30 am and the Germans
come on in massed waves, these Australian soldiers of the 4th Brigade
are without mercy as the succeeding lines are simply 'broken by Lewis
gun and rifle fire'.[20]

The next company along from Lieutenant Aherne is commanded by
Captain Daniel Aarons, and they, too, have their hands full keeping an
entire German battalion at bay – while managing it without problem.

'The [first wave] got so knocked about that the balance of the attack
seemed to be on hands [and knees], along saps, go as you please. Sort
of Anzac rules.'[21]

Traditionally, the Australians do well with such rules – at the least
defending their tryline with some ferocity – and so it proves here. The
Germans simply cannot move forward, and remain pinned down for
the entire day before deciding discretion to be the better part of valour
and withdrawing with the dark.

Germany's 126th Infantry Regiment, which had been holding the
German front trench while watching their assaulting force pass through
en route towards the Australians, now sees them coming back cowed,
beaten and bloodied. As their battalion history would faithfully record:
'The 5th Bavarian Reserve Division, attacking south of Hébuterne,
made absolutely no headway.'[22]

The Australian machine-gun fire, meanwhile, would be reported
by the 10th Bavarian Reserve Regiment as 'most unpleasant'. And
moreover, 'The attack had *kein* prospect whatever of success unless the
enfilade fire of enemy machine guns was eliminated by the preliminary
bombardment.'[23]

Worse for the Germans, the Australians aren't going anywhere. After dark, a messenger brings Colonel Douglas Marks of the 13th Battalion a note from Brigadier Charles Brand, his brigade commander.

> Dear Marks.
>   The Corps Commander is afraid to let the defence of Hébuterne out of our hands . . .[24]

In short, the 4th Brigade must stay there for the foreseeable future, ensuring that the Germans are definitively blocked from getting access to Doullens.

———

Though the Germans aren't renewing the attack on Villers-Bretonneux and *Höhe 104*,[25] Height 104 – or, as the British call it, Hill 104 – they are sending out patrols to find out how far forward the Australians are among the farmhouses and hedges along the Somme.

The day before at Vairé, at around 3 pm, Brigadier Pompey Elliott had positioned four men for'ard of the Lewis gun that had unleashed a murderous maelstrom on the attacking Germans – to prevent there being any chance of Fritz sneaking up on the Lewis Gun crew. Those four men are still in position in their trench – actually a drainage ditch in this very swampy farmland by the Somme – on the afternoon of the 5th when, at 2 pm, they spy with their little eyes something beginning with 'G'. A German officer in the lead of 30 German soldiers are coming out from Hamel and heading their way, until . . .

Jeder, um auf den Boden! Everyone, get on the ground!

The Australians have been spotted and the Germans quickly set up a machine gun, bringing fire upon them.

Not particularly perturbed, the man in charge, Corporal Doug Sayers, leaves two of his men to return fire while he and the remaining soldier creep into a drain he has already reconnoitred and move in on the Germans from behind.

The Germans never know what hits them when the duo cut a

bloody swathe through the pack. Crawling, dragging their wounded with them, the Germans retreat towards a sunken road where the mad Australians cannot get at them.

They think.

Corporal Sayers has still not had enough of it and orders his men to charge, leading the way from his new position, firing from the hip and bringing down the officer, at which point the German soldiers get up and charge . . . away.

As a proud Pompey Elliott will shortly recount to his cousin Milly, in the face of his boys the Germans 'skedaddled for their lives, shedding arms and accoutrements as they ran. They never stopped till they got out of sight and our fellows [were] laughing so hard they could hardly shoot . . .'[26]

The final tally in this encounter between four Australians and 30-odd Germans: 'six Germans were killed and two who were left wounded were brought in by the Australians, none of whom was hurt.'[27]

And there is a bonus: 'The information gained from documents found on the dead officer, and from the wounded, was of greatest value to our side.'[28]

———

At Dernancourt, the battle rages on.

Lieutenant George Mitchell of the 48th Battalion, occupying a support line some 500 yards back from his comrades in the front-line, becomes more than aware of just how bad things are getting when the gully to his left – occupied by A Company of the 48th – simply disappears for minutes at a time 'neath plumes of billowing smoke coming from the explosions of German shells landing in what has become a witch's cauldron of flying shrapnel. But even more terrifying, around noon 'a machine gun spewed somewhere on the right close *behind* . . .'

Obviously, at least parts of the line must have disintegrated for the Germans to get through to there.

And now, at 1.15 pm, Lieutenant Mitchell looks up to see 'strings of [Australian soldiers] coming over the hill, many of them wounded'.

'"The *Boche* have overwhelmed the 52nd," they raggedly advise. "Rushed artillery into the gap, and blew us out of our positions."'[29]

The 48th Battalion, those hardy bastards from Adelaide and regional South Australia, stay firm, for all that, though more and more men of the 52nd and 47th fall back. 'Bodies of desperate men were coming back, shooting, running, and falling.'[30]

Mitchell is soon overwhelmed with differing emotions, realising that not only has the first line been almost entirely overwhelmed, but the support line he is currently in – which it is his duty to hold – will also fall unless they bring the stragglers together quickly to provide the firepower they need.

'With tears of rage, grief and injured vanity in my eyes,' Mitchell would recount, 'I went out to a 47th Captain to arrange a defence . . .' For it is the men of the 47th they need, and the stragglers will be more likely to obey one of their own. Working his way along the trench, enlisting the help of Sergeants and Corporals, Mitchell manages to restore some kind of line, with some kind of firepower once more.

Walking over a slight rise, he is confronted by bullets whistling around his ears, coming from the enemy at close range, and the haunting vision of the dead and wounded men of the 47th Battalion everywhere he looks. Those few men of the 47th still alive and fighting shout to him: 'Keep down or die! Everyone standing up has been shot!'[31]

And now he realises that an explosion off to his right, just behind, must mean a shell has hit very close to the trench he has just left. 'A horrible black shrapnel bursting a few feet from the ground obliterated part of my line.'[32]

The 48th, too, now has no choice but to fall back to the point that its open right flank – vacated by the shattered 47th – can be closed.

'A man fell a few yards in front of me. He got up and came on limping . . . I congratulated him on his wound, shook hands with him, took his bandolier of ammunition and told him to get for his life.'[33]

And now the Huns are swarming again, 'coming on gamely in groups under cover of heavy M.G. fire'.[34]

The Australians do their best.

'Our men were shooting like the devil, but we were being badly enfiladed.'[35]

Several groups of German soldiers close to within 150 yards of Lieutenant Mitchell's position. Mitchell takes over, exhorting group after group of Australian riflemen with their .303 Lee-Enfields: 'Shoot like hell at them! Now hop it back . . .'

And so they do, emptying their ten-round magazines at the oncoming groups before withdrawing on the specific orders of their officer. Finally, one last gunner remains, with the Germans now just 100 yards away: Lance-Corporal William James Connaughton and his trusty Lewis gun.

'How many magazines?' Mitchell shouts over the chattering roar of the German machine guns getting closer.

'Three,' Connaughton shouts back.

'Rip them in.'[36]

Connaughton rips 'em in all right, seeming to make every burst of the 47-round magazines count. Before their eyes, as German soldier after German soldier goes down, Fritz's advance stops, with the survivors lying flat on the grass!

'What now?' Connaughton says after the first magazine.

'Sweep the ground,'[37] says Mitchell.

Connaughton sweeps back and forth until the magazine is empty.

'Now get back!'[38]

Mitchell waits to see precisely what the Germans are going to send at them now.

Oh.

Now he sees.

Stormtroopers. Rising up from the grass!

One of them, seeing Mitchell on the skyline, raises his rifle. He's so close that Mitchell can make out his features.

As a point of honour, Mitchell does not throw himself to the ground or run away – for that would be displaying fear and not playing the game. No. Instead he begins 'to walk at right angles to minimise his chance of [getting hit]'. [39]

A puff of smoke comes from the German's rifle. Mitchell steels himself . . . only for the bullet to go harmlessly by. He has won this part of the game!

Still, no use in being silly about it, what?

'I walked quickly away. Bullets were sizzling around my ears, but a fold in the ground soon protected me.'[40]

Somewhere on the other side of the fold, he knows, there is a German stormtrooper gnashing his teeth and probably not telling his comrades about the one that got away.

Still barely crediting he is alive, Lieutenant Mitchell is overjoyed to reach the back-up trench – all of it protected by rolls of 'tanglefoot' and filled with those very Australian soldiers who had previously fallen back, now getting ready to fight again.

Perhaps the Huns have at last got the message – *you bastards can go this far, but no further* – for 1000 yards away, down the slope, Fritz can be seen digging in. The opportunity is too good to miss. 'Various flares were shooting up. Suddenly our artillery got on them with a beautiful shrapnel barrage and shifted things.'[41]

—

Fritz's advance has faded away. Now it is time to counter-attack. The officers of the 48th Battalion double over as they make their way along the shallow trench and give the word.

'Prepare to advance . . .'[42]

The 49th and the 45th have come up to join the attack. They'll all be going over the top in about 30 minutes, meaning the men have just enough time to get some tucker into them. While they are wolfing it down – it is either a very late lunch or a slightly early dinner – one Digger has a friendly word of warning for the others as he rips into a tin of pork and beans he's knocked off from somewhere.

'Don't eat *too* much,' he cautions, for all the world as if he is a concerned mother whose already-full kids get stuck into the Christmas pudding just before going for a swim in the dam. 'A bayonet in a full tucker box is dangerous.'[43]

His mates would have been a tad more inclined to follow the advice if the Digger in question hadn't practically licked his own tin clean like a hungry dog, but, still, it is the thought that counts.

It is nearly 5.15 pm, the time set for the hop-over. Now all the banter stops and each man is alone with his thoughts, wondering if he has just minutes, maybe *seconds*, to live. Nervously, many of the men pat their top left pocket to see that the regulation field dressing is there, or pull back the bolt on their .303 to check they have a round in the chamber. Such tension is unbearable. There is even 'a surge of relief'[44] when the whistle blows and they go over the top, 'cos, whatever else, they are no longer waiting.

With a roar, the men of the 48th are now charging at the Germans – a roar that is, alas, lost as machine guns open up on them, each one spitting ten bullets a second.

'Men start dropping everywhere. Still we advance,' Private Eddie Lynch records. 'Still that perfect parade ground formation is kept despite flying bullets and falling mates, kept when each man knows each step may be his last, kept without an order or a direction given. Yet they say the Australians lack discipline – the biggest lie of jealous lying criticism.'[45]

Still they keep running down the hill, straight into the teeth of that devastating fire, knowing that their only hope is speed, that the Germans can't shoot them all, and the quicker they get to them the fewer Australians will die. Now they are close enough to see the German helmets popping out above the rifles pointed at them from yonder trench, those rifles that are also exacting a terrible toll.

'On we go,' Lynch chronicles. 'The man next to me spins and gives a soft, surprised gasp. The poor wretch staggers in front of me . . . He's down. I step over him like a man in a dream . . . The men begin to yell and shout. I'm running on with the rest, doing a desperate bayonet charge over the last hundred yards.'[46]

And now, it happens. They are getting close to the bastards, about to get to grips with Fritz, when some of them start to run away! And then more of them! And now *all of them*!

Again, the reputation of the Australians precedes them. For the Germans know where they come from, all right, and know there will be no mercy shown. And rather than face more mad Australians with their still flashing, slashing bayonets, they run.

'A tremendous rush and with a roar we're into the trench. We're all calling, shouting, roaring, laughing from the reaction and excitement . . .'

They're alive. They're *alive!* And the bloody Germans are running – can yers believe it?!

Now to secure the line. While some of the Diggers climb to the other side of the trench so they can shoot at the fleeing Germans, Private Lynch, with his mates 'Darky' and 'Snow', charge along the trench to their right, to where the 47th were forced to give way. There are bound to be Germans there.

There!

Only 100 yards along the trenches, three German soldiers suddenly appear and go at Darky, who is in the lead, with their bayonets.

Two shots ring out – one from Lynch, one from Snow – and two of the Germans go down. Darky trips over one of the dead men while Lynch leaps over the other, bringing his bayonet forward to do the business. The remaining German does the same. The bayonets clash, a test of strength that the Australian wins, forcing the German's blade away from him. And it is amazing the difference that manoeuvre makes. In the space of a second, Fritz goes from wanting to end Digger Lynch's life by forcing a bayonet into his belly to screaming *'Kamerad!',*[47] all while dropping his rifle and throwing his hands in the air.

They let him live. Snow takes his rifle and Darky takes Fritz in hand.

Some 200 yards to the right of Snow, Darky and Lynch, Sergeant McDougall – him again – leads his platoon in a similar mad counter-attack straight at the German positions and is quickly among the enemy,

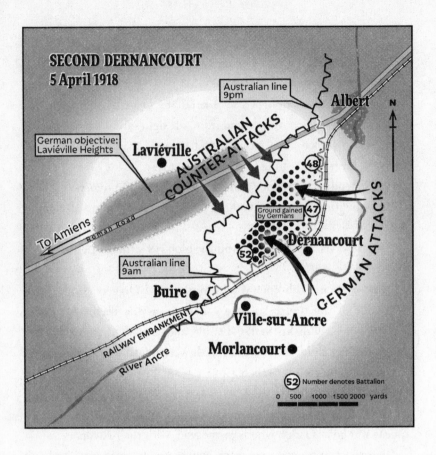

SECOND DERNANCOURT
5 April 1918

Australian line
9pm

Albert

N

German objective:
Laviéville Heights

Laviéville

AUSTRALIAN
COUNTER-ATTACKS

48

To Amiens

Roman Road

Ground gained
by Germans

47

Dernancourt

52

Australian line
9am

GERMAN ATTACKS

Buire

Ville-sur-Ancre

RAILWAY EMBANKMENT

Morlancourt

River Ancre

52 Number denotes Battalion

0   500   1000 1500 2000 yards

first firing with his rifle and then using his bayonet on a succession of
German soldiers who fall to its blade, displaying a 'contempt of danger'
that is simply 'amazing' to those who witness it. The Tasmanian is a
blur of movement, seemingly with six arms and as many bayonets –
thrusting, parrying and stabbing – and often as not supported by the
platoon coming in tightly behind and thrusting forward themselves at
any German soldier who manages to resist McDougall for longer than
a few seconds as he works his way along the bloody trench.

Finally, it is over. The Australian 12th and 13th Brigades have driven
the Germans back no fewer than 1000 yards, in the process reclaiming
the key trench and rubbing Fritz's nose in it – he will not be getting the
Laviéville Heights.

'The trench is ours,' Private Edward Lynch of the 48th Battalion exults. 'We've hunted the enemy! . . . We are still working in this captured trench wondering if they'll come on again, though somehow we feel they won't and their gallop to Amiens is at an end.'[48]

For the moment, it is.

———

All up, in this 'Second Battle of Dernancourt', as it would become known, the Australians have suffered 1233 casualties, of which a quarter have been killed. The Germans have fared much worse, with some 2000 casualties, of which one-third have been killed and a handful taken as prisoners. (One of the latter, a Sergeant of the 50th Reserve Division, could not help himself and, still stunned by the counter-attack, says the Australian charge was '*sehr schneidig*, very dashing.')[49]

For the German forces, the loss of two men for every yard gained in their mere 1000-yard advance from the embankment up the slope towards Laviéville Heights is an extremely heavy price to have paid, with the Australians as heavily dug in as ever and stopping their further advance.

As to what might happen on the morrow at Dernancourt, however, General Maclagan is clear: 'I don't think . . . we shall be able to hold the line.'[50]

———

By the evening of 5 April, at Hébuterne, Dernancourt and Villers-Bretonneux, all is quiet once more, as the battered and shattered Germans have retreated, defeated. As ever more reports come in to General von Kuhl, the Chief of Staff of the Rupprecht Army, in his HQ at Mons, the scale of the defeat dawns.

Every time Operation Michael has hit *die Australier* on either side of the Somme, just as it had yesterday at Villers-Bretonneux and today at Dernancourt, it has come to an ignominious halt.

This might need *ein* rethink.

Surveying the whole last fortnight of operations, including today's setbacks, it is even worse.

'Strategic success,' von Kuhl would recount, 'was denied to the Michael offensive and . . . the great tactical success [of an advance of 40 miles on a 50 mile front] had cost heavy casualties, some ninety divisions in all [almost half the whole German army on the Western Front] having had to be engaged. The conclusion of the fighting . . . left our troops in very unfavourable positions . . .'[51]

In sum, it is his view that the failure of his forces to take Villers-Bretonneux is so significant that it means nothing less than this: 'Germany's last chance to strike a decisive blow against the British [at Amiens] had just passed.'[52]

And he reports as much to General Ludendorff in his HQ at Avesnes.

Putting all of the reports together, Ludendorff bows to the inevitable. At 7.25 pm his message goes out to his two army group commanders, Bavarian *Kronprinz* Rupprecht and *Kronprinz* Wilhelm:

The supply situation does not allow the continuation of [Operation Michael] . . . the attack is henceforth temporarily discontinued . . .[53]

In the course of the night, the Germans move into defensive positions only. The troops at Dernancourt are particularly devastated with the course of the day's events, even being described as 'bitterly depressed',[54] while a German war correspondent on site at Dernancourt notes, 'The Australians and Canadians are much the best troops that the English have.'[55]

'The Allies had offered a particularly obstinate resistance . . . and it was no longer possible to throw the enemy back . . . the final result . . . is the unpleasant fact that our offensive has come to a complete stop, and its continuation without careful preparation promises no success.'[56]

And so Operation Michael is over.

For the rest of his life, von Hindenburg would regret the failure to push harder for Amiens. 'We ought to have shouted in the ear of every single man,' he would recall, "Press on to Amiens. Put in your last ounce. Perhaps Amiens means decisive victory. Capture Villers-Bretonneux whatever happens, so that from its heights we can command Amiens with masses of our heavy artillery!"[57]

———

Wo bin ich? Where am I?

Was ist los? What's happening?

Is he still alive?

He must be.

Now, in the silent watch of night, Private Hubert Schroeter of the 3rd *Jäger* Battalion slowly comes to, aware both of the terrible pain in his left arm and just how light-headed he is from loss of blood. Not sure if he is behind German or Australian lines, nor caring, he knows what he needs and now calls for it in the night with as much strength as he can muster.

Hilfe! Hiiilfe! Help! *Heeelp!'*

There! A movement in the darkness. And it proves to be Corporal Fehlau, a soldier from his company! Having heard Schroeter's cries, Fehlau has moved forward, ducking from tree to tree for extra cover, until he gets to his *Freund*. With a grunt and a heave, he soon has Schroeter on his back and carries him to the safe side of the railway embankment where, using his own first-aid dressings, he quickly cleans and binds Schroeter's wounds by the light of the moon.

And now they are on their way once more, with Fehlau carrying his friend through Albert, all while vengeful English shells roar down into buildings and streets. It is a miracle they get as far as they do without being hurt by shrapnel or falling debris. Finally, Fehlau can support his friend's weight no more, at which point a second miracle occurs for Schroeter. In a basement window they see a light, and upon investigation Fehlau finds German Army doctors, orderlies and an equipped field hospital!

Private Schroeter is soon receiving first-class care, and yet so grave are his wounds that he asks the obvious: 'Will I lose my arm?'[58]

'*Lieber Freund*,' the kindly doctor working on him says, '*das ist möglich. Aber jedenfalls wirst du am Leben bleiben.* Dear friend, that is possible. But at least you will stay alive.'[59]

And that really is something.

—

General Haig's own problem, meanwhile, is acute. It is one thing to have been able to stop, for the moment, the German thrust to Amiens in the south, but for how long? Are the Germans just pausing before going again? Or are they about to attack elsewhere? There is no doubt that aerial reconnaissance, captured German prisoners and intelligence reports confirm a building up of the Kaiser's forces before both Amiens and Hazebrouck. Is Hazebrouck the likely new assault target? Or perhaps the Germans will attack on both fronts *at once*?

Hence the acute problem. There are only so many troops to go around, and the German assault, Operation Michael, has already cost Haig 178,000 casualties so far, rendering half his divisions nearly useless in terms of further fighting value.

And, yes, there has at last been a flood of soldiers coming from Britain – 101,000 of them arriving by 4 April[60] – but bitter experience has shown that the lack of experience of these 18- and 19-year-olds makes them almost more of a liability than an asset to the war effort. Already, thousands of the new drafts to the 14th and 18th Divisions have turned on their heels and run away rather than face the Germans in front of Villers-Bretonneaux on 4 April.

For the moment, Haig's general hunch is that the most likely next thrust will once more be at Amiens, and it is with that in mind that he has already ordered the last Australian division he has in reserve at Messines Ridge, the 1st Division, to move south to help their brethren defend Amiens. The Australians have done so well in the battles of Dernancourt, Morlancourt, Hébuterne and Villers-Bretonneux, it only makes sense to keep them together.

—

That word so well known by troops across the British and French Empires over the centuries – *reveille* – is, of course, French for, 'Time to get up and get moving, soldier/*soldat*.'

But what is the word when the call comes like this, at two o'clock in the bloody morning? Some blokes have barely got to sleep yet, let alone need to wake up. Such is the grumbly mood among the men of the 1st Division, the last of the Australians still in the north, as they are loudly woken by the bawling bastards otherwise known as 'Sergeants' in these wee hours and told that within 60 minutes they must have their kit packed and be ready to march for three hours to Godewaersvelde before catching the train to take them south.

'Here,' Archie Barwick would record, 'we had breakfast, & then entrained in horse trucks. We had a cold ride for the next ten hours when we arrived at the storm centre, Amiens.'[61]

—

The news breaks in Paris with an exclusive account by one of the special correspondents 'with the British army . . . at the front' in the *Echo de Paris* under the headline '*Les Australiens Se Sont Couvert De Gloire*, The Australians Covered Themselves with Glory':

> *At Villers-Bretonneux . . . the German rush was impetuous. Without stopping, the waves of assault renewed themselves, breaking every time against our lines. The machine guns, functioning without stopping, literally mowing the assailants down. The combat lasted 20 hours, and the enemy realised that for their small gain they had paid extremely dear. The Germans fired so many shells that Villers-Bretonneux*

is near completely destroyed.

At Albert, the battle was still more terrible. Our positions were defended by Australian troops who had to fight against an enemy four or five times more numerous. The order was to not cede any terrain: almost none fell. Some of the gunners were killed; others avenged them, as thousands of dead Germans littered the terrain after the combat. The Australians covered themselves in glory and, afterwards, one of their leaders was able to say to them:

What our troops have this done this week assures our children the right to call themselves 'Australians,'...[62]

—

All up, it is a typical example of what the author of the history of the 19th Battalion would describe as a military manoeuvre that has come about by 'waving large hands over small maps'.[63]

While it was one thing for Marshal Foch and General Haig to conceive their plans and give orders for the 'Fourth Army to clean up the woods and ravine north and north-east of Hangard'[64] simply by scanning maps in their comfortable headquarters far to the rear – without much consideration to the ground itself or actual battlefield conditions – it is quite another thing to actually execute those orders.

And yet, the Fourth Army must try to do exactly that, and so straighten out that troublesome German bulge into the British line left over by the last German push on Villers-Bretonneux. With the Germans holding Hangard Wood just 3000 yards south of Villers, if Fritz attacks again they can do so from both the east and the south, allowing them a pincer movement. Recapturing the wood will allow the Allies to severely clip one arm of the pincer before they start.

No rest for the wicked. And particularly not when you are needed to fight the more wicked still. Though the AIF's 2nd Division has only arrived on the Somme yesterday – with the 5th and 6th Brigades immediately marched forward to relieve the totally knackered 9th Brigade – already some of them are being thrown into action.

On this crisp dawn, one-and-a-half companies of the 5th Brigade's 19th Battalion – just 250 men in all – have been assigned the task of clearing the remaining Germans from the northern half of Hangard Wood, right below Villers-Bretonneux. A similar force from 20th Battalion will take on the southern half. It is a task that should not be too difficult, as aerial reconnaissance has established that the wood is only 'lightly held'.[65]

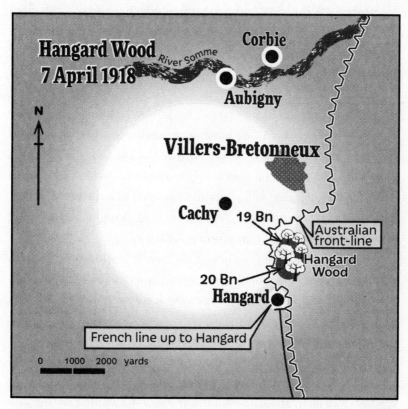

At the fore of the 19th Battalion is Captain Clarence Wallach's B company, and after an exhausting march through the night they are in position, just before dawn.

Now, *quietly*, lads.

On the sharp order of the newly promoted Wallach – the tallest man in the Battalion, he is one of six Bondi surf lifesaver brothers in the AIF and already famous for the fact that his sterling Wallaby career as a second rower had been cut short by the war – they are up and moving, padding lightly over the open country that slopes gently down to the wood. In fact, they have so diligently obeyed the order to be quiet that they have left no less than their second-in-command, Lieutenant Percy Storkey, behind, asleep, at the starting line! (The same has happened to several other soldiers, the penalty for having been roused at midnight to mount the attack.)

Storkey, a Kiwi-born Australian officer who has risen quickly from the ranks since joining the AIF as a private – just two days after the news of the Gallipoli landing had broken – rises even more quickly now.

A 'well-knit figure with dark hair and eyes . . . a laughing face and dare-devil, happy-go-lucky ways',[66] he is not laughing now. Twice wounded in this war to date but entirely undaunted by that fact and only keen to return serve, he is devastated at his own dereliction of duty in having nodded off, and is only relieved that he has woken up in time – to see the backs of his men disappearing into the gloom ahead, approaching Hangard Wood. Without running outright, as that would draw attention to himself, he moves quickly and . . .

Just a few yards from the last of his men, a machine gun secreted right on the edge of the wood opens up and dozens of his men go down, flopping like puppets with their strings suddenly cut.

Inevitably, the survivors follow suit.

Down! *Down! Everyone* . . . DOWN!

Among those shot in the initial onslaught is Captain Wallach, who has taken bullets to both knees – surely the end of his time with the mighty Wallabies, should he survive the war. Crawling forward, still under heavy fire, Storkey instantly assesses the situation and knows he has to move quickly. Barking orders over the gun fire from both sides, Storkey, who has four men by him, orders another officer, Lieutenant Fred Lipscomb, who has six men under his lead, to follow him. They crawl well off to the left, through the bush and a jungle of abandoned telephone wires, hopefully without the Germans seeing them.

Once clear and at last able to stand in the forest – filled with the thick and tawny undergrowth that France so specialises in, most of it over head-high with taller saplings scattered about – Storkey takes the lead. He and his men make good time through the gloom, and within minutes they know they must be close by the guttural shouts and roar of the machine guns up ahead.

There they are! Just twenty yards off, in a clearing. There are a *hundred* of them, German soldiers in half-a-dozen makeshift trenches, firing machine guns *nineteen* to the dozen 'at the survivors of Wallach's company, still struggling across the open ground'.[67]

So much for Hangard Wood being only 'lightly held'! As it turns out, these are two companies of the 133rd Infantry Regiment of the 24th Saxon Division, the same unit from which the old German soldier had crossed No-Man's Land for a bit of a chat with the Australians a few months earlier.

No such friendliness is apparent now, and Storkey does not hesitate. The key, of course, is to get as close as possible before opening fire, and it is with that in mind that Storkey charges forward, still without saying a word.

Alas, one of Storkey's men cannot help himself and utters his own kind of guttural war cry, which alerts the Germans to their presence. They turn around, aghast.

Time to change tack.

In a dead sprint now, Storkey runs straight at the Germans, 'shouting as if the whole battalion was following',[68] as one of his companions would describe it, firing his Webley revolver while the men with him fire rifles and roll their exploding 'eggs' into trenches full of Germans before following up with savage fighting at close quarters.

These madmen are battling as if they are the pointy end of a spear borne by 1000 men. It never occurs to the Germans that they are being attacked by no more than a dirty dozen scoundrels with – dot four, carry five, subtract six – *no* back-up at all. And just as 'he who hesitates is lost', it can also be very grim for a whole bunch of soldiers who do the same, as the Australians get in 'quickly, with bombs, bayonet and revolver'.[69] Caught in an attack from in front and behind, the Germans are trapped, a dire situation that is compounded when the remaining soldiers of 19th Battalion, aware of what is happening, surge forward themselves. A fearful battle without mercy quickly ensues, and in the end it is no contest.

Amid the slaughter, some Germans throw their hands in the air in the internationally recognised symbol for, *You bastards have got us, and we know it.* They are spared, and Storkey quickly calls on the other Germans to do the same, using one or another or all of the phrases they have been taught to shout, phonetically, in precisely this situation: 'Hender Hoch!' 'Airgaben zee zisch!' 'Oder ish sheesser!' 'Kommen zee here!' 'Revolver veck!' All of which the Germans will hear, in very bad accents, as *'Hände hoch!' 'Ergeben Sie sich!' 'Oder ich schieße!' 'Kommen Sie hier!' 'Revolver weg!'* ... otherwise known as 'Hands up!' 'Surrender!' 'Or I shoot!' 'Come here!' 'Throw away your revolver!'[70]

Some obey and they, too, are spared.

But when three of the German soldiers turn their weapons on Storkey, he shoots all three with his revolver, at which point it jams ... He is only saved from being killed himself when some of his men behind hurl grenades into the trench holding those German soldiers who are still fighting. They throw themselves to the ground an instant before the shattering roar of the explosions, followed by German screams, fill the fog. By the time the Australians jump back to rejoin the furious fray, it is all over.

A staggering 30 Germans lie dead or wounded at their feet.

'Many [of our dead] were hit through the head and clubbed – some from behind,' the 133rd Regimental History will bitterly record. 'An evil enemy had been at work.'[71]

No fewer than 50 shaken prisoners are led away, relieved to still be alive, albeit in the hands of the monster.

Done now?

No. As Storkey knows, they still have not achieved their objective, which is to push on through the wood and establish a new line on its eastern side so the lines on the Generals' maps could be neat once more. While two men take the 50 prisoners and one captured machine gun to the rear, Storkey and ten soldiers start to push through the woods, looking for more Germans to kill.

It does not take long for them to realise that, contrary to the intelligence report, Hangard Wood is swarming with Germans. In fact, there are – with a good *two battalions* of Saxons – over 1000 Squareheads, and so the counter-attack that quickly comes is savage. It is soon obvious that no number of ruses or amount of shouting will trick them into thinking the Australians' dirty dozen are in fact a thousand strong. The detachments of both the 19th and 20th Battalions have no choice but to withdraw, leaving Hangard Wood holus-bolus with Fritz.

But, oh, what devastation they leave in their wake.

Germany's 133rd Regimental history records the damage the Australians have caused: 'an extraordinarily high number of casualties', around the 300 mark, most of them from the two companies that Storkey and his men have hit, practically wiping them out.

But a low drone is heard overhead.

—

The circus is in town – specifically Baron von Richthofen's Flying Circus.

They are as busy as ever in the heavens above Villers-Bretonneux that now offer such splendid hunting opportunities. The day before, the Red Baron had shot from the skies a Sopwith Camel that had, as he records, 'crashed burning near the little wood north-east of Villers-Bretonneux, where it continued to burn on the ground'.[72] He has returned today in the hope of finding more.

And here is one now. Actually . . . many.

A singularly impressive *eighteen* Sopwith Camels are seen below – a 'full squadron show', as the British call it – heading east on an 'OP', offensive patrol, looking for Germans to shoot down. Among them is Lieutenant Albert Gallie, who is proceeding at an altitude of 10,000 feet when, within seconds, he meets von Richthofen, and very nearly his maker. It all happens so quickly that Gallie barely knows what hits him.

'The aeroplane,' the Baron would record, 'smashed into the ground and I saw that it crashed into splinters. This occurred 500 metres east of Hill 104.'[73] Extraordinarily, Lieutenant Gallie, the Baron's 77th victim, walks away shaken but unscathed and is quickly taken prisoner.

Just 30 minutes later, another British pilot, Lieutenant Ronald Adams, flying a Sopwith Camel, is equally sent plummeting earthwards courtesy of the Baron's guns, crashing four miles east of VB, right on the Roman road. And he survives, too, to be quickly captured and then cared for at a German medical post.

Lieutenant Adams is resting comfortably later that evening, covered in fresh bandages and contemplating what life will be like as a prisoner, when an orderly brings him a message: '*Freiheer* von Richthofen's compliments, you are his 78th victim.'[74]

The honour is all his.

7 APRIL 1918, AMIENS, BROTHERS REUNITED

Now in their billets in the villages near Amiens, after travelling all of the previous day on the railway, passing by roads clogged with French refugees and retreating British forces, the 1st Division are very pleased to at last be close to their brother units of the AIF, ready to do their bit.

'The morning broke nice and sunny,' Archie Barwick would record. 'The sun is pouring down. In the distance Amiens lies, a great white patch in a sea of green & she looks very pretty with the sun glistening on the roofs & spires . . . Things are very busy round the billet, getting ready for the line . . . At the present moment there is a great rattle of artillery. The old Hun must be attacking again.'[75]

7 APRIL 1918, AMIENS, VIEWS BEAN CHANGED

Charles Bean's perceptions have changed in the course of this war. At the outbreak of hostilities he had been almost 'more British than the British', convinced of the inherent superiority of all things emanating from those small islands. But the more the war has gone on, the more he has felt proud of things quintessentially *Australian*, starting with the Australian soldier, just as his eyes have been opened to the failings of the British officer class. It is for this reason that the piecemeal breaking up of the Australian Corps since the beginning of this latest battle has not sat easily with him, and why he is thrilled with the news that, from this morning, the Australian Corps will be coming back together to fight as the one unit, under General Rawlinson's Fourth Army. It's a welcome change from the constantly changing and multiple British Corps command. It coincides with the entire front of the Fourth Army, from Albert to Hangard Wood – the principal screen defending Villers-Bretonneux – now being held only by Australians.

General Rawlinson – ensconced in his new HQ at Flixecourt, in what would have been a pleasant little village on the western side of Amiens, but for the overpowering smell coming from the local jute weaving factory – is nothing if not pleased. He notes as much in his diary: 'I feel happier about the general situation as I now have three brigades of Australians in reserve [the 1st Division], so I think I shall be able to keep the *Boche* out of Amiens. I am to take over the Australian Corps on the 8th, with a front up to Albert. Hurrah!'[76]

———

Hurrah! Hurrah! Hurrah!

How good is life in Villers-Bretonneux at this time? And another three cheers for good measure.

Yes, it is sad that the French inhabitants have had to leave, but never let it be said that the new folks in town – or at least those camped near its western outskirts and able to duck in – the Australians, aren't enjoying themselves as never before.

Now it *is* true that the town is being constantly shelled by the angry Germans, and at night huge German bombers, Gothas, roar overhead, dropping their seeds of death.

'Sometimes when these night bombers flew,' Edmund Street would recount, 'it was possible to see their blurred outline and it seemed to me that they were black ghouls from Hell.'[77]

And no doubt about it, the aerial combat overhead never stops, and you have to be on the lookout for planes tumbling down and killing everyone within coo-ee.

But ignore all that! The Diggers mostly do. They are mere annoyances to the main game. 'Souveniring!'[78] Other unkind souls might call it looting, but not most of them – certainly not the party of half-a-dozen that Edmund Street enters the town with on this day. Things do get a bit hairy when a shell lands on the roof and rains debris over them, followed shortly afterward by another that blows out a wall of a house that has already been mostly demolished. Deadly bricks fly everywhere.

'We scooted across to the other side of the street to escape the rolling bricks and stone as they spread across the road,' Street would recall.

Keep going, Diggers. Souvenirs ahead!

As they proceed, they can see the devastation wrought by the shells. No house has escaped at least some damage.

'Here a roof was blown in, and there a wall blown out. Beds, chairs, tables, pianos and other furnishings lay scattered and broken, revealed from the roadside view by holes in the walls, or by the walls missing altogether.'[79]

And, yes, of course they help themselves to whatever wine, food and easily portable treasures they find. But for Edmund Street and his mates, there is something they are looking for above all else – a hot bath!

It ain't easy – baths are not that common in this country – and it is only on their second excursion to the town that they find one on the second floor of an imposing house. They get a fire going, boil some water taken from the pump in the yard, and are soon calling *Robert* their *oncle*, every bit as much as Bob's their uncle back home.

Ah, but now comes the true delight! Out of the bath, pink and glowing for the first time in yonks – *rub-a-dub-dub* – and having already gone through Madame's drawers, they are able to don precisely the undergarment they were searching for. 'As it was springtime we chose silk. Being silk the garments were nearly all of the type belonging to women. Silk attracted us further because [lice] usually shunned the wearer of the material.'

Can life ever get any better than this?

'We donned our bloomers and underskirts, put on our uniforms and marched out new men, far, far cleaner than we went in.'

And, of course, they are not the only ones.

As Edmund Street and his mates head off to see what else they can find – simply luxuriating in the feel of silk against their skin – they come across a sight they will never forget.

'Near the centre of the town a tall, a wild looking woman staggered out of a café with her hat on one side, waving a bottle and singing. The hilarious lady presented a truly strange sight. Another lady staggered out waving a bottle in each hand. In a loud raucous voice she sang the latest song from London stage, while her friend applauded loudly . . .'

On they go, and now there are still more of them!

'Some were quite sober, others were rolling and singing. Some had lips and cheeks painted a brilliant red and wore Paris creations, others the usual dress of the village maidens. They kissed each other and us brazenly and without the semblance of a blush. For the sake of the fair ladies of France it must be explained that the ladies were Diggers in disguise. They wore outrageous busts, and huge hips. A kiss from one of the ladies with a ten days' growth of beard served only to remind us that we were far from soft sweet lips and cheeks.'[80]

CHAPTER FOURTEEN

OPERATION GEORGE

After our first attack on the British and for a while at least it need not be anticipated that the French will run themselves off their legs and hurry at once to the help of their Entente comrades. They will first wait and see if their own front is not attacked also, and decide to support their ally only when the situation has been quite cleared up.[1]

Major Hans Fehr, Staff Officer of General von Hutier's 18th Army, before the beginning of the battle

7 AM, 8 APRIL 1918, AVESNES, BY GEORGE, THE GERMANS ADVANCE

It is with some grim satisfaction that General Ludendorff gives the orders that see the German military machine rumble into place in preparation for the start of Operation George, now due to launch on the morning of 9 April – his 53rd birthday.

Yes, there have been some disappointments in the *Kaiserschlacht* to date, including the failure to take Villers-Bretonneux because of the cursed Australians, but such disappointments are to be expected in war. As he has long learned, the key is to probe, to keep pushing forward on all fronts, with as strong a force as you can muster, and find the spot where they are weakest.

Hence, Operation George, first conceived six months earlier at

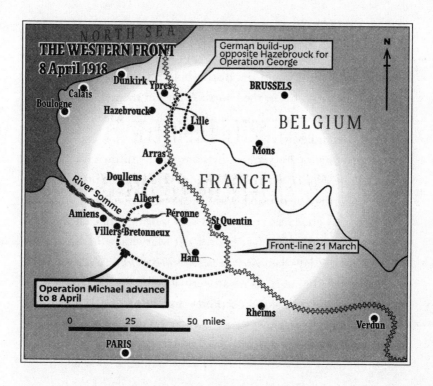

Kronprinz Rupprecht's headquarters at Mons, has a very simple overall goal: get to the Channel ports of Calais, Dunkirk and Boulogne, and thus destroy the entire British operation in France. All else being equal, the task should be a lot easier because, despite its disappointments, Operation Michael has drawn the best colonial troops south of the Somme.

Operation George will start with a barrage of 2210 artillery pieces, and more than 1000 mortars will send down 1.4 million rounds over four-and-a-half hours. No fewer than 750,000 German soldiers will attack along a front ten-miles wide. They will push to the north-west, with the 6th Army leading the way from Fromelles. Their aim will be to first cross the Lys River and capture the town of Hazebrouck – a key railway hub, nearly as important as Amiens – some 15 miles from their starting point. Once that falls, Calais and Dunkirk on the coast are just another 25 miles further. And of course the British will fight hard to hold them off, but . . . with what?

German intelligence has it that nearly all of the British reserves have been used up in the south trying to stop the push of Operation Michael. And even should the British hold off the initial thrust, the next day, *die vierte Armee*, the Fourth Army, on the right of *die sechste Armee*, the Sixth Army, will attack Messines Ridge, widening the front by another ten miles.

All up, a total of 26 German divisions will be thrown into the fray, with ten more in reserve, all of them hurled at just eight British divisions and a sole Portuguese division, with three British divisions in reserve.

It is for very good reason that the attack is being framed here, where the Australians are not, as General von der Marwitz, writes in a letter:

'Today is the day when . . . *eine neue Druckoffensive*, a new offensive [at Hazebrouck] has started. We are very hopeful, but we cannot know of course how it'll turn out . . . We know that the best English divisions, Canadians and Australians, were drawn before my front [down here]; that encourages the hope that up there good divisions will be missing.'[3]

8 APRIL 1918, FLEURBAIX, GHOSTS OF FROMELLES

The hundreds of dead Australian soldiers who still lie out in No-Man's Land? The loyal sons of Murwillumbah, Mooloolaba, Mooney Mooney and myriad places across Australia? As their remains have been there for most of the last two years, since that dreadful night of 19 July 1916 – when Australia had lost 1900 soldiers in less than 14 hours over the course of the Battle of Fromelles – they are by now more a part of the landscape than simply lying in it. But, still, they are testament to what can happen when a mass of men come face to face with German machine guns, with no escape. And Brigadier Frank Crozier, the Commanding Officer of the 119th Brigade of the 40th Division, whose troops are now positioned in the same trenches that the Australians had first launched from, is not only all too aware of it – sometimes, when digging new company toilets or communication trenches, they uncover dead Australians – but tonight he is more than a little worried.

Everything is quiet . . . maybe a little too quiet.

It is either a sixth sense or commonsense that tells the canny Crozier that the silence is 'uncanny'[4] – and the strong instinct of the British officer is that nowhere is it so silent as right in front their gallant allies, the Portuguese 2nd Division on his right. Surely that must be where the Germans will attack?

Quietly, Crozier heads over to where an infamous old German bunker known as 'the Sugarloaf' is situated, to ensure all is in order with the Portuguese, only to find them '. . . *all* asleep, bootless, minus equipment, with dirty cartridge cases and rifles, jammed Lewis guns, insufficient wire and filth surrounding them'.

Crozier immediately dashes off a report to be sent to his divisional commander, General John Ponsonby while – look here! – demanding to see the Portuguese commander, the magnificently named General Manuel de Oliveira Gomes da Costa.

'He's not available.'

'Why not?'

'He is suffering from venereal disease and cannot come.'[5]

Crozier takes his hat and his coat, and storms off in all directions.

8 APRIL 1918, LECHELLE, EIN KOLOSSALER SUCCESS

In his canvas quarters by the airfield, the Red Baron sits at a small table and writes exhaustedly, but still proudly, to a friend: 'Here in the last few days was *ein ganz kolossaler Betrieb*, quite a colossal operation. *Staffel 11* has shot down 49 Englishmen since 21.3. In all, since I started flying with them, [*Staffel*] *11* has shot down 264 Englishmen. The men who I have trained for me, are all contenders for the [highest German bravery award] and their successes almost give me more pleasure than my own.'[6]

—

Sure enough, in the wee hours of the following morning, the German Army does indeed launch Operation George – about half the size of

Operation Michael – with a bombardment by 2000 guns and over 1000 mortars raining down the shells of Hell unimagined, along a front extending for ten miles from Armentières to Givenchy, with the near centre of the attack focused on the infamous battlefield of Fromelles, held by the Portuguese division – before the stormtroopers attack in force, followed by 750,000 German soldiers[7] from 36 divisions, hurtling forward in now-familiar fashion.

At Fleurbaix, the German's artillery positioned around Fromelles starts pounding at 4.15 am – just as it does across the entire battlefront

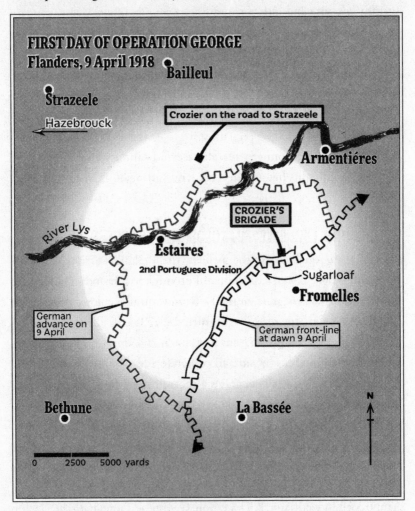

FIRST DAY OF OPERATION GEORGE
Flanders, 9 April 1918
Bailleul
Strazeele
Hazebrouck
Crozier on the road to Strazeele
Armentiéres
River Lys
CROZIER'S BRIGADE
Éstaires
2nd Portuguese Division
Sugarloaf
•Fromelles
German advance on 9 April
German front-line at dawn 9 April
Bethune
La Bassée
N
0   2500   5000 yards

– and within little more than an hour the first of the Portuguese soldiers are abandoning their positions amid the shattering roar. Crozier receives the report of the Portuguese abandonments at 7 am, and by 8.15 am the Portuguese artillery are reporting the same – significant, as the artillery knows that without their own infantry in front of them they have little protection. So why should the Portuguese battery crews hold their positions?

Good question.

They don't.

At 8.45 am, when the 35th and 42nd German Divisions storm down from Fromelles Ridge, it is all over very quickly and the stormtroopers are into the Portuguese trenches within 15 minutes – after what the Germans themselves will characterise as 'feeble resistance'[8] – to capture and kill the remaining soldiers of the Portuguese 2nd Division.

In fact, the relieved Portuguese soldiers – delighted that for them the war is over and they are still alive – surrender in such numbers, emerging from their dugouts with their hands in the air, that there is initially difficulty in coping with them all. (The final tally is 6000 Portuguese soldiers surrendered, over half of all the infantry in the 2nd Portuguese Division.) Some are given shovels and told to repair the roads, others are used as stretcher-bearers for their own wounded, since there are practically no German casualties in this initial thrust.

'The Portuguese,' the German medico with the 35th Division would note, 'looked rather strange in their light blue uniforms with corrugated tin hats, which resembled dustbin lids.'[9]

Not all of them surrender to the Germans, and some try to get away by moving through the British lines, particularly that of Crozier's 40th Division. This flood of Portuguese so exposes the right flank of the 119th Brigade that Brigadier Crozier feels he must act and goes so far as to order, as he would recount, 'the shooting, by machine gun fire, of many Portuguese in order to stem the tide. Had a complaint been lodged against me and had I been tried for murder, would Sir Douglas Haig have ordered my execution?'[10]

He will never know. Although many fleeing Portuguese are mown down on his orders, no complaint is made. And yet so overwhelming is the German attack and so exposed are the British now on both flanks that it soon becomes apparent to Crozier that his own 40th Division must also stage a 'tactical withdrawal' – a much nicer phrase than that dreadful word 'retreat' – and are soon obliged to swim from one shore of the Lys River to the other, a distance of some 50 yards. It all happens so quickly that it is hard to comprehend, but the bottom line remains.

The ground that 1900 Australian soldiers had given their lives for two years earlier has fallen to the rampaging Germans in just a few minutes, with barely a whimper of resistance offered.

———

Still wet from having swum the river, only minutes after the bridge had fallen and two of his staff officers had been shot dead before his eyes, Crozier is now standing in his shirtsleeves on the Strazeele Road, appalled to see British soldiers fleeing in panic, with every bit as much cowardice as the Portuguese had displayed just hours earlier. What's worse, even British *officers* are fleeing, something that Crozier simply cannot abide.

It must be stopped and the cowards made an example of, and he is just the man to do it. Here is a panic-stricken young British Lieutenant, his face a complete agony of fear, of mindless terror.

What to do?

'It was a desperate emergency,' Crozier would later say, justifying his actions. 'I had to shoot him myself, along with a German who was running after him. My action *did* stem the tide; and that is what we were there for . . .'[11]

No sooner has he shot his countryman – without trial, without hesitation – than a British staff car drives up.

'Is all well?'[12] a British officer asks as he leans out the window, looking rather pointedly at the dead Lieutenant at Crozier's feet and the still-smoking revolver in his right hand.

Crozier laughs.

Yes, all is well. At least as well as it can be when you have just been obliged to kill one of your own men. But he has no regrets. He reasons that his duty is 'to hold the line *at all costs*', and if one of those costs is to kill a coward as a demonstration to other cowards that they may as well stand and fight because they will be shot anyway if they run away, then so be it.

'Panic spreads so easily when the madness of a moment assails you,' he will later note. 'And a running man is a dangerous madness.'[13]

Whatever else, enough British soldiers do make a stand so that, for the moment, the German push is stopped on the shores of the west bank of the Lys.

A great day, nevertheless, for the Germans, with *Kronprinz* Rupprecht, who is in command, noting in his diary that so far Operation George 'has been successful, and the first three trenches of the enemy position are in our possession. According to the statements of prisoners, the attack came as a complete surprise. The Portuguese suffered the greatest losses, due to our *Minenfeuer*, shell fire.'[14]

Of course, he does not expect every day to be like this. Yet whatever the difficulties of the next part of the push, when 'dragging the artillery behind them will probably cause great difficulties due to the condition of the soil'[15] and where it is crucial that they keep pushing on to 'the high ground beyond the Lys',[16] if they succeed in setting up there the game is won.

Much of that high ground beyond the Lys is around the small village of Strazeele, where at this time there is little more happening than a rise in apprehension among the village folk that the booms from the east are getting louder. Strazeele is just a small, picturesque settlement, precisely as France specialises in. While in peacetime its loftiness brings the breeze and little more, it is that very same loftiness that is now attracting the winds of war, and they are starting to blow ever stronger.

—

Though it doesn't come easily, Haig now sees the truth: he really was

... *wrong*. Though he'd positioned many of his forces according to the belief that the Germans would thrust again at Amiens, in fact they have sharply struck towards Hazebrouck with overwhelming firepower and shattered the Allied lines. He'd been hopeful that it was no more than a feint, but by now, on the evening of 9 April, it is clear that Hazebrouck itself is threatened and he urgently needs to get more troops there. But which ones? And from where?

There is one obvious answer ... and after the paperwork has shuffled its way from desk to desk in Haig's HQ at Montreuil and been dispatched by motorcycle courier to Australian Corps HQ in Bertangles, it finally gets to the senior officers of 1st Division, whose men are now in billets at Amiens and getting ready to move into the line: **WIRE RECEIVED FROM AUSTRALIAN CORPS WARNING THE DIVISION TO BE PREPARED TO ENTRAIN TOMORROW. THIS EVIDENTLY (CONCERNS) OUR MOVE TO THE SCENE OF THE NEW GERMAN OFFENSIVE (AIMED AT HAZEBROUCK).**[17]

Of all the bloody things! The 1st Divvie, of course, has just arrived in the south, yet to fire a shot in anger, and even before they can go into the line they must now head back north whence they came!

Still, just as Alfred Lord Tennyson would have it: *Theirs not to reason why. Theirs but to do and die.*

—

Another day, another devastating German attack – this one on the second day of Operation George, 10 April, hurtling forth along a ten-mile front that links neatly with the northern end of the previous day's attack, going from Armentières all the way to Messines – meaning Operation George is now surging forward along a 20-mile front overall.

And, just as happened on the first day, what British resistance is offered is fragile at best, disgraceful at worst – with one notable exception. On Messines Ridge the 9th Scottish Division – the one that Winston Churchill had visited on the eve of Operation Michael, and the same one that the Australians had relieved at Dernancourt on 27 March, sent to Messines to recuperate – fight to the bitter end.

When the battle is finished, so is this brave unit of Scots as a fighting force, with their losses in killed, wounded and missing totalling 3800. By the evening of 11 April, Messines Ridge is captured, while, further south at Armentières, the Germans have pushed their line forward 4000 yards.

10 APRIL 1918, BEF HQ, MONTREUIL, HAIG HAS HIS BACK TO THE WALL

The situation is desperate, and getting worse. After having used up all his reserves, like the Australians, to stop the first major German attack on Amiens, General Haig is now confronted by a new breach in the Allied line, pushing towards Hazebrouck . . . In just two days of this latest German assault, they have advanced 12 miles, almost halfway to Hazebrouck from their starting point. On current projections, they will reach that key town by 13 or 14 April, perhaps earlier – already a disaster, now teetering on catastrophe.

If the Germans do capture Hazebrouck, there is little to stop them pushing on from there to the Channel ports. At that point, the British Expeditionary Force will have little choice but to surrender, with nearly three-quarters of their supply of materiel cut off. With the BEF consuming 1000 tons of food and 10,000 tons of artillery ammunition *every day*, Haig would have to surrender within a week at most, or face the total destruction of his 1.5-million-strong force. Without the British, the French would soon fall and the war would be over and Germany victorious.

All of this and more – that he might be the man with his name in the bottom right-hand corner of the greatest military defeat the world has ever seen – weighs heavily.

The solution, for Haig, is readily apparent. The British need the French to commit Divisions to stop this latest German thrust, and they need them now. Which is why Haig now calls by rushed letter for an urgent meeting with Foch.

'The anxiety which this letter revealed,' Foch would recount, 'caused me to leave at once for Montreuil.'[18]

And *voilà*! The dark car with the fluttering French flag on one side of the bonnet and Foch's pennant on the other pulls into the driveway of the château. The swish of the tyres on wet gravel and the sight of the flag and pennant instantly alert one of Haig's staff officers to charge down the stairs and open the door for *le Généralissime*. Word is quickly passed to 'the Chief', as Haig is known, that General Foch is here, and within minutes the two are standing face to face in Haig's study, before a roaring fire. To Foch's eyes, Haig seems quite shaken and is 'still under the influence of the blow he had received [from Operation Michael]'.[19] To Haig, Foch looks as self-assured as ever, with nothing in his bearing to give the first clue that he cares if the entire war now hangs in the balance. Is it perhaps that he just does not understand that? Or that the only thing that truly counts for him is saving Paris?

The problem here, of course, is that Marshal Foch, with Haig's own blessing, is no less than his Commanding Officer, the 'Supreme Commander of the Allied Armies on the Western Front, *le Généralissime*'. Haig is not quite free to vent the enormous frustration he feels.

But he does feel it, all right.

Carefully, if desperately, Haig lays out the position. In the German assault to date, around Amiens, they have lost 40 miles of ground, which, though devastating, hasn't yet cost them the war. If exactly the same happens in this current assault and they lose 40 miles, then the Germans will have the Channel ports, the British Expeditionary Force will be up to their knees in the English Channel, France will collapse next, and the war will be lost. Haig needs fresh French divisions placed in the line, and he needs them *maintenant*, now.

Marshal Foch barely blinks.

The same man who a fortnight earlier had replaced Pétain on the very grounds that he refused to cede an inch to the Germans apparently seems so unconcerned by the possible loss of the Channel ports that he all but refuses to come to Britain's aid, even when they are in real danger of collapse!

'Our reserves must be engaged sparingly,' he insists to Haig. 'In the meantime, Sir Douglas, you and the British will have to depend on your own resources.'[20]

Monstrous!

The best Foch can offer Haig is to send French forces north within 48 hours if the British get in real trouble.

Haig blanches, which is about as far as he goes in demonstrating emotion, but with a few tight words thrown in – for his British forces are already in REAL trouble – the extent of his displeasure is nevertheless apparent.

'Sir Douglas Haig . . .' Foch would delicately summate the Scotsman's views, 'impressed by the enemy's furious onslaughts against the British lines, considered these measures inadequate.'[21]

In the end, so insistent is Haig on more help that Foch finally, reluctantly, agrees to send a single French division immediately, and others as they become available.

Finally, after midnight, Foch leaves and Haig is alone with his thoughts, considering his position: 'I am glad that the French are at last beginning to realise the object of the Germans [is to wipe out the BEF]. The French losses in this battle [since 21 March] are about 20,000 to 25,000, ours are 160,000 and will be more. This shows their share in the fight so far! But personally I have come to the conclusion that Foch is afraid to put any French division into the battle, and that he won't do so until force of circumstances, as a last resort, compel him.'[22]

What to do, then?

It is this question that Haig sits pondering for the next three hours after Foch has left, turning it all over. What is clear is that beyond, perhaps, that sole division that Foch has promised, the French will put their own interests first. So the British must save themselves, and such forces as he does have must be galvanised, inspired to rise to the occasion.

Finally, knowing sleep to be impossible, in the wee hours of the night and indeed in the bleak 3 am of his soul, Haig sits down at his desk in the wee hours to draft, in *his careful and precise handwriting,* an Order of the Day to be read out by his Commanders to all the Allied troops on the morrow.

SPECIAL ORDER OF THE DAY
By FIELD-MARSHAL SIR DOUGLAS HAIG
K.T., G.C.B., G.C.V.O., K.C.I.E.
Commander-in-Chief, British Armies in France

To ALL RANKS OF THE BRITISH ARMY IN FRANCE AND FLANDERS

Three weeks ago to-day the enemy began his terrific attacks against us on a fifty-mile front. His objects are to separate us from the French, to take the Channel Ports and destroy the British Army
. . .

There is no other course open to us but to fight it out. Every position must be held to the last man: there must be no retirement. With our backs to the wall and believing in the justice of our cause each one of us must fight on to the end. The safety of our homes and the Freedom of mankind alike depend upon the conduct of each one of us at this critical moment. Be of good cheer, the British Empire will win in the end.[23]

(Signed) D. Haig F.M.
Commander-in-Chief
British Armies in France
General Headquarters
Tuesday, April 11th, 1918[24]

It is all so neat when written down like that. A little too neat perhaps. So Haig makes one change. Taking his pen, he draws a line through the final sentence: ~~Be of good cheer, the British Empire will win in the end.~~.

Of course, that is still his hope. And they are doing everything possible to achieve it. But perhaps this is more a time for a sober call to arms than a vainglorious prediction of victory.

—

Despite the German's brilliant beginning to Operation George, and the sense that their forces, after bursting through the initial defences, are about to throw the blow that will send the Allies reeling all the way back to the Channel ports . . . there is a pause.

Not because of a lack of men or munitions or materiel so much as a surfeit of cellars, waiting to be emptied. And empty them they do.

When the offenders are found, it is less a matter that their excuses don't stand up, it is that they can't . . . for most are *sturzbetrunken*, dead drunk.

A few hours to sleep it off and then they can go again, at last pushing on to Hazebrouck.

11 APRIL 1918, AMIENS, THE 1ST DIVISION TURNS AROUND
All abooooooard!

'We had been warned that we were moving off today & nearly certain for the north again,' Archie Barwick notes in his diary. 'Oh, she's a lovely war, & what a time we're having. We have just dumped our packs, in preparation for a forced march, where to I don't know, nor care much either, for it's all the same to us no matter where you go – we will eventually be shot into the thick of it.'[25]

12 APRIL 1918, AT AVESNES, LUDENDORFF LAYS DOWN THE LAW

Yes, this is nominally a meeting to decide important matters, but there proves to be little in the way of an exchange of ideas – there rarely is when General Ludendorff presides. And when the Chief of Staff of the German Army is meeting at his HQ as their superior officer, with General Hermann von Kuhl, Chief of Staff for *Kronprinz* Rupprecht's Army Group, and General Friedrich von der Schulenburg for *Kronprinz* Wilhelm's Army Group, it is almost their job to agree with him.

At least General Ludendorff makes clear what the issue is: now that Operation George is off to such a good start in the area east of Hazebrouck, it is a matter of urgency that the British not reinforce their lines there to stop that German advance. And how better to stop them 'milking' divisions from quiet areas in the south than by ensuring the areas are not quiet, by the German Army redoubling their efforts at Villers-Bretonneux and getting 'as close to Amiens as possible'.[26]

Ludendorff is confident that Villers will fall if they attack in the right way – this time with *tanks*, which are being moved forward – and then so too will Amiens. And even if it doesn't fall, holding it will lock the British forces down and keep them away from defending Hazebrouck.

With 60,000 men from the 228th Division, 4th Guards Division and 77th Reserve Division – the last due to arrive in about a week from Russia – the Germans should, at worst, be able to take Villers-Bretonneux and begin pinpoint shelling on Amiens. At best, they'll be able to crush all opposition before them and break through to Amiens the next day.

At the meeting's conclusion it is decided that the attack on Villers-Bretonneux will take place on the morning of 20 April, by which time, it is hoped, the 77th Reserve Division will have arrived.

12 APRIL 1918, HAZEBROUCK, THE AMIENS OF THE NORTH

The train slows and these first of the men of the 1st Division rouse themselves as best they can, with those who are too slow being roused on by their Corporals and Sergeants for their trouble. Get up, you lazy bastards! For the word has passed around, sent by officers to make sure all of them are ready for what used to be called 'getting off the train' but the military is pleased to call 'detraining'.

They are here, at the railway station of the town they are to help defend – Hazebrouck. It is a place already well known to, and beloved by, most of the soldiers. It was to this town that they had frequently come when off front-line duty at Messines, just ten miles to the north-east. It's awash with cosy estaminets, beer made cold, just for them, more point blank *vin blanc* than you could drink, and more soft French girls than you could poke a stick at. But you tried, anyway . . . But now, once they get into the town proper, it is clear that everyone has *gorn*. Worse, the Rue Notre Dame, the main street by the station, is also empty, and all of their favourite estaminets closed down. *Napoo* Charlotte, *napoo* Carole, *napoo* Emmanuelle! Gone, all gone!

What is more, the fact that the Australians have arrived only just in time is made apparent by the fact that as they gather their kit and step out on the siding they can hear the regular boom of German guns in the distance. The veterans among them – and there are a lot, like Archie Barwick, who've 'been there since Anzac', the reverential reference for those who've served from Gallipoli onwards – reckon the front must be just ten miles away, at most.

Just as the first of the soldiers of the 1st Division are forming themselves up by company on the station platform, one of the 1st Division staff officers arrives a'gallop – a 'rosella' with bright red tabs on his collars and hatband – and quickly calls all the senior officers of the 8th Battalion, including Major William Joynt, VC, to gather around him on the platform. The news is not good, and urgent action is required.

'The Germans are attacking towards Hazebrouck right now,' he says, 'and we need you to defend it by taking up this position . . .'[27] He takes the blue pencil in his right hand and slashes a line across the map along the high ground, extending north from Hazebrouck Forest – a rectangle of beech, oak and chestnut trees, three miles long by two miles wide – which lies four miles south-east of where they are standing . . .

The officers lean in closer, almost a rugby scrum of brass, tightly packed and pushing forward, trying to get on top of the situation as they peer down at the map, noting the dangerously long front they will have to hold.

And, uh, where exactly are the British forces they are to replace?

Exactly.

None of the British brass seem to know. It is as if their men have vanished.

But the Germans are there, all right, likely girding their Teutonic loins for another big push, only waiting after their ammunition supplies and the like have been replenished, together with fresh reserves coming forward. And so it goes from there, with the senior officers briefing their underlings, who brief the men.

In Sergeant Archie Barwick's case, as soon as the roll call is completed the Captain of his company tells his men what he knows of the situation – three-fifths of bugger-all, as it turns out – and then gives them the usual spiel on how they must 'hold to the last . . . never surrender', which is a total waste of time in Archie's view. 'For the Australians always fought up to their reputation, & needed no telling about it.'[28]

He and his mates are eager to get to it now. Within 20 minutes of arriving, at least they are on their way, 'alley toot sweet', with all the rest . . .

By the riiiiight . . . quiiiiick . . . march!

'When a lot of old people saw we were Australians,' Archie would note in his diary, 'they stopped on the road and some of them even turned back, such faith they have in our chaps. More than one old lady I heard say *"Bravo Australia, Australia bon"* & some of the old people actually cried with joy and relief when they saw the lads coming up with that firm easy swinging stride which belongs to us alone when marching in columns. Here, they thought, were troops who would give Fritz a fight for it, come what may.'[29]

The mood among these men of the 1st Division as they leave Hazebrouck – marching in 200-strong columns of companies, with half a mile between each one – to move down the cobblestone byways, through villages and hamlets, is close to exuberant. There is a keen awareness that the other divisions have already done very well for themselves, most particularly the 3rd Division at Morlancourt and Villers-Bretonneux, and now is their chance to show what they can do, too.

Marching on in the moonlight along the ancient, cobbled road leading to the town of Strazeele – positioned 5000 yards north of Hazebrouck Forest – lined by hedges on both sides in country that is as flat as a billiard table, albeit a little greener, even in the light thrown by the golden orb that hangs above. In the distance, for once, there is no boom of artillery, and beyond the clumping of their boots, the noisiest thing is the regular mooing of cows. It has all fallen so quiet that you could almost forget for a moment there is a war on and they will very soon likely be fighting for their very lives.

And now company commanders gather their men around in the darkness to read some words from General Haig himself. 'Every position must be held to the last man,' the Captains softly intone. 'There must be no retirement. With our backs to the wall and believing in the justice of our cause each one of us must fight on to the end . . .'[30]

Barely a word needs to be spoken thereafter.

'The famous appeal,' Captain Bean would note, 'had precisely the result intended – that of stringing them to the highest pitch of determination.'[31]

By midnight, Major Joynt's 8th Battalion is in position near the northern edge of Hazebrouck Forest, and the mood is even stronger.

'With 1000 yards to defend with 120 bayonets,' Major Joynt would record of his own A Company, 'the men were proud as punch. The Australian units in the south had demonstrated what they could do and 1st Division was quite sure it could do equally well . . .'[32]

No matter that they are exhausted after a long day. There are careless soldiers and there are veteran soldiers, but the rule of blistered thumb is that there are no careless veteran soldiers. Make the effort. Dig *in*, Digger. And so they do.

'Pick your own line and wait for the Fritzes,' Joynt tells the men as he walks along, inspecting their work.

'By cripes,' they respond happily, by his characterisation, 'this will do us.'[33]

Still, the Australian soldiers have a very strong presentiment. 'All of them are keenly [aware] there was nothing between us and the Channel Ports, and we felt "It's on us!"'[34]

The men of Archie Barwick's 1st Brigade, meanwhile, have not been called on to go to establish the front-line – that job has been given to 2nd and 3rd Brigades – and so may settle into the tiny village of Pradelles, just 1000 yards west of Strazeele and two miles east of Hazebrouck. And settle in they do, comfortably, quickly spreading out to the surrounding farmhouses and cottages and more than making themselves at home after their long march.

Oh, she's a lovely war.

Fritz, though, waits for no man and continues to push forward in the night. Just after dawn the next morning, Archie and his 1st Battalion must move forward themselves to stop him, positioning themselves in a line 1000 yards east of Strazeele, along a gentle rise, with Hazebrouck three miles behind them.

After four days of advancing in leaps and bounds, and booms and endless rattling of machine-gun fire, Fritz, in the form of *Herr* Dr Stephen Westmann and the German 35th Division, are closing in on the town of Strazeele, and on a collision course with the 1st Australian Division.

'The assault battalion stormed on,' *Herr* Dr Westmann would recount, 'occasionally fired on by German guns because a stupid artillery observer who should have been with the forward troops lagged behind and thought that the soldiers he saw through his glasses were British or Portuguese.'

Whoever they are, there are not many of them. Much of the resistance seems to have so suddenly vanished that some of the German soldiers even find an abandoned column of British lorries, all with full petrol tanks.

'The way to the Channel Ports lay open – the road which led through the Forest of Hazebrouck to St Omer and Calais . . .'[35]

Now it can only be a matter of roaring forth before the Allies can compose their defences once more.

———

Such is the way of this war.

You not only have to fight it, you also have to write endless reports on it. On this late morning, Colonel Henry Goddard and Colonel John Milne of the 35th and 36th Battalions are working together in Milne's HQ at Bois de Blangy, three miles west of VB, with a couple of their staff officers, writing their reports – a week after the event – of exactly what had happened on the late afternoon of 4 April, when their men had combined to lead that extraordinary counter-attack to defend Villers-Bretonneux.

> Report on Operations carried out by 36th Battalion
>   . . . At 5.15 pm the counter-attack was launched,
> the Battalion moved forward with great dash and
> in fine formation . . . the rapidity of their advance
> thoroughly demoralized the enemy who were
> advancing . . .[36]

Both men have admired the role of the other, but perhaps it is Goddard who is most deeply admiring of the work of Milne, the hard man from Queensland who had seized the moment and driven back the Germans in a brilliant charge, saving both the day and Villers-Bretonneux.

When the report is finally done, in the absence of breakfast the senior officers have a cup of tea together, at which point Goddard and his Staff Officer take their leave, eager to make a quick visit to the men of the 35th Battalion's D Company, who are nearby. Just a few minutes later, however, there is that familiar screaming whistle as a shell descends, followed by a pause as everyone holds their breath. Have their last moments on this earth come? The higher the pitch of the whistle, they know, the closer to them it will land. And this one, Colonel Goddard and his Staff Officer realise, is clearly going to be close. In fact, it lands with a thunderous blast just 150 yards or so to their right.

Goddard and his officer look to each other, aghast, and say it in the same breath: 'That's on headquarters. I wonder if it got them.'[37]

Racing back the same way they had come, they are not long in finding the answer. The shell has scored a direct hit on 36th Battalion HQ.

Colonel Milne lies dead, his shattered body crumpled at an impossible angle, with his dead officers all around. One officer, Major John McDowell, though badly wounded – blinded – will survive. Ten men have been killed outright.

It is with an extremely heavy heart that Colonel Goddard reports the news to Brigadier Rosenthal's 9th Brigade HQ, where it is quickly arranged for Major Walter Fry to take command. 'The news soon spread,' Colonel Goddard would sorrowfully write that night, 'and the men were very much heartbroken.'[38]

It is, in fact, a grief that will not dissipate, as one Digger, Sydney Young, would note in his diary: 'This is the most drastic event in the history of the Battalion. As all three [officers], especially the colonel, were loved by the battalion as it is the fortune of few officers to be. For coolness, gallantry, ability and consideration the colonel could not be excelled.'[39]

On the spot, the Digger pens a poem:

War takes its toll of bravest and best of men they say,
And true it is for all our hopes were garnered in a day,
The colonel, major, adjutant, were shattered by a shell,
As gentlemen they lived and as heroes all they fell.

Yes they got our brave old colonel still I guess he's marching on
To a greater path of glory just as such as he has won,
And the boys who used to follow when the enemy defied,
Will be prouder still to follow when they cross the great divide[40]

And I bet he's somewhere watching his battalion as of old,
And his spirit still shall guide us and his eye serene and bold,
Will lead us on to triumph still again against the foe
So we'll keep his memory sacred, Colonel Milne D.S.O.[41]

———

By the morning of 13 April, the 1st Division is well dug in defending Hazebrouck, with two brigades occupying the trenches that run north from Hazebrouck Forest past Strazeele for a total length of 7000 yards.

On their flanks they have the British 40th Division – Colonel Crozier's unit – and the British 33rd on their left. Under the circumstances, it is a real worry for the Australians to be so dependent on the now notoriously brittle British, but at least on their immediate left is the 1st Battalion of the Cameronian Regiment, who are Scots, so that is different. The Scots don't run, they fight.

Oh, and a full fortnight after Foch has promised he will send a French division to the aid of the British, they have at last arrived and settled in, just west of Hazebrouck, well back from the front-lines. It is no more than a tokenistic offering, with just 5000 cavalrymen of the 4th French Cavalry Division, but it is *something*.

That evening, Archie's company is sent forward once again to bolster the newly established line east of Strazeele and batten down the hatches before the storm of stormtroopers breaks upon them. Archie and his mates hop to it, distributing .303 ammunition, pushing 'listening posts' out into No-Man's Land so they will get as much warning as possible of German advances, and positioning Lewis guns and their crews where they will have a good field of fire while still being well protected and hard for the Hun to spot.

Throughout, Archie confides to his diary that he feels 'rotten, worse than I ever remember feeling . . . before, but I dare not show it for I had to appear as calm as I could.'[42]

It is with this in mind that he walks along the parapet of the hastily dug trenches of the night before, cracking jokes with the Privates, hoping to keep their minds off what is very likely about to happen – some of them are about to die horrible, violent deaths – and it seemingly works for them. But not Archie.

'I had a nasty feeling about me, as if something was going to happen to me . . . but by exerting my willpower I crushed this feeling utterly & carried on.'[43]

———

And yet, the British still have some sting left in them, some ability to resist. That much is apparent to Dr Westmann as he and his orderlies take shelter in a dugout near Vieux-Berquin. Tending to the wounded, they are suddenly overrun by British soldiers and given orders: 'Take off our [trouser] belts and wait until you can be escorted to the rear'.[44] (A simple expedient, it means prisoners' hands must always be occupied, defending their modesty.)

In fact, rather than years spent as prisoners of war, as Dr Westmann and his colleagues had feared, after just an hour the German counter-attack completely overwhelms their captors, who suddenly have to put *their* hands up. It is Dr Westmann himself who takes charge of three 'Scottish prisoners in their kilts, which aroused the curiosity of our men as to what they wore underneath them'.[45]

SHORTLY AFTER MIDNIGHT, 14 APRIL 1918, HAZEBROUCK FOREST, NOT ENOUGH HORSES FOR THE COURSES

After such a promising start for Operation George, things have slowed. While it had been one thing to have the road 'wide open', it had been quite another to have the horsepower to move an entire army of 750,000 men and 2200 guns forward. The normal number of horses per division had been 4000. Now they are down to just 600, hauling artillery and wagons night and day, literally worked to death on the many trips back and forth. In the course of Operation Michael to the south – making an average advance of five miles a day – it has already cost 29,000 horses dead, with just under 2000 a day being slaughtered. In Operation George the rate has moved even higher, and so the advance is down to just three miles a day at best.

Still, this particular company of Germans from the 35th Division probe forward, being under the command of one *Leutnant* Frey, who has taken over this unit just the day before and is still getting his bearings, in every sense of the word.

It is their singular misfortune, this misty midnight, to be heading along a lane that goes straight towards where a platoon from the AIF's 8th Battalion, under the command of Lieutenant Ivan Murdoch, are dug in just to the east of Hazebrouck Forest and settling down for a kip – if not so engaged already – leaving only sentries on duty.

But those sentries hear it, all right – the unmistakable, rhythmic sound of clodhoppers on cobblestones. It is the sound of men, marching. A *lot* of them. And it is coming from . . . *over there*. Where?

There! Those with keen senses of both hearing and danger point to the east, in the direction of a country lane that passes right along the front of this part of the Australian front-line, just on the other side of a hedge.

Germans!

Sure enough, within 30 seconds – which is just enough time to wake everyone and have their rifles pointing in the right direction, not to mention their already carefully positioned Lewis gun primed and ready to go – the marchers appear. An entire company of Germans!

Murdoch, the younger brother of the famed correspondent Keith Murdoch, is a natural leader of men himself. Using hand signals only, he has his men bring the Lewis gun and their rifles to bear once more, but hold their fire until he gives the signal. And . . . and . . . and . . . NOW!

Murdoch shouts 'Fire!' and the night is instantly filled with death flying forth at the speed of bullets. The Germans – who had been allowed to get within 20 yards of the Australian trench – are suddenly torn apart by a ferocious fusillade of lead. Many fall, mortally wounded. Those who can, flee.

When it is quiet once more, bar the groaning of the grievously wounded, Murdoch takes some of his men forward and find they have killed a German officer, *Leutnant* Frey,[46] and 20 soldiers of Germany's 141st Regiment. Most happily, they are able to snaffle five German machine guns, always highly prized for their deadly efficiency. It will be a great pleasure to turn them on the Germans themselves.

And, as they all know, that will likely be soon.

———

By dawn on this 14th day of April, no fewer than 4000 soldiers of the AIF's 1st Division are now well dug in across 7000 yards of front, with their ammunition supplies well secured in for'ard positions. After clashes along the line, such as that of Lieutenant Ivan Murdoch's crowd, all of them are sure that the main German attack is about to hit them . . . which is as well, for that is precisely what happens. At 6.30 am, the barrage begins. Strangely, however, this time it lasts for just 15 minutes, and the shells fall on the village of Strazeele, 1000 yards *behind* the Australians.

Corporal Percival Turvey of the 3rd Battalion, 1st Brigade, Gallipoli veteran and the son of the publican of Wagga Wagga's Bridge Hotel – in which Percy had been born 26 years before in an upstairs room – makes a key decision. After giving it some thought, he positions himself and his Lewis gun team a bit forward of their previous position, at a spot the Diggers call Gutzer Farm, right atop a small rise. This vantage point allows them a great view to the east, from where they presume the Germans will come.

Sure enough, only minutes after they have arrived and dug themselves in, just before 10 am, Turvey and his men are gazing forth over the superbly picturesque country – a rich mosaic of carefully tended fields bounded by hedges, through which lovely lanes crisscross – when they see the most extraordinary thing.

It is . . . it is . . . '*miles* of infantry slowly but surely goose-stepping towards us'.

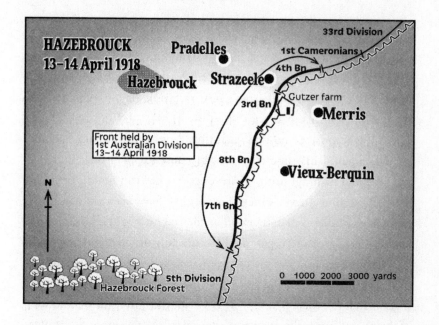

Hundreds of them. *Thousands* of them! *Goose*-stepping! No greater contrast with the Australian amble could exist.

Beside the long *feldgrau*, field-grey lines, German officers on even greyer horses are riding up and down, watching over the men as they make this momentous push west to where the Channel ports lie – clearly unaware that the Australians have come so far forward and now hold the high ground. Up to this point, all these soldiers of Germany's 42nd Division have seen is first Portuguese and then British soldiers *retreating*.

Corporal Turvey sends one of his men racing back to his company commander with the message that Fritz will be on the doorstep very shortly, and then gives his orders. Much in the manner that Lieutenant Murdoch had done two nights earlier, his men are told not to fire, nor give away their position in any manner, until the Germans are right upon them, and he gives the word.

That word is not long in coming once the goose-steppers are within 200 yards of them, and that word is 'FIRE!'

'It was like firing into a haystack,' Turvey would recount. 'One could not miss.'[47]

Within minutes, all that these shattered and now scattered remnants of the 42nd Division of the 6th Army can do is take to the only shelter available – some abandoned British trenches out in front of the Australians, together with some nearby farmhouses – desperate for their reinforcements to arrive.

To the surprise of no one, just after 2 pm the Germans launch a second assault. This time they are not goose-stepping but alternately crawling and rushing, using whatever cover they can find to try to get forward, around Turvey's men, just as they have been trained to do. And the Australians pick them off as they come, not at all intimidated by the new tactics and eager to add to the tally of the morning's work.

Yes, these are real, live men they are shooting, but they might as well be sitting ducks. Once the Germans emerge from the farmhouses and shallow trenches there is simply no cover for them to speak of, and most of the Australians really are expert shots, particularly at this close range.

Still, through it all, one particular German stands out. A brave officer, on foot, at the head of his men, urging them . . . What is that word he is repeating?

'*Forwich! Forwich!*'[48] is what it sounds like to Turvey's ears.

In fact, it is '*Vorwarts! Vorwarts!*' as in 'Forwards! Forwards!' In any case, the meaning is clear as he oh-so-courageously keeps coming, as do his men, surely shamed to hang back when one so brave is leading them.

Even when a united volley of fire from the Australians brings the German officer and the most forward of the *forwich* soldiers to ground, still it doesn't stop him. As Turvey observes closely, it is not that the officer springs up, for clearly he has been hit, but he *does* struggle to his feet and gurgle the cry once more . . . 'forwich'.

'Another volley sent him in a heap,' Turvey would recount, 'and it seemed that he was done. But, to our utter amazement, he gallantly struggled to his feet, and, lurching from one side to the other to get his balance, called again 'Forwich, Forwich.' This time he took the full count.[49]

And – *napoo* Germans! – that is the end of the attack, for today at least. If so bold a German officer as that, backed by his men, can't get through the Australians there, where can they? The answer: nowhere.

To the far right of Corporal Turvey's 1st Brigade is the 2nd Brigade, which includes Major Joynt's 8th Battalion, and they are able to beat off a remarkably similar attack. The German troops had included a fresh elite unit, the Alpine Corps, used as conventional infantry in this battle. Writing after the war, one officer would ruefully recall, 'We were accustomed to definite success in attaining our objectives everywhere, in Serbia, in front of Verdun, in Rumania and Italy. For the first time . . . [we failed]. I think I may say that the defenders on the British front in April 1918 were the best troops of the many with whom we crossed swords in the course of the four and a quarter years.'[50]

In fact, 14 April is just one more disappointing day for the Germans, in no small part because they have come up against Australians who simply have not moved – just as has happened at Hébuterne, Morlancourt, Villers-Bretonneux and Dernancourt, *twice*.

Right now, what stands between the Germans and victory in this war is the 100,000 soldiers of the Australian Corps.

—

General Ludendorff, of course, is mightily displeased. While this is not an uncommon occurrence for this most important of German military figures, on this evening of 14 April, he is particularly grim.

General Ferdinand von Quast, the commanding officer of the 6th Army, which has been fighting the Australians of the 1st Division, gives him the news. And it is *nicht gut*, not good.

'The offensive today has, to all appearances, fizzled out, and the troops are completely exhausted . . . We need any further offensive to be postponed until a proper deployment of trench mortars and artillery can be arranged . . .'[51]

As disappointed as he is, General Ludendorff has no choice but to accept it. Experience has shown just in the last fortnight that redoubling efforts against dug-in Australians only results in a redoubling of the casualty lists and little in the way of advances. He agrees that the 6th Army should not resume its offensive north of the Hazebrouck Forest, against Meteren and Strazeele, until 17 April, at which point they should have the weaponry and ammunition needed. Perhaps then they will be able to crack the Australian nut.

——

Conversely, down on the Somme, General Rawlinson is thrilled with these extraordinary men under his Fourth Army command and goes to the effort of visiting senior Australian officers this same evening. Returning, he records in his diary, 'I went round the divisions of the Australian Corps today, and found them in excellent heart. They are a splendid body of men, and Hobbs and Monash are both very good commanders. They are ready for any emergency, which is comforting.'[52]

And General Rawlinson would like to think he is equally prepared, even telling Monash, 'I have staked my reputation on holding Villers-Bretonneux . . .'[53]

——

The following afternoon, Archie Barwick is just having a yarn to his cousin Bill, who is in a nearby unit, when he hears shelling start up nearby. Cocking his ear, Archie reckons he has it placed.

'That's among my Company,' he says brightly. 'I must get back as quickly as possible.'[54]

Hoo-roo, Bill.

Hurrying to where his mates of the 1st Battalion, 1st Brigade, 1st Division are dug in around Strazeele, 300 yards from where Corporal Turvey had performed so wonderfully well the day before – Archie and his men had been in reserve for that battle – the country boy from Tassie quickly reaches his men and orders them to get out from under the hedge they have been secreted in and 'get down into the sunken road for safety'.[55]

He is only just in time for 'shells, big ones at that [were] . . . falling thick and fast and quite a number were getting knocked'.[56]

And then he hears it – the shell that is higher pitched than all the others. Archie stands stock still, awaiting his fate, and the next thing he knows he feels it: 'A frightful red-hot searing pass across my right side & I staggered from the blow. I knew I was hit but I did not know how badly.[57]

His first thought as he feels the rush of his own warm blood pouring down his body is that he has been effectively disembowelled and his stomach is hanging out, as he has seen happen to so many other blokes – a death sentence, if ever there was one. But, no, one of his mates, Jackie Hayes, can see it is not as bad as that and Archie might be saved. Hayes scoops him up and starts carrying him to the regimental aid post until Archie is in such agony that he begs to be put down. Jack obliges.

'The funniest part of all is that I never heard the explosion of the shells. I suppose the shock of getting hit took that away but I remember on looking around seeing 3 or 4 more chaps who had been hit & 1 dead alongside me.'[58]

The truth? Archie is thrilled, and his mates envious. The large gash in his right side, nearly exposing several ribs, is one they all instantly recognise as a 'Blighty', a wound bad enough that he will have to be sent to England for treatment. But he will live!

'Oh she looked a beauty,' he would exult, '[and] did not trouble me in the slightest once I saw it was bad enough to get me to [England.] When the lads heard I was hit they came crowding around . . . They were all of the same opinion as myself & that was I was a lucky dog to get out of it for a while.'[59]

His mates will have to stop the Germans without him.

16 APRIL 1918, ALBERT, WITHER YONDER VIRGIN

At least *some* of the signs are good.

On this morning, Captain Frederick Petch, MC, is with his British artillery unit of the 5th Corps, within sight of German-held Albert, when his field telephone rings. Over the sound of a chattering machine gun coming down the line, he can just make out the voice of a panicked Infantry Colonel positioned right on the front-line on the edges of Albert, shouting that his men are being ripped apart by a heavy machine gun atop the cathedral.

'Can you blow the place to blazes?'[60] the Colonel asks plaintively.

Yes, well, as it happens, a recent Army order has been put out to the effect that NO MORE BUILDINGS IN ALBERT ARE TO BE DEMOLISHED BY GUNFIRE,[61] as it is feared that even if the Allies take the old town back there will be nothing to hand over to the French. Captain Petch has no superior officer he can refer to – both his General and Brigade Major are away on other business. Thus, the decision is his and his alone.

In an instant, Petch, a clever man with an ability to work the angles on more than just artillery matters, finds the answer. Giving his crew the coordinates for some imaginary trenches that lie directly on the other side of yonder cathedral, he orders the Major of this battery to 'fire a couple of hundred rounds',[62] and then waits for the inevitable results as the gun starts to roar.

Sure enough, within minutes, the cathedral tower is blown to hell, including the troublesome machine gun. Among the tumbling rocks and bell, of course, comes the leaning Virgin Mary with the child.

The French understand the significance of it. The war will soon be over!

What remains to be seen, of course, is just which side will win that war.

16 APRIL 1918, NEAR HAZEBROUCK, QUELLE SURPRISE, THE FRENCH ARE HERE?

Could today be the day of the expected next big German attack towards Hazebrouck? It seems likely to the men of the 1st Battalion when every man is issued with two grenades and three bandoliers of ammunition, some 280 rounds altogether, and told to be 'ready to move into action at five minutes' notice'.[63] They soon move forward into the front-line positions for the third time to take over from the 4th Battalion, who are due a spell.

Among those moving forward is 2nd Lieutenant Tom Richards, an officer already famous before the war for playing international rugby for both the Wallabies and the British Lions (1908–1912), not to mention being an Olympic gold medallist in rugby and a *Sydney Morning Herald* journalist who had played club rugby in France. A veteran of Gallipoli, awarded the Military Cross for bravery displayed at Bullecourt, Richards – a muscly six-footer, all of 13 stone, though of curiously fine facial features rare in a rugby player – is nothing if not capable, and quite calm, even though in areas near and far panic is going cheap. As a German barrage comes down upon the men, he understands the situation entirely, including the fact that, miracle of all miracles, their left flank is now guarded by the French 32nd *Chasseurs à Pied* of the 133rd Division – resplendent in their dark blue with gay yellow edgings – meaning that General Foch is at last contributing a significant force to the line.

'It seems that Strazeele is the key to Hazebrouck,' Richards writes in his diary, 'and that the 1st Australian Division has sworn to defend it to the very last.'

This they prepare to do, as the German storm before them darkens, as the German barrage becomes heavier and the planes swooping on them strafe and drop bombs more frequently. The certainty grows that they are about to face Fritz's full fury. All Lieutenant Richards and the 6000 soldiers of the 1st Division, now in the front-line, can do is dig their trenches deeper, ensure their weaponry is ready, their Lewis guns positioned and their lines of communication open, all while pursuing whatever other defensive measures they can. This includes hooking empty tin cans with a couple of stones in them onto the barbs of the wire. Just let Fritz try to sneak through the wire in the dark and they'll know about it soon enough – and it won't be just the tins filled with holes.

'It is awfully dark laying down barbed wire,' Richards dashes off in his diary, 'and a little discouraging when the Hun puts down his barrage at intervals.'[64]

Still, it is done. Along with his mates in the 1st Battalion, he is finally able to get some kip at 2.30 am on the morning of the 17th, until the alarms sound for a gas attack shortly afterwards and they must don their masks. It can only be a matter of hours now, if that.

—

The German attack finally hits the Allied lines at 10 am, after a one-hour bombardment. No fewer than eight German divisions, some 100,000 men in all, storm forth across an eight-mile front, with the southern tip against the 1st Division Australians in the south at the edge of Hazebrouck Wood to the British 19th Division in the north at Mt Kemmel.

Germany's 35th and 12th Divisions throw everything they have at the Australian 1st Division, 'but were met with such a volume of fire from the 4th and 1st Australian battalions on the left, that they at once desisted. Opposite the 3rd Battalion the Germans hardly left their shallow jumping off trenches . . . So secure did the Australians feel that they did not report the attacks until the end of the day.'[65]

The Germans try again in the afternoon. If at first you don't succeed . . .

In the thick of it, as ever – just as he had always been on the international rugby field – is Lieutenant Tom Richards. Notwithstanding that one of his closest friends in the army, Private Norman McGill, is shot through the head and killed right by his side, only a short time before his batman, Private Alfred Lucas, is killed, Richards keeps firing coolly at every German he can sight in range.

He can mourn men and personally bury them when all this is over. For now, he must take his revenge on the Germans who did this and ensure that he is not another victim of their cruel attentions.

'I think I got four for certain with my own rifle,' he would matter of factly note in his diary. 'I only have a Lewis gun and nine riflemen as a platoon now . . .'[66]

Their position as the Germans continue to swarm becomes close to untenable – Richards is in a 1st Battalion spot as forward as it is isolated, with little natural cover. But the orders they have received are firm: 'There must be no retiring.'[67]

And so they, as Richards would describe it, 'fight on and on'.

So do his comrades of the Australian 1st Division down the line, and the result is splendid.

'At nightfall,' Richards records on 17 April, the fourth day of German attacks against the Australians, 'we had the Hun as tame as a caged canary, and afraid to look over the top at all . . .'[68]

For Richards, the most immediate task he faces is to bury McGill and Lucas, which he does just outside the post, only a few yards from where they had been killed, carefully marking their graves with make-shift crosses and a notation on a rock as to who lies below.

—

For the German military leadership, there is simply no getting past it, any more than their troops can get past the Australians who've been defending Hazebrouck, despite four days of trying: Operation George has been only half a success so far.

In this time of crisis, at his HQ in Avesnes, Ludendorff gathers the commanders of his Armies to him, to work out the next step.

The meeting begins with General Fritz von Lossberg, the Chief of Staff of the Fourth Army, who gravely informs General Ludendorff that, when it comes to the attack on Hazebrouck, 'the situation is very bad'.[69] And though that applies across the board, perhaps most significant is that the 35th and the 12th Divisions have made no progress at all against the Australians between Hazebrouck Wood and Strazeele.

Many of the German divisions 'are quite played out,'[70] Lossberg adds. It is clear they need fresh divisions, but on that front the Chief of Staff of the Prince Rupprecht Army Group, General von Kuhl, is clear. There will be none available for a week.

Another factor that must come into their reckoning, as noted by one of Ludendorff's staff officers, is that the morale among the troops has markedly declined, and it is affecting the attitude of their commanders and troop leaders as well.

In sum, there is no way around it. Though Operation George still has life in it, for the moment they must stop attacking Hazebrouck and redouble their efforts against the British further north between Mont Kemmel – where they are making fair progress – and Ypres.

In the end, Ludendorff puts off a decision about what to do until the morrow.

EVENING 17–18 APRIL, NOT OUT OF THE WOODS, WEST OF VILLERS

Moroccans in the moonlight . . .

Soldiers of the *la Division Marocaine* from French North Africa have come to this part of the woods, Bois l'Abbé, on the western edge of the same high plateau as Villers-Bretonneux, just a mile from the outskirts of town, because they have heard tell of the most extraordinary thing.

Tanks! Three British Mark IV tanks, no less than 29 tons each, bristling variously with cannon and machine guns, placed here against the strong possibility of a German attack on Villers-Bretonneux. The commander of this platoon of tanks, Lieutenant Frank Mitchell, watches with some bemusement as these men from Casablanca and surrounds 'gingerly creep up to the tanks to touch them with their fingers – as if to make sure that they were real – and then slink away again. In the same wood there were also detachments of the famed Foreign Legion . . . and Australian troops in their picturesque slouch hats . . .'[71]

And what is *that?*

Oh.

Christ!

The soldiers of the British Tank Corps, the members of the French Foreign Legion, a few stray Moroccans and Australia's 9th Brigade are just settling down for the night when, suddenly, they hear the most extraordinarily unnerving thing.

It is not just that shells are landing among them . . .

It is that they don't explode in regulation manner. Instead, there is what the troops describe as 'the unmistakable *plop, plop,*' of gas shells landing to emit the equally unmistakable 'burnt-potato or onion smell . . . followed by a foul stench, a poisonous odour, that made your eyes water and your nose run instantly'.[72]

Among the usual high-explosive shells, the German artillery opposite are firing a different kind of shell. They're called *die Senfgasgranaten*, mustard gas shells, and this is the most devastating gas of all. As odourless as it is deadly once ingested, the strangest thing is that it is slow working. Initially, for those caught without their gasmasks on, all seems fine. Several hours later, severe blistering of the skin begins, while the lungs become congested and the mucous membrane is hacked up in severe coughing fits. Those suffering from its effects would frequently be in so much pain that they had to be strapped to their beds for fear of them scratching their blisters as they slowly turn into splattering, spluttering, suffering, putrescent messes of men – blind and useless as far as further soldiering goes. The luckiest die within days.

Most devastating, militarily, is that, once dropped, mustard gas lingers on the battlefield for days, and a stray platoon simply walking through it could be all but wiped out, while it lingered longest in underground dugouts . . .

The quickest of the men manage to whip their gasmasks on in time. Many of those men are too slow, however, and beyond their weeping eyes, they begin to vomit as the gas does its work and toxic chemicals enter their bodies through their eyes, nose and mouth

The English poet Wilfred Owen would capture the horror of mustard gas and its effects in his poem, '*Dulce et Decorum est*':

> *Gas! Gas! Quick, boys! – An ecstasy of fumbling,*
> *Fitting the clumsy helmets just in time;*
> *But someone still was yelling out and stumbling,*
> *And flound'ring like a man in fire or lime . . .*[73]

Within minutes, just under 1000 Australian soldiers are suffering the effects. Also affected are some of the tank crews, whom Lieutenant Frank Mitchell soon finds to have 'eyes swollen and weeping and faces and bare knees heavily blistered'.[74]

For the moment, all the soldiers and crew must be evacuated from the woods until the gas dissipates – which might be a matter of days. Left behind are the results, as detailed by Lieutenant Mitchell: 'Dead horses, swollen to enormous size, and birds with bulging eyes and stiffened claws lay everywhere. In the tree-tops the half-stifled crows were hoarsely croaking. The gas hung about the bushes and undergrowth and clung to the tarpaulins.'[75]

The results among the men are the most appalling of all. And it is the 33rd Australian Battalion of the 9th Brigade that is the most affected.

'The men were asleep,' their war diary records, 'and a number were gassed before respirators could be adjusted . . . Our casualties to gas were heavy, 13 officers, 26 NCOs, 268 men.'[76] In one fell swoop, the 33rd have lost half a battalion to this one gas attack.

One of the first unaffected Australians on the scene is sapper Henry William Dadswell, who goes forward to repair the telephone line to the 54th Battalion HQ that has gone dead, and he is shocked by what he finds.

'Nearly everyone was gassed, many of them dying later,' he would recount. 'The gas had destroyed the sense of smell and the gas sergeant had told them to put their helmets on. Later he tried the air and couldn't smell anything, so gave the all clear, with tragic results. We then went on to the 53rd Bn and found the same thing there. Our Brigade had about 800 casualties for the day.'

And never would he be able to forget the suffering.

'It was awful to see the poor beggars. The gas had affected their eyes and a dozen or twenty would link arms and only two or three could see. One would be at each end and perhaps one in the middle, they would guide the others out and along the road.'[77]

The township has equally been plastered with gas shells, with inevitable results.

'The type of gas directed on us was vile,' Edmund Street would recount. 'We called it "Dead Dog Gas". Apart from its chemical effect, the terrific odour compelled one to spew violently. For days afterwards Villers Bret was unsafe, the reek of gas was everywhere, in the streets, in the tumbled piles of bricks, in broken houses and in cellars.'[78]

And still the Germans are only getting warmed up.

18 APRIL 1918, LUDENDORFF HQ AT AVESNES, NO RUSHING FROM RUSSIA

General Ludendorff, after a quick, staccato conversation with General Hermann von Kuhl, puts the phone down.

He has told von Kuhl that Operation George is still going well enough to be worth pursuing, so it is more important than ever to get the attack at Villers-Bretonneux underway as quickly as possible to stop the British sending their troops north to stop them. If it goes well, then they can move on to Amiens the next day. If it doesn't, it should *still* make the British think twice.

The bad news for General Ludendorff, however, is that *still* the 77th Reserve Division – one of the four divisions earmarked to attack Villers – has been delayed on their trip from Russia. So a new launch date has been decided on. They will attempt to claim Villers-Bretonneux in the early morning of 23 April.

In the meantime, the Germans continue to build up their troops in the trenches in front of Villers-Bretonneux. Among them are the soldiers of the 478th Regiment, Württembergers, men from the rugged forests between the Rhine and the Danube, who'd fought well enough in the first week of Operation Michael to be withdrawn from the line for several weeks of rest, recuperation and the absorption of new recruits . . . only to find themselves suddenlyputbackintheline!

Of course the troops themselves know nothing of the urgent imperatives of the situation.

'These strategic complexities were not of course known to the *"Frontschwein"*, "front-line pigs",' the Württemberger Regiment's official history would note with rather stark honesty, 'and the officers and men grumbled once again to their hearts' content about going into the line once more.'[79]

And not the well-provisioned, superbly engineered trenches they had occupied for most of this war to date . . .

'The fortifications, if one can speak of such at all [are poor],' their history records. 'There are some holes that offer protection, but only from weather . . . Some of these holes are even connected by knee-deep trenches. The wire obstacle exists only in written reports. So it is the same as always when the regiment came to a new position, it had to *bauen, buddeln, graben*; build, burrow, dig.'[80]

Still, the main thing is that the build-up of troops before Villers-Bret continues. The Germans ready for their make-or-break thrust on that key plateau overlooking Amiens.

In his own quarters in Dury, the Commanding Officer of the British Fourth Army, General Rawlinson, comes to the conclusion that the Germans are about to try for exactly that, and writes to his superior in London, the Chief of the Imperial General Staff, General Sir Henry Wilson: *There can be no question that the Amiens area is the only one in which the enemy can hope to gain such a success as to force the Allies to discuss terms of peace.*[81]

18 APRIL 1918, ON THE FIELDS WEST OF PRADELLES, LET THE DOG SEE THE RABBIT, AND THE AUSTRALIANS SEE THE HARE

On a brief visit to the north on this day, to check on how the 1st Division are faring as they continue to do their bit to hold the Germans from securing Hazebrouck, Charles Bean sees something that pleases him greatly.

In one of the areas well back from the front-lines, he spies two Australian artillerymen, strolling through the wheat, carrying their rifles under their arms the way a mother holds a baby with natural ease.

Clearly, they are out hunting hares.

'You will see this wherever you go in France, where our men are,' he notes in his diary. 'The British troops are too much afraid of their officers to do this – but if there are Australians about our men go out and get food for the mob . . . Our own officers, I think, wink at it in order to keep the men in good spirits.'[82]

And in general good spirits the Australians mostly prove to be, with one notable exception.

'Our men,' an Australian officer tells him, 'are getting very tired of reading in the press all about "magnificent rear guard actions [of the British forces]" and "enormous German losses" and that sort of thing.'

'What are the British correspondents to write?' Bean replies archly. 'Would you have them say that "the men threw down their arms and ran away"?'[83]

Point taken.

20 APRIL 1918, 2ND ARMY HEADQUARTERS AT GUISE, THE GERMANS SEEK TO CHANGE THE CHANNEL

The news from the north is mixed. While Operation George is continuing to make fair progress and may yet get to the Channel ports, there is no doubt that it has slowed considerably from the spectacular leaps of the first few days. What is more, a familiar danger is emerging. That is, to stop the progress the German forces are making in Flanders to the north, up around Hazebrouck, there is a real likelihood the Allies will 'milk' their forces from the south and move them up there.

In fact, it is already happening. Through intelligence and captured prisoners, the Germans have been able to establish that units such as the 1st Australian Division had disappeared from the line at Messines around 5 April, showed up around Amiens in the south on 8 April and has now reappeared back north, in the line east of Hazebrouck, on 13 April!

The possibility, nay probability, of the British doing this en masse commits Ludendorff to a particular course of action.

On this bitterly cold morning, he orders the Commanding Officer of the 2nd Army, General Georg von der Marwitz, to attack

Villers-Bretonneux once more. And this time they must hit it with such massive force – including the 14 tanks that have at last arrived in the area for the first time – that they will surely break the defences, occupy the town and at last be able to bring their artillery to bear on Amiens. And even if the attack doesn't do exactly that, it still should prevent *die Tommys* from moving their divisions north.

Sixty miles to the west of von der Marwitz at much the same time, the British commanders of seven Whippet light tanks, tucked away west of Bois l'Abbé, some 1000 yards further to the west than Lieutenant Frank Mitchell and the three Mark IV tanks, are also advised that their services will likely be required soon. Though the Whippets, with only half an inch of armour, would be completely hopeless against the German tanks, the fact that they are half the weight and more than twice as fast and armed with four machine guns means they are perfect against German infantry. And it looks like there is *plenty* of that coming forward!

—

The base rule of warfare, of physical conflict, has never altered.
Hard men flourish and endure, softer men wither and perish. Hence why Charles Bean is so shocked as, near the front-line at Villers-Bretonneux, he witnesses the hard men streaming back from the front on which the fate of the battle rests and the soft men streaming forward.

What is going *on?*

Keen to place his own imprimatur on the structure of the defences, General Rawlinson is removing the Australians to hold 14 miles of line to the left of Villers-Bretonneux – from Albert, via Dernancourt and Morlancourt, to Hill 104 – and replacing them with General Heneker's British 8th Division, now bolstered by the 5000 newly arrived 18- and 19-year-olds of the draft.

'For two days companies of infantry have been passing us on the roads,' Bean confides to his diary, 'companies of children, English children; pink faced, round cheeked children, flushed under the weight of unaccustomed packs, with their steel helmets on the backs of their heads and straps hanging loosely on their baby rounded chins.'[84]

And look how *tiny* they are. Sure, both in Australia and Great Britain, the previous rule that all soldiers had to be taller than 5 foot 4 inches had been abandoned, and the Brits had even raised whole 'bantam battalions' of wee ones, from 4 foot 10 to 5 foot 4. But in the case of these kids it looks more like they haven't grown yet because they're barely shaving!

Can these kids, come to replace the 5000 veterans of the 8th who had so tragically fallen in the last month, really stop the marauding Germans? Bean would be most surprised.

The 55th Battalion's Edmund Street feels the same when, just before dark on the night of 20 April, it is his job to wait for the Tommies coming forward and lead them to the positions they are to take over from the 55th Battalion. Escorting them through the gloom, he, too, is shocked.

'98% of this Battalion [of the 23rd Brigade] was composed of boys of 18 and 19 years of age. None had ever been in the line before. Fine, wholesome fresh faces, blue-eyed boys they were. I felt sorry for them. I had just turned twenty-one and felt an old man beside them . . .'[85]

Nearly there. The Australian trenches are just up ahead. Which leaves still more time for the kids to ask him ever more questions.

'Are there many shells?'

'Is Jerry going to attack?'

'Will you Australians be near?'

'Is there any barbed wire?'

'These shells landing up ahead and bullets flying – who do you suppose has fired them?'

'And whose flares are going up?'

Street answers all the questions the best he can, as cheerfully as he can.

But the truth?

'I felt a sharp pang of sorrow when they asked me what were the scattered shell holes.'[86]

He has no doubt they are pretty much all 'going to their doom'.[87]
He walks away, shaking his head.

After all, *'Who has fired the bullets and shells we can hear?'* Really? He is convinced they will find out soon enough. And through no fault of their own, they won't last long when they do find out.

———

It is a close call, but of all those appalled at the decision to remove the Australians defending Villers-Bretonneux and replace them with these kids, it is likely the 15th Brigade's Pompey Elliott who is most outraged of all.

Not only have the British decided to replace his men with mere boys, but there are simply not enough of these boys in key positions! Why, Colonel John Scanlan of the 59th Battalion had been holding a key spot in the trenches dug into Bois l'Abbé with all of his 600 men, only to find the Brits had sent forward one sole platoon of the Durham Light Infantry – just 40 men of a pioneer battalion more usually devoted to

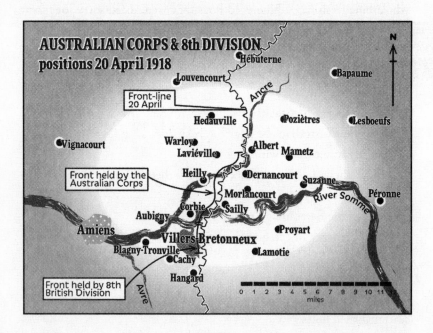

digging trenches than holding them – to replace them! Madness. And dangerous madness for his 15th Brigade specifically, who are defending the Aubigny Line just to the left of Bois l'Abbé. If Bois l'Abbé falls – *when* it falls – then his men will be taking flanking fire from just 200 yards away.

'The security of Bois l'Abbé,' he would note, 'was absolutely vital to the preservation of our position.'[88]

In desperation, Pompey contacts the Commanding Officer of the 5th Division, General Hobbs, and suggests the 59th be sent back to support them, but Hobbs demurs. General Heneker has decided to send forth a platoon of Durhams for that particular trench. So who are the Australians to say they are not happy? In short, Hobbs says it is 'impossible that we should move into the 3rd Corps area to do their job for them'.[89]

Pompey is *not* happy.

Convinced that the lives of his men depend upon it, Pompey – with the reluctant agreement of Hobbs – insists his men put considerable energy into building yet one more trench. This one goes due west from the Aubigny Line and will protect his southern flank once the Germans push through Villers-Bretonneux and further take Bois d'Aquenne and Bois l'Abbé. Between them, Elliott and Hobbs agree that they will tell the British that this trench is for 'communication' purposes, so as to hide the truth.

It is their full expectation that the British will fail to hold both Villers-Bretonneux and the key woods surrounding it, and they want to be ready when that happens.

CHAPTER FIFTEEN
'ALL ROADS LEAD TO STOUSH'

The AIF have hitherto accomplished nothing to be
compared in importance with the work they have in
hand just now . . . we turned the tide that threatened to
sweep over everything to Paris and the sea . . . Australia
should be proud of our boys . . . I was never so proud of
being an Australian as I am today . . . The gallant bearing
and joyous spirit of the men at the prospect of a fight
thrills you through and through . . . you simply cannot
despair or be downhearted, whatever the odds against
you, when you feel their spirits rising the more danger
seems to threaten. It is glorious indeed to be with them.[1]
Brigadier Pompey Elliott of the 15th Brigade
to his wife, Kate, on 17 April 1918

I fear that the English reputation of being 'bulldogs'
is entirely lost. Both here and on the Somme, a few
Australians restored the line the moment they got
in position and had the finest sport of their lives
. . . It is hard to believe but it seems quite clear
the English refused to fight and ran away.[2]
Lieutenant Tom Richards, 1st Battalion, 1st Brigade, 1st Division

MORNING 21 APRIL, MARCHING ON VILLERS-BRETONNEUX

Los! Los! Los!

Get going! Get *going!*

At last, with the arrival of the 77th Reserve Division from Russia, the attacking force is complete. Together with the soldiers of the 228th Division and the 4th Guards Division – some 50,000 troops in all – these men of General Georg von der Marwitz's 2nd Army can begin their march to Villers-Bretonneux, to be ready to launch their attack on the morning of the 23 April.

Los! Los! Los!

This is no walk in the country, for all that. Fully aware of what is at stake, *die Tommys* send over their bombers, and the experience of the 5th Guards Grenadier Regiment, as recorded by their regimental history is typical: 'Whilst 1st and 2nd Companies were marching up the Roman road on the 21st they were attacked by aircraft: Both company commanders, all platoon commanders and twenty other ranks were severely or lightly wounded by bombs.' And even then they are not free of it as, four hours later, just as they're approaching Marcelcave two miles east of Villers-Bretonneux, the British artillery joins in. 'Suddenly British shells fell on the marching column of the 1st Company and there were fresh losses.'[3]

Right behind them, 3rd Company lose 26 members from one devastating shell. Still, the German tide continues to flood forward, ready to engulf Villers-Bretonneux.

———

At Cappy Aerodrome, the Red Baron gives his final briefing. Personally, he is in a very good mood, having just the day before notched up, staggeringly, his *80th* victory. He had been so pleased with the feat that he had flown down low over the German troops so they could see it was indeed him, the nation's hero in his red plane, and cheer him to the echo, throwing their hats and helmets in the air. After he had landed, he smacked his hands together and exulted:

'Donnerwetter! Golly! Eighty is a respectable number.'[4]

And so it is. But not as good as 81 or 82 or . . . perhaps even *100?*

He must shake off the celebrations of yesterday, of course, and focus once more on the task at hand, as must his squadron. There is not even time to think of Käte.

In the wake of Allied airborne attacks on German troops moving into position to attack Villers-Bretonneux, the *Rittmeister* is personally aggrieved, as it is the specific responsibility of *Jagdgeschwader 1* to have stopped exactly this from happening, as the *Landser,* German soldiers, came up along the Roman road towards Villers-Bretonneux. It must not happen again. Today, *JG1* are to patrol along that same section of road leading west to the town and attack any enemy aircraft seen. The German troops *must* be given protection.

Ach so, und noch was . . . One thing more.

Addressing his remark to his young cousin, *Leutnant* Wolfram von Richthofen, the *Rittmeister* tells him that if they get into a dogfight, Wolfram will have to climb and watch from above. Manfred has seen too many young pilots go to their early deaths by engaging in a battle when they are on their first mission or two. He tells his cousin straight out: for the moment, your job is to survive, not fight. And, yes, you have already won the Iron Cross earlier in the war for your bravery on the ground with the 4th Silesian Hussars, but today is a day for caution. (Such is Richthofen's deep affection for Wolfram, he has already booked sleepers on a train for them in a week, so they can take their precious leave together and, for relaxation . . . go hunting for deer in the Black Forest, as they used to before the war.)

So today, Wolfram . . . *kreise oben drüber,* circles above. Watch and learn.

Jawohl.

Moving now outside to where their gaily coloured planes await, all the men are disappointed to see that the fog has not yet lifted, but at least that gives the *Rittmeister's* dear friend and long-time flying companion, *Oberleutnant* Karl Bodenschatz, the chance he has been looking for to take him aside.

Manfred, Bodenschatz says quietly, after all you have accomplished, all the risks you have taken and triumphed over, perhaps it really is time to take up the government's long-time offer and become . . . the Inspector of German Fighter Aviation. With such a role you could place your expertise and prestige at the service of all pilots, seeing that they receive the resources they need, the best training, the best aircraft, not to mention the morale value to Germany by keeping you alive, Manfred.

'A paper-shuffler?' Von Richthofen dismisses his friend's kindly suggestion out of hand. '*Nein!* I'm staying at the front.'[5]

This is where he is meant to be, in the thick of the action, adding to his victories and being with his men, these knights of the sky, with whom there is even a little time for skylarking. When *Leutnant* Richard Wenzl decides to profit from the delay this day by grabbing a quick bit of shut-eye, *ein Schläfchen*, it is the *Rittmeister* himself who tips over his cot, to the high hilarity of all. By way of mock revenge, another pilot ties a wheel chock to the tail of the Richthofen's dog, a superb Great Dane by the name of Moritz. Oh, how they laugh as Moritz runs hither and thither, the wheel chock clanking back and forth. It is all such good fun that Wenzl takes two photos, including one of Richthofen. The photo is highly prized for it is of the rarest kind – the Baron, for once, seems so light and carefree, the worries of his world having lifted this morning with the mist.

The sun has come out.

Within minutes, Baron von Richthofen's Flying Circus is winging its way to the western skies, the Baron's red triplane leading the way. Wolfram's green Fokker Dr.1 with red cowling stays close off his cousin's right wing.

—

Twenty-five miles to the west on this same morning, at Bertangles Aerodrome, Captain Roy Brown is giving his final briefing to 15 pilots of his own unit, the Royal Air Force's No. 209 Squadron – many of whom are fellow Canadians – who are about to fly east over enemy territory.

They are to go on a 'high offensive patrol' at an altitude of some 15,000 feet and make it as far as 20 miles into enemy territory within 'the St Quentin sector', seeking to intercept enemy reconnaissance aircraft before they can cross the lines.

Oh, and one more thing.

Captain Brown now addresses his remarks to the one novice pilot among them, Lieutenant Wilfrid 'Wop' May, who is about to go out on his first actual patrol of his wartime flying career.

Lieutenant May, if we run into any enemy aircraft over there, you are *not* to get involved, are we clear? Watch and learn.

Very clear, sir . . .

No matter that Captain Brown is an old school friend of May's. This is a formal military briefing, in front of their military peers, so at least a rough kind of protocol has to be followed – and all the more so when he needs to make a point. It is not a request to a school friend; it is an order to an underling.

And he means it. At a time when the attrition rate in squadrons is three pilots killed a week, it would be madness for May to join the dogfight before he has learned the slightest thing about aerial combat. No, for now, he must let those among them who are more experienced deal with the threat.

—

It is two hours later on this crisp, clear morning. Two old Australian planes from No. 3 Squadron Australian Flying Corps – RE8s both – are well into their three-hour reconnaissance above enemy territory just east of Villers-Bretonneux. Reports have come in of a build-up of German troops in the area, and their job has been to take many photos, which can be earnestly examined upon their return and compared with photos from the day before. Suddenly, the observer in the lead Australian plane has no sooner spotted a problem – when they are two miles north-east of Villers-Bretonneux, over Hamel, at 7500 feet – than he is furiously slapping his pilot on the shoulder and shouting, 'Huns!'[6]

Oh. Gawd.

Up on high they can see no fewer than nine – count 'em *nine* – multicoloured Fokkers. And look at the colour of the one in the lead – all red.

And now, clearly, just as they have seen the Germans, so too have the Germans seen them. Two of the planes above peel off from the formation and bear down directly upon the Australians. (Only two are dispatched by hand signals from the Red Baron, because that is all the force needed for such easy meat as two old, slow RE8s – the others need not give up the tactical advantage represented by their height unnecessarily.)

Struth!

The observer in the lead Australian aircraft takes out a Very flare pistol from where it is secured on the rack in his cockpit. Snapping it open, he carefully slides a flare cartridge into the breech, points it high into the sky and, with shaking hands – careful to point it well away from the aircraft – cocks the pistol hammer and pulls the trigger.

With a fizz and a whizz swallowed whole by the roar of the engines, the flare shoots skywards, bursting red against the low clouds that abound all around – an urgent SOS to any friendly fighters who might happen to be nearby.

It is something, anyway. But they all know it: short of a miracle, they have little chance of surviving. Their two-seater RE8s are older, slower and notoriously difficult to manoeuvre. But perhaps there is a God, for, sure enough, a miracle indeed appears. It comes, naturally, from the heavens above.

At that instant, Captain Roy Brown's squadron of Sopwith Camels from No. 209 Squadron appears from high altitude to engage the Germans, including the two going after the Australians.

———

Also at this moment, driving east on the Bray–Corbie Road, Bean's great friend, AIF photographer Hubert Wilkins, looks up to see an aerial dogfight of stunning size and intensity with five . . . six . . . hang on, ten, no, more . . . make that 15 . . . and now as many as *30* planes involved! He immediately pulls over.

One of the planes, he notes, is an entirely red triplane . . .

Could it be?

It is.

Rittmeister Manfred von Richthofen is now leading his squadron back to the honeypot of Villers-Bretonneux, which lies near the tip of the big bulge the Germans have made in the Allied lines. The British will be sending reconnaissance planes to Villers, to see if another push towards Amiens is planned, and where there are reconnaissance planes there will be Royal Flying Corps[7] fighters – always the Red Baron's preferred targets – not far behind. And the Flying Circus has found them all right, or, perhaps more to the point, *they* have been found and engaged by *14* Sopwith Camels.

And it really is '*ein erbitterter Luftkampf,* a fierce air battle'.[8] Wilkins and the troops on the ground gaze, awestruck, at these caterwauling, screaming knights of the sky as they twist and turn, side-slip and skid, dive and destroy, and go at each other again and again in something as ferocious as it is, somehow, beautiful – nothing less than an 'aerial ballet'.

And look at the red plane go! And yet . . . what is he doing now, seemingly breaking away?

———

In all the sheer adrenalin-surging excitement of the situation, and despite the admonition of the captain of his squadron that morning – his old schoolmate, Captain Roy Brown – Lieutenant Wilfrid May just can't help himself.

As soon as he saw the dogfight break out with the German planes, he knew it just wasn't in him to leave his comrades behind, to cut and run.

And so he feels justified in ignoring his orders and getting involved . . .

For there, now, he sees one of the German planes, clearly less skilfully flown than the others, hovering above the fight, as is he. This is his chance!

With adrenalin surging, he goes after the green Fokker Dr.1 with red cowling flown by *Leutnant* Wolfram von Richthofen, and even fires his guns at the retreating German.

The Red Baron has been keeping an eye on his cousin from below – the beloved son of his Uncle Wolfram and Aunt Therese – just as his brother Lothar has been keeping an eye on both of them and is first pleased to see young Wolfram break away . . . and then alarmed to see a Sopwith Camel in pursuit! Pulling back on the joystick, Baron von Richthofen puts his Fokker into a steep climb, trying to squeeze out every last ounce of power his *Oberursal Ur II* engine can produce, which is considerable. One of the best features of these new Fokkers is that they can, in von Richthofen's words, 'climb like monkeys'.[9]

—

Goddamn it!

Lieutenant May's twin Vickers machine guns – each of them belt-fed with 500 rounds available when they work – *jam,* as they are ever wont to do.

Lieutenant May keeps pressing the triggers furiously, praying they will release, but achieves nothing.

His previous bravado instantly disappears, and he suddenly realises what he is up against. Now, *now* he is sure that discretion really is the better part of valour and it is time to get away. Within seconds he has dived out of the battle and is racing to the west, back to his own lines.

Alas, the young Canadian had not yet learned enough to know that a plane of his type, flying at that speed and altitude, on its own, away from a dogfight, suddenly transforms into the equivalent of a fat chicken in a farmyard waddling away from a ravenous fox with a toothache . . .

—

Manfred von Richthofen's Fokker is closing fast now, moving in for the kill. He simply swoops from on high, hurtling downwards, accelerating all the while, embarked on a flight to the death. He watches with satisfaction as the Sopwith Camel starts to loom large in his gun-sights . . .

Unbeknownst to the Red Baron, however, disengaging from the dogfight at that moment just above him is Captain Roy Brown, and therein lies a tale. For while Brown is an accomplished pilot – with six victories of his own to his credit – never in his adult life has he been in worse shape than now, as the strain of days and now months dealing in life and death has taken its toll. In the last two months he has lost 25 pounds, his eyes are permanently bloodshot and, though he is still only 24 years old, his hair has suddenly gone grey. All this, and he is recovering from a recent case of food poisoning. Completely exhausted, his friends have insisted he must go and see the squadron doctor and ask for a break.

Most of this is forgotten as Brown sums up the situation in an instant. His Sopwith Camel hurtles down after the Red Baron in the hope that he can prevent the certain death of his compatriot and old school friend.

Rally, School!

—

Ruhig, ruhig, ruhig . . . Steady, steady, steady . . .

Just a few hundred feet from his target now, as the neat green quilt of the French farmlands loom before him, the Red Baron is doing what he always does in such circumstances – holding his fire until he just can't miss. Other pilots are satisfied if they hit any part of an enemy plane, but not him. A student of his art, he knows that at the front of any aircraft is a vulnerable area that contains the fuel tank, pilot and engine, in that order from the rear. Of those, the most vulnerable thing is the pilot, and that is the bullseye he always aims for, knowing that with just one bullet in the right spot, he will win. Five hundred feet away now . . . 400 . . . 300 . . . 200 . . .

As ever, his finger tightens on the trigger and the twin Spandaus suddenly leap into life, his whole plane vibrating in a pleasing fashion. Amazingly, however, this time his first burst of fire doesn't bring his quarry down.

But Lieutenant May knows he is there, all right, and looks around to see a red triplane right on his hammer!

OH.

Holy Mother of God . . .

For *Rittmeister* Manfred von Richthofen, however, things have suddenly become problematical.

The Camel pilot, now warned that he is under attack, begins desperate evasive actions, twisting and turning clumsily from side to side and going ever lower, racing for the Allied lines with every ounce of speed he can muster from his tortured engine. In terms of performance capacity, the Sopwith Camel and the Fokker *Dr.1* have maximum speeds of about 113 miles per hour, with the slight edge going to the Camel, but the fact that Lieutenant May is so inexperienced means that narrow advantage is much more than neutralised.

The Red Baron, embracing the chase, follows closely, anticipating every move the Sopwith pilot makes before he makes it. Yet he keeps getting it wrong! Time and again von Richthofen fires where the terrified young Canadian pilot *would* have been, had May been experienced, only to find that he isn't there . . . *He isn't there!*

Time after time, the Red Baron fires off a burst . . . . only to find that . . . . his target has moved an instant earlier in an entirely unexpected direction.[10]

'I didn't know what I was doing myself,' May would recount, 'and I do not suppose Richthofen could figure out what I was going to do.'[11]

Worse for the Red Baron, the two planes have now flashed over Australian lines, towards 11th Australian Brigade HQ. Pushed along by an unusual easterly wind, which nudges the German along from behind and likely puts him much further into the dangerous west than he has realised – the German pursuer is now the intruder, not the Canadian.

From well above, another pilot from the Flying Circus, Hans Wolff, is not quite as bemused as he is concerned.

'I looked . . .' he would recount, 'and saw that he was at an extremely low altitude over the Somme near Corbie, right behind an Englishman. I shook my head instinctively and wondered why [our leader] was following an opponent so far on the other side.'[12]

If *der Rittmeister* does realise that he is above enemy guns, it is surprising that he continues the fight. For his previous admonition to his fellow pilots, that *one should never obstinately stay with an opponent who, through bad shooting or skilful turning, one has been unable to shoot down, when the battle lasts until it is far on the other side of the front and one is alone and faced by a greater number of opponent*,[13] seems now forgotten. (Which is doubly surprising, as Richthofen had only submitted his writing for that textbook to *Generalfeldmarschall* von Hindenburg's Supreme HQ just two days earlier.)

He is not only breaching his own dictum but, even worse, he is flying just 100 feet above enemy trenches now, breaking *das oberste Gebot*, the Cardinal Rule to beat them all.

But with the blood-lust upon him, compounded by his frustration at not yet bringing his quarry down, knowing that another victory is only a second or two away, the Red Baron stays right on the tail of Lieutenant May as the Canadian twists and turns up the valley of the Somme River, just 50 feet above the surface of the water.

———

Oh . . . *God*.

Though May momentarily thinks that he has shaken the German, he is shocked to find that his pursuer has simply hopped over a hill on a river bend and is now coming down on him. This time, there is no escape. This time, trapped by the sides of the narrow valley, he can't dart to the left or to the right. He is as good as dead. The Canadian tenses, waiting for the blast he knows is coming, and even wonders if he should end it himself by jamming the stick forward and hitting the river.

—

A deadly burst of fire rings out, tearing into the aircraft's wings.

The Red Baron had just been coming in to fire off his own deadly final burst at the Camel, knowing he can't miss, when . . .

Suddenly he sees the couple of tears in his wing.

Mein Gott.

Now, *he* is under attack from above! Taking instant evasive action, he twists the red Fokker triplane away, which, as fate would have it, takes him towards a hill held by the AIF's 53rd Battery of the 5th Division.

Atop this particular hill, an Australian artilleryman by the rank and name of Gunner Robert Buie – an oyster farmer before the war, from Brooklyn, just north of Sydney – has watched the whole distant dogfight with fascination and is now amazed to see the red plane that had broken away from the scramble to pursue a Camel heading in his rough direction. It is soon only a few hundred feet away, at an altitude of just 50 feet or so! This is too good an opportunity to miss, and Buie has not been prone to miss a target that close, ever since those days growing up on the Hawkesbury River, when he had honed his shooting skills by knocking sea eagles out of the sky when they tried to steal fish from his net.

Aiming his Lewis gun upwards, he fires at the plane, just as from a nearby hill Sergeant Cedric Popkin of the Australian 24th Machine Gun Company fires his Vickers machine gun . . .

'I observed at once that my fire took effect,'[14] Popkin would later tell Bean, backed up by the No. 2 on his Vickers, Private Rupert Weston.

Nearby, still another Australian soldier fires a Lee-Enfield .303 at the plane . . . and yet *another* Australian, Gunner 'Snowy' Evans, also fires a burst from his Lewis gun.

In the end, there is no doubt that a blizzard of bullets is whizzing around, and into, the Fokker. Nevertheless, Robert Buie, for one, is absolutely certain that his bullets hit right where the German is sitting, as he can see the fragments from the cockpit flying off as he keeps shooting . . . Gunner Frank Wormald, standing just four yards from Buie, is also sure that it is Buie's bullets that hit the red plane, and later recounted that he could see, 'plain as daylight . . . the Baron sort of shrug and sit up. I could *see* him'.[15]

Yet one more witness is the sapper William Dadswell, who is right there at the time, not 200 yards away: 'We thought our poor chap had had it but as they flew fairly low over a battery of guns, a machine gun opened up and we saw the German plane going down.'[16]

An instant after the fusillade of bullets flies forth, the Red Baron's plane – for so long a bright red streak of death, the terror of the western skies – suddenly staggers in the air, slows and then quickly turns, beginning a rapid descent.

Unfortunately, George Wilkins misses this final part of the action. He is still back on the Bray–Corbie Road, and it had been a few moments earlier that the red Fokker had 'side-slipped' downwards behind a hill, momentarily obscuring the photographer's vision. Wilkins does not witness the Red Baron's plane finally coming to ground 'like a wounded bird', right in front of the men of the 33rd Australian Field Artillery Battery of the 5th Division, who are dug in on the high ground west of Morlancourt Ridge and peeping over their sand bags. As soon as they are sure there are no more German planes coming their way, spitting death, some of the Diggers rush forward and . . .

And Christ almighty! His bus is 'bright red and very light, rotary engine, single prop',[17] just like . . .

It couldn't be, could it?

They find the pilot slumped in his cockpit, barely alive if at all, and certainly dead within seconds.

It is 11.45 am on a cool, windy day.

'A fair haired rather good looking pilot'[18] rests before them. Going through his pockets, they find his name on papers he is carrying:

Rittmeister Freiherr M. von Richthofen[19]

Stone the bloody crows . . .

It really *is* von Richthofen!

They have got him at last![20]

'Richthofen's Flight,' a thrilled General Monash would note, 'circled around overhead four or five times and then majestically flew away. Such was the requiem for this doughty warrior.'[21]

In fact, there is another tribute, with the 14th Australian Infantry Brigade war diary of Gunner Robert Buie and Gunner Snowy Evans noting proudly:

> 21 April. The division was fortunate in disposing of the enemy's most famous airman today, BARON VON RICHTHOFEN, who was crashed by one of the A.A. Lewis of the 53rd Battery. There was considerable controversy of who was the owner of the bag, but indisputable evidence was produced confirming that the battery mentioned was responsible.[22]

———

High in the sky, Lieutenant Alec S. Paterson, the observer of the third plane of the Australian reconnaissance patrol – which had been behind the other two when they'd struck the Flying Circus – had watched the engagement right to the point where 'the two planes disappeared into a haze over the Somme Valley near Corby . . .'[23]

He is fearful for the fate of the Sop, but mightily relieved to see it, and only it, emerge from the haze a few minutes later. Having by now completed their patrol, the Australians fly back to their aerodrome at Poulainville, where they are startled to find mechanics rushing up to them the second the engine is cut, wanting to know who shot down the Baron.

'It was the first intimation we had that Von Richthofen was the Pilot of the German plane: they also stated that our [truck] had gone to bring in his remains.'[24]

For Captain Lothar Richthofen, the situation is, of course, the exact opposite. 'I looked around for [my brother], but saw no-one else except *Oberleutnant* Karjus . . . Then I became a bit uneasy, as I certainly should have seen [my brother]. We circled the area for a time . . . but of [my brother] there was no trace.'[25]

———

At his residence in Amiens, Charles Bean notes the result of his key interview on the subject: *Aust Major-General James Harold Cannan, from Townsville, commander of 11th Brig of 3rd Div . . . is convinced it was our Lewis gunner who shot him down.*[26]

———

Wo ist der Rittmeister?

All of Baron von Richthofen's squadron has returned safely from their mission to their aerodrome at Cappy, but from the first there is concern that the Baron's plane is *nicht*, not among those returning.

A group of anxious mechanics and pilots soon gathers by the small wooden hut by the aerodrome's canvas hangars that serve as the communications centre, hoping that a phone call will came from one of the front-line units: *haben Sie keine Angst*, don't be afraid, we have him and he is safe. But no call comes. All they can do for the moment is earnestly gaze to the western skies, straining their ears, praying for that famous red speck to appear in the distance. Quick discussion among the pilots establishes that the Baron was last seen in pursuit of a Camel, flying low and to the west over enemy lines. Lothar von Richthofen – to whom they all defer with elaborate sensitivity, so devastated is he – has seen that himself.

They wait, and wait, but there is nothing.

Finally, in desperation, the pilots Wenzl, Wolfram and Karjus take off once more and fly to the last spot their leader was seen, hoping for some sign, even red wreckage on the ground that might indicate his fate.

As they take off, the phone starts ringing!

Alas, it proves to be senior officers wanting to know the situation. A report is circulating that *der Rittmeister* is missing. Is it true?

Ja, it is true. The greatest hero in Germany is missing and has, in all likelihood, been shot down.

After two hours, Wenzl, Wolfram and Karjus return, and again the others crowd round, even before they have turned off their engines, praying for a miracle. But, no, they have seen nothing.

—

Of course, the news spreads even more quickly on the Allies' side, powered by the confirmed news that Richthofen has actually, definitely, been killed.

Corporal Noel Keating of 13th Battalion records in his diary:

> *Rather an exciting message came through during the morning. Capt Baron von Reichtofen the famous Hun airman who claims so many victims of our English aviators was shot to the ground by one of our Brigade Gunners. A bullet had passed thro' his body and he crashed to the ground.*[27]

—

In desperation for some news, *any* news, General Georg von der Marwitz, the commander of the 2nd Army, even gives permission for a radio message to be sent to the British in plain, uncoded text: RITTMEISTER VON RICHTHOFEN LANDED ON YOUR SIDE, REQUEST NEWS ABOUT HIS FATE.[28]

With no reply, one of von Richthofen's fellow pilots, who had been with him on the last mission, *Leutnant* Hans Joachim Wolff, writes a note to Lothar, giving details of their optimism.

After all, reports had come in that 'a red triplane had landed smoothly north-west of Corbie . . . There were two possibilities . . . the engine had quit [or] shots fired from the ground had hit the engine. But he had to be alive . . . Indeed we were happy for his parents, who would be able to see their great son again after the war.'[29]

And yet, for *Oberleutnant* Karl Bodenschatz – who had tried to persuade Manfred to take the desk job that very morning – a dreadful certainty grows. Alive or dead, the *Rittmeister* is not going to magically reappear. Their absolute best hope is that he has been taken prisoner, otherwise they would have heard by now.

A cold wind of doom strengthens from that most hated direction.

'This thrice accursed east wind! It drives everything that can no longer resist it to the west, towards France. And anyone whose engine failed will be driven by it, [and] without the east wind, it would have been possible for him . . . but such dreams are futile.'[30]

Reluctantly, but knowing it is now his duty, *Oberleutnant* Bodenschatz goes to the *Rittmeister's* quarters and retrieves the small metal box he knows Manfred has left, with instructions that it is to be opened if he does not return. Taking out the grey envelope that lies within, and removing the note dated 10 March 1918, he reads:

Should I not return then *Oberleutnant* Reinhard
should succeed to command of the squadron.[31]

Once notified, *Oberleutnant* Reinhard dispatches Bodenschatz to go and tell *der Rittmeister's* father, Major Albrecht von Richthofen – who is the garrison commander at Lille, some 20 miles away – that his son is missing.

And who will tell the Red Baron's mother, and his nurse and love, Käte Otersdorf?

That remains to be seen.

—

Among those waiting closely on events is Crown Prince Rupprecht, who refuses to believe Richthofen could have been shot down but notes in his diary:

'Yesterday Captain von Richthofen achieved his 80th victory in the air. Today he had to, because of engine defect, land on the enemy's side, gliding down. The loss of Richthofen is extremely painful for us: the sight of[32] his dreaded red airplane appeared alone intimidating to the enemy aircraft.' [33]

—

And now the body of Baron von Richthofen has been brought back to the aerodrome where the Australian No. 3 Squadron are, and many of the pilots, observers and mechanics crowd around to look at this legend of the skies.

'He was about 5 foot 7,' Lieutenant Alec Paterson records, 'well proportioned, fair hair closely cropped and small hands and feet and although dead, had a smile on his face... I noticed several small punctures in his face apparently caused by small splinters off a bullet which had probably hit the metal work of his plane and a larger wound about the size that would be caused by a .303 bullet in the lower part of his chest and travelling upwards in the direction of his heart, but I did not see any other injury.'[34]

Another small parenthesis here. Paterson's testimony was one of many that the bullet appeared to have come from *below*, not above. That very afternoon an autopsy is held, which shows that the German pilot who had personally shot down 126 Allied airmen in 80 aircraft had himself been killed by a single bullet that had entered his body below his right armpit towards his back, gone through his heart, and exited next to his left nipple. The direction that the bullet came from is crucial to the controversy that would rage for the next century as to who, precisely, killed the Red Baron. The fact that the bullet came from below and from the side is firm indication that it was fired by one of the Australians, rather than the Canadian pilot, the worthy Captain Roy Brown, who was awarded the official victory for shooting him down. Close parenthesis.[35]

At the completion of the autopsy, the body of Manfred von Richthofen is treated with elaborate ritual and respect. As his hands are joined on his chest in the supplicatory biblical pose that his mother would surely want. The commanding officer of the Australian Flying Corps' No. 3 Squadron, Major David Blake, bears responsibility for organising a full military funeral, and he does so with great care.

That evening the Red Baron effectively lies 'in state', in an open coffin in one of No. 3 Squadron's hangars, and a long line of his former opponents and many of their ground crew come by to pay their final respects. Yes, he had killed many of their comrades, but he had been an honourable opponent and had only done to the Allied pilots what they had been trying to do to him. In their deadly common calling, he was the best.

—

Late that night, Corporal Mechanic Joe Porter of No. 3 Squadron Australian Flying Corps can barely believe it. Manfred von Richthofen is the most famous person in the war, and now, he's been told, the German pilot is right here in a hangar at Bertangles Aerodrome, his body being guarded by his own mates!

Of course those mates let him in to have a gander. Another soldier who had gazed on the pilot's body would report, 'He looked very insignificant lying there in his plain stained overalls,'[36] but Joe's primary emotion is one of awe. And he notices something that interests him: von Richthofen's very fine boots, which are clearly handmade and of the finest leather. Even *more* interesting? They look to be about Joe's size!

A few minutes later, Joe walks away with an unaccustomed swagger, in the footsteps of a legend, with some very big boots to fill.

And Manfred von Richthofen lies there, still, now wearing the boots of Joe Porter of Morningside, Brisbane.[37]

—

Yet another visitor before the body of the Red Baron on this night is the Canadian fighter pilot Captain Roy Brown.

'He looked so friendly, blond, silk-soft hair, like that of a child fell from the broad high forehead. His face, particularly peaceful, had an expression of gentleness, goodness, of refinement. Suddenly I felt miserable, desperately unhappy, as if I had committed an injustice . . . I went away. I didn't feel like a victor.'[38]

Later, Brown would write to his parents in Canada: 'They had a medical examination of the body. It is a terrible thing when you think of it that they should examine the body to see who should have the credit of killing him. What I saw that day shook me up quite a lot as it was the first time I have seen a man whom I know I have killed.'[39]

22 APRIL 1918, RUPPRECHT ARMY GROUP HQ, MONS, EIN 'NEIN' FOR AN IMMEDIATE ATTACK ON VB

Ja. Ja. Ja. Nein. Ja. Nein. Nein.

Die Kronprinz Rupprecht puts the phone down, disappointed but not surprised, with the news subsequently recorded in his diary.

The attack of the 2nd Army at Villers-Bretonneux–Cachy was postponed to 24 April due to the very slow progress of the Munitionierung, ammunitioning.[40]

—

'We stood to attention as six of our pilots carried [the Baron] out to the car,'[41] one of the Australian Flying Corps mechanics would recall of the scene as Richthofen's body is moved from where he had been examined to where he would be buried at Bertangles Cemetery.

To bear the coffin of Baron von Richthofen, Major David Blake has chosen six captains of the Australian Flying Corps – the same rank as von Richthofen. An honour guard from the other ranks is also formed, comprising 14 Australian soldiers in service dress, and each of these men uses spit and Blanco to be impeccable for the occasion. Respectful attention to detail has been maintained to the point that, courtesy of three squadron mechanics, Richthofen's coffin even bears 'a small zinc plate'[42] inscribed in English and German, nailed to the top.

> Cavalry Captain Baron Von Richthofen
> Aged 25
> Killed in Aerial combat
> Sailley-le-Sec Somme France
> 21-4-18.[43]

There are three wreaths, one of which has been offered by the Australian 5th Division HQ, with flowers in the German Empire colours of black, white and red, and a card that reads: To a worthy and valiant foe[44]. The other two wreaths are from the Royal Air Force and the Australian Flying Corps' No. 3 Squadron.

Yes, there are some private quibbles among those present, noting, 'It seemed a downright shame that such a fuss should be made over an enemy airman.' But even they acknowledge, 'Our men say he always fought fair.'[45]

The men stand to attention as the Baron is laid beneath the sod in the overgrown Bertangles Cemetery, with the propeller of an RE8 plane serving as the cross at the head of the grave. As a final salute, a 14-man firing party thunders a three-volley salute. Photos are taken, and copies of these will be dropped by an English pilot above a German aerodrome, together with a note confirming von Richthofen's death.

> To the German Flying Corps,
>
>   Rittmeister Baron Manfred von Richthofen was killed in aerial combat on April 21st 1918. He was buried with full military honours.
>
>   From,
>
>   British Royal Air Force.[46]

This respect proffered by the Allies does not extend to the French villagers, who, that evening, desecrate the grave – scattering the flowers and destroying the cross – under the erroneous impression that Richthofen had personally carried out the night bombings against them that had killed so many of their number. In response, the mechanics of the Australian Flying Squadron fashion a new cross while General John Monash thunders his disgust to the local mayor. Monash makes clear that if any such thing happens again, the Australian Corps headquarters will be moved away from Bertangles. The mayor understands the threat that the village economy will suffer a severe blow if the Australians leave.

There is no more desecration.

—

Major Wilhelm Haenhelt of the 2nd Army Air Staff breaks the news to the pilots of *JG1*, with a singularly heavy heart: *Der Rittmeister ist tot*, dead.

They have received confirmation from the English that he had been shot down and killed the previous morning.

'If the fatal shot came from the ground,' *Leutnant* Hans Wolff would record, 'then he could no longer land a tri-plane smoothly. But there were Australians who had seen how the British shot [him] down . . . No, it was not to be imagined . . .'[47]

—

At rest once more in the tiny French village of Quiquery on this day – his unit has been going back and forth with the ebb and flow of battle – *Leutnant* Herbert Sulzbach sees another version of the Army bulletin that had gone out three weeks earlier. 'A high reward has been offered by a very senior person for information . . . leading to the whereabouts . . . of a pilot in Flying Group 29.'[48]

He has been meaning to check that out. A month earlier, he had seen a burned-out German plane just by the old Roman road, on the way to Villers-Bretonneux. Could that be the same one? As that spot is no more than a couple hundred yards from where he now sits, Herbert decides to go and have a quick look.

Sure enough, the grave is still there beside the wreck. And on the back of the fuselage he sees that the identification mark mentioned in the Army Order is the same.

Gott im Himmel. Searching the wreckage, he finds a small silver purse, undoubtedly belonging to one of the crew. Racing back to his battery headquarters at Nesle, he quickly gets the message through by *Funkentelegraph*, wireless telegraph, and soon hears the astonishing news. He has discovered the final resting place of none other than the stepson of the most powerful man in the German Army, General Erich Ludendorff.

—

Herr General . . .?

Herr General, I beg to report . . .

I beg to report, the wreck of Lieutnant Erich Pernet's plane has been found. Ashen-faced, General Ludendorff immediately orders a car to be ready straightaway – *Schnell!* – so that he may go there personally to identify the body of dear Erich.

Ludendorff picks up the phone with a heavy hand. For the second time in just over six months, he calls his wife to break her heart. The ringtone cuts short as Margarethe answers and then slightly fumbles the receiver. Even in a situation like this, Ludendorff shuns pleasantries and gets straight to it.

'The local commander at Nesles,' he tells her, incapable of softening such news, 'reports they have discovered the grave of two unknown aviation officers in his area.'[49]

Margarethe Ludendorff's heart shatters in an instant, just as her husband had known it would, and whatever she says is incoherent. General Ludendorff hangs up the phone, walks outside and hops in the car. He doesn't utter a word.

Overhead, as ever, there is the familiar drone of planes, never more frequent than right now, as both sides send droves of squadrons forward to fight, harass and reconnoitre.

But how lucky *those* pilots are to still be alive!

Two hours later, the General arrives at an open field by the village of Nesle, where a group of grim-faced German officers await, snapping to attention the instant Ludendorff emerges from the car. They lead him to an open grave, just 50 yards away, at the head of which is a makeshift wooden cross. Ludendorff bends down to read it: Here rest two German flying officers.[50]

They lead him another few steps away, where two lumps are visible under an otherwise flat tarpaulin. One of the officers leans down and lifts back one end, revealing the two bodies, still in shrouds.

General Ludendorff – with his hat removed – catches his breath as one of his men pulls back 'the linen, which the Englishmen had wrapped him in',[51] to reveal the beloved face and slender, boyish body underneath.

Now one cannot become a great General without at least a certain iciness in the soul. One must be able to take decisions that send thousands of good men to their deaths and not be overly troubled. It has to be done. Someone has to bear responsibility for the decision, and you have become that man for many reasons, including that sliver of iciness. General Ludendorff is all that and more.

But there is an enormous difference between taking decisions in HQs distant from the battle, filled with maps, orderlies and hovering officers, and this . . . gazing down on to the face of one he loves so well, 'my son'.

The General does not cry out, but the emotion nearly overwhelms him.

After a month in the French soil, Erich's skin is a blotchy, putrescent green – while the rest is badly burned – but, there is no doubt.

It is my *Piekchen*. It is my little spike.

And the English have cared for him, wrapping him in that linen shroud, closing his eyes and crossing his hands on his chest. In those hands the General recognises the scarf that his wife had so lovingly knitted for him, a gift before he returned from his last leave.

So many wonderful memories. Such terrible tragedy.

Finally, Ludendorff walks away, snapping off an order as he goes for the body to be brought with him to his HQ at Avesnes. Once arrived, General Ludendorff, staying close to his dead son, oversees the body being reinterred, 'under laurel trees and flowering plants. Here he slept, while outside roared the guns, and the fighting continued raging.'[52]

Within the hour, General Erich Ludendorff writes to Margarethe, giving her details of the discovery and adding, 'One thing I can tell you, I have had the boy to love. The last we had time together, he even told me, "Father, I have had a beautiful youth" . . .'[53]

Finally, the German General stops all of this self-indulgence. Settles himself. The war calls, as it is always calling. There is much to be done.

Tomorrow morning, among many other actions, the German forces will be attacking Villers-Bretonneux, hopefully not only taking it but *keeping* it.

———

What the *blazes* is that?

A pilot in a British reconnaissance plane on this afternoon, flying above the area east of Hangard Wood, looks down to see something more than passing strange.

They are large 'square objects, thought to be wagons',[54] though he cannot be quite sure. What else the hell could they be?

Roaring forth like the blitzing, bristling behemoth it is, *Leutnant* Wilhelm Biltz's lead tank, *Nixe,* ushers forward the rest of his section as they get into their *Ausgangsstellungen,* initial position, behind Lancer Wood, ready for the battle that is to come on the morrow. They are part of a *Sturm Panzerkraftwagen Abteilungen,* Armoured Assault Vehicle Detachment, of 14 tanks – less one that has broken down two miles earlier – which is to be deployed for the attack, operating in four groups. Biltz's group is the southern-most of the four. The main group, including the tank called *Mephisto,* moves into cover in the fields west of Marcelcave.

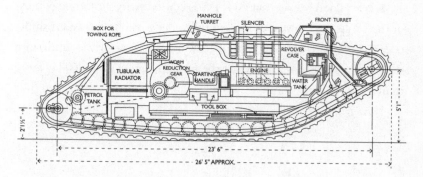

The British tank, Mark IV, used at Villers-Bretonneux

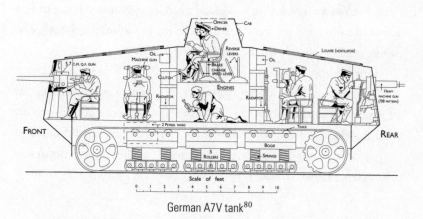

German A7V tank[80]

The tanks have been unloaded from the train at Guillaucourt, five miles east of Villers-Bretonneux, and perhaps it would have been wiser to move them forward by night to avoid reconnaissance. But it is now a matter of urgency to get them forward, come what may. Not for nothing do the impressed German soldiers give the noisy brutes a wide berth as they roar by. Just look at them! These massive A7V machines are 24-feet long, 10-feet wide, 11-feet high and weigh 35 tons, in part courtesy of the inch-thick armour that covers them. The only thing that can move such a mechanical mass is two Daimler-Benz 100-horse-power, four-cylinder engines, but they do it well, with the tanks able to rise to a maximum speed of ten miles per hour on the road and four miles per hour going cross-country. Yes, extraordinary machines, but very hot and shockingly uncomfortable in the interior.

It is for good reason that on this unaccustomedly pleasant day most of the 18-strong crew sit atop the tanks, enjoying the spring sunshine, occasionally banging on the roof to warn the poor driver inside of a shell hole up ahead – as they are the natural enemy of tanks, far more than mere soldiers.

Vorwärts! Vorwärts!

—

Flying on, the pilot in the British reconnaissance plane now sees something even more interesting . . . A long grey caterpillar is making its way across the shattered terrain. He looks closer . . . Could that be what he thinks it is? Nosing down, he realises it is exactly that.

German troops!

Thousands of them, a grey swarm moving west, clearly building for an assault. It is the job of the observers now to estimate how many columns there are and their length, so an estimate can be made of exactly how many soldiers are on the march. (The preliminary estimate is somewhat easier: '*Heaps.*')

—

Meanwhile, in the trenches around Villers-Bretonneux, and just to the west where the British reserves are situated, there are even more significant signs that the Germans are preparing to do something. These include several gas shells landing on the outskirts of Aubigny throughout the day and then, at 6 pm, simply 'raining into the village a hundred a minute'.[55]

Donning their gasmasks is not enough, and the Australians must actually abandon Aubigny for the moment and get into the open fields where the air is clear.

Corporal Herbert Harris of the 55th Battalion – a one-time lift operator at Sydney's Grace Brothers department store – notes in his diary, '[It is] a couple of hours after he has finished before we can go back. The buildings are being knocked silly. Got back at 10-30 p.m.'[56]

Returning to Aubigny, it is Harris who finds himself on the first two-hour shift as 'Gas Guard', charged specifically with sounding the warning if another gas attack comes. An empty shell case hangs on a rope from a branch. He is given a huge spanner and told at the first whiff of gas that he must beat the shell case like a mad thing.

There is practically no doubt that the Germans will soon be coming at the Allies. Nosing around in 5th Divisional HQ, Charles Bean is informed as much. After a day in which movement had been reported on all the roads to the east that lead to Villers-Bretonneux, 'The attack is expected tomorrow morning.'[57]

It worries Bean, and he is far from certain that those fresh-faced British boys he had seen a couple of days earlier would actually be able to hold anything against a concerted veteran German attack. These kids are so young they even wear their helmets on the back of their heads, as it is the only way their slender necks, like young chickens heading to the slaughterhouse, can bear the weight.

—

General George Grogan is equally certain that the Germans are about to attack and carefully oversees his young soldiers of the British 8th Division's 23rd Brigade as they move forward to relieve their brother

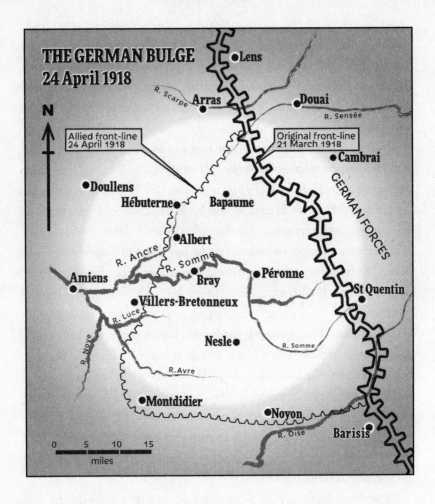

brigade, which has been there for the last two days, and take over the front-line positions right in front of Monument Wood.

Yes, 8th Division HQ has specifically warned him that 'a heavy attack is believed to be imminent next morning',[58] but Grogan is not particularly worried.

'The troops,' he would recount, 'though very young and quite new to the game . . . were in very good spirits. The trenches we took over were good, and all ranks were confident that we would be able to hold our own.'[59]

—

Baroness von Richthofen can barely stand it. First she had heard two days ago that Manfred had been missing, then that he had survived and been captured by the English. And *now*? She knows not. Only that her son has been the talk of all Germany since, that her phone never stops ringing, that rumours continue to swirl, that every minute feels like an hour . . . and that she must *will* herself to keep going, to not do what she most wants to do, which is simply collapse. And now the mailman has come and she must retrieve the enormous bundle of letters he has deposited. Just outside her gate, a large group of children is standing, staring with their large round eyes.

Composed as best she can, she walks down the garden path to the mailbox, only to hear one child say, clearly, 'Is it true then, *Frau Baroness*, that the *Herr Rittmeister* has fallen?'

The Baroness stops, stricken.

'What kind of nonsense do you speak?' she asks the child. 'The *Herr Rittmeister* is captured – but not fallen.'[60]

'But it is posted on *The Ring*,' the child persists, naming a local publication, 'with a thick black band around it.'

'Who said that?' the Baroness screams. 'Have you seen it?'

'My brother told me.'[61]

Rushing back inside, she snatches up the telephone, asking to be put through to the local newspaper: 'The *Rundschau*, please!'

But the journalists have all gone home, and a call to the post office only reveals that no telegram of that nature has been received . . . but . . . there is something in the man's voice that sounds guarded, hesitant . . . Is it pity, sadness?

'Get me the *Bürgermeister*, mayor, please!'[62] she now insists, her sense of dread rising still further.

It takes some time, and the Mayor is even more hesitant, but finally it comes out. Both local papers have in fact brought out extra editions bearing the news that Manfred has been confirmed . . . killed . . .

The Mayor's voice slowly . . . fades away. . .

The Baroness stands there, completely numb, unable to move or scream, even to collapse. And now the young girl who has come to help with the house steps towards her and silently, but with infinite sorrow, hands her the extra edition of one of the papers, indeed with the front page ringed with black, and the big headline blacker still:

'𝕽ittmeister 𝕱reiherr von 𝕽ichthofen
dead[63]

> *Berlin, 23 April. Official. On April 21, Rittmeister Manfred Freiherr von Richthofen did not return from a patrol along the Somme... By the English report, Richthofen was buried in a churchyard in the area of his landing place on April 22, with military honours...[64]*

She stares at it for seconds that turn into minutes that seem like hours, still trying to grasp the contents.

'Manfred is dead... My boy is dead... I am alive... Manfred is dead.'[65]

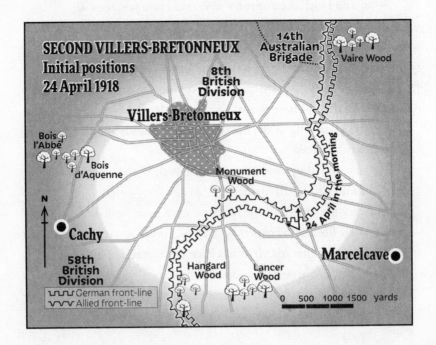

CHAPTER SIXTEEN

THE SECOND BATTLE OF VILLERS-BRETONNEUX

> Villers-Bretonneux is most important and
> Rawlinson told Monash that he had staked
> his reputation on our keeping it.[1]
> *Charles Bean in his diary entry on 22 April 1918*

> The Diggers comprised a civilisation picked up and
> transported 12,000 miles from home. We were a piece
> of Australia in a foreign land, and we naturally formed
> a community, always ready to fraternise and enjoy life
> to the full, but always a piece of Australia in France.[2]
> *Edmund Street, a runner in the 55th Battalion, writing in his diary*
> *while at the front-line at Villers-Bretonneux, mid-April 1918*

EVENING, 23 APRIL 1918, BOIS L'ABBÉ, STEEL RABBITS IN THE WOODS

The drone of the planes goes all night long.

It is Fritz, flying high over Amiens and surrounds, dropping bombs and sowing havoc, as he is ever wont to do, perhaps softening the Allies for a blow about to fall?

'I counted 16 searchlights stabbing the sky looking for him,'[3] one

Digger will recount, but it is all in vain. Even when they spot Fritz, he is too high for the Ack-Ack gun to reach.

Ah, but at least to a certain extent Fritz can see them as reconnaissance planes continue to drop Very lights, which slowly float down and illuminate the countryside nearly as bright as day. And it is not just those who are caught in the open for whom it is a problem.

Hiding under green camouflage nets in the gas-drenched wood of Bois l'Abbé, just to the west of Villers-Bretonneux, are three British tanks that have been moved into position against the possibility of a German attack.

Under the command of Lieutenant Frank Mitchell, they are British Mark IVs, one 'male' and two 'females' of No. 1 Section, A Company, 1st Battalion Tank Corps. That is, while the male tank has two six-pounder guns protruding from its sides – capable of firing artillery shells – and three Lewis guns, the female tank simply has five Lewis guns protruding from all sides and is designed as an anti-infantry armament *par excellence*. And all of those armaments protruding from their sides now show up as two German planes flying very low over the woods drop flares in their midst to get a good look at them, which, as Mitchell would recount, 'showed up the bulky outlines of the tanks in vivid relief. We were discovered!'[4]

This is a real problem. Beyond everything else, the intent had been to use these tanks as part of what is known as the tactic of 'the savage rabbit',[5] whereby, once the enemy soldiers are surging forward, the tanks suddenly emerge from their 'burrows' to destroy them. Now all element of surprise is lost, and they will just have to do the best they can, to follow the orders they've been given, to 'prevent the enemy from gaining a foothold in the Cachy Switch'.[6]

As a precaution, fearing that Fritz will give them some extra attention now that he knows they are here, Mitchell – who, though just 23 years old and a former bank clerk from Guernsey in the Channel Islands is already a tank veteran, having switched from the infantry in 1916 and going on to first command a tank in the Cambrai attack in November 1917 – gives his own orders. The men must move the tanks away from where they are now.

'An hour later,' Mitchell would later recount, 'when clouds hid the moon, three huge, toad-like forms, grunting and snorting, crept out of the wood to a spot some hundred yards to the rear.'[7]

Mitchell and his men then return to their previous sleeping spots. For they are not out of the woods yet.

———

This night sees the end of the old pre-war Villers-Bretonneux. In the first attempt to capture the town, almost three weeks ago, the German artillery had avoided destroying all the houses, thinking they'd be useful to shelter their own troops after the battle. The Red Château, presumably earmarked for a generals' headquarters, was spared. But now the gloves were off. A thousand high-explosive shells an hour pummelled the streets, and by dawn a battered but intact town and château had become a ruin.

Meantime, Fritz, of course, is also moving forward in enormous numbers, getting into position to attack Villers-Bretonneux at dawn.

After their long haul by rail from Russia, the boots of Germany's 77th Reserve Division have barely touched the ground when they find themselves marching in the middle of the night. All hope that their attack might be a surprise has faded as they receive 'from the muzzles of the British artillery' what their regimental historian records as, 'a most impressive object lesson in the fighting methods of the Western Front'.[8]

Even well back from the Front, all the approach roads to their starting point lie 'under continuous accurate fire'. The only way forward is to get off those roads, spread out and make detours across the fields.

'In pitch darkness they felt their way along . . .' an officer of 1st *Jager Battalion* would record of their experience. 'At one place a half section stumbled head over heels in a shell hole full of water; at another, the remains of a wire entanglement tore trousers, coat and skin. Meanwhile salvoes of eight to twelve shrapnel shells broke like lightning through the night and drove us all struggling painfully . . . to press our faces into the slimy earth . . .'[9]

Sometimes it helps, more often it doesn't.

'It was however quite immaterial where one lay; heavy shells came down almost vertically. They struck straight like hammers and crushed out life . . . with the same rage and indifference. There was nothing for the *Jager* to do but lie as close as possible to the damp clayey earth and wait . . . an eternity.'[10]

Also moving into position on this night are the veterans of the 4th Guards Infantry Division, with the 93rd Infantry Regiment, as ever, at their prow, ready to attack along the southern edge of Villers-Bretonneux and through to the woods on the far side to be sure no British lurk therein. They are filled with confidence, as always. And why wouldn't they be?

Throughout all of the war, the 4th Guards in general, and the 93rd Regiment in particular, have been in the thick of the action. As Britain's official history of the Great War would ruefully record, they had bagged 'an outstanding share of the victories'.[11] This had included huge gains on the opening days of Operation Michael, from which they had been removed and rested. They are now being thrown back into the fray.

Not for nothing has their commander, General Graf Finck von Finckenstein, and all three of his regimental commanders, been awarded Germany's highest military honour – in recognition of the extraordinary achievements of the troops they command – just as many of those troops boast Iron Crosses for extraordinary bravery demonstrated in the heat of battle.

And such valuable troops, of course, are not to be sent forward alone.

'Flamethrowers and tanks would support the attack,' the official history of the 93rd Regiment records. 'The artillery were to fire tear gas . . .'[12]

Their orders are clear:

The 4th Guard Infantry Division shall first take
the English positions south-east and south of
Villers-Bretonneux, then by advancing on both

sides of the railroad to Amiens ... continue the attack up to the western edge of the Aquenne Forest. Seven *Panzerwagen*, armored cars, are allocated to the division, because strong resistance is to be expected.[13]

And while the 4th Guards Division take the southern half of the town, the 228th Division will take the north!

—

Under the light of an almost-full moon, with just the occasional storm cloud to obscure it, the German tanks roar to life. It is 2 am and they have been positioned behind Marcelcave, just two miles from Villers-Bretonneux. Some of Germany's finest, the 5th Guards Grenadiers, are in old British trenches 300 yards away and still a mile from the German front-line. While the tanks turn their engines over, just to make sure all will be fine in the morning, the Grenadiers are being given their orders to pack their *Tornister* knapsacks and 'move forward ... into the *Bereitschaftsstellungen*, standby position',[14] from which they are due to launch at 7 am when the planned barrage is over.

As the 5th Guards Grenadiers move forward, they come under sporadic British artillery 'harrassing fire', like the fists of a blind man in a fight, throwing out punches and just hoping to connect with a vulnerable point.

'But the Englishman has bad luck, he does not hit them.'[15]

When the Grenadiers arrive, it is to find that the trenches awaiting them are only knee-deep, and so, as a precaution, they dig deeper. They know that once the German barrage begins, the British will make further reply, hoping to kill precisely the likes of them, a mile in front of the British lines.

Other German units have similar experiences. Nevertheless, by 4 am it is done. Just over 60,000 German soldiers are in position – five divisions in all – ready to attack. And all may take comfort from the fact that each division is supported by two, three or four of the new German tanks that have just started coming into front-line attacks – some 13 machines in total.

———

As dawn approaches on 24 April, off on the eastern horizon, those tiny flashes in the night that represent the German artillery – followed by the usual low, angry rumbling of cannon fire rolling forth – start to twinkle as never before. Instead of the light peppering of bridges and crossroads that has been going all night long, the actual German barrage begins.

'The *Höllenlärm*, hellish noise,' the 93rd Regiment's history records, 'becomes increasingly mightier . . .'[16]

For now, look closer as the 550 heavy guns and 40 mortars of the German artillery, lined up in scattered groups, side by side – ideally in spots hard to see from the air, 'with gun-teams stripped to the waist [and] relief teams standing by each gun in order to keep up a continuous service of the guns'[17] – go at it, focusing specifically on front-line positions. Each of those pleasant twinkles in the distance is, up close, a roaring, belching beast, spitting fire and raining down death. And some of that can even be slow death – the wind, rare for this time of the year, is coming from the east, meaning the Germans can add gas shells without fear of it blowing back upon them.

All of the German artillery commanders are singing from the same hymnal – backed by a full orchestra – and a minutely calibrated one it is:

0445–0515 – Gassing of enemy artillery.
0515–0530 – Bombardment of V.B. with all kinds of gas shell.
0530–0600 – Gassing of enemy arty.
0600–0630 – Engage enemy positions,- front lines/, during last fifteen minutes.
0630–0635 – Bombard enemy Inf. [infantry] *and arty.*
0645–0700 – Gas Hill 104 and enemy arty. Drum fire on

enemy front line positions for last five minutes.
0700 – Inf. attack commences. Barrage advances 300 metres.
0706 – Barrage on defence lines in rear.
0706–0715 – Further advance of barrage on north edge of V.B.
Barrage stops here until 0745.
0745 – Barrage to station road.
0750 – Barrage as far as church[18]

'Our artillery, with their destruction hurricane,' the official history of the Württemberger Regiment would report, 'rained on the enemy trenches and batteries. The mortars of our regiment . . . hurled bomb after bomb into the next enemy trenches, [as] raging iron hail came down on the English positions. . .'[19]

—

For the men of General Grogan's 23rd Brigade, in their trenches in front of Villers-Bretonneux, things go from calm to catastrophic in the time it takes for thousands of shells and mortar rounds to suddenly start raining down upon them, tearing everything asunder. Parapets, trenches, bodies – bits and pieces of all of them start flying. Men whimper as heads are sliced neatly from torsos, to fall at dead feet before the body collapses upon them, and men are splattered with the pulverised persons of their once-best friends.

Further back, at least for those British soldiers in Bois d'Aquenne just behind Villers-Bretonneux, it seems, mercifully, that there are no devastating explosions among them, no shells sending out lethal shrapnel followed by the usual screaming and death rattles of comrades.

But again, for those awake to hear it, there is something else, in many ways even more frightening, that lethal . . . *plop . . . plop . . . plop.*

Frank Mitchell is camped with his men beside their tanks in the undergrowth of those woods when he is half-woken around 4.45 am by 'a tremendous deluge of shells' landing all around them in the woods, followed an instant later by a violent shaking.

'Gas, sir! Gas!' his orderly is shouting. Now alarmed, realising the Germans had had no problem locating their tanks despite their evasive precautions, Mitchell struggles to extract himself from his groundsheet and shallow indentation in the ground that that same orderly had prepared the night before, making the mistake of taking the instinctive deep breath all humans do when suddenly confronted with danger. He instantly realises his mistake as soon as he inhales the mustard gas – his eyes start to run and his breathing becomes laboured. Whipping on his gasmask before any further damage can be done, he can now hear trees crashing to the ground all around as further German shells – both gas and high-explosive – start to fall.

For a moment or two he is stricken with fear – 'confused thoughts chased wildly through my mind'[20]– but soon pulls himself together, realising what his priority must now be.

In the near-blackness, leavened only by the faintest blood-red glimmer from the rising sun that comes through the wood, Mitchell and two others grope their way forward, holding hands, each breathing heavily through his mouthpiece. There is shouting all around and trees still crashing down from the shelling. All they know is that, in the flickering light from all the explosions, the darkest blob in the darkness must be their tanks. They keep going until a half-choked hoarse cry comes from the panicked orderly: 'My mouthpiece is broken, sir!'[21]

'Run like mad for the open!' shouts Mitchell's section commander.

The orderly does not have to be asked twice, and within a second he has let go of their hands and can be heard 'crashing away through the undergrowth like a hunted beast'.[22]

Mitchell and his section commander make their way to the tanks, at much the same time as others in their section. Removing the camouflage tarpaulin, they find the small oblong doors on the tank open for airing, just as they had left them, and the interior unoccupied.

Feeling around in the dark, it doesn't take long for Mitchell to find what he is looking for – something warm and fleshy that grunts when he prods it.

'It was one of the crew lying full length [under a tarp of his own],'

Mitchell would recount, 'wearing his mask, but dazed by gas.'[23]

It is time to gather the crew for what awaits. It will likely be action. Nearby, right on the edge of the wood, 'a battery of artillery was blazing away, the gunners in their gas masks feverishly loading and unloading like creatures of a nightmare.'[24]

—

The British artillery does its best to counter the German attack, but as the official history of the 93rd Regiment records, it is not enough to turn the tide of the battle: 'The answer by the enemy is inevitable. First, the English artillery replied briskly. It shoots partially with *Gasgranaten*, gas grenades. Then the enemy fire diminishes more and more. The German destruction fire lies well on the English infantry positions.'[25]

—

And so it has come . . . precisely as Brigadier Pompey Elliott had feared it would. Awoken by the barrage in his HQ at Blagny, the Commanding Officer of the 15th Brigade is quick to order both the 59th and 60th Battalion to send forth patrols. *Find out how far the Germans have got and where our front-line is now, if we still have one.*

It is a move, he will later acknowledge, that is 'entirely anticipatory and (it may as well be said plainly) in expectation of the British [8th Division] retiring. Unfortunately our previous experience of them had left us fully prepared for this sort of thing.'[26]

Elliott's second lot of orders are for the 59th and 60th Battalions to move forward to a valley a mile north-west of Villers-Bretonneux and prepare to counter-attack with a flanking movement along the north side of the town, then turn south-east as far as the Roman road. Meanwhile, his 57th Battalion can also get themselves in position to push from the south side. Once they reach the Roman road, the Germans inside will be cut off – unable to be resupplied with ammunition and reserves

– and the town can be retaken. The 58th Battalion is in reserve.

All of it is obvious to Pompey. The town will soon fall to the Germans and have to be retaken by the Allies, and his men are the obvious ones to do it – so he may as well give the provisional orders now. All he needs is permission from on high and his men will be in position to take care of it.

Yet he is not entirely confident that the British command will see it his way. As he will later note, his previous experience with them in just the last few days – sending in 40 teenagers to replace his 600 men at Bois l'Abbé, and insisting on it despite his protests – 'forbade us to hope that any intelligent military action could reasonably be expected from any of them from the Corps Commander down.'[27]

All he can do is give orders to his men to get ready, and agitate for orders from his superiors to allow him to let them loose. In the later words of Charles Bean, 'From the very first news of attack [Brigadier Pompey Elliott] was straining at the leash to be able to counter-attack.'[28]

And that is putting it mildly – a word rarely associated with Pompey Elliott.

—

In the British front-lines, all is carnage as the precisely targeted German shells continue to rain down upon them. Captain Mayberly Esler, a Medical Officer of the 23rd Brigade, is at his aid post in Bois l'Abbé, just behind the front-line, when a shell comes and wipes out most of his stretcher-bearers. The survivors cannot hold on, and the Captain soon finds himself with 180 others, mostly soldiers, who simply up sticks and move back.

'I have never known such a barrage of shell fire,' he would recount. 'It was like walking through Dante's Inferno.'[29]

Every 50 yards or so, more shells take out more men, till they are down to 100, then 50, then just Esler and a couple of dozen others are left.

He is frightened of course, and shocked, but he also has a profound sense of unreality. This can't really be happening, can it? All he can do for the moment is keep pushing back, with, by now, five wounded men clinging to him, one of whom has half his jaw blown away. And now another shell explodes, neatly slicing off both legs of the Sergeant walking beside him. When the smoke clears, there he is, sitting on his bottom with both stumps waving in the air. All Esler can do is carry him to the side of the road in the hope that when the *Boche* come through they will care for him.

'You are not going to leave me here?' the shocked Sergeant asks. 'I felt a real heel,' Esler would recall, 'but could not explain that we had nothing to carry him in, and if we stayed, we should all die. Luckily, most of the wounded were beyond asking for help and most were beyond caring.'[30]

—

And now, together with the shattering shells, comes something new. From 6.30, mixed with those high-explosive and gas shells, come smoke[31] shells, emitting billowing plumes of dirty white vapour – a sure sign that German infantry will soon be on their way.

But hang on, what the HELL is this?

Instead of the ethereal figures emerging from the mist that the 23rd Brigade expect, there is now something far more ominous. They are enormous, roaring, *hulks* of things. Can it be? Is it possible?

It is.

Horrified soldiers of one company shout to their Captain, 'Tanks, my God!'

The Captain cannot believe it and replies, 'No, lads, that's not a tank, it's only a ruddy molehill . . .'[32]

Something, anything, but not what it bloody well looks like, not molehills, but mountains on the move – yes, *tanks!*

In fact, across the line there are a dozen of them. Just after 7 o'clock, they appear through the mix of mist and smokescreen and head straight for the British lines with the German troops for the moment still lurking behind – their northern flank touching the Somme and their southern flank extending just to the south of Hangard Wood.

This time, in their advance, the Germans are using a newly developed tactic, broadly lining up with one platoon behind another, rather than side by side, advancing as an arrow that only spreads out once it hits the British lines, rather than a wave. This presents two benefits ... (I) CASUALTIES BY M.G., ARTILLERY FIRE ARE AVOIDED. (II) THE ATTACKERS APPEAR TO BE LESS STRONG THAN THEY REALLY ARE . . .[33]

And, certainly, the casualties the Germans are taking on this morning are minimal, particularly among those able to take shelter behind the tanks.

'As the fog clears,' the official history of the German 93rd Regiment records, 'the *deutsche Panzerwagen*, German tanks, become visible. With outstanding cunning the tanks enter the battle. They perform better than the English colossuses. At the bow they have a skull displayed. One finishes off the M. G. nest in front of the 6th Company, so that this can also advance further.'[34]

—

Right in the spot where the German attack is at its strongest, the 23rd Brigade's Captain Colin Brodie is sheltering with his men in their trench, keeping their heads down as furious machine-gun fire flies overhead, when he is suddenly aware that the fire has stopped.

Risking a quick look, Brodie pokes his head above the parapet for a split-second, only to see the most terrifying sight of the fight, and his life. It is an 'enormous and terrifying iron pill-box, bristling with automatic weapons, bearing straight down on [me]'.[35]

Ducking back down, Brodie is just in time as the German tank passes over the top of the trench, just three feet above his face. Once it is clear, Brodie rises again and fires his .32 automatic pistol at the machine gun at the stern of the tank. A sudden roar and he realises another tank is just behind!

For the men of General Grogan's 23rd Brigade, defending Villers-Bretonneux is a disaster as the tanks come at them in a line from just north and south of Monument Wood, advancing behind an iron curtain of creeping barrage.

'Despite the storm of rifle and machine-gun fire that was opened on them,' Grogan will regretfully recount, 'there was no metal heavy enough to damage or stop them . . . No one had ever thought that there was a possibility of the Germans employing this weapon, so no provision had been made to stop them, by the placing forward of anti-tank guns to knock them out by direct fire.'[36]

Runners are sent back to report to General Heneker's 8th Divisional HQ what has happened, arriving at 7.20 am, but Heneker is one of many who simply do not believe it. Tanks? The Germans don't have *tanks* in this area! They barely have them at all. There must be some mistake.

(A somewhat difficult character, Heneker. Still with the light Canadian lilt of one who had been born and raised there some 50 years earlier, he had begun his soldiering for Great Britain in India and West Africa a decade before the turn of the century, and he had risen steadily from there. He is a martinet like they don't make them anymore, and one of his officers would note, 'His eagle eye could detect an unshaven chin, the need for a haircut, a grease stain, or an unpolished button, at a considerable distance. His comments were clear, vividly expressed and long remembered.'[37] He is, in short, the embodiment of precisely the kind of officer Australians of all stripes, and no stripes at all, *don't* like.)

In this case, he does not believe there can be tanks, and that is that. If only.

But whatever HQ might want to believe, up front there is just no stopping the German armour. As General Grogan would note of his men's experience with them, '[German tanks] were soon across the 23rd Infantry Brigade's front-line trenches, enfilading them with gunfire and lachrymatory gas, running up and down them.'[38]

Oh, but it's about to get so much worse. From out of the smoke, no fewer than five German divisions quickly advance on British lines already shattered by the dreadful hammering they have taken from the barrage and completely confused by the tanks.

All this carnage is compounded by the German machine gunners, who have come with the tanks, together with crews bearing that most horrifying of all weapons, the *flammenwerfer*, flamethrowers. Operated by three men – one directing the nozzle, another supporting the pipe attached to the gas cylinder that shoots out propellant with petrol and the third wheeling the cylinder around – it is capable of throwing a flame 30 yards. There is a sudden roar followed by a hissing sound, and then the defenders see a crimson glare billowing madly towards them, before they are on *fire* and screaming – only to be left within seconds

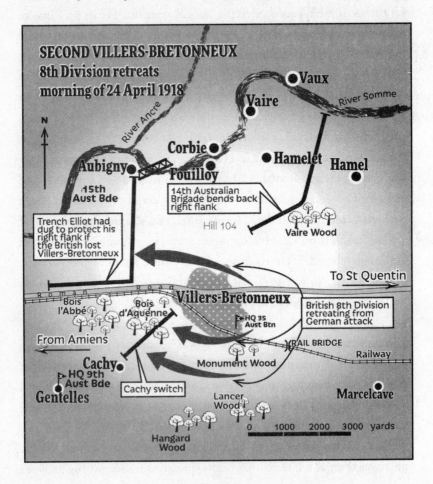

as flaming human torches, 'with ghastly wounds: hair and eyebrows singed, almost not human anymore, black creatures with bewildered eyes . . .'[39]

Many, oh so many, of those bewildered human torches are those 18-year-olds whom Private Edmund Street had led forward to the front-lines just four days earlier, the ones he would ever recall as 'fine, wholesome fresh faces, blue-eyed boys . . .'[40]

Oh, the *tragedy* of what has become of them.

And even those fortunate few who survive the flames must face the hundreds of bayonet-wielding German soldiers that follow, only too keen to finish them off.

Brodie, as he would recount, 'acting on the assumption that he who fights and runs away lives to fight another day', takes to his heels, together with the few men still surviving from the 150 soldiers who'd been in his company when the attack began. And it really is a 'few', with just five men still able to get away after the second and third tanks have done their bloody work.

'Under *schweren blutigen Verlusten*, severe bloody losses then,' the 93rd Regiment history would record, 'the English battalions flood back . . .'[41]

The three German tanks keep moving forward, creating havoc as they go, with one of them, *Mephisto*, with *Leutnant* Heinz Theunissen and the soldiers accompanying it, being particularly successful in rounding up British prisoners, some 250 in all. For now, *Mephisto* splits off from the other two and heads off to help the 5th Guards Grenadier Regiment finish off enduring pockets of British resistance in Monument Wood. (The resistance of the Yorkshiremen in the wood ended very shortly after one tank burst through the wall around the wood.)

The other two tanks continue west, causing carnage among whatever resistance they come across – and subduing that resistance. By 8 am, even General Heneker at 8th Division can no longer deny it. The Germans have tanks and they are destroying his men and his defences. In the face of it all, no fewer than half the soldiers of the 8th Division break and run . . .

———

Clearly now, finally, it is come. Or at least coming.

For the men of the 5th Division, 15th Brigade, 57th Battalion, in position on the Aubigny Line just back from Villers-Bretoneux, that is what it feels like as they come under scattered enemy shelling. Most of the damage seems to be falling in front of them, and, as one of their number, Jimmy Downing, would record, 'We had few casualties, but the thunder of doom rolled and boomed along the front.'[42]

Now if Brigadier Pompey Elliott had had his way, Jimmy, his platoon, company, battalion and entire brigade would be already right in the middle of that dooming and booming. But it is not to be. He has received an answer back from the commander of his 5th Division, General Joseph Hobbs, to his request to move his men forward: no. It is a matter of military protocol. The area Elliott wanted to move the 15th Brigade into is clearly marked on the map as being in the bailiwick of the 8th. The Australians could only go in if the Commanding Officer of the 8th Division makes 'an urgent request'.[43] No such request from General Heneker has come, and so the hands of Hobbs are tied.

Ol' Pompey. He's going to blow.

General Hobbs – in the same spirit he might note that Ayers Rock is 'big' – notes that Brigadier Elliott 'was very upset because he was not allowed to take part in the fighting'.[44]

It rankles with Pompey more than somewhat. He is already jack with the 'most unfair discrimination' that has been displayed against his men since the war began.

'For four years almost we have had to endure in silence albeit with writhing souls the comments of all and sundry British Officers on our lack of discipline, and all they have had to base it on was our men's lack of saluting and their free and independent manners.'[45]

When it came to the actual fighting, however, they were nothing less than magnificent. And yet now, when it really counts, he is not being allowed to unleash them to do what so obviously needs to be done.

And so Pompey fumes, even as his men can now see heading their way the remnants of the poor bastards who had been the focus of the attack. Among the British passing through Elliott's men, soon enough, is a runner, staggering back from the British 24th Brigade at Bois l'Abbé, bearing a message from an officer in 24th Brigade HQ:

> A man from the battalion which was in the line
> in front of Villers-Bretonneux has come through
> to here and reports enemy has advanced through
> our frontline with tanks and flammenwerfers and
> that enemy infantry were in open order. Nearly all
> communications have been cut. This seems fairly
> reliable. Enemy are reported advancing towards
> Villers-Bretonneux . . .[46]

Of course they are. Pompey Elliott's worst fears are now being realised: the Germans keep surging forward.

'At first,' the 93rd Regiment's history of the 4th Guards Division records, '*verlief alles wie am Schnürchen*, everything went without a hitch. The tanks drove across the enemy trenches, which were then cleaned out by the infantry and the *Flammenwerfern*. Numerous prisoners were taken. Unstoppable, the companies went forward, some of them already beyond their objectives.'[47]

———

At least for the moment the Australian lines in the trenches that run north of Villers-Bretonneux, in front of Hill 104 and all the way to the Somme, manned by 14th Brigade, are holding well. 'Fritz hopped over,' one of the Diggers of the 14th Brigade would recount, 'wave after wave of them. Our S.O.S shot up then down came our artillery barrage on No Man's Land and our machine gunners worked till their guns ran hot. In a few minutes his attack was broken. The Hun dead lying in heaps in No Man's Land. Again and again he sent his troops to meet the same fate. Our artillery broke up two of his attacks before they left their trenches. We never gave ground anywhere.'[48][49]

The German soldiers of the 478th Regiment, the Württembergers, are now more than just frustrated. While their bristling brethren to the immediate south have clearly been going so well against the lines defending Villers-Bretonneux, they are still unaccountably being held up by the Australians of the 14th Brigade defending Hill 104.

Wave after wave has been sent at them, for no result.

'For as long as only one of the enemy machine guns covers our lines from a so favourable higher-flanking position,' the Württemberger's report of the fate of their 478th Regiment would read, 'it made it impossible for any living being to advance towards the enemy without any cover.'[50]

The only way forward has to be to quell the Australian machine guns, and it is with that in mind that the *Regimentskommandeur*, Major Bürger, now calls for renewed artillery fire on the Australian lines before Hill 104.

'Again roars the iron hail on the rumpled Height 104, excellently directed by the commander of the artillery, Captain Schlösser. This fine artillery regiment *schon so manche harte Nuß geknackt hat*, "has previously cracked some hard nuts".'[51]

But not this time. After their intense attack, the Germans are indeed able to take a small portion of the lower slopes, yet the heights of Hill 104 are still denied them. For the shocked 478th Württembergers, who have been attacking the Australians in the lines immediately north of Villers-Bretonneux, there is no choice, as their official history records, 'The battalion must grudgingly, after severe losses, return to their starting position.'[52]

The Australians cheer at the sight of their backs.

Next time, Fritz, send in the *men!*

Alas, to the right of the Australians of the 14th Brigade, it is obvious the Germans are now pouring through the British lines. Within minutes, the first of the attackers enter Villers-Bretonneux, charging down the cobbled streets on its outskirts. Reaching the first of the houses, the

German troops of the 228th and 4th Guards Divisions, in small groups of five and six soldiers, make their way up both sides of a street, house by house. Working steadily westward, instead of knocking they throw a grenade through the window and then burst through the door and hunt room by room. Particular attention is paid to the cellar, which cops another grenade, as it is the most likely place for these mostly young Tommies of the 8th Division to secrete themselves before coming out later.

'About 450 prisoners,' the official history of Infantry Regiment No. 48 would recount, 'remain in our hands. The Regiment digs into the position gained. Communications are established and contact made with neighbouring units.'[53]

While the Australians holding the line just to the north of the German breakthrough – the 14th Brigade of the 5th Division – don't give an inch either back or to the left, the British forces on their right flank retreat to the Aubigny Line, while the British forces further to the right pull back to the Cachy Switch, carefully making their way through the heavy rolls of barbed wire that have been placed before it as an added defensive measure. All the 14th Brigade can do to defend their right flank is to bring forward a reserve battalion to dig in along an east–west line facing the town.

—

With Monument Wood now fallen, *Mephisto*, still under the command of *Leutnant* Heinz Theunissen, heads off west once more through the smoke and mist to join the other two tanks when . . . through bad luck or bad management, perhaps both, it falls into an enormous hell hole of a shell hole. Theunissen tries everything – roaring the engines to within an inch of their life, rocking back and forth, trying to pivot in the mud – but nothing will move that tank. It is stuck, and they must abandon it.

—

From atop Hill 104, just after 8.30 am, an artillery observer with 5th Australian Division affirms that he can see Germans in the streets of Villers-Bretonneux and, what is more, some German soldiers are now moving on Corbie from VB! Everywhere he looks, he sees the 8th Division's 25th Brigade – which had been in reserve – falling back.

Clearly, when even your reserves are running, the situation is getting out of hand and something must be done, whatever the assurances of the 8th Division's General Heneker that his men could handle it. (In fact, even this early, one attempt to counter-attack by the 8th has just failed.)

Clearing the town house by house has taken the Germans a while, but now the east, north and south of Villers-Bretonneux is secure. The obvious direction beckons to the Germans – west and the way to Amiens. The key obstacle in their way is the Cachy Switch, the trench that runs along the south-eastern side of the Bois d'Aquenne between Cachy and Villers-Bretonneux.

If they can take that, Amiens will be wide open to them!

Certainly, the Germans would have even gone on from the town this instant, but they come out on the western side to find the brave Royal Horse Artillery galloping up in the nick of time to fire their 13-pounder 'horse guns' upon the marauding Germans at a distance of 1000 yards and hold them off long enough that the 'Tommies were steadied in the trenches they had fallen back into'.

A pod of four tanks, *Abteilung III,* is assigned to the task, and starts to push west towards the Cachy Switch, with the soldiers of the 77th Division tightly in behind.

As ever, the leading German tank is *Nixe,* under the tight command of 41-year-old *Leutnant* Wilhelm Biltz – *Professor* Wilhelm Biltz at Clausthal University before the war – who is as courageous as he is intelligent, which is no small thing.

—

For the 23-year-old Lieutenant Frank Mitchell and his crew, with their tanks in the Bois l'Abbé still awaiting orders, the tidings are grim. First they see a trickle of wounded men coming back, and then a steady stream.

Mitchell expects at any time that he and his tanks will be thrown into a counter-attack, which is problematic, as by now two of his eight-man crew have so suffered the effects of the gas attack – spitting, coughing and turning purple in the face – that they are completely disabled. Instead of taking their place in the tank, one is led away to an aid station, while the second man cannot manage even that and is left 'sprawling limply in a wheel barrow found in the wood'.[55]

Meanwhile, it becomes ever more obvious that things are going badly for the defenders of Villers-Bretonneux. The shelling up ahead grows in intensity, and more and more wounded men and shocked soldiers with haunted eyes appear, all fleeing. Some tell of the growing menace behind.

'Villers-Bretonneux had been captured and with it many of our own men,' they say. 'The *Boche* have almost broken through.'[56]

Still uncertain what to do, both with his own tank and the two other tanks also under his command, Mitchell is relieved when there now appears, in the company of two orderlies, Brigadier Clifford Coffin, VC, the commanding officer of the 25th Brigade – in reserve for the 8th Division – who, apprised of the situation, says he will go forward to investigate, accompanied by one of Mitchell's men, a Captain, and a couple of runners who can bring back messages.

No more than ten minutes later, one of the runners is back, his message writ in the blood gushing from his leg – things are getting very willing just up ahead. Another ten minutes pass and the message from the second runner arrives, writ even more graphically in the blood gushing from what used to be his intact left arm. Fritz's artillery is clearly doing damage.

And now, finally, walking back through the barrage untouched, is Brigadier Clifford Coffin, VC, himself.

There is very bad news and a glimmer of good.

It is doubly confirmed that both the trenches defending Villers-Bretonneux and the town itself have been lost to the Germans, and the

8th Division has 'suffered heavy losses'.[57] And yet, *and yet*, there are still some infantry holding on!

They are in the southern end of the Cachy Switch, between Cachy and Villers-Bretonneux – the Germans have taken the northern end – and are in urgent need of help.

After a quick consultation with Lieutenant Mitchell, Coffin gives him a direct order: 'Proceed to the Cachy switch-line and hold it at all costs.'[58]

Yes, sir!

Donning their masks, Mitchell and his men head to their tank through the wood. Alas, as four of the men crank the huge handle to get it started, the tortured lungs of one of Mitchell's crew give up the ghost for the moment and he collapses. All the rest can do is prop him up against the tree, with some tablets to battle the effects of the gas, while they head off to the task at hand – holding the Cachy Switch – operating their tank with a five-man crew, all of them with red-rimmed, bulging eyes and wheezing lungs.

Mitchell's massive male tank – weighing 29 tons and powered by

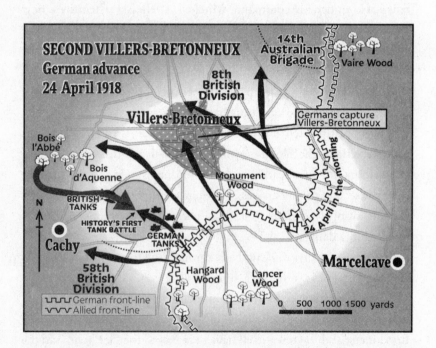

a strained Daimler-Foster engine, oddly similar to the Daimlers inside their German opponents' tanks – is in the lead. It is an extraordinary 26-feet long and 13-feet wide, with steel sides.

The other two tanks quickly fall in behind as they all emerge, engines roaring, from Bois l'Abbé, setting off over the open ground towards Cachy, for the moment trying to ignore the iron curtain formed by the German barrage, 'like a wall of fire in our path'.[59]

—

In the face of it all, General Rawlinson, surrounded by anxious staff officers in his Flixecourt HQ, some 20 miles from Villers-Bretonneux, moves quickly. The previous week, in a conversation with Monash, General Rawlinson had said, 'I have staked my reputation on holding Villers-Bretonneux,'[60] and now he must do everything in his power to get both it and that reputation back. Thus, at 9.30 am – once it is confirmed that the town has fallen – he issues an order to his army reserve, Brigadier William Glasgow's 13th Brigade. They must immediately leave their billets at Querrieu and march eight miles to the south to assist in the recapture of Villers-Bretonneux, which is imperative for the security of Amiens . . .[61]

As to timing, Rawlinson is firm from the first: 'Villers-Bretonneux must be retaken by tonight at the latest.'[62] Which is one thing. Getting that order through is another. The bombardment has destroyed all the telephone lines to the 13th Brigade HQ, meaning Glasgow is yet to get the message.

—

At *last*, at least the way Brigadier Pompey Elliott sees it, General Hobbs gets the message.

Something has to be done, and the 15th Brigade are just the mob to do it. Just after 9.30 am, Pompey gets permission from General Hobbs to bring the 15th Brigade forward to their projected start-line, to launch a flanking movement on the north side of the town.

At this time, Jimmy Downing is with his mates of the 15th Brigade's 57th Battalion in their position on the south side of the Somme, by Corbie, and they are gazing with the steely hardness of grizzled veterans at the stream of severely wounded men that continues to pass by, coming back from the front east of Villers-Bretonneux, courtesy of stretcher-bearers.

From the grim-faced stretcher-bearers and some of the wounded who could still speak, they manage to glean something of what had happened: 'They had been almost annihilated by the weight of metal.'[63]

It had not just been the shelling, though God knows that had been bad enough. It had been the tanks! Huge metal monsters, rolling right over the top of them, destroying all in their path. And then, of course, the German troops, thousands of them, charging forward. The Australian line of the 5th Division's 14th Brigade had held, but not so these men who had been defending Villers-Bretonneux. It had been *impossible*, don't you understand? Shelling! Tanks! *Thousands* of German soldiers!

And make no mistake, the Germans have not stopped there.

Atop yonder hill, the Australians can suddenly see German infantry.

And now come the first of the orders, direct from Pompey himself. Still outraged at how many Brits are falling back without fighting, he has put it in language where there can be no mistaking his intent:

ALL BRITISH TROOPS TO BE RALLIED AND REFORMED AS OUR TROOPS MARCH THROUGH THEM BY SELECTED OFFICERS AND ON ANY HESITATION TO BE SHOT.[64]

Jimmy Downing and his mates don't have to be asked twice. From that point on, all those making their way back from the front are given a weapon and posted in lots of a dozen among the Australian infantry.

'We were not sorry thus to reinforce our weak platoons,' Downing would recount. 'The Tommies proved themselves good men . . . and we thanked our stars we had escaped the hell that they had already endured. Nevertheless, we would have preferred Australians.'[65]

No disrespect n'all, but at least with Australians they could be sure they'd fight. These British coves are worthy n'all, but so many of them are so young, and they've simply been plucked from England and thrown forward without anything like proper training. And a lot of them are shocked by what they have already endured. Could they be counted on if the Germans come again?

Mercifully, the Australians now start hearing artillery coming from behind. Our blokes!

The shells of the Australian artillery are, in effect, also shots across the German bow, giving fair warning against them pushing forward. That and the fact that the Germans are now aware of the Aubigny Line, the trench system dug just west of Villers-Bretonneux as something of a *cordon sanitaire* to still hold the Germans back should they take the town. It indeed gives the attackers pause.

And now, among the Australians, word goes out. We are to move forward! We're going to have a go at Fritz!

Sure enough, Brigadier Elliott himself soon appears on his horse, moving back and forth among his troops, shouting orders, encouragement and threats in fairly equal measure, 'brandishing a revolver, threatening to shoot the gunners if they pulled out . . .'[66]

To the Tommies who have just – involuntarily – joined his ranks, Pompey is nothing if not encouraging, telling them, 'I will show you how Australians fight.'[67]

———

Perhaps it is a lucky shell, or perhaps, under the circumstances, there are so many shells falling on Villers-Bretonneux that one of them just *has* to hit a target so large, but it is around this time that the towering Red Château, on the northern edge of the town, takes a direct hit and immediately bursts into flames.

Everything goes up – centuries-old furniture, paintings, carpets, birds in the aviary. Billowing black smoke mixed with feathers tells something of the tale.

—

At 10 o'clock, the designated attack battalions of the 15th Brigade – the 59th and 60th – have only been on the move for 15 minutes when the word comes directly from General Hobbs to Pompey.

'The British are going to try to restore the line. Our Division will stand fast pending further orders.'[68]

Companyyyyyy . . . . halt!

General Heneker has changed his mind.

Hobbs has been told firmly and perhaps even a little sniffily by the General that, in response to Hobbs's offer to have his own men do the job, no, Heneker's own 8th Division 'was quite capable to deal with the situation',[69] thank you very much. Hobbs even had the impression that the Australian 'offer was unwelcome'.[70]

What can Pompey Elliott do?

The obvious. As Bean would faithfully record, 'Elliott could now only wait fuming while the 8th div all day telegraphed to them its postponed or revised plans for counter-attack.'[71]

In the meantime, the men of the 15th Brigade settle down just 500 yards forward of the Aubigny Line, still two miles from the start-line that Elliott had designated for the attack he had wanted to launch.

And nor is Hobbs happy.

The order to stand down the 15th Brigade because the Brits can handle it comes at almost exactly the same time that Hobbs receives a confirmed report from the liaison officer with the 14th Brigade: ENEMY HOLDS VILLERS . . . ENEMY TANKS REPORTED WEST OF VILLERS.[72]

For the life of them, for the lives of their men, for the sake of the war, neither Hobbs nor Elliott can work out why Heneker and his superior officer, General Richard Butler of the III Corps, appear to be saying that they don't need the Australians, when clearly they do.

—

At 10.15 am the telephone lines have been fixed by the brave men of one of the signalling companies, and the order arrives from General Rawlinson for Brigadier William Glasgow to have his 13th Brigade **READY TO MOVE AT A MOMENT'S NOTICE.**[73]

A 'moment's notice', in military terms for an entire brigade, is about one hour, and this suits Brigadier Glasgow and the 13th Brigade well. On the previous evening, Glasgow and his senior officers had been discussing 'what might be organised at short notice to celebrate Anzac Day. They went to bed without having made a decision and woke to find the Germans had made it for them.'[74]

Now Glasgow quickly gives orders of his own, and within minutes those orders are on their way to the four battalions of the 13th billeted around Querrieu, north of the Somme. They must be in marching formation in one hour, call it 11.15 am.[75]

In short order, no fewer than 4000 men are loading their personal belongings and blankets onto the general service wagons, receiving newly issued ammunition, filling their water bottles and sorting out their haversacks, as well as – most crucially – cleaning their rifles and sharpening their bayonets.

Moving among them, of course, are their Captains and Lieutenants, overseeing that all is as it should be.

In C Company of the 51st Battalion, Captain Billy Harburn, a 24-year-old former bank clerk from WA, embodies the Australian way of leadership. A gentle word here, a pointed look there, his ease of command makes it easy for his men to return the respect they would deny, just on principle, to officious bastards who demanded it by virtue of their position in the military hierarchy. Beside Harburn, the newly promoted Lieutenant Cliff Sadlier is cut from much the same cloth, if not quite so distinguished looking. Still, within the strict confines of Australian manhood, which rather stunts the expression of warm emotion, Sadlier is deeply admired by the men he leads.

Harburn and Sadlier are veterans of Gallipoli, as well as many battles of the Western Front. They have seen trouble before, bad trouble, and now that it is come again, they know that the younger ones who might be facing it for the first time will be looking to them for the lead, and they provide it. They are calm, purposeful, no-nonsense.

Mounted officers meantime, report to Brigade HQ, seeking 'details as to route and destination'.[76]

They are told to head south across the Somme, to the flat ground just west of Bois l'Abbé to await further orders.

———

By 10.30 am, *Abteilung III*, the four tanks led by *Leutnant* Biltz in *Nixe*, has progressed far enough west that they have gone past the monument on the southern side of Villers-Bretonneux and are now heading for the Cachy Switch.

Just as they have been trained not to do, the four tanks – *Nixe*, *Elfriede*, *Seigfried* and *Schnuk* – lose each other in the dim visibility and proceed independently. *Nixe* is now just 1000 yards or so from Bois d'Aquenne, with no friends in sight. After all the mustard gas the Germans have put down on the wood, it is 'full of dead and dying birds, and the gas [hangs] about in the trees and bushes'.[77]

———

Closing in on the Cachy Switch, the impatient Lieutenant Mitchell orders a shift into top gear. The driver presses the pedal to the metal and gets the mobile monster to full speed – all the way up to 4 mph – as he sets a zigzag course through the iron curtain. Though shells fall close by, and inside the tank they hear the fearful ring of shrapnel hitting hard, both they and the other tanks avoid a direct hit. Miracle of all miracles, they are all through the worst of the shelling!

The strange thing, though? As they approach the Cachy Switch, there are no soldiers apparent . . . and Mitchell is momentarily confused until, from seemingly right out of the ground, just ten yards ahead of him, an infantryman suddenly rises up as if from the grave . . . waving his rifle *furiously*.

Mitchell brings his tank to a shuddering halt, allowing the soldier to charge forward and shout, 'Look out! Jerry tanks about!'[78] Just as swiftly, the soldier runs back and dives into his trench.

And now Lieutenant Mitchell sees it.

Coming straight at him from out of the smoke is the vision horrid of a massive German tank, with 𝔑𝔦𝔵𝔢 written in Gothic script on its boilerplate. As a matter of fact, it almost looks like a conglomerate of four tanks. It looks, Mitchell would record, 'just like an iron tortoise with the armour-plating hanging down around the tracks like a skirt almost touching the ground.'[79]

No matter that the mustard gas from several days before is still very badly affecting many of his tanks' crews, who have congested lungs, streaming and puffed up eyes and terribly itchy blisters on their exposed skin. When Lieutenant Mitchell tells his crew the news, that they are going to go after German tanks, the reaction is universal.

'A great thrill ran through us all,' Mitchell would chronicle.

Peering through the vision slit positioned before his eyes, he looks out . . . and there it is! Just 300 yards away and closing, 'a round squat looking monster'.

Extraordinary! While they had heard, of course, that the Germans had tanks, none of them had the slightest clue what they would look like. And now they know: Huge. Ugly. Menacing. A strong sense of noisy evil about them.

Right behind the tank he can see lines of German infantry, advancing with it the way chicks might stay close to a mother hen. And behind them again, out to the left, are two more tanks, also heading towards them.

'So we had met our rivals at last!' Mitchell would record. 'For the first time in history, tank was encountering tank!'[81]

Sitting in front of Mitchell, in the belly of their roaring beast, their backs against the engine cover, the gunners of the six-pounder guns – capable of delivering six-pound shells a distance of 4000 yards, but only

1000 yards with any real accuracy – adjust the gun's elevation, keeping it aimed at where the enemy might appear. Hoping to maintain visual contact with the German tanks, and being lightly thrown from side to side, Mitchell tries to identify terrain features to keep the tank on course, even while giving instructions to the driver – mostly by first bashing a heavy spanner on the steel wall in front of him to get his attention, and then using prearranged hand signals. It is almost impossible to make yourself heard above the roaring engine. Occasionally he refers to the rough map he has on his lap, and in this manner the British tanks manage to get through the small gaps that have been left between the trenches the British soldiers have dug the previous night.

The two pods of tanks close on each other, like ships of medieval times, the British crew eagerly aware that the fate of the battle will likely lie with the one who can shoot straightest.

In Mitchell's leading British tank, the left gunner, Sergeant McKenzie, peers through his telescopic sight. His hands a blur of movement, first he selects a round to insert into the breech – not case-shot for firing at infantry but armour-piercing rounds. Then he turns the two small wheels on the gun – one controlling elevation, the other to traverse the barrel left or right – until the sights are on the target. He can make out the great black monster he wants to hit, hundreds of yards across the fields, and centres it in his crosshairs.

Perfect.

He brings pressure to bear on the pistol grip trigger, remarkably like the trigger and stock of an ordinary pistol, but the result is far from ordinary . . .

There is a roar, the six-pounder recoils and a shell bursts forth, hurtling at 500 yards a second with tightly packed explosives in its head, complete with six pounds of metal to tear apart whatever it hits . . . only to go over the top of the tank and explode some 50 yards beyond it. In response, McKenzie simply tugs on the breech and the shell casing ejects onto the floor. The Lewis gunner, also trained as a loader, places another shell in the breech, and McKenzie pauses for just a second so the Lewis gunner can get his fingers out of the way before slamming the breech shut once more. After some more dialling of the wheels, and another rough sighting through his now grossly swollen right eye, McKenzie fires once more. This one lands just to the left.

A cry, and the Lewis gunner is holding his right leg, from which blood is now pouring, making the floor of the tank sticky. A machine-gun bullet has penetrated the tank, possibly through a vision slit, and hit him hard. Still, he can function, and that is all that counts.

The tanks keep rumbling towards each other, with no reply yet from the lead German AV7, whose occupants apparently remain unaware that the British tanks have spotted it, let alone that they are eager for a spot of sport, what?

Ah, but it won't be long.

Inside the *Nixe*, *Leutnant* Wilhelm Biltz is oblivious to the English tanks for only a short time, despite being narrowly missed both times. In all the artillery smoke of battle, he simply keeps his tank rumbling forward, getting his bearings from the sight of Cachy off to his front left at a 45-degree angle and, more importantly, Bois d'Aquenne straight ahead, where he is heading. Suddenly, the Mark IVs appear from out of the tree line and artillery smoke off his port bow!

Zurück! Reverse!

Nixe's supremely powerful twin Daimler-Benz engines roaring, its whole structure vibrates with the effort as he attempts to quickly get 35 tons of machinery into better position.

Behind *Nixe*, the German assault infantry who have been carefully advancing behind the tank's protective skirts, must now scramble while mother engages in a fight for her life. For a minute or so they follow orders and stay close to their tanks, but now that a battle against other tanks has broken out, the German soldiers fall back behind whatever shelter they can find to watch, as best they can, the unfolding drama of history's first tank-on-tank engagement.

Again the British gun roars, again there is a recoil, and this time the shell lands just to *Nixe*'s right.

And look there, how the lead German tank has stopped to get a clear shot in . . . With a mighty roar, *Nixe*'s 57-mm cannon unleashes a shell with a trail of flame behind it, streaking straight towards the foremost British tank – a pell-mell of hell hurtling forth.

Inside Mitchell's tank – by now, courtesy of the roaring engine and cramped space, suffocatingly hot, noisy and choked with acrid smoke and engine fumes – they are suddenly hit by a 'hurricane of hail' that sees sparks fly, together with potentially lethal steel splinters. Luckily, the crew are wearing 'splatter masks' – very similar to the chain-mail hoods worn by medieval soldiers – to protect their head and neck from 'spall'. A new phenomenon to go with the new weaponry, spall is the hundreds of small splinters of steel that tend to come off the insides of a tank when it is hit by a shell – even those that don't penetrate, like this one – and then ricochet through the crew compartment, often causing devastating wounds as it rips into soft flesh.

Above the roar of the engine, Mitchell can hear some of the spall striking the helmet of his driver, just as his own face starts to sting from the small fragments. The rest of the crew are mostly unhurt, too, but they have still thrown themselves to the floor of the tank for safety's sake. Not the driver. *Annoyed*, he simply ducks his head a little as a nod to safety's sake. Pulling hard on the steering handles on each side of his knees so that both tracks are running at the same speed, the driver then halts the tank under instruction from Mitchell, who hopes a stationary shot might at last be an accurate shot. 'We kept going up and down like a ship in a heavy sea, which made accurate shooting difficult.'[82]

And now they keep going.

In one horrifying moment, some of the British soldiers look likely to become more than spectators as Mitchell's tank zigs left then zags right, trying to keep clear of the enemy shells, only to find itself roaring straight for a trench crammed with men on his own side!

Mitchell is able to roar the order to turn, 'avoiding catastrophe by a second'.[83]

And now comes still worse.

'Above the roar of our engine sounded the staccato *rat-tat-tat-tat* of machine guns and another furious jet of bullets sprayed our steel side, the splinters clanging against the engine cover. The Jerry tank had just treated us to a broadside of armour-piercing bullets.'[84]

Erroneously believing the lead British tank – the dangerous male with the protruding cannons – is done for, *Leutnant* Biltz now shifts his fire to the females, scoring hits immediately.

The two tanks that had been backing Mitchell's lead tank now withdraw, limping and lumbering away – German shells have rent great tears in their sides, leaving the crews defenceless against machine-gun bullets. And so now it is just their sole male tank against however many German behemoths are out there. Only one is in sight for the moment, Biltz's *Nixe*.

'We were treated here to a real thrill,' one Australian soldier, Private Walter Kennedy, would later recount, 'for right in the open between the two lines, a British armoured tank, and a German tank, fought it out to the death.'[85]

All this while the British and German infantry have been firing at each other, at the same time 'tensely watching the duel like spectators in the pit of a theatre'.[86]

Biltz now sees Mitchell's tank is still firing and determines to finish him off. *Nixe* rakes them with another broadside of armour-piercing bullets. Again there is a hurricane of hail, and this time their rear Lewis gunner cries out in pain as bullets hit both of his legs. There is no time to even attempt to patch him up, and all they can do – as he lies groaning on the floor beneath the right-hand six-pounder, among the clanking empty shell cases, in a pool of his own blood – is keep going, keep firing, all while the interior of their tank fills with the stifling fumes of petrol and cordite and the sickly stench of hot blood, and the shattering cacophony of their own roaring guns. While they are yet to take out the enemy tank, they at least have the satisfaction of cutting a swathe through the formation of German infantry.

And now Mitchell's own left gunner suddenly sees the outline of *Nixe* through the smoke.

And fie, the cannon's roar!

The conning tower of the Jerry tank explodes and the monster shudders to a standstill. A second shot hits Jerry! The British gunner, peering through his telescopic sight – and his weeping eyes – cries out in triumph, and can even take a little more time now to take precise aim, before . . .

There is a roar, the six-pounder recoils and a shell bursts forth . . .

Bullseye! The Jerry tank explodes and reels over to one side. A direct hit!

Inside *Nixe*, all is smoke, blood, death and destruction. Men are wailing, the gunner is clearly dead, and two other crew are mortally wounded. For good measure, McKenzie fires two more shots right at it, both of which find their mark.

Mitchell and his men are now close enough to observe their hand-iwork: 'A door opened and out ran the crew. We had knocked the monster out!'[87]

Still not satisfied, Mitchell orders his remaining Lewis gunner to pour a blizzard of machine-gun bullets into the retreating figures. Mitchell now looks to the other two German tanks, which are still coming forward, while his 'six-pounder gunners spread havoc in the ranks of the advancing German infantry with round after round of case-shot'.[88]

As the two German tanks close on them, Mitchell is certain that the end is nigh, for if they both concentrate their fire it will be impossible to survive . . . but in the interim he is determined to fire on the closest Jerry tank.

And then it happens.

The iron tortoise is slowing. It has taken punishment and is hurt. It is reversing. It is backing away!

The British tank keeps pouring round after round into it, and suddenly not only is the Jerry tank retreating, but so is the second one! 'In a few minutes,' Mitchell would record with a great deal of satisfaction, 'they had both disappeared, leaving our tank the sole possessor of the field.'[89]

True, it is not long before the German artillery gets a bead on Mitchell's tank and they take a bad hit too, meaning they have to evacuate and scramble into the nearest infantry trench, dragging their bleeding Lewis gunner with them as they go. By now it scarcely matters. The German tank attack has been beaten off, and the British have won the first tank battle in the history of the world – one on which, perhaps, the fate of a hugely important battle turned.

As Mitchell and his men are making their way back to camp on foot at Bois l'Abbé a short time later, they come across a young officer on horseback, driving forward a team of gunners, with a team of horses, all of them, 'wildly dragging an 18-pounder gun across an open field'.

What is this then?

'I say, old man,' says the young fellow on horseback, 'I've been sent forward to knock out a German tank. Is that the blighter over there?'

Lieutenant Mitchell follows his gaze to the still-smoking ruin of the German tank *Nixe,* glowering out in the field.

'You're a bit late,' the exhausted Lieutenant replies lightly. 'It's already knocked out.'[90]

'Oh,' says the officer. 'I see. Well . . . thank you very much.'

He turns his team around and then, yes, a'gallops, a'gallops, a'gallops . . . awaaaaay . . .[91]

Whatever else, the British tank victory has helped put a little lead in the pencil of the British soldiers, and bullets back into the breeches of their rifles – *once more into the breech, dear friends, once more* – as they realise both the Germans and their tanks *are* stoppable.

Such is confirmed, just a short time later, when seven of the light British tanks known as Whippets – armed only with machine guns – charge straight at the oncoming 77th Division infantry in front of Cachy. They run over so many Germans that, although four of those tanks are stopped by *Siegfried* and *Schnuck,* as well as field guns – the three surviving Whippets return with 'their tracks dripping with blood'.[92] Those German soldiers who have escaped their attentions run away, and as a direct result two of the 77th's infantry battalions are stopped cold.

CHAPTER SEVENTEEN

HIGH NOON

Villers-Bretonneux marked the crisis of the war . . .[1]
General Monash

With pride, each man of [Germany's] 74th [Infantry
Regiment] can look back on the days of 24–26 [April
1918], which belong to the most difficult ones of the
entire war and are a *Glanzleistung*, brilliant performance,
and [they] bear witness of *Mannesmut und Opferwillen*,
manly courage and the will to sacrifice, for our *schwer
ringendes Vaterland*, hard wrestling homeland.[2]
Major Kurt Gabriel, 74th Regiment

NOON, 24 APRIL 1918, HENEKER'S HQ, WHO WILL BELL THE CAT?

While the news that the German tanks have been turned back is of
course welcome, the fact remains – Villers-Bretonneux, all of it, is now
in German hands.

General Heneker has been trying to organise counter-attacks, and
has in fact ordered four battalions of the 8th Division in different
locations to do the job. Of these, only one has even got underway, to
be quickly blown apart by German rifle and machine-gun fire, and a
shattering barrage of 5.9-inch guns. Instead of capable troops roaring
forth from the 8th Division, the only thing emitted has been ever more

orders from Heneker that, like his soldiers, go nowhere and do nothing.

As noon approaches, General Rawlinson has had enough. Losing faith that the 8th Division will be able to retake Villers, he *orders* Heneker to make contact with the 5th Division's General Hobbs and seek the assistance of the Australians, perhaps attacking at 2 pm. Though reluctant and rejecting the idea of an attack by that time (for one thing, his men simply can't be ready by then), Heneker has no choice but to follow orders. He even embraces an expansion of Pompey Elliott's original plan, namely that 'the attack should be launched by two brigades, one on each side of the town, ignoring the town itself and meeting beyond it'.[4]

Effectively, it would be a pincer starting from the west, a thumb and forefinger curling around both flanks, to meet on the far side of town and squeeze the life out of the German lice found in Villers-Bretonneux.

As to who will attack on the south side, Heneker remains hopeful that he will be able to put together a force from the 8th Division, but other options are strengthening.

—

High noon finds the Australians of the 13th Brigade a good couple of miles into their eight-mile march south to Villers-Bretonneux. By any measure they are a fine body of soldiers and officers, vastly experienced, highly trained, with a string of solid successes on their record – Mouquet Farm, Messines and 2nd Dernancourt. Beyond that, they boast many Gallipoli veterans in their number.

One of them, Colonel Robert Christie, the commander of Western Australia's 51st Battalion, had been a mere private when he'd hit that legend of a landing – three years earlier, less a day – and risen from there, courtesy of his capacity for leadership. Equally regarded is the Commanding Officer of the 52nd Battalion, Colonel John Whitham, the cool Tasmanian who at Dernancourt, having prepared his battalion for the German attack, read his newspaper while waiting for the battle to begin.

Both men are on horseback, leading their battalions, as, singing on this clear, cold spring day, their men march down a pretty valley 'side a boggy little stream you could spit across, meandering south to the Somme, which it has all good intentions of meeting two miles west of Corbie. (Sometimes it floods.)

In the meantime, the 13th Brigade's Commanding Officer, Brigadier William Glasgow, having gone ahead by car, is just pulling up at the 8th Division HQ at Glisy. General Heneker, if he is not shaken, should be.

Heneker quickly apprises Glasgow of the situation. Villers-Bretonneux has fallen to the Germans and urgent action is necessary. You, Brigadier Glasgow, must be ready to move at a moment's notice and position three of your battalions just south of Bois l'Abbé, from

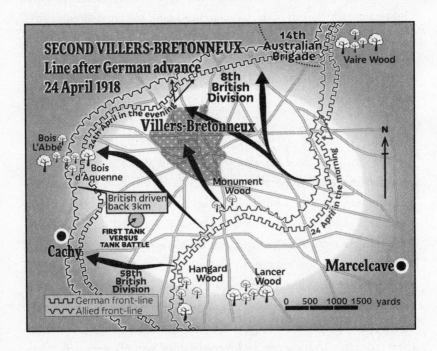

where they must prepare to make a counter-attack. The other battalion can be kept in reserve.

For Glasgow, there will be no ordering his men to do anything – and he means it – until he has 'a clear notion of the situation, and is completely satisfied with the plans'.[5]

'Are the Cachy Switch and the Bois l'Abbé held by the British?' he asks pointedly, naming the spot that Heneker says they might have to launch from.

'We have troops through the wood here,' Heneker replies, pointing to the map, 'and here – and others in Cachy Switch here – but of course the situation is changing from moment to moment. I can't be sure of it.'[6]

'Oh, I can easily find out about that, sir,' Glasgow replies equably. 'I'll go up there myself and come back and see you.'[7]

Simple as that. This is the way the Australians fight. We try to survey the ground ourselves, first.

Heneker has no option but to agree, and Glasgow is quickly on his way.

—

In the meantime, no one is in any doubt that the fate of the battle, and perhaps the war, hangs in the balance. That much is confirmed by a cable arriving in the late morning from a very anxious General Foch himself, telling General Rawlinson what he already knows: Villers-Bretonneux *must* be retaken. And, as if that is not enough, the cable is followed shortly afterwards by a personal visit from General Haig to Rawlinson at his HQ, ensuring that everything that can be done is being done.

Haig comes away pleased at the way Rawlinson is 'arranging for a counter-attack to retake the village of Villers-Bretonneux . . .'[8]

In London, the matter is being followed closely, with the Chief of the Imperial General Staff, Sir Henry Wilson, receiving a cable from General Rawlinson in the early afternoon, advising that Villers-Bretonneux has been lost by British forces, COMPOSED OF YOUNG BOYS UNDER FIRE FOR THE FIRST TIME . . . THE VILLAGE IS OF THE HIGHEST TACTICAL IMPORTANCE . . . WE MUST GET IT BACK WHATEVER HAPPENS . . .[9]

Rawlinson further advises that the Australians are on the job.

If the Australians are on the job, Wilson cannot ask for more.

—

No matter that Glasgow and his two staff officers discover the area where General Heneker wants the 13th Brigade to start from under a bombardment of German shells. Still, Glasgow does not flinch.

'The Old Man,' one of those staff officers would recount, 'said we must set an example and on no account duck for shells; so he, Morell and I walked steadily through the bombardment, and by the grace of God got through unscathed.'[10]

Now, the key thing for Brigadier Glasgow is to ensure that the Germans are not yet into Bois l'Abbé or the Cachy Switch – both of which, he is reassured to see now that he is here, appear to be in British hands. But that is not enough for him. If these places fall to the Germans in the next few hours, his men will be massacred if they try to attack here.

Can the line hold?

Right on cue, as if sent by providence, there now arrives a young staff officer, an English chap who, as he takes off his helmet, exhibits a forehead glistening with sweat. There is just something about his air of calm competence mixed with honest effort that impresses Glasgow. This is a fellow traveller, a man after his own heart.

'Here's the man I want,' Glasgow says, taking him aside. 'You may be able to tell me. I want to know if you have troops in this Cachy Switch, south of the wood? Have you been up there?'

'Yes, I have just come back from there.'

'Are your men in it?'

'Yes.'

'Can I be certain they'll hold?'

'Yes, I'm sure they will.'

'Well, how about this trench through the wood? Are you there?'

'Yes, there are a lot of men in it.'

'Well, I want you to get someone through to them to tell them to hang on whatever they do. There'll be troops up to them in two hours' time.'[11]

And sometimes, even in war – perhaps particularly in war – it is just like that. They are dealing with a matter of life or death. They will likely never see each other again, and both know it. They talk for no more than two minutes, but Glasgow has an instinct that he can trust this English officer to do all possible to hold the Cachy Switch and, *in extremis*, is prepared to back his instinct. The Englishman, in turn, knows the gravity of the trust that has been placed in him – and accepts it.

The two men salute and take leave of each other.

Making his way back to Heneker, Glasgow happens to come over the last rise above the Somme River at the very moment the first Australian soldiers of his 13th Brigade are crossing on the makeshift bridges the Australian engineers have just put across to allow the column to pass more quickly. It is with an expert, appraising eye – and perhaps even a glistening one – that Old Man Glasgow gets a close look at them, here on what he knows is the eve of a very big battle. Standing by the end of the bridge, he takes the casual salute of those who particularly notice him but is not fussed otherwise, having a friendly word with many as they pass. Not long to go now, men, just a couple more miles. And there will likely be action tonight.

They are young, many of them, their eyes shining with the prospect of battle ahead, their helmets cocked at a jaunty angle, the rollie cigarettes dangling stylishly but unaffectedly from the corners of their mouths, and a swagger in their step that they actually have no right to. 'Poor chaps,' Glasgow thinks to himself. 'They're in for a tougher time than they realise.'[12]

The veterans, on the other hand, have the look of men who are steeling themselves for another turn at Hell. They know what awaits.

They have faced it before. They are facing it again. If they live, they will face it again and again. They have no time for affectation of any nature. With veterans who have been battling since the landing at Gallipoli, they can have a 2000-yard stare on a 500-yard horizon, for they really have seen Hell on earth, and can't quite believe they are still here. For the moment.

Glasgow's attention comes back to the young'uns. They are obviously the new recruits, brought in to replace the men lost at Dernancourt. It is not just the Brits who have had to fill the ranks of the lost with men perhaps not yet quite up to it.

The Brigadier now seeks out his battalion commanders to give them his impression of the lay of the land and tell them what they might be facing:

The 13th is going in. Our brigade has been given the task of counter-attacking along the south side of Villers-Bretonneux. I'm about to go back to Heneker to lock in the details, but the start-line will likely be positioned somewhere between Cachy and Bois l'Abbé. So return

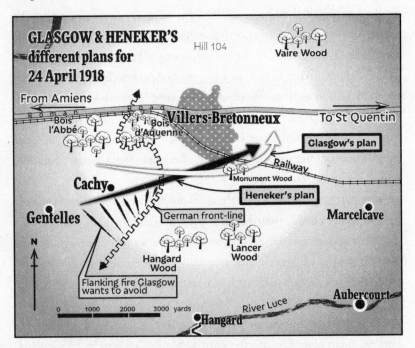

GLASGOW & HENEKER'S different plans for 24 April 1918

Hill 104 · Vaire Wood · From Amiens · Roman Road · Bois l'Abbé · Bois d'Aquenne · Villers-Bretonneux · To St Quentin · Glasgow's plan · Railway · Monument Wood · Heneker's plan · Cachy · Gentelles · German front-line · Marcelcave · Lancer Wood · Hangard Wood · Flanking fire Glasgow wants to avoid · Aubercourt · River Luce · Hangard

0 1000 2000 3000 yards · N

to your men and halt the brigade two miles west of there. Issue extra ammunition and make the usual preparations. I'll be back with more as soon as I can.

The battalion commanders return to their men and push off, heading across these flats of the Somme in artillery formation, spread out.

And again there is a soft drone overhead. Looking up, the men of the 13th Brigade spot German reconnaissance planes patrolling back and forth, clearly interested in their presence. From half a mile up, those planes briefly spray the marching columns with a few bursts of machine-gun fire, more on principle than in any expectation of inflicting casualties. Some of the Australian troops offer return fire in the same spirit.

—

Brigadier Glasgow, meanwhile, arrives back at General Heneker's 8th Division HQ at 2.30 to discuss where the plan now stands – and to be told for the first time that while the 13th Brigade will be attacking from the south, it is the 15th Brigade who will be the northern part of the pincer.

Glasgow is enormously pleased. With Pompey Elliott's men on the job, it will be a serious attack, and that is what is necessary if the pincer movement is to work. And yet when it comes to where the 13th Brigade will be starting from, Glasgow does not budge. Yes, he will send his 13th Brigade forth, with a start-line that runs north–south between Bois d'Aquenne and Cachy village.

'But you can't do that,' Heneker replies. 'The Corps Commander says the attack is to be made from Cachy.'

'Why, it's against all the teaching of your own army, sir,' Glasgow replies, 'to attack across the enemy's front. They'd get hell from the right.'

Glasgow is sure of his ground and precisely which ground he wishes to attack from. By having his men start where he wants, there will be no flanking fire coming from the right. If they get attacked from the left, they can put companies to the task of quelling that fire, dropping them as they go to deal with the Germans in the wood, allowing the rest of the brigade to proceed with the attack.

'Tell us what you want us to do, sir,' Glasgow says firmly, in a tone that is polite yet unyielding, 'but you *must* let us do it our own way.'[13]

It is a hard point to argue against, coming from an even harder man, and Heneker really has no choice but to give way. After all, he is asking the Australians to do what his own British troops have already tried to do and failed. The manner in which Glasgow says it gives firm indication that, when push comes to shove – Heneker *may* push, but the Australian *will* shove back if necessary – Glasgow's men will be doing it Glasgow's way, say what Heneker may. Something upon which Glasgow is equally firm is that there is to be 'no preliminary bombardment or creeping barrage', as this would merely warn the Germans that they are coming. No, their best chance is to try to maximise the surprise. All they want of the artillery is just to hit Villers-Bretonneux itself, starting as they leave their positions and continuing for 60 minutes, to wreak carnage generally. After that hour, as his men approach Villers, the barrage could move further forward, on to the old British front, and prevent German reinforcements coming forward.

It is also agreed that the British 54th Brigade will advance on Glasgow's right, with the dual goal of protecting the right flank of the 13th Brigade and securing the north tip of Hangard Wood. Finally, the 8th Division will contribute two battalions, one each to follow behind the 13th and 15th Brigades, with the idea that as the brigades pass the north and south sides of the township, these battalions will drop off and turn into the town, to protect the flanks of the 13th and 15th from any German forces emerging.

But to the key. The 13th Brigade must keep pushing on, past Villers-Bretonneux on the left, through Monument Wood on the right, and then turn north towards the Roman road, where they will meet the 15th Brigade right where the old British front-line trenches had been, some 500 yards north of the railway, mid-way between the railway and the Roman road. (A slight variation on Pompey Elliott's original plan – and much bigger for the fact it involves two brigades and not just one – it means the 15th Brigade have to travel 500 yards further than the Roman road, instead of just to it, and the 13th Brigade will travel 500 yards less.) Once they meet up, the Germans in Villers will be cut off, and it should then be a fairly simple matter for the battalions of the 8th Divvie to mop them up.

Oh, and one more thing.

They need to settle on what time Glasgow's 13th Brigade will begin their attack.

'What time do you propose?' Heneker asks.

'Half-past-ten [tonight],' Glasgow replies.

'That will not do. Can you start at eight?'

'But at that hour,' Glasgow replies, knowing that full dark does not come until ten o'clock, 'the light will be still too clear, indeed only a few minutes after sunset.'

'But the Corps Commander wishes it done at eight.'

Really? The III Corps Commander, you say, who commands the 8th Division, and therefore – as the 8th has been given command of the Villers-Bretonneux situation – the 13th Brigade? General Richard Butler? Glasgow's answer brooks no opposition.

'If it was God Almighty who gave the order,' old man Glasgow bursts forth, 'we couldn't do it in daylight. Here is your artillery largely out of action and the enemy with all his guns in position.'[14]

It would be madness to do it in daylight, and he *won't* do it.

'Well then, eight thirty perhaps?'

'No.'

'Nine o'clock?'

'No.'

'Nine thirty?'

'No.'

'Ten o'clock?'

'All right.'[15]

With 'zero hour' now set, Brigadier Glasgow hurries off to inform his men, who are due to be arriving at their designated bivouac area.

—

And *now* things start to move over at 5th Division!

General Heneker calls Hobbs and finally puts him in the picture, telling him that 5th Division's 15th Brigade must prepare to attack on the north side of Villers-Bretonneux. In other words, the very plan that Heneker had derailed hours earlier is now back on.

How on earth is it, by the by – and sigh the sigh – that the Australian attack is to go in under the command of General Heneker, who had not only commanded the 8th Division troops that had lost Villers-Bretonneux in the first place, but has also proven himself so far incapable of mounting a counter-attack to win the town back again?

Once advised of the situation, that is just what Pompey Elliott would like to know, now and forevermore, till death do him part. And he would ever after have only one explanation for it.

It was done, in his view, 'to save the face of the [British command]' who ultimately made the decision. The 5th Australian Division was handed over to the 3rd Corps for the purpose of making the attack, and, ultimately, the 15th Brigade was placed under the orders of the Commander of the 8th Division. 'I myself cannot see the object of this unless it was for the purpose suggested.'[16]

But in the here and now, his primary feeling is relief that his men have been so called upon. But can the British command really order just 6000 men to attack two German divisions, more than double their own numbers, with many more in reserve? Well, they are going to try.

Oh. And one more thing has been worked out. Pompey receives shortly afterwards a direct order, that the command he had put out at 9.05 am – ALL BRITISH TROOPS TO BE RALLIED AND REFORMED AS OUR TROOPS MARCH THROUGH THEM BY SELECTED OFFICERS AND ON ANY HESITATION TO BE SHOT[17] – be immediately cancelled.

Pompey Elliott, of course, obeys the order and withdraws his previous command, but he will make no apology for it. By his account it had been the very thing that had restored order to the panicky British troops. No one had actually been shot, but, 'Firmly informed what the orders were, and by association with our men [they] were at once restored to discipline and sanity.'[18]

———

In Villers-Bretonneux itself this afternoon, all is victory and celebration as the German soldiers who have made it this far start to enjoy the spoils of victory. These include gazing close-up at the many vanquished English prisoners before they are led away and examining the many captured artillery batteries – but there are also more obvious pleasures.

'This rather large place was still inhabited until a few days ago by the civilian population,' the 93rd Regiment's history would record. 'The stores and magazines were full, albeit partially destroyed. We saw units from different regiments with sacks full of coffee, with large bales of fabrics, with food and other things coming from the place. Also there was in the cellars a blood-red, viscous wine in large quantities, so that there were also drunks appearing . . .'[19]

———

After their vigorous march on this sunny but cold day, the 13th Brigade arrive at their destination – west of Bois l'Abbé, two miles west of Villers-Bretonneux.

'The march had been without incident,' the commander of the 52nd Battalion, Colonel John Whitham, would recall, 'and morale ran high.'[20]

First things first, Colonels Whitham and Christie send forth reconnaissance patrols to Bois l'Abbé and Bois d'Aquenne, to get a feel for the land and the likely sources of danger.

———

Interesting. A report has just come in to General Friedrich von Gontard, the Commander of XIV German Corps, the force attacking Villers-Bretonneux, from the reconnaissance *flieger*, airmen: 'Different columns of all arms are on the march to the endangered front.'[21] Perhaps as many as 4000 men have crossed the Somme and are now approaching the area just west of Villers-Bretonneux. The evidence mounts that *die Tommys* are building for a big counter-attack.

———

For Charles Bean, it is not luck. It is hard work. It is his instinct to always want to be in the middle of things, to see events unfold first-hand, to be with the Australian soldiers even when they go over the top and to be with their commanders when key decisions are made and transmitted.

And here he is now, just before three o'clock in the afternoon, with Hobbs in the 5th Division HQ at Bussy-lès-Daours, when the phone rings. On the other end of the line is the Commanding Officer of III Corps, General Richard Butler, who tells Hobbs his 5th Division is to help Heneker's 8th Division make a counter-attack on Villers-Bretonneux. The wheels of officialdom are just beginning to catch up with decisions that have effectively been taken three hours earlier.

As the conversation goes on, it is clear that Pompey Elliott's Brigade is to attack on the north side, and Butler even maintains to Hobbs that the 8th Division will make the principal attack on the south side of Villers-Bretonneux.

But, listening closely, Bean does not believe it for a minute. Nodding to one of the General's 5th Division staff officers, Colonel John Peck, as Hobbs continues talking, Bean whispers, 'This is what it will be . . .'[22]

With his finger, Bean traces on the map the two routes he predicts will be taken by the two Australian Brigades, the 15th and the 13th.

Sure enough, there are many phone calls that follow over the next 60 minutes, but by 4 pm Brigadier Elliott has got the call from General Hobbs.

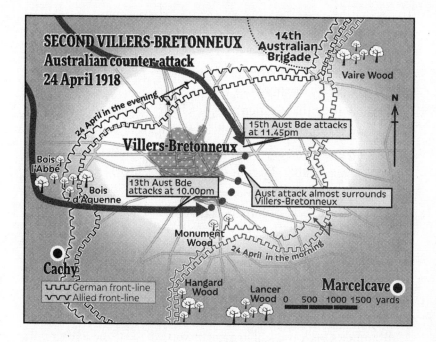

SECOND VILLERS-BRETONNEUX
Australian counter-attack
24 April 1918

14th Australian Brigade

Vaire Wood

24 April in the evening

Villers-Bretonneux

N

15th Aust Bde attacks at 11.45pm

Bois l'Abbé

Bois d'Aquenne

13th Aust Bde attacks at 10.00pm

Aust attack almost surrounds Villers-Bretonneux

Monument Wood

24 April in the morning

Cachy

⎍⎍⎍ German front-line
⋁⋁⋁ Allied front-line

Hangard Wood

Lancer Wood

Marcelcave

0   500   1000 1500 yards

It is *on*.

For now, Brigadier, you are to move your 4000 men to the small dip in the ground that lies just a mile or so north-west of the edges of Villers-Bretonneux, ready to move when the order comes. In short, some five hours after Pompey Elliott had been stopped from bringing his men forward as he had wanted to, he is now told to move them forward once more.

Ropable?

No. No one can rope Pompey in when he is in a mood like this. And certainly not General Heneker. Arriving unannounced at Heneker's HQ, the rambunctious Australian Brigadier quickly makes his views felt, just a notch down from outright insubordination. His 15th Brigade will cooperate, but his manner is truculent.

Heneker, struggling for the nominal control that has been bestowed upon him, tells the Australian as he leaves that he wants progress reports on how the 15th Brigade is faring, 'at least every hour'.

Oh, *really?*

'You'll be bloody lucky to hear from me before morning,'[23] Pompey Elliott tosses back over his shoulder as he strides out the door, prickly as a burr of blackberry bush in winter.

Still following the situation closely, Charles Bean is appalled at the very notion that the Australians will be placing their lives on the line in such an obviously difficult attack, under such command as this, for he knows that the British officer in question is not highly regarded. *The attack will be under Gen. Henniker of 8th Div who is a failure. . .*[24]

As to the practicalities of the operation: *It is a question if Elliott can do it by moonlight.*[25]

At least the answer to that question is soon provided when Pompey calls through to Hobbs, while Bean is still there, to advise he 'is glad 13th Bde will be on his right; that he was ready to attack by moonlight and that he would prefer an attack without artillery preparation'.[26]

Bean takes his leave, still extremely worried about the likely result, and heads back to Amiens. On his way, he passes the nigh-legendary 48th Battalion as they march through Montigny.

'As we passed the grand battalion,' Bean records, 'I could not help feeling very sour and disinclined to talk. They are being sent down there to be ready for the failure of the British army on which Rawlinson staked his precious reputation.'[27]

How has it come to this?

I suppose the poor Tommies [who abandoned VB] were scared by those prancing German tanks . . . The poor Tommies up there on the flat had. as far as I know. no plan. no instructions,- and certainly no means of fighting them . . . The tanks would have their way at will to do as they liked . . . until 3 of our tanks were sent up there.[28]

—

At the request of General Haig, an approach is also made to the French to contribute the French Moroccan Division to the composite force, but the answer comes back: *'Non.'*

Not tonight, Josephine. Perhaps tomorrow.

—

After a long day's fighting, the soldiers of Germany's 93rd Regiment are finally able to fulfill their orders and get themselves dug into Bois d'Aquenne on the western side of Villers-Bretonneux.

'Around 5 pm we reached our objective [in the wood],' their official history records. 'There, the brave men dig themselves in. The regiment thus stands 10 km before Amiens! Also the southern edge of the D'Aquenne Wood is occupied by parts of the 1st and 3rd Machine Gun Companies . . .'[29]

The men of those companies, with their light and heavy *Maschinengewehrs*, are soon digging themselves into the edges of the Bois d'Aquenne.

—

And what now?

Suddenly, at 5 o'clock, news comes for the senior officers of the 13th Brigade. Colonel Whitham of the 52nd Battalion and Colonel Christie of the 51st have a car sent for them and are soon taken to 8th Division HQ at Glisy, where they are ushered into the presence of . . . their own Brigadier Glasgow, who advises them that the 13th Brigade is to be a part of a major operation this night with the 15th Brigade. Their two battalions are to be in the prow of the attack, with the 50th Battalion forming a second line. He carefully explains what will be required of Whitham, Christie and their men, where they are to start from, the kind of country they will have to cover, where the Germans are expected to be, and where they will need to get to. It requires a quick march of 4000 yards over open country to get to the starting line, and then a further 3000-yard attack at high speed. Whatever happens, you must keep in touch with your flanking units and keep pushing forward. And now he waits. His question is unspoken but obvious. Can they manage it?

'One saw the relief in his eyes,' Whitham would recount, 'when, after careful examination of the distances to be covered and the several hazards involved, Christie and I were able to assure him that we could carry out our tasks.'

Right then.

The principal concern of both battalion commanders now is to get back to their company commanders before dark sets in, get them briefed and give them time to 'paint the picture' to their platoon leaders. By 7 o'clock they are on their way back, armed with maps and their attack order: A COUNTER-ATTACK TO RECOVER VILLERS-BRETONNEUX AND RESTORE THE LINE AS HELD UP TO THIS MORNING WILL BE DELIVERED TONIGHT IN CONJUNCTION WITH 53RD BDE ON RIGHT AND 15TH AUST BDE ON LEFT. ATTACK WILL START AT 10 PM.[30]

A similar process has been underway with the 15th Brigade. After receiving final confirmation at 7 pm that the attack is definitely going ahead, Pompey Elliott confers with his battalion commanders for the next hour and orders them to have their men ready to move into position at the start-line, two miles away, at 8.30 pm.

Pompey also gives orders that the men must wear white armbands covered with black cloth – that cloth to be ripped off once the attack proper begins, so they can identify each other in the gloom. And of course, 'All rules for night operations . . . [are to be] enforced until dawn.'[31] That means silence on the approach march, no smoking, no officers getting out their torch to check a map and so forth. (Most of the more astute officers, in any case, will have been holding up their compasses to the sunlight during the day, against this very likelihood that they would attack at night, just as many of the soldiers now rip sandbags to pieces and wrap the hessian around those bayonets, for the opposite effect: to prevent them gleaming in the moonlight.)

In the meantime, intelligence officers of both brigades prepare to head off with eight scouts apiece, well ahead of the main body of their soldiers – with compasses, maps and luminescent tape well in hand – to lay out those start-lines so the men will have no trouble finding the spots in the darkness.

As night falls, the Australian soldiers of the 13th and 15th Brigades busy themselves for what lies ahead.

—

As above, so below . . .

Above, the forces of light, represented by the near-full moon, are in a fight for control against the forces of darkness in the form of clouds. Below, the Australians and Germans are moving towards the same struggle, disagreeing only on who is good and who evil, and who will triumph.

And now . . .

Was zur Hölle? What the hell?

For the German soldiers of the 4th Guards Division, dug into the edge of Bois d'Aquenne, the vision is almost dream-like. Off there in the mid-distance, they can see, in the wan light thrown by the struggling moon, soldiers laying out luminescent tape on the ground 200 yards to their south-west. This, it seems, is fair warning of what they are about to face.

'At 9 pm,' the division's official history would record, 'it is observed that the Englishman prepares for a counter-attack.'[32]

The word goes out. Extra men are brought forward, extra guns and extra belts of bullets. Let them come.

—

Arriving back at their HQs, Whitham and Christie are able to brief their company commanders. All of their faces are illuminated by candlelight as they huddle over the map, and Whitham and Christie relate what must be done in a manner that would make the adjutant of the 2nd Northamptons, Major Hubert Essame, later recount how he was 'much impressed by the calmness of the Australian officers'[33] as they gave their orders. From here, these same company commanders now have just ten minutes to brief the Lieutenants, Sergeants and Corporals. By the light of a torch and the map spread before them on the ground, they go through it. And now the men themselves have to be addressed.

In C Company of the 51st Battalion, once that is done, Captain Billy Harburn gathers all 175 soldiers around him and, with Lieutenant Cliff Sadlier by his side, gives them their last, key, order.

'The Monument is your goal,' Captain Billy Harburn tells them flatly, 'and nothing is to stop you getting there. Kill every bloody German you see, we don't want any prisoners, and God bless you.'[34]

Similar orders are given to the other companies: no prisoners.

A brutal order, yes, but there is little choice. Sparing the lives of their enemy – to either ferry prisoners back or leave wounded Germans behind – would in the first instance limit their manpower to go on with the attack and in the second instance allow the possibility of those wounded Germans shooting them in the back after they have passed. It has to be done.

And one other thing is particularly important, and all the men of the 51st Battalion – due to lead the attack on the left flank, closest to Bois d'Aquenne and Villers-Bretonneux – are told it. The ground slopes down from right to left as they proceed, and there will be a natural tendency in the darkness to drift towards the southern outskirts of Villers-Bretonneux and the railway bank, where the Germans have also positioned many machine guns that could enfilade them at close quarters. So be careful.

Now, get yourselves ready. We are to move soon.

Quickly, quietly, as darkness falls the soldiers of the 51st and 52nd Battalions – the 13th Brigade's finest – prepare to march to the start-line positioned south of the Bois l'Abbé, just 500 yards west of the Cachy Switch.

The English officer who had assured Brigadier Glasgow that his men would hold the southern end of the Cachy Switch, in order to give his men a clean start, has been as good as his word. As they set off, Lieutenant Cliff Sadlier steadies his men of C Company, up the front on the left, encouraging them to keep tight to each other despite the boggy ground they're moving over, which tends to break them up.

And now, sure enough, at 9 pm, it is time for the two attack battalions of the 13th Brigade to get moving, with each company heading off independently to get to the start-line in their own manner. As Christie's men walk through the fields, all is quiet, bar the roar of German artillery shells landing in the small village of Cachy up ahead on the right.

———

For the men of the 15th Brigade, still in the shallow valley a mile northwest of town, where they have been waiting for hours, it has been a confusing and oft disappointing day. Orders have continued to come down the line, as have rumours, followed by counter-orders and counter-rumours. And then more of the same.

Finally, however, in the fading light just after 8 o'clock, they are told to fall in and are given the definite word. She's *on*, mate. The 15th Brigade are going to flank VB on the north, the 13th on the south, and together they're going to bite the bastard off!

Private Edwin Need – a 22-year-old from the Dandenong Ranges who had tried to enlist *14* times before finally succeeding when the standards came down to meet one with such bad teeth as him – is with his mates of the 59th Battalion. He would report how, after the briefing, 'the talk began as to the job in hand . . . all in a high pitch of excitement, we being filled up with plenty of hot stew, as much as we could stuff into us, later being loaded up with three bombs each, 150 extra rounds, extra dry rations, and two white arm bands to distinguish one another in the dark during the attack . . .'[35]

Inevitably, the talk dies down as the evening cools, and perhaps the shadow of death passes over the souls of a few of them – or at least there is the contemplation that they *might* have just hours to live.

'The men too serious to talk much,' Need chronicles, 'everyone thinking of the job in hand, and if they were to be one of the lucky ones . . .'[36]

And yet if the Four Horsemen of the Apocalypse are now starting to snort in the distance, drawing ever closer as the darkness deepens, so too is there a real horseman among them – Brigadier Pompey Elliott himself. His ever-ruddy cheeks now bright red with the emotion of it all, he explains one last time their orders, first to the men of the 59th Battalion.

We are attacking along the northern flank of Villers-Bret, boys. You of the 59th will be closest to the town, with the 60th on your left and the 57th in support. Don't stop for anything. Don't waste time taking prisoners. And, in the course of doing your duty, you must 'think of those back in Australia, and keep up the good name of the Anzacs . . .'

Pompey Elliott makes further promises: 'If you take your objectives you will be relieved before morning.'[37]

—

Alas, there is a delay. In this man's army there is *always* a delay. This one is in no small part due to the fact that, as it had only been confirmed at 4 pm that the 15th Brigade was required, the requisite meetings, preparations, distributions of weapons and ammo simply couldn't fit into four hours, and it is going to take just a little longer. Still, for men who have been expecting a move a whole day ago, waiting another half-hour is neither here nor there, and in the face of it they do the obvious. The horse-drawn company cookers come up and they have a cup of tea. It helps keep them warm, and it is – just maybe – a reminder of home and what they are fighting for in the first place. Contrary to the British practice, the Australians can have rum *after* the battle.

If they are still alive.

At 8.30, the first battalions of the 15th Brigade grab their rifles and their haversacks, their grenades and their bandoliers of ammunition, and – in the company of a dozen or so British stragglers who've lost their units, *choom*, but are nevertheless genuinely eager to fight – begin the two-mile march to their starting position, a line that has been laid out for them on yonder slope, the landmark to look out for being 'a stumped tree on a rise'.[38] By 9.10 pm, the last of them are also on their way.

'Along the valley,' Walter Downing would recount, 'we walked in single file towards Bois l'Abbé.'[39]

The advance is more difficult than expected. It is very dark as they proceed up the open valley, with just the full moon occasionally peeking through the clouds before it falls dark again. There are many obstacles, such as hedges, that keep breaking up their formations, platoons keep getting lost, and, soon enough, one of the advancing companies is 'warned by a sentry that a depression ahead had been drenched by German gas-shells'.[40] They divert accordingly, only to become even more lost in the dark – as does the company behind, which had been following their lost lead.

Further complicating things is the ongoing, if still sporadic, German shelling that continues to fall in their rough environs. Finally, however, the worst of it seems over; the German barrage moves on. And so they rise once more, moving across the countryside in the moonlight, the 60th on the left, the 59th on the right, with the 57th behind.

———

To the south, as the soldiers of the 13th Brigade proceed towards their start-line, they pass enormous numbers of shattered British soldiers of General Grogan's 23rd Brigade of the 8th Division – the ones who, though young, Grogan had still been confident would hold up – still straggling back from the positions they had lost that morning.

'Jerry's coming . . .' says one.

'Give 'em hell, Aussie,' says another. 'They've knocked us rotten.'[41]

The men of the 13th Brigade, with the companies of the 52nd Battalion in the lead, keep slowly pushing on in the darkness until finally, up ahead in the gloom, they come to 'a long straggling line of men seated on a white tape',[42] its left end ribboning off into the darkness towards the rather ominous dark patch in the darkness of Bois d'Aquenne.

But dontchers worry. Right now the Tommies are clearing those woods of any Germans who might lurk there.

It is 9.35 pm. The first companies of the 13th have made it in time to have a 'smoko' before the zero hour of 10.00, when the plan is for the two lead battalions of the 13th to set off together. The 13th Brigade's Machine Gun Company and 50th Battalion will be behind them.

'Great joy was felt,' Colonel Whitham of the 52nd Battalion would document, 'when all our sub-units reached the tape line and were deployed in their battle formation some ten minutes before "zero" – a tribute to the leadership and control of company and platoon officers.'[43]

Word also comes back that the British composite brigade, the 54th, is in position out on their right.

Alas, other companies have been delayed in the darkness, and when the 51st Battalion arrives, 23 minutes late, at 9.53 pm, Colonel Christie quickly goes in search of the 52nd's Colonel Whitham, and between them they arrange to delay departure by ten minutes to allow the men of the 51st to complete the deployment – a place for each platoon, and every platoon in its place – before setting off.

Suddenly, a German flare from up ahead soars high and bursts lazily against the night, casting them all in the smallest of deathly glows. As if awoken in the night by the flare, and upset by it, an angry enemy machine gun starts chattering up ahead on the left.

At ten o'clock exactly, British artillery shells start landing on Villers-Bretonneux and its surrounds, and what had been at best an irregularly seen dark silhouette up ahead on the Australians' left now becomes an angry, throbbing glare on the near horizon. The Germans quickly return serve with several shells of their own lobbed into the darkness where they clearly presume the British forces are likely to be gathering. None come close enough to do any major damage to either the 13th or 15th Brigades.

—

In his rough quarters at Amiens, just ten miles from Villers-Bretonneux, Charles Bean listens to the 'heavy firing of cannon' coming from that direction with some trepidation.

The preparation has been so hurried. The Germans in Villers-Bretonneux are no doubt already well dug in, as will be the Germans in the trenches that snake out from both sides of the town – the whole German line has moved forward. And now the light is going to make it hard for the Australians. Though the previous dark night had been promising for an attack, a glance through his window reveals the moon starting to push through the ever-thinning cloud cover, causing *a diffused moonlight . . . [meaning] a man would be visible at 30 yards.*

Bean pauses, and then jots his summation in his diary:

> *One cannot help but think of our 13th Bde going over, as they may be doing now. I don't believe they have a chance. No one worth anything to left or right. 5000 yards to go through the enemy, another Brigade to meet in the dark. Hobbs and Peck think they will. I scarcely think it will come off – surely.*[44]

Bean goes to bed, in his own words, *thoroughly depressed . . . feeling certain that this hurried attack would fail hopelessly.*[45]

———

It is coming time. They all know it. They stand quietly, just a little light movement here and there. The Corporal takes a last swig of cold tea, the private dashes off a note to the folks at home, just in case. The bombers check their Mills grenades in the sacks they are to carry over their shoulders, ten in each sack. The Lieutenant opens the chamber of his Webley revolver – for the second time – to check that he really has loaded it properly.

'Boys,' one of the officers is heard to say in the darkness, 'you know what you have to do. Get on with it.'[46]

Right up the front, on the left, Lieutenant Cliff Sadlier, a 25-year-old commercial traveller from Western Australia's Subiaco, who is Harburn's second-in-command, steadies his platoon and repeats the word of warning that has been passed down from on high about the woods 800 yards ahead on the left.

'If you hear any noise in the woods,' he says, 'don't "get the wind up" – it will only be a few Tommies cleaning up the Germans there.'[47]

Righto then.

Among the men getting ready, not a little goggle-eyed at everything they are witnessing, are two reinforcement drafts recently arrived from Australia, and they include many young fellows, like 18-year-old Bertie Denman, a mill-hand from Perth who is about to undergo his baptism of fire.

Such men, the 51st Battalion's history would note, 'had not yet faced the death rattle of hostile machine guns or the devastating and mind destroying power of incoming artillery fire. Every man hoped earnestly to acquit himself well in his first action, but until he went over the top and charged into blistering fire no man could say how he would be affected . . . The veterans knew what to expect.'[48]

Those veterans include Cecil Burt and Reg Helyar, country boys from Solomontown, South Australia, and Nanup, Western Australia, and while they are thick with each other, lately the young'un Bertie is never far away, gravitating to their wizened nous, as new chums have been ever wont to do.

All of them are told that their objective is to get to Monument Wood and push through. 'After you get away from the tapes and over the top of the hill you will see the wood and must make for that. The direction is due east . . .'[49]

At 10.10 pm, the word goes out: 'Advance.'[50]

With this, the soldiers of the 13th Brigade, the 51st Battalion on the left and the 52nd on the right – some 1500 men in all, arranged in two successive waves, two companies in each wave, spaced 200 yards from each other – start off in the darkness. In final support, the 50th Battalion follows 1000 yards behind. At the last instant, Colonel

Whitham decides to accompany his men of the 52nd.

The night would be as black as a Brigadier's heart, bar the fact that the heavy cloud cover is less thick in places, meaning that some sad, bare luminescence of the moon does manage to seep through. It is still dark enough that for some time the runners they send out in front struggle to find the signals and medical posts that have been set up in the darkness ahead, but still they keep moving.

German artillery shells are falling around them, with a few bringing death and destruction, but Brigadier Glasgow had obviously been right. The darkness really is their friend – for the moment. For the first few hundred yards, the men of the 13th struggle across soil freshly ploughed, primed to reap a terrible harvest of death if they get caught on it.

From Villers-Bretonneux, yet more flares now lazily arc up into the sky, illuminating the soldiers on the move in a kind of deathly twilight. They push on regardless, the dark and menacing outline of Bois d'Aquenne soon looming ever larger on their left, its roots on the slopes that drift down from Cachy plateau.

On the edge of those woods, observing them closely, are hundreds of Prussian Guards of the 5th Guard Grenadier Regiment, German soldiers who have escaped the attention of the British soldiers who had been meant to clean them out.

Following the lead of their commander, the Germans hold their fire, waiting until the attackers' course brings them to a distance of just 200 yards away.

Komm nur. . . Komm nur. . . Keep coming . . . Keep coming . . . .

—

Where have they gone?

At the starting line of the 15th Brigade, a mile north of the 13th Brigade on the western side of Hill 104, the Commanding Officer of the 60th Battalion, Colonel Norman Marshall, is trying to sort things out. This one-time welterweight boxing champion of all Victoria is no-nonsense, I said NO-nonsense!

He quickly works out the situation. After his own 60th Battalion had been delayed leaving their bivouac by a last-minute meeting of officers, and then struggling forward, they had arrived at the starting line at 10.15 pm – already 15 minutes after their scheduled departure. What is more, only half of the 59th Battalion is there, and no sign at all of the 57th Battalion. He has no choice. Assuming command of an otherwise chaotic situation, he insists that the attack of the 15th Brigade *cannot* go ahead until the missing troops are located and brought forward, and he sends out trusted officers to do exactly that. They will wait until the last of the soldiers of the 15th have arrived and then, and only then, will they launch their counter-attack.

Fritz won't be going anywhere, after all.

Meantime, they send their scouts forward to try to work out exactly where the German defences are.

—

The 13th Brigade keep moving east.

Komm nur. . . Komm nur. . .

Very close now. The fingers of the Prussian Guards in Bois d'Aquenne itch to whiten and tighten on the trigger, waiting for the command to fire. Several flares are sent soaring.

They burst right above the Australians and, for the Germans, illuminate the shrouded figures in the near distance better than ever.

'Still!'[51] cries an Australian officer, as ever on the reckoning that, caught beneath a flare, your best chance is to lie doggo if you're on the ground and stand like a statue if upright.

Of course, it is too late . . .

Jetzt! Now!

For the Australians, it starts as an ominous thudding out to their left – is this the British clearing out the Germans in the woods that they'd been told about? – Then men start to fall.

'The darkness in front started to *tap, tap, tap*,' one officer would recount, 'and bullets whistled round and the line shuffled forward with rifles at the ready like men strolling into fern after rabbits.'[52]

And there are shells, too!

'We had not gone far,' another officer would recount, 'before the dark lit up in a one mile long blaze like a row of footlights, and as these faded the shells arrived. We melted into shell-holes.'[53]

As the first burst of shells slacken, the Australians are up and moving once more, 'leaving the shell-bursts behind us as we went forward'.[54]

And then the fusillade goes from light rain to a heavy downpour as it now roars into an unending *TAPPITY-TAP-TAP-TAP-TAP*. The German bullets simply tear into them and gaps appear in the Australian line.

Some cry out. Most fall for their country 'without a sound'.[55]

Far and away the worst hit is the platoon right next to the wood, the men of Captain Billy Harburn's company, under the command of Lieutenant Cliff Sadlier.

Sadlier is shocked. He had been told that any shooting from that section of the woods would be the British cleaning out the Germans! And yet, within seconds, '39 out of the 42 in my platoon were in mud either dead or wounded'.[56]

It is a miracle that he is still alive. But there are at least a handful of others in the same position. The platoon to their immediate right has also been hit hard, but another miraculously spared is a tall, dark, likely sort of bloke, Sergeant Charlie Stokes, who now crawls over to Sadlier and asks him straight out: 'What are you going to do?'

'Carry out the order,' Sadlier replies, 'go straight to our objective.'

'You can't do it,' Stokes replies. 'You'll all be killed.'

'Well, what can we do?'

'Collect your bombers and go into the wood and bomb those guns out.'[57]

Sadlier considers it. After all, Stokes makes ghastly sense. Going forward, as he had intended, they can only be killed. Stopping here and doing nothing means the advance of the 51st Battalion is also stopped and the whole plan of recapturing Villers-Bretonneux threatened. And with the bombers – specially trained infantry who carry bags of grenades and work in pairs, one carrying, one throwing – they really could give the enemy some how's-your-mother?

Yes, there is no way around it.

'I knew,' he would later recount, 'that if we did not clean out the edge of that wood, the 51st Battalion would be sitting ducks.'[58]

Fortunately, he finds near him a couple of bombers by the names of Wilfred Guthrie and John Collins – good mates who'd first met aboard HMAT *Aeneas* when they'd sailed out of Fremantle in April 1916 as part of the 2nd Reinforcement for 51st Battalion – who are also still kicking, and just beyond them another couple of ordinary privates. And, of course, Charlie Stokes will join them, having taken a bag of grenades from a dead bomber, determined to do his fair share and more to see out the idea he has come up with.

—

At his command post behind the 51st, Colonel Whitham gets the message from a runner. C Company is in SERIOUS DIFFICULTY ON ITS LEFT FLANK, DUE TO ENEMY FIRE FROM THE WOODS TO THE NORTH.[59]

The word is it will take ten minutes to sort out. In the meantime, the two battalions keep moving, as it is obvious that, whatever else, Sadlier's men will be drawing all the fire.

—

After giving orders for the Lewis guns to come forward and designating exactly where he wants them, Sadlier gathers his men to him and gives brief instructions.

Now, Lewis gun team. Give covering fire. While you are keeping the Squareheads down, we will loop out to the left and right, to be out of your firing line while we throw bombs. Then when you see us go in, cease fire.

The rest of you, stay with me. Take the ripped bits of sandbag off your bayonets – there is no point, we are spotted. Taking the bombers with us, we need to get close enough – through quick bursts – so that we can hurl our grenades at them.

Yes, sir.

As a last move before getting stuck into it, Sadlier sends a runner to find Captain Billy Harburn, to tell him of the disaster that has occurred. His platoon will 'clear the woods' regardless, though they 'might be late at the objective'.[60]

Showing the way, as ever, Sadlier is on his feet and running straight at the dark wood, lightly illuminated by the flares, clenching the two grenades in his hands as he goes. Charlie Stokes is seen to be running just off his right shoulder, toting the heavy bag of bombs . . . only for all of them to come under heavy machine-gun fire after just 30 yards.

Again, Sadlier and his men must go to ground, but at least now they are close enough to see exactly where the German machine-gun post is – those flashes in the wood, about 80 yards off.

Sadlier waits for his moment, and then gives the signal.

And . . . *now!*

In an instant the Lewis gun opens up, spitting out 30 bullets in three seconds, and Sadlier and his men are loping forward, their grenades in their throwing hands, holding down the lever which, the instant they release it, will mean the bomb has seven seconds to explode.

They run and, following Sadlier's cue, Charlie Stokes and the others hurl their grenades with every bit of enthusiasm as back in the old days, when beating the Albany kids at the cricket carnival seemed like the most important thing in the world.

But this is different . . .

And throw! And throw! And throw!

Seven seconds later, the grenades explode all around the German machine-gun post.

Come in, spinner!

Within seconds Sadlier and his men are into the woods and able to use the trees for some cover as they rush to get among the pan-icked Germans – notwithstanding that Sadlier had felt 'a burning pain in my leg'[61] the instant they got in the wood – and a furious hand-to-hand fight breaks out. Australian bayonets wreak bloody havoc. Screams fill the night, along with cries for mercy: '*Kamerad!*' '*Kamerad!*' '*KAMER . . .*'

A bloody gurgle, and *Kamerad* is no more.

That machine-gun post is quickly destroyed, and now that the Australians are among the trees, they can also attack two nearby machine-gun posts that are soon flashing at them. Yes, Sadlier is now bleeding quite badly from the leg. 'It did not give too much trouble,' he would recall, 'so I kept going, hurling grenades and firing my pistol. I concentrated on one machine gun that seemed to be doing a lot of damage. Probably more by good luck than good management, I cleared out the post and took the gun. But another machine gun bullet smashed into my forearm, paralysing it.'[62]

Sadlier urges his men forward to attack the third machine-gun post. Right by it, one enormous German soldier is holding up his left hand in surrender, while shouting out '*Kamerad*' and firing his gun with his right hand! Sadlier guns him down with his revolver, just before he is shot again, this time in the arm. He goes down hard and is dragged to the rear, but his few remaining men finish the job, capturing six machine guns in all.

The advance of the 13th Brigade can now continue with no risk of taking murderous fire from its left flank. Sadlier is bandaged up at a Regimental Aid Post to stem the blood flow and sent to a rear area where he can be evacuated.

—

Half a mile south-east of Sadlier, *Leutnant* Roßbach is on a mission: racing in a westerly direction, crouched over from shell hole to shell hole towards the German front-line, which lies fair in the path of the 13th Brigade moving east. He has been ordered to find a *Leutnant* Brosig of 11th Company of the Guards Grenadiers and arrange to replace Brosig's men with his own 7th Company of the Foot Guards, and . . .

Here he is now, in a shell hole just back from the Cachy wire, and as far from happy as they are far from Germany. Brosig reels off his complaints. They simply don't have enough men, with just 40 of them defending 150 yards of trenches. The company on his right are in equally *arger Bedrängnis*, desperate straits, but at least they are there to do what they can. On his left, the company from the 77th Division is nowhere to be seen. Those trenches are empty! 'He feared,' Roßbach would recount, 'that a counter-attack was imminent and said that his men were in no condition to meet it.'[63]

Under the circumstances, it is no surprise that Brosig is anxious for Roßbach to bring his own men forward immediately, but Roßbach demurs, insisting he must reconnoitre the position first. That completed – things are every bit as dire as reported – he returns and tells Brosig that he will return with his company shortly, once they have eaten. Roßbach disappears into the night, returning from whence he came, shell hole to shell hole, until he reaches his own men once more, in the second German line 500 yards to the east.

—

Though Colonel Marshall has ordered the 15th Brigade to stand fast on the start-line until he can sort out the mess, in all of the confusion there is a blunder and the scouts are sent forward – one of them is the redoubtable Private Edwin Need.

Need soon finds himself in the moonlight, with another mate, Ted Wiley, 20 yards out to his right. Like the two antennae of a snail – though they are actually moving at a brisk pace – their job is to look for signs of the enemy first, which, one way or another, will warn the battalion where they are.

It is, and no mistake, a *shit* job, but someone has to do it for the good of the battalion. A single scout, of course, can be much quieter than a platoon of 40 men, so Need has every chance of hearing the enemy talking or digging before they hear or see him. Secondly, if things go wrong, it is a much better outcome that one scout is shot dead than a whole platoon. It is a *shit* job.

Need and Wiley keep going, as quietly as they can, both keenly aware that every step might be their last, because if the Germans have sentries out to counter their scouts, it is their own foreheads that are most likely the first thing to explode with the night and . . .

There!

Ahead in the gloom, Need can see dim figures putting out rolls of wire in front of a newly dug trench, an instant before a voice rings out: '*Alt!*'

Need doesn't need any more 'signs' and cries out to where – mistakenly – he presumes the rest of the battalion is right behind him: 'Look out boys, they're Fritz's!'[64]

Need can see the Germans tumbling back into their own trench. Diving into the first shell hole he can find, he can plainly hear the guttural sounds of the German officers snapping orders at their men. He has not the first clue what those orders are, but he is fairly certain they involve an attempt to terminate the life of one Private Edwin Need of the Dandenong Ranges. Sure enough, within seconds, a tempest of machine-gun bullets is flying above his hidey-hole, together with grenades. If just one grenade drops short and into his hole, he will never see Australia again.

'I hugged mother earth as close as I possibly could, and admit I had the wind up then if I ever did . . .'[65]

———

The mighty 13th Brigade is now free to get about its business, to push through on the south side of town and get within 500 yards of the Roman road, where they are due to meet up with the 15th Brigade.

The Australians keep moving forward and soon come upon soldiers just ahead!

The call goes up: 'Bomb the bastards!'[66]

A couple of grenades are hurled forward before a second cry goes up: '*Wait!*

TOMMIES!'

And it's true. Rather than marauding Fritzes, these men prove to be battered British soldiers of the 2nd Devon and 1st Worcester Regiments who, despite having Australian grenades whistling around their ears – mercifully no one is wounded – are nearly overcome with sheer relief that the oncoming soldiers in the darkness are Australians and not Germans, as they thought they were being attacked from the rear.

These English soldiers are holding the Cachy Switch, a perfect place for the medical officer of the 52nd Battalion, Captain Robert Forsyth, a Melburnian MD before the war, to set up his advanced aid post behind a large heap of mangold-wurzel.

Bent low to the ground, the 13th Brigade are able to keep going relatively unscathed, right to the point where the flashes in the dark just ahead – mixed with the throaty roar of dozens of machine guns being pointed at them – show that they have come upon a line of enemy outposts.

The call goes up one more time: 'Bomb the bastards!'

This time, the bullets coming their way leave no doubt that they are courtesy of the Germans, and a dozen grenades are hurled from Australian hands at the flashes coming from *Leutnant* Brosig's men of the 11th Company of Guard Grenadiers.

The difficulty now is to get at these Germans through the barbed wire that had been set up to stop them in the first place . . . but is now providing them with a useful obstacle through which the Australians must pick their way like bugs trying to get to the other side of a vicious spider's web. For the retreating Brits, it had been relatively easy to navigate through it in the daytime, but now it is Hell's own job for them to make their way past en masse on this dark night.

As the Australians manoeuvre through, it turns out the Germans have positioned a lot of their *Maschinengewehr 08/15* machine guns on the perimeter *exactly* there. Once they set off their flares, they open up on the Australians, exacting a heavy toll.

No fewer than half a dozen of these machine guns are roaring. Most devastating is an especially accurate gun aimed at a particularly dense entanglement of wire out on the far left flank, where it dips into a hollow and the men caught there can move neither backwards nor forwards They cannot even throw themselves to the ground, as that would be onto the rolls of barbed wire. And who are the Australian soldiers so unfortunate as to be on that far left? The remains of Lieutenant Cliff Sadlier's platoon, who have just caught up after their quick demolition of the *Boche* in the *bois*, only to be under heavy fire once more. Again, it is Sergeant Charlie Stokes who must rise to the occasion.

Leading his fellow survivors on a crawl forward, Stokes is able to launch a counter-attack that, by virtue of grenades and then guns, takes those *Maschinengewehr* out one by one.

In the meantime, realising that the wire would hold them up forever if they didn't take action, it is Captain Billy Harburn, the commander of C Company – already awarded the Military Cross with Bar for heroism in battle – who once again takes matters into his own hands. Blowing his whistle, shouting and leaping forward, he leads a charge through gaps in the wire. The shouting, swearing soldiers of the 13th Brigade stream through, just as Brosig's terrified men send so many Very flares soaring into the skies that it is briefly as bright as day.

'The enemy,' Charles Bean would document, 'a weak line of machine-gun posts in small bits of trench, was killed, surrendered or ran away, and the advance continued.'[67]

The Australians are now moving forward again, in force.

—

Five hundred yards east of Brosig, and directly in the path of the Australians, is *Leutnant* Roßbach, now back at the German second line after his visit to the outpost line.

Roßbach is seeing to the feeding of his men when he catches 'the sound of a loud cheer. That settled all doubt – the expected counter-attack had been launched.'[68]

Sausages, black bread and ersatz coffee fly everywhere as the soldiers race to their guns. Out there in the dark on the outpost line, Roßbach realises his one brief meeting with *Leutnant* Brosig 15 minutes ago is likely to be the only time they ever meet – by now the nervous *Leutnant* is probably dead. Then the shooting stops, and within a couple of minutes dozens of guardsmen with wild eyes come racing back out of the darkness, gurgling the terrifying news.

Feindlichen Soldaten . . .! Tausende von ihnen!

Enemy soldiers . . .! Thousands of them!

Der Tommy kommt!

—

As the Australian advance passes beyond the German outpost line, the wounded from that clash start to make their agonising way back towards Forsyth's aid post in the Cachy Switch.

'From every side,' he would record, 'boys came crawling in . . . and I started to tie up and send back anyone that could crawl . . .'[69]

From out of the dark behind them comes another line of Australian soldiers of the 13th Brigade, led by a Lieutenant brandishing a revolver, who has no sooner sighted the medical officer and the wounded men all around than he howls at them to 'Get on!'

There are to be no stragglers on this night, not among the Australians, and it is all the medical officer can do to explain that they are not stragglers – these men have actually been hit.

The second Australian wave soon heads out after the first, at which point much of Villers-Bretonneux appears to burst into flames, a massive bonfire in the night, throwing its immediate borders into much the same kind of crossover twilight world that many of the dying soldiers from both sides are now entering. For the surviving Australians of the 13th Brigade moving forward, it provides, nevertheless, a sure beacon in the night to guide their path, and also means that many of the German soldiers defending the town are now silhouetted by the flickering flames behind.

. . .

. . .

Back at the medical post, Captain Robert Forsyth sees the third wave of the 13th Brigade go through, picking up some new casualties in need of attention along the way, again with a Corporal making sure that all men here are genuinely wounded. Taking Forsyth's assurances that they are, they continue on.

Shortly afterwards, the first of the soldiers of the 2nd Northamptons come through – the British soldiers assigned to follow the 13th – then turn north to attack the south side of Villers-Bretonneux.

'The church was on fire, illuminating the field,' one of them would recall. 'There were many black blobs which were not shell holes. They were obviously deceased Aussies.'[70]

For the young British soldiers in particular, it is confronting, even terrifying, but with one exception they push on. The odd man out is a small young British soldier who sits down in front of Captain Forsyth and confesses that he has not been hit but has just got the wind up him, what with all the shells landing all around and bullets whizzing past.

'Well,' Forsyth says in his kindly manner, 'we are all going [forward] in a minute. With one of these shells you are just as safe with the boys.'[71]

'I believe you're right,' the lad says, nodding slowly, and goes out after his mates.

('He was,' Forsyth would observe, 'the only boy I saw hesitate that night.')

But wait, what's this?

Now into the aid post comes a weeping Tommy Corporal – really, crying like a ten-year-old – holding his wounded arm.

'Pain bad?' asks Captain Forsyth.

'No, sir,' the Corporal squeaks, 'this is nothing, but I can't get the boys to go forward.'

Clearly, the poor bastard has been trying to get his platoon of equally young British soldiers to move forward, all while nursing his arm, but he just can't manage it.

Mercifully, an older wounded Digger in the aid post takes pity on him. 'Never mind, kid,' sez he, 'the boys will hunt Fritz without youse kids.'[72]

—

The men of the 13th continue to push forward, and now, several hundred yards east of the Cachy wire, they are relieved that the fire upon them has somewhat diminished – which is to say only a few of their number are now being killed and grievously wounded, instead of a lot. Off to their right, they note the dark bulk of an abandoned German tank, stuck in a shell hole. Those closest to it can even see its name: 𝕰𝔩𝔣𝔯𝔦𝔢𝔡𝔢.

—

With the German flares still rising, it doesn't take long to find the next German line some 500 yards ahead, based around a series of shell holes and shallow trenches. Of course, the German soldiers can see them approaching, too.

Leutnant Roßbach and his men prepare to meet them.

The Australians can determine the position of this next obstacle fairly precisely by the fact that it has about eight machine guns firing upon them from trenches spread across a front of about 200 yards, all while the Germans are sending flare after flare soaring into the night sky as the brutes call in their artillery to plaster the ground the Australians are now covering.

Right, then. The men of the 13th throw themselves down and use the skills honed at the rifle ranges back at Pontville in Tassie and Eagle Farm in Queensland, moving forward in short bursts and aiming for the flashes in the night, knowing that German gunners are just on the other side.

Now the Lewis gunners bring withering fire on all eight German machine guns at once. 'There they are, boys!'[73] Lieutenant Rogers shouts, and he does not have to ask twice. The finest sons of Queensland and Tassie are on their feet, rushing en masse with wild yells . . . *straight* at the German positions.

—

Out of the darkness emerges a murderous mob of cheering, shooting, grenade-hurling Australian soldiers just 100 yards away . . . and heading straight for them. Roßbach's men fire their rifles and their eight machine guns at the attackers, and they have the satisfaction of seeing them going to ground, to take emergency cover in shell holes . . . only . . . only to see them *still* moving forward!

Ahead in the gloom, the now-alarmed German soldiers can see low movement right in front of them as the Australians make short rushes from shell hole to shell hole, even as more flitting shadows out to their left show the Australians are outflanking them. *Leutnant* Roßbach switches the two heavy machine guns to fire at the attackers and is quick to ensure his men launch as many flares as possible.

But still the attackers keep coming!

And now the Germans' ammunition is running short!

And every flare reveals more Australians breaking through on the left!

And now on the right, too!

And there are yet more cheers in their strange language, now louder than ever over the machine-gun fire.

Get the bastards!

Into 'em!

Stick 'em!

'The right gave way . . .' the commander of the platoon next to Roßbach, *Leutnant* Walter Elfeldt, would recount. 'The last belt of machine gun ammunition has now to be used . . . The leading men fall but others charge on . . . These too are mown down, but new waves always come on cheering . . . Their Lewis guns hammer with tracer bullets into the German line . . . [Our] fusillade was drowned in an [Australian] cheer . . . The defenders gave way . . . The [Australians] followed hard on our heels. With great uproar they sweep through the dark night . . .'[74]

'Only the machine guns hold, stuck like a wedge in the enemy advance . . . The attackers come on, we are bypassed left and right . . .

The ammunition is running out . . . We must slow the rate of fire. There are now more and more attackers, a second wave closely following the first . . . The enemy in front of us charging forward . . .'[75]

Most unnervingly, they *never* stop their cheering!

'Some fall, mown down, others rush on but always new waves appear rushing forward into our machine gun fire. [The enemy's Lewis guns] are hammering into our line . . . We can't hold them back . . . The left and right wings back away under the onslaught . . .'

Every time they look up, there are still more of them coming! And now we Germans have run out of ammunition for our machine guns!

'With a loud roar . . . the assault waves roll against us. Only the machine gun fire has held them down so far. Now that it is extinguished . . . Our line staggers . . . backwards. . . backwards . . . There seems to be no stopping our men from going backwards . . .

'All around you can hear only the loud cheers . . . The [enemy] is hard on the heels. With great noise and confusion, the crowds roll through the dark night.'[76]

One wounded Tommy soldier, taken prisoner earlier by the Germans and now in their trenches, will later report how when one of the German officers in the face of the hard-charging 13th Brigade 'tried to get them forward . . . they shot him and [ran]'.[77]

Now that the Australians are right upon them, many of the brave remaining Germans give in to the reality of their situation and throw their hands into the air. But it is too late. Among the savaged survivors of the 51st Battalion, who have suffered most at the hands of German soldiers on this night, there is no mercy, and nor do their officers want them to show any.

Captain Billy Harburn, still right in the middle of his distinctly thin ranks of C Company, even reminds them of what he had said just as they stepped off, about taking no prisoners. And none are taken. Those who fight are shot. Those who surrender are shot.

'I did not know what to do with them,'[78] Harburn would say afterwards of the Germans who wished to surrender.

Beyond everything else, the Australians have long had problems with

Germans who tried to kill you right to the instant when you were about to kill them, and who *then* thought their surrender would save them.

'Strike me pink the squareheads are dead mongrels,' one Australian soldier had previously written home. 'They will keep firing until you are two yards off then drop their rifle and ask for mercy. They get it too, right where the chicken gets the axe . . . when the bayonet goes in their eyes bulge out like prawns.'[79]

And so it is on this night. The Germans are killed in their hundreds.

In the face of merciless carnage, the *Leutnants* Roßbach and Elfeldt are among those who do the obvious – they fall back fast (some would say flee) in the hope of making a stand further back at the third German line at Monument Wood. They are among hundreds of Germans now running with the wild men of the far south on their tails.

Agonised screams fill the night.

—

Dug in on the south side of Villers-Bretonneux, along the railway and not quite in the path of the 13th Brigade's advance – and now deeply alarmed at the sounds in the night, the obvious tumult of battle coming closer – is Captain Adolf-Helmut von Gadow of Germany's 93rd Infantry Regiment. And he is far from the only one feeling the strain. For now here is Major Wegehaupt, the leader of 1st Battalion, who suddenly jumps into his hole, crying out, '*Hören Sie mal, hier links von uns reißt ja alles aus!* Listen, here on our left everyone's running away!'[80]

And he's right. Von Gadow and Wegehaupt can hear shouts and the sound of men running. Rushing to a point where they can get a better view, they can now see the mess as well.

'We saw by the light of flares all [the men] in wild flight,' Captain von Gadow would recount. 'It was a real panic.'[81]

Trying to keep calm in spite of everything, von Gadow sends a runner to bring forward the Reserve Company, telling them they 'must come immediately and intervene'.[82]

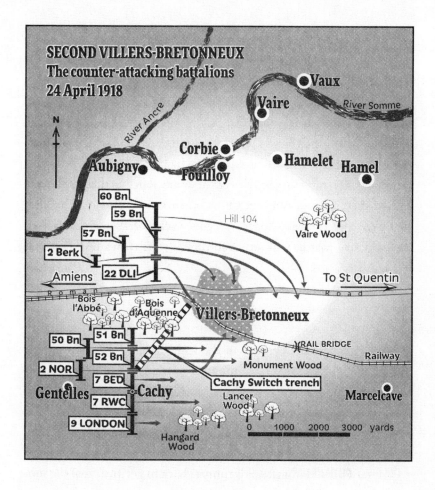

In the third German line extending through and south of Monument Wood, the 700 soldiers of the 5th Foot Guards – their numbers increased by the 3rd Machine Gun Company's 100 men and 12 machine guns – have listened to the events of the last two hours unfold with growing alarm, all too aware that their own time will come. And the problem they have now, in their deep trenches dug just south of the wood, is that although the darkness is suddenly *wimmelt es von Männern*, 'seething with men',[83] it is not immediately clear who they are.

Ach, but now the shouts come in the darkness '*Nicht schießen! Wir sind Deutsche.* Don't fire, Germans here!'[84]

The shattered Germans arrive, bearing terrifying testament to what must be behind them. Merciless, marauding, murderous Australians. In the face of it, the commander of 10 Company, *Leutnant* Iversen, would recall the carnage wrought by the Australians the last time the 5th Foot Guards had faced them at Passchendaele, and so now prays he and his men are 'not in for an experience like that'.[85]

What they most urgently need now are flares to illuminate the enemy; they have all run out. On his own initiative, one of Iversen's young ensigns, von Falkenhayn, has gone back to get some, and Iversen can only pray that he will return in time, before they are all engulfed by the Australians.

—

And now the forward elements of the 13th Brigade are coming to the third German defensive line, running north–south on the western edge of Monument Wood. And yet, as triumphant as they have been through the night so far, inevitably they, too, have taken casualties that have thinned their line. Nowhere is it thinner than among C Company of the 51st Battalion, which has been in the thick of it from the first.

Captain Billy Harburn sends runners back to get men from the support company of the 51st to come forward, to replace the fallen, as well as one company of the follow-up battalion for this purpose, the 50th.

It is as well, for as the midnight hour approaches and all of the 13th Brigade get close to Monument Wood, the Germans resistance really does stiffen. Yet only a small part of that stiffening comes from those who have fled and are now turning to make a stand. Among the German officers trying to get his men to do exactly that is *Leutnant* Elfeldt, along with other survivors of the 7th Company who had fallen back until they reached the trenches on the west side of Monument Wood, occupied by a Fusilier Battalion and 200 yards north of *Leutnant* Iverson.

'Once we have crossed this line, a defence is formed. We manage to bring the . . . waves to a halt. It won't be so easy for the enemy to overrun the Fusilier battalion . . . From [my] 7th Company I can only find seven men in this vicinity.'[86]

Of the Fusiliers, however, there are at least 700 men and they are fresh, with plenty of ammunition.

For the Australians of the 13th Brigade, it is not just that the fire from in front is now furious, but on their left flank – positioned behind the railway embankment that runs on the southern edges of Villers-Bretonneux – they are copping heaps.

Who are *those* bastards?

—

At the railway embankment, ashen-faced messengers had come back to Captain von Gadow once, and then *twice*. They swear there is *no* reserve company. In any case, it is by now almost beside the point. The enemy has moved past them, towards Monument Wood. That meant the enemy's left flank was exposed and, whatever else, von Gadow was still gratified to have two heavy *Maschinengewehr 08/15s*, and a mortar with their crews, *die glänzend wirkten*, working brilliantly, with one man – Sergeant Wunderlich – in charge of them all and fighting well.

These are the men von Gadow has unleashed, firing right into the 13th Brigade's left flank. It even encourages some of the fleeing Germans to come to them, 'astonished to find German troops still here'.[87]

The Australians on that left flank bring their own fire to bear in turn, placing von Gadow and his men in *eine heikle Lage*, a precarious position, but they hold on and keep firing.

—

While von Gadow and his men are able to keep the Australians at bay on their own section of the perimeter of Villers-Bretonneux, the line out to their right is so thin that two foraging privates of the 51st Battalion – Cecil Burt and Reg Helyar – actually get into the town, the streets lit by the wavering light thrown by the flares of the battle behind them and the burning buildings in front. Turning a corner, they suddenly come face to face with some 40 Germans, who are only yards away! Quick flash, Helyar takes a grenade and hurls it at them to give him and Cec time, as they duck back around the corner, to work out what to do next. Flee or go the bastards? But the Lewis gun they are carrying has just about had it – a German bullet had buggered the firing mechanism, meaning rapid fire is no longer possible. They can only get off single shots by pulling the cocking handle each time. But what the hell – they *go* the bastards. Rushing back around the corner just moments after the grenade has exploded right in the midst of the Germans – causing many casualties – they are right on them in seconds, with Burt furiously pointing the Lewis gun at all 40 of them.

Hender Hoch! Hender Hoch! Hender Hoch, you bastards!

Stunned, the Germans put their hands up, just as Helyar and Burt are joined by the young'un, Bertie Denman, the 18-year-old who had joined the 51st Battalion only a week earlier and is now being welcomed to First Grade in style.

Bursting with blood-lust, Denman is beside himself and brandishes his rifle and bayonet menacingly, shouting, 'What will we do with them? Shoot them, stick them?'

'For God's sake, shut up,' Helyar growls back. 'Cec's gun is useless and my bombs are *napoo*. This crowd could *eat* us if they liked.'[88]

But they don't. With their hands firmly in the air, the Germans have had the stuffing completely knocked out of them and are quickly escorted to the rear . . . *Hender hoch.*

—

At Monument Wood, the battle goes on, with the 13th Brigade still pressing forward the best they can, making ready to charge in the darkness on this last key German line.

Just up ahead, in those lines, *Leutnant* Iversen, commander of 10 Company, turns to see the young ensign von Falkenhayn dripping with sweat but triumphant, with three flares! Alas, just as the young officer-in-training hands them over, a bullet pierces both the night and von Falkenhayn's chest, and the young man falls, hard.

Yet the blinding light that now appears before him is not – or at least not exclusively – the first sign of the death he is now fast approaching. Rather, it is the first of the flares, taken from his dying hands and now sent soaring skywards. Instantly, the ground in front of the 5th Foot Guards and the 3rd Machine Gun Company is illuminated to reveal 'a dense crowd of khaki uniforms . . .' into which the German machine-gunners now fire their furious fusillades, exacting a heavy toll.

To *Leutnant* Iversen's amazement, that still doesn't stop them outright.

'But the Englishman, too, is tough,' he would recount, using the German generic term for all enemies who spoke English. 'His bombs fall thick as hail . . . and with all his own daring he brought up a swarm of machine gunners into position immediately ahead of us.'[89]

—

Among the Australians, Captain Billy Harburn is still pressing his men to follow up their earlier success and keep going! As thin as they are in number, as appalling as the fire now upon them is, they are still a force to be reckoned with as Harburn juggles his command to fill gaps in the line. He 'grabbed every man he could get, formed small parties of ten . . . and pushed them up to the left.'[90]

Crawling forward, Major William Craies, who has come with the reserve company of the 52nd Battalion, following the call of Captain Harburn, must make a decision. The well-ordered Australian waves of an hour ago are now more like choppy surges – their casualties have been heavy and concentrated in particular parts. Meanwhile, the British 54th Brigade on their right have not kept up. The Germans in the wood in front of them are putting out a wall of fire, and his men are still taking heavy fire from Germans on their left, on the railway embankment.

Keep pushing to the designated objective, the other side of Monument Wood, or bow to reality? Even if they can get there, it would be with too few men to make a difference once they arrived at the meeting point with 15th Brigade.

The obvious choice is to consolidate the extraordinary gains they have made, dig in, and bring fire to bear anyway on all forces that might try to enter or leave Villers-Bretonneux by that road.

Major Craies pulls the men back 100 yards to a more easily defensible line, just west of Monument Wood. It is not as good as actually being on their objective 500 yards south of the Roman road, but as they have advanced 2500 yards in their night's work and are now within 1000 yards of that objective, it is a great start.

If 15th Brigade do their job, Villers-Bretonneux will be all but cut off – most importantly from the heavy artillery the Germans would be wanting to bring forward today to start shelling Amiens.

Why lose more lives when far and away the most important thing is to secure what they have and not risk losing it?

And so Major Craies gives the order: Dig in, Diggers!

'The III Battalion,' *Leutnant* Iversen would report, 'held its ground and the advance at this point was stopped.'[91]

CHAPTER EIGHTEEN

ANZAC DAY 1918 – THE DAY OF RECKONING

I don't think there is much use
preaching mercy to my men.[1]
Colonel John McArthur, 29th Battalion

It will ever be remembered for perhaps the greatest
individual feat of the war – the successful counter-
attack by night across unknown and difficult ground,
at a few hours' notice, by the Australian soldier.[2]
General George Grogan, the British Commander of the 23rd Brigade

There was a howling of demons as the 57th, fighting
mad, drove through the wire, through the 59th,
who sprang to their sides – through their enemy.[3]
Jimmy Downing

ANZAC DAY EVE, HILL 104, WITH YOUR PIKE UPON YOUR SHOULDER BY THE RISING OF THE MOON

Finally, it is time.

With the arrival of most of the 59th Battalion just after 11.30 pm – one company is still missing, but Colonel Norman Marshall orders another company forward from the second line to replace it – at last the 15th Brigade is *enough* present and accounted for that, at 11.45 pm, the word is passed along the line: 'All detachments are in position.'[4]

It is time to move, Dig.

Good.

For the last two bloody hours most of the 15th Brigade have been listening to the firing in the distance, hoping that the men of the 13th are getting the best of it. But they are eager to get to it themselves. The one-hour bombardment of their objectives at 10 pm that would have helped them has been and gone. Never mind . . .

The order hisses out and spreads along the line: Advance!

Up and at 'em. It is rising midnight and the battle knell is nigh. Their scouts, like Edwin Need, have gone out an hour earlier, by accident – not aware that the brigade was going to be held up – and presumably will be in position to give them fair warning of whatever trouble lies ahead.

In short order, and in good order, no fewer than 3000 Australian soldiers of the 15th Brigade – formed up in two waves across a 2000-yard front, with each battalion splitting up into two companies per wave – begin their flanking movement proper on the north side of Villers-Bretonneux.

Advancing in the moonlight, with the 60th on the left, the 59th on the right and the 57th following behind, they soon arrive at a sunken road where the officers check their compass bearings before moving off again.

For the moment, at least, they must proceed carefully, both to give no warning that they are coming and because the landscape offers many obstacles in the tepid light. As far as they know, their starting point is still 1000 yards behind the remaining British line, and so they keep expecting to come across a line of 8th Division soldiers, but, oddly, there are no soldiers apparent.

Only shortly after starting, they stumble over difficult ground. After midnight, the moon sinks behind the clouds. The houses still burning in the town off to their right, including the Red Château, act as a kind of beacon, always enabling them to get their bearings in the darkness.

One way or another, they keep moving.

The significance of the day is not lost on any of them.

'It's Anzac Day,'[5] they mutter to each other, smiling. Three years earlier, near the beginning of the war, Australian soldiers in the Dardanelles had proved to the world just how good they were, and they have proved it many times since. But now, they must do it again.

'The die was now cast,' Jimmy Downing would recount of the mood of the 15th Brigade. 'It seemed that there was nothing to do but go straight forward and die hard.'[6]

For the moment things remain fairly quiet, bar some sporadic German artillery fire. Some of the shells land close enough to the marching Australians that the 15th suffers its first casualty – a Corporal from Edwin Need's 59th Battalion is killed – with others being wounded here and there.

—

The lost company of the 59th Battalion at last arrives at their starting line, in the wake of the main body of the 15th Brigade, only to find that everyone's . . . *gorn*. All the company can do is proceed to the east themselves, in the hope they will be on the right track and catch up.

Not that it's going to be easy to find them – or anyone!

'A heavy fog . . .' one officer would document, 'magnified the size of minor objects [and] made identification of localities difficult.'[7]

It is unnerving, and they have the distinct impression that they are entirely on their own, until, out of the darkness they can hear it.

Bloody thing!

It fucking hurts!

It is a wounded Australian soldier who has taken a stray bullet and is now expressing his views on the matter, the very way he had learned west of Woop Woop. Tough for him, but at least he is there, and no doubt with the rest of the brigade.

The sound of that wounded Australian, one Digger would note, 'was very reassuring to us'.[8] The company continue, a little faster, confident they are on the right track and eager to catch up.

—

Sixty minutes after first taking cover there, Private Edwin Need is still in his shell hole, glad to be still alive, but is shattered that the attack – *which was meant to be right behind him!* – has so clearly failed that he tears off his white arm bands in the now clear moonlight. No point in giving the Germans something to aim at if he makes a run for it. For if they don't see him by that bright moon, they will by the glare thrown by those parts of Villers-Bretonneux now *truly* in flames, 'lighting up the whole countryside'.[9]

The obvious danger, Need thinks, is that the Germans will come forward, at which point his best hope would be to be taken prisoner . . .

—

Despite the odd shot in the dark – and despite what has happened on the south side of town – mercifully, it seems that the Germans on the north side have not yet twigged what the 15th Brigade is up to. Though the 15th keep advancing, everything is generally so quiet that they can even hear glass shattering in the distance as the fires in the houses continue their devouring path.

As they get close to the north-eastern edge of Villers-Bretonneux, right on the outskirts, two companies of the 57th Battalion are detached with specific instructions to stay and gun down any Germans who try to leave the town this way, while the rest of the men continue to move east and tighten the noose on Fritz's neck that way.

They don't have to wait long. Suddenly, many furious fusillades to the right of the main body of Australians indicates that those two companies have come across some German outposts and have exchanged greetings in the traditional manner.

And now the main body of the 15th Brigade encounters strategically placed rolls of barbed wire, forcing them to bunch up from their previous formation so they can struggle through the entanglements when it happens …

The Germans in the old British trenches ahead, on the other side of the wire, become aware of their presence – or at least a worrying noise – and fire a flare. Hey, ho, and up she rises, trailing sparks across the night sky, and down she comes . . . illuminating the scene. And now come more, and then ever more again!

'German flares of all kinds shot into the air,' Downing would recount, 'reds, whites, greens, bunches of golden rain.'[10]

A couple of seconds hang suspended – two ticks on the clock in real time, but an eternity of shocked silence for both the German and Australian soldiers. And now the flares burst to fully reveal them, a body of 3000 men advancing in lines.

Gott im Himmel!

Thousands of German machine-gun bullets are instantly flying in their direction. Most of the Australians are able to throw themselves to the ground in time. Others die hard.

One Lieutenant with the 59th Battalion, a particularly beloved figure with the name – no, really – of Alison O'Brien, goes down, shot.

'Carry on, boys,' he shouts to his men. 'I'm hit!'[11]

They carry on, roaring, as they roar forth.

—

And now Edwin Need hears it.

'Stick it in him!'

'You fuckers!'

'Come 'ere, you bastards!'

'Fuck you, Fritz!'

'No prisoners!'[12]

Music to his ears. Balm for his soul. Australian shouts in the night! The curses are followed by the familiar rifle-shots of massed .303s, and better still, the chatter of Lewis guns! The attack is clearly back on. Fritz obviously gets it as now still *more* flares soar high in the hope they can give their machine gunners more time to see *die australischen Teufel*, the Australian devils, before they are in their trenches.

Unbeknownst to Need, the 15th Brigade's advance had been delayed but has finally come on. For now, Need keeps his head down, the shouting and firing from behind 'getting closer until it was like hell let loose'.[13]

——

The German machine gunners are doing their best, firing their belt-fed light and heavy machine guns, the *Maschinengewehr 08/15* and *08s*, straight at the oncoming waves of soldiers in the night. Yet, despite the heavy fire upon the Australians, there is no panic in the ranks of the main body of the 15th Brigade. These are veteran troops. They know bullets at that distance are like snakes in long grass back home. They can kill you, sure. But the main thing you need to work out – if you can't keep clear of them – is how to kill them first. They know, too, that scared troops fire too high at night, as do inexperienced ones, and if they keep as low as a snake's bellybutton moving forward, they should be okay.

Now, where are the bullets coming from? That much becomes obvious from careful observation of the sparks flying from the German machine guns straight in front and on the right flank. The Australians quickly revert to their training, employing the tactic of 'fire and movement'. Some fire, some move. The Lewis guns ensure the Huns keep their heads down while the riflemen and bombers crawl closer. When they are within range, the bombers will throw grenades and then the riflemen can charge, their bayonets pointed towards the Germans.

As one Lieutenant of the 59th Battalion would recall, the clear voice of an officer rang out: 'Charge!'[14]

Oh, they do that, all right – there, and all along the line.

Almost as one, the Australians rise and run straight for the Germans, all with a guttural growl of wild exultation. They are going to get to the brutes at last, unleashing 'a savage, eager yell'.[15]

626

—

Nearly teary with joy, Edwin Need, the worthy scout still hiding in his shell hole before the German line, can hear his countrymen getting closer now. Timing his move to fit with the oncoming attack, Need takes his grenade, pulls the pin and lets it fly at where he knows the Germans are no more than 20 yards away. He still dare not raise his head to see if it has hit, but he can hear 'our fellows cursing and swearing, yelling like madmen, enough to put fear into the gamest Fritz on the Western Front . . .'[16]

And one other person besides . . . For back in 1808, the Duke of Wellington, after surveying the British troops sent to him in Spain, is reputed to have said: 'I don't know what effect these men will have on the enemy, but by God, they terrify me.'[17] Edwin Need feels much the same as he turns to see an enormous soldier of the 60th Battalion now bearing down with a bayonet, clearly intent on letting moonlight into his gizzards.

'*Australian!*' Need roars just in time.

Now that the Australian flood has reached him, he is at last able to grab his rifle and bayonet and 'join in the business, everyone mad for a fight, the whole affair a bedlam, the bursting of shells, firing of flares, the town burning fiercely, and our fellows, cursing and yelling, charging on, the Fritzs flying for their lives, having very little recollection of the charge, just stabbing and thrusting with the bayonet at any thing that came in the way, and on again, taking no prisoners . . .'[18]

—

From the northern outskirts of Villers, the 'machine gun fire was intense but all very high, causing few casualties'.[19] And even then, when it comes to both 'fury' and 'wild', those guns have nothing on the Australians.

From that instant, the Australian official history would record, 'There was no holding the attack. The bloodthirsty cry was caught up again and again along the line, and the whole force was off at the run.'[20] The cry goes on, as one Digger would describe it, in a manner 'that would have turned a tribe of Red Indians green with envy . . .'[21]

There is no more mucking about with direction now; it is obvious which way to go – straight at the Germans.

'Into the bastards, boys!'[22]

The results are as savage as have ever been recorded in the annals of Australian military history. And it is at the hands not just of isolated pockets of the Australians, but the whole lot of them, even those in the follow-up companies.

'A snarl came from the throat of the mob, the fierce low growl of tigers scenting blood,' Jimmy Downing would memorably describe it. 'There was a howling of demons as the 57th, fighting mad, drove through the wire, through the 59th, who sprang to their sides – through their enemy.'

Australians on the charge, all of them yelling with a primal passion that comes from a place perhaps long ago. In an instant, the sounds of this bursting blood-lust spread as the men of the 59th and the 60th out on the left join in.

'Baying like hell hounds, they also charged.'[23]

It is a roar that only gets ever *louder*.

'A yell from a thousand throats split the night,'[24] one officer would recount. All up, the sound of the 15th Brigade, brothers in arms on the charge, released as never before from the hellish cramped life of the trenches, month after sodding month, year after fucking *year*, and now able, at last, to get at the Germans, man on man, in open space . . . carries all the way to the 13th Brigade some 1500 yards away on the south side of Villers-Bretonneux.

'Cheering, our men rushed straight to the muzzles of machine guns . . .'[25]

It doesn't take long.

'There was a wild rush, a short sharp clash of arms – then pandemonium.'[26]

———

Ach . . . mein . . . GOTT!

The German soldiers stare, momentarily transfixed by the vision before them of some 3000 wild men from the far south of the planet, running, screaming, hurling grenades extraordinary distances, now exploding among them, firing from the hip . . .

'The [Australians] were magnificent,' one stunned German officer would later recall. 'Nothing seemed to stop them. When our fire was heaviest, they just disappeared in shell holes and came up as soon as it slackened.'[27]

And though, yes, in some parts the German gunners cut down whole rows of Australians, they can't get them all, and it takes a steely nerve beyond most of them to keep shooting straight in front when to your left and right you can see enormous men charging forth with flashing bayonets, who you know will be coming straight for you, if you don't run now . . . *run now* . . . RUN NOW. . .

Too late. The Australians are on them, shooting, throwing grenades, swinging the butts of their rifles to crack heads, slashing and thrusting with their bayonets to raise geysers of German blood that spurt forth and just as quickly settle.

'They had not had such a feast with their bayonets before,'[28] one officer would comment.

Even had the officers *wanted* to control their soldiers, it would have been beside the point. 'For the time being their men had thrown off the restraints of civilised intercourse and were what the bayonet instructors of all armies aimed at producing by their tuition – primitive, savage men.'[29]

No matter that the Germans heavily outnumber the Australians. Or that they are in entrenched positions, and under normal circumstances it would be no contest. In the face of so many Australians charging at them so fast, so furiously, some of the Germans give in to sanity and turn and run. Those who don't are quickly engulfed.

'[The Germans],' Jimmy Downing would record for posterity,

without fear or favour or mercy, 'had no chance in the wild onslaught of maddened men, who forgot no whit, in their fury, of their traditional skill. The latter were bathed in spurting blood. They killed and killed. Bayonets passed with ease through grey-clad bodies, and were withdrawn with a sucking noise. The dozen English we had with us, mere boys, and without arms till they could find a rifle, were fighting with fists and boots, happy so long as they knew where to find the Australian put in charge of them.'[30]

Mocking Australian voices ring out, just before they kill their German counterparts.

'Coming *mit* a flare, *Herman!*'

'*Vos* you *dere, Fritz?*'[31]

Many of the Germans scream for mercy, but it is a sentiment in singularly short supply on the night.

The Australians simply cut them down or shoot to kill. By Downing's count, some Australians were so devastating with their Lewis guns at close quarters on massed Germans, followed up by grenades and bayonets, that they may have killed, individually, 'twenty and thirty and more'.[32]

Some do it so intensely and for so long that they even require a 'smoko', a brief pause to refresh themselves, before they go at it again, and . . .

The cry goes up!

'The Germans ran,' one Digger would report with no little satisfaction.

'There they go, there they go!' some Diggers shout as some German soldiers who have been taking shelter in a nearby trench decide to make a break for it and run for their lives. And off after them they go, in hot pursuit, with one enormous Australian seen to be running after them even while firing a Lewis gun *from the shoulder* – no small feat for a weapon weighing 28 pounds. And the ruthless slaughter goes on.

True, in pockets, some Germans are standing their ground. As Downing would document, 'Several times, Germans and Australians stood up to each other in the open and fought with grenades, the former tugging the strings in the handles of their canister bombs, then flinging them at their adversaries, the latter pulling out the pins of Mills grenades with their teeth and bowling them overarm.'[33]

But mostly, now, the Germans are running, and the Australians are chasing them.

And *there!*

A German up ahead on the right rises from a shell hole with his hands in the air, only to be first shot down and then bayoneted for good measure.

And over there on the left!

A resilient German gun crew is holding on, still firing at the marauding Australians right in front of them. But we riddle them with bullets too, and they fall, with the tiniest sign of movement being rewarded with several bayonets.

And there!

Far ahead, some Fritzes are spied running like scalded cats. The sharpshooters with the .303s bring their rifles to bear, take careful aim . . . and bring them down.

And now, on again! Forward! Forward! Chasing. Chasing.

—

As the Australians continue to push, they get to the German second line. Here, the resistance is stronger as the Germans have rushed reserve troops forward to make a stand, and of course they are better protected in the trenches but . . .

This time, much of the fight has gone out of the Germans – they've seen hundreds of their own fear-crazed men race past – and once the Australians rush those trenches, it doesn't take long before the Fritzes start surrendering in droves. In fact, there are so many that the Australians tire of killing them and actually take prisoners.

But careful!

Sergeant John Naylor of the 59th Battalion now comes face to face with a German officer and his men who are 'standing with their hands over their heads signifying that they had surrendered'.[34]

Naylor shows mercy, lets them live and indicates for them to pass to the rear with their hands in the air, only for the German officer to suddenly draw a hidden revolver and shoot him in the side. Naylor will live, which is a mercy. His mates, however, show none, and take quick revenge. The German officer is dead before he hits the ground, which is within seconds.

As the Germans try to flee, they inevitably get caught in the rolls of wire that had been set up on the other side of those trenches by the English. As the wire catches them, the Australians quickly set upon them, stabbing with their bayonets so viciously that it is the lucky ones who are shot and die quickly.

It is an image that will stay with Need ever afterwards, as he would recount, 'By the light of the flares, the Fritzs running ahead, the poor devils frantic to get away, the whole thing being too tragic to be amusing, we keeping close on their heels, until we reached our final objective . . .'[35]

That final objective is south of the Roman road. They just have to keep fighting their way towards it.

—

For Germany's XIV Corps HQ, positioned at Proyart, the first worrying reports come through at 1.20 am. The enemy has successfully counter-attacked. The 5th Foot Guard has been forced back, the southern edge of Villers-Bretonneux is now threatened. The obvious thing to do would be to send forward their reserve division . . .

If they had one.

Alas, the last of the Corps reserve had been used in taking Villers-Bretonneux, and so the best the Foot Guard can do is scrape together a battalion from here and there and send them forward. In the middle of the night, the men are woken – *Los! Los! Los!* – and ordered to be ready to march within minutes. Villers-Bretonneux is under attack and they must move forward. Even as this is underway, however, a second series of messages is received at XIV Corps HQ. Now the *north* side of

Villers-Bretonneux is under attack, too! The 228th Division is believed to be resisting fiercely, but there is no doubt that the enemy is launching a major operation on them. In the case of the 228th, they at least have two battalions of the 35th Fusiliers in reserve nearby – but they, too, must be woken and moved forward.

—

For the men of the 13th Brigade, now digging into their new line in front of Monument Wood, the sounds of the night are promising. Though things have gone quiet on their front, when they cock their ear to the breeze, and they do, they can hear that that is not the case with the 15th Brigade. From precisely the direction their battling brethren of the 15th are meant to be coming, the 13th can hear it all – shots, machine guns, grenade explosions and screams. And the best they can work out, those sounds are getting closer, meaning the 15th must be making headway!

—

The Australians of the 15th Brigade push on, across the ground and through the night, slashing and firing and throwing – getting their bearings from the burning buildings of Villers-Bretonneux until it becomes apparent that they have reached the point where they must change direction. Instead of continuing due east, they must veer to the right, to get to the Roman road. The 59th Battalion lead the way, with the 60th Battalion following up hard.

Still, there is scattered fight from brave German soldiers who have refused to run.

Those who continue to resist are killed, while those who flee are pursued – some so vigorously that whole platoons of Australian soldiers cross the Roman road without realising it, and they keep going until they come to 'the huts and big canvas hangars of the old aerodrome'.[36]

It is now about 4 o'clock in the morning, one of the officers of the 59th realises they have gone too far, and he shouts to his men that they must pull back. 'The men were excited, unearthing a handful of Germans and British captives in some houses near the Roman Road, and searching for Germans in the hangars, but . . .'

Bit by bit control is established and the Australians indeed pull back.

Back at the Roman road, things are getting organised by the officers as the survivors of all the companies – who are grouped together once more – are now spread out north-east to south-west across the road in a defensive line, with the 60th Battalion on the left, the 59th in the centre and 57th on the right, closest to the town.

For the first time, the officers are able to do a headcount and work out just how many of their own men have been lost – about 150, at first count. It is remarkably few given the night they've had and the ground they've gained.

A good night's work, so far. They have advanced 3000 yards and are little more than 1000 yards from the 13th Brigade dug into the line just before Monument Wood to the south-west.

—

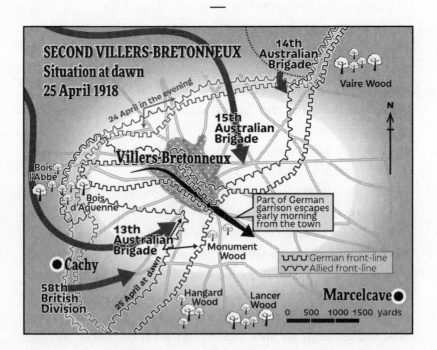

Now that the men have reached the road, things have quietened a little. It is possible for the Australians of the 15th Brigade to take German prisoners and, as Edwin Need would put it, 'souvenir them' – another way of saying 'shake them down for whatever they have'.

This even includes wedding rings, but when one German soldier *begs* to be allowed to keep his, Private Need acts as his mother would want him to and allows him to keep it.

Only to look around a few minutes later to see another Australian soldier, Private Len Doody, relieving Fritz of his ring and giving him in exchange a really good – feel the quality! – kick in the arse.

In the end, beyond souveniring, the more urgent matter of surviving beckons, for it will surely not be long before the Germans themselves counter-attack, and the Australians' only hope will be to be well dug in. Now that the carrying parties have arrived with picks and shovels, the men of the 15th Brigade begin furiously digging their trenches, interrupted only by three figures suddenly looming out of the darkness, crying out, '*Kamerad! Kamerad!*'

They are German soldiers wanting to surrender.

'One little chap with spectacles,' Need records, 'was half in tears, afraid he might be run through with a bayonet, and quite justified too, for some of our fellows were not too particular on that point . . .'[37]

As it happens, these three Germans have presented themselves at the right time, and to their infinite relief they are spared and sent to the rear.

—

The signal wires have now been laid and Colonel Christie of the 13th Brigade's 51st Battalion is able to get a circuitous message through to Major George Wieck on the staff of Brigadier Elliott's 15th Brigade to advise him of the situation. They have advanced about 2500 yards from the starting position and are placed a mile beyond the recent German line. Though they are still about 1000 yards short of their objective, they can lay down some fire upon any bastard trying to get in or out of VB – so long as the 15th Brigade have reached it, or are equally close.

What is unclear to the Australians is just where the two battalions of the 8th Division, the Durhams and the Northamptons, are. They had been meant to attack from the north and south by now, to go in and mop up the newly isolated German resistance left in VB. The Australian commanders had assumed that this would be 'a comparatively easy task',[38] given that the German defenders would realise their only hope of survival would be to completely surrender, as their ammunition would be limited.

And yet, as the night wears on and there appears to be no diminution in Fritz's fire either from Villers-Bretonneux or even Bois l'Abbé, the Australians gain the distinct impression that the Brits have not launched on VB at all!

At 4.15 am Brigadier Pompey Elliott makes his first report to General Heneker in the 12 hours since the commander of the 8th Division had told him he wanted reports 'at least every hour'.[39]

It is brief.

My 15th Brigade has accomplished its task and is now dug in. There is no sign whatsoever, however, of your Durham Battalion attacking from the north side of VB, as ordered. I suspect they have not moved at all.

Yes, well.

Heneker acknowledges that is indeed the case – the Durhams had funked it, never budging from where they had been left. But he has just ordered the 2nd Royal Berkshire Regiment forward to do the job in their stead. Regarding the situation on the south side, the 2nd Northamptonshire, trailing the 13th Brigade, has also struggled. After being late in leaving their starting point, their Commanding Officer had been killed, and his second-in-command, Major Hubert Essame – who, two hours earlier, had been 'much impressed by the calmness' of the 13th Brigade officers[40] – had been gravely wounded. After crossing first the Cachy Switch and then the barrier of barbed wire that had helped protect it, they had, as planned, turned north-east towards the railway station, only to be stopped by withering German fire just before reaching the railway.

They have formed a defensive flank on its southern fringes by the railway embankment and have prevented any possibility of a German breakout into the rear of the 13th Brigade. But, no, they have not been able to move into the town at all . . .

Pompey puts the phone down and assumes the usual position: disgust.

The disappointment at the British effort aside, there is no doubt that the night's achievements have been enormous. The key now is to squeeze the life out of the German lice that have so infested Villers-Bretonneux, and press along the seams once more. Hopefully, the British battalions will come into their own with the dawn, around six o'clock, when the mopping up operation is due to begin.

—

At 5.20 am, even worse reports come back to German XIV Corps HQ: things have gone from bad to worse, to worse still at Villers-Bretonneux. For the first time, the shocked Corps Commander, General Friedrich von Gontard, is advised of the fact that the enemy has reached the Roman road *east* of Villers-Bretonneux and that his men are in danger of being cut off.

—

With the first dull rays of dawn, the 15th Brigade can see more clearly their achievement. They have advanced an extraordinary 3000 yards in the night, across a front 2000-yards wide. They continue to dig in and snipe at any German within coo-ee trying to escape from the town and . . .

Look out! There are headlights heading our way, from the east!

Sure enough, all of the 15th Brigade dug in by the Roman road can see the approaching headlights and hear the growing rumbling.

Everyone get ready!

Out of the gloom they soon spot some German trucks coming along – clearly driven by men who do not understand the situation – heading towards town, no doubt with more guns, ammunition and reinforcements.

It doesn't take long. Following the growled orders of one of the Captains, the soldiers hold their fingers on the triggers until the order comes – 'FIRE!' – and a dozen weapons open up at once, barking death to the drivers in the front cabin, and soon enough to most of those on the hooded trays behind.

In the words of one Digger, 'Fritz could not believe their eyes to see our troops in such a position behind their lines. They were shot. One Hun was unfortunate enough to be driving a flying pig *Minenwerfer*. He did not live two seconds.'[41]

Still, it is as well for the soldiers of the 57th, 59th and 60th Battalions of Elliott's 15th Brigade that they are now well dug in on either side of the Roman road, for the fire upon them now becomes furious, most particularly from town, where the German soldiers of the 48th Infantry Regiment are able to shoot from relatively close by.

If there is some satisfaction for the Australian survivors of these fusillades, it is that every bullet fired by the Germans from now, every grenade thrown, will diminish their overall supply of ammo. If the Australians can successfully shut down the escape route via the railway, which is where a gap remains between the 15th and the 13th, there will be no chance of the Germans getting resupplied from outside.

With the town now cut off, the next job is to clean out the Germans who remain within, and this job is soon begun by the two companies of the 57th left on the north-east side of town to prevent Fritz coming out in 15th Brigade's rear. They push directly south into the houses. Their orders are to go through 'the eastern half of the town and finally [emerge] from its eastern edge to take up a line in front of it'.[42]

The 2nd Berkshire Regiment, meanwhile, sweeps around to the north of the town in the dawn and turns their attack south, while the Durham Light Infantry finally move in from the west and the

Northamptonshires push forth from the south, mopping up as they go, all moving from street to street, house to house.

Where they do find resistance, as in a machine gun opening up on them from one of the buildings, 'Mr Lewis' is sent forward to do the door-knocking, first plastering every window and door, ensuring every bastard inside will have to take cover from a blizzard of bullets, splinters and flying glass, even as other men from the platoon race around and throw bombs through the back to give those inside something to really think about. It's the Diggers' version of *Guten Morgen* on the day.

'On finding themselves surrounded, the Germans surrendered.'[43]

And so they all keep moving.

The way Private Jimmy Downing of the 15th Brigade would later explain it, there are four 'spears' of soldiers, all pushing towards the centre of town. Other British soldiers, with tank assistance, start to clean Bois d'Aquenne of the now completely cut-off Germans found therein – the luckiest of whom are able to meekly surrender.

They keep moving . . .

For the bulk of the Germans inside Villers-Bretonneux, the sound of shooting suddenly breaks out from four directions at once, getting progressively closer.

On the western end of the village, a panicked German soldier rushes up to the men of the 6th Company of the 35th Fusilier Regiment, to shout that enemy soldiers have broken through the perimeter between the 11th and 12th Companies of his regiment. Of course, the 6th Company at once counter-attacks and is able to retake the line, but even as they do so they become aware that the 5th Company to their right is also under heavy attack. This, too, is beaten off, with heavy losses, but only with the German officers themselves taking over the machine guns. They soon realise that the entire town is now under attack, and inevitably they must fall back under the weight.

'Fritz was taken completely by surprise,' one Digger would note of the clean-out. 'Companies of them did not know what was happening until our men appeared at their billets throwing bombs and shooting right and left. Over 1000 prisoners were captured and 600 were killed . . .'[44]

One piece of welcome news is that the Tommy soldiers now come into their own.

'The Sergeants who had charge of the Tommies,' the same Digger would recount, 'say that those boys fought like tigers . . . Chasing Fritz down streets, into houses, out again through windows and doors, having the time of their lives with rifle, bomb and bayonet.'[45]

———

The Germans are now surrendering in such numbers that it is hard to know what to do with them all without weakening the Australian force, but the problem is solved when hundreds of prisoners are put into the care of a company of Durhams and a company of Berkshires, who take them to the rear while the men of the 57th continue their left wheel through the town.

In the middle of the madness, a brave German officer of the 228th Division's 35th Fusilier Regiment, *Leutnant* Krause, actually manages

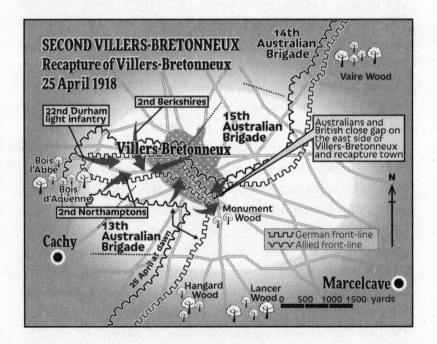

to make his way into Villers-Bretonneux and successfully seeks out the ranking German officer in the town, a battalion commander of Infantry Regiment 48, Captain Rudolf Teichmann.

Teichmann, a 32-year-old career officer of no little ability, is quick to give him the message, which Krause returns to his superior officers outside Villers-Bretonneux with: I ASK URGENT RELIEF AS I AM SURROUNDED. ATTACK AS QUICKLY AS POSSIBLE ON BOTH SIDES OF THE ROMAN ROAD. THE ENEMY WILL THEN BE DRIVEN INTO MY ARMS.[46]

—

With the growing light, the dog can see the rabbit better than ever, and the fighting inside Villers-Bretonneux becomes more vicious. Some resilient German snipers take their toll, while others recognise the impossibility of their situation and surrender easily. The men of the two companies of Pompey Elliott's 57th Battalion make great headway from the first, managing to ambush a German patrol of a dozen, killing half, taking the rest prisoner and capturing two heavy machine guns. One patrol of four men, all of them aces, comes back with the full deck – 52 German prisoners who have meekly surrendered!

Inside the rest of Villers-Bretonneux and Bois d'Aquenne there is a growing unease among the German soldiers of the 4th Guards and 228th Division as the terrible truth becomes apparent. They are *trapped* – or at least very nearly so. Patrols heading out from all points around Villers-Bretonneux report a solid line of enemy soldiers waiting for them in every direction, bar one. There is still a small opening 1000 yards to the south of the Roman road, along the path taken by the railroad cutting.

Inevitably, the word spreads and more and more of the German soldiers start to push in that direction. After a terrible night, *Leutnant* Walter Elfeldt of Roßbach's 7th Company of the 5th Foot Guards Regiment can now see soldiers from other companies heading that way. Those who can are evacuating Villers-Bretonneux.

'A skirmish line from 93rd Regiment comes out of the village and hurries back,' Elfeldt would describe. 'Others follow . . . Some fall down exhausted just east of the village, others go back further. Why? . . . Individuals run back . . . many escape . . .'[47]

Everything is confused. Panicky. Miserable. And very, very unstable. No one is sure what is going to happen. Where the remnants of his own 7th Company are right now, Elfeldt has no idea. In the course of the night so many units inside Villers-Bretonneux have become mixed up that it is hard to work out what is what and who is who.

There is still just enough cohesion left with the 93rd Regiment that two brave officers, Major von Kriegsheim and *Leutnant* von Leyser, try to stop the tide and turn back the men attempting to leave, to get them to fight, to hold on.

'But it's no use,' *Leutnant* Elfeldt documents, 'the repeated commands to face to the front have no effect . . . morale has been lost . . . The line staggers back further to the east . . .'[48]

Some of the most fierce resistance, however, still comes from the soldiers of 48th Regiment, right in the path of the two companies of the 57th Battalion. They hold the houses in the north-east section of town, and so once the outer perimeter of defence has fallen they come under direct attack from the 57th pushing south. Running out of ammunition, they are exhausted, outnumbered and surrounded in the dawn.

'Under these circumstances,' the 48th Regimental history would record, 'Captain Teichmann gives the order to vacate the present position and to occupy the eastern edge of the village. Bombarded from all sides, the battalion has the heaviest losses, a large proportion of men who have hesitated to retreat or who received the order to retreat late, got captured.'[49]

Occasionally, there is negotiation. At one point, when four Australian soldiers of the 57th Battalion call to German soldiers inside a building that they must surrender, a voice comes back in perfect English: 'You will only shoot us if we come out . . .'

'No,' one of the Australians replies. 'You are prisoners.'[50]

Did someone say, *prisoners*? As in, we *won't* be shot?!

That is all the Germans need to hear. From inside the building comes an immediate clatter of rifles and equipment being thrown down, and before the Australians' very eyes, out come no fewer than 20 Huns with their hands in the air, 'all very meek and docile and quite pleased with their fate'.[51]

Extraordinary scenes abound all around as the spearheads of Australian and British soldiers continue to push into the heart of the German defences. One Digger of the 59th Battalion who enters the town at this point with his platoon is confronted first by the vision of Australian soldiers 'chasing Fritz with the bayonet and others running and throwing bombs'.

One of the Australian Sergeants, seemingly drunk on blood-lust, or maybe actually drunk – there has been a lot of it about – takes an admittedly unfamiliar Hun automatic pistol, points it at the head of a surrendering Hun with his hands high in the air, fires three times . . . and *misses!* He is about to try his luck again when one of Corporals of the 59th Battalion's platoon sings out: 'Give him a go, Sarge!'[52]

In response, the Sergeant turns to the man who has called out and . . . laughs. You're probably right. Instead of shooting the Hun dead, he turns him around and gives him a kick in the arse, heading him towards another group of German prisoners.

'The Hun was very much relieved.'[53]

Once the four spears meet in the centre, they unite to turn east and start to sweep the remaining Germans out of the town towards the guns that wait on both sides of the railway gap, leaving a tattered group of German prisoners behind to be brought out shortly, once the rest of the town is subdued.

(Among those prisoners, one of the German staff officers says to an Australian Colonel with sincere congratulations: 'This was to have given us victory. Now I can only congratulate you on the quality of your regiments.' The German is awed to find out that the 10,000 German soldiers holding Villers-Bretonneux have been overcome by an attacking force consisting of no more than 6000 Australians.)

The remaining problem is the German soldiers, most of them under the command of the worthy Captain Teichmann – an officer already recognised for his 'outstanding bravery'[54] – who has, meanwhile, established a temporary HQ in a house by the station.

In extremis, he manages to get a message to his superiors:

WERDE VON ALLEN SEITEN ANGEGRIFFEN, HALTE BIS ZUM LETZTEN MANN. AM UNDER ATTACK FROM ALL SIDES, HOLDING TO THE LAST MAN.[55]

The bulk of his soldiers are still resisting, having now congregated in the south-eastern sector of the town, by the railway cutting. That railway cutting, with the broad swathe of land beside it – which passes through the gap where the 13th and 15th Brigades have not yet met – remains the principal means by which other Germans continue to escape, helped by the still misty morning. In order to keep that thoroughfare open, Teichmann has given orders for his men and the men of the 5th Company of the 35th Fusiliers to line the railway and fight any who would try to secure it.

—

Meanwhile, other parties of Australians from the main body of the 15th Brigade now head back to the scene of last night's major battles, looking to find, hopefully alive, mates who have fallen in battle and attend to them at last. Many devastating scenes occur as the Australians walk among the brutal aftermath: so many dead cobbers staring at them with unseeing eyes, their faces all too often contorted in agonised expressions. Sometimes, there is happiness, as when a group of the 57th go back to where they had left Lieutenant O'Brien the night before, after he had told them, 'Carry on boys, I'm hit.'[56]

They call for him, and a weak answer mercifully breaks the dawn: 'Over here . . .'[57]

In two shakes of a lamb's tail they get to him, bind the worst of his wounds and carry him back on a stretcher to the Regimental Aid Post.

'Here we parted,' one of his rescuers would recount, 'with many expressions of goodwill and hopes for a speedy recovery.'[58]

—

For those brave German soldiers who still remain in Villers-Bretonneux – and there are several hundred still, who are armed, dangerous and determined – their best chance remains the possibility that Captain Teichmann's messages have got through and that their still well-armed and well-munitioned brethren from outside can counter-attack. They have not given up, and around seven o'clock they are given some hope.

From outside Villers-Bretonneux, the Germans unleash an extraordinary storm of artillery shells on the Australians in the front-line positions – most particularly those of the 15th and 13th Brigades, who have been trying in vain to close the gap between them.

'A terrific barrage,' Private Edwin Need would note in his diary, 'not a man expecting to come out alive . . . a shell landing in the trench six feet from me, killing one man, badly shell shocked another . . . and blowing the butt clean off the Lewis gun . . . Lieutenant Dave Fair running about on top from one post to another with orders and handing out rum in big doses, heedless of shells . . .'[59]

And here come the last reserve the Germans have! It is the 3rd Battalion of the 35th Fusilier Regiment – less than 1000 men – charging forward along the south side of the Roman road in the growing morning light, 'with orders to attack the southern flank of the Australian line there'.[60]

'But after going 300 yards under artillery and machine-gun fire, finding no German troops to right or left, [they] stop . . .'[61] The attack is called off, with the survivors instead used to bolster the German line in front of Villers-Bretonneux, to try to prevent the Australians from pushing any further east from there.

For the Australians, the time is right. With that German advance to the west stopped, and the barrage ending after eight o'clock, the men of the 57th Battalion, who are now completing their left wheel through the town and emerging on the eastern edge of Villers-Bretonneux, are indeed able to establish a line extending halfway from the Roman road to the railway. It means the last remaining German escape route is now tightened by hundreds of yards. The last way for the fleeing Germans to escape is through the railway cutting.

That, clearly, must be closed, and it is with this in mind that one of the 57th's finest officers, Lieutenant James Falconer, moves forward with his platoon, steering for a house near the railway station which a German prisoner has told them is the key German HQ. Perhaps, if they can take that, all organised resistance in the town can stop. Fighting their way forward, they are just getting near the house when a furious exchange of fire breaks out just to its left at the end of the street, where a bridge crosses the railway cutting . . .

—

Inside the house by the railway, meanwhile, even the valiant Captain Rudolf Teichmann understands that the position is hopeless. If he and his immediate staff are ever going to get away, it is now or never.

He gives the order: '*Rückzug!* Withdraw!'

At the last possible moment, the withdrawal 'was carried out fighting . . .'[62]

Though nearly surrounded, Teichmann and his men are able to make their way out of the back of the house and join the trickle of German soldiers still making their way along the railway tracks, to the east, to safety. As good as his word – of defending to 'the last man' – Teichmann's proud Divisional Commander will report that after '*schwerem Häuserkampf,* heavy urban warfare, on the eastern edge of the village . . . Captain Teichmann left last'.[63]

From there, Teichmann and his fellow survivors from the last stand get to the nearest secure German trenches, held by their brethren of the 5th Foot, in a trench running east–west, halfway between Monument Wood and the railway station. From here they can bring fire on any further move by the enemy to push even further east.

Watching them go with growing dismay is *Leutnant* Walter Elfeldt of the 5th Guard Infantry Regiment. For hours now he has been hoping for a counter-attack, hoping that his fellow soldiers will stop deserting and stand and fight instead. But he now realises the gamble hasn't paid off. '*So kommt Villers-Bretonneux in die Hand des Gegners*,' he would finish his account. 'So Villers-Bretonneux is left to our enemy . . .'[64]

———

And now that Lieutenant Falconer and his men have made it to the bridge over the railway, they realise why the fighting is so vicious. They find six Australian soldiers firing down on 25 Germans below who are attempting to flee east. The Diggers are dominating, in no small part due to Lewis gunner Corporal Walter Patten and his crew. Just a few bursts turns the cutting into a scything, whistling, screaming cauldron of death, before Patten swings his Lewis gun around and turns it on 200 other Germans soldiers he can see in the distance, making their way across the open country to the south, in the last gap that lies between the 13th and the 15th Brigade.

The British soldiers of the Durham Light Infantry, meanwhile, have been more than coming into their own as they continue to move through the village, cleaning out German resistance as they go. By around 10 am the Durhams have emerged at the east end of the village, right by where Lieutenant Falconer, Corporal Patten and their men continue to hold the bridge. The orders for the Durhams now are to help to close what remains of the gap.

Again, the remaining German resistance at this point is strong, and the Durhams lose no fewer than 16 men but are finally able to dig in by the railway station. The 2nd Northamptons, meanwhile, have also done well. They begin to advance towards the town with a starting point 750 yards south-west of the station bridge. With the Australians now in control of that bridge, the key is for them to push forward and completely close the gap. As part of this effort, Brigadier Glasgow, at 10 am on Anzac Day, orders his support battalion, the 50th, to come forward – a disaster as the Germans still in Monument Wood and Hangard Wood are able to bring heavy fire upon them as they attempt to cross '400–800 yards of open plateau'.[65] The plan is abandoned. Mercifully, the 2nd Northamptonshire, however, are able to rise to the occasion. From a much closer position, they only have to traverse 150 yards of level plateau – running flat out – to get to the required positions.

As Bean would delicately note, 'This was an occasion on which English athletics proved valuable, most of the distance being covered before the Germans realised what was happening.'[66]

The gap still remains between the 15th and 13th Brigades, but thanks to the worthy Brits it has been closed considerably – a matter less significant now, as the last of the Germans have clearly left Villers-Bretonneux. That gap might be more easily closed in the dark, when they can move forward without making such easy targets.

—

Filled with a sense of dread, Charles Bean goes for breakfast to 5th Division Headquarters, almost afraid to ask if the attack had gone forward.

(For one thing, 18 months earlier he had been at Amiens on 20 July 1916, when blithely told at breakfast by an English officer, 'The 5th Division had their little show last night.'[67] That had proved to be the Battle of Fromelles, where the 5th Division had 1900 Australian soldiers killed in a single night, the worst night in Australian history.)

But of course he must ask, and so he does.

'Well,' Colonel John McColl of 5th Division HQ staff replies carefully, 'they say that 15th and 13th Brigades are east of Villers-Bretonneux. It appears that there is still a German remnant within Villers-Bretonneux . . .'[68]

East of Villers-Bretonneux?

They've done well! Bean wolfs down his breakfast and hurries away, eager to capture the story.

—

Back at the HQs of the 13th and 15th Brigades, the reports have been flooding in, getting progressively better, with the first significant one from the 13th reading:

> Operations successful . . . German prisoners
> brought in bearing marks of battle and trenches.
> Further messages say that Villers-Bretonneux now
> in our hands. More prisoners. Our casualties are
> beginning to come in. Very heavy. A fitting but sad
> anniversary of the landing on ANZAC. The price is
> a heavy one to pay for the Tommies' failure.[69]

And yet now the Germans make a move that the Australians have simply not been expecting. In the mid-morning, two German officers, 'blindfolded and carrying a white flag', who had approached the left flank of the 13th Brigade positions, are brought to the HQ trench of Colonels Whitham and Christie. The senior German, a Sergeant-Major who speaks remarkably good English, has a message for them:

'My commander has sent me to tell you that you are confronted by superior forces and surrounded on three sides. There are two Guards Divisions and another Division. He desires to know whether you will surrender and avoid a big loss of life. If you do not surrender he will blow you to pieces by turning the heavy artillery on to your trenches.'[70]

Really? A *very* interesting proposal! The Australians, after the triumphs they have wrought against the German forces through the night, should now throw their hands in the air and surrender? And even on a day such as *this* day?

'He seemed,' Colonel Whitham would note, 'to have no knowledge of Anzac Day.'[71]

And nor does a third German who arrives, a Private this time, with – just like the first two – a message from his superior officers, this one a roughly worded note written on the back of a German signal form:

The officer who commands the troops there has to come at once . . . with the German soldier.
Commander von Linsingen. [72]

Again, the Colonels Whitham and Christie are somewhere between bemused and outright stunned at the presumption of the Germans that the *Australians* are the ones who are in trouble here, not the Germans who've just lost Villers-Bretonneux!

Still, they faithfully pass on his message to Brigadier Glasgow while they keep the German emissaries talking, so as to glean as much information as they can about what unit they are from and what the state of the divisions lined up against them are. And here now is Brigadier Glasgow, coming to them over a crackly phone line, with his official, considered response after taking all factors into account.

'Tell them to go to Hell.' [73]

Yes, sir.

Pompey Elliott could not have said it better.

However, instead of telling the Germans to go to Hell, they tell them that they are now prisoners. They have seen too much of the Australian set-up to risk sending them back.

The German Sergeant-Major is initially upset at the prospect, gravely warning, 'I must return to my commander as he will be annoyed . . .'[74] but still seems to brighten up at the obvious implications that he is likely to survive this war after all.

The third German, however, makes not the slightest pretence of dismay or disgust at being told that his services are now required to help the hard-pressed stretcher-bearers and he won't be returning to his unit, even exulting, 'Me prisoner! *Bon!*'[75]

—

Few could be more pleased with the result than Pompey Elliott, while still embittered that it had to come to this when it had all been so avoidable.

'We have given the *Boche* an awful hiding,' he will write to his wife, Kate, shortly afterwards. 'Regular "Bouquets" of praise have been showered on us . . . So far it has only gone as far as the Commander in Chief [Haig]. I suppose Gen. Foch and the President and the King maybe will have a say in it yet. Some people say it is the absolute best thing done in the war . . . Our boys certainly did well. Some wonderful things were done.'[76]

—

Now catching up, Charles Bean arrives at the Bussy-lès-Daours Château, where the 5th Division HQ is situated, to find the front lawn completely covered with shattered – but relieved to be alive – German prisoners. (*Donnerwetter!* Golly! The things they have seen this night! And, somehow, they are still alive.)

The latest, Bean hears, is that the two Australian Brigades are 'still east of town, the 15th trying to get touch with the 13th. Prisoners were being fetched out of town everywhere.'[77]

And so begins what will be a long process for Bean of doing what he does best – working out precisely what happened by interviewing as many key witnesses at all levels of the operation that he can. One of those he will soon interview is General Ewen Maclagan, the Commander of the AIF's 4th Division, who has found out that General Heneker's 8th Division 'had a more or less fresh brigade of their own which they did not put in to the V/Bretonneux counter attack'. When Maclagan had asked why, in such a crucial battle, with everything in the balance, they had not thrown in the fresh brigade, the answer had come back: 'We thought the Australians could do it.'[78]

—

And so they have, as it turns out. After a day of low-level jousting between the defending Australians and the Germans, who make several half-hearted efforts to oust them, on this evening of 25 April, at his HQ next to the Flixecourt jute factory, General Rawlinson writes in his diary:

> The [Australian] counter-attack last night succeeded beyond my expectations. We have, by dusk, recaptured the whole of Villers-Bretonneux . . . The 15th and 13th Australian brigades did brilliantly; especially the former, attacking round the north of the village . . . The counter-attack was . . . exceedingly well carried out by the Australians.[79]

At 1 am on 26 April, when two patrols of the 50th Battalion carefully move out from both sides of the gap, they are able to meet in the middle and dig in. Two companies of the 49th Battalion move forward, to also dig in and take over the position.

'Thus by the small hours of April 26th,' Charles Bean would proudly record, 'the line east of Villers-Bretonneux was complete.'[80]

By the next day again, Bean records, 'The Australian Corps has now taken over the whole Fourth Army front. The 4th Div goes into the line south next to the French up to V/B; the 5th Div . . . extended north of the Somme; the 3rd Division takes [it up to] Dernancourt. The 2nd Division extends up north of Albert.'[81]

In sum, what had been a thin line of British soldiers covering 15 miles from Albert to Hangard Wood on 27 March, when the Australians had arrived on the scene, is now a solid line of Australians – and they ain't shifting. The German plan to drive a wedge between the British and French Armies is thwarted.

'So ended happily,' General Grogan of the 23rd Brigade would note, 'what, at one time, threatened to be a serious disaster to the British lines in France, and which was only averted by Australian valour and Australian arms.'[82]

True.

Within three weeks, Operation George would go the same way

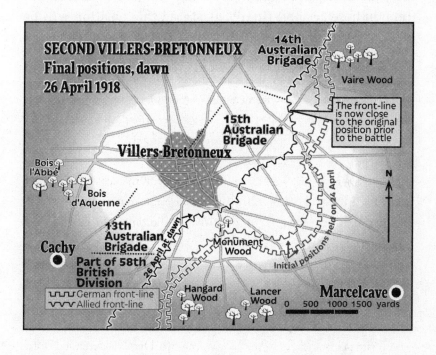

as Operation Michael – a slow stalling all the way down to miserable defeat – and ultimately, the *Kaiserschlacht* was a failure, thanks in no small part to the efforts of the Australians.

The Australians, on 12 occasions in the course of that campaign

– in five positions over five weeks – had been attacked. And on 12 out of 12 times, the Australians had held their positions, in a manner to do Lieutenant Frank Bethune proud – **If the section cannot remain here alive, it will remain here dead, but in any case it will remain here . . . and finally, as stated this position will be held**[83] – and triumphed each time.

All along the line, the Australians really *had* held those bastards, averting Allied defeat in the First World War and staving off what would likely have otherwise been a German victory in the whole war because of it.

EPILOGUE

Due to violent [Australian] counter-attacks – that
had mostly already begun at 2.30 at night – serious
setbacks occurred in Villers-Bretonneux, which
continued in the morning of 25 April; the enemy
was able to recapture the important place . . .
Our own losses amounted to 8000 men . . . The attack
. . . had failed. Thus it has damaged the morale of the
troops on the German side, just as it has brought the
opponent the feeling of superiority on this front section.[1]
German Official History on the result of the
Second Battle of Villers-Bretonneux[2]

Now the bleedin' war is over
Oh, how happy was I there
Now old Fritz and I have parted
Life's one everlasting care
No more Estaminets to sing in
No ma'moiselles to make me gay
Civvie life's a bleedin' failure
I was happy yesterday[4]
A. Tiveychoc, There and Back

To my countrymen from all parts of our wide Empire
I say: Think of what it meant to you, this band of men
who stood unflinchingly between you and all that
defeat meant. And realise that many thousands of the
survivors live today, passing unnoticed in a civilian

crowd, unhonoured and unknown. Acknowledge their
valour as and when you can; it is too easy to forget.[5]
General Sir Hubert Gough, The Fifth Army, 1931

The general lack of British acknowledgement for Australia's staggering
valour and feat of arms at Villers-Bretonneux?

Don't get me started.

But the tone was set, as detailed by Pompey Elliott, with a message
of congratulations which arrived from GHQ shortly after the victory:
'The brilliant idea of the [British] 3rd Corps for the recapture of Villers-
Bretonneux was ably carried out by the [British] 8th Division, assisted
by the 13th and 15th Australian Infantry Brigades.'[6]

No, really, they shouldn't have.

And they really didn't.

In fact, as Bean would note in his diary, the idea for the 'converging
attack on V/B . . . was suggested by [Pompey] before the bombardment
had finished'.[7]

As the aggrieved Elliott would also note, while he was directly
told to limit the number of Distinguished Service Orders awarded to
members of the 15th Brigade to just three, '8th Division . . . who were
soundly beaten, received thirteen DSOs'.[8] He would also note that all
of the machine guns and artillery 'captured by the Australian brigades
have been credited to III Corps and not the Australian Corps'.[9] Most
outrageous of all to him, most likely, was the subsequent suggestion that
the idea for the successful pincer movement had come from a Colonel
Armitage, the Chief of Staff of Heneker's 8th Division, as opposed to
being his own idea, floated from the first hours of the battle.

'I can say myself,' he wrote to Colonel John Treloar, in an effort to
set the record straight, 'that Colonel Armitage's contribution to the victory was a hare-brained suggestion that we should advance to Warfusee
[four miles east of VB].'[10]

Ol' Pompey! Run for your lives, he's going to blow.

In the final analysis, neither Amiens nor Hazebrouck nor any of
the Channel ports fell. While Operation Michael was over on 5 April

1918, the last Operation George attack was launched on 29 April 1918, resulting in such a total failure that General Ludendorff had no choice but to call the whole thing off that very night. The *Kaiserschlacht* dribbled on for another couple of months, as Ludendorff then changed tack to attack the French from May to July, but he and his forces failed there too.

In the end, such were the times that the Australians' valour – in all of their actions opposing Operation Michael and subsequent operations in France till the end of the war – did not always receive their due.

The same British press who, as Bean had already noted, were very reluctant to write of so many of their own men who 'threw down their arms and ran away',[11] were even more reluctant still to throw plaudits to the Australians.

While Bean himself was extraordinary in his effort to document the Australians' astonishing efforts through all of Dernancourt, Morlancourt, Hèbuterne, Hazebrouck and Villers-Bretonneux – tabulating them very carefully in his Official History as well as his seminal account, *Anzac to Amiens* – the battles never quite gripped the Australian imagination, never really became a talking point, a point of pride. Many of the men who fought there and survived, like my wife's grandfather, returned to their lives after the war, resumed their civilian careers and barely spoke of it again – at least not of the fear, nor the blood . . . and certainly not to those who weren't there as well.

For the wider public, in any case, up against the enduring legend of Gallipoli, Villers-Bretonneux was never remotely close to the headline act of the Great War. To this day, while many Australians recognise that Villers-Bretonneux was one of the most legendary Australian battles of the Great War – with the likes of Gallipoli, Fromelles, Pozières, Passchendaele, Le Hamel, Mont St Quentin, Beersheeba and the Hindenburg Line – there is little recognition of how crucial the Australian effort was in retrieving the whole situation from what could have been, had Amiens or Hazebrouck fallen, outright Allied defeat.

But the French? They recognised the feat from the first.

After the battle was over, no less than *Le Figaro* exulted:

> *These Australians ... are amongst the most*
> *magnifiques soldats de l'armee britannique.*
> *They are the famous ANZACs of the*
> *terrible battle of GALLIPOLI. It is*
> *nearly four years since they left their distant*
> *lands and what losses they have sustained*
> *... But their spirit has remained the same*
> *as during the first days of the War. They*
> *would not defend their villages other than*
> *they are defending ours. Our Country has*
> *become theirs. All the ideal nobility of our*
> *common cause dwells in the broad bosoms*
> *of these bronzed men, who have come from*
> *the Antipodes and resemble the warriors*
> *of the bas-reliefs of Aegina. They and*
> *their leaders when spoken to of AMIENS*
> *repeat the immortal words of the 'poilus' at*
> *VERDUN - 'They will not pass'.*[12]

(Personally, I'll bet 'We'll stop these bastards' was closer to the money, but still.)

While the possibility of capturing, or at least shelling, Amiens from Villers-Brettoneux was denied the Germans, at least one part of the German plan worked – because of the attack, it was indeed well over a week before British GHQ dared to move any divisions from the south to the north to block Operation George.

After playing their part in defeating the *Kaiserschlacht*, the Australians went on to cover themselves in glory, most particularly during the Battle of Le Hamel on 4 July, when the Australian Corps, with brigades from 2nd, 3rd, 4th and 5th Divisions – under the stewardship of General John Monash – captured well over two miles of the German line in 90 minutes. Three days after that battle, the delighted

French Prime Minister, Georges Clémenceau, journeyed to the French village and asked to address the men of the 4th Australian Division who had accomplished the feat.

'I am glad to be able to speak at least this small amount of English,' he told them in his thick accent, 'because it enables me to tell you what all French people think of you. They expected a great deal of you because they have heard what you accomplished in the development of your own country. I should not like to say that they are surprised that you have fulfilled their expectations. By that high standard they judge you, and admire you that you have reached it. We have all been fighting the same battle of freedom in these old battlegrounds. You have all heard the names of them in history. But it is a great wonder too, in history, that you should be here fighting on the old battlefields, which you never thought, perhaps, to see. The work of our fathers, which we wanted to hand down unharmed to our children, the Germans tried to take from us. They tried to rob us of all what is dearest in modern human society. But men were the same in Australia, England, France and Italy, and all countries proud of being the home of free people. That is what made you come; that is what made us greet you when you came. We knew you would fight a real fight, but we did not know that from the very beginning you would astonish the Continent with your valour. I have come here for the simple purpose of seeing the Australians and telling them this. I shall go back tomorrow and say to my countrymen: I have seen the Australians; I have looked into their eyes. I know that they, men who have fought great battles in the cause of freedom, will fight alongside us, till the freedom for which we are all fighting is guaranteed for us and our children.'[13]

And that glory, glory, hallelujah continued in the last 100 days of the war, as, with the Canadians, the Australians were the shock troops leading the advance all the way through breaking the Hindenburg Line, Germany's last line of defence.

Revealingly, after such a long string of major Australian battles in France, when the time came to choose a site to build the Australian National Memorial for the First World War – to honour *all* Australian dead in France and Belgium – the Australian military leaders chose Hill 104 overlooking Villers-Bretonneux. Built with stone quarried in Australia, the towering monument stands before the cemetery that contains the remains of many of the Australians who gave their lives for the town, while the monument itself honours the names of the 10,738 Australians who died in France whose actual final resting place remains unknown. The top of the tower offers particularly clear views of much of the route taken by the 15th Brigade in their counter-attack starting on the eve of Anzac Day 1918. If you see it in the moonlight – and I have – you can imagine them surging forth up that same slope, which remains virtually unchanged since 1918.

———

Of all the senior Australian officers involved in the Great War, it was **General Sir John Monash, GCMG, KCG, VD, MID**, who would go on to become the most revered Australian military leader of all time, leading the most powerful Corps in the British Army – the Australian Corps, numbering 120,000 Australian soldiers – to victory after victory from July to October 1918.

Deep respect for him extended beyond our shores, with none other than Brigadier Frank Crozier writing of him – after tearing down the British Generals as jumped-up polo players who should have been sacked – 'That is why the Australian Monash, a fine man and a good soldier, a civil engineer by profession and a soldier at birth, could have commanded the armies of the Empire in France with success. And more – he would have staffed the whole army with suitable men, chosen for battle and not for bridge.'[14]

Field Marshal Bernard Montgomery, perhaps the most highly regarded of the British Second World War military leaders, would agree, firmly claiming Monash as 'the best general on the Western Front in Europe . . .'[15] Returning to Australia after the war, Monash became one of the most prominent and important leaders in the country, and from 1925 onwards led Melbourne's Anzac Day march. The cause closest to his heart was the Shrine of Remembrance, for which he was the prime founding force. When he died in 1931, his soldiers and their families, and the Australian people, turned out in droves a quarter of a million strong as his flag-laden coffin was pulled on a gun carriage through the streets of Melbourne.

—

Brigadier Harold 'Pompey' Elliott, CB, CMG, DSO, DCM, VD, would be proud of the success of his men at Villers-Bretonneux for the rest of his days. As I noted in the epilogue to my book *Fromelles and Pozières: In the Trenches of Hell*, for the rest of the war Pompey continued on as a successful officer, loved by his men, and yet, despite in the course of the war being mentioned in dispatches seven times for his valour, was never given a division to command.

'The reason for this,' his Intelligence Officer, Lieutenant David Doyle, would state more than 20 years later in a letter to the Editor of *Reveille*, 'was General Elliott's inability to get on with British Officers. He couldn't understand them, and they couldn't understand him . . .'[16]

After the war, Elliott entered politics, becoming a Victorian Senator for the Nationalist Party for all of the 1920s. Much of his energy also went to helping returned soldiers in any way he could – and yet, he was a man who desperately needed help himself.

Likely suffering from post-traumatic stress, in March 1931 the 52-year-old Elliott took his own life. His state funeral was attended by several thousand returned servicemen, who followed the gun carriage bearing his coffin from his home at East Camberwell to his grave at Burwood Cemetery, standing to attention as his coffin was lowered into the grave and a 13-gun salute was fired. There was such an outpouring of emotion that the former Prime Minister Stanley Bruce would say of it, 'I have never seen a greater tribute.'[17]

—

Brigadier Sir William Glasgow, KCB, CMG, DSO, VD, was promoted in June to the rank of Major-General and became the Commanding Officer of the 1st Division, leading it through many successful battles to the end of the war. Knighted upon his return to Australia for his wartime achievements, he quickly entered the nation's parliament as a Senator for the Nationalist Party, going on to become the Minister for Home and Territories and then Minister for Defence – where he most notably expanded both the Australian Army and Royal Australian Air Force – before losing his seat in 1931.

For the rest of the 1930s, he returned to his pastoral and business interests before, in 1939, being appointed as Australia's first High Commissioner to Canada. After the Second World War he again returned to Queensland, to engage in more pastoral and business pursuits for the next decade. He died on 4 July 1955, survived by his wife, Annie, and two daughters – and was given a state funeral. A statue of him now stands in Brisbane.

———

In May 1918, **Brigadier Charles Rosenthal, CB, CMG, DSO**, took over command of the 2nd Division, being promoted to Major-General in the process, and worked closely once more with the newly installed Commanding Officer of the Australian Corps, General John Monash, in the legendary attack at Hamel on 4 July 1918. Rosenthal and his men most particularly distinguished themselves in the famed battle of Mont St Quentin for three days from 31 August.

After a brief stint in charge of repatriating the Australian troops following the war, he returned to Australia in 1920 and resumed an extremely successful practice as an architect, as well as doing a couple of brief stints as a Nationalist politician in the NSW Parliament. He attracted attention in 1926 for publicly advocating that a law should be passed banning alcohol in the newly built national capital because, as the newspapers characterised it, 'Canberra would only become one of the finest cities of the world if the residents all remained sober.'[18] The idea did not gain traction. He went on to become the administrator of Norfolk Island, which he governed throughout the Second World War. He died on 11 May 1954, survived by his second wife and two sons.

—

Colonel Sir Leslie James Morshead, KCB, KBE, CMG, DSO, ED, was awarded the *Légion d'Honneur* in August 1918 for his valour in leading the 33rd Battalion in the 1st Battle of Villers-Bretonneux. He went on to even greater fame in the annals of Australian military lore, including being the commander of the joint British–Australian garrison that held Tobruk for eight months from April 1941 – against General Erwin Rommel and the Afrika Korps. Known as 'Ming the Merciless' to his men, Morshead was the direct opponent of Rommel four times in North Africa – including twice in the Battles of El Alamein – and was victorious on all four occasions.

Towards the end of the war he commanded the 1st Australian Corps against the Japanese. Knighted for his services in defending Tobruk, after the war Morshead returned to civilian life and threw himself into the world of business, becoming the manager for the Orient Line of cruise ships as well as chair of David Jones Ltd. He died on September 26, 1959, just a few days after turning 70.

—

Captain Percy Storkey was awarded the Victoria Cross 'for most conspicuous bravery, leadership and devotion to duty when in charge of a platoon in attack'.[19] Wounded in action once again in May 1918, he returned to Australia in November of that year, returned to his university studies and graduated with a law degree in 1921 – just before he married an English-born divorcee, Minnie Gordon – and went on to a sterling legal career as a Crown prosecutor and then District Court judge from 1939, until his retirement in 1955. He died on 3 October 1969, aged 77, survived by his wife.

—

Captain Arthur 'Harry' Cobby, OBE, DSO, DFC, GM, kept flying missions for the Australian Flying Corps (he shot down three aircraft in one day on 28 June 1918) despite soon becoming frustrated with the diminished desire of the Germans to take to the air from July onwards as the Allies dominated ever more heavily. Cobby and the men under his command began to engage in the practice of swooping in low over enemy aerodromes, to drop, yes, old boots upon them, with messages inside addressed to 'the footsore aerial knights of Germany', inviting them to quit their cowardly ways and come up and have a go. More than a few German pilots, seething with rage, did exactly that, and were shot down for their trouble, allowing Cobby to take his final tally of victories up to 29.

After being awarded the Distinguished Flying Cross in June 1918, he was awarded 'another two Bars to the D.F.C. in July, the Distinguished Service Order in August, and was mentioned in dispatches,'[20] before heading to England to become an instructor. Chosen to lead the Australian Flying Corps fly-past in London on Anzac Day 1919, he dived on the crowd and over the head of the Prince of Wales. Cobby said, 'It was the most foolish thing I have ever done.'[21]

After the war he returned to Australia, married Hilda Urban and, in 1921, became one of the foundation members of the newly formed Royal Australian Air Force. Cobby continued to rise to the point that, when he resigned in 1936, he had the rank of Wing Commander – the broad equivalent of an Army Colonel. When the Second World War began, Cobby returned to the RAAF, rising further to the rank of Air Commodore – like an Army General – going on to win the George Medal in 1943 for heroism displayed while rescuing survivors after a plane on which he was travelling as a passenger crashed. Despite such glory, and such a pure flying pedigree, in April 1945 Cobby fell out with his superiors in the RAAF after something of a mutiny was mounted against him by senior pilots reporting to him on the Dutch East Indies island of Morotai. He was peremptorily sacked from that position, leaving the RAAF the next year. In his later years, Cobby returned to the Department of Civil Aviation, before dying suddenly on 11 November 1955, aged 61. He was survived by his wife, son and daughter.

—

As I noted in the epilogue of my book *Gallipoli*, in the course of the war **Captain Charles Bean** filled 226 notebooks, which formed the foundation stone for his work for the next 23 years after the war, as he compiled 12 volumes – of which he wrote the first six – of the *Official History of Australia in the War of 1914–1918,* with the twelfth and final volume being published in 1942. In 1946, Bean released a separate single volume account of the war titled *Anzac to Amiens.*

Beyond his writings, Bean's other great legacy, of course, was the Australian War Memorial, for which he was the driving force and served as its first Acting Director. The building itself opened its doors on 11 November 1941. He died aged 88 on 30 August 1968, survived by his wife, Ethel, a one-time Queanbeyan nurse, and their daughter, grandson and granddaughter – the latter two of whom I warmly thank again for allowing me to quote so extensively from his diaries and notebooks.

—

Lieutenant George Mitchell, MC, DCM, returned to Australia after the war and lived something of a peripatetic existence thereafter, moving through all of South Australia, Victoria, Queensland and New South Wales for the next two decades, working any number of jobs, from estate agent to garage-owner, motorcar salesman, journalist and author. I have drawn heavily for this account on his great book *Backs to the Wall*, which was published in 1937.

He also rose to be his state's representative of the Returned Sailor's and Soldier's Imperial League of Australia, and represented the seat of Oxley in the Legislative Assembly of New South Wales from 1941 (when he married for the first time) to 1944. He took up with the Australian Army once more and only attended parliament for three sitting days before returning to civilian life as soon as the war was over. At the age of 67, he died of cancer on 11 January 1961 at Darlinghurst, Sydney, and was survived by his second wife and a son.

—

Lieutenant Cliff Sadlier, VC, was still recuperating from his heroics at Villers-Bretonneux, receiving treatment on his severely wounded arm at South Kensington Hospital in London, when a rumour came to his ears that he was going to be awarded the Distinguished Service Order.

'I'll believe it when I see it,' Sadlier told his mates. Surely a humble commercial traveller from Subiaco would not be awarded something so, well, *distinguished* as a Distinguished Service Order?

Not bloody likely.

He continued to pass his days receiving treatment, getting movement back into his arm and playing bridge with the boys, when, one day, a reporter with a notepad suddenly appeared and asked: 'Which one of you is Sadlier?'

Wordlessly laying down his bridge hand, Sadlier stood up.

'You've been awarded the Victoria Cross,' the reporter told him, simply.

Stunned, Sadlier sat down again.

'It was the proudest moment of my life,'[22] he would recount. But two weeks later ran it close, when he turned up for the investiture at Buckingham Palace, and King George V *himself* pinned the Victoria Cross on him. The King was about to shake the brave Australian's right hand before noticing that it was still in a sling and graciously offering his left hand instead, which Cliff Sadlier, VC, shook heartily.

Sadlier returned to Australia just before the war was over, married his sweetheart, worked as a manufacturer's agent through the 1920s, had an unsuccessful tilt at politics, divorced in 1934, remarried in 1936 and worked for well over another decade as a clerk in the Repatriation Department in Perth. He retired to Busselton and died on 28 April 1964. He was survived by his second wife.

———

There would be some ill-feeling, however, that **Sergeant Charlie Stokes**, who was in turn awarded the Distinguished Conduct Medal for his own derring-do with the 13th Brigade on the night of 24 April – as he had come up with the idea for the attack and been heavily involved in the most brutal parts of it, taking command for the rest of the night after Sadlier had been wounded – was not awarded the VC himself. (After all, following the battle Stokes had been formally recommended for the DCM while the recommendation for Sadlier had been one step lower, for the Military Cross.) Needless to say, it was controversy with which Stokes himself never remotely engaged. He returned to Subiaco in Perth after the war to his wife, Ellen, and bought a truck to cart wheat from farms to Fremantle. They had two children. He died in Subiaco in 1969, a grand old man of 83.

———

Sergeant Stanley Robert McDougall – the great man! – was awarded a Victoria Cross for his actions on the morning of 28 March at Dernancourt, specifically, 'for most conspicuous bravery and devotion to duty when the enemy attacked our line and his first wave succeeded in gaining an entry . . . The prompt action of this non-commissioned officer saved the line and enabled the enemy's advance to be stopped.'[23]

His brother's wish before Stan left Tassie that he 'win the Victoria Cross'[24] had been fulfilled.

As for McDougall's heroics on the same ground eight days later, he was awarded a Military Medal.

After the war, McDougall returned to Tassie and married. At the first reunion of the 47th Battalion in Hobart in 1921, he was the

Guest of Honour, and such honours would continue with a street in Canberra named after him, while his VC and uniform are on display at the Australian War Memorial. When Bean tried to talk to McDougall about just what had happened in both Dernancourt actions, assembling material for his *Official History*, he found it very hard going. 'The boy wouldn't talk about himself – was most modest.'[25]

In 1956, when all recipients of the Victoria Cross were invited to go to London to commemorate the centenary of the medal, McDougall was one of the attendees. Three hundred VC recipients came from all over the Commonwealth, including Australian James Rogers, who had received his VC in 1901 during the Boer War.

In his career beyond the army, after the war, McDougall was a long-serving officer with the Tasmanian Forestry Department. His bravery in the face of fire with southerly busters behind them was every bit as on display as when he was under fire from the Germans, and he became locally famous anew as Inspector-in-Charge of Forests in north-east Tasmania for his work during bushfire periods. He died in 1968, aged 79, and was survived by his wife, Martha.

—

Private Edwin Need was wounded at Mont St Quentin in September 1918. He returned home to marry his sweetheart, Violet, to whom he had been writing throughout the war, and together they raised three kids. He initially worked with his father and brothers in a painting and decorating business, and all went well until the business collapsed in the Depression. It was at this point, in 1933, that Need began to assemble all of his diaries into a manuscript in which he 'remembers best of all that true comradeship that existed towards one another . . . strengthened by danger and discomfort, even death, each being judged by his essential qualities rather than by his graces, men from the slums, from the land, and public schools, all on the one footing . . . all equal, I missing all this when I walked out into civilian life once again, the reason I suppose why I, as do the others, look forward to the reunions on Anzac day, when we lapse back into the same spirit as existed in those years, if only for a few hours, and it is hard to realise that such a state of affairs should have to exist to give a man that experience.'[26]

In the Second World War he joined the Volunteer Defence Corps, before becoming ill. He died in 1954 in Melbourne.

—

General Hubert Gough, GCB, GCMG, KCVO, never again took active command of a battlefield force. Retiring from the military in 1922, much of his energies postwar went into trying to rehabilitate his reputation. More than anything, he appeared to be hurt by people not understanding what he and his men had been through, and after the war he wrote in an introduction to the book, *The Fifth Army*, 'Why my country failed to realize or to appreciate the splendid valour and great results achieved by the men of the Fifth Army is a difficult and perhaps a delicate matter for me to touch upon.'[27]

But he would, at length, succeed to the point that he was knighted in 1937. He died at home in 1963 at the age of 92, one of the longest lived of the British Commanders of the Great War.

—

The newly promoted **Marshal Ferdinand Foch** considered the Versailles Peace Treaty of 1919 to be useless, as it did not permanently weaken Germany, claiming, prophetically, 'This is not peace. It is an armistice for twenty years.'

Heaped with honours from France and her Allies, he retired the same year and died in 1929. He is buried in Les Invalides, close to Napoleon.

—

Operation Michael and Operation George proved to be the beginning of the end for the once all-powerful 'Duo' of *Generalfeldmarschall* **Paul von Hindenburg** and **General Erich Ludendorff**.

'By the end of April,' Ludendorff would note, 'the offensive begun on 21st March had come to an end . . .'[28]

There would be other attacks launched by the Germans in the Summer of 1918, but none of them worked either – the less so because by the middle of the year the arrival of the American troops en masse really did swing the balance the Allies' way – and by August it was only a matter of time before Germany would be defeated.

On 26 October 1918, Ludendorff tendered his resignation, only for von Hindenburg to beg him 'not to desert the Emperor and the army at this time'.[29]

No matter, in a conversation with the Kaiser the next day, as Ludendorff would recall, 'I said respectfully to His Majesty that I had gained the painful impression that I no longer enjoyed his confidence, and that I accordingly begged most humbly to be relieved of my office. His Majesty accepted my resignation.'[30]

Ludendorff walked back to his office alone to clean out his desk, and upon arrival, after he had announced his resignation to his officers, added, 'In a fortnight, there will no longer be an Emperor in Germany.'[31]

His staff agreed and all were proved right, as on 9 November 1918, a weeping General Friedrich von Gontard, who had commanded XIV Corps at Villers-Bretonneux, was obliged to tell the Kaiser that both His Imperial Majesty and the Crown Prince had been deposed by the government.

The next day, Kaiser Wilhelm crossed the border into exile in the Netherlands. He learned Dutch and wrote his memoirs, defending his conduct in the First World War. He died at Doorn, Holland, in 1941, never having set foot back in Germany.

Following the war, General Ludendorff threw in his lot with the rise of his one-time junior soldier Adolf Hitler, including being involved with his only surviving stepson, Heinz, in the infamous Beer Hall Putsch of 1923, which was a miserable failure – but Ludendorff's name and enduring prestige lent the Nazis a credibility they would not otherwise have enjoyed.

In 1925, the Duo definitively split, as Ludendorff stood against Hindenburg for the presidency of Germany, even claiming that von Hindenburg had taken credit for the victories in Russia, which, properly, should have been credited to Ludendorff himself.

Von Hindenburg won, meaning his former Chief of Staff attacked him all the harder – but Ludendorff did so without the grieving Margarethe by his side. She never recovered from the loss of her youngest son, a double body blow after the loss of her firstborn that sent her reeling and left her always 'sick and sorry'.

Of her lad Erich, she would later recount, 'A concise route was attributed to him. He went straight through, his soul is pure and undefiled, gone home to God. My consolation was that he was spared disappointments and painful years. My happiness and my pride is that I possessed such children . . .'[32]

Margarethe and her husband divorced in 1926, and he quickly married again.

In the years that followed, Ludendorff's association with Hitler waxed and waned. In his later years he became a pacifist, despite Hitler offering him the position of *Generalfeldmarschall* in his army.

Ludendorff died on 20 December 1937 at age 72. Against his wishes, he was given a state funeral, organised and attended by the Chancellor of the Third Reich, Adolf Hitler. Margarethe had died alone, in comparative obscurity, the year before. The last member of Ludendorff's family left alive, his second son Heinz, would go on to live a long life, dying in 1973, aged 77.

—

All up, *Generalfeldmarschall* **Paul von Hindenburg** proved to be the greatest survivor of his generation. He did not resign at the same time as Ludendorff at the end of the First World War, and was there till the bitter end. It affected naught his national popularity, and though he retired from the military in 1919, by 1925 he was back on the national stage as President of the Weimar Republic – a position he retained for most of the next decade, even as the rise of Hitler as Chancellor made the role progressively smaller and weaker. Von Hindenburg died in office on 2 August 1934, aged 86.

—

Crown Prince Rupprecht finished the war as the most highly regarded of the Royal Commanders, only to see a revolution break out straight afterwards that swept away the reign of his father as King of Bavaria – and along with it his chance at succession. Nevertheless, Rupprecht maintained a 'court' with money from his estate throughout the Weimar Republic, and was regarded by many as King of Bavaria for all of the rest of his life – including his self-imposed exile in Italy from 1938 to 1945. He died at Schloss Leutstetten in Bavaria in 1955, aged 86.

—

The Red Baron, **Manfred von Richthofen's** story had some curious angles to it that extended well beyond his death. His whole family attended the memorial service for him in Berlin on the 2 May 1918, and were seated next to none other than *der Kaiserin*, Kaiser Wilhelm's wife, Auguste Victoria. The Commander of the *Deutsche Luftstreitkräfte*, German Air Force, General Ernst von Hoeppner, told the Baron's mother, 'That he could definitely assure me that Manfred had taken a chance hit from the ground,' before adding, 'We have no replacement for your son in the whole Air Force.'[33]

The closest they could get, at least in leadership, and even then it would take three months, was a German ace with 18 victories to his credit, one *Oberleutnant* **Hermann Göering**, who took over as Commander of *Jagdgeschwader 1*, a stepping stone to the enormous fame that was to come for him as the *Reichsminister* of Aviation, President of the Reichstag and Vice Chancellor of Adolf Hitler.

Shortly after the war, in 1921, Richthofen's body was moved from Bertangles to a German military cemetery on the outskirts of the French town of Fricourt, just outside Albert. It was from there, in 1925, that his younger brother, Bolko, claimed it, as his mother wished to bury him in the family plot at Schweidnitz cemetery – beside his father, who had died of natural causes in 1920, and his brother, Lothar, who had been killed when his plane crashed in 1922.

And yet once the German government became aware that one of the Fatherland's most famous sons was returning to German soil, it managed to persuade Bolko to have Manfred buried in the Invalidenfriedhof Cemetery in Berlin, a place where most of Germany's greatest military heroes and leaders are interred.

In 1938, Göering, by then Hitler's Minister for Economic Affairs and given the responsibility for the German rearmament program, added a massive monument atop the grave.

When the Berlin Wall was built in 1961, it transpired that the Invalidenfriedhof was in the Communist Russian eastern sector, meaning that the von Richthofen family, who lived in the western sector, could only visit the gravesite with special permission. It was because of this that Bolko applied for permission from the East German government to once again reclaim his brother's body, and this time do what he had intended to do in 1925 and bury him in the family plot. Though this did not happen before Bolko died in 1971, the final burial did take place in 1975, and that is where Manfred von Richthofen lies today, in the family's tomb in Wiesbaden.

The controversy over who actually was responsible for the fatal shot on the Red Baron goes on to this day. It would even include staggering – though nonsensical – allegations.

In the May 1932 edition of the German soldiers' magazine *Der Frontsoldat Erzahlt*, Hermann Bink of the 3rd Grenadier Regiment recounted how he saw it all through his telescope from Hamel, just a mile away: '[Richthofen] landed . . . we saw him climb out of the aeroplane alive! Several brown forms fell on him with drawn daggers – or with shiny side-arms – and presumably stabbed him. They were British colonial troops which were opposite us.'[34]

More reliably, the German war correspondents who were on the spot at the time and inquired into the circumstances of his death were resolute in their conviction, best expressed by the journalist on the spot for *Vossische Zeitung:* 'As Richthofen as the persecutor of his opponent cannot be hit well in the air, he seems to have fallen victim to a *Zufallstreffer*, fluke from the ground.'[35]

But who fired the shot? Within a day of it occurring, the 5th Division's General Hobbs asked Charles Bean to try and get to the bottom of it, which Bean essays to do, despite resenting expending his energies on 'so trivial a matter'.[36]

Still, Bean cooperates and interviews, among others **Gunner Robert Buie** and **Gunner 'Snowy' Evans**, who were firing 'the two Lewis guns about 130 yards apart. English plane first appeared over top of the hill, then the German after him, hidden by him. [Then] the German plane came about 15 feet above other plane and both gunners fired a burst at him at about 100 yards. The plane wobbled at once and swerved to the German's right and speared towards the earth.'[37]

Upon further examination, however – such is the interest – Bean will eventually write nine pages of analysis on it at the end of Vol. V of his *Official History*. He concludes it was the Sydney carpenter **Sergeant Cedric Popkin** of the Australian 24th Machine Gun Company, while Bean placed Captain Roy Brown as an unlikely second choice.

For his part, in 1964, Popkin would tell the Brisbane *Courier* that, while he was fairly sure he was the one who shot down the Red Baron, it was impossible to be certain. After the war, Popkin went back to carpentry, living in Tweed Heads for the rest of his life, before dying there in 1968.

———

Gunner Robert Buie returned from the war to live a relatively gentle life, fishing and oyster farming on the Hawkesbury River where he had grown up. A certain renown followed him as 'the man who had shot down the Red Baron', and I remember my own mother proudly telling me that the man who had accomplished that feat had lived not far from our family farm at Peats Ridge, an hour north of Sydney. He lived for nigh on half a century longer than von Richthofen until finally, on Anzac Day 1964, Robert Buie, aged 71, was found dead in his boat, adrift on the Hawkesbury. His headstone in Brooklyn cemetery has the simple epitaph: *He shot down the Red Baron.*[38*]

—

You will recall, too, **Corporal Joe Porter**, the mechanic with No. 3 Squadron Australian Flying Corps, who swapped his boots for those of the Red Baron the night before the German pilot was buried at Bertangles. He returned to Australia after the war, had a daughter with his wife, Margaret, and got on with his life as a car mechanic. But something kept bothering him. Those boots. They did not rightly belong to him. As detailed in the *Independent* of Deniliquin, New South Wales, 6 April 1934, a decade and a half after the war was over, he finally wrote to the Red Baron's mother and arranged to personally return the boots, journeying to Germany by ship for the purpose and travelling by train to the 'the picturesque old world town of Schweidnitz', where the Baroness gratefully received him, and her late son's 'high topped boots, patched and worn . . . of regulation German aviation pattern'.[39]

—

Captain Roy Brown, who was – in my view, mistakenly – credited with shooting down Baron von Richthofen, only remained on flying duties for another nine days after the Baron's fall before being sent to hospital with 'nervous exhaustion'. He never flew again as a fighter pilot.

After the war Brown was restless, moving through all of accountancy, the aviation business, journalism, politics and farming, most with varying degrees of failure before moving on to the next. He died in

1944, shortly after buying a farm in Ontario, Canada, and was survived by his wife and his two daughters.

—

Captain Rudolf Binding continued with the Germany Army, almost to the end of the war, collapsing with trench fever and dysentery just before the Armistice on 11 November 1918. On 14 November he returned home amid throngs of men in field grey doing exactly the same thing.

Binding's diary and letters, combined in one book, *A Fatalist at War*, was published in 1927. In the early 1930s, he fell in love with his private secretary, Elisabeth Jungmann, but was prevented from marrying the Jewish woman by the Nuremberg Laws. In October 1933, Binding, with 87 other German writers and poets, signed the *Gelöbnis treuester Gefolgschaft*, declaring loyalty and support to Hitler. He died in 1938 in Starnberg, Germany, aged 72.

—

After serving in the Great War as a Jewish German citizen, ***Leutnant Herbert Sulzbach*** fled the Nazis in 1938 with his wife and family – and served in the Second World War in the British army, fighting against his oppressors.

After the war, he became Cultural Attaché in the German Embassy in London, staying in the role until 1981, just four years before his death at the age of 91.

—

On 18 May 1918, **Captain Rudolf Teichmann** was awarded the highest German military honour for bravery – the curiously named *Pour le Mérite* – specifically for his heroism at Villers Bretonneux.

—

At the conclusion of the war, the anti-aircraft gunner **Leutnant Fritz Nagel** went back to Germany, where he witnessed the violence of the revolution. Still with his beloved Dorothy, and now with a young son, he emigrated to the United States in 1921, settling in Kentucky. His entry visa was obtained with the assistance of his brother, who had spent the war in America.

In 1962, exactly half a century after he first joined the German field artillery as a one-year volunteer in 1912, Fritz Nagel began writing down his experiences as a soldier of the First World War. Called *Fritz: The World War I Memoir of a German Lieutenant*, it was a comprehensive account, which I have drawn on for this book. He died in 1986 aged 94 in the city of Louisville, Kentucky.

—

Private Baier, the one-time German officer who, after shooting dead the man he'd discovered in bed with his wife – and being busted down to Private – went on to be so notably courageous on the opening day of the *Kaiserschlacht*, survived that day. But, as *Feldwebel* Wilhelm Prosch of 463rd Regiment would report, 'He was killed in action several months later at the *Chemin des Dames* area. I was with him when he died'[40]

—

All up, the Australian heroics at Villers-Bretonneux would not be forgotten, and the key keepers of the flame would be the villagers themselves. *To this day*, the very name of Australia is revered in the picturesque French town. When my wife and I visited the local primary school *L'Ecole Victoria* in October 2015, we were greeted as honoured guests – simply because we were Australians – and shown the classrooms. Above every blackboard, written in big letters, are the words every Villers-Bretonneux *enfant* knows from the moment they can read:

'N'oublions jamais l'Australie.'

Never forget Australia.

That school was rebuilt after the war by the collected proceeds of Victorian school children being encouraged to donate a penny apiece. On the outside wall of the school is affixed a bronze plaque:

> This school building is the gift of the schoolchildren of Victoria, Australia, to the children of Villers-Bretonneux as a proof of their love and good will towards France. Twelve Hundred Australian soldiers, the fathers and brothers of these children, gave their lives in the heroic recapture of this town from the invader on 24th April 1918 and are buried near this spot. May the memory of great sacrifice in a common cause keep France and Australia together in bonds of friendship and mutual esteem.

No fewer than 91 years later, when the Black Saturday bushfires devastated Victoria, Villers-Bretonneux returned the favour. Out of the blue on a black day, the Principal of Strathewen Primary School in regional Victoria, which had burned to the ground, was contacted by the Mayor of Villers-Bretonneux, saying his people would like to contribute to the cost of rebuilding. Beyond everything else, there was a certain symmetry to the proposal, as the Principal, Jane Hayward AM, has a great-uncle, Edmund King, lying for eternity in Grave 26 in the cemetery at Villers-Bretonneux.

A further connection, of course, was that so many of the Australian soldiers who died on the Western Front, like her great-uncle, had come from the Strathewen area, just 40 miles north of Melbourne. She gratefully accepted the kind offer, and the Mayor started a small fund, which soon turned into a big fund as many villagers became involved.

Astounded that so much money was coming from so far away, in honour of an event so long ago, Principal Hayward put the money towards re-establishing the grounds of the school, including cricket nets and a 'French courtyard' – a paved outdoor area with a giant chess set and a pavement plaque recognising the relationship between the two schools, and Strathewen's appreciation.

The following year, on Friday 28 October 2011, the great day came when a coach-load of visitors from Villers-Bretonneux, led by Mayor Patrick Simon, arrived for what was intended to be an hour-long morning tea to meet the students and families and see where VB's funds had been spent.

The kids of Strathewen – *all in their places, with bright shining faces* – lined up, waving French flags, as the bus pulled up. As the villagers of Villers-Bretonneux emerged, blinking in the sunlight, the kids sang the songs in French they had been practising for so long, and then each child took one of the visitors by the hand to show them around, including to the beautiful courtyard of the school where the visitors gazed with teary eyes on the plaque, forevermore embedded in the tiles.

This chess courtyard is a gift from the people of Villers-Bretonneux who generously supported Strathewen Primary School after the devastation of Black Saturday 2009.

We shall carry our historic connection into the future.

'N'oublions jamais nos amis de Villers-Bretonneux, France.'

A morning tea with pumpkin scones and lamingtons was served.

No matter that none of the visitors spoke English, and none of the kids or staff spoke French. What was happening was beyond words anyway, and all knew it.

'No one wanted the morning to end,' Principal Hayward notes. 'And it really never did. Since then we've kept in even closer touch. We've sent special treasures over to the school and they've sent things back. We have photos from the Villers-Bretonneux school on display and a framed map of the Somme, which they presented us with. The French flag sits proudly alongside the Australian flag in our school entrance.'

All of the Strathewen kids know the story behind the support their school has been shown and are very proud of the link. Each year the Grade 6 students head into the Shrine of Remembrance in Melbourne, as invited and honoured guests, to attend a special French–Australian service the day before Anzac Day and lay a wreath to the Australian soldiers who fell in France a century ago . . .

Lest We Forget.

Villers-Bretonneux certainly has not.

NOTES AND REFERENCES

EPIGRAPH

1. Monash, p. 63.
2. Essame, p. 3.
3. Frank Fischer, Letter to his siblings, 1 April 1918, AWM 1DRL/0288, p. 3.

BACKGROUND AND ACKNOWLEDGEMENTS

1. Bean, *Official History of Australia in the War of 1914–1918*, Vol. V, p. 110.
2. Bean, *Anzac to Amiens,* p. 415.
3. Bean, *Official History of Australia in the War of 1914–1918*, Vol. V, p. 177.

PROLOGUE

1. Hart, *1918: A Very British Victory*, pp. 257–8.
2. Newton, p. 79.
3. Walther Schwieger, English translation of 'His Majesty's Submarine U-20 War Diary', 7 May 1915, National Archives Record Group 45: Naval Records Collection of the Office of Naval Records and Library, 1691–1945, National Archives Identifier: 785591, p. 5, https://catalog. archives.gov/id/833792?q=lusitania
4. It included 52 tons of shrapnel shells, more than 3000 percussion fuses and 4200 cases of Remington rifle cartridges.
5. There were, in fact, 1257 passengers and 702 crew, together with three stowaways. Of the 1962 on board, 1191 lost their lives.
6. Walther Schwieger, English translation of 'His Majesty's Submarine U-20 War Diary', 7 May 1915, National Archives Record Group 45: Naval Records Collection of the Office of Naval Records and Library, 1691–1945, National Archives Identifier: 785591, p. 5, https://catalog. archives.gov/id/833792
7. A. A. Hoehling and Mary Hoehling, pp. 189–190.

8. Rappaport, pp. 46–47.

9. Wilhelm, *The Memoirs of the Crown Prince of Germany*, p. 154.

10. Bean, *Official History of Australia in the War of 1914–1918*, Vol. III, p. 953.

11. Ibid., p. 958.

12. John Monash to Hannah Monash, Letter, 15 January 1917, AWM 3DRL/2316, Series 1, Box 1, Wallet 1, p. 268.

13. Mitchell, George D., *Backs to the Wall*, p. 70.

14. Barwick, p. 231.

15. Ibid., p. 232.

16. Meyer, p. 416.

17. Ludendorff, Erich, *My War Memories: 1914–1918*, Vol. I, p. 318.

18. Mombauer, p. 202.

19. Görlitz, *The Kaiser and His Court: The Diaries, Notebooks and Letters of Admiral Georg Alexander von Müller, Chief of the Naval Cabinet 1914–1918*, p. 230 (reported speech changed to direct speech).

20. Ibid., p. 228–229.

21. Lutz, (ed.), p. 279.

22. Hindenburg, *The Great War*, p. 130.

23. Tsar Nicholas II, Diary, 15 March 1917, Extracts from the 1917 Diary of Nicholas II, Alexander Palace Archives, www.alexanderpalace.org/palace/ndiaries1917.html.

24. Ibid.

25. Alexander Kerensky and Robert Browder (eds), p. 103.

26. Lauryssens, p. 35.

27. Zeman, p. 26, https://archive.org/stream/Germany-and-Revolution-in-Russia-1915-1918/GermanyAndRevolutionInRussia1915-1918-DocumentsFromArchivesOfGermanForeignMinistry_djvu.txt

28. Berg, p. 440.

29. Görlitz, *The Kaiser and His Court: The Diaries, Notebooks and Letters of Admiral Georg Alexander von Müller, Chief of the Naval Cabinet 1914–1918*, p. 255.

30. Pearson, pp. 77–78.

31. Ibid.

32. Krupskaya, p. 287.

33. Pearson, pp. 126–127.

34. Ibid., p. 128.

35. Ibid.

36. Churchill, p. 73.

37. Tucker, p. 131.

38. Wells, p. 23.
39. Lloyd George, *War Memoirs of David Lloyd George*, p. 6.
40. The other name for this battle is the Third Battle of Ypres.
41. *Daily Herald* (Adelaide), 31 July 1914, p. 5, http://trove.nla.gov.au/ndp/del/article/105632670
42. Downing, *To the Last Ridge*, p. 84.
43. Until February 1918, Russia used the Julian calendar, which fell 13 days behind the Gregorian calendar used widely in western Europe at the time and to this day. As such, these events occurred on 25 October, according to the Russian calendar, and led to the name the 'October Revoultion'.
44. Wade, p. 240.
45. Frankel, p. 154.

CHAPTER ONE: THE CALM BEFORE THE STORMTROOPERS . . .

1. Ghiz, p. 16.
2. Mitchell, George D., *Backs to the Wall*, p. 73.
3. Bean, *Diaries and Notebooks*, October–November 1917, AWM38, 3DRL 606/92/1, p. 38. www.awm.gov.au/collection/RCDIG1066660/?image=38.
4. Bean, *Official History of Australia in the War of 1914–1918*, Vol. V, p. 13.
5. Major G. I. Adcock, Typed extracts of letters and diary entries, 2nd Australian Tunnelling Company, AWM 2DRL/0123.
6. *Western Mail* , 20 April 1933, p. 2.
7. Brahms, p. 15.
8. Bean, *Official History of Australia in the War of 1914–1918*, Vol. V, p. 13.
9. Callwell, p. 42.
10. Ibid.
11. Bailey, p. 76.
12. Maurice, Sir Frederick, *The Life of General Lord Rawlinson of Trent from His Journals and Letters*, p. 203.
13. Ibid., p. 200.
14. Bernard Ulrich and Benjamin Ziemann (eds), pp. 99–100.
15. Zabecki, p. 99.
16. Ibid.
17. Ibid.
18. Louis Avery , Diary, 8 December 1917, SLSA, Part 3, Record b2186690, PGR500, p. 24.
19. Edgar, p. 185.
20. Oldham, p. 9.

21. Kent, pp. 143–144.
22. Ibid., p. 127.
23. Major G. I. Adcock, Typed Extracts of Letters and Diary Entries, 2nd Australian Tunnelling Company, AWM 2DRL/0123, pp. 48–49.
24. Mitchell, George D., *Backs to the Wall,* pp. 200–204.
25. Louis Avery, Diary, 14 December 1918, SLSA, Part 3, Record b2186690, PGR500, p. 42.
26. John Monash to Hannah Monash, Letter, 30 December 1917, Papers of General Sir John Monash, AWM 3DRL/2316, Series 1, Box 1, Wallet 2, p. 356.
27. Mitchell, George D., *Backs to the Wall,* pp. 200–204.
28. Downing, *To the Last Ridge*, pp. 90–91.
29. Ibid.
30. Hartnett, p. 51.
31. *Aussie: The Australian Soldiers' Magazine*, March 1918, p. 14.
32. Edmund Street, Typed memoirs, AWM PR85/179, Folder 5, p. 57.
33. Ibid., p. 59.
34. Bernard Ulrich and Benjamin Ziemann (eds), p. 123.
35. Binding, p. 198.
36. Ibid, p. 199.
37. Bean, *Official History of Australia in the War of 1914–1918*, Vol. V, p. 106.
38. Hindenburg, *Out of my Life,* p. 333.
39. Timothy Lupfer, 'The Dynamics of Doctrine: The Changes in Tactical Doctrine During the First World War', Leavenworth Papers, No. 4, Combat Studies Institute, 1981, p. 46.
40. Major Christopher Ghiz, 'Specialised Assault Units of the First World War', Master of Military Art and Science thesis, 2010 p. 29.
41. Wilhelm, *My War Experiences,* p. 291.
42. Ibid.
43. Middlebrook, p. 181.
44. Wilhelm, *My War Experiences,* p. 296.
45. German General Staff, *Der Angriff im Stellungskrieg*, translation B. E. F Intelligence as *The Attack in Position Warfare,* 1 January 1918, GHQ 1918, p. 3.
46. Ibid., p. 4.
47. Wilhelm, *My War Experiences*, p. 297.
48. Westman, pp. 160–161
49. Rupprecht, p. 307
50. Cobby, p. 35.
51. Ibid., p. 34.

52. Ibid., p. 35.

53. Cutlack, p. 215.

54. Jones, pp. 191–192 (reported speech changed to direct speech). Although Mick Mannock himself did not train No. 4 Sqadron this early in 1918, it is expected that this is the type of training and advice they would have received.

55. Cobby, p. 38.

56. Ibid., p. 39.

57. Ibid.

58. Ibid.

59. Ibid.

60. Görlitz, *The Kaiser and his Court: the Diaries, Notebooks and Letters of Admiral Georg Alexander von Müller, Chief of the Naval Cabinet 1914–1918*, p. 324.

61. Ibid.

62. Zabecki, p. 29.

63. Samuels, p. 273.

64. Ludendorff, Erich, *Ludendorff's Own Story*, p. 221.

65. Bernard Ulrich and Benjamin Ziemann (eds), p. 156.

66. Ibid., pp. 156–157.

67. Ibid. p. 157.

68. Ludendorff, Erich, *My War Memories: 1914–1918*, p. 587

69. Reported speech changed to direct speech.

70. Reported speech changed to direct speech.

71. Streissguth, p. 17.

72. Barwick, p. 302.

73. Bean, *Diaries and Notebooks*, February 1918, AWM38, 3DRL 606/98/1, pp. 18–19, www.awm.gov.au/collection/RCDIG1066666.

74. Ibid., p. 27.

CHAPTER TWO: EIN MANN MIT EINEM PLAN – A MAN WITH A PLAN

1. Beckett, p. 212.

2. Maurice, Sir Frederick, *The Life of General Lord Rawlinson of Trent from His Journals and Letters*, pp. 204–205.

3. Lloyd George, p. 212.

4. John Monash to Felix Meyer, Letter, 3 April 1918, Papers of General Sir John Monash, AWM 3DRL/2316, Series 1, Box 1, Wallet 2, p. 391.

5. German Official History, Vol. XIV, p. 301.

6. Rupprecht, *In Treue fest: Mein Kriegstagebuch*, p. 326.

7. Ludendorff, Mathilde, *Erich Ludendorff: Sein Wesen und Schaffen (Erich Ludendorff: His Character and Work)*, p. 129.
8. Ludendorff, Margarethe, *Als ich Ludendorffs Frau war (When I was Ludendorff's Wife)*, pp. 131–132.
9. Zabecki, p 60.
10. Gough, p. 225.
11. Durwood, p. 25.
12. Kilduff, Peter, *Richthofen: Beyond the Legend of the Red Baron*, p. 174.
13. Wohl, p. 228.
14. Kilduff, Peter, *Richthofen: Beyond the Legend of the Red Baron*, p. 194.
15. Fischer (ed.), pp. 157, 160.
16. Molkentin, p. 43.
17. Cobby, p. 39.
18. Molkentin, p. 43.
19. Sufrin, p. 242.
20. Ibid.
21. Taylor, p. 53.
22. Cutlack, p. 215.
23. Cobby, p. 40.
24. Ibid.
25. Cutlack, p. 214.
26. Cobby, p. 36.
27. Ibid.
28. Ibid.
29. Görlitz, *The Kaiser and His Court: The Diaries, Notebooks and Letters of Admiral Georg Alexander von Müller, Chief of the Naval Cabinet, 1914–1918*, p. 332.
30. In fact, Lenin was not brought to a final agreement to end the war in the east until 3 March 1918, after a small German force had marched on St Petersburg in February and the Bolsheviks found themselves unable to seriously oppose the German advance.
31. Ludendorff, Erich, *My War Memories: 1914–1918*, Vol. II, p. 588 (reported speech changed to direct speech).
32. Ibid.
33. Hindenburg, *The Great War*, pp. 327–328.
34. Bean, *Diaries and Notebooks*, 16 February 1918, AWM38 3DRL 606/100/1, pp. 32–34, www.awm.gov.au/collection/RCDIG1066808.
35. Ibid., pp. 34–37.
36. Sulzbach, p. 142.
37. Ibid.

38. German General Staff, *Der Angriff im Stellungskrieg*, translation B. E. F Intelligence as *The Attack in Position Warfare*, 1 January 1918, GHQ 1918, p. 16.
39. Ibid., p. 22.
40. Sulzbach, p. 144.
41. Edgar, p. 186.
42. Ibid.
43. Ibid. p. 226.
44. Grant, p. 47.
45. Nagel, p. 64.
46. Ibid., p. 3.
47. Ibid., p. 64.
48. Hindenburg, *Out of My Life*, p. 330.
49. Gary Sheffield and John Bourne (eds), pp. 336–337.
50. Reported speech changed to direct speech.
51. Downing, *To the Last Ridge*, p 96.
52. Ibid.
53. Ibid.
54. Ibid., p. 97.
55. McMullin, pp. 355–356.
56. Cobby, p. 47.
57. Cutlack, p. 215.
58. Ludendorff, Margarethe, *Als ich Ludendorffs Frau war* (*When I was Ludendorff's Wife*), p. 150.
59. Ibid., p.154.
60. Ibid.
61. Ibid., p. 150.
62. Ibid., p. 154.

CHAPTER THREE: THE HUN IS AT THE GATE

1. Jones (ed.), p. 341.
2. Lee, p. 54.
3. Edmonds, p. 107.
4. Gough, pp. 237–238 (reported speech changed to direct speech).
5. Ibid., p. 238 (reported speech changed to direct speech).
6. Bean, *Official History of Australia in the War of 1914–1918*, Vol. V, p. 109.
7. Sulzbach, p. 156.
8. Zabecki, p. 70.
9. Bishop, p. 139.

10. Ibid.
11. Ibid., p. 140.
12. Joynt, pp. 1–2.
13. Rupprecht, p. 326.
14. Ibid.
15. Ibid.
16. Feuchtwanger, p. 84.
17. Zabecki, p. 186.
18. Cobby, p. 48.
19. Cutlack, p. 224.
20. Bean, *Official History of Australia in the War of 1914–1918*, Vol. V, p. 109.
21. Ibid., p. 110.
22. Gary Sheffield and John Bourne (eds), p. 387 (reported speech changed to direct speech).
23. Reid, p. 410.
24. Sulzbach, p. 146.
25. Ibid.
26. Guttman, p. 68.
27. Cutlack, p. 225.
28. Ibid.
29. Sulzbach, p. 147. I have expanded the words of the song, from the couple of lines Sulzbach cited.
30. Ibid., p. 148.
31. MacDonald, pp. 68–69.
32. Cutlack, p. 225.
33. Hart, *Aces Falling*, p. 48.
34. Kilduff, *Red Baron: Life and Death of an Ace*, p. 202.
35. Hindenburg, *Out of My Life*, p. 343.
36. Sulzbach, p. 148.
37. Walter (ed.), p. 196.
38. Barwick, p. 12.
39. Monash, pp. 20–21.
40. Australian Corps Intelligence Summary, From 6 pm 18 March to 6 pm 19 March 1918, Australian Corps Intelligence Headquarters, Unit Diary, AWM4 1/36/3, p. 72.
41. Ibid. p. 73.
42. Sulzbach, p. 148.
43. Ibid. pp. 148–149.
44. Wodehouse, p. 50.
45. Churchill, p. 766.

46. Ibid.
47. Gough, p. 251.
48. Ibid.
49. Ibid., p. 255.
50. Sulzbach, p. 149.
51. Ibid.
52. Zabecki, p. 138 (reported speech changed to direct speech).
53. Hindenburg, *The Great War*, p. 173.
54. Cobby, p. 48.
55. Ibid. (reported speech changed to direct speech).
56. Ibid. (reported speech changed to direct speech).
57. Sulzbach, pp. 159–160.
58. Ibid., p. 149.
59. McDonald, p. 8.
60. Hindenburg, *The Great War*, p 173.
61. MacDonald, p. 78.
62. Ibid., p. 70.
63. Churchill, p. 768.
64. Binding, p. 204.
65. Churchill, p. 768.
66. Gough, p. 256.
67. Ibid. (reported speech changed to direct speech).
68. Maze, p. 278.
69. Delacour, p. 18.
70. MacDonald, p. 78.
71. Ibid.
72. Ibid., p. 79.
73. Gough, p. 259.
74. Stark, p. 29.

CHAPTER FOUR: THE KAISERSCHLACHT – THE KAISER'S BATTLE – BEGINS

1. Robertson, p. 144.
2. MacDonald, p. 71.
3. Zabecki, p. 85.
4. Clausewitz, p. 101.
5. Middlebrook, p. 172.
6. Middlebrook, p. 174.
7. MacDonald, p. 81.
8. Middlebrook, p. 155.

9. Ibid., p. 156.
10. MacDonald, p. 83.
11. Ibid.
12. Ibid., p. 82.
13. Ibid.
14. The lumps and shards of metal that are thrown in all directions by the blast of a high-explosive shell are not, strictly speaking, called shrapnel. However, I have sometimes called it shrapnel as that's what the Australian infantryman often called any fast flying bit of metal from an artillery shell that was liable to tear him in two, and I tend to embrace the language of the Digger.
15. Sulzabach, pp. 160–161.
16. Churchill, p. 767.
17. Farrar-Hockley, p. 275.
18. Ibid.
19. Gough, p. 260.
20. Ibid.
21. Farrar-Hockley, p. 275.
22. Sparrow, p. 64.
23. Reported speech changed to direct speech.
24. Maze, p. 281.
25. Ibid.
26. Ibid.
27. Stark, p. 29.
28. Middlebrook, p. 156.
29. Cobby, p. 48.
30. Ibid.
31. Ibid., p. 49.
32. MacDonald, p. 84.
33. Ibid. (reported speech changed to direct speech).
34. Ibid.
35. Feldwebel Wilhelm Prosch in Martin Middlebrook, *The Kaiser's Battle*, p. 168.
36. German General Staff, *Der Angriff im Stellungskrieg*, translation B. E. F. Intelligence as *The Attack in Position Warfare*, 1 January 1918, GHQ 1918), p. 16.
37. MacDonald, p. 85.
38. Middlebrook, p. 181
39. Jünger, *The Storm of Steel*, p. 255.
40. Ibid.

41. Jünger, *Kriegstagebuch (War Diary), 1914–1918*, p. 380.
42. Jünger, *The Storm of Steel*, p. 258.
43. Ibid.
44. MacDonald, Lyn, *To the Last Man: Spring 1918*, p. 92.
45. Ibid.
46. Ibid., p. 93.
47. German General Staff, *Der Angriff im Stellungskrieg*, translation B. E. F. Intelligence as *The Attack in Position Warfare*, 1 January 1918, GHQ 1918, p. 4.
48. MacDonald, p. 93.
49. Hart, Peter, *1918: A Very British Victory*, p. 94.
50. Ibid.
51. Sulzbach, p. 161.
52. Ibid.
53. Middlebrook, p. 187.
54. Ibid.
55. Emden, p. 335.
56. Ibid., p. 336 (reported speech changed to direct speech).
57. Sulzbach, p. 161.
58. General Staff, Headquarters Australian Corps, War Diary, March 1918, AWM4 1/35/3, p. 8.
59. Murland, p. 111.
60. Gary Sheffield and John Bourne (eds.), p. 341.
61. Bean, Diary, 21 March 1918, *Diaries and Notebooks*, AWM38 3DRL 606/102/1, pp. 13–14, www.awm.gov.au/collection/RCDIG1066653.
62. Ibid., p. 14.
63. Ibid., p. 16.
64. Ibid., p. 17.
65. Hindenburg, *The Great War*, p. 173.
66. Ibid., p. 174.
67. Private John Parkinson in Martin Middlebrook, *The Kaiser's Battle*, p. 192.
68. Ibid.
69. Ibid.
70. Hart, *1918: A Very British Victory*, p. 98.
71. Rupprecht, p. 344.
72. Ibid.
73. Wilhelm, *My War Experiences*, p. 301.
74. Ibid., p. 302.
75. Middlebrook, p. 185.
76. Ibid., p. 292.

77. Jünger, *Storm of Steel*, p. 263.

78. Binding, p. 205.

79. John Hardie, Handwritten War Narrative, AWM PR00519, p. 11.

80. Downing, *To the Last Ridge*, p. 101.

81. McMullin, p. 360.

82. 9th Brigade, Unit Diary, March 1918, AWM 23/9/17, p. 8.

83. General Staff Headquarters, 3rd Australian Division, Unit Diary, March 1918, AWM4 1/46/17 PART 2, Appendix 10a, p. 9, https://www.awm.gov.au/images/collection/bundled/RCDIG1011421.pdf.

84. John Hardie, Handwritten War Narrative, AWM PR00519. pp. 11–12.

85. Middlebrook, *The Kaiser's Battle*, p. 299.

86. Private Arthur Flindt in Middlebrook, p. 299.

87. Ibid.

88. Middlebrook, *The Kaiser's Battle*, p. 303.

89. Hart, *A Very British Victory*, p. 103.

90. Gough, p. 270.

91. Ibid., p. 271 (reported speech changed to direct speech).

92. Ibid. (reported speech changed to direct speech).

93. Ibid. (reported speech changed to direct speech).

94. Ibid. (reported speech changed to direct speech).

95. Wilhelm, *My War Experiences*, p. 302.

96. Ibid. p. 303.

97. Gary Sheffield and John Bourne, p. 390.

98. Pedersen, *Villers-Bretonneux*, p. 85.

99. Alun Thomas, 'British 8th Infantry Division on the Western Front, 1914-18', PhD Thesis, Centre for First World War Studies, The University of Birmingham, p. 277, http://etheses.bham.ac.uk/599/1/thomas10PhD.pdf.

100. Asprey, p. 167.

101. Middlebrook, p. 322.

102. Görlitz, *The Kaiser and his Court: the Diaries, Notebooks and Letters of Admiral Georg Alexander von Müller Chief of the Naval Cabinet 1914–1918*, pp. 343–344.

103. Hindenburg, *The Great War*, p. 174.

CHAPTER FIVE: AUX ARMES AUSTRALIENS, FORMEZ VOS BATAILLONS!

1. Cobby, p. 50.

2. Lieutenant Ben Champion, Diary, www.awm.gov.au/images/collection/bundled/RCDIG0000977.pdf.

3. The original quote is, 'Then imitate the action of the tiger; Stiffen the sinews, summon up the blood,' from William Shakespeare's *Henry V*, Act 3, Scene 1.

4. Charles Rosenthal, Diary, 22 March 1918, SLNSW, MLMSS 2739/, Vol. I, p. 398, http://acms.sl.nsw.gov.au/_transcript/2014/D27827/c00585.html.

5. Castan, *Der Rote Baron*, p. 218.

6. Ludendorff, *My War Memories*, p. 602.

7. Friedrich (ed.), p. 151.

8. Gough, p. 278.

9. Ibid., p. 264.

10. Edmonds, p. 265.

11. Edwards, taken from Chapter One.

12. John Hardie, Handwritten War Narrative, AWM PR00519, p. 12.

13. Ludendorff, Margarethe, *Als ich Ludendorffs Frau war* (*When I was Ludendorff's Wife*), p. 155 (reported speech changed to direct speech).

14. Hindenburg, p. 174.

15. Miller, p. 97.

16. Ibid., p. 20.

17. Ibid. p. 25.

18. Horn (ed.), *War Mutiny and Revolution in the German Navy: The World War I Diary of Seaman Richard Stumpf*, p. 396.

19. Sulzbach, p. 163.

20. Bean, Diary, 24 March 1918, Diaries and Notebooks, AWM38 3DRL/606/102/1, p 34. https://www.awm.gov.au/collection/RCDIG1066653.

21. Hughes (ed.), p. iii.

22. Edmonds, pp. 396–397.

23. Mark Whitmore, 'Transport and Supply During The First World War', IWM, www.iwm.org.uk/history/transport-and-supply-during-the-first-world-war.

24. Zabecki, p. 150.

25. Edmonds, p. 397.

26. Gary Sheffield and John Bourne (eds), p. 391.

27. Ibid.

28. Farrar-Hockley, p. 292.

29. Ibid.

30. Ibid. (reported speech changed to direct speech).

31. Ibid., p. 292.

32. Need, p. 117.

33. Ibid.

34. Deayton, p. 199.
35. George Mitchell, Diary, 23 March 1918, Vol. IV, AWM 2DRL/0928 (no page number).
36. Binding, p. 206.
37. Gary Sheffield and John Bourne (eds), p. 391.
38. Lloyd George, *War Memoirs*, p. 2842.
39. Görlitz, *The Kaiser and His Court: The Diaries, Notebooks and Letters of Admiral Georg Alexander von Müller Chief of the Naval Cabinet 1914–1918*, p. 344.
40. Ibid.
41. Görlitz, *Regierte der Kaiser? Kriegstagebücher, Aufzeichnungen und Briefe des Chefs des Marine-Kabinetts Admiral Georg Alexander von Müller, 1914–1918* (*Did the Emporer Reign? War Diaries, Notes and Letters of the Chief of the Naval Cabinet Admiral Georg Alexander von Müller, 1914–1918*), p. 365.
42. Edmonds, p. 393.
43. *The Western Australian*, 23 August 1918, p. 8, http://trove.nla.gov.au/newspaper/article/27487655.
44. John Hardie, Handwritten War Narrative, AWM PR00519, p. 14.
45. *The Sydney Morning Herald*, 26 January 1935, p. 13.
46. Charles Rosenthal, Diary, 23 March 1918, SLNSW, MLMSS 2739/, Vol. I, p. 399. http://acms.sl.nsw.gov.au/album/albumView.aspx?acmsID=844177&itemID=1122617.
47. J. Delahunty, Diary, 24 March 1918, AWM PR03651 (no page numbers).
48. Edmund Street, Typed Memoirs, AWM PR85/179, Folder 5, p. 85.
49. Ibid.
50. Leonard Bartlett, Diary, 24 March 1918, SLNSW, MLMSS 959, Item 3, p. 19.
51. Barwick, p. 309.
52. Ludendorff, *My War Memories*, p. 602.
53. Bean, *Diaries and Letters*, 26 March 1918, AWM38, 3DRL606/103/1, p. 6, www.awm.gov.au/collection/RCDIG1066548.
54. Ibid.
55. Bean, Diary, 16 January 1918, *Diaries and Notebooks*, AWM38 3DRL 606/96/1, p. 36, www.awm.gov.au/collection/RCDIG1066664.
56. G. I. Adcock, 'Notes from War Diary', March 1918, AWM 2DRL/0123, p. 61.
57. Ibid.
58. Lynch, p. 255.

59. Ibid.

60. Ibid., 255–256.

61. Ibid., p. 256.

62. Ibid.

63. Mitchell, George D., *Backs to the Wall*, p. 208.

64. Ibid.

65. Bean, *The Official History of Australia in the War of 1914–1918*, Vol. V, p. 115.

66. Ibid., p. 116.

67. Gary Sheffield and John Bourne (eds.), p. 392.

68. Ibid., p. 391.

69. Ibid., p. 392 (reported speech changed to direct speech).

70. Ibid. (reported speech changed to direct speech).

71. Ibid.

72. Edmonds, pp. 448–50 (reported speech changed to direct speech).

73. Sheffield, p. 274.

74. Bean, *Diaries and Notebooks*, March 1918, AWM38 3DRL 606/102/1, p. 39., www.awm.gov.au/collection/RCDIG1066653.

75. Ibid., p. 42.

76. Ibid.

77. Ibid., p. 44.

78. *An Album of Digger Songs: Songs the Diggers Sang*, NLA, MUS N m 783.2421599 A345, p. 5. http://nla.gov.au/nla.obj-176560073/view#page/n6/mode/1up.

79. George Mitchell, Diary, 25 March 1918, AWM 2DRL/0928 (no page numbers).

80. Mitchell, George D., *Backs to the Wall*, p. 208.

81. Ibid., p. 209.

82. George Mitchell, Diary, 25 March 1918, AWM 2DRL/0928 (no page numbers).

83. Mitchell, George D., *Backs to the Wall*, p. 209.

84. Ibid.

85. 'A.I.F. Leaders: Their Nicknames', *Reveille*, 1 Septmeber 1932, p. 12.

86. Green, p. 112 (reported speech changed to direct speech).

87. Ibid.

88. John Hardie, Handwritten War Narrative, AWM PR00519, p. 15.

89. Bean, *Official History of Australia in the War of 1914–1918*, Vol. V, p. 119.

90. Ibid.

91. Ibid., p. 120.

92. Nagel, p. 79.
93. Maurice, P. A., *The Supreme Command: 1914–1918,* p. 787.
94. George Mitchell, Diary, 25 March 1918, AWM 2DRL/0928 (no page numbers).
95. Bean, *Official History of Australia in the War of 1914–1918,* Vol. V, p. 121.

CHAPTER SIX: THE EMPIRE STRIKES BACK

1. G. I. Adcock, Typed extracts of letters and diary entries, 'Notes from War Diary', March 1918, AWM 2DRL/0123, p. 65.
2. Lydia O'Neil in '51st Battalion Newsletter', September 1966, No. 43, p. 8.
3. Binding, p. 207.
4. Ibid.
5. Ibid.
6. Ibid.
7. Ibid.
8. Ibid. (reported speech changed to direct speech).
9. Ibid. (reported speech changed to direct speech).
10. 4th Infantry Brigade War Diary, March 1918, AWM 23/4/30, p. 8.
11. Görlitz (ed.), *The Kaiser and his Court: the Diaries, Notebooks and Letters of Admiral Georg Alexander von Müller Chief of the Naval Cabinet 1914–1918,* p. 345.
12. John Monash to Hannah Monash, Letter, 2 April 1918, Papers of General Sir John Monash, AWM 3DRL/2316, Series 1, Box 1, Wallet 2, p. 381.
13. Ibid.
14. Ibid. p. 382.
15. Ibid.
16. Ibid.
17. Gough, p. 299.
18. Ibid., p. 203.
19. Bann, p. 46.
20. Williams, p. 182 (reported speech changed to direct speech).
21. Keegan, p. 432 (reported speech changed to direct speech).
22. Foch, p. 299 (reported speech changed to direct speech).
23. Tuchmann, p. 46.
24. Raymond Recouly and Mary Cadwalader Jones, p. 112.
25. Barnett, p. 358. In the actual quote, it says 'Marshal' Foch, but that could not be the case, as he was not promoted to Marshal until August 1918.
26. Doughty, p. 408.
27. Callwell, p. 78.

28. Gough, p. 291.
29. Bean, Diary, March–April 1918, *Diaries and Notebooks*, AWM38 3DRL 606/104/1, p. 61, www.awm.gov.au/collection/RCDIG1066549.
30. Bean, *Official History of Australia in the War of 1914–1918*, Vol. V, p. 115.
31. MacDonald, p. 263.
32. Reid, Richard, p. 46.
33. George Mitchell, Diary, 26 March 1918, AWM 2DRL/0928 (no page numbers).
34. Ibid. (reported speech changed to direct speech).
35. Ibid.
36. Ibid.
37. Barwick, p. 310.
38. Foch, p. 299.
39. Ibid. p. 300.
40. Ibid.
41. Asprey, p. 381.
42. Brahms, p. 62.
43. Brahms, p. 62.
44. Henry Goddard, Diary, 26 March 1918, AWM 3DRL/2379, Series 1: *Diaries and Notebooks of Henry Arthur Goddard*, p. 67. https://www.awm.gov.au/collection/RCDIG0000784/?image=67.
45. Ibid.
46. Ibid., p. 68.
47. Ibid.
48. Paul Feenan, Unpublished Monograph, 1989, 35th Battalion draft outline of history obtained from records held at the local history section of the Newcastle Region Public Library, p. 33.
49. Ibid., p. 34.
50. John Hardie, Handwritten War Narrative, AWM PR00519, p. 16.
51. I have changed Hardie's text from 'two kilometres' to 'just over a mile' in keeping with the imperial system of measurement used throughout the book.
52. John Hardie, Handwritten War Narrative, AWM PR00519, p. 16.
53. Ibid., p. 17.
54. Monash, John to Hannah Monash, Letter, 2 April 1918, Papers of General Sir John Monash, AWM 3DRL/2316, Series 1, Box 1, Wallet 2, p. 382.
55. Charles Rosenthal, Diary, 26 March 1918, MLMSS 2739/, Vol. 1, p. 399. http://acms.sl.nsw.gov.au/_transcript/2014/D27827/c00585.html.
56. John Monash to Hannah Monash, Letter, 2 April 1918, Papers of

General Sir John Monash, AWM 3DRL/2316, Series 1, Box 1, Wallet 2, p. 383.

57. Brahms, p. 62.

58. Paul Feenan, Unpublished Monograph, 1989, 35th Battalion draft outline of history obtained from records held at the local history section of the Newcastle Region Public Library, p. 34 (reported speech changed to direct speech).

59. Ibid.

60. Fraser-Tytler, pp. 229–233.

61. W. E. Duncan, Photocopy of Unpublished Autobiography, Liddle Collection, Leeds University Library, LIDDLE/WW1/GS/0478, pp. 64–65.

62. Essame, p. 47.

63. Callwell, p. 78 (reported speech changed to direct speech, tenses changed).

64. Bean, *Official History of Australia in the War of 1914–1918*, Vol. V, p. 273.

65. Gough, p. 299.

66. Sparrow, p. 136.

67. Gough, p. 305.

68. Ibid., 306 (reported speech changed to direct speech).

69. Ibid., (reported speech changed to direct speech).

70. Ibid., p. 307.

71. Ibid.

72. Ibid.

73. Bean, *Anzac to Amiens,* pp. 414–415

74. Harry Murray was a temporary colonel until May 1918, when his rank was confirmed.

75. Maurice, pp. 213–214.

76. John Monash to Hannah Monash, Letter, 2 April 1918, Papers of General Sir John Monash, AWM 3DRL/2316, Series 1, Box 1, Wallet 2, p. 384.

77. Walter Kennedy, Unpublished Memoir, *From Anzac Cove to Villers-Bretonneux*, AWM PR02032, p. 63.

78. Bean, *The Official History of Australia in the War of 1914–1918,* Vol. V, p. 122.

79. Ibid., p. 123 (reported speech changed to direct speech).

80. Ibid.

81. White, p. 122.

82. Bean, *The Official History of Australia in the War of 1914–1918*, Vol. V, p. 123.

83. Ibid., p. 124.
84. White, p. 122.
85. Bean, *The Official History of Australia in the War of 1914–1918,* Vol. V, p. 124 (reported speech changed to direct speech).
86. White, p. 122.
87. Bean, *The Official History of Australia in the War of 1914–1918,* Vol. V, p. 125.
88. 4th Infantry Brigade War Diary, March 1918, AWM 23/4/30, p. 8.
89. 'The Old Brig', *Reveille,* 1 August 1933, p. 16.
90. Ibid. It is my presumption that this was the expletive used, as he was a known heavy swearer.
91. 'The Old Brig', *Reveille,* 1 August 1933, p. 16.
92. Bean, *The Official History of Australia in the War of 1914–1918,* Vol. V, p. 126.
93. White, p. 124.
94. Ibid.
95. Bean, *The Official History of Australia in the War of 1914–1918,* Vol. V, p. 128.
96. Rupprecht, p. 357.
97. Ibid., p. 358.
98. Ibid.
99. Ibid.
100. Mitchell, George D., *Backs to the Wall,* p. 210.

CHAPTER SEVEN: 'FINI RETREAT – BEAUCOUP AUSTRALIENS ICI'

1. Essame, p. 117.
2. John Monash to Hannah Monash, Letter, 2 April 1918, Papers of General Sir John Monash, AWM 3DRL/2316, Series 1, Box 1, Wallet 2, p. 385.
3. Brahms, p. 62.
4. Mitchell, George D., *Backs to the Wall,* pp. 210–211.
5. Mitchell, George D., *Backs to the Wall,* p. 211.
6. 48th Infantry Battalion War Diary, 26 March 1918, AWM4 23/65/26, p. 20.
7. Callwell, p. 78.
8. Mitchell, George D., *Backs to the Wall,* pp. 212–213.
9. Ibid.
10. Emden, p. 323.
11. John Monash to Hannah Monash, Letter, 2 April 1918, Papers of

General Sir John Monash, AWM 3DRL/2316, Series 1, Box 1, Wallet 2, p. 385.

12. Ibid.

13. Ibid.

14. Ibid, p. 386.

15. 47th Infantry Battalion War Diary, 26 March 1918, AWM 23/64/22, p. 15.

16. Bean, Diary, 27 March 1918, *Diaries and Notebooks*, AWM38 3DRL 606/185/1, p.48, www.awm.gov.au/collection/RCDIG1066801.

17. Mitchell, George D., *Backs to the Wall*, p. 212.

18. George Mitchell, Diary, 27 March 1918, AWM 2DRL/0928, (no page numbers).

19. Mitchell, George D., *Backs to the Wall*, p. 211.

20. Ibid.

21. Hardie, p. 19.

22. Ibid.

23. Ibid., p. 20.

24. White, p. 125.

25. Bean, *The Official History of Australia in the War of 1914–1918*, Vol. V, p. 128.

26. Ibid., p. 129.

27. Ibid., p. 130.

28. Cooper, p. 9.

29. Downing, *Digger Dialects*, p. 23.

30. Sutherland, p. 167 (reported speech changed to direct speech).

31. Middlebrook, p. 56.

32. 47th Infantry Battalion War Diary, 27 March 1918, AWM 23/64/22, p. 16.

33. Mitchell, George D., *Backs to the Wall*, p. 214.

34. 48th Infantry Battalion War Diary, 27 March 1918, AWM4 23/65/26, p. 20.

35. Mitchell, George D., *Backs to the Wall*, p. 213.

36. John Monash to Hannah Monash, Letter, 2 April 1918, Papers of General Sir John Monash, AWM 3DRL/2316, Series 1, Box 1, Wallet 2, p. 386.

37. Ibid., p. 378.

38. Ibid., p. 386.

39. Hardie, p. 20.

40. Henry Goddard, Diary, 27 March 1918, AWM 3DRL/2379, Series 1: *Diaries and Notebooks of Henry Arthur Goddard*, p. 69, www.awm.gov. au/collection/RCDIG0000784/?image=69

41. Hardie, p. 20.
42. Nagel, p. 82.
43. Ibid. (reported speech changed to direct speech).
44. Ibid., pp. 82–83 (reported speech changed to direct speech).
45. Ibid., p. 83 (reported speech changed to direct speech).
46. Ibid. (reported speech changed to direct speech).
47. Nagel, p. 83.
48. The Red Baron commanded *Jagdgeschwader 1* with a maximum strength of fifty aircraft. The *Jagdgeschwader* was divided into *Jastas* 4, 6, 10 and 11.
49. Nagel, p. 88.
50. Ibid.
51. Ibid., p. 89.
52. Ibid.
53. Ibid.
54. MacDonald, p. 276.
55. Ibid.
56. Bean, *Anzac to Amiens,* p. 415.
57. Ibid.
58. *The Sydney Morning Herald*, 22 June 1907, p. 6., http://trove.nla.gov.au/ndp/del/article/14868292
59. Bean, *The Official History of Australia in the War of 1914–1918,* Vol. V, p. 177 (extemporised).
60. Though Bean doesn't specifically indicate that it was an old lady with a wheelbarrow on this occasion, diaries and letters indicate them as the most common sight they saw at this late stage, as most families and younger ones had already gone, and that is indeed what fits with the comment.
61. Bean, *The Official History of Australia in the War of 1914–1918*, Vol. V., p 177.
62. Douglas Gray Marks, Diary, 27 March 1918, SLNSW, MLMSS 2879, p. 158, http://acms.sl.nsw.gov.au/album/albumView.aspx?acmsID=872435&itemID=1087264
63. Bean, Charles, *The Official History of Australia in the War of 1914–1918*, Vol. V, p. 132.
64. Ibid., p. 130.
65. John Monash to Hannah Monash, Letter, 2 April 1918, Papers of General Sir John Monash, AWM 3DRL/2316, Series 1, Box 1, Wallet 2, p. 387.
66. Brahms, p. 64.
67. Ibid., p. 65.

68. Charles Bean, Diary, 27 March 1918, *Diaries and Notebooks* AWM38, 3DRL 606/103/1, p. 17. www.awm.gov.au/collection/RCDIG1066548.

69. Ibid., p. 28 (reported speech changed to direct speech).

70. Ibid., p. 29.

71. Ibid.

72. Ibid., pp. 28–29.

73. Ibid., p. 31.

74. Hart, *Aces Falling: The War Above the Trenches, 1918*, p. 126.

75. Udet, p. 48.

76. Guttman, p. 56.

77. Ibid.

78. Downing, *To The Last Ridge*, p 102.

79. Ibid.

80. Edmund Street, AWM PR85/179, p. 85.

81. Churchill, p. 768.

82. Relief begins at 9.30 pm, 27 March, and is complete by 1.30 am, 28 March.

83. 47th Infantry Battalion War Diary, 27 March 1918, AWM 23/64/22, p. 16.

84. Ibid., p. 17.

85. Ibid.

86. Ibid.

87. Rupprecht, p. 360.

88. Ibid.

89. Bean, *The Official History of Australia in the War of 1914–1918*, Vol. V, p. 198.

90. Niebelschütz (ed.), *Reserve-Infanterie-Regiment Nr. 230: Zusammengestellt nach den amtlichen Kriegstagebüchern und privaten Aufzeichnungen* (*Reserve Infantry Regiment 230: Compiled from Official War Diaries and Private Records*), pp. 215–216.

91. Ibid., p. 216.

92. Binding, p. 208.

93. Ibid.

94. Ibid.

95. Charles Bean, Diary, March 1918, *Diaries and Notebooks*, AWM38 3DRL 606/103/1, p. 39, www.awm.gov.au/collection/RCDIG1066548.

96. Ibid., p. 40.

CHAPTER EIGHT: HOLD THOSE BASTARDS

1. John Monash to Hannah Monash, Letter, 2 April 1918, AWM 3DRL/2316, Series 1, Box 1, Wallet 2, p. 381.
2. Longmore, *Eggs-a-Cook: The Story of the Forty-Fourth*, p. 90.
3. MacDonald, p. 291.
4. Mitchell, George D., *Backs to the Wall*, p. 219.
5. The word 'bastard' was blanked out, and that is my presumption of what was said.
6. Mitchell, George D., *Backs to the Wall*, p. 218.
7. Ibid., pp. 218–219.
8. 48th Infantry Battalion War Diary, 27 March 1918, AWM4 23/65/26, p. 21, https://www.awm.gov.au/images/collection/bundled/RCDIG1006496.pdf.
9. 47th Infantry Battalion War Diary, 27 March 1918, AWM4 23/64/22, p. 18, https://www.awm.gov.au/collection/RCDIG1006486/?image=18.
10. Niebelschütz (ed.), *Reserve-Infanterie-Regiment Nr. 230: Zusammengestellt nach den amtlichen Kriegstagebüchern und privaten Aufzeichnungen (Reserve Infantry Regiment 230: Compiled from Official War Diaries and Private Records)*, p. 216.
11. Charle Rosenthal, Diary, 27 March 1918, SLNSW, MLMSS 2739/ Vol.1, p. 400., http://acms.sl.nsw.gov.au/_transcript/2014/D27827/c00585.html
12. Hardie, pp. 22–23.
13. Edmund Street, Typed Memoirs, AWM PR85/179. Folder 5.
14. Ibid.
15. Ibid.
16. Ibid.
17. Eric Russell, Letter, 17 November 1918, AWM PR01479, p. 2.
18. Binding, p. 209.
19. Ibid.
20. Ibid.
21. Ibid. (reported speech changed to direct speech).
22. Ibid.
23. Ibid.
24. Mercury , 1 May 1918, http://trove.nla.gov.au/newspaper/article/11392788.
25. Bean, *The Official History of Australia in the War of 1914–1918*, Vol. V, p. 194.
26. Ibid.
27. Statement by Captain Symons, 1 April 1918, in John Monash Papers, AWM 3DRL/2316, Series 3, Folder 56, p. 49, www.awm.gov.au/

images/collection/bundled/RCDIG0000628.pdf.

28. Statement by Sgt. James C. Lawrence, 28 March 1918, in McDougall, NAA, Service Number 4061, p. 46. http://discoveringanzacs.naa.gov. au/browse/records/125997/46

29. Bean, *The Official History of Australia in the War of 1914–1918*, Vol. V, p. 195.

30. Statement by Sergeant Brown, 30 March 1918, in John Monash Papers, AWM 3DRL/2316, Series 3, Folder 56, p. 11, www.awm.gov.au/ images/collection/bundled/RCDIG0000628.pdf

31. George Dean Mitchell, Diary, 28 March 1918, AWM 2DRL/0928, Notebook 14, p. 28.

32. Binding, *A Fatalist at War*, p. 219.

33. Bean, *The Official History of Australia in the War of 1914–1918*, Vol. V, p. 197.

34. Fritz Nagel dates his account of this day 27 March 1918. In fact, cross-referencing with other historical records confirms that these events actually took place on the following day.

35. Nagel, p. 85.

36. Ibid.

37. Ibid., p. 88.

38. Ibid., p. 86.

39. Ibid.

40. Ibid., p. 87.

41. Ibid.

42. Ibid.

43. Ibid.

44. Ibid.

45. Ibid., p. 88.

46. Ibid., p. 89.

47. Downing, *To the Last Ridge*, p. 102.

48. Pedersen, *Villers-Bretonneux*, p. 28.

49. Maze, pp. 309–310 (reported speech changed to direct speech).

50. Officially the Fourth Army was not renamed Fifth Army until 2 April, but in practice the change took place on 28 March.

51. Maze, pp. 309–310.

52. Ibid.

53. Ibid.

54. Gough, p. 317.

55. Edmund Street, Typed Memoirs, AWM PR85/179, Folder 5, p. 86.

56. Ibid.

57. Ibid.

58. Ibid.

59. Ibid., p. 87.

60. Niebelschütz (ed.), p. 218.

61. Rupprecht, p. 361.

62. Ibid.

63. Ludendorff, *Ludendorff's Own Story*, p. 232.

64. Sulzbach, p. 166.

65. Bean, *The Official History of Australia in the War of 1914–1918*, Vol. V, p. 217.

66. Ibid., 220–221.

67. John Monash to Hannah Monash, Letter, 28 March 1918, Papers of General Sir John Monash, AWM 3DRL/2316, Series 1, Box 1, Wallet 2, p. 378.

68. Ibid.

69. Edmonds, p. 51.

70. Hart, *A Very British Victory*, p. 198.

71. 2/7 Battalion Royal Warwickshire Regiment, War Diary, 28 March 1918, TNA, WO 95/3056/3, p. 50.

72. Edmund Street, Typed Memoirs, AWM PR85/179. Folder 5, p. 87.

73. Ibid. (tense changed).

74. Edmund Street, Typed Memoirs, AWM PR85/179. Folder 5, p. 87.

75. Henry Goddard, Diary, 29 March 1918, AWM 3/DRL 2379, p. 71.

76. Ibid.

77. Ibid., p. 72 (reported speech changed to direct speech).

78. Henry Goddard, Diary, 29 March 1918, AWM 3/DRL 2379, p. 72.

79. Bean Vol. 5, p. 301.

80. 9th Infantry Brigade UNIT Diary, 29 March 1918, AWM4 23 23/9/17, p. 14, www.awm.gov.au/collection/RCDIG1016534/?image=14.

81. Hardie, p. 24.

82. Hardie, p. 25.

83. *The Sydney Morning Herald*, 4 May 1934, p. 9, http://trove.nla.gov.au/newspaper/article/17066933

84. Downing, *To the Last Ridge*, p. 103.

85. Ibid.

86. Gary Sheffield and John Bourne, p. 396.

87. John Monash to Hannah Monash, Letter, 24 May 1915, SVL, MS 13875, Box 4083/1, p. 67.

88. John Monash to Hannah Monash, Letter, 2 April 1918, Papers of General Sir John Monash, AWM 3DRL/2316, Series 1, Box 1, Wallet 2, p. 390.

89. Ibid., p. 389.

90. Ibid., p. 390.

91. John Monah to Hannah Monash, Letter, 2 April 1918, Papers of General Sir John Monash, AWM 3DRL/2316, Series 1, Box 1, Wallet 2, p. 389.

92. Ibid.

93. Ibid., p. 390.

94. Ibid.

95. Delacour, *The Living Air: The Memoirs of an Ornithologist*, p. 39.

96. Ibid., p. 39.

97. Görlitz, p .346.

98. Zabecki, p. 217.

99. Downing, *To the Last Ridge*, p. 104.

100. McMullin, p. 369.

101. Downing, *To the Last Ridge*, p. 104.

CHAPTER NINE: THE FIRST BATTLE OF VILLERS-BRETONNEUX

1. Bean, Diary, 4 April 1918, *Diaries and Notebooks*, AWM38 3DRL 606/105/1, p. 33, www.awm.gov.au/collection/RCDIG1066550.

2. Charles Rosenthal, Diary, 30 March 1918, MLMSS 2739, Vol. 1, p. 401.

3. John Hardie, Handwritten War Narrative, AWM PR00519, p. 25.

4. Ibid.

5. Ibid.

6. Ibid., pp. 25–26.

7. Henry Goddard, Diary, 30 March 1918, AWM 3DRL/2379, p. 72.

8. Ibid.

9. John Hardie, Handwritten War Narrative, AWM PR00519, p. 26.

10. Ivor Novello, 'Keep the Home Fires Burning', 1914.

11. Henry Goddard, Diary, AWM 3DRL/2379, p. 101.

12. Maze, p. 316.

13. Ibid., p. 317.

14. Charles Rosenthal, Diary, 30 March 1918, SLNSW, MLMSS 2739, Vol. 1, p. 401, http://acms.sl.nsw.gov.au/_transcript/2014/D27827/c00585.html

15. Bean, *The Official History of Australia in the War of 1914–1918*, Vol. V, p. 301.

16. Ibid.

17. Leslie Morshead, 'Counter Attack Operation: Afternoon and Evening,

March 30th 1918, 33rd Battalion A.I.F', in 33rd Battalion Unit Diary, March 1918, AWM4 23/50/17, Part 2, p. 32, www.awm.gov.au/collection/RCDIG1005120/?image=32 (reported speech changed to direct speech).

18. Bean, *The Official History of Australia in the War of 1914–1918*, Vol. V, p. 302.

19. John Hardie, Handwritten War Narrative, AWM PR00519, p. 26.

20. Ibid.

21. Ibid., p. 27.

22. Ibid.

23. Bean, *The Official History of Australia in the War of 1914–1918*, Vol. V, pp. 302–303 (reported speech changed to direct speech).

24. Leslie Morshead to Charles Bean, Letter, April 1931, AWM38 3drl 3953/3, Part 1. *Official history 1914–1918 War Records of Charles E. W. Bean correspondence 1929–1939*.

25. Bean, *The Official History of Australia in the War of 1914–1918*, Vol. V, p. 301.

26. Leslie Morshead, 'Comments by Lieutenant Colonel L. J. Morshead, 33rd Battalion, Villers-Bretonneux, 4th April, 1918', p. 1, in Bean, *Official history 1914–1918 War Records of Charles E. W. Bean correspondence 1929–1939*, AWM38 7953/30, Part 1.

27. Bean, *The Official History of Australia in the War of 1914–1918*, Vol. V, p 304.

28. Leslie Morshead, 'Counter Attack Operation: Afternoon and Evening, March 30th 1918, 33rd Battalion A.I.F', in 33rd Battalion Unit Diary, March 1918, AWM4 23/50/17, Part 2, p. 32, www.awm.gov.au/collection/RCDIG1005120/?image=32.

29. John Hardie, Handwritten War Narrative, AWM PR00519, p. 27.

30. Bean, *The Official History of Australia in the War of 1914–1918*, Vol. V, p. 307.

31. Shakespeare, *Henry IV*, Part 1, Act 5, Scene 4: 115–121.

32. Leslie Morshead, 'Counter Attack Operation: Afternoon and Evening, March 30th 1918, 33rd Battalion A.I.F', in 33rd Battalion Unit Diary, March 1918, AWM4 23/50/17, Part 2, p. 34, www.awm.gov.au/collection/RCDIG1005120/?image=32.

33. Harms, p. 356.

34. John Hardie, Handwritten War Narrative, AWM PR00519, pp. 28–29.

35. Leslie Morshead, 'Counter Attack Operation: Afternoon and Evening, March 30th 1918, 33rd Battalion A.I.F', in 33rd Battalion Unit Diary,

March 1918, AWM4 23/50/17, Part 2, p. 34, www.awm.gov.au/collection/RCDIG1005120/?image=32.

36. Ibid.
37. John Hardie, Handwritten War Narrative, AWM PR00519, p. 29.
38. Ibid.
39. Leslie Morshead, 'Counter Attack Operation: Afternoon and Evening, March 30th 1918, 33rd Battalion A.I.F', in 33rd Battalion Unit Diary, March 1918, AWM4 23/50/17, Part 2, p. 34, www.awm.gov.au/collection/RCDIG1005120/?image=32.
40. Henry Goddard, Diary, 30 March 1918, p. 73.
41. Ibid., pp. 73–74.
42. Ibid., p. 74.
43. Ibid.
44. Leslie Morshead, 'Counter Attack Operation: Afternoon and Evening, March 30th 1918, 33rd Battalion A.I.F', in 33rd Battalion Unit Diary, March 1918, AWM4 23/50/17, Part 2, p. 34, www.awm.gov.au/collection/RCDIG1005120/?image=32.
45. Ibid.
46. Ibid.
47. John Hardie, Handwritten War Narrative, AWM PR00519, p. 30.
48. Ibid.
49. Ibid.
50. Ibid., p. 31.
51. Ibid., p. 32.
52. Ibid.
53. Pederesen, *Villers-Bretonneux*, p. 42.
54. Bean, *The Official History of Australia in the War of 1914–1918*, Vol. V, p. 313.
55. Ibid., (reported speech changed to direct speech).
56. John Monash, Letter, 4 April 1918, *War letters of General Monash: Volume 2*, AWM 3DRL/2316, RCDIG0000570, p. 394, www.awm.gov.au/collection/RCDIG0000570/?image=100.
57. John Hardie, Handwritten War Narrative, AWM PR00519, p. 32.
58. Ibid.
59. Ibid.
60. Leslie Morshead, 'Counter Attack Operation: Afternoon and Evening March 30th 1918, 33rd Battalion A.I.F', March 1918, in 33rd Battalion Unit Diary, AWM4 23/50/17, Part 2, p. 34, www.awm.gov.au/collection/RCDIG1005120/?image=34.
61. Ibid.

62. Ibid.

63. John Hardie, Handwritten War Narrative, AWM PR00519, p. 33.

64. Longmore, *Eggs-a-Cook: The Story of the Forty-Fourth*, p. 90.

65. Brahms, pp. 66–67.

66. Longmore, *Eggs-a-Cook: The Story of the Forty-Fourth*, p. 90.

67. Brahms, pp. 66–67 (tense changed).

68. Bean, *The Official History of Australia in the War of 1914–1918*, Vol. V. p 223.

69. Brahms, pp. 66–67.

70. Longmore, *Eggs-a-Cook: The Story of the Forty-Fourth*, p. 90.

71. Bean, *The Official History of Australia in the War of 1914–1918*, Vol. V, p 233.

72. Harold Grimwade, Diary, 30 March 1918, AWM PR00778 (no page numbers).

73. Brahms, pp. 66–67.

74. John Monash to Hannah Monash, Letter, 2 April 1918, AWM 3DRL/2316, Series 1, Box 1, Wallet 2, p. 388.

75. R. L. Mullens to John Monash, Letter, 10 April 1918, in 33rd Infantry Battalion Unit Diary, AWM4 23/50/18, p. 61, www.awm.gov.au/collection/RCDIG1005121/?image=61.

76. John Monash to Hannah Monash, Letter, 31 March 1918, AWM 3DRL/2316, Series 1, Box 1, Wallet 2, p. 378.

77. Passingham, *All the Kaiser's Men*, p. 213.

78. Jürgensen (ed.), pp. 214–215.

79. Edmonds, p. 107.

80. Ibid., p. 101.

81. Ibid., p. 107.

82. The original plan for Operation George was modified and renamed Georgette on 29 March 1918. Here, for the sake of simplicity, it has been called Operation George throughout.

83. Rupprecht, p. 366.

84. Gary Sheffield and John Bourne, p. 346 (reported speech changed to direct speech).

CHAPTER TEN: STORM ON THE HORIZON

1. Pedersen, *Villers-Bretonneux*, pp. 13–14.

2. Henry Goddard, Diary, 31 March 1918, AWM 3DRL/2379, Series 1, p. 82, www.awm.gov.au/collection/RCDIG0000784/?image=82 (reported speech changed to direct speech).

3. Ibid.
4. Ibid., p. 80.
5. Ibid.
6. Ibid.
7. Ibid. (reported speech changed to direct speech).
8. 33rd Infantry Battalion Unit Diary, 31 March 1918, AWM4 23/50/17 PART 1, p. 7.
9. Hardie, p. 33.
10. Ibid.
11. Ibid., pp. 33–34.
12. Ibid., p. 34.
13. Thomas Louch, Papers of Thomas Louch, 'In the Ranks', Part III, PR85/363, p. 21 (reported speech changed to direct speech).
14. Ibid.
15. Ibid.
16. *Reveille*, 31 July 1929, p. 20.
17. McMullin, p. 374.
18. Ibid., p. 370.
19. Ibid., pp. 370–371.
20. Henry Goddard, Diary, 31 March 1918, AWM 3DRL/2379, p. 80, www.awm.gov.au/collection/RCDIG0000784/?image=80
21. Ibid., p. 82.
22. Barwick, p. 312.
23. Hardie, p. 34.
24. Sydney Young, Diary, 2 February–1 September 1918, MLMSS 985, Item 6, p. 23, http://acms.sl.nsw.gov.au/_transcript/2011/D11976/a2748.htm.
25. Harms, p. 356.
26. Hindenburg, *Out of my Life*, p. 351.
27. Harms (ed.), p. 356.
28. Zabecki, p. 158 (reported speech changed to direct speech).
29. Hindenburg, *Out of my Life*, p. 350.
30. Gary Sheffield and John Bourne (eds), p. 396.
31. Ibid.
32. Bean, Diary, 1 April 1918, *Diaries and Notebooks*, AWM38 3DRL 606/104/1, p. 12, www.awm.gov.au/collection/RCDIG1066549.
33. Ibid., p. 55.
34. Ibid., p. 60.
35. Ibid., p. 64.
36. Hart, *Voices from the Front: An Oral History of the Great War*, pp. 333–334.

37. Ellis, pp. 287–288.

38. Mooney, p. 41.

39. Ibid.

40. Ibid.

41. Charles Rosenthal, Diary, 1 April 1918, SLNSW, MLMSS 2739, Vol. I, p. 402, http://acms.sl.nsw.gov.au/_transcript/2014/D27827/c00585.html.

42. John Monash to Hannah Monash, Letter, 2 April 1918, AWM 3DRL/2316, Series 1, Box 1, Wallet 2, p. 389.

43. Leslie Morshead, 'Report on Defensive Operations East of Villers-Bretonneux, April 4th–5th 1918', in 33rd Battalion Unit Diary, AWM4 23/50/18, p. 56, www.awm.gov.au/collection/RCDIG1005121/?image=56.

44. Hardie, pp. 35–36.

45. Pedersen, *Villers-Bretonneux*, p. 59.

46. Alfred Holton, Typed Narrative, AWM PR05317, p. 30.

47. Hardie, p. 37.

48. Ibid.

49. Charles Rosenthal, Diary, 3 April 1918, SLNSW, MLMSS 2739, Vol. I, p. 403, http://acms.sl.nsw.gov.au/_transcript/2014/D27827/c00585.html.

50. Ibid.

51. Henry Goddard, Diary, 3 April 1918, AWM 3DRL/2379, p. 89, www.awm.gov.au/collection/RCDIG0000784/?image=89.

52. Charles Rosenthal, Diary, 3 April 1918, SLNSW, MLMSS 2739, Vol. I, p. 403, http://acms.sl.nsw.gov.au/_transcript/2014/D27827/c00585.html.

53. George Mitchell, Diary, 3 April 1918, Vol. IV, AWM 2DRL/0928 (no page numbers).

54. MacDonald, p. 335.

55. Noel Keating, Diary, 3 April 1918, AWM PR00561 (no page numbers).

56. Tschischwitz (ed.), p. 287.

57. Rupprecht, p. 370.

58. Ibid., p. 371.

59. Alfred Holton, Typed narrative, AWM PR05317.

60. Sydney Young, Diary, 2 February–1 September 1918, MLMSS 985, Item 6, p. 21, http://acms.sl.nsw.gov.au/_transcript/2011/D11976/a2748.htm.

61. Bean, *The Official History of Australia in the War of 1914–1918*, Vol. V. p 317 (reported speech changed to direct speech).

62. Ibid.

CHAPTER ELEVEN: A DAY OF RECKONING

1. Francis Fairweather, Letter, 4 April 1918, AWM 2DRL/0207, p. 26.
2. Essame, *The Battle for Europe 1918*, p. 3.
3. *Vossische Zeitung*, 6 April 1918, Morning Edition, p. 1.
4. Henry Goddard, 'Villers-Bretonneux: March 30–April 6, 1918', in Papers relating to narrative history of the 35th Battalion, AWM 3DRL/2379, RCDIG0000808, p. 5, www.awm.gov.au_collection_RCDIG0000808_.pdf.
5. Bean, *The Official History of Australia in the War of 1914–1918*, p. 319.
6. Kaupert, p. 93.
7. Ibid., p. 94.
8. Möller, p. 406.
9. Kaupert, p. 94.
10. Henry Goddard, 'Villers-Bretonneux: March 30–April 6, 1918', in Papers relating to narrative history of the 35th Battalion, AWM 3DRL/2379, RCDIG0000808, p. 8, www.awm.gov.au_collection_RCDIG0000808_.pdf.
11. Ebeling, p. 179.
12. Ibid.
13. Ibid.
14. Ibid.
15. Henry Goddard, 'Villers-Bretonneux: March 30–April 6, 1918', in Papers relating to narrative history of the 35th Battalion, AWM 3DRL/2379, RCDIG0000808, p. 8, www.awm.gov.au_collection_RCDIG0000808_.pdf.
16. Ibid., p. 15.
17. Leslie Morshead, 'Report on Defensive Operations East of Villers-Bretonneux, April 4th–5th 1918', in 33rd Battalion Unit Diary, AWM4 23/50/18, p. 56, www.awm.gov.au/collection/RCDIG1005121/?image=56.
18. Ibid.
19. Henry Goddard, 'Villers-Bretonneux: March 30–April 6', in Papers relating to narrative history of the 35th Battalion, AWM 3DRL/2379, RCDIG0000808, p. 15, www.awm.gov.au/collection/RCDIG0000808/?image=15 (tense changed).
20. Ibid.
21. James Stevens, 'Battle Honours of the 58th Battalion', AWM MSS 1993, p. 13.
22. Henry Goddard, 'Villers-Bretonneux: March 30–April 6', in Papers relating to narrative history of the 35th Battalion, AWM

3DRL/2379, RCDIG0000808, p. 16, www.awm.gov.au/collection/
RCDIG0000808/?image=15.

23. Leslie Morshead, 'Report on Defensive Operations East of
Villers-Bretonneux, April 4th–5th 1918', in 33rd Battalion Unit
Diary, AWM4 23/50/18, p. 57, www.awm.gov.au/collection/
RCDIG1005121/?image=57.

24. Charles Rosenthal, Diary, 3 April 1918, SLNSW, MLMSS 2739, Vol.I,
pp. 404–405.

25. Hindenburg, *Out of My Life*, p. 351.

26. 15th Australian Infantry Brigade War Diary, 4 April 1918,
AWM4 23/15/26, Part 1, p. 5, www.awm.gov.au/collection/
RCDIG1008004/?image=5.

27. Ibid. (reported speech changed to direct speech).

28. Ibid.

29. McMullin, p. 374.

30. James Stevens, 'Battle Honours of the 58th Battalion', AWM MSS
1993, p. 12.

31. Leslie Morshead, 'Report on Defensive Operations East of
Villers-Bretonneux, April 4th–5th 1918', in 33rd Battalion Unit
Diary, AWM4 23/50/18, p. 57, www.awm.gov.au/collection/
RCDIG1005121/?image=57.

32. Ibid.

33. Charles Rosenthal, Diary, 4 April 1918, p. 404.

34. Alfred Holton, Memoir, AWM PR05317, p. 32.

35. Ibid.

36. Alfred Fell, Memoir, AWM RCDIG0000445, p. 4.

37. Ibid.

38. Ebeling, p. 179.

39. Ibid.

40. Ibid.

41. Ibid., p. 180.

42. McMullin, p. 375.

43. Henry Goddard, 'Villers-Bretonneux: March 30th–April 6th 1918',
in Papers relating to narrative history of the 35th Battalion, AWM
3DRL/2379, RCDIG0000808, p. 16, www.awm.gov.au/collection/
RCDIG0000808/?image=16.

44. Ibid.

45. Bean, *The Official History of Australia in the War of 1914–1918*, Vol. V.,
p. 301.

46. Henry Goddard, 'Villers-Bretonneux: March 30–April 6 1918', in

Papers relating to narrative history of the 35th Battalion, AWM 3DRL/2379, RCDIG0000808, p. 5, www.awm.gov.au/collection/RCDIG0000808.

47. Alfred Fell, Memoir, AWM RCDIG0000445, p. 4.

48. Shakespeare, *Henry V*, Act 3, Scene 1.

49. Leslie Morshead, 'Report on Defensive Operations East of Villers-Bretonneux, April 4th–5th 1918', in 33rd Battalion Unit Diary, AWM4 23/50/18, p. 57, www.awm.gov.au/collection/RCDIG1005121/?image=57.

50. Ebeling, p. 180.

51. Alfred Holton, Typed narrative, AWM PR05317, p. 32.

52. 35th Infantry Battalion War Diary, 4 April 1918, AWM 23/52/10, p. 4, www.awm.gov.au/images/collection/bundled/RCDIG1003996.pdf (reported speech changed to direct speech).

53. Ebeling, p. 180.

54. 35th Infantry Battalion War Diary, 4 April 1918, AWM 23/52/10, p. 4, www.awm.gov.au/images/collection/bundled/RCDIG1003996.pdf (reported speech changed to direct speech).

55. Gammage, p. 209.

56. Bean, *The Official History of Australia in the War of 1914–1918*, Vol. V, p. 336.

57. Ibid.

58. 34th Australian Infantry Battalion Unit Diary, 4 April 1918, AWM4 23/51/18, p. 6, www.awm.gov.au/collection/RCDIG1005643/?image=6.

59. Alfred Fell, Memoir, AWM RCDIG0000445, p. 4.

CHAPTER TWELVE: A TWILIGHT OF FIGHT

1. Robert Goldrick, Letter, 10 April 1918, SLNSW, MLMSS 3013, Item 1, p. 1.

2. Bean, *The Official History of Australia in the War of 1914–1918*, Vol. V, p. 337.

3. Ibid. (reported speech changed to direct speech).

4. Ibid.

5. Henry Goddard, 'Villers-Bretonneux: March 30–April 6, 1918', in Papers relating to narrative history of the 35th Battalion, AWM 3DRL/2379, RCDIG0000808, pp. 16–17, www.awm.gov.au/collection/RCDIG0000808/?image=16.

6. Ibid. (reported speech changed to direct speech).

7.   Ibid.

8.   34th Australian Infantry Battalion Unit Diary, 4 April 1918,
     AWM4 23/51/18, p. 6, www.awm.gov.au/collection/
     RCDIG1005643/?image=.

9.   Leslie Morshead, 'Report on Defensive Operations East of
     Villers-Bretonneux, April 4th–5th 1918', in 33rd Battalion Unit
     Diary, AWM4 23/50/18, p. 57, www.awm.gov.au/collection/
     RCDIG1005121/?image=57.

10. Ibid., p. 58.

11. Bean, Diary, AWM38 3DRL 606/105/1, p. 20, www.awm.gov.au/
     collection/RCDIG1066550.

12. Ibid., p. 21.

13. Ibid., p. 22.

14. Ibid., pp. 23–24 (reported speech changed to direct speech).

15. Ibid., p. 24.

16. Bean, Diary, April 1918, *Diaries and Notebooks*, AWM38 3DRL
     606/105/1, p. 25, www.awm.gov.au/collection/RCDIG1066550.

17. Ibid., p. 26.

18. Ibid.

19. Ibid., p. 32.

20. Ibid., p. 33.

21. Ibid.

22. Bean, *The Official History of Australia in the War of 1914–1918*, Vol. V,
     p. 339.

23. *Sydney Mail*, 5 September 1917, http://trove.nla.gov.au/newspaper/
     article/160629066

24. 36th Australian Infantry Battalion Unit Diary, 4 April 1918, AWM4
     23/53/18, p. 3, www.awm.gov.au/collection/RCDIG1004121/?image=3
     (reported speech changed to direct speech).

25. Ibid., p. 4 (reported speech changed to direct speech).

26. Ibid. (reported speech changed to direct speech).

27. Ibid. (reported speech changed to direct speech).

28. Bean, *The Official History of Australia in the War of 1914–1918*, Vol. V,
     p. 340.

29. Ibid.

30. Ibid.

31. Alexander Milne, 'Report on Operations Carried Out by 36th
     Battalion A.I.F., 4th April–6th April', in 36th Infantry Battalion
     Unit Diary, AWM4 23/53/18, p. 15, www.awm.gov.au/collection/
     RCDIG1004121/?image=15.

32. Bean, *The Official History of Australia in the War of 1914–1918*, Vol. V, p. 340.

33. Alfred Holton, Typed narrative, AWM PR05317, p. 32.

34. Bean, *The Official History of Australia in the War of 1914–1918*, Vol. V, p. 340.

35. T. G. Cooper, 'Saving Amiens: April 4th Attack', *Reveille*, 1 September 1933, p. 11, (reported speech changed to direct speech).

36. Bean, *The Official History of Australia in the War of 1914–1918*, Vol. V, p. 338.

37. Henry Goddard, 'Villers-Bretonneux: March 30–April 6, 1918', in Papers relating to narrative history of the 35th Battalion, AWM 3DRL/2379, RCDIG0000808, p. 17, www.awm.gov.au/collection/RCDIG0000808/?image=17.

38. Alexander Milne, 'Report on Operations Carried Out by 36th Battalion A.I.F., 4th April to 6th April', in 36th Infantry Battalion Unit Diary, AWM4 23/53/18, p. 15, www.awm.gov.au/collection/RCDIG1004121/?image=15.

39. 36th Australian Infantry Battalion Unit Diary, 4 April 1918, AWM4 23/53/18, p. 4, www.awm.gov.au/collection/RCDIG1004121/?image=4.

40. Ibid.

41. Alfred Holton, Typed narrative, AWM PR05317, p. 32.

42. Ibid.

43. Ibid., p. 33.

44. Ibid.

45. Ibid.

46. Ibid.

47. Ibid.

48. Alexander Milne, 'Report on Operations Carried Out by 36th Battalion A.I.F., 4th April to 6th April', in 36th Infantry Battalion Unit Diary, AWM4 23/53/18, p. 15, www.awm.gov.au/collection/RCDIG1004121/?image=15.

49. 36th Australian Infantry Battalion Unit Diary, 4 April 1918, AWM4 23/53/18, p. 4, www.awm.gov.au/collection/RCDIG1004121/?image=4.

50. Ibid.

51. Alexander Milne, 'Report on Operations Carried Out by 36th Battalion A.I.F., 4th April to 6th April', in 36th Infantry Battalion Unit Diary, AWM4 23/53/18, p. 16, www.awm.gov.au/collection/RCDIG1004121/?image=16.

52. Ibid.

53. T. G. Cooper, 'Saving Amiens: April 4th Attack', *Reveille*, 1 September 1933, p. 11.

54. Alfred Holton, Typed narrative, AWM PR05317, p. 33.

55. Reported speech changed to direct speech.

56. Alfred Holton, Typed narrative, AWM PR05317, p. 34.

57. Ibid.

58. Pedersen, *Villers-Bretonneux*, p. 65.

59. Kaupert, p. 95.

60. 36th Australian Infantry Battalion Unit Diary, 4 April 1918, AWM4 23/53/18, p. 4, www.awm.gov.au/collection/RCDIG1004121/?image=4.

61. Bean, *The Official History of Australia in the War of 1914–1918*, Vol. V, p. 345.

62. Charles Rosenthal to John Monash, Letter, 5 April 1918, 3DRL/2316, Series 3, RCDIG0000628, p. 64.

63. Ibid.

64. Bean, *The Official History of Australia in the War of 1914–1918*, Vol. V, p. 355.

65. Alfred Holton, Typed narrative, AWM PR05317, p. 34.

66. Charles Rosenthal, Diary, 3 April 1918, SLNSW, MLMSS 2739, Vol. I, p. 405.

67. Ebeling, p. 178.

68. Passingham, *The German Offensives of 1918*, p. 87.

69. Henry Goddard, 'Villers-Bretonneux: March 30–April 6, 1918', in Papers relating to narrative history of the 35th Battalion, AWM 3DRL/2379, RCDIG0000808, p. 6, www.awm.gov.au/collection/RCDIG0000808.

70. Rosenthal, Diary, 4 April 1918, p. 405.

71. Henry Goddard, 'Villers-Bretonneux: March 30–April 6, 1918', in Papers relating to narrative history of the 35th Battalion, AWM 3DRL/2379, RCDIG0000808, p. 6, www.awm.gov.au/collection/RCDIG0000808.

72. Ibid.

73. Charles Rosenthal to John Monash, Letter, 5 April 1918, 3DRL/2316, Series 3, RCDIG0000628, p. 64.

74. The 35th Infantry Battalion War Diary, 5 April 1918, p. 8, AWM4 23/52/10, www.awm.gov.au/collection/RCDIG1003996/?image=8.

75. Charles Rosenthal, Diary, 4 April 1918, p. 405.

76. Henry Goddard, 'Villers-Bretonneux: March 30–April 6, 1918', in Papers relating to narrative history of the 35th Battalion, AWM 3DRL/2379, RCDIG0000808, p. 10, www.awm.gov.au/collection/RCDIG0000808/?image=10.

77. McMullin, p. 381.
78. Charles Rosenthal, Diary, 4 April 1918, p. 405.
79. *Vossische Zeitung*, 5 April 1918, Morning Edition, p. 1.
80. *Vossische Zeitung*, 6 April 1918, Morning Edition, p. 1.

CHAPTER THIRTEEN: THE SECOND BATTLE OF DERNANCOURT

1. Thomas Louch, 'In the Ranks', Papers of Thomas Louch, Part III, PR85/363, p. 17.
2. Deayton, p. 225.
3. Bean, *The Official History of Australia in the War of 1914–1918*, Vol. V, p. 366.
4. Bean, Diary, March 1918, *Diaries and Notebooks*, AWM38 3DRL 606/184/1, p. 31, www.awm.gov.au/collection/RCDIG1066800.
5. George Mitchell, Diary, 4 April 1918, Vol. IV, AWM 2DRL/0928 (no page numbers).
6. George Mitchell, Diary, 5 April 1918, Vol. IV, AWM 2DRL/0928 (no page numbers).
7. Ibid.
8. MacDonald, p. 349.
9. George Mitchell, Diary, 5 April 1918, Vol. IV, AWM 2DRL/0928 (no page numbers).
10. Lynch, *Somme Mud*, p. 211.
11. MacDonald, p. 348.
12. Ibid., p. 349.
13. Ibid.
14. Thomas Louch, 'In the Ranks', Papers of Thomas Louch, Part III, PR85/363, p. 17.
15. Bean, Diary, March 1918, *Diaries and Notebooks*, AWM38 3DRL 606/184/1, p. 26–27, www.awm.gov.au/collection/RCDIG1066800.
16. *Commonwealth Gazette No. 185*, 27 November 1918, p. 2264.
17. Ibid.
18. Lynch, p. 212.
19. Bean, *The Official History of Australia in the War of 1914–1918*, Vol. V, p. 414.
20. Longmore, *The Old Sixteenth: Being a Record of the 16th Battalion AIF, During the Great War, 1914–1918*, p. 169.
21. Bean, *The Official History of Australia in the War of 1914–1918*, Vol. V, p. 416.
22. Ibid., p. 415.

23. Ibid., p. 416.

24. White, p. 130.

25. Elfeldt, p. 509.

26. McMullin, pp. 377–378.

27. Bean, *The Official History of Australia in the War of 1914–1918,* Vol. V, pp. 526–527.

28. 58th Australian Infantry Battalion Unit Diary, April 1918, AWM4 23/75/27, Appenidx 19, p. 67, www.awm.gov.au/collection/ RCDIG1006037/?image=67

29. George Mitchell, Diary, 5 April 1918, Vol. IV, AWM 2DRL/0928, (no page numbers, reported speech changed to direct speech).

30. Ibid.

31. Ibid. (reported speech changed to direct speech).

32. Ibid.

33. Ibid.

34. Ibid.

35. Ibid.

36. Ibid.

37. Ibid.

38. Ibid.

39. Ibid.

40. Ibid.

41. Ibid.

42. Lynch, p. 212.

43. Ibid., p. 213 (the first sentence is reported speech changed to direct speech).

44. Ibid.

45. Ibid., p. 214.

46. Ibid.

47. Ibid.

48. Ibid., pp. 214–215.

49. Bean, Diary, 6 April 1918, *Diaries and Notebooks,* AWM38 3DRL 606/106/1, p. 19, www.awm.gov.au/collection/RCDIG1066551.

50. Bean, *The Official History of Australia in the War of 1914–1918,* Vol. V, p. 406.

51. Edmonds, p. 137.

52. Zabecki, p. 159.

53. Edmonds, p. 137.

54. Bean, *The Official History of Australia in the War of 1914–1918,* Vol. V, p. 417.

55. Ibid.

56. Passingham, *The German Offensives of 1918*, p. 87.

57. Hindenburg, *Out of My Life*, p. 350.

58. Reported speech changed to direct speech.

59. MacDonald, p. 351.

60. Gray, p. 88.

61. Barwick, p. 312.

62. *L'Echo de Paris*, 9 April 1918, p. 3, http://gallica.bnf.fr/ark:/12148/ bpt6k809228f/f3.item.

63. Wayne Mathews and David Wilson, p. 309.

64. Bean, *The Official History of Australia in the War of 1914–1918*, Vol. V, p. 503.

65. Percy Storkey to Charles Bean, Letter, April 1931, AWM38 3drl 3953/3, Part 1, *Official History 1914–1918 War Records of Charles E. W. Bean Correspondence 1929–1939*.

66. 'Lieut. Percy Storkey, V.C.', *Hermes: The Magazine of the University of Sydney*, No. 1, June 1918, p. 55, http://sydney.edu.au/arms/archives/ hermes%201918%20June%20Vol%20XXIV%20No%201.pdf.

67. Wayne Mathews and David Wilson, p. 312.

68. Ibid., p. 313.

69. Bean, *The Official History of Australia in the War of 1914–1918*, Vol. V, p. 507.

70. Henry Goddard, Diary, AWM 3DRL 2379, p.101, www.awm.gov.au/ collection/RCDIG0000784/?image=101.

71. Bean, *The Official History of Australia in the War of 1914–1918*, Vol. V, p. 512.

72. Kilduff, *Red Baron: The Life and Death of an Ace*, pp. 209–210.

73. Jon Guttman, p. 59.

74. Ibid., p. 58.

75. Barwick, pp. 313–314.

76. Maurice, p. 216.

77. Edmund Street, Memoir, AWM PR85/179, Folder 6, p. 97.

78. Ibid., p. 99.

79. Ibid., p. 97.

80. Ibid., p. 101.

CHAPTER FOURTEEN: OPERATION GEORGE

1. Bean, *The Official History of Australia in the War of 1914–1918*, Vol. V, p. 258.

2. Tschischwitz (ed.), p. 290.

3. Crozier, p. 81.
4. Ibid. (reported speech changed to direct speech).
5. *Vossische Zeitung*, 24 April 1918, Morning Edition, p. 4.
6. Zabecki, pp. 184–185.
7. Edmonds, p. 168.
8. Westman, p. 157.
9. Crozier, p. 35.
10. Ibid., p. 39.
11. Reported speech changed to direct speech.
12. Crozier, p. 40.
13. Rupprecht, p. 375.
14. Ibid., pp. 375–6.
15. Ibid., p. 376.
16. General Staff Headquarters 1st Australian Division War Diary, 10 April 1918, AWM4 1/42/39, Part1.
17. Foch, p. 326.
18. Ibid., p. 324.
19. Ibid., p. 325 (reported speech changed to direct speech).
20. Ibid.
21. Gary Sheffield and John Bourne, p. 401.
22. Thompson, p. 126.
23. Ibid., p. 126.
24. Barwick, pp. 314–315.
25. Zabecki, p. 190.
26. Bean, *The Official History of Australia in the War of 1914–1918,* Vol. V, p. 455 (reported speech changed to direct speech).
27. Barwick, p. 316.
28. Ibid., p. 316–317.
29. Thompson, p. 126.
30. Bean, *The Official History of Australia in the War of 1914–1918*, Vol. V, p. 473.
31. Ibid., p. 456.
32. Ibid.
33. Ibid.
34. Westmann, p. 158.
35. Bean, *The Official History of Australia in the War of 1914–1918*, Vol. V, p. 345.
36. Henry Goddard, *Tour of a Company on the Front Line*, AWM 3DRL/2379, p. 9.
37. Ibid.
38. Sydney Young, Diary, 12 April 1918, MLMSS 985, Item 6, 2

February–1 September 1918, p. 32, http://acms.sl.nsw.gov.au/_
transcript/2011/D11976/a2748.htm.

39. Ibid., p. 79.

40. Ibid., p. 80.

41. Barwick, p. 320.

42. Ibid.

43. Westman, p.161.

44. Ibid.

45. For the record, I note that as the Australian account has it that they
killed a German officer, and the German records (from the *Bayerischen
Armeemuseum*/Bavarian Army Museum in Ingolstadt) say Leutnant
Frey was ever after MIA from this date. Frey was indeed killed in this
action.

46. Bean, *The Official History of Australia in the War of 1914–1918*, Vol. V,
p. 467.

47. Ibid., p. 469.

48. Ibid.

49. Edmonds, p. 304.

50. Ibid., p. 344 (reported speech changed to direct speech).

51. Maurice, p. 217.

52. Bean, *The Official History of Australia in the War of 1914–1918*, Vol. V,
p. 535.

53. Barwick, p. 321.

54. Ibid.

55. Ibid.

56. Ibid.

57. Ibid., p. 322.

58. Ibid.

59. Frederick Petch, Letter to the Editor, *Air Pictorial Magazine*, Vol. 30,
p. 249.

60. Ibid.

61. Ibid. (reported speech changed to direct speech).

62. Richards, p. 199.

63. Ibid.

64. Edmonds, pp. 343–344.

65. Richards, p. 200.

66. Ibid.

67. Ibid.

68. Zabecki, p. 194 (tense changed).

69. Edmonds, pp. 355.

70. Mitchell, Frank, *Tank Warfare*, p. 185.
71. MacDonald, p. 82. The quotation refers to a bombardment several weeks before 17 April, but it accurately describes the sounds and smells of gas bombardments in 1918.
72. Kendall (ed.), p. 83.
73. Mitchell, Frank, *Tank Warfare*, p. 185.
74. Ibid.
75. 33rd Infantry Battalion War Diary, April 1918, AWM 4 23/50/18.
76. Henry Dadswell, Diary, *Diary of a Sapper*, AWM MSS 0828, p. 100.
77. Edmund Street, Memoir, AWM PR85/179, Folder 6, p. 103.
78. Graf (et al), p. 93.
79. Ibid.
80. Zabecki, p. 168.
81. Bean, Diary, April 1918, *Diaries and Notebooks*, AWM38 3DRL 606/107/1, pp. 83–84, www.awm.gov.au/collection/RCDIG1066552.
82. Ibid., p. 78.
83. Bean, *The Official History of Australia in the War of 1914–1918*, Vol. V, p. 540.
84. Edmund Street, Memoir, AWM PR85/179, Folder 6, p. 104.
85. Ibid. (reported speech changed to direct speech).
86. Ibid. (reported speech changed to direct speech).
87. McMullin, p. 390.
88. Ibid. (reported speech changed to direct speech).
89. Handwritten Diary, April 1918, Vol. 24, p. 1.

CHAPTER FIFTEEN: 'ALL ROADS LEAD TO STOUSH'

1. McMullin, p. 380.
2. Richards, p. 201.
3. Edmonds, pp. 383–4.
4. Guttman, p. 65.
5. Ibid.
6. Molkentin, p. 253.
7. On 1 April 1918, the Royal Flying Corps had become the Royal Air Force, but for ease of narration I have kept it as Royal Flying Corps throughout.
8. *Vossische Zeitung*, 24 April 1918, Morning Edition, p. 4.
9. Karl Bodenschatz, *Hunting with Richthofen*, p. 35.
10. *Aviation Magazine*, 12 June 2006.
11. McGuire, p. 143.

12. Guttman, p. 67.

13. Kilduff, *Richthofen: Beyond the Legend of the Red Baron*, p. 239.

14. Bean, *The Official History of Australia in the War of 1914–1918,* Vol. V, p. 701.

15. Mark Day, 'Unsung No. 1 with a Bullet', *The Australian,* 11 April 2007, www.theaustralian.com.au/in-depth/anzac-day/unsung-no1-with-a-bullet/story-e6frgdaf-1111113322520.

16. William Dadswell, *Diary of a Sapper,* AWM MSS 0828, p. 101.

17. John Alexander, Diary, Undated, AWM PR86/133 (no page numbers).

18. Bean, Diary, 22 April 1918, *Diaries and Notebooks*, AWM38 3DRL 606/107/1, p.89, www.awm.gov.au/collection/RCDIG1066552.

19. Ibid., p. 90.

20. 'Report on the Death of Captain Baron Von Richthofen', 21 April 1918, John Monash Papers, AWM 3DRL/2316, Series 3, Folder 57, p. 1, www.awm.gov.au/images/collection/bundled/RCDIG0000629.pdf.

21. MacDougall, p. 182.

22. 14th Australian Infantry Brigade War Diary, April 1918, AWM4 23/14/25.

23. Alec Paterson, Letter, Undated, AWM, 3DRL/3389, p. 2.

24. Ibid.

25. Guttman, p. 67.

26. Bean, Diary, 22 April 1918, *Diaries and Notebooks*, AWM38 3DRL 606/107/1, pp. 90–91, www.awm.gov.au/collection/RCDIG1066552.

27. Corporal Noel Keating, 13th Brigade Headquarters, Handwritten diary, AWM PR00561.

28. Kilduff, *Red Baron: The Life and Death of an Ace,* pp. 224–225.

29. Ibid.

30. Bodenschatz, *Jagd in Flanderns Himmel*, p. 84.

31. Kilduff, *Red Baron: The Life and Death of an Ace,* p. 227.

32. Rupprecht, p. 387.

33. Ibid, p. 388.

34. Alec Paterson, Letter, Undated, AWM, 3DRL/3389, p. 4.

35. Captain Brown was awarded the victory and still holds it officially.

36. Frank Rawlinson, Unpublished Memoir, *Wood and Fire,* AWM MSS0770, p. 49.

37. Molkentin, p. 255.

38. Mackersey, p. 256.

39. Ibid., p. 258.

40. Rupprecht, p. 388.

41. John Alexander, Diary, Undated, AWM PR86/133 (no page numbers).

42. Titler, p. 210.
43. Alec Paterson, Letter, Undated, AWM, 3DRL/3389, p. 1.
44. Ibid.
45. Ibid.
46. Joy, p. 99.
47. Kilduff, *Red Baron; The Life and Death of an Ace*, p. 224–225.
48. Sulzbach, p. 176.
49. Ludendorff, Margarethe, *Als ich Ludendorffs Frau war* (*When I was Ludendorff's Wife*), p. 155.
50. Goodspeed, p. 200.
51. Ludendorff, Margarethe, *Als ich Ludendorffs Frau war* (*When I was Ludendorff's Wife*), p. 156.
52. Ibid.
53. Uhle-Wettler, p. 338.
54. Pedersen, *Villers-Bretonneux*, p. 86.
55. Herbert Henry Harris, Diary, 23 April 1918, SLNSW MLMSS 2772/ Item 4, p. 84, http://acms.sl.nsw.gov.au/_transcript/2013/D23223/ a4627.html.
56. Ibid.
57. Bean, Diary, 24 April 1918, *Diaries and Notebooks*, AWM38 3DRL 606/108/1, p. 8, www.awm.gov.au/collection/RCDIG1066553 (reported speech changed to direct speech).
58. G. W. Grogan, 'Villers-Bretonneux, April 24 1918', *Reveille*, 1 August 1936, p. 9.
59. Ibid.
60. Fischer (ed.), p. 167.
61. Ibid.
62. Ibid.
63. Ibid., 168.
64. Ibid.
65. Ibid.

CHAPTER SIXTEEN: THE 2ND BATTLE OF VILLERS-BRETONNEUX

1. Bean, Diary, April–May 1918, *Diaries and Notebooks*, AWM38 3DRL 606/107/1, p. 95, www.awm.gov.au/collection/RCDIG1066552.
2. Edmund Street, Memoir, AWM PR85/179, Folder 6, p. 103.
3. John Turnbull, Diary, 24 April 1918, AWM PR91/015, RCDIG0001110, p. 45.
4. Mitchell, Frank, *Tank Warfare*, p. 186.
5. Fletcher, pp. 33–34.

6. Alun Thomas, 'British 8th Infantry Division on the Western Front, 1914–18', PhD Thesis, Centre for First World War Studies, p. 297, http://etheses.bham.ac.uk/599/1/thomas10PhD.pdf.

7. Mitchell, Frank, *Tank Warfare*, p. 186.

8. Edmonds, p. 384.

9. Ibid.

10. Ibid.

11. Ibid. p. 254.

12. Sievers (ed.), p. 255.

13. Stosch, p. 516.

14. Walter Elfeldt, 'In the Battle of Villers-Bretonneux: Diary Pages from Walter Elfeldt, Former Platoon Leader of 1st Platoon 7th/5th Guards Infantry Regiment', from *Das Ehrenbuch der Garde* (*The Guards' Book of Honour*), p. 507.

15. Ibid., p. 508.

16. Stosch, p. 517.

17. G. W. Grogan, 'Villers-Bretonneux, April 24 1918', *Reveille*, 1 August 1936, p. 9.

18. Alun Thomas, 'British 8th Infantry Division on the Western Front, 1914–18', PhD Thesis, Centre for First World War Studies, p. 302, http://etheses.bham.ac.uk/599/1/thomas10PhD.pdf.

19. Graf (et al), p. 94.

20. Mitchell, Frank, *Tank Warfare*, p. 186.

21. Ibid.

22. Ibid., p. 187.

23. Ibid.

24. Ibid.

25. Stosch, p. 517.

26. Harold Elliott, 'Report on Operations of 15th Australian Infantry Brigade During Period from 25th to 27th April 1918 at Villers-Bretonneux', AWM252 A159, p. 3.

27. Ibid.

28. Bean to Edmonds, Letter, 15 September 1931, Relates to the British Official Accounts of the Campaign in France, AWM38 7953/30, Part 1, p. 2.

29. Alun Thomas, 'British 8th Infantry Division on the Western Front, 1914–18', PhD Thesis, Centre for First World War Studies, p. 304–305, http://etheses.bham.ac.uk/599/1/thomas10PhD.pdf

30. Ibid.

31. G. W. Grogan, 'Villers-Bretonneux, April 24 1918', *Reveille*, 1 August 1936, p. 9.
32. Ibid.
33. LMEGI I don't know where that quote is from
34. Stosch, p. 517.
35. Pedersen, *Villers-Bretonneux*, p 91.
36. G. W. Grogan, 'Villers-Bretonneux, April 24, 1918', *Reveille*, 1 August 1936, p. 9.
37. Pedersen, Peter, *Villers-Bretonneux*, p. 85.
38. G. W. Grogan, 'Villers-Bretonneux, April 24, 1918', *Reveille*, 1 August 1936, p. 9.
39. Such as it was most memorably described, at the first real unveiling of that weapon, on the first day of the Battle of Verdun.
40. Edmund Street, Memoir, AWM PR85/179, Folder 6, p.104.
41. Stosch, p. 517.
42. Downing, Walter, *To the Last Ridge*, p. 114.
43. McMullin, p. 393.
44. Comments by Lieutenant General Talbot Hobbs, 5th Australian Divisions, in Bean, *Records of Charles E. W. Bean, Correspondence 1929–1939*, Relates to the British Official Accounts of the Campaign in France, AWM38 7953/30, Part 1.
45. Harold Elliott, 'Report on Operations of 15th Australian Infantry Brigade During Period from 25th to 27th April 1918 at Villers-Bretonneux', AWM252 A159, p. 2.
46. Ibid.
47. Sievers, p. 255.
48. John Turnbull, Diary, 24 April 1918, AWM PR91/015, Digital RCDIG0001110, p. 45.
49. Ibid.
50. Graf (et al), p. 93.
51. Ibid.
52. Ibid., 95.
53. Kaupert, p. 97.
54. Mitchell, Frank, *Tank Warfare*, p. 187.
55. Ibid. (reported speech changed to direct speech, tenses changed).
56. Mitchell, Frank, *Tank Warfare*, p. 188.
57. Ibid.
58. Ibid.
59. Bean, *The Official History of Australia in the War of 1914–1918*, Vol. V, p. 535.

60. Ibid., p. 568.
61. Ibid., p. 569.
62. Downing, *To the Last Ridge*, p. 114.
63. Bean, *The Official History of Australia in the War of 1914–1918*, Vol. V, p. 549.
64. Downing, *To the Last Ridge*, p. 114.
65. Scott (ed.), p. 132.
66. John Turnbull, Diary, 24 April 1918, AWM PR91/015, Digital RCDIG0001110, p. 49 (reported speech changed to direct speech).
67. Harold Elliott, 'Report on Operations of 15th Australian Infantry Brigade During Period from 25th to 27th April 1918 at Villers-Bretonneux', AWM252 A159, p. 10.
68. Bean, *The Official History of Australia in the War of 1914–1918*, Vol. V, p. 551.
69. Ibid.
70. Ibid.
71. Harold Elliott, 'Report on Operations of 15th Australian Infantry Brigade During Period from 25th to 27th April 1918 at Villers-Bretonneux', AWM252 A159, p. 7
72. Bean, *The Official History of Australia in the War of 1914–1918*, Vol. V, p. 568.
73. Edgar, p. 223.
74. Whitham, p. 3.
75. Ibid.
76. Foley, p. 180.
77. Ibid., p. 182.
78. Ibid.
79. Tank diagrams courtesy of Simon Williams, illustrated by Midland Typesetters.
80. Foley, p. 182
81. Mitchell, Frank, *Tank Warfare*, p. 190
82. Ibid.
83. Ibid.
84. Private Walter Kennedy, Typed narrative, 'From Anzac Cove to Villers-Bretonneux', AWM PR02032, p. 63.
85. Mitchell, Frank, *Tank Warfare*, p. 190.
86. Foley, p. 184.
87. Ibid.
88. Ibid.
89. Ibid.

90. Ibid.
91. Mitchell, Frank, *Tank Warfare*, p. 194.

CHAPTER SEVENTEEN: HIGH NOON

1. *Argus* (Melbourne), 9 October 1931, p. 7.
2. Gabriel, *Das 1. Hannoversche Infanterie-Regiment Nr. 74 im Weltkriege*, p. 414.
3. Bean, *The Official History of Australia in the War of 1914–1918*, Vol. V, p. 571.
4. Ibid. (reported speech changed to direct speech).
5. Ibid., p. 572.
6. Ibid.
7. Gary Sheffield and John Bourne, pp. 406–407.
8. Jeffrey (ed.), pp. 39–40.
9. Edgar, p. 226.
10. Bean, *The Official History of Australia in the War of 1914–1918*, Vol. V, p. 573.
11. Ibid., p. 537.
12. Ibid., p. 574.
13. Ibid., p. 575.
14. Ibid. (reported speech changed to direct speech).
15. Harold Elliott to John Treloar, Letter, 7 July 1918, AWM252 A158, p. 1.
16. Bean, *The Official History of Australia in the War of 1914–1918*, Vol. V, p. 549.
17. Harold Elliott, 'Report on Operations of 15th Australian Infantry Brigade During Period from 25th to 27th April 1918 at Villers-Bretonneux', AWM252 A159, p. 9.
18. Sievers (ed.), *R.I.R. 93: Geschichte eines Regiments im Weltkriege*, p. 256.
19. Whitham, p. 3.
20. Graf (et al), *Das Württembergische Infanterie-Regiment Nr. 478*, p. 93.
21. Bean, Diary, April–May 1918, *Diaries and Notebooks* AWM38 3DRL 606/108/1, p. 16, www.awm.gov.au/collection/RCDIG1066553.
22. McMullin, p. 403.
23. Bean, Diary, April–May 1918, *Diaries and Notebooks* AWM38 3DRL 606/108/1, p. 18, www.awm.gov.au/collection/RCDIG1066553.
24. Ibid.
25. Ibid., p. 19.
26. Ibid., p. 20.
27. Ibid., p. 22.

28. Stosch, p. 518.
29. Edgar, p. 231.
30. Bean, *The Official History of Australia in the War of 1914–1918*, Vol. V, p. 598.
31. Stosch, p. 522.
32. Pedersen, *Villers-Bretonneux*, p. 181.
33. Bean, *The Official History of Australia in the War of 1914–1918*, Vol. V, p. 580.
34. Need, p. 133.
35. Ibid., p. 134.
36. Ibid.
37. Ibid.
38. Downing, *To the Last Ridge*, p. 117.
39. Bean, *The Official History of Australia in the War of 1914–1918*, Vol. V, p. 601.
40. Ibid., p. 581.
41. Ibid.
42. Whitham, p. 3.
43. Bean, Diary, April–May 1918, *Diaries and Notebooks*, AWM38 3DRL 606/108/1, p. 24, www.awm.gov.au/collection/RCDIG1066553.
44. Ibid.
45. G. W. Grogan, 'Villers-Bretonneux, April 24, 1918', *Reveille*, 1 August 1936, p. 11.
46. Bean, *The Official History of Australia in the War of 1914–1918*, Vol. V, p. 582.
47. Browning, p. 155.
48. Bean, Diary, April–May 1918, *Diaries and Notebooks*, AWM38 3DRL 606/108/1, pp. 45–46, www.awm.gov.au/collection/RCDIG1066553 (reported speech changed to direct speech).
49. Bean, *The Official History of Australia in the War of 1914–1918*, Vol. V, p. 582 (reported speech changed to direct speech).
50. Ibid. (reported speech changed to direct speech).
51. Ibid.
52. Captain R. L. Forsyth, 'Villers Bret. A Medical Officer's Impressions', *Reveille*, 1 April 1939, p. 32.
53. Ibid.
54. Bean, *The Official History of Australia in the War of 1914–1918*, Vol. V, p. 582.
55. Pedersen, *Villers-Bretonneux*, p. 115.

56. Bean, *The Official History of Australia in the War of 1914–1918*, Vol. V, p. 583.
57. Pedersen, *Villers-Bretonneux*, p. 115.
58. Whitham, p. 4.
59. Bean, *The Official History of Australia in the War of 1914–1918*, Vol. V, p. 583.
60. Pedersen, *Anzacs on the Western Front*, p. 342.
61. Ibid.
62. Bean, *The Official History of Australia in the War of 1914–1918*, Vol. V, p. 589.
63. Scott (ed.), p. 136.
64. Ibid., p. 137.
65. Bean, *The Official History of Australia in the War of 1914–1918*, Vol. V, p. 585.
66. Ibid., p. 587.
67. Ibid., p 590.
68. Ibid., p. 585.
69. Pedersen, *Villers-Bretonneux*, p. 126.
70. Bean, *The Official History of Australia in the War of 1914–1918*, Vol. V, p. 586.
71. Ibid.
72. Ibid., p. 588.
73. Ibid., pp. 590–591. Again, I note that the Germans tended to refer to all English-speaking enemies as the English. To avoid confusion in this instance, I have placed 'Australians' in square brackets.
74. Elfeldt, p. 511.
75. Ibid., p. 511.
76. Bean, Diary, April–May 1918, *Diaries and Notebooks*, AWM38 3DRL 606/108/1, pp. 80, www.awm.gov.au/collection/RCDIG1066553.
77. Bean, *The Official History of Australia in the War of 1914–1918*, Vol. V, p. 591.
78. Gammage, p. 259.
79. Sievers (ed.), p. 257.
80. Ibid.
81. Ibid., p. 258.
82. Bean, *The Official History of Australia in the War of 1914–1918*, Vol. V, p. 595.
83. Ibid.
84. Ibid.

85. Elfeldt, p. 512.
86. Sievers (ed.), p. 258
87. Browning, p. 164.
88. Bean, *The Official History of Australia in the War of 1914–1918*, p. 595.
89. Ibid., p. 591.
90. Ibid., p. 595.

CHAPTER EIGHTEEN: ANZAC DAY 1918 – THE DAY OF RECKONING

1. James McWilliams and R. James Steel, *Amiens: Dawn of Victory*, p. 47.
2. G. W. Grogan, 'Villers-Bretonneux, April 24 1918', *Reveille*, 1 August 1936, p. 8.
3. Downing, *To the Last Ridge*, p. 118.
4. Ibid., p. 117 (reported speech changed to direc speech).
5. Bean, *The Official History of Australia in the War of 1914–1918*, Vol. V, p. 582.
6. Downing, *To The Last Ridge*, p. 117.
7. Whitham, p. 5.
8. Bean, *The Official History of Australia in the War of 1914–1918*, Vol. V, p. 602.
9. Scott, p. 136.
10. Downing, *To The Last Ridge*, p. 118.
11. Bean, *The Official History of Australia in the War of 1914–1918*, Vol. V, p. 604.
12. Such are the imprecations that Australian soldiers are documented to shout at such times, and we know from Need's account that he heard precisely this kind of shouting.
13. Scott, p. 136.
14. J. J. McKenna, Papers, in K. Schneider's *Pompey Elliott's Left Hand Man: Lieutenant Colonel Charles Denehy*', p. 247.
15. Bean, *The Official History of Australia in the War of 1914–1918*, Vol. V, p. 602.
16. Scott, p. 136.
17. The actual quote is: 'As Lord Chesterfield said of the Generals of his day, "I only hope when the enemy reads the list of their names, he trembles as I do."'.
18. Scott, pp. 136–137.
19. Colonel J. J. Scanlon, in R. Corfield's *Give Me Back My Dear Old Cobbers: The Story of the 58th and 59th Australian Infantry battalions 1913–1942*, p. 218.

20. Bean, *The Official History of Australia in the War of 1914–1918*, Vol. V, p. 602.
21. Ibid., p. 603.
22. Ibid.
23. Downing, *To the Last Ridge*, p. 118.
24. J. J. McKenna, Papers, in K. Schneider's *Pompey Elliott's Left Hand Man: Lieutenant Colonel Charles Denehy*, p. 247.
25. Downing, *To the Last Ridge*, p. 118.
26. J. J. McKenna, Papers, in K. Schneider's *Pompey Elliott's Left Hand Man: Lieutenant Colonel Charles Denehy*, p. 247.
27. Browning, p. 157.
28. Bean, *The Official History of Australia in the War of 1914–1918*, Vol. V, p. 603.
29. Ibid.
30. Downing, *To The Last Ridge*, p.118.
31. Ibid., p.118–119.
32. Ibid., p. 119.
33. Ibid.
34. Arthur Rusden, Private Record, AWM 1DRL.0559 p. 2.
35. Scott, p. 137.
36. Bean, *The Official History of Australia in the War of 1914–1918*, Vol. V, p. 605.
37. Scott, p. 138.
38. Bean, *The Official History of Australia in the War of 1914–1918*, Vol. V, p. 613.
39. McMullin, p. 403.
40. Pedersen, *Villers-Bretonneux*, p. 181.
41. Driver John Turnbull, Handwritten diaries, 24 April 1918, AWM PR91/015 (Digital RCDIG0001110), p. 50.
42. Bean, *The Official History of Australia in the War of 1914–1918*, Vol. V, p. 616.
43. Ibid.
44. Driver John Turnbull, Handwritten diaries, 24 April 1918, AWM PR91/015 (Digital RCDIG0001110), p. 50.
45. Ibid., p. 51.
46. Bean, *The Official History of Australia in the War of 1914–1918*, Vol. V, p. 620.
47. Elfeldt, p. 514.
48. Ibid..
49. Kaupert, p. 98.

50. Arthur Rusden, Private Papers, AWM 1DRL.0559, p. 2.
51. Ibid.
52. Driver John Turnbull, Handwritten diaries, 24 April 1918, AWM PR91/015 (Digital RCDIG0001110), p. 51.
53. Ibid.
54. Möller, p. 406.
55. Ibid.
56. Arthur Rusden, Private Papers, AWM 1DRL.0559, p. 1.
57. Ibid., p. 2 (reported speech changed to direct speech).
58. Ibid., p. 2.
59. Scott, p.139.
60. Bean, *The Official History of Australia in the War of 1914–1918*, Vol. V, p. 620.
61. Ibid.
62. Ibid.
63. Möller, p. 406.
64. Elfeldt, p. 514.
65. Bean, *The Official History of Australia in the War of 1914–1918*, Vol. V, p. 628.
66. Ibid.
67. Bean, Diary, 20 July 1916, *Diaries and Notebooks*, AWM38 3DRL 606/52/1, p. 10, www.awm.gov.au/collection/RCDIG1066752.
68. Bean, Diary, April–May 1918, *Diaries and Notebooks,* AWM38 3DRL 606/108/1, p. 25, www.awm.gov.au/collection/ RCDIG1066553 (last sentence reported speech changed to direct speech).
69. Corporal Noel Keating, Handwritten diary, AWM PR00561.
70. Bean, *The Official History of Australia in the War of 1914–1918*, Vol. V, p. 625.
71. Whitham, p. 6.
72. Ibid.
73. Ibid.
74. Ibid.
75. Ibid.
76. McMullin, p 415.
77. Bean, Diary, April–May 1918, *Diaries and Notebooks*, AWM38 3DRL 606/108/1, p. 25, www.awm.gov.au/collection/RCDIG1066553.
78. Ibid., p. 64.
79. Maurice, Sir Frederick, *The Life of General Lord Rawlinson of Trent from his Journals and Letters*, p. 219.

80. Bean, *The Official History of Australia in the War of 1914–1918*, Vol. V, p. 629.

81. Bean, Diary, April–May 1918, *Diaries and Notebooks*, AWM38 3DRL 606/108/1, p. 25, www.awm.gov.au/collection/RCDIG1066553.

82. G. W. Grogan, 'Villers-Bretonneux, April 24 1918', *Reveille*, 1 August 1936, p. 9.

83. Bean, *The Official History of Australia in the War of 1914–1918*, Vol. V, p. 110.

EPILOGUE

1. The German Official History usually refers to all British forces as English, but the counter-attack mentioned here was conducted almost entirely by Australians.

   The German casualty reporting system didn't record lightly wounded, as the British and the Australians did. This means 10 per cent at least should be added to German casualty reports to get the equivalent, so in the British/Australian understanding of casualties, it was likely closer to 9000.

2. Tiveychoc, pp. 261–262.

3. Gough, p. 329.

4. Harold Elliott to John Treloar, Letter, AWM252 A158, p. 2.

5. Bean, Diary, April–May 1918, *Diaries and Notebooks*, AWM38 3DRL 606/108/1, pp. 60–61, www.awm.gov.au/collection/RCDIG1066553.

6. Harold Elliott to John Treloar, Letter, AWM252 A158, p. 2.

7. Ibid.

8. Ibid.

9. Bean, Diary, April–May 1918, *Diaries and Notebooks*, AWM38 3DRL 606/108/1, p. 67, www.awm.gov.au/collection/RCDIG1066553.

10. *Le Figaro,* Friday, 10 May 1910.

11. Monash, p. 63.

12. Crozier, p. 74.

13. Montgomery, p. 494.

14. David Doyle to John Black, Letter, 6 July 1937 in Bean, *Diaries, Notebooks and Folders*, AWM38 3DRL 606/276/1, p. 144, www.awm.gov.au/collection/RCDIG1066752.

15. Ross McMullin, 'Pompey Elliott: Our Most Revered Fighting General?', *The Sydney Morning Herald*, 22 April 2011.

16. *The Canberra Times*, 14 October 1926, p. 9.

17. *The London Gazette*, 4 June 1918.

18. Australian Dictionary of Biography, http://adb.anu.edu.au/biography/cobby-arthur-henry-5700

19. Odgers, p. 43.

20. Clifford Sadlier, 'Interview with Clifford Sadlier in the 1960s', in Walsh, *The Battle for Villers-Bretonneux and How It was Nearly Lost*, p. 9, www.amosa.org.au/schools/mhp/ww1/The%20battle%20for%20VB.pdf.

21. Supplement to the *London Gazette,* 30 April 1918, p. 5354.

22. *Mercury*, 11 May 1918, http://trove.nla.gov.au/newspaper/article/11392788.

23. Bean, Diary, March 1918, *Diaries and Notebooks*, AWM38 3DRL 606/184/1, p. 6, www.awm.gov.au/collection/RCDIG1066800.

24. Scott, pp. 178–179.

25. Sparrow, p. xii.

26. Ludendorff, Erich, *My War Memories*, p. 763.

27. Ibid.

28. Ibid.

29. Ibid., p. 764.

30. Ludendorff, Margarethe, *Als ich Ludendorffs Frau war* (*When I was Ludendorff's Wife*), p. 156.

31. Kilduff, *Red Baron: Life and Death of an Ace*, p. 235.

32. Ibid., p. 218.

33. *Vossische Zeitung*, 23 April 1918, Evening edition, p. 1.

34. Bean, Diary, April–May 1918, *Diaries and Notebooks,* AWM38 3DRL 606/108/1, p. 56, www.awm.gov.au/collection/RCDIG1066553.

35. Ibid., p. 58.

36. *The Australian*, 11 April 2007, www.theaustralian.com.au/in-depth/anzac-day/unsung-no1-with-a-bullet/story-e6frgdaf-1111113322520.

37. *The Independent,* Deniliquin, 6 April 1934, p. 4., http://trove.nla.gov.au/ndp/del/page/10985860?zoomLevel=1

38. Feldwebel Wilhelm Prosch, 463rd Regiment, in Martin Middlebrook's *The Kaiser's Battle*, p. 293.

BIBLIOGRAPHY

Initials used:

AWM	Australian War Memorial, Canberra
IWM	Imperial War Museum, London
ML	Mitchell Library, Sydney
NAA	National Archives of Australia, Canberra
NLA	National Library of Australia, Canberra
SLNSW	State Library of New South Wales, Sydney
SLV	State Library of Victoria, Melbourne
TNA	The National Archives, Kew, England
WO	War Office records held at the National Archives, Kew, England

BOOKS

Asprey, Robert, *The German High Command at War*, William Morrow, New York, 1991

Bailey, Frederick, *The Kingdom of Individuals*, Cornell University Press, Ithaca, 1993

Bann, Stephen, *The Inventions of History*, Manchester University Press, Manchester, 1990

Barnett, Corelli, *The Swordbearers: Studies in Supreme Command in the First World War*, Macmillan, London, 1966

Barwick, Archie, *In Great Spirits: The WWI Diary of Archie Barwick*, HarperCollins, Sydney, 2013

Bean, Charles E. W., *Anzac to Amiens*, Australian War Memorial, Canberra, 1968

— *The Official History of Australia in the War of 1914–1918*, Vol. V, Angus & Robertson, Sydney, 1937

Beckett, Ian, *The Making of the First World War*, Yale University Press, New Haven, 2012

Berg, A. Scott, *Wilson*, Simon & Schuster, London, 2013

Binding, Rudolf, *A Fatalist at War*, Houghton Mifflin Company, Boston/New York, 1929

Bishop, Bert, *The Hell, the Humour and the Heartbreak: A Private's View of World War I*, Kangaroo Press, Kenthurst, 1991

Bodenschatz, Karl, *Hunting with Richthofen*, Grub Street, London, 1996

— *Jagd in Flanderns Himmel: aus den sechzehn Kampfmonaten des Jagdg-eschwaders Freiherr von Richthofen*, Knorr & Hirth, Munich, 1935

Brahms, Vivian, *Spirit of the Forty-Second*, Naval and Military Press, Uckfield, 1938

Browning, Neville, *Fix Bayonets: The History of the 51st Battalion, AIF*, Bayswater, Perth, 2000

Callwell, Sir C. E., *Field Marshal Sir Henry Wilson: His Life and Diaries*, Vol. II, Cassell, London, 1927

Castan, Joachim, *Der Rote Baron: die ganze Geschichte des Manfred von Richthofen* (*The Red Baron: The Whole Story of Manfred von Richthofen*), Klett-Cotta, Stuttgart, 2007

Cecil, Hugh and Liddle, Peter (eds), *Facing Armageddon: The First World War Experienced*, Pen & Sword, Barnsley, 1996

Churchill, Sir Winston L., *The World Crisis 1911–1918*, Free Press, New York, 2005

Clausewitz, Carl von, *On War*, Princeton University Press, Princeton, 1976

Cobby, Arthur Henry, *High Adventure*, Robertson & Mullens, Melbourne, 1942

Cooper, Albert, *Character Glimpses: Australians on the Somme – Boys of the Bulldog Breed*, Waverly Press, Sydney, 1920

Crozier, Frank Percy, *The Men I Killed*, Doubleday, Doran, New York, 1938

Cutlack, Frederic Morley, *The Australian Flying Corps in the Western and Eastern Theatres of War 1914–1918*, Angus & Robertson, Sydney, 1933

Deayton, Craig, *Battle Scarred: The 47th Battalion in the First World War*, Big Sky Publishing, Newport, 2011

Delacour, Jean, *The Living Air: The Memoirs of an Ornithologist*, Country Life, London, 1966

Doughty, Robert A., *Pyrrhic Victory*, Belknap Press, London, 2005

Downing, Walter Hubert, *Digger Dialects*, Oxford University Press, Melbourne, 1990

— *To the Last Ridge*, Grub Street, London, 2013

Drew, George, *Canada's Fighting Airmen*, MacLean, Toronto, 1930

Durwood, Heinrich, *Attack out of the Sun*, Universe, Bloomington, 2010

Ebeling, Fritz, *Geschichte des Infanterie-Regiments Herzog Friedrich Wilhelm von Braunschweig (ostfriesischen) Nr. 78 im Weltkriege: Bearbeitet auf Grund der amtlichen Kriegstagebücher auf Veranlassung des Reichsarchivs* (*History of the Infantry Regiment Herzog Friedrich Wilhelm von Braunschweig (East Frisian) No. 78 in the World War. Edited based on official war diaries at the instigation of the National Archives*), Gerhard Stalling, Berlin, 1924

Edgar, Peter, *To Villers-Bretonneux with Brigadier-General William Glasgow*

DSO and the 13th Australian Infantry Brigade, Australian Military History Publications, Loftus, 2006

Edmonds, Sir James Edward, *Military Operations: France and Belgium 1918, March–April: Continuation of the German Offensive*, Vol. I, Macmillan, London, 1937

— *Military Operations: France and Belgium 1918; The German March Offensive and its Preliminaries*, Vol. I, Macmillan, London, 1935

— *Military Operations: France and Belgium, 1918*, Vol. I, Macmillan, London, 1935

— *Military Operations: France and Belgium, 1918, March–April: Continuation of the German Offensives*, Vol. II, Macmillan, 1937

— *Military Operations: France and Belgium, 1918*, Vol. II, Macmillan, 1937

Edwards, John, *Never a Backward Step: A History of the First 33 Battalion AIF*, Beetong Books, South Grafton, 1996

Elfeldt, Walter, *In der Schlacht von Villers-Bretonneux: Tagebuchblätter von Walter Elfeldt, ehemals Zugführer des 1. Zuges 7./5. Garde-Regt. z. F. (In the Battle of Villers-Bretonneux: Pages of Walter Elfeldt's Diary, Former Platoon Leader of 1st Platoon 7th/5th Foot Guard Regiment)*, Kindle edition, originally published in *Das Ehrenbuch der Garde (The Guards' Book of Honour)*.

Ellis, A. D., *The Story of the Fifth Australian Division*, Hodder and Stoughton, London, 1919

Emden, Richard van, *The Soldier's War: The Great War Through Veterans' Eyes*, Bloomsbury, London, 2008

Essame, Hubert, *The Battle for Europe: 1918*, Batsford, London, 1972

Farrar-Hockley, Anthony, *Goughie: The Life of General Sir Hubert Gough*, Hart-Davis, MacGibbon, London, 1975

Fischer, Suzanne Hayes (ed.), *Mother of Eagles: The War Diary of Baroness von Richthofen*, Schiffer Military History, Atglen, PA (USA), 2001

Fletcher, David, *Landships: British Tanks in the First World War*, HMSO, London, 1984

Foch, Ferdinand, *The Memoirs of Marshal Foch*, William Heinemann, London, 1931

Foley, John, *The Boilerplate War*, Star, London, 1963

Frankel, Benjamin, *History in Dispute: Revolutionary Russia, 1890–1930*, Vol. 21, St James Press, London, 2005

Fraser-Tytler, Neil, *Field Guns in France: With a Howitzer Battery in the Battles of the Somme, Arras, Messines & Passchendaele, 1915–1918*, Tom Donovan, Brighton, East Sussex, 1995

Gabriel, Kurt (ed.), *Das 1. Hannoversche Infanterie-Regiment Nr. 74 im*

*Weltkriege: Nach amtlichen Unterlagen und Berichten von Kriegsteilneh-
mern unter Mitarbeit der im Vorwort genannten Kameraden, Selbstverlag
der kameradschaftlichen Vereinigung des ehemaligen 1. Hannoverschen
Infanterie-Regiments Nr. 74* (*The 1st Hanoverian Infantry Regiment No. 74
in the World War: According to official documents and reports of comrades,
self-published by the comradely association of the former 1st Hanoverian
Infantry Regiment No. 74*)

Gammage, Bill, *The Broken Years, Australian Soldiers in the Great War*, Penguin, Harmondsworth, 1975

Gemmingen-Guttenberg-Fürfeld, Karl von (Colonel, retired), *Das Württem-
bergische Infanterie-Regiment Nr. 478 und seine Stammtruppen: Brigade-Er-
satz-Bataillone Nr. 51, 52, 53 und Ersatz-Infanterie-Regiment Nr. 51* (*The
Württemberg Infantry Regiment No. 478 and its Core Troops: Brigade Reserve
Battalions No. 51, 52, 53 and Reserve Infantry Regiment No. 51*), Chr. Belser,
Stuttgart, 1924

George, David Lloyd, *The Great Crusade: Extracts from Speeches Delivered
During the War*, George H. Doran Company, New York, 1918

— *War Memoirs of David Lloyd George*, 1917–1918, Vol. V, Nicholson &
Watson, London, 1936

German General Headquarters, *Der Angriff im Stellungskrieg: Entwurf,
Geheim! 1 January 1918*, translation B. E. F Intelligence as *The Attack in
Position Warfare* (G. H. Q. 1918)

Ghiz, Christopher, *Specialised Assault Units of the First World War*, Master of
Military Art and Science thesis, Fort Leavenworth, Kansas, 2010

Goodspeed, D. J., *Ludendorff: Soldier, Dictator, Revolutionary*, Rupert
Hart-Davis, London 1966

Görlitz, Walter (ed.), *Regierte der Kaiser? Kriegstagebücher, Aufzeichnungen
und Briefe des Chefs des Marine-Kabinetts Admiral Georg Alexander von
Müller, 1914–1918* (*Did the Emperor Reign? War Diaries, Notes and
Letters of the Chief of the Naval Cabinet Admiral Georg Alexander von
Müller, 1914–1918*), Musterschmidt-Verlag, Göttingen, 1959

— *The Kaiser and his Court: The Diaries, Notebooks and Letters of Admiral
Georg Alexander von Müller, Chief of the Naval Cabinet 1914–1918*,
Macdonald, London, 1961

Gough, Hubert, *The Fifth Army*, Hodder and Stoughton, Bath, 1968

Grant, Neil, *The Lewis Gun*, Osprey, Oxford, 2014

Gray, Randal, *Kaiserschlacht 1918: The Final German Offensive*, Osprey,
London, 1991

Green, Frank C., *The Fortieth: A Record of the 40th Battalion, A.I.F.*, printed
for the 40th Battalion Association by J. Vail, Hobart, 1922

Guttman, Jon, *Sopwith Camel vs Fokker Dr I: Western Front 1917–18*, Osprey, Oxford, 2008

Hankey, Maurice Pascal Alers, *The Supreme Command: 1914–1918*, Vol. II, Allen & Unwin, London, 1961

Harms, Heinrich (ed.), *Die Geschichte des Oldenburgischen Infanterie-Regiments Nr. 91: Mit Unterstützung von Kriegskameraden, nach den amtlichen Kriegstagebüchern und persönlichen Aufzeichnungen bearbeitet (The History of Oldenburg Infantry Regiment No. 91: Edited with the Support of War Comrades, According to the Official War Diaries and Personal Records)*, Gerhard Stalling, Berlin, 1930

Hart, Peter, *1918: A Very British Victory*, Phoenix, London, 2009

— *Aces Falling: The War Above the Trenches, 1918*, Phoenix, London, 2008

— *Voices from the Front: An Oral History of the Great War*, Profile Books, London, 2015

Hartnett, H. G., *Over the Top: A Digger's Story of the Western Front*, Allen & Unwin, Crows Nest (Sydney), 2011

Hindenburg, Paul von, *Out of My Life*, Forgotten Books, London, 2013

— *The Great War*, Cassell and Company, London, 1920

Hoehling, A. A., and Hoehling, Mary Duprey, *The Last Voyage of the Lusitania*, Madison Books, Lanham, 1956

Horn, Daniel (ed.), *War Mutiny and Revolution in the German Navy: The World War I Diary of Seaman Richard Stumpf*, Rutgers University Press, New Brunswick, 1967

Hughes, Daniel J. (ed.), *Moltke on the Art of War: Selected Writings*, Random House Ballantine Publishing Group, 1993

Jeffrey, Keith (ed.), *The Military Correspondence of Field Marshal Sir Henry Wilson, 1918–1922*, Bodley Head, London, 1985

Jones, Ira, *King of Airfighters: Biography of Major 'Mick' Mannock DFC*, Casemate, Philadelphia, 2009

Jones, R. T. (ed.), *The Collected Poems of Rudyard Kipling*, Wordsworth Editions, Ware, 1994

Joy, William, *The Aviators*, Shakespeare Head Press, Sydney, Australia, 1971

Jünger, Ernst, *Kriegstagebuch: 1914–1918 (War Diary: 1914–1918)*, Klett-Cotta, Stuttgart, 2010

— *The Storm of Steel*, Howard Fertig, New York, 1975

Jürgensen, Wilhelm (ed.), *Das Füsilier-Regiment 'Königin' Nr. 86 im Weltkriege: Nach den amtlichen Kriegstagebüchern, privaten Aufzeichnungen und persönlichen Erinnerungen*, Oldenburg, Berlin, 1925.

Kaupert (no first name), *Das Infanterie-Regiment von Stülpnagel (5. Brandenburgisches) Nr. 48: Nach den amtlichen Kriegstagebüchern (The Infantry*

Regiment of Stülpnagel (5th Brandenburg) No. 48: According to the official war diaries), Gerhard Stalling, Berlin, 1921

Keegan, John, *The First World War*, Hutchinson, London, 1998

Kendall, Tim, *The Oxford Handbook of British and Irish War Poetry*, Oxford University Press, Oxford, 2009

Kent, David, *From Trench and Troopship: The Experience of the Australian Imperial Force, 1914–1919*, Hale & Ironmonger, Maryborough, 1999

Kerensky, Alexander and Browder, Robert (eds); *The Russian Provisional Government 1917: Documents*, Vol. I, Stanford University Press, Stanford, 1961

Kilduff, Peter, *Red Baron: The Life and Death of an Ace*, David & Charles, Devon, 2008

— *Richthofen: Beyond the Legend of the Red Baron*, Arms and Amour Press, London, 1999

Krupskaya, Nadezhda, *Memories of Lenin: Nadezhda Krupskaya Lenin's Widow*, Panther, London, 1970

Lauryssens, Stan, *The Man Who Invented the Third Reich: The Life and Times of Arthur Moeller van den Bruck*, Sutton, Stroud, Gloucestershire, 1999

Lee, Arthur S. Gould, *No Parachute: A Classic Account of War in the Air in WWI*, Grub Street, London, 1968

Longmore, Cyril, *Eggs-a-Cook: The Story of the Forty-Fourth*, Colortype Press, Perth, 1920

— *The Old Sixteenth: Being a Record of the 16th Battalion A.I.F., During the Great War, 1914–1918*, Naval and Military Press, Uckfield, 2009

Ludendorff, Erich, *Ludendorff's Own Story: August 1914–November 1918: The Great War from the Siege of Liege to the Signing of the Armistice As Viewed from the Grand Headquarters of the German Army*, Vol. II, Harper & Brothers, New York, 1919

— *My War Memories: 1914–1918*, Vol. I, Hutchinson, London, 1919

— *My War Memories: 1914–1918*, Vol. II, Hutchinson, London, 1919

Ludendorff, Margarethe, *Als ich Ludendorffs Frau war (When I was Ludendorff's Wife)*, Dreimasken Verlag, Munich, 1929

Ludendorff, Mathilde, *Erich Ludendorff: Sein Wesen und Schaffen (Erich Ludendorff: His Character and Work)*, Ludendorffs Verlag, Munich, 1938

Lutz, Ralph (ed.), *The Fall of the German Empire 1914–1918*, Vol. I, Stanford University Press, Stanford, 1932

Lynch, E. P. F., *Somme Mud: The War Experiences of an Infantryman in France 1916–1919*, Random House Australia, North Sydney, 2008

MacDonald, Lyn, *To the Last Man: Spring 1918*, Carroll & Graf, New York, 1999

Macdougall, Tony, *War Letters of General Monash*, Duffy and Snellgrove, Sydney, 2002

Mackersey, Ian, *No Empty Chairs: The Short and Heroic Lives of the Young Aviators Who Fought and Died in the First World War*, Phoenix, London, 2013

Mathews, Wayne and Wilson, David; *Fighting Nineteenth: History of the 19th Battalion, AIF, 1915–1918,* Australian Military History Publications, 2011

Maurice, Sir Frederick, *The Life of General Lord Rawlinson of Trent from his Journals and Letters*, Cassell, London, 1928

Maze, Paul, *A Frenchman in Khaki*, Heinemann, London, 1936

McGuire, Frank, *The Many Deaths of the Red Baron*, Bunker to Bunker Publishing, Calgary, 2001

McMullin, Ross, *Pompey Elliott*, Scribe, Melbourne, 2008

McWilliams, James and Steel, R. James, *Amiens: Dawn of Victory*, Dundurn, Toronto, 2001

Meagher, Norman R. T., *With the Fortieth: Lieutenant Norman Meagher, 40th Battalion, Australian Imperial Force Abroad*, Hobart, 1918

Meyer, G. J., *A World Undone: The Story of the Great War, 1914 to 1918*, Delacourte Press, New York, 2006

Middlebrook, Martin, *The Kaiser's Battle*, Penguin, Harmondsworth, 1978

Miller, Henry Willard, *The Paris Gun: The Bombardment of Paris by the German Long-range Guns and the Great German Offensives of 1918*, George Harrap, London, 1930

Mitchell, Frank, *Tank Warfare: The Story of the Tanks in the Great War*, Thomas Nelson and Sons, London, 1933

Mitchell, George D., *Backs to the Wall: A Larrikin on the Western Front*, Allen & Unwin, Crows Nest (Sydney), 2007

Molkentin, Michael, *Fire in the Sky: The Australian Flying Corps in the First World War*, Allen & Unwin, Crows Nest (Sydney), 2010

Mombauer, Annika and Deist, Wilhelm (eds); *The Kaiser: New Research on Wilhelm's Role in Imperial Germany*, Cambridge University Press, Cambridge/New York, 2011

Monash, Sir John, *The Australian Victories in France in 1918*, Imperial War Museum, London, 2005

Mooney, Charles James, *The History of the Ninth Australian Field Ambulance*, John Sands, Sydney, 1919

Murland, Jerry, *Retreat and Rearguard: Somme 1918, The Fifth Army Retreat*, Pen & Sword Military, Barnsley, 2014

Nagel, Fritz, *Fritz: The World War I Memoirs of a German Lieutenant*, Der

Angriff Publications, Huntington, 1981

Neiberg, Michael S., *The World War I Reader*, New York University Press, New York, 2007

Newton, L. M. p. 79. *The Story of the 12th: A Record of the 12th Battalion, A. I. F. During the Great War of 1914–1918*, The University of Michigan, 2006.

Niebelschütz, Günther von (ed.), *Reserve-Infanterie-Regiment Nr. 230: Zusammengestellt nach den amtlichen Kriegstagebüchern und privaten Aufzeichnungen* (*Reserve Infantry Regiment No. 230: Compiled based on Official War Diaries and Private Records*), Gerhard Stalling, Berlin, 1926

Odgers, George, *The RAAF: An Illustrated History*, Child & Associates, Frenchs Forest (Sydney), 1989

Oldham, Peter, *Messines Ridge: Ypres*, Pen & Sword, Havertown, 1990

Passingham, Ian, *All the Kaiser's Men: The Life and Death of the German Army on the Western Front*, History Press, Stroud, Gloucestershire, 2011

— *The German Offensives of 1918: The Last Desperate Gamble*, Pen & Sword, Barnsley, 2008

Pearson, Michael, *The Sealed Train*, Macmillan, London, 1975

Pedersen, Peter A., *Anzacs on the Western Front*, Wiley, Melbourne, 2012

— *Villers-Bretonneux*, Pen & Sword Military, Barnsley, 2004

Rappaport, Armin, *The British Press and Wilsonian Neutrality*, Stanford University Press, Stanford, 1951

Recouly, Raymond and Jones, Mary Cadwalader; *Foch: The Winner of the War*, New York, C. Scribner's Sons, 1920

Reichsarchiv Potsdam, *Der Weltkrieg 1914 bis 1918: Die militärischen Operationen zu Lande* (*The World War 1914 to 1918: Military Operations*), Vol. 14.1, E. S. Mittler & Sohn, Berlin, 1931

Reid, Richard (et al.), *Beaucoup Australiens Ici: The Australian Corps in France 1918*, Commonwealth Department of Veterans' Affairs, Canberra, 1998

Reid, Walter, *Douglas Haig: Architect of Victory*, Birlinn, Edinburgh, 2006

Richards, Tom, *Wallaby Warrior: The World War I Diaries of Australia's Only British Lion*, Allen & Unwin, Sydney, 2013

Richthofen, Manfred von, *Der Rote Kampfflieger, The Red Fighter Pilot*, Red and Black Publishers, New York, 2007

Robertson, James, *Tenting Tonight: The Soldier's Life*, Time-Life Books, 1994

Rupprecht, Maria Luitpold Ferdinand (Crown Prince of Bavaria), *In Treue fest: Mein Kriegstagebuch*, Vol. II, E. S. Mittler & Sohn, Berlin, 1929

Samuels, Martin, *Command or Control? Command, Training, and Tactics in the British and German Armies, 1888–1918*, Frank Cass, London/Portland, OR (USA), 1995

Scott, Joan (ed.), *A Soldier on the Somme: The Diary of Private Henry Need, 59th Battalion, 15th Brigade, 5th Division, Australian Imperial Force*, Victoria Joan Scott, Castlemaine, 2014;

Sheffield, Gary, *The Chief: Douglas Haig and the British Army*, Aurum, London, 2012

— with Bourne, John (eds), *Douglas Haig: War Diaries and Letters, 1914–1918*, Weidenfeld & Nicolson, London, 2005

Sievers, Adolf (ed.), *R.I.R. 93: Geschichte eines Regiments im Weltkriege, Im Auftrage des Vereins ehemaliger Kameraden des Res.-Inf.-Reg. 93 zu Berlin im Reichsbund 4. Gardisten* (*R.I.R. 93: History of a Regiment in the World War, on Behalf of the Association of Former Comrades of the Reserve-Infantry-Regiment 93 to Berlin in the Reichsbund 4th Guards*), Buchdruckerei von Johann Schwarck Söhne, Wilster in Holstein

Sparrow, Walter Shaw, *The Fifth Army in March*, John Lane (Company), London/New York, 1921

Stark, Rudolf, *Wings of War*, London, Hamilton, 1933

Stosch, Albrecht von, *Das Garde-Grenadier-Regiment Nr. 5 (1897–1918): Nach amtlichen Kriegstagebüchern und Mitteilungen von Mitkämpfern bearbeitet* (*The Grenadier Guards Regiment No. 5 (1897–1918). Edited According to Official War Diaries and Messages from Comrades*), Gerhard Stalling, Berlin, 1925

Streissguth, Thomas, *The Christmas Truce of 1914*, Essential Library (an imprint of Abdo Publishing), Minneapolis, 2016

Sufrin, Mark and Smith, Richard; *The Brave Men: Twelve Portraits of Courage*, Platt & Munk, New York, 1967

Sulzbach, Herbert, *With the German Guns: Four Years on the Western Front*, Pen & Sword Military, Barnsley, South Yorkshire, 2012

Taylor, Sir Gordon, *Sopwith Scout 7309*, Cassell, London, 1968

Thompson, Julian, *Call to Arms: Great Military Speeches*, Quercus, London, 2009

Titler, Dale M., *The Day the Red Baron Died*, Ian Allan Ltd, 1973

Tiveychoc, A. (pseud.), *There and Back: The Story of an Australian Soldier*, Returned Sailors and Soldiers' Imperial League of Australia, Sydney, 1935

Tschischwitz, E. von (ed.), *General von der Marwitz: Weltkriegsbriefe* (*World-War Letters*), Steiniger-Verlage (part of Verlag Reimar Hobbing), Berlin, 1940

Tuchmann, Barbara Wertheim, *The Guns of August*, Penguin, London, 2014

Tucker, Spencer, *The Great War: 1914–18*, UCL Press, London, 1998

Udet, Ernst, *Mein Fliegerleben*, Ullstein, Berlin, 1935

Uhle-Wettler, Franz, *Erich Ludendorff in seiner Zeit: Soldat – Stratege – Revolu-tionär; eine Neubewertung* (*Erich Ludendorff in his Time: Soldier – Strategist – Revolutionary; a Reappraisal*), Kurt Vowinckel, Berg, 1992

Ulrich, Bernd and Ziemann, Benjamin (eds), *German Soldiers in the Great War: Letters and Eyewitness Accounts,* Pen & Sword Military, Barnsley, 2010

Wade, Rex A., *The Russian Revoltuion: 1917,* Cambridge University Press, 2005

Walter, Friedrich (ed.), *Leutnant Schmidt und seine Kompanie: Ein Soldat-enschicksal, Aus den Tagebüchern des Kriegsfreiwilligen, Vikars Dr. Erich Schmidt, gefallen als Leutnant im Juli 1918* (*Lieutenant Schmidt and His Company: A Soldier's Fate, From the Diaries of the Military Volunteer, Vicar Dr Erich Schmidt, Fallen as Lieutenant in July 1918*), Ernte-Verlag, Potsdam (Berlin), 1930

Wells, E., *Reflections of Gallipoli, France and Flanders*, G. A. Jones (printer), Sydney, 1919

Westman, Stephen Kurt, *Surgeon with the Kaiser's Army*, Kimber, London, 1968

White, Thomas Alexander, *The History of the Thirteenth Battalion, A.I.F.*, Tyrells for the 13th Battalion, A.I.F. Committee, Sydney, 1924

Whitham, J. L., Villers Bretonneux, April 1918, *Stand To*, June–July 1932

Wilhelm (Crown Prince William of Germany), *My War Experiences*, Hurst and Blackett, London, 1922.

Williams, Charles, *Pétain,* Little, Brown, London, 2005

Wodehouse, Pelham Grenville, *What Ho! The Best of P. G. Wodehouse*, Arrow Books, London, 2011

Wohl, Robert, *A Passion for Wings: Aviation and the Western Imagination, 1908–1918*, Yale University Press, New Haven, 1994

Zabecki, David T., *The German 1918 Offensives: A Case Study in the Opera-tional Level of War*, Routledge, London/New York, 2006

Zeman, Z. A. B. (ed.), *Germany and the Revolution in Russia 1915–1918: Documents from the Archives of the German Foreign Ministry*, Oxford University Press, London, 1958

DIARIES, LETTERS, PAPERS AND REPORTS

1st Australian Division (General Staff Headquarters), Unit War Diaries, AWM4 1/42/39, Part 1, https://www.awm.gov.au/collection/RC-DIG1009666/

2/7th Battalion Royal Warwickshire Regiment, War Diary, The National Archives, UK, WO 95/3056/3

3rd Australian Division (General Staff Headquarters), Unit War Diaries, AWM4 1/46/17, Part 2 (March 1918), https://www.awm.gov.au/collection/RCDIG1011421/

4th Infantry Brigade, Unit War Diaries, AWM4 23/4/30 (March 1918), https://www.awm.gov.au/collection/RCDIG1008431/

9th Infantry Brigade, Unit War Diaries, AWM4 23/9/17 (March 1918), https://www.awm.gov.au/collection/RCDIG1016534/

15th Australian Infantry Brigade, Unit War Diaries, AWM4 23/15/26, Part 1, https://www.awm.gov.au/collection/RCDIG1008004/

33rd Infantry Battalion, Unit War Diaries, AWM4 23/50/17, Part 1 (March 1918, Appendices), https://www.awm.gov.au/collection/RCDIG1005119/

33rd Infantry Battalion, Unit War Diaries, AWM4 23/50/17, Part 2 (March 1918, Appendices), https://www.awm.gov.au/collection/RCDIG1005120/

33rd Infantry Battalion, Unit War Diaries, AWM4 23/50/18 (April 1918), https://www.awm.gov.au/collection/RCDIG1005121/

34th Infantry Battalion, Unit War Diaries, AWM4 23/51/18 (April 1918), https://www.awm.gov.au/collection/RCDIG1005643/

35th Infantry Battalion, Unit War Diaries, AWM4 23/52/10 (April 1918), https://www.awm.gov.au/collection/RCDIG1003996/

36th Infantry Battalion, Unit War Diaries, AWM4 23/53/18 (April 1918), https://www.awm.gov.au/collection/RCDIG1004121/

47th Infantry Battalion, Unit War Diaries, AWM4 23/64/22 (March 1918), https://www.awm.gov.au/collection/RCDIG1006486/

48th Infantry Battalion, Unit War Diaries, AWM4 23/65/26 (March 1918), https://www.awm.gov.au/collection/RCDIG1006496/

58th Infantry Battalion, Unit War Diaries, AWM4 23/75/27 (April 1918), https://www.awm.gov.au/collection/RCDIG1006037/

Adcock, Garnet Ingamells, Letters and 'Notes from War Diary' (March 1918), AWM, 2DRL/0123, https://www.awm.gov.au/collection/2DRL/0123/

Alexander, John A. R., Papers (Diary), AWM, PR86/133, https://www.awm.gov.au/collection/PR86/133/

Australian Imperial Force (General Staff, Headquarters Australian Corps), Unit War Diaries, AWM4 1/35/3 (March 1918), https://www.awm.gov.au/collection/RCDIG1008738/

Australian Imperial Force (Intelligence, Headquarters Australian Corps), Unit War Diaries, AWM4 1/36/3 (March 1918), https://www.awm.gov.au/collection/RCDIG1009244/

Avery, Louis Willyama, Papers (WWI Diary), SLSA, PGR500, http://www.slsa.sa.gov.au/archivaldocs/prg/PRG500_1-6_Avery_papers_transcript.pdf

Bartlett, Leonard V., Diary, MLMSS 959, Item 3, http://acms.sl.nsw.gov.au/item/itemdetailpaged.aspx?itemid=900704

Barwick, Archie, Diary (5 March – 12 April 1918), MLMSS 1493, Box 2, Item 12, http://acmssearch.sl.nsw.gov.au/search/itemDetailPaged.cgi?itemID=844565

Bean, Charles, Official History, '1914–18 War: Records of C E W Bean, Official Historian' (Diaries and Notebooks), AWM38 3DRL 606/52/1 (July 1916), https://www.awm.gov.au/collection/RCDIG1066816/

— AWM38 3DRL 606/92/1 (October–November 1917), https://www.awm.gov.au/collection/RCDIG1066660/

— AWM38 3DRL 606/96/1 (January 1918), https://www.awm.gov.au/collection/RCDIG1066664/

— AWM38 3DRL 606/98/1 (February 1918), https://www.awm.gov.au/collection/RCDIG1066666/

— AWM38 3DRL 606/100/1 (February 1918), https://www.awm.gov.au/collection/RCDIG1066808/

— AWM38 3DRL 606/102/1 (March 1918), https://www.awm.gov.au/collection/RCDIG1066653/

— AWM38 3DRL 606/103/1 (March 1918), https://www.awm.gov.au/collection/RCDIG1066548/

— AWM38 3DRL 606/104/1 (March–April 1918), https://www.awm.gov.au/collection/RCDIG1066549/

— AWM38 3DRL 606/105/1 (April 1918), https://www.awm.gov.au/collection/RCDIG1066550/

— AWM38 3DRL 606/106/1 (April 1918), https://www.awm.gov.au/collection/RCDIG1066551/

— AWM38 3DRL 606/107/1 (April 1918), https://www.awm.gov.au/collection/RCDIG1066552/

— AWM38 3DRL 606/108/1 (April–May 1918), https://www.awm.gov.au/collection/RCDIG1066553/

— AWM38 3DRL 606/184/1 (March 1918), https://www.awm.gov.au/collection/RCDIG1066800/

— AWM38 3DRL 606/185/1 (1915–1918), https://www.awm.gov.au/collection/RCDIG1066801/

— AWM38 3DRL 606/276/1 (1928–1937), https://www.awm.gov.au/collection/RCDIG1066716/

Dadswell, Henry William (Sapper), Papers ('Diary of a Sapper'), AWM, MSS0828, https://www.awm.gov.au/collection/MSS0828/

Delahunty, John Patrick (Sapper), Private Record (Diary), AWM, PR03651, https://www.awm.gov.au/collection/PR03651/

Fairweather, Francis Edward, Private Record (Letters), AWM, 2DRL/0207, https://www.awm.gov.au/collection/2DRL/0207/

Fell, Alfred James, Private Record, AWM, 3DRL/6608 (RCDIG0000445), https://www.awm.gov.au/collection/3DRL/6608/

Fischer, Frank Reinhardt, Private Record (Letters), AWM, 1DRL/0288, https://www.awm.gov.au/collection/1DRL/0288/

Goddard, Henry Arthur, Diary ('1918 Diary related to Henry Arthur Goddard'), AWM, 3DRL/2379, https://www.awm.gov.au/collection/RCDIG0000784/

— 'Papers relating to narrative history of the 35th Battalion compiled by Henry Arthur Goddard' ('Account of Villers-Bretonneux, 30 March to 6 April 1918'), AWM, 3DRL/2379 (RCDIG0000808), https://www.awm.gov.au/collection/RCDIG0000808/

— Document ('Tour of a Company on the Front Line'), AWM, 3DRL/2379, https://www.awm.gov.au/collection/RCDIG0000808/

Goldrick, Robert Austen, Letters, MLMSS 3013, Item 1, http://acmssearch.sl.nsw.gov.au/search/itemDetailPaged.cgi?itemID=982584

Grimwade, Harold William, Private Record (Diary), AWM, PR00778, https://www.awm.gov.au/collection/PR00778/

Hardie, John, Private Record (War Narrative), AWM, PR00519, https://www.awm.gov.au/collection/PR00519/

Harris, Herbert Henry, Diary (transcript), MLMSS 2772/Item 4, http://acms.sl.nsw.gov.au/_transcript/2013/D23223/a4627.html

Holton, Alfred Edward, Private Record, Memoir (handwritten and transcribed), AWM, PR05317, https://www.awm.gov.au/collection/PR05317/

Keating, Noel Michael, Private Record, Diary (handwritten), AWM, PR00561, https://www.awm.gov.au/collection/PR00561/

Kennedy, Walter Scott, Private Record, Memoir (handwritten and transcribed), 'From Anzac Cove to Villers Bretonneux: The Story of a Soldier in the Fifteenth Battalion 1st AIF (Dedicated to Alf Stein Killed at Gallipoli, 2 May 1915'), AWM, PR02032, https://www.awm.gov.au/collection/PR02032/

Louch, Thomas Steane, Private Record (Manuscript 'In the Ranks'), AWM, PR85/363, https://www.awm.gov.au/collection/PR85/363/

Marks, Douglas Gray, War Diary, MLMSS 2879, http://acmssearch.sl.nsw.gov.au/search/itemDetailPaged.cgi?itemID=872435

McDougall, Stanley Robert, Service Records, NAA, No. 4061, http://discoveringanzacs.naa.gov.au/browse/records/125997/1

Mitchell, George Deane, Private Record (Notebooks), AWM, 2DRL/0928, https://www.awm.gov.au/collection/2DRL/0928/

Monash, Sir John, Papers, AWM, 3DRL/2316, Series 1 ('Personal Letters, 1914–1918'), Box 1, Wallets 1 and 2, Vol. 1 ('24 December 1914–4

March 1917'), https://www.awm.gov.au/collection/RCDIG0000568/

— Papers, AWM, 3DRL/2316, Series 1 ('Personal Letters, 1914–1918'), Vol. 2 ('4 March 1917 – 28 December 1918), AWM, 3DRL/2316 (RCDIG0000570), https://www.awm.gov.au/collection/RCDIG0000570/

— Papers, AWM, 3DRL/2316, Series 3 ('First World War Papers, 1914–1918'), https://www.awm.gov.au/collection/RCDIG0000572/

Paterson, Alec S., Private Record, AWM, 3DRL/3389, https://www.awm.gov.au/collection/3DRL/3389/

Rawlinson, Frank Ronald, Manuscript (Narrative 'Wood and Fire'), AWM, MSS0770, https://www.awm.gov.au/collection/MSS0770/

Rosenthal, Sir Charles, Diary, MLMSS 2739/Vol. 1, http://acms.sl.nsw.gov.au/_transcript/2014/D27827/c00585.html

Rusden, Arthur Stuart Keylock, Private Record (Papers), AWM, 1DRL/0559, https://www.awm.gov.au/collection/1DRL/0559/

Russell, Eric, Private Record (Letters), AWM, PR01479, https://www.awm.gov.au/collection/PR01479/

Schwieger, Walter, 'English Translation of His Majesty's Submarine U-20 War Diary' National Archives, Record Group 45 ('Naval Records Collection of the Office of Naval Records and Library, 1691–1945'), https://catalog.archives.gov/id/833792?q=lusitania

Stevens, James Arthur, Manuscript ('Battle Honours of the 58th Battalion A.I.F. 1914–1918'), AWM, MSS1993, https://www.awm.gov.au/collection/MSS1993/

Street, Edmund Harrington, Private Record (Service Narrative and Typescript), AWM, PR85/179, Wallets 5 and 6, https://www.awm.gov.au/collection/PR85/179/

Turnbull, John Henry Llewellyn, Private Record (Diary), AWM, PR91/015,

Young, Sydney B., War Diary, MLMSS 985/Item 6 (2 February – 1 September 1918), http://acms.sl.nsw.gov.au/_transcript/2011/D11976/a2748.htm

NEWSPAPERS

The Argus (Melbourne)
The Australian
The Canberra Times
Daily Herald (Adelaide)
Daily Telegraph (Sydney)
L'Echo de Paris
Le Figaro
Sydney Mail

The Mercury (Hobart)
The Sydney Morning Herald
The West Australian
Vossische Zeitung
Western Mail

JOURNALS AND MAGAZINES
Air Pictorial, Vol. 30, 1968
Aussie: The Australian Soldiers' Magazine, March 1918
Aviation Magazine, 12 June 2006
Commonwealth Gazette No. 185, 27 November 1918
Leavenworth Papers, No. 4 (Lupfer, Timothy T., 'The Dynamics of Doctrine:
    The Changes in Tactical Doctrine During the First World War'),
    Combat Studies Institute, Fort Leavenworth, Kansas, 1981, seen in:
    http://usacac.army.mil/cac2/cgsc/carl/download/csipubs/lupfer.pdf
London Gazette, 30 April 1918
Reveille, 31 July 1929
— 1 August 1933
— 1 September 1933
— 1 August 1936
The London Gazette, 4 June 1918
The Magazine of the University of Sydney, June 1918

ONLINE SOURCES
http://history-world.org/battle_of_verdun.htm
http://adb.anu.edu.au/biography/brand-charles-henry-5338
http://usacac.army.mil/cac2/cgsc/carl/download/csipubs/lupfer.pdf
https://catalog.archives.gov/id/785591
Nicholas II (Tsar), Diary, Alexander Palace Archives, http://www.alexander-
    palace.org/palace/ndiaries1917.html
Thomas, Alun Miles, PhD Thesis ('British 8th Infantry Division on the
    Western Front, 1914–18'), University of Birmingham, Centre for
    First World War Studies, Birmingham, 2010, http://etheses.bham.
    ac.uk/599/1/thomas10PhD.pdf
Walsh, Matt, *The Battle for Villers-Bretonneux and How it was Nearly Lost*,
    Defence Reserves Association (NSW) Inc and the Military Police As-
    sociation of Australia Inc., Canberra, 2008 http://www.amosa.org.au/
    schools/mhp/ww1/The%20battle%20for%20VB.pdf

INDEX